ScottForesman
LITERATURE
AND INTEGRATED STUDIES

Middle School: Grade Six

Middle School: Grade Seven

Middle School: Grade Eight

Forms of Literature

World Literature

American Literature

English Literature

The cover features a detail of Sam Adoquei's *Portrait of Rockney C.* (1992), which appears in full on this page. Born in the West African country of Ghana, Adoquei was primarily a landscape painter until the mid-1980s, when his "love of people" brought him to portrait painting.

ScottForesman
LITERATURE
AND INTEGRATED STUDIES

Grade Eight

Senior Consultants

Alan C. Purves
State University of New York at Albany

Carol Booth Olson
University of California, Irvine

Carlos E. Cortés
University of California, Riverside (Emeritus)

Judith A. Brough
Gettysburg College, Gettysburg

Edward N. Brazee
University of Maine

ScottForesman

Editorial Offices: Glenview, Illinois
Regional Offices: San Jose, California • Tucker, Georgia • Glenview,
Illinois • Oakland, New Jersey • Dallas, Texas

Visit ScottForesman's Home Page at http://www.scottforesman.com

ACKNOWLEDGMENTS

Texts

xxv "A Mother in Mannville" from *When the Whippoorwill* by Marjorie Kinnan Rawlings. Copyright © 1936, 1940 Marjorie Kinnan Rawlings; copyright renewed © 1964, 1968 Norton Baskin. Reprinted by permission of Scribner, a Division of Simon & Schuster, Inc. **6** "Viva New Jersey" by Gloria Gonzalez. Copyright © 1993 by Gloria Gonzalez. From *Join In, Multiethnic Short Stories* by Donald R. Gallo, Ed. Reprinted by permission of Delacorte Press, a division of Bantam Doubleday Dell Publishing Group, Inc. **18** "Stop the Sun" by Gary Paulsen, *Boy's Life,* January 1986. Copyright © 1986 Gary Paulsen. Reprinted by permission of Jennifer Flannery Literary Agency. **27** "The Dust Will Settle" by Luci Tapahonso. Reprinted by permission of the author. **28** "Forgotten Language" from *Where the Sidewalk Ends* by Shel Silverstein. Copyright © 1974 by Evil Eye Music, Inc. Reprinted by permission of HarperCollins Publishers. **29** Two lines from "The Dust Will Settle" by Luci Tapahonso. Reprinted by permission of the author. **31** "Prisoner of My Country" from *The Invisible Thread* by Yoshiko Uchida. Copyright © 1991 Yoshiko Uchida. Reprinted by permission of Simon & Schuster Books for Young Readers. **39** "Home" from *Maud Martha* by Gwendolyn Brooks. Copyright © 1991 by Gwendolyn Brooks. Published by Third World Press, Chicago, 1991. Reprinted by permission of the author. **45** "The Kid Nobody Could Handle" from *Welcome to the Monkey House* by Kurt Vonnegut, Jr. Copyright © 1961 by Kurt Vonnegut, Jr. Reprinted by permission of Delacorte Press/Seymour Lawrence, a division of Bantam Doubleday Dell Publishing Group, Inc. **56** From "I'm the Luckiest Person I Ever Met" by Patricia Sellers, *Fortune,* August 10, 1992, p. 93. Copyright © 1992 Time Inc. All rights reserved. Reprinted by permission of Fortune Magazine. **60** From "Be Your Own Cheerleader" from *Current Health ®,* September 1993. Copyright © 1993 by Weekly Reader Corporation. All rights reserved. Reprinted by permission of Weekly Reader Corporation. **64** Hal May & James G. Lesniak, *Contemporary Authors,* Vol. 29. Detroit: Gale Research Inc., 1990, p. 95. **65** "Liverwurst and Roses" from *I Love You, I Hate You, Get Lost* by Ellen Conford. Copyright © 1994 by Conford Enterprises, Ltd. Reprinted by permission of Scholastic Inc. **78** "A President's Wife" from *Eleanor Roosevelt: A Life of Discovery* by Russell Freedman. Text copyright © 1993 by Russell Freedman. Reprinted by permission of Clarion Books/Houghton Mifflin Co. All rights reserved. **82** From "Milestones" from *The Autobiography of Eleanor Roosevelt* by Eleanor Roosevelt. Copyright © 1937, 1949, 1958, 1961 by Anna Eleanor Roosevelt. Copyright © 1958 by Curtis Publishing Company. Reprinted by permission of HarperCollins Publishers, Inc. **88** "Fable for When There's No Way Out" by May Swenson. Copyright © 1967. Reprinted with permission of the Literary Estate of May Swenson. **93** From *Back There* by Rod Serling. Copyright © 1960 by Kayuga Productions, Inc. Reprinted by permission of International Creative Management, Inc. **106** Linda Metzger, *Contemporary Authors,* Vol. 13. Detroit: Gale Research Inc., 1984, p. 80. **107** "The Passing of the Buffalo" from *Keepers of the Animals* by Michael J. Caduto and Joseph Bruchac. Copyright © 1991 Michael J. Caduto and Joseph Bruchac. Reprinted by permission of Fulcrum Publishing. **109** Doreen Rappaport, *American Women: Their Lives in Their Words.* New York: Thomas Y. Crowell, 1990. **130** "Who You Are" from *Hey World, Here I Am!* by Jean Little. Copyright © 1986 by Jean Little. Reprinted by permission of HarperCollins Publishers and Kids Can Press. **135** "The Mechanical Mind" from *Local News* by Gary Soto. Copyright © 1993 by Gary Soto. Reprinted by permission of Harcourt Brace and Company. **142** "The Parsley Garden" from *The Assyrian and Other Stories* by William Saroyan. Copyright 1950 by William Saroyan. Reprinted by permission of the William Saroyan Foundation. **152** From *I Know Why the Caged Bird Sings* by Maya Angelou. Copyright © 1969 by Maya Angelou. Reprinted by permission of Random House, Inc.

continued on page 794

ISBN: 0-673-29453-6

Copyright © 1997
Scott, Foresman and Company, Glenview, Illinois
All Rights Reserved. Printed in the United States of America.

http://www.sf.aw.com

5 6 7 8 9 10 DR 03 02 01 00 99

Senior Consultants

Alan C. Purves
Professor of Education and Humanities, State University of New York at Albany; Director of the Center for Writing and Literacy. Dr. Purves developed the concept and philosophy of the literature lessons for the series, consulted with editors, reviewed tables of contents and lesson manuscript, wrote the Assessment Handbooks, and oversaw the development and writing of the series testing strand.

Carol Booth Olson
Director, California Writing Project, Department of Education, University of California, Irvine. Dr. Olson conceptualized and developed the integrated writing strand of the program, consulted with editors, led a team of teachers in creating literature-based Writing Workshops, and reviewed final manuscript.

Carlos E. Cortés
Professor Emeritus, History, University of California, Riverside. Dr. Cortés designed and developed the multiculturalism strand embedded in each unit of the series and consulted with grade-level editors to implement the concepts.

Judith A. Brough
Chair, Department of Education; Professor of Education; Supervisor of Student Teachers; Gettysburg College, Gettysburg.

Edward N. Brazee
Associate Professor of Education, University of Maine. Founder and Director, Middle Level Education Institute; Founder and Executive Director, Maine Association for Middle Level Education.

Drs. Brough and Brazee advised on middle school philosophy, the needs of the middle school student, and requirements of the middle school curriculum. In addition they reviewed selections, tables of contents, and lessons and developed prototypes and outlines for all middle school unit projects.

Series Consultants

Visual and Media Literacy/Speaking and Listening/Critical Thinking
Harold M. Foster. Professor of English Education and Secondary Education, The University of Akron, Akron. Dr. Foster developed and wrote the Beyond Print features for all levels of the series.

ESL and LEP Strategies
James Cummins. Professor, Modern Language Centre and Curriculum Department, Ontario Institute for Studies in Education, Toronto.

Lily Wong Fillmore. Professor, Graduate School of Education, University of California at Berkeley.

Drs. Cummins and Fillmore advised on the needs of ESL and LEP students, helped develop the Building English Proficiency model for the program, and reviewed strategies and manuscript.

Life Skills/Personal Development
David J. DePalma. Partner, Life Skills Consultants; developmental psychologist.

Charlotte Wright DePalma. Partner, Life Skills Consultants; former high school and university teacher.

Andrea Donnellan White. Partner, Life Skills Consultants; former elementary school teacher.

W. Brent White. Partner, Life Skills Consultants; former middle school teacher.

The Whites and DePalmas conceptualized the Life Skills sequence for the program and wrote pupil book activities as well as the Life Skills book for each middle school grade.

Reviewers and Contributors

Pupil Edition/Teacher Edition
Valerie Aksoy, El Dorado Intermediate School, Concord, California   Sylvia Alchediak, Burney Simmons Elementary School, Plant City, Florida   Doris Ash, Dolan Middle School, Stamford, Connecticut   Camille Barnett, Pioneer Middle School, Cooper City, Florida   Beverly Bradley, W. Mack Lyon Middle School, Overton, Nevada   Candice Bush, O'Callaghan Middle School, Las Vegas, Nevada   Colleen Fleming, Charles Shaw Middle School, Gorham, Maine   Philip Freemer, Hall High School, West Hartford, Connecticut   Ellen Golden, Hammocks Middle School, Miami, Florida   Anita Hartgraves, Martin Middle School, Corpus Christi, Texas   Lea Heyer, Burney Simmons Elementary School, Plant City, Florida   Linda Holland, Medinah Middle School, Roselle, Illinois   Mary Howard, Valley Center Middle School, Valley Center, California   Kathy Jesson, Hammocks Middle School, Miami, Florida   Christina Kenny, Hill Middle School, Long Beach, California   Kathy Knowles, Alamo Junior High School, Midland, Texas   J. Chris Leonard, Southridge Middle School, Fontana, California   Sandra Litogot, O.E. Dunckel Middle School, Farmington Hills, Michigan   Sue Mack, Gregory

CONTENTS

MODEL FOR ACTIVE READING AND DISCUSSION

Marjorie Kinnan Rawlings   A Mother in Mannville ◆ short story   xxii

UNIT 1

CHANGE

THEME OVERVIEW   2

PART ONE: WHY IS THIS HAPPENING TO ME?

Literature

Gloria Gonzalez	6	Viva New Jersey ◆ short story
	16	**WRITING MINI-LESSON** Setting Up Your Working Portfolio
Gary Paulsen	18	Stop the Sun ◆ short story
Luci Tapahonso	27	The Dust Will Settle ◆ poem
Shel Silverstein	28	Forgotten Language ◆ poem
Yoshiko Uchida	31	Prisoner of My Country ◆ autobiography
Gwendolyn Brooks	39	Home ◆ short story
Kurt Vonnegut, Jr.	45	The Kid Nobody Could Handle ◆ short story

Integrated Studies

	56	**INTERDISCIPLINARY STUDY** High Jumpers
		Ben Carson: A Man of Action by Patricia Sellers ◆ sociology
		Jumping the Hurdles ◆ mathematics
		Be Your Own Cheerleader ◆ psychology
	62	**READING MINI-LESSON** Using Comparison and Contrast

PART TWO: THE MANY FACES OF CHANGE

Literature

Ellen Conford   65   Liverwurst and Roses ◆ short story

Russell Freedman   78   A President's Wife ◆ biography

Eleanor Roosevelt   82   from The Autobiography of Eleanor Roosevelt ◆ autobiography

   86   LANGUAGE MINI-LESSON   Commonly Misspelled Words

May Swenson   88   Fable for When There's No Way Out ◆ poem

Georgia Douglas Johnson   89   Your World ◆ poem

Rod Serling   93   Back There ◆ play

Exploring the Theme through American Folklore

Michael J. Caduto and Joseph Bruchac   107   The Passing of the Buffalo ◆ Kiowa folk tale

Integrated Studies

109   INTERDISCIPLINARY STUDY   Trailblazers
Survival of the Stronghearted by Anna Howard Shaw ◆ U.S. history
A New Life on the Frontier ◆ U.S. history

114   READING MINI-LESSON   Visualizing

115   WRITING WORKSHOP   Narrative Writing
Assignment   Traveling Through Time
Revising Strategy   Writing Realistic Dialogue
Editing Strategy   Correct Format for a Play

121   BEYOND PRINT   Technology Skills
Electronic Research

122   LOOKING BACK
Projects for Collaborative Study
Read More About Change

UNIT **2**

CHALLENGES

THEME OVERVIEW   **126**

PART ONE: SEARCHING FOR THE REAL YOU

Literature

Jean Little	130	Who You Are ◆ interior monologue
Gary Soto	135	The Mechanical Mind ◆ short story
William Saroyan	142	The Parsley Garden ◆ short story
	150	WRITING MINI-LESSON Showing, Not Telling
Maya Angelou	152	from I Know Why the Caged Bird Sings ◆ autobiography
Diane Mei Lin Mark	162	Rice and Rose Bowl Blues ◆ poem
Lillian Morrison	163	The Sidewalk Racer ◆ poem
Julio Noboa Polanco	164	Identity ◆ poem

Integrated Studies   167   INTERDISCIPLINARY STUDY   Brainstorms
Corn Flake Kings: The Kellogg Brothers by Meredith Hooper ◆
U.S. history/health
19th-Century U.S. Inventions ◆ U.S. history
Now You Invent a Cereal! ◆ health

173   READING MINI-LESSON   Main Idea and Supporting Details

PART TWO: OUTSIDE FORCES

Literature

Jack London	176	To Build a Fire ◆ short story
	192	LANGUAGE MINI-LESSON Placement of Modifiers
James Berry	194	The Banana Tree ◆ short story
Dionne Brand	201	Hurricane ◆ poem
Ann Petry	205	from Harriet Tubman ◆ biography
Anonymous	213	Go Down, Moses ◆ traditional song

Exploring the Theme through American Folklore

Irwin Shapiro	217	Strong but Quirky: The Birth of Davy Crockett ◆ North American tall tale
Judith Ortiz Cofer	220	Aunty Misery ◆ Puerto Rican folk tale

Integrated Studies

224	INTERDISCIPLINARY STUDY Forces of Destruction
How Does a Hurricane Develop? by Howard Smith ◆ earth science
Hurricanes ◆ earth science
228	READING MINI-LESSON Taking Notes and Outlining
229	WRITING WORKSHOP Expository Writing
Assignment   Characters Inside and Out
Revising Strategy   Writing Focused Paragraphs
Editing Strategy   Clear Pronoun Reference
235	BEYOND PRINT Visual Literacy
Images of You
236	LOOKING BACK
Projects for Collaborative Study
Read More About Challenges

UNIT 3

CONFLICT

THEME OVERVIEW   **240**

PART ONE: MOMENTS OF TRUTH

Literature

Gish Jen	244	The White Umbrella ◆ short story
Langston Hughes	254	Thank You, Ma'am ◆ short story
	260	**WRITING MINI-LESSON** Point of View
Edgar Allan Poe	262	The Tell-Tale Heart ◆ short story
James D. Houston	270	Elegy Written at the County Junkyard ◆ essay
Julia Alvarez	274	Dusting ◆ poem

Exploring the Theme through American Folklore

Virginia Hamilton	278	He Lion, Bruh Bear, and Bruh Rabbit ◆ African American folk tale

| **Integrated Studies** | 284 | **INTERDISCIPLINARY STUDY**   Reformers
Jacob Riis: Exposing the Truth ◆ photography
Jane Addams by Deborah Gore Ohrn ◆ U.S. history |
| | 289 | **READING MINI-LESSON**   Varying Your Reading Rate |

Part Two: Things Are Not As They Seem

Literature

Gayle Pearson	292	At the Avenue Eatery ◆ short story
	300	LANGUAGE MINI-LESSON Subject-Verb Agreement
Bruce Brooks	302	Animal Craftsmen ◆ essay
Deloras Lane	309	Keepsakes ◆ poem
Alice Walker	310	Without Commercials ◆ poem
Jacqueline Balcells	315	The Enchanted Raisin ◆ short story

Integrated Studies

324 **INTERDISCIPLINARY STUDY**   Deceiving to the Eye
Camouflage: The Big Cover-Up by Mary Batten ◆ life science
Patterns in Nature ◆ life science
What Is a Tessellation? ◆ mathematics

330 **READING MINI-LESSON**   Classifying Ideas

331 **WRITING WORKSHOP**   Narrative Writing
Assignment   Examining Points of View
Revising Strategy   Using Transitional Devices
Editing Strategy   Confusing Adjectives with Adverbs

337 **BEYOND PRINT**   Critical Thinking
Living with Commercials

338 **LOOKING BACK**   Projects for Collaborative Study
Read More About Conflict

UNIT 4

RELATIONSHIPS

THEME OVERVIEW   **342**

PART ONE: WORKING THINGS OUT

Literature

Judie Angell	346	Dear Marsha ◆ short story
Walter Dean Myers	362	The Treasure of Lemon Brown ◆ short story
Phillip Hoose	374	Beni Seballos ◆ biography
William Carlos Williams	382	This Is Just to Say ◆ poem
Kenneth Koch	383	Variations on a Theme by William Carlos Williams ◆ poem
	386	WRITING MINI-LESSON Maintaining Your Working Portfolio

Exploring the Theme through American Folklore

Zora Neale Hurston	388	How the Snake Got Poison ◆ African American folk tale
Gayle Ross	390	Strawberries ◆ Cherokee legend
Carl Sandburg	392	Primer Lesson ◆ poem

Integrated Studies

Integrated Studies	395	INTERDISCIPLINARY STUDY In Harmony In Balance with Nature by Vine Deloria, Jr. ◆ anthropology Native American Spirituality ◆ art
	401	READING MINI-LESSON Generalizing

PART TWO: APPRECIATING EACH OTHER

Literature

Merrill Markoe   404   Greeting Disorder ◆ play

Rosalie Moore   406   Catalogue ◆ poem

Robert Cormier   410   The Moustache ◆ short story

420   **LANGUAGE MINI-LESSON**   Punctuating for Clarity

Carol Saline   422   Coretta and Edythe: The Scott Sisters ◆ letters

Robert Frost   429   A Time to Talk ◆ poem

Teresa Palomo Acosta   430   My Mother Pieced Quilts ◆ poem

Virginia Driving
Hawk Sneve   435   The Medicine Bag ◆ short story

Gerald Haslam   446   The Horned Toad ◆ short story

Integrated Studies

456   **INTERDISCIPLINARY STUDY**   Generations Together
They Won't Let Me Grow Up by Lauren Tarshis ◆ psychology
Search for Your "Roots": Interviewing Your Grandparents
by Ann Elwood and Carol Orsag ◆ history

462   **READING MINI-LESSON**   Recalling Details

463   **WRITING WORKSHOP**   Expository Writing
Assignment   Letter of Thanks
Revising Strategy   Sentence Variety
Editing Strategy   Form for a Friendly Letter

469   **BEYOND PRINT**   Effective Listening
Feel Like You're Talking to a Wall?

470   **LOOKING BACK**
Projects for Collaborative Study
Read More About Relationships

UNIT 5

*J*USTICE

THEME OVERVIEW   474

PART ONE: LIFE'S NOT ALWAYS FAIR

Literature

Ophelia Rivas	479	Indians ◆ poem
Nereida Román	480	Inequalities ◆ essay
Judith Ortiz Cofer	481	The Changeling/Transformación ◆ poems
Daniel Keyes	485	Flowers for Algernon ◆ short story
	516	LANGUAGE MINI-LESSON Sentence Conciseness

Exploring the Theme through American Folklore

Rudolfo A. Anaya	518	The Boy and His Grandfather ◆ Mexican American folk tale
Dell J. McCormick	522	Paul Bunyan Digs the St. Lawrence River ◆ North American tall tale
Anonymous	524	John Henry ◆ American folk ballad

Integrated Studies

	528	INTERDISCIPLINARY STUDY All Work, No Play
		Mother Jones Seeks Justice for the Mill Children by Penny Colman ◆ U.S. history
		Too Much Work = Poor Grades by Rahul Jacob ◆ sociology
		Child Labor and Rules of Reason ◆ sociology
	534	READING MINI-LESSON Distinguishing Between Fact and Opinion

PART TWO: THE TRIUMPH OF THE SPIRIT

Literature

Frances Goodrich and
Albert Hackett   538   **The Diary of Anne Frank** ◆ play

611   **WRITING MINI-LESSON**   Summarizing Information

Integrated Studies

612   **INTERDISCIPLINARY STUDY**   Unshackled
A Spirit Unshackled by Frederick Douglass ◆ U.S. history
Music, Art, Crafts ◆ fine arts
Kin by James S. Kunen ◆ sociology

618   **READING MINI-LESSON**   Using Cause-and-Effect Relationships

619   **WRITING WORKSHOP**   Narrative Writing
Assignment   Research Report
Revising Strategy   Vivid Language and Imagery
Editing Strategy   Works Cited

625   **BEYOND PRINT**   Media Literacy
Designing a Scale Model of a Set

626   **LOOKING BACK**
Projects for Collaborative Study
Read More About Justice

UNIT 6

JOURNEYS

THEME OVERVIEW   630

PART ONE: REACHING FOR YOUR DREAM

Literature

Esmeralda Santiago	634	A Shot at It ◆ autobiography
	645	LANGUAGE MINI-LESSON Checking Your Spelling
Emma Lazarus	648	The New Colossus ◆ poem
Wing Tek Lum	648	Chinese Hot Pot ◆ poem
Langston Hughes	650	Dreams ◆ poem
Langston Hughes	650	The Dream Keeper ◆ poem
Langston Hughes	650	I, Too ◆ poem
Naomi Shihab Nye	652	My Father and the Figtree ◆ poem
Abraham Lincoln	656	The Gettysburg Address ◆ speech
Walt Whitman	657	O Captain! My Captain! ◆ poem
Ved Mehta	661	from Sound-Shadows of the New World ◆ autobiography

Integrated Studies

672	INTERDISCIPLINARY STUDY School Days Frontier Students ◆ U.S. history Frontier Schools by Russell Freedman ◆ U.S. history Frontier Trivia ◆ mathematics
678	READING MINI-LESSON Using Graphic Aids

PART TWO: DECISIVE JOURNEYS

Literature

Washington Irving   681   **Rip Van Winkle ◆ play** (dramatized by Adele Thane)

Henry Wadsworth
Longfellow   695   **Paul Revere's Ride ◆ poem**

Arthur C. Clarke   702   **"If I Forget Thee, Oh Earth . . ." ◆ short story**

May Swenson   707   **Orbiter 5 Shows How Earth Looks from the Moon
◆ poem**

Exploring the Theme through American Folklore

Donna Rosenberg   711   **The Creation of Music ◆ Aztec myth**

716   WRITING MINI-LESSON   Preparing Your Presentation Portfolio

Paul Yee   718   **Spirits of the Railway ◆ Chinese American folk tale**

Li-Young Lee   723   **I Ask My Mother to Sing ◆ poem**

Integrated Studies

726   INTERDISCIPLINARY STUDY   Polar Journeys
Follow Your Dreams by Louise Tolle Huffman ◆ history
Six Across Antarctica by Will Steger ◆ history
A New Global Outlook by Michael Woods ◆ earth science
The North and South Poles ◆ geography

732   READING MINI-LESSON   Understanding Sequence

733   WRITING WORKSHOP   Descriptive Writing
Assignment   Exploring Personal Changes
Revising Strategy   Active and Passive Voice
Editing Strategy   Comparative Forms of Adjectives and Adverbs

739   BEYOND PRINT   Effective Speaking
Esmeralda Santiago on Television

740   LOOKING BACK
Projects for Collaborative Study
Read More About Journeys

GLOSSARIES, HANDBOOKS, AND INDEXES

Understanding Fiction 744
Understanding Nonfiction 746
Understanding Poetry 748
Understanding Drama 750
Glossary of Literary Terms..........752
Glossary of Vocabulary Words 756
Language and Grammar Handbook 765
Index of Skills and Strategies....................783
Index of Fine Art and Artists....................790
Index of Authors and Titles 792
Text Acknowledgments 794
Illustration Acknowledgments 796

GENRE OVERVIEW

Short Stories

A Mother in Mannville xxv
Viva New Jersey 6
Stop the Sun 18
Home 39
The Kid Nobody Could Handle 45
Liverwurst and Roses..............................65
The Mechanical Mind 135
The Parsley Garden 142
To Build a Fire.................................176
The Banana Tree.................................194
The White Umbrella 244
Thank You, Ma'am.................................254
The Tell-Tale Heart.................................262
At the Avenue Eatery.................................292
The Enchanted Raisin 315

Dear Marsha.................................346
The Treasure of Lemon Brown 362
The Moustache.................................410
The Medicine Bag 435
The Horned Toad.................................446
Flowers for Algernon 485
If I Forget Thee, Oh Earth.................................702

Nonfiction

Prisoner of My Country 31
A President's Wife 78
from The Autobiography of
    Eleanor Roosevelt.................................82
Who You Are.................................130
from I Know Why the Caged Bird Sings 152
from Harriet Tubman.................................205
Elegy Written at the County Junkyard 270
Animal Craftsmen.................................302
Beni Seballos.................................374
Coretta and Edythe: The Scott Sisters 422
Inequalities.................................480
A Shot at It 634
The Gettysburg Address 656
from Sound-Shadows of the
    New World 661

Poetry

The Dust Will Settle.................................27
Forgotten Language 28
Fable for When There's No Way Out............88
Your World 89
Rice and Rose Bowl Blues.................................162
The Sidewalk Racer.................................163
Identity.................................164
Hurricane 201
Go Down, Moses.................................213
Dusting 274
Keepsakes.................................309
Without Commercials.................................310

This Is Just to Say 382

Variations on a Theme by William
    Carlos Williams 383

Primer Lesson 392

Catalogue 406

A Time to Talk..............................429

My Mother Pieced Quilts...............430

Indians 479

The Changling/Transformación 481

John Henry 524

The New Colossus 648

Chinese Hot Pot 648

Dreams 650

The Dream Keeper 650

I, Too...650

My Father and the Figtree.............652

Oh Captain! My Captain!...............657

Paul Revere's Ride 695

Orbiter 5 Shows How Earth Looks from
    the Moon..............................707

I Ask My Mother to Sing 723

Drama

Back There 93

Greeting Disorder 404

The Diary of Anne Frank................538

Rip Van Winkle 681

Folklore

The Passing of the Buffalo 107

Strong but Quirky: The Birth of
    Davy Crockett 217

Aunty Misery................................220

He Lion, Bruh Bear, and Bruh Rabbit..........278

How the Snake Got Poison 388

Strawberries 390

The Boy and His Grandfather 518

Paul Bunyan Digs the
    St. Lawrence River................522

John Henry 524

The Creation of Music 711

Spirits of the Railway....................718

FEATURE OVERVIEW

Interdisciplinary Studies

High Jumpers 56

Trailblazers..................................109

Brainstorms 167

Forces of Destruction 224

Reformers 284

Deceiving to the Eye 324

In Harmony 395

Generations Together 456

All Work, No Play...........................528

Unshackled..................................612

School Days 672

Polar Journeys.............................726

Reading Mini-Lessons

Using Comparison and Contrast.................62

Visualizing...................................114

Main Idea and Supporting Details.............173

Taking Notes and Outlining 228

Varying Your Reading Rate.............289

Classifying Ideas 330

Generalizing.................................401

Recalling Details 462

Distinguishing Between Fact
    and Opinion 534

Using Cause-and-Effect Relationships 618

Using Graphic Aids 678

Understanding Sequence 732

Writing Mini-Lessons

Setting Up Your Working Portfolio 16

Showing, Not Telling......................150

Point of View 260

Maintaining Your Working Portfolio 386
Summarizing Information 611
Preparing Your Presentation Portfolio 716

Language Mini-Lessons

Commonly Misspelled Words........................86
Placement of Modifiers 192
Subject-Verb Agreement 300
Punctuating for Clarity.................................420
Sentence Conciseness.................................516
Checking Your Spelling 645

Writing Workshops

Indicates workshops found in the Unit Resource Books—Teacher's Resource File

Guide to Your School (Expository) ....*
Traveling Through Time (Narrative)..............115
A Symbol of Yourself (Descriptive)...................*
Characters Inside and Out (Expository) 229
The Rest of the Story (Narrative).....................*
Examining Points of View (Narrative) 331
Describing a Conflict (Descriptive)...................*
Letter of Thanks (Expository) 463
Problems and Solutions (Persuasive) ....*
Research Report (Narrative) 619
Catalogue of Dreams (Descriptive) ....*
Exploring Personal Changes
    (Descriptive) 733

Beyond Print

Electronic Research (Technology Skills)......121
Images of You (Visual Literacy) 235
Living with Commercials
    (Critical Thinking) 337
Feel Like You're Talking to a Wall?
    (Effective Listening).............................469
Designing a Scale Model of a Set
    (Media Literacy) 625
Esmeralda Santiago on Television
    (Effective Speaking) 739

Model for Active Reading

Good readers tend to read actively. They jump right in, getting involved, picturing the action, and reacting to the characters or ideas. They question, evaluate, predict, and in other ways think about the story or article they are reading. These three eighth-grade students agreed to let us in on their thoughts as they read "A Mother in Mannville." You might not have the same questions or ideas that they did about this story. However, their ways of responding will give you ideas for how *you* can get actively engaged as you read literature.

BEN KIM Well, I like playing all sorts of sports . . . anything . . . baseball, soccer, football. I like to read science fiction books.

RICHARD SAMAYOA Mostly I like to read magazines about science and stuff like that—technical things about different countries, volcanoes and earthquakes, that kind of thing. I like tackle football and soccer.

Matthew Stanislawski I like music computers. I like listening to music. I like to read a lot—mostly science fiction novels. I like to play basketball, football, baseball.

Six Reading Strategies

Following are some of the techniques that good readers use, often without being aware of them.

Question Ask questions that come to mind as you read.

Example: What is the narrator doing at this orphanage? What kind of work does she do? What is she writing?

Clarify Clear up confusion and answer questions.

Example: Oh, I see what's going on. This woman is staying in a cabin near this orphanage for a short time, to write—a book or something.

Summarize Review what has happened so far.

Example: The woman is becoming good friends with Jerry. He doesn't just chop wood for her. He stays to talk with her every day, and he takes care of her dog when she's away.

Predict Use what has happened so far to make reasonable guesses about what might happen next.

Example: The narrator and the boy seem to really like each other. Maybe she'll decide to adopt him.

Evaluate Use your common sense and evidence in the selection to arrive at sound opinions and valid conclusions.

Example: This boy seems very humble. I don't think he's gotten much love or attention so far in his life.

Connect Compare the text with something in your own experience, with another text, or with ideas within the text.

Example: I know how relaxing it is to sit by a fire and stare into the flames. If I was sitting by the fireplace with a friend, *I* would feel like confiding secrets too.

▲ *Albert's Son,* painted by Andrew Wyeth in 1959, is a portrait of a boy Wyeth knew whose mother had recently died and whose father was planning to send him to an orphanage. The boy stands at the barn door, his face to the sun, his back to the darkness and barred window. What do you think he is feeling?

A Mother in MANNVILLE

Marjorie Kinnan Rawlings

The orphanage is high in the Carolina mountains. Sometimes in winter the snowdrifts are so deep that the institution is cut off from the village below, from all the world. Fog hides the mountain peaks, the snow swirls down the valleys, and a wind blows so bitterly that the orphanage boys who take the milk twice daily to the baby cottage reach the door with fingers stiff in an agony of numbness.

"Or when we carry trays from the cookhouse for the ones that are sick," Jerry said, "we get our faces frostbit, because we can't put our hands over them. I have gloves," he added. "Some of the boys don't have any."

He liked the late spring, he said. The rhododendron was in bloom, a carpet of color, across the mountainsides, soft as the May winds that stirred the hemlocks. He called it laurel.

"It's pretty when the laurel blooms," he said. "Some of it's pink and some of it's white."

I was there in autumn. I wanted quiet, isolation, to do some troublesome writing. I wanted mountain air to blow out the malaria from too long a time in the subtropics. I was homesick, too, for the

RICHARD What is going on here? Who is Jerry? What is this story about? (question)

RICHARD This kid seems weird. Most people don't like to sit quietly and watch things. (evaluate; connect)

flaming of maples in October, and for corn shocks and pumpkins and black-walnut trees and the lift of hills. I found them all, living in a cabin that belonged to the orphanage, half a mile beyond the orphanage farm. When I took the cabin, I asked for a boy or man to come and chop wood for the fireplace. The first few days were warm, I found what wood I needed about the cabin, no one came, and I forgot the order.

I looked up from my typewriter one late afternoon, a little startled. A boy stood at the door, and my pointer dog, my companion, was at his side and had not barked to warn me. The boy was probably twelve years old, but undersized. He wore overalls and a torn shirt, and was barefooted.

He said, "I can chop some wood today."

I said, "But I have a boy coming from the orphanage."

"I'm the boy."

"You? But you're small."

"Size don't matter, chopping wood," he said. "Some of the big boys don't chop good. I've been chopping wood at the orphanage a long time."

I visualized mangled and inadequate branches for my fires. I was well into my work and not inclined to conversation. I was a little blunt.

"Very well. There's the ax. Go ahead and see what you can do."

I went back to work, closing the door. At first the sound of the boy dragging brush annoyed me. Then he began to chop. The blows were rhythmic and steady, and shortly I had forgotten him, the sound no more of an interruption than a consistent rain. I suppose an hour and a half passed, for when I stopped and stretched, and heard the boy's steps on the cabin stoop, the sun was dropping behind the farthest mountain, and the valleys were purple with something deeper than the asters.

The boy said, "I have to go to supper now. I can come again tomorrow evening."

I said, "I'll pay you now for what you've done," thinking I should probably have to insist on an older boy. "Ten cents an hour?"

"Anything is all right."

We went together back of the cabin. An astonishing amount of solid wood had been cut. There were cherry logs and heavy roots of rhododendron, and blocks from the waste pine and oak left from the building of the cabin.

"But you've done as much as a man," I said. "This is a splendid pile."

I looked at him, actually, for the first time. His hair was the color of the corn shocks, and his eyes, very direct, were like the

RICHARD She thought he was weak—stereotyping. (evaluate)

MATTHEW She doesn't fully trust him, but it's not important enough to think about. (clarify)

BEN "Go ahead and see what you can do." She talks as if she doesn't believe he could do it. (clarify)

BEN "Anything is all right." Shows honesty. (evaluate)

BEN She compliments him. (clarify)

mountain sky when rain is pending—gray, with a showing of that miraculous blue. As I spoke a light sun had touched him with the same suffused glory with which it touched the mountains. I gave him a quarter.

"You may come tomorrow," I said, "and thank you very much."

He looked at me, and at the coin, and seemed to want to speak, but could not, and turned away.

"I'll split the kindling tomorrow," he said over his thin ragged shoulder. "You'll need kindling and medium wood and logs and backlogs."

MATTHEW The boy seems very humble at this point. (evaluate)

At daylight I was half awakened by the sound of chopping. Again it was so even in texture that I went back to sleep. When I left my bed in the cool morning, the boy had come and gone, and a stack of kindling was neat against the cabin wall. He came again after school in the afternoon and worked until time to return to the orphanage. His name was Jerry; he was twelve years old, and he had been at the orphanage since he was four. I could picture him at four, with the same gray-blue eyes and the same—independence? No, the word that comes to me is "integrity."

MATTHEW It looks like she is starting to care about him. (summarize)

The word means something very special to me, and the quality for which I use it is a rare one. My father had it—there is another of whom I am almost sure—but almost no man of my acquaintance possesses it with the clarity, the purity, the simplicity of a mountain stream. But the boy Jerry had it. It is bedded on courage, but it is more than brave. It is honest, but it is more than honesty. The ax handle broke one day. Jerry said the woodshop at the orphanage would repair it. I brought money to pay for the job and he refused it.

"I'll pay for it," he said. "I broke it. I brought the ax down careless."

"But no one hits accurately every time," I told him. "The fault was in the wood of the handle. I'll see the man from whom I bought it."

BEN This shows integrity. (clarify)

It was only then that he would take the money. He was standing back of his own carelessness. He was a free-will agent and he chose to do careful work, and if he failed, he took the responsibility without subterfuge.

And he did for me the unnecessary thing, the gracious thing, that we find done only by the great of heart. Things no training can teach, for they are done on the instant, with no predicated experience. He found a cubbyhole beside the fireplace that I had not noticed. There, of his own accord, he put kindling and "medium" wood, so that I might always have dry fire material ready in case of sudden wet weather. A stone was loose in the

MATTHEW He doesn't want her to have to pay for what he thinks he's responsible for. (clarify)

rough walk to the cabin. He dug a deeper hole and steadied it, although he came, himself, by a short cut over the bank. I found that when I tried to return his thoughtfulness with such things as candy and apples, he was wordless. "Thank you" was, perhaps, an expression for which he had had no use, for his courtesy was instinctive. He only looked at the gift and at me, and a curtain lifted, so that I saw deep into the clear well of his eyes, and gratitude was there, and affection, soft over the firm granite of his character.

He made simple excuses to come and sit with me. I could no more have turned him away than if he had been physically hungry. I suggested once that the best time for us to visit was just before supper, when I left off my writing. After that, he waited always until my typewriter had been some time quiet. One day I worked until nearly dark. I went outside the cabin, having forgotten him. I saw him going up over the hill in the twilight toward the orphanage. When I sat down on my stoop, a place was warm from his body where he had been sitting.

He became intimate, of course, with my pointer, Pat. There is a strange communion between a boy and a dog. Perhaps they possess the same singleness of spirit, the same kind of wisdom. It is difficult to explain, but it exists. When I went across the state for a weekend I left the dog in Jerry's charge. I gave him the dog whistle and the key to the cabin, and left sufficient food. He was to come two or three times a day and let out the dog, and feed and exercise him. I should return Sunday night, and Jerry would take out the dog for the last time Sunday afternoon and then leave the key under an agreed hiding place.

My return was belated and fog filled the mountain passes so treacherously that I dared not drive at night. The fog held the next morning, and it was Monday noon before I reached the cabin. The dog had been fed and cared for that morning. Jerry came early in the afternoon, anxious.

"The superintendent said nobody would drive in the fog," he said. "I came just before bedtime last night and you hadn't come. So I brought Pat some of my breakfast this morning. I wouldn't have let anything happen to him."

"I was sure of that. I didn't worry."

"When I heard about the fog, I thought you'd know."

He was needed for work at the orphanage and he had to return at once. I gave him a dollar in payment, and he looked at it and went away. But that night he came in darkness and knocked at the door.

RICHARD He needs to talk to someone. It's like him talking to his mother. (evaluate)

RICHARD "There is a strange communion between a boy and a dog." I don't think that's true. I don't like dogs. They bark all the time. They make too much noise. (connect)

RICHARD He needs a companion. The dog is a companion. (evaluate)

BEN He could be lonely during that time, so he makes friends with the dog. (evaluate)

MATTHEW Worried that, now that he's really working for her, she might think he's responsible for more than chopping wood. (evaluate)

"Come in, Jerry," I said, "if you're allowed to be away this late."

"I told maybe a story," he said. "I told them I thought you would want to see me."

"That's true," I assured him, and I saw his relief. "I want to hear about how you managed with the dog."

He sat by the fire with me, with no other light, and told me of their two days together. The dog lay close to him, and found a comfort there that I did not have for him. And it seemed to me that being with my dog, and caring for him, had brought the boy and me, too, together, so that he felt that he belonged to me as well as to the animal.

"He stayed right with me," he told me, "except when he ran in the laurel. He likes the laurel. I took him up over the hill and we both ran fast. There was a place where the grass was high and I lay down in it and hid. I could hear Pat hunting for me. He found my trail and he barked. When he found me, he acted crazy, and he ran around and around me, in circles."

We watched the flames.

"That's an apple log," he said. "It burns the prettiest of any wood."

We were very close.

He was suddenly impelled to speak of things he had not spoken of before, nor had I cared to ask him.

"You look a little bit like my mother," he said. "Especially in the dark, by the fire."

"But you were only four, Jerry, when you came here. You have remembered how she looked, all these years?"

"My mother lives in Mannville," he said.

For a moment, finding that he had a mother shocked me as greatly as anything in my life has ever done, and I did not know why it disturbed me. Then I understood my distress. I was filled with a passionate resentment that any woman should go away and leave her son. A fresh anger added itself. A son like this one—The orphanage was a wholesome place, the executives were kind, good people, the food was more than adequate, the boys were healthy, a ragged shirt was no hardship, nor the doing of clean labor. Granted, perhaps, that the boy felt no lack, what about the mother? At four he would have looked the same as now. Nothing, I thought, nothing in life could change those eyes. His quality must be apparent to an idiot, a fool. I burned with questions I could not ask. In any, I was afraid, there would be pain.

"Have you seen her, Jerry—lately?"

"I see her every summer. She sends for me."

I wanted to cry out. "Why are you not with her? How can she let you go away again?"

MATTHEW Maternal instinct really shows here. (evaluate)

BEN She's shocked. (clarify)

RICHARD She really cares—she is real angry about this mother. (clarify)

He said, "She comes up here from Mannville whenever she can. She doesn't have a job now."

His face shone in the firelight.

"She wanted to give me a puppy, but they can't let any one boy keep a puppy. You remember the suit I had on last Sunday?" He was plainly proud. "She sent me that for Christmas. The Christmas before that"—he drew a long breath, savoring the memory—"she sent me a pair of skates."

"Roller skates?"

My mind was busy, making pictures of her, trying to understand her. She had not, then, entirely deserted or forgotten him. But why, then—I thought, "But I must not condemn her without knowing."

"Roller skates. I let the other boys use them. They're always borrowing them. But they're careful of them."

What circumstance other than poverty—

"I'm going to take the dollar you gave me for taking care of Pat," he said, "and buy her a pair of gloves."

I could only say, "That will be nice. Do you know her size?"

"I think it's eight and a half," he said.

He looked at my hands.

"Do you wear eight and a half?" he asked.

"No. I wear a smaller size, a six."

"Oh! Then I guess her hands are bigger than yours."

I hated her. Poverty or no, there was other food than bread, and the soul could starve as quickly as the body. He was taking his dollar to buy gloves for her big stupid hands, and she lived away from him, in Mannville, and contented herself with sending him skates.

"She likes white gloves," he said. "Do you think I can get them for a dollar?"

"I think so," I said.

I decided that I should not leave the mountains without seeing her and knowing for myself why she had done this thing.

The human mind scatters its interests as though made of thistledown, and every wind stirs and moves it. I finished my work. It did not please me, and I gave my thoughts to another field. I should need some Mexican material.

I made arrangements to close my Florida place. Mexico immediately, and doing the writing there, if conditions were favorable. Then, Alaska with my brother. After that, heaven knew what or where.

I did not take time to go to Mannville to see Jerry's mother, nor even to talk with the orphanage officials about her. I was a

RICHARD Who cares about her size? (question)

BEN I think that's pointless. But it describes the woman. You could imagine how tall or short she is. (clarify)

trifle abstracted about the boy, because of my work and plans. And after my first fury at her—we did not speak of her again—his having a mother, any sort at all, not far away, in Mannville, relieved me of the ache I had had about him. He did not question the anomalous relation. He was not lonely. It was none of my concern.

MATTHEW She feels less responsible for him now, knowing he has a mother. (summarize)

He came every day and cut my wood and did small helpful favors and stayed to talk. The days had become cold, and often I let him come inside the cabin. He would lie on the floor in front of the fire, with one arm across the pointer, and they would both doze and wait quietly for me. Other days they ran with a common ecstasy through the laurel, and since the asters were now gone, he brought me back vermilion maple leaves, and chestnut boughs dripping with imperial yellow. I was ready to go.

I said to him, "You have been my good friend, Jerry. I shall often think of you and miss you. Pat will miss you too. I am leaving tomorrow."

He did not answer. When he went away, I remember that a new moon hung over the mountains, and I watched him go in silence up the hill. I expected him the next day, but he did not come. The details of packing my personal belongings, loading my car, arranging the bed over the seat, where the dog would ride, occupied me until late in the day. I closed the cabin and started the car, noticing that the sun was in the west and I should do well to be out of the mountains by nightfall. I stopped by the orphanage and left the cabin key and money for my light bill with Miss Clark.

"And will you call Jerry for me to say goodbye to him?"

"I don't know where he is," she said. "I'm afraid he's not well. He didn't eat his dinner this noon. One of the boys saw him going over the hill into the laurel. He was supposed to fire the boiler this afternoon. It's not like him, he's unusually reliable."

BEN Where is he? Maybe he ran away. (predict)

I was almost relieved, for I knew I should never see him again, and it would be easier not to say goodbye to him.

I said, "I wanted to talk with you about his mother—why he's here—but I'm in more of a hurry than I expected to be. It's out of the question for me to see her now. But here's some money I'd like to leave with you to buy things for him at Christmas and on his birthday. It will be better than for me to try to send him things. I could so easily duplicate—skates, for instance."

She blinked her honest spinster's eyes.

"There's not much use for skates here," she said.

Her stupidity annoyed me.

"What I mean," I said, "is that I don't want to duplicate things his mother sends him. I might have chosen skates if I didn't know she had already given them to him."

"I don't understand," she said. "He has no mother. He has no skates."

BEN Oh, here's the realization. He has no mother. How does she feel now? (summarize; question)

Discussion After Reading

Once they've finished a selection, active readers reflect and respond in a variety of ways. Following are these students' personal reactions and literary responses to "A Mother in Mannville," along with the connections they make to their own experiences. After a general discussion, they answer the kinds of questions that you will find following the other selections in this book.

General Comments

RICHARD At the beginning of the story I really didn't understand what they were talking about. (question)

BEN Yes, it was really hard to understand what the theme of the story was at the beginning. But when you get into the story more it explains what the problem is. (clarify)

MATTHEW Even though it started abruptly, as it went on it got more understandable. Basically it was interesting from the beginning. I liked the part about how she didn't really trust him and she underestimated him. (summarize)

MATTHEW My impression of the boy was he was hard-working, humble, and honest, even in the situation he was in, at an orphanage. (evaluate)

BEN He didn't complain or anything. He's honest, wholesome, he can be trusted. The main part is trust. (evaluate)

MATTHEW I think the reason he lied about having a mother is that, since he knew the narrator cared about him, he didn't want her to worry. (clarify)

BEN That was really actually a good lie, in a way. (evaluate)

RICHARD You can't really blame the kid. Everyone wants to have a mother, and everyone wants to be able to say that I have all these things, all this nice stuff, and he really doesn't have anything. (connect)

RICHARD The ending was too short. I wanted to read more. (evaluate)

BEN If there was a little more you'd feel better. (evaluate)

RICHARD The narrator—she really cared. She got really angry when she thought he had a mother. (clarify)

BEN At the end, she acted like she really cared about Jerry—that's why she was mad. (clarify)

MATTHEW She really seemed to have a strong maternal instinct toward him. (evaluate)

What would you like to say to the narrator at the end of the story?

RICHARD I'd tell her to look for the kid, not just leave—because he just ran off somewhere. The way she feels, she's going to want to know something about him, where he is.

MATTHEW I'd like to say that she really cared about him so much. She should take responsibility for him, maybe even adopt him.

BEN I'd like to ask how she felt, if she thought about whatever happened after this ending. She's going to feel different. It would be nice to know if he's all right.

Do you think the story Jerry tells makes him more a person of integrity, or less so? Explain.

MATTHEW I think his intentions were good, but the result wasn't what he planned. He wanted her not to worry about him. I think he's selfless.

RICHARD He just really didn't want to hurt her feelings. Maybe he didn't want to be asked many questions. So I think he's still honest most of the time.

BEN He's still helpful and trusting.

What message do you think this story has for anyone who wants to help abandoned or orphaned children?

BEN I think the message is somebody can help even if it's so small. Orphans need to be loved, cared for by someone.

RICHARD You would feel a lot better helping someone, if you had the chance. People always need someone to be loved by. They need to do something, help someone. That was the only one he had, so he went to her and helped her out.

MATTHEW It's about taking responsibility for someone. A child like this really would need a parent to care for him, to love him.

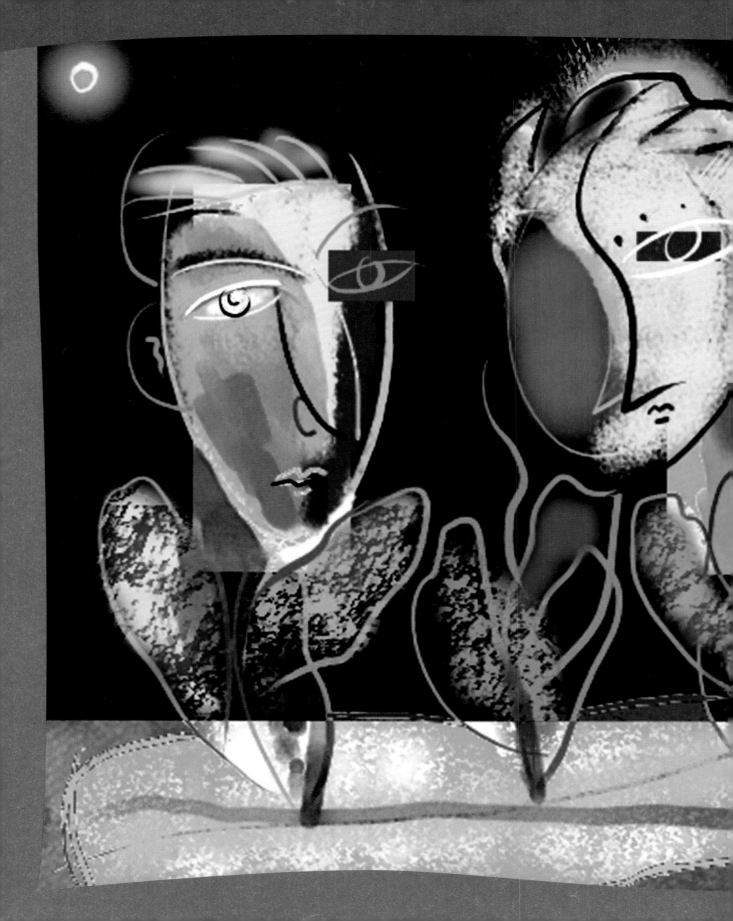

Change

Why Is This Happening to Me?
Part One, pages 4–62

The Many Faces of Change
Part Two, pages 63–123

Talking About
CHANGE

Change is unavoidable. It happens every day, and it is part of the condition of being human. Change happens in the environment, in the political leadership of countries throughout the world, and in our personal lives. Sometimes change is for the good, but other times it is difficult to handle.

Young people from across the country talk about what change means to them. Match their comments with the quotations from the literature you will read.

"Change to me is moving to a new home or a new school."

Nicholas – Houston, TX

The teenager, tall and slight of build with long dark hair that reached down her spine, was uncomfortable among her new classmates, most of whom she towered over.

from "Viva New Jersey" by Gloria Gonzalez, page 8

"People our age would probably enjoy this theme, because our lives are going through serious changes, and we could see how others cope with changes."

Su – San Francisco, CA

Childhood lingered in his features, but when he paused to rest, his fingers went hopefully to the silky beginnings of sideburns and a mustache.

from "The Kid Nobody Could Handle" by Kurt Vonnegut, page 46

"Change happens every day, and you can't stop it."

Gabe – St. Louis, MO

Through the rest of the night in the rain in the paddy, I thought I could do it. I could stop the dawn.

from "Stop the Sun" by Gary Paulsen, page 22

"Change is good when it is for the better. Unfortunately, it's not always for the better."

Melissa – Rochester, MN

What had been wanted was this always, this always to last, the talking softly on this porch....

from "Home" by Gwendolyn Brooks, page 39

Part One

Why Is This Happening to Me?

Sometimes events occur that are out of your control. You might wonder, "Why is this happening to me?" or "What did I do to cause this?" Realizing that you are not at fault for these events is all a part of growing up. Sometimes things just happen. Despite this fact, there are ways you can respond to improve any situation.

Multicultural Connection **Change** may involve dealing with the new experiences that occur when you move from one cultural situation into another. Such cultural changes force you to react, and in the process you yourself may change! As you read the following selections, ask yourself: What changes do the characters in these selections face, and how do they deal with them?

Literature

Gloria Gonzalez   **Viva New Jersey** ◆ short story 6

     Writing Mini-Lesson ◆ Setting Up Your Working Portfolio 16

Gary Paulsen   **Stop the Sun** ◆ short story 18

Luci Tapahonso   **The Dust Will Settle** ◆ poem 27

Shel Silverstein   **Forgotten Language** ◆ poem 28

Yoshiko Uchida   **Prisoner of My Country** ◆ autobiography 31

Gwendolyn Brooks   **Home** ◆ short story 39

Kurt Vonnegut, Jr.   **The Kid Nobody Could Handle** ◆ short story 45

Interdisciplinary Study   High Jumpers

Ben Carson: A Man of Action by Patricia Sellers ◆ sociology 56

Jumping the Hurdles ◆ mathematics 59

Be Your Own Cheerleader ◆ psychology 60

     Reading Mini-Lesson ◆ Using Comparison and Contrast 62

Before Reading

Viva New Jersey

by Gloria Gonzalez

Gloria Gonzalez
born 1940

Gloria Gonzalez grew up in New York City and lived for many years in West New York, New Jersey, where "Viva New Jersey" takes place. Her father is from the Canary Islands in Spain, and she grew up speaking Spanish at home. She began her writing career as a newspaper reporter, before turning to play writing. She enjoys writing plays, she says, because of the immediate feedback. Her plays, one of which was named one of the Best Short Plays of 1976, have been produced in the United States and Europe. In addition, Gonzalez has written novels for teenagers as well as adults.

Building Background

The Cuban Connection As you can see from the map, Cuba is an island about ninety miles south of Florida. In 1959 Fidel Castro took power and many Cubans who did not agree with his politics left. In recent years, more people have left Cuba by boat, seeking a better life in the U.S. Some of those who managed to survive the difficult journey stayed with other Cubans in Florida. Others moved north to the New York City area. In both places there were large Cuban communities where people could help each other find shelter and jobs.

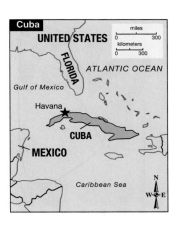

Getting into the Story

Writer's Notebook The story "Viva New Jersey" is about a girl who has just arrived in the U.S. from Cuba. It is the first selection in a unit called "Change." In your notebook, write about what changes you think must be happening to the main character in this story. You may want to draw on your own experiences— maybe you've changed schools, moved to a new town, or perhaps you've been to a party where you didn't know anyone.

Reading Tip

Predicting Good readers tend to **predict** what will happen next in a story. To do so, they must pay attention to events and details in the story and use this information to predict what will happen next. Read the first three paragraphs of the story. Then write down what you think will happen. Support your ideas by explaining what information you used to make your predictions.

Viva New Jersey

Gloria Gonzalez

As far as dogs go, it wasn't much of a prize—a hairy mongrel[1] with clumps of bubble gum wadded on its belly. Pieces of multicolored hard candies were matted in its fur. The leash around its neck was fashioned from a cloth belt, the kind usually seen attached to old bathrobes. The dog's paws were clogged with mud from yesterday's rain, and you could see where the animal had gnawed at the irritated skin around the swollen pads.

The dog was tied to an anemic tree high above the cliffs overlooking the Hudson River and the majestic New York City skyline.

Lucinda traveled the route each day on her way to the high school, along the New Jersey side of the river. The short walk saddened her, despite its panoramic vista of bridges and skyscrapers, for the river reminded her of the perilous[2] journey six months earlier, when she and her family had escaped from Cuba in a makeshift boat with seven others.

They had spent two freezing nights adrift[3] in the ocean, uncertain of their destination, till a U.S. Coast Guard cutter towed them to the shores of Key West.

From there they wound their way north, staying temporarily with friends in Miami and finally settling in West New York, New Jersey, the most densely populated town in the United States. Barely a square mile, high above the Palisades, the town boasted a population

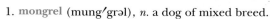

---

1. mongrel (mung′grəl), *n.* a dog of mixed breed.
2. perilous (per′ə ləs), *adj.* dangerous.
3. adrift (ə drift′), *adj.* floating without direction.

An untitled painting by Romare Bearden, done in the 1930s, shows a city neighborhood much like Lucinda's. What cultural **changes** would Lucinda face in moving from the Cuban countryside to a large U.S. city?

of 85,000. Most of the community was housed in mammoth apartment buildings that seemed to reach into the clouds. The few private homes had cement lawns and paved driveways where there should have been backyards.

Lucinda longed for the spacious front porch where she'd sat at night with her friends while her grandmother bustled about the house, humming her Spanish songs. Lucinda would ride her bike to school and sometimes not see a soul for miles, just wild flowers amid a forest of greenery.

Now it was cement and cars and trucks and motorcycles and clanging fire engines that seemed to be in constant motion, shattering the air with their menacing roar.

Lucinda longed painfully for her grandmother. The old woman had refused to leave her house in Cuba, despite the family's pleas, so she had remained behind, promising to see them again one day.

The teenager, tall and slight of build with long dark hair that reached down her spine, was uncomfortable among her new classmates, most of whom she towered over. Even though the majority of them spoke Spanish and came from Cuba, Argentina, and Costa Rica, they were not like any of her friends back home. These "American" girls wore heavy makeup to school, dressed in jeans and high heels, and talked about rock singers and TV stars that she knew nothing of. They all seemed to be busy, rushing through the school corridors, huddling in laughing groups, mingling freely with boys, and chatting openly with teachers as if they were personal friends.

It was all too confusing.

Things weren't much better at home. Her parents had found jobs almost immediately and were often away from the tiny, cramped apartment. Her brother quickly made friends and was picked for the school baseball team, traveling to nearby towns to compete.

All Lucinda had were her memories—and now this dog, whom she untied from the tree. The animal was frightened and growled at her when she approached, but she spoke softly and offered a soothing hand, which he tried to attack. Lucinda persisted, and the dog, perhaps grateful to be freed from the mud puddles, allowed her to lead him away.

She didn't know what she was going to do with him now that she had him. Pets were not allowed in her building, and her family could be evicted.[4] She couldn't worry about that now. Her main concern was to get him out of the cold.

Even though it was April and supposedly spring, the weather had yet to top fifty degrees. At night she slept under two blankets, wearing warm socks over her cold feet. Another night outdoors, and the dog could freeze to death.

Lucinda reached her building and comforted the dog, "I'm not going to hurt you." She took off her jacket and wrapped it quickly around the animal, hoping to disguise it as a bundle under her arm. "Don't make any noise," she begged.

She waited till a woman with a baby stroller exited the building and quickly dashed inside, unseen. She opted not to take the elevator, fearful of running into someone, and instead lugged the dog and her schoolbag up the eight flights of stairs.

Lucinda quickly unlocked the apartment door and plopped the dog on her bed. The animal instantly shook its hair free and ran in circles atop her blanket.

"Don't get too comfortable," Lucinda cautioned. "You can't stay."

She dashed to the kitchen and returned moments later with a bowl of water and a plate of leftover chicken and yellow rice.

---

4. **evict** (i vikt′), *v.* remove from a building by legal means.

The dog bolted from the bed and began attacking the food before she even placed it on the floor. The girl sat on the edge of the bed and watched contentedly as he devoured[5] the meal.

"How long has it been since you've eaten?"

The dog swallowed the food hungrily, not bothering to chew, and quickly lapped up the water.

It was then, with the dog's head lowered to the bowl, that Lucinda spotted the small piece of paper wedged[6] beneath the belt around its neck. She slid it out carefully and saw the word that someone had scrawled with a pencil.

"Chauncey. Is that your name?"

The dog leaped to her side and nuzzled its nose against her arm.

"It's a crazy name, but I think I like it." She smiled. Outside the window, eight stories below, two fire engines pierced the afternoon with wailing sirens. Lucinda didn't seem to notice as she stroked the animal gently.

Working quickly, before her parents were due to arrive, she filled the bathtub with water and soap detergent and scrubbed the animal clean. The dog didn't enjoy it—he kept trying to jump out— so Lucinda began humming a Spanish song her grandmother used to sing to her when she was little. It didn't work. Chauncey still fought to get free.

Once the animal was bathed, Lucinda attacked the clumps of hair with a scissor and picked out the sticky globs of candy.

"You're white!" Lucinda discovered. While using her brother's hair blower, she ran a quick comb through the fur, which now was silvery and tan with faint traces[7] of black. "You're beautiful." The girl beamed.

The dog seemed to agree. It picked up its head proudly and flicked its long ears with pride.

Lucinda hugged him close. "I'll find you a good home. I promise," she told the animal.

Knowing that her parents would arrive any moment, Lucinda gathered up the dog, covering him with her coat, and carried him down nine flights to the basement. She crept quietly past the superintendent's apartment and deposited the animal in a tiny room behind the bank of washing machines.

The room, the size of a small closet, contained all the electrical levers that supplied power to the apartments and the elevator.

Chauncey looked about, confused. He jumped up as if he knew he was about to be abandoned again. His white hairy paw came dangerously close to hitting the protruding, red master switch near the door.

Lucinda knelt to the animal. "I'll be back. Promise."

She closed the door behind her, praying the dog wouldn't bark, and hurried away. An outline of a plan was taking shape in her mind.

Ashley.

The girl sat in front of her in English and always went out of her way to say hi. She didn't seem to hang out with the other kids, and whenever they passed in the corridor, she was alone. But what really made her even more appealing was that she lived in a real house. Just a block away. Lucinda had seen her once going in. Maybe Ashley would take Chauncey.

Lucinda's parents arrived from work, and she quickly helped her mother prepare the scrumptious fried bananas. Her father had stopped at a restaurant on his way home and brought a *cantina* of food—white rice, black

"Don't get too comfortable," Lucinda cautioned. "You can't stay."

---

5. **devour** (di vour′), *v.* eat very hungrily.

6. **wedge** (wej), *v.* squeeze.

7. **trace** (trās), *n.* very small amount; a little bit.

beans, avocado salad, and meat stew. Each food was placed in its own metal container and clipped together like a small pyramid. The local restaurant would have delivered the food to the house each day, if the family desired, but Lucinda's father always liked to stop by and check the menu. The restaurant also made fried bananas, but Lucinda's mother didn't think they were as tasty as her own. One of the nice surprises of moving to New Jersey was discovering that the Latin restaurants supplied *cantina* service.

"How was school today?" her mother asked.

"Okay," Lucinda replied.

The dinner conversation drifted, as it always did, to Mama's problems at work with the supervisor and Papa's frustration with his job. Every day he had to ride two buses and a subway to get to work, which he saw as wasted hours.

"You get an education, go to college," Lucinda's father sermonized for the thousandth time, "and you can work anywhere you like—even in your own house, if you want. Like a doctor! And if it is far away, you hire someone like me, with no education, to drive you."

Lucinda had grown up hearing the lecture. Perhaps she would have been a good student anyway, for she certainly took to it with enthusiasm. She had discovered books at a young age. School only heightened her love of reading, for its library supplied her with an endless source of material. She excelled in her studies and won top honors in English class. She was so proficient at learning the English language that she served as a tutor to kids in lower grades.

Despite her father's wishes, Lucinda had no intention of becoming a doctor or lawyer. She wasn't sure what she would do—the future seemed far too distant to address it—but she knew somehow it would involve music

and dance and magnificent costumes and glittering shoes and plumes in her hair.

They were talking about her brother's upcoming baseball game when suddenly all the lights in the apartment went out.

"*¡Qué pasó!*"[8] her father exclaimed.

Agitated[9] voices could be heard from the outside hallway. A neighbor banged on the door, shouting. "Call the fire department! Someone's trapped in the elevator!"

Groups of tenants[10] mingled outside their apartments, some carrying candles and flashlights. The building had been pitched into darkness.

"We'll get you out!" someone shouted to the woman caught between floors.

Lucinda cried: "Chauncey!"

He must've hit the master switch. She could hear the distant wail of the fire engines and knew it was only a matter of minutes before they checked the room where the dog was hidden.

"I'll be right back!" Lucinda yelled to her mother as she raced out the door. Groping onto the banister, she felt her way down the flights of steps as people with candles hurried to escape.

The rescuers reached the basement before she did. Two firemen were huddled in the doorway checking the power supply. Lucinda looked frantically for the dog, but he was gone.

> ### "Call the fire department! Someone's trapped in the elevator!"

---

8. *¡Qué pasó!* (kä pä sō′), Spanish for "What happened?"
9. agitated (aj′ə tāt əd), *adj.* disturbed, upset.
10. tenant (ten′ənt), *n.* person who rents the place where he or she lives.

Señorita #1 was painted by Diana Ong, a contemporary Chinese American artist. How did the artist create a lively, happy mood? ➤

She raced out into the nippy night, through the throng of people crowded on the sidewalk, and searched for the dog. She was afraid to look in the street, expecting to see his lifeless body, the victim of a car.

Lucinda looked up at the sound of her name. Her mother was calling to her from the window.

"Come home! What are you doing?"

The girl shouted, "In a minute!" The crowd swelled about her as she quickly darted away.

Lucinda didn't plan it, but she found herself in front of Ashley's house minutes later. She was on the sidewalk, with the rest of her neighbors, gazing up the block at the commotion in front of Lucinda's building.

"Hi," Lucinda stammered.

Ashley took a moment to place the face and then returned the smile. "Hi."

Lucinda looked about nervously, wondering if any of the adults belonged to Ashley's family. She didn't have a moment to waste.

"What happens," she blurted out, "when a dog runs away? Do the police catch it?"

The blond, chubby teenager, with light green eyes and glasses with pink frames, shrugged. "Probably. If they do, they only take it to the pound."

"What's that?" It sounded bad, whatever it was.

"A shelter. Where they keep animals. If nobody claims 'em, they kill 'em."

Lucinda started to cry. She couldn't help it. It came upon her suddenly. Greatly embarrassed, she turned quickly and hurried away.

"Wait up!" The blonde hurried after her. "Hey!"

Lucinda stopped, too ashamed to meet her eyes.

"Did you lose your dog?" Ashley's voice sounded concerned.

Lucinda nodded.

"Well, let's go find him," Ashley prodded.

They searched the surrounding neighborhood and checked underneath all the cars parked in the area in case he was hiding. They searched basements and rooftops. When all else failed, they walked to the park along the river, where Lucinda pointed out the tree where she had found him.

The girls decided to sit on a nearby bench in case Chauncey reappeared, though they realized there was little hope.

Lucinda knew her mother would be frantically worried.

"She probably has the police looking for me," she told Ashley.

"You've only been gone an hour."

"It's the first time I've left the house, except to go to school, since we moved here," she revealed.

It was a beautiful night, despite the cold tingling breeze that swept up from the river. The New York skyline was ablaze with golden windows silhouetted against dark, boxlike steel structures. You could make out the red traffic lights along the narrow streets. A long, thin barge sailed down the river like a rubbery snake.

Lucinda learned that Ashley's mother was a lawyer, often away from home for long periods, and her father operated a small business in New York's Chinatown, which kept him busy seven days a week. An only child, she spent her time studying and writing letters.

"Who do you write to?" Lucinda asked.

"My grandmother, mostly. She lives in Nevada. I spend the summers with her."

Lucinda told her how lucky she was to be able to see her grandmother. She felt dangerously close to tears again and quickly changed the subject. "I never see you with any friends in school. Why?"

Ashley shrugged. "Guess I'm not the friendly type. Most of the girls are only interested in boys and dates. I intend to be a famous writer one day, so there's a lot of books I have to read. Just so I know what's been done."

It made sense.

"What are you going to be?"

Lucinda admitted she had no ambition.[11] No particular desire. But maybe, if she had her choice, if she could be anything she wanted, it would probably be a dancer.

"My grandmother used to take me to her friend's house who used to be a famous ballerina in Cuba. She'd let me try on her costumes, and she'd play the records and teach me the steps. It hurt my feet something awful. Hers used to bleed when she first started, but she said it got easier after the first year."

Ashley told her, "You have the body for it. I bet you'd make a wonderful dancer."

When it became apparent that Chauncey would never return, the girls walked home together.

Despite all that had happened, Lucinda found herself sad to have the evening end. For the first time since leaving her homeland, she felt somewhat at peace with herself. She now had someone to talk to. Someone who understood. Someone who carried her own pain.

"Wanna have lunch tomorrow?" Ashley asked her. "I usually run home and eat in front of the television. I'm a great cook. My first book is going to be filled with exotic recipes of all the countries I plan to visit. And if you want," she gushed excitedly, "after school we can go to the library. You can get out a book on how to be a ballerina."

Lucinda agreed immediately, "That would be wonderful!"

The girls parted on the sidewalk and Lucinda raced home where her irate father and weeping mother confronted her angrily.

"Where have you been! I was only going to wait five more minutes and then I was calling the police! Where were you?"

Before she could stammer a reply, the lights went out.

"Not again!" her mother shrieked.

Lucinda's heart throbbed with excitement. Chauncey was back!

She ran out of the apartment, unmindful of the darkness, with her mother's screams in the air: "Come back here!"

This time Lucinda made it to the basement before the firemen, and she led her pal safely out the building. She reached Ashley's doorstep just as the first fire engine turned the corner.

For the first time since leaving her homeland, she felt somewhat at peace with herself.

_____

11. ambition (am bish′ən), *n.* desire to rise to a high position.

After Reading

Making Connections

1. Draw two lines in your notebook, with a 1 on the left and a 5 on the right:

1	2	3	4	5		1	2	3	4	5

A "1" means "not at all" and a "5" means "very much." Now, for the first line, circle how much you identified with Lucinda at the beginning of the story, just before Lucinda hid the dog. For the second line, circle how much you identified with Lucinda at the end of the story. Did your answers change? Explain why you circled the number you chose for the second line.

2. Look at the predictions you made before reading the story. Were they correct? Or were you surprised by how things turned out?

3. The **theme** for this group of selections is "Why Is This Happening to Me?" Why does "Viva New Jersey" belong to this group?

4. Lucinda experienced many cultural **changes** in her move from Cuba to the United States. What seemed to you to be the most difficult change for her? Is there a way in which finding the dog helped her cope with this change?

5. Reread what Lucinda had to say about the other girls in her school. How do you think they would describe her?

6. Lucinda made friends with Ashley because she was worried about the dog. What are some other ways that a stranger can make friends in a new school?

7. Lucinda's father said that when you get an education you can work where you like. Why do you think he said this? Do you agree?

Literary Focus: Plot

The **plot** is the organization of events in a story. In almost every story, characters make decisions that affect what will happen next. Look through the story to find some decisions Lucinda made and decide how they affected the plot of the story. Then use a chart like the one started below to organize your ideas.

Character	Decision the Character Made	How it Affected the Story
Lucinda	untied the dog	

Vocabulary Study

perilous
adrift
agitated
ambition
devour
evict
mongrel
tenant
trace
wedge

On a separate sheet of paper, write the word from the list that best fits each blank below.

A. There was tension in the apartment building. A __(1)__ in the building was angry. A young girl feared that he would get the other residents __(2)__ . One person, a tall man with a __(3)__ of silver in his black hair, called a meeting. "These are __(4)__ and dangerous times!" he shouted, "and the landlord will not help us! When we ask for better locks on our doors and better lighting in the parking lots, he threatens to __(5)__ us! Well, we won't take it! We have dreams! We have plans! We have __(6)__ ! And we will make this building safe for our families!"

B. The poor __(7)__ was cold and wet. He had been __(8)__ on a raft for three days. Suddenly, he felt the raft bang into something. He watched the raft __(9)__ itself between two rocks at the end of a beach. Slowly, he wobbled off the raft and onto the rocks. He saw a nest with some eggs in it, which he proceeded to __(10)__ in a second. Then he rested on the beach.

Expressing Your Ideas _____

Writing Choices

A Letter to Grandmother Pretend you are Lucinda. Write a **letter** to your grandmother in Cuba, describing your school and your family life in New Jersey.

So What Happened Next? Write a **continuation of the story** "Viva New Jersey." What happened at school the next day? Did Ashley and Lucinda become friends? What about Chauncey?

Be a Teacher In small groups, pool your knowledge about dog care. Call or interview a veterinarian if necessary. Then write a set of **directions** for Ashley, giving her detailed instructions on how to take care of a dog. Explain to her how to feed him and to understand what he may need in terms of walks, baths, medical attention, and affection.

Other Options

Recipes from Afar Ashley says that her first book will be "filled with exotic recipes." Alone or with a group, collect recipes from different countries and produce your own **recipe book.** Perhaps you could include information, pictures, a folk tale, or a song about the country.

Mutt Makeover Go back to the story and find descriptions of the dog. Then use this information to draw **before and after pictures** of the dog. The first picture will be Chauncey when Lucinda first discovered him. The second picture will be Chauncey after his bath.

Brick or Stucco? Use your imagination as well as information from the story to draw a **diagram** of Lucinda's building. Be sure to include the basement.

Writing Mini-Lesson

Setting Up Your Working Portfolio

What Is a Working Portfolio? A working portfolio is a collection of the writing you've done throughout the school year. Think of your working portfolio as a road map. It can show you and others where you've been and where you're heading as a writer as you continue through school. Later in the year, you'll create a presentation portfolio to display your best writing.

What to Keep in Your Working Portfolio

- Working drafts of your writing, including lists, charts, other planning pieces, and first drafts

- Final drafts of your writing, including pieces that have been revised and edited as a record of your completed work

- Other completed assignments that are not pieces of writing, such as videotapes or audiotapes

- Self-evaluations in which you examine ways you've improved and ways you can still improve as a writer

- Reflections in which you consider how the writing you've done has helped you to grow as a student and as a person

How to Get Started

Start by setting some writing goals. Find out from your teacher what the course goals are for the first grading period. Then, get together with a group of students and discuss how you plan to meet those goals. Where do you think you need to work the hardest? Write a statement of goals to post at the front of your portfolio. Then decide what to use for your working portfolio. You might try a three-ring binder, an expandable folder, or a report folder. You, your group, or your teacher might have other ideas.

Finally, create a cover for your portfolio. You could draw it, use a photograph, or make a collage. In planning your cover illustration, think about how to show who you are as a person and as a writer. Consider the cover illustration a working draft as well, as you may decide to change it later in the year.

Before Reading

Stop the Sun

by Gary Paulsen

Gary Paulsen
born 1939

Gary Paulsen could be called a "jack of all trades." He has been a teacher, soldier, actor, farmer, truck driver, professional archer, singer, and sailor. He has even competed in the Iditarod—the grueling, annual Alaskan dog-sled race run over 1,000 miles of rugged, snow-covered terrain. Today, he spends much of his time writing. A popular author of young adult novels, Paulsen has won the prestigious Newbery Honor for three of his books, *Dog Song, Hatchet,* and *The Winter Room.*

Building Background

Good-bye Vietnam The Vietnam War (1957–1975) took place in Vietnam, a country in Southeast Asia. Its battles were mainly fought in thick jungles, where it was easy for the well-hidden enemy to strike with little or no warning. American soldiers were not trained to fight in this way, and the constant tension of this type of warfare took its toll on many of them. When the soldiers returned home after their tour of duty, some found that the moments of terror could not be forgotten. They began to have *flashbacks*—that is, vivid moments when memories of the war returned and seemed to be happening again. Sometimes these flashbacks develop into a serious mental condition called *post-traumatic syndrome.*

Getting into the Story

Discussion Many doctors believe that it is good for a person to talk about his or her problems. There are many kinds of therapy (treatment) that rely on talking to make a person well. As a class, discuss how you think talking about a problem may, or may not, help a person feel better and resolve his or her problems.

Reading Tip

Character Development Characters grow and change as things happen in the story. This is called **character development**. After you've read the first few pages of the story, take a moment to jot down some words in your notebook that describe Terry, his father, and his mother. Use a chart like the one below. Explain why you chose those words. Then, at the end, review your list of words. Are there any you want to add or delete? Did the characters change?

Terry	Father	Mother
persistent		

Gary Paulsen

Terry Erickson was a tall boy, 13, starting to fill out with muscle but still a little awkward. He was on the edge of being a good athlete, which meant a lot to him. He felt it coming too slowly, though, and that bothered him.

But what bothered him even more was when his father's eyes went away.

Usually it happened when it didn't cause any particular trouble. Sometimes during a meal his father's fork would stop halfway to his mouth, just stop, and there would be a long pause while the eyes went away, far away.

After several minutes his mother would reach over and take the fork and put it gently down on his plate, and they would go back to eating—or try to go back to eating—normally.

They knew what caused it. When it first started, Terry had asked his mother in private what it was, what was causing the strange behavior.

"It's from the war," his mother had said. "The doctors at the veterans'[1] hospital call it the Vietnam syndrome."[2]

"Will it go away?"

"They don't know. Sometimes it goes away. Sometimes it doesn't. They are trying to help him."

"But what happened? What actually caused it?"

"I told you. Vietnam."

"But there had to be something," Terry persisted. "Something made him like that. Not just Vietnam. Billy's father was there, and he doesn't act that way."

"That's enough questions," his mother said sternly. "He doesn't talk about it, and I don't ask. Neither will you. Do you understand?"

"But, Mom."

"That's enough."

And he stopped pushing it. But it bothered him whenever it happened. When something bothered him, he liked to stay with it until he understood it, and he understood no part of this.

Words. His father had trouble, and they gave him words like Vietnam syndrome. He knew almost nothing of the war, and when he tried to find out about it, he kept hitting walls. Once he went to the school library and asked

---

1. **veteran** (vet′ər ən), *n.* person who has served in the armed forces.
2. **syndrome** (sin′drōm), *n.* a group of symptoms considered together to be characteristic of a particular disease or condition.

A *Hard Listening* was painted in 1994 by Richard Dana. What type of mood has the artist created? Does the painting reflect the feelings of the father or the son?

for anything they might have that could help him understand the war and how it affected his father. They gave him a dry history that described French involvement, Communist involvement, American involvement. But it told him nothing of the war. It was all numbers, cold numbers, and nothing of what had *happened*. There just didn't seem to be anything that could help him.

Another time he stayed after class and tried to talk to Mr. Carlson, who taught history. But some part of Terry was embarrassed. He didn't want to say why he wanted to know about Vietnam, so he couldn't be specific.

"What do you want to know about Vietnam, Terry?" Mr. Carlson had asked. "It was a big war."

Terry had looked at him, and something had started up in his mind, but he didn't let it out. He shrugged. "I just want to know what it was like. I know somebody who was in it."

"A friend?"

"Yessir. A good friend."

Mr. Carlson had studied him, looking into his eyes, but didn't ask any other questions. Instead he mentioned a couple of books Terry had not seen. They turned out to be pretty good. They told about how it felt to be in combat. Still, he couldn't make his father be one of the men he read about.

And it may have gone on and on like that, with Terry never really knowing any more about it except that his father's eyes started going away more and more often. It might have just gone the rest of his life that way except for the shopping mall.

It was easily the most embarrassing thing that ever happened to him.

PREDICT: What do you think will happen to Terry at the shopping mall?

It started as a normal shopping trip. His father had to go to the hardware store, and he asked Terry to go along.

When they got to the mall they split up. His father went to the hardware store, Terry to a record store to look at albums.

Terry browsed[3] so long that he was late meeting his father at the mall's front door. But his father wasn't there, and Terry looked out to the car to make sure it was still in the parking lot. It was, and he supposed his father had just gotten busy, so he waited.

Still his father didn't come, and he was about to go to the hardware store to find him when he noticed the commotion.[4] Or not a commotion so much as a sudden movement of people.

Later, he thought of it and couldn't remember when the feeling first came to him that there was something wrong. The people were moving toward the hardware store and that might have been what made Terry suspicious.

There was a crowd blocking the entry to the store, and he couldn't see what they were looking at. Some of them were laughing small, nervous laughs that made no sense.

Terry squeezed through the crowd until he got near the front. At first he saw nothing unusual. There were still some people in front of him, so he pushed a crack between them. Then he saw it: His father was squirming along the floor on his stomach. He was crying,

looking terrified, his breath coming in short, hot pants like some kind of hurt animal.

It burned into Terry's mind, the picture of his father down on the floor. It burned in and in, and he wanted to walk away, but something made his feet move forward. He knelt next to his father and helped the owner of the store get him up on his feet. His father didn't speak at all but continued to make little whimpering sounds, and they led him back into the owner's office and put him in a chair. Then Terry called his mother and she came in a taxi to take them home. Waiting, Terry sat in a chair next to his father, looking at the floor, wanting only for the earth to open and let him drop in a deep hole. He wanted to disappear.

Words. They gave him words like Vietnam syndrome, and his father was crawling through a hardware store on his stomach.

When the embarrassment became so bad that he would cross the street when he saw his father coming, when it ate into him as he went to sleep, Terry realized he had to do something. He had to know this thing, had to understand what was wrong with his father.

When it came, it was simple enough at the start. It had taken some courage, more than Terry thought he could find. His father was sitting in the kitchen at the table and his mother had gone shopping. Terry wanted it that way; he wanted his father alone. His mother seemed to try to protect him, as if his father could break.

Terry got a soda out of the refrigerator and popped it open. As an afterthought, he handed it to his father and got another for himself. Then he sat at the table.

His father smiled. "You look serious."

"Well . . ."

It went nowhere for a moment, and Terry was just about to drop it altogether. It may be

---

3. browse (brouz), *v.* look at casually.
4. commotion (kə mō′shən), *n.* bustle or confusion.

the wrong time, he thought, but there might never be a better one. He tightened his back, took a sip of pop.

"I was wondering if we could talk about something, Dad," Terry said.

His father shrugged. "We already did the bit about girls. Some time ago, as I remember it."

"No. Not that." It was a standing joke between them. When his father finally got around to explaining things to him, they'd already covered it in school. "It's something else."

"Something pretty heavy, judging by your face."

"Yes."

"Well?"

I still can't do it, Terry thought. Things are bad, but maybe not as bad as they could get. I can still drop this thing.

"Vietnam," Terry blurted out. And he thought, there, it's out. It's out and gone.

"No!" his father said sharply. It was as if he had been struck a blow. A body blow.

"But, Dad."

"No. That's another part of my life. A bad part. A rotten part. It was before I met your mother, long before you. It has nothing to do with this family, nothing. No."

So, Terry thought, so I tried. But it wasn't over yet. It wasn't started yet.

"It just seems to bother you so much," Terry said, "and I thought if I could help or maybe understand it better. . . ." His words ran until he foundered,[5] until he could say no more. He looked at the table, then out the window. It was all wrong to bring it up, he thought. I blew it. I blew it all up. "I'm sorry."

But now his father didn't hear him. Now his father's eyes were gone again, and a shaft of something horrible went through Terry's heart as he thought he had done this thing to his father, caused his eyes to go away.

"You can't know," his father said after a time. "You can't know this thing."

Terry said nothing. He felt he had said too much.

"This thing that you want to know—there is so much of it that you cannot know it all, and to know only a part is . . . is too awful. I can't tell you. I can't tell anybody what it was really like."

It was more than he'd ever said about Vietnam, and his voice was breaking. Terry hated himself and felt he would hate himself until he was an old man. In one second he had caused such ruin. And all because he had been embarrassed. What difference did it make? Now he had done this, and he wanted to hide, to leave. But he sat, waiting, knowing that it wasn't done.

EVALUATE: Do you think it was a mistake for Terry to ask his father about Vietnam?

His father looked to him, through him, somewhere into and out of Terry. He wasn't in the kitchen anymore. He wasn't in the house. He was back in the green places, back in the hot places, the wet-hot places.

"You think that because I act strange, that we can talk and it will be all right," his father said. "That we can talk and it will just go away. That's what you think, isn't it?"

Terry started to shake his head, but he knew it wasn't expected.

"That's what the shrinks say," his father continued. "The psychiatrists tell me that if I talk about it, the whole thing will go away. But they don't know. They weren't there. You weren't there. Nobody was there but me and some other dead people, and they can't talk because they couldn't stop the morning."

Terry pushed his soda can back and forth, looking down, frightened at what was happening. *The other dead people,* he'd said,

---

5. founder (foun′dər), *v.* fail.

as if he were dead as well. *Couldn't stop the morning.*

"I don't understand, Dad."

"No. You don't." His voice hardened, then softened again, and broke at the edges. "But see, see how it was. . . ." He trailed off, and Terry thought he was done. His father looked back down to the table, at the can of soda he hadn't touched, at the tablecloth, at his hands, which were folded, inert on the table.

"We were crossing a rice paddy[6] in the dark," he said, and suddenly his voice flowed like a river breaking loose. "We were crossing the paddy, and it was dark, still dark, so black you couldn't see the end of your nose. There was a light rain, a mist, and I was thinking that during the next break I would whisper and tell Petey Kressler how nice the rain felt, but of course I didn't know there wouldn't be a Petey Kressler."

He took a deep, ragged breath. At that moment Terry felt his brain swirl, a kind of whirlpool pulling, and he felt the darkness and the light rain because it was in his father's eyes, in his voice.

"So we were crossing the paddy, and it was a straight sweep, and then we caught it. We began taking fire from three sides, automatic weapons, and everybody went down and tried to get low, but we couldn't. We couldn't get low enough. We could never get low enough, and you could hear the rounds hitting people. It was just a short time before they brought in the mortars and we should have moved, should have run, but nobody got up, and after a time nobody *could* get up. The fire just kept coming and coming, and then incoming mortars, and I heard screams as they hit, but there was nothing to do. Nothing to do."

"Dad?" Terry said. He thought, maybe I can stop him. Maybe I can stop him before . . . before it gets to be too much. Before he breaks.

"Mortars," his father went on, "I hated mortars. You just heard them *wump* as they fired, and you didn't know where they would hit, and you always felt like they would hit your back. They swept back and forth with the mortars, and the automatic weapons kept coming in, and there was no radio, no way to call for artillery. Just the dark to hide in. So I crawled to the side and found Jackson, only he wasn't there, just part of his body, the top part, and I hid under it and waited, and waited, and waited.

"Finally the firing quit. But see, see how it was in the dark with nobody alive but me? I yelled once, but that brought fire again, so I shut up, and there was nothing, not even the screams."

His father cried, and Terry tried to understand, and he thought he could feel part of it. But it was so much, so much and so strange to him.

"You cannot know this," his father repeated. It was almost a chant. "You cannot know the fear. It was dark, and I was the only one left alive out of 54 men, all dead but me, and I knew that the Vietcong were just waiting for light. When the dawn came, 'Charley'[7] would come out and finish everybody off, the way they always did. And I thought if I could stop the dawn, just stop the sun from coming up, I could make it."

Terry felt the fear, and he also felt the tears coming down his cheeks. His hand went out across the table, and he took his father's hand and held it. It was shaking.

"I mean I actually thought that if I could stop the sun from coming up, I could live. I made my brain work on that because it was all I had. Through the rest of the night in the rain in the paddy, I thought I could do it. I could stop the dawn." He took a deep breath. "But you can't, you know. You can't stop it

---

6. **rice paddy**, the flooded field where rice is grown.
7. **Charley**, American word for the North Vietnamese and the Vietcong, who were allied against the Americans during the Vietnam War.

from coming, and when I saw the gray light, I knew I was dead. It would just be minutes, and the light would be full, and I just settled under Jackson's body, and hid."

He stopped, and his face came down into his hands. Terry stood and went around the table to stand in back of him, his hands on his shoulders, rubbing gently.

"They didn't shoot me. They came, one of them poked Jackson's body and went on, and they left me. But I was dead. I'm still dead, don't you see? I died because I couldn't stop the sun. I died. Inside where I am—I died."

Terry was still in back of him, and he nodded, but he didn't see. Not that. He understood only that he didn't understand, and that he would probably never know what it was really like, would probably never understand what had truly happened. And maybe his father would never be truly normal.

But Terry also knew that it didn't matter. He would try to understand, and the trying would have to be enough. He would try hard from now on, and he would not be embarrassed when his father's eyes went away. He would not be embarrassed no matter what his father did. Terry had knowledge now. Maybe not enough and maybe not all that he would need.

But it was a start.

▲ This collage by Lauren Ling is comprised of a variety of elements that reflect the Vietnam War experience. Note that the background is a photograph of a portion of the Vietnam War Memorial in Washington, D.C. What do you think is the significance of the painting in the middle of the collage?

After Reading

Making Connections

1. What are the most memorable images in the story? Quote the passages from the story that moved you the most, and explain why they were memorable.

2. If this story were a movie, what theme song would you choose? Why?

3. How would the story have been different if Terry hadn't asked his father about the war?

4. Why would Terry's mother not want to talk about the father's experience in Vietnam?

5. In the hardware store, people reacted to Terry's father with curiosity and with "small, nervous laughs." Why would people react this way?

6. When veterans returned from the Vietnam War, they found little sympathy, honor, or support from other Americans. Why do you think that was so? Do you think that made it harder for them to come to terms with the violence they had experienced? Explain.

7. We haven't all fought in a war, but many of us have experienced violence or trauma in our lives. What do you think a person can do to deal with trauma?

Literary Focus: Character Development Through Dialogue

As you were reading you may have noticed that Terry's father changes when he begins to talk about his experiences in the war. You can see some of the changes by the way he speaks. On a chart like the one below, make note of what Terry's father says. Put his comments in one box. Then, in the other box, explain how what the father says gives clues to his **character**.

You don't have to write everything the father says. Most of the important clues are in the comments he makes to Terry, such as when he smiles and says, "You look serious." In fact, that comment could be your first entry on the chart. What do you think of a man who smiles and says "You look serious" to his son?

What Terry's Father Said	What That Tells Me About Him
• "You look serious."	• He wants to talk.
•	•
•	•

Vocabulary Study

veteran
syndrome
browse
commotion
founder

For each number, write a word from the list that best fits in the context.

The highly decorated _(1)_ of the Vietnam War arrived at his doctor's office. While waiting for the doctor he began to _(2)_ through a rack of magazines. When the doctor appeared and escorted him to her office, she told her patient she thought he was suffering from a common _(3)_ that affects many people who have fought in wars. The patient reacted by leaving the office in a rage, causing quite a _(4)_ in the lobby. Although the doctor never expected the session to _(5)_ this badly, she was optimistic that she would eventually be able to help him.

Expressing Your Ideas

Writing Choices

Flashback! Flashbacks are interesting literary devices because they allow a writer to go back and forth from the present to the past. Write a **story** about a person who is experiencing flashbacks. Why are they happening? What are they like? How are they affecting this person's life?

Imagine Write a short **prediction,** telling what the father and son's relationship will be ten years later.

Be the Doctor Imagine that you are in charge of planning a therapy program for Terry and his father. Write a **prescription** of things the two of them can do to help each other live happier, fuller lives.

Other Options

Short and Sweet The Vietnam War is a big topic, but it can be summarized in about five minutes—and you are just the person to do the job. Find out what the war was about and why people in the United States were so divided about it. Explain what you have discovered in an **oral report.**

Talk It Out With some of your classmates, prepare a **skit** with little action but a great deal of dialogue. The purpose of the skit is to have a person change, and to have the change become evident in his or her speech. Begin by brainstorming possible situations in which a person might change his or her tone during a conversation.

Bring Out the Artist in You Draw or paint an **illustration** for one of the scenes from this story. First, imagine one of the scenes that really stood out for you. As you draw, try to catch an interesting perspective, such as a close-up of two faces, or the scene in the hardware store from the father's perspective.

Before Reading

The Dust Will Settle by Luci Tapahonso

Forgotten Language by Shel Silverstein

Luci Tapahonso
born 1953

Luci Tapahonso is a Navajo Indian who has taught courses in Native American literature. She was born in Shiprock, New Mexico.

Shel Silverstein
born 1932

Shel Silverstein has been a cartoonist, composer, and songwriter. He usually doesn't give interviews about the meaning of his poetry because he believes that "if you're a creative person, you should go about your business, do your own work, and not care about how it's received."

Building Background

Stages of Change As exciting as change can be, it usually also means experiencing a loss of some sort. This loss can lead to feelings of grief and anger. In fact, Dr. Elisabeth Kübler-Ross, who worked with people who were dying, found that there were five stages of facing, not just death, but any change:

1. Denial (when you don't want to believe what's happening)
2. Anger
3. Bargaining (when you think: "If I do this, then maybe I can stop this from happening.")
4. Depression
5. Acceptance

The poems you are about to read express strong feelings about change and loss.

Getting into the Poetry

Discussion Lots of people get nervous when reading or discussing poetry because they think that they have to find "the real meaning." Actually, poetry is often nothing more than what it appears to be: a celebration of life, a way of remembering, or an outlet for feelings. Before you begin reading, brainstorm with your classmates other reasons why someone might create a poem.

Reading Tip

Reading Poetry Traditionally, poems are read aloud. Sometimes they are even sung. This means that, although the idea behind a poem is important, the *language* of a poem is also crucial. So, when you get a chance, read each poem aloud. Sing it whenever appropriate. Figure out what words to stress and what you think the **rhythm** of the poem should be. After you finish reading each poem, close your eyes for a second. What images does the poem bring to mind? What is the overall feeling of the poem? Write your reactions in your notebook.

The Dust Will Settle

Luci Tapahonso

I

my grandmother
I cried to see you sitting
leaning against the hard strength
of the rocks when your strength
5 has failed you.

how is it that
we have come to this?
we are dirt-poor in a world
where land, sheep and songs
10 haunt us still.

the dusty smell of
gallup[1] parking lots will be
the memories of the children—
their dreamless nights
15 long days waiting.

II

my uncle
you laugh too quick
and talk too loud yet
the children wait quietly watching
20 huddled in the pickup with
the 5-pound bag of oranges
you bought this morning.

they remember your voice
strong, clear on quiet nights
25 as you sang them to sleep easily.

we will wait.

1. **gallup,** a reference to Gallup, New Mexico,
   where there are Navajo, Hopi, and Zuñi Indian
   reservations.

▲ *Her Precious Time*, by Redwing T. Nez, is a portrait of the Navaho artist's grandmother. How do you think the artist feels about his grandmother?

III

what have i for you?
i curse my helplessness,
this frustration of having
30 nothing more than they.

i can cry and feel this hard anger
and know

grandmother
uncle

35 this will change
this will change

the winds will shift.
the dust will settle.

this will change.

Forgotten Language

Shel Silverstein

Once I spoke the language of the flowers,
Once I understood each word the caterpillar said,
Once I smiled in secret at the gossip of the starlings,[1]
And shared a conversation with the housefly
5   in my bed.
Once I heard and answered all the questions
               of the crickets,
And joined the crying of each falling dying
               flake of snow,
10 Once I spoke the language of the flowers. . . .
               How did it go?
               How did it go?

---

1. **starlings,** dark-colored birds that gather in big groups in fields and trees.

After Reading

Making Connections

1. For each poem, draw a circle. Surround each circle with labels of all the things you think are affecting the narrator of the poem.

2. How old is the narrator of "Forgotten Language"? Why do you think so?

3. What characters from literature, movies, TV, or comics can "talk to the animals"? Why is this a topic that people like to write about?

4. What does it mean to say, "the dust will settle" or "as soon as the dust settles"? Why do you think this is the title of the first poem?

5. 🐾 On a scale of 1 to 10, with 10 being the greatest, how much do you think being Native American affects Luci Tapahonso's poem? Explain your choice.

6. 🐾 The poem "The Dust Will Settle" contrasts Native American life in the past with its present reality. What **changes** does the poem describe in the lives of Native Americans? Cite lines from the poem to support your answers.

7. Think of a recent movie, story, cartoon, song, or comic that featured a Native American. How was that person similar to or different from the person in "The Dust Will Settle"?

Literary Focus: Repetition

Repetition in a poem or song creates rhythm and emphasis. Both poems use repetition. In your notebook, draw a chart like the one shown. Write down the repeated phrases and explain what impact or effect they have on the poem.

Poem	Phrase	Impact

Expressing Your Ideas

"Land, Sheep and Songs . . ." Luci Tapahonso is Navaho, and her poem is about her people. Find out more about the Navaho people to share with your classmates. You might want to research Navaho art and prepare an **exhibit** of typical Navaho designs. You might want to write a **report** on the history of the Navaho people or their traditional way of life. You might want to search for recordings of Navaho **music** to play for the class.

Before Reading

Prisoner of My Country

by Yoshiko Uchida

Yoshiko Uchida
1921–1992

Yoshiko Uchida was a student at the University of California in Berkeley when she and her family were sent to an internment camp in 1942. She taught elementary school during part of her internment and for a period after the war. When teaching began to interfere with her writing, she became a secretary to free up some of her time. Uchida wrote many novels about Japanese Americans for young people, including *Journey to Topaz, Journey Home,* and *A Jar of Dreams.* She said she wrote especially for third-generation Japanese Americans, "to give them the kinds of books I'd never had as a child."

Building Background

Prisoners in Their Own Country On December 7, 1941, Japan bombed Pearl Harbor, an American naval base in Hawaii. The U.S. then declared war on Japan and entered World War II. As the U.S. went to war against Japan, Germany, and Italy, prejudice against Japanese Americans began to build in the United States. Several groups spread fears that Japanese Americans were planning various acts that posed a threat to the war effort. Although evidence of these plans never existed, President Roosevelt ordered more than 110,000 Japanese Americans to leave their homes and businesses and relocate to internment camps in isolated parts of California, Arizona, and several other states. The barbed-wire enclosed camps were like prisons.

Getting into the Selection

Writer's Notebook Write a brief account of an injustice in which someone got blamed or punished for something that wasn't his or her fault. It could be something that happened to you, or to someone you know, or something you heard about on the news. If possible, try to tell both sides of the story. That is, try to see the event from the viewpoint of the person who did the injustice, as well as from the viewpoint of the person who was treated badly.

Reading Tip

Tracking Change Many things change in this selection. As you read, make note of some of the changes, which can be physical (such as the change from a house to Barrack 16) or emotional. When you have finished the selection, make a list of before and after characteristics of Yoshiko's life.

YOSHIKO UCHIDA

PRISONER
OF *my* COUNTRY

Papa's beautiful garden was now full of gaping holes. Mama had dug up a few favorite plants to give to her friends, and the others were given to people like the woman who stopped by one day to ask if she could have some gladiolas. "Since you're leaving anyway . . ." she said, smiling awkwardly.

Our rented house was now a barren shell, with only three mattresses left on the floor. In the corner of Mama's room was a large shapeless canvas blanket bag that we called our Camp Bundle. We tossed into it all the things we were instructed to take with us—sheets, blankets, pillows, dishes, and eating utensils. We also added our own list of necessities—boots, umbrellas, flashlights, teacups, a hot plate, a kettle, and anything else we thought might be useful in camp.

"You know, we're supposed to bring only what we can carry," Kay warned.

We practiced lifting our suitcases and found that we could each carry two. But what were we to do about the Camp Bundle? Each day it grew and bulged like some living thing, and we had no idea how we would ever get it to camp.

Still, there was nothing we could do but continue to fill it, and to hope that somehow things would work out.

The night before we left, our Swiss neighbors invited us to dinner. Mrs. Harpainter made a delicious chicken dinner, served on her finest china and linens, reminding me of all the company dinners we'd had in our own house in happier days.

When we got home, Marian and Solveig came from next door to say good-bye, bringing gifts for each of us.

They hugged us, saying, "Come back soon!"

"We will," we answered. But we had no idea when or if we would ever come back.

The next morning Mrs. Harpainter brought us breakfast on a tray full of bright colorful dishes. She then drove us to the First Congregational Church of Berkeley, designated as the Civil Control Station where we were to report.

We said our good-byes quickly, unable to speak many words. Already the church grounds teemed with hundreds of bewildered Japanese Americans, clutching bundles tagged with their names and family number. Parked at the curb were rows of trucks being loaded with the larger baggage that could not be hand-carried.

"I wish they had told us there'd be trucks," Kay muttered. "We could have been spared all that worry about our Camp Bundle."

But the army didn't seem to care whether we worried or not. To them we were simply prisoners. They had stationed armed guards all around the church, their bayonets mounted and ready. It was only when I saw them that the full horror of the day struck me. My knees felt weak, and I almost lost my breakfast.

The First Congregational Church had been good to us. Many of its families had offered to store belongings for the departing Japanese Americans, and now the church women were serving tea and sandwiches. But none of us could eat.

We were soon loaded onto waiting buses and began our one-way journey down familiar streets, across the Bay Bridge, and down the Bayshore Highway. Although some people wept quietly, most of us were silent. We kept our eyes on the window, watching as familiar landmarks slipped away behind us one by one.

And then we were there—at the Tanforan Racetrack[1] Assembly Center, one of fifteen such centers created at racetracks and fairgrounds along the West Coast to <u>intern</u>[2] the Japanese Americans.

From the bus window I could see a high barbed-wire fence that surrounded the entire area, and at each corner of the camp was a guard tower manned by soldiers.

The gates swung open to receive the buses, and armed guards closed them behind us. We were now locked in and under twenty-four-hour guard.

We had always been law-abiding citizens. We had done nothing wrong. And yet, we had now become prisoners of our own country.

There was an enormous crowd gathered around the grandstand. One would have thought the horses were running, except that all the people there were Japanese of all ages, sizes, and shapes.

We scanned the crowd for familiar faces and were relieved to find several friends who had arrived a few days earlier from Oakland.

"Hey, Kay and Yo! Over here!"

They steered us through the crowds to an area where doctors peered down our throats and pronounced us healthy. Then they helped us find our way to Barrack 16, Apartment 40, to which we had been assigned.

"We get apartments?" I asked.

"Not the kind you're thinking of, Yo. Wait, you'll see." My friend knew I was in for a rude awakening.

Mama was wearing her hat, gloves, and Sunday clothes, simply because she never would have thought of leaving home any other way. In her good Sunday shoes, she was carefully picking her way over the puddles left in the muddy track by rain the day before.

The army had hastily constructed dozens of tar-papered <u>barracks</u>[3] around the track and in the infield <u>to house</u> the eight thousand "evacuees," as we were called. Each barrack was divided into six rooms, one family to a room. But our barrack was not one of these.

Barrack 16 turned out to be nothing more than an old stable, with twenty-five stalls facing north, back to back with the same number facing south. Our so-called apartment was a small, dark horse stall, ten feet by twenty feet. I couldn't believe what I saw.

Dust, dirt, and wood shavings littered the linoleum, and I could still smell the manure that lay beneath it. There were two tiny windows on either side of the door (our only source of daylight), and the stall was divided into two sections by a Dutch door worn with teeth marks.

One the walls I saw tiny corpses of spiders and bugs that had been permanently whitewashed to the boards by the army painters. A single light bulb dangled from the ceiling, and three folded army cots lay on the dirty floor. This was to be our "home" for the next five months.

One of our friends found a broom and swept out our stall, while two of the boys went

---

1. **Tanforan Racetrack,** a race track converted into an internment camp for thousands of Japanese Americans.
2. intern (in tėrn′), *v.* force to stay in a certain place.
3. barrack (bar′ək), *n.* a large, plain building in which many people live.

Military police in San Francisco help Japanese Americans board a bus that will take them to one of the internment camps.

to pick up our mattresses. Actually, they'd had to stuff the tickings with straw themselves.

Another friend loaned us some dishes and silverware since our big bundle hadn't yet been delivered. "We'd better leave soon for the mess hall before the lines for supper get too long," she warned.

Until smaller mess halls could be built throughout the camp, all meals were being served in the basement of the grandstand. Clutching our plates and silverware, we made our way back down the muddy track.

When we arrived at the grandstand, there were already several long weaving lines of people waiting to get in, and we were soon separated from our friends. Mama, Kay, and I took our places at the end of one line and huddled together to keep warm. A cold, piercing wind had begun to blow as the sun went down, and it scattered dust and debris[4] in our faces.

I felt like a refugee standing in a soup line in some alien and forbidding land. It was not only degrading[5] and humiliating, it seemed totally unreal—like some horrible nightmare.

Since we had missed lunch, I was eager for a nice hot meal, but supper consisted of a piece of butterless bread, two canned sausages, and a plain boiled potato. Everything was dropped onto our plates by two cooks, who picked up the food with their fingers from large dishpans.

We ate at picnic tables in the cold, damp basement crowded with hundreds of people, and even though I was still hungry, I couldn't wait to get back to our stall.

It was dark now, and the north wind was blowing into our stall from all the cracks around the windows and the door. We bundled up in our coats and sat on our prickly mattresses, too miserable even to talk.

Kay and I worried that the cold air would aggravate Mama's neuralgia, which caused terrible pain in her facial nerves.

"Are you OK, Mom?" we asked.

But Mama wasn't thinking about herself. "I wonder how Papa San[6] is?" she said softly.

Then we heard a truck outside, and a voice called, "Hey Uchida! Apartment 40!"

As Kay and I rushed to the door calling, "That's us!" we saw two baggage boys wrestling our big Camp Bundle off their truck.

"What ya got in here anyways?" they asked good-naturedly. "Didja bring everything in your whole damn house?"

I was embarrassed. Our bundle was clearly the biggest and bulkiest object in their truck.

"It's just our pet rhinoceros," I quipped. And while the boys were still laughing, we dragged our monstrous bundle into the stall and quickly untied all the knots we'd labored over just that morning.

Everything we had tossed into its obliging depths now tumbled out looking like old friends.

"I'll go get some water," I volunteered.

I grabbed the kettle and hurried to the women's latrine-washroom about fifty yards from our stable. Kay and Mama, in the meantime, retrieved our sheets and blankets to make up the cots.

I had news for them when I returned.

"There're no doors to the toilets or showers," I reported, horrified. "And we have to wash up at long tin sinks that look like feeding troughs."

I had also taken a look at the laundry barrack with its rows of washtubs, where everything, including sheets and towels, were to be washed by hand. They were still empty, but by morning there would be long lines of people waiting to use the tubs.

---

4. debris (də brē′), *n.* litter.
5. degrading (di grā′ding), *adj.* bringing into dishonor or contempt.
6. **Papa San** (pä pä sän), *San* is a Japanese word that is often added to the names of both men and women as a polite form of address. Kay and Yoshiko's father was being held in an internment camp in Montana.

Mama diverted our attention to matters at hand. "Well, we can at least make some tea now," she said.

We plugged the hot plate into a double socket we'd had the good sense to bring and waited for the water to boil.

Then came the first of many knocks we'd be hearing at our door, as friends discovered where we lived.

"Hey, Kay and Yo. Are you home?"

Four of my college friends had come by to see how we were doing, bringing along the only snack they could find—a box of dried prunes. Even the day before, I wouldn't have given the prunes a second look. But now they were as welcome as a box of the Maskey's chocolates Papa used to bring home from San Francisco.

We gathered around the warmth of the hot plate, sipping the tea Mama made for us, wondering how we had gotten ourselves into such an intolerable[7] situation.

We were angry that our country had so cruelly deprived[8] us of our civil rights.[9] But we had been raised to respect and trust those in authority. Resistance or confrontation such as we know them today was unthinkable, for the world then was a totally different place.

There had yet been no freedom marches or demonstrations of protest. No one had yet heard of Martin Luther King, Jr. No one knew about ethnic pride. Most Americans were not concerned about civil rights and would not have supported us had we tried to resist the uprooting.[10]

We naively[11] believed at the time that cooperating with the government was the only way to prove our loyalty and to help our country. We did not know then, as we do today, how badly our leaders betrayed us and our country's democratic ideals.

They had imprisoned us with full knowledge that their action was not only unconstitutional,[12] but totally unnecessary. They knew

The author's family posed for this photograph on the day they were allowed to leave the internment center.

there was no military necessity for the mass uprooting, although that was the reason given for incarcerating us.

How could America —our own country— have done this to us? we wondered. And trying to cheer ourselves up, we talked about steaks and hamburgers and hot dogs as we munched on the cold dried prunes.

---

7. **intolerable** (in tol′ər ə bəl), *adj.* too much to be endured, unbearable.
8. **deprive** (di prīv′), *v.* keep from having.
9. **civil rights** (siv′əl rīts), the rights guaranteed to all citizens.
10. **uprooting** (up rüt′ ing, up rút′ ing), *n.* removal from one's home.
11. **naively** (nä ēv′ lē), *adv.* without question, like a child.
12. **unconstitutional** (un′kon stə tü′shə nəl), *adj.* against the Constitution of the United States, which guarantees certain rights.

After Reading

Making Connections

1. Did this selection surprise you? Explain.

2. If you were a movie director, how would you film this piece? On which scenes would you concentrate?

3. If you had been a prisoner at Tanforan, which of the difficulties of the situation would have bothered you most? Why?

4. What does the author mean when she writes, "We gathered around . . . wondering how we had gotten ourselves into such an intolerable situation"? How had they gotten into this situation? Had they done anything wrong?

5. 👣 As the political climate in the U.S. **changed,** the author's family—and other Japanese Americans during the same period—experienced injustice and racism. They reacted with understandable anger and bitterness, but also with humor, acceptance, and even loyalty to their country. Give an example from the selection for each of these reactions.

6. In 1988 Congress granted a payment of $20,000 to each Japanese American who had been interned in a camp during the war. In addition, Japanese Americans received a formal apology from the government for violating their civil rights. What is your feeling about this payment and apology? Were they necessary? Was the amount too much or too little? Should other groups also be compensated for past injustices?

7. Could something like this happen today? Think beyond the borders of the United States.

Literary Focus: Setting

The **setting** of a piece of literature is where and when it happens. The setting may be specific and detailed and introduced at the very beginning of the selection, or it may be merely suggested through the use of details scattered throughout the selection. In some stories the setting is vital to the narrative: it may have an effect on the events of the plot, reveal character, or create a certain atmosphere. In other pieces of literature the setting is relatively unimportant.

The setting for this selection is California, 1942, at an internment camp. Write down important details from the piece to help you picture the camp; then write a description or draw a picture of how you see the place.

Vocabulary Study

barrack
civil rights
debris
degrading
deprive
intern
intolerable
naively
unconstitutional
uprooting

A. Match each word on the left with its synonym on the right.

1. barrack   **A.** confine

2. debris   **B.** quarters

3. intern   **C.** humiliating

4. degrading   **D.** unbearable

5. intolerable   **E.** trash

B. With a small group, make up a story containing all of the following vocabulary words: *unconstitutional, civil rights, uprooting, naively,* and *deprive.* One student can begin by saying a sentence that contains one of the words; the next student should continue the story with a new sentence, using a second word; and so on.

Expressing Your Ideas

Writing Choices

Decisions, Decisions! Make a **list** of what you would pack if you could only take one suitcase with you to a new home. Explain your choices.

Dust and Wind Soon after the events described in this selection, the Uchida family was sent to a concentration camp in Topaz, Utah, located in a desert. While there, Yoshiko painted this scene of a dust storm— a frequent occurrence at Topaz. Write a **description** of what is happening in the painting from the point of view of someone living there.

Other Options

The Walls Around Us Work in a small group to design a **mural** that commemorates the Japanese American internment of the 1940s. Find a quote or poem that can be included in the design.

The Other Side of the Story Why did the government feel it was necessary to intern Japanese Americans? **Interview** someone who is familiar with this time in history and ask about the other side of the story. Explain the other side to your classmates.

Media Mania If the Japanese American internment happened today, it would be thoroughly covered by the media. With a group, improvise a TV **news panel show** with a moderator and journalists of opposing points of view. "Journalists" may want to research their positions before the panel makes its presentation to the class.

Before Reading

Home

by Gwendolyn Brooks

Gwendolyn Brooks
born 1917

Gwendolyn Brooks is a well-known poet and novelist. Her book *Maud Martha,* in which this story appears, is about a woman who is concerned with being seen as ugly, but who learns to stand up for herself. Brooks, the first African American author to win a Pulitzer Prize, says that she doesn't like the term African American. She prefers "B-L-A-C-K, which comes right out to meet you, eye to eye."

Building Background

Home, Sweet Home Part of the American Dream is owning your own home. Because homes are expensive, banks lend people the money to buy them. This loan is called a **mortgage**. People have to repay the bank. If they can't, the bank can legally take the house back. Sometimes, though, a bank will allow a person a little extra time to make a payment that is overdue. This period can be a very scary, tense one for people who are waiting to find out if they will still be homeowners.

Getting into the Story

Discussion One of the main points in the story is the importance of having your own place. Brainstorm with the class a list of possible reasons why a person or family might have to give up their home. Mark which reasons are within a person's control, and which reasons are not.

Reading Tip

Family Bonds There are four people in this story. In order to keep track of them, write down their names in your notebook and try to figure out how they are related. Use an equal sign (=) to show marriage and a line to show children. As an example, you could try to diagram your own family or a family you know.

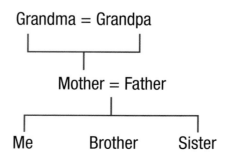

HOME

Gwendolyn Brooks

What had been wanted was this always, this always to last, the talking softly on this porch, with the snake plant in the jardiniere in the southwest corner, and the obstinate[1] slip from Aunt Eppie's magnificent Michigan fern at the left side of the friendly door. Mama, Maud Martha and Helen rocked slowly in their rocking chairs, and looked at the late afternoon light on the lawn, and at the emphatic[2] iron of the fence and at the poplar tree. These things might soon be theirs no longer. Those shafts and pools of light, the tree, the graceful iron, might soon be viewed possessively by different eyes.

---

1. obstinate (ob′stə nit), *adj.* hard to control.
2. emphatic (em fat′ik), *adj.* strongly expressed.

▲ *Adam's House* was painted in 1928 by Edward Hopper. Does this house resemble the one you imagined as you began reading the story? How is it similar? different?

Papa was to have gone that noon, during his lunch hour, to the office of the Home Owners' Loan. If he had not succeeded in getting another extension,[3] they would be leaving this house in which they had lived for more than fourteen years. There was little hope. The Home Owners' Loan was hard. They sat, making their plans.

"We'll be moving into a nice flat somewhere," said Mama. "Somewhere on South Park, or Michigan, or in Washington Park Court." Those flats, as the girls and Mama knew well, were burdens on wages twice the size of Papa's. This was not mentioned now.

"They're much prettier than this old house," said Helen. "I have friends I'd just as soon not bring here. And I have other friends that wouldn't come down this far for anything, unless they were in a taxi."

Yesterday, Maud Martha would have attacked her. Tomorrow she might. Today she said nothing. She merely gazed at a little hopping robin in the tree, her tree, and tried to keep the fronts of her eyes dry.

---

3. **extension** (ek sten′shən), *n.* an additional amount of time.

"Well, I do know," said Mama, turning her hands over and over, "that I've been getting tireder and tireder of doing that firing. From October to April, there's firing to be done."

"But lately we've been helping, Harry and I," said Maud Martha. "And sometimes in March and April and in October, and even in November, we could build a little fire in the fireplace. Sometimes the weather was just right for that."

She knew, from the way they looked at her, that this had been a mistake. They did not want to cry.

But she felt that the little line of white, somewhat ridged with smoked purple, and all that cream-shot saffron, would never drift across any western sky except that in back of this house. The rain would drum with as sweet a dullness nowhere but here. The birds on South Park were mechanical birds, no better

"YOU KNOW," HELEN SIGHED, "IF YOU WANT TO KNOW THE TRUTH, THIS IS A RELIEF."

than the poor caught canaries in those "rich" women's sun parlors.

"It's just going to kill Papa!" burst out Maud Martha. "He loves this house! He *lives* for this house!"

"He lives for us," said Helen. "It's us he loves. He wouldn't want the house, except for us."

"And he'll have us," added Mama, "wherever."

"You know," Helen sighed, "if you want to know the truth, this is a relief. If this hadn't come up, we would have gone on, just dragged on, hanging out here forever."

"It might," allowed Mama, "be an act of God. God may just have reached down, and picked up the reins."

"Yes," Maud Martha cracked in, "that's what you always say—that God knows best."

Her mother looked at her quickly, decided the statement was not suspect,[4] looked away.

Helen saw Papa coming. "There's Papa," said Helen.

They could not tell a thing from the way Papa was walking. It was that same dear little staccato[5] walk, one shoulder down, then the other, then repeat, and repeat. They watched his progress. He passed the Kennedys', he passed the vacant lot, he passed Mrs. Blakemore's. They wanted to hurl themselves over the fence, into the street, and shake the truth out of his collar. He opened his gate—the gate—and still his stride and face told them nothing.

"Hello," he said.

Mama got up and followed him through the front door. The girls knew better than to go in too.

Presently Mama's head emerged. Her eyes were lamps turned on.

"It's all right," she exclaimed. "He got it. It's all over. Everything is all right."

The door slammed shut. Mama's footsteps hurried away.

"I think," said Helen, rocking rapidly, "I think I'll give a party. I haven't given a party since I was eleven. I'd like some of my friends to just casually see that we're homeowners."

---

4. suspect (sus′pekt, sə spekt′), *adj.* open to suspicion.
5. staccato (stə kä′tō), *adj.* when the beats of a rhythm (such as a person's footsteps) are abrupt and disconnected.

After Reading

Making Connections

1. Let's say you were on the front porch with Maud Martha, Helen, and Mama, casually listening in on the conversation. What are you doing? What is your reaction to the conversation?

2. How do you picture the **setting** of this story? What time of year is it? What is the furniture like? How are the characters sitting?

3. Why is it important for Helen to be a homeowner?

4. Why do you think the author chose to make this story mostly **dialogue?**

5. 👏 Cultural **change** can affect a whole country. What national issues would affect people's abilities to pay for and own a home?

6. Change is often very stressful. On a scale of one to ten, with ten representing the most difficult, how would you rank being forced to move from your home in terms of stress? Explain your choice.

Literary Focus: Dialogue

Sometimes **dialogue** can be an effective way to show what characters in a story are feeling. Look through the story at what people are saying. Are they saying what they really mean? Or are they saying what they wish they meant? In this story, the characters often say things they don't mean. Why would they do that?

In a chart like the one below, note what people say and what you think they really mean.

Character	What He/She Said	What He/She Really Meant
Mama	"We'll be moving to a nice flat somewhere."	At least we'll have a home, even if we don't own it.

Vocabulary Study

On a sheet of paper, write the word or phrase that does not belong with each group. Read across.

obstinate
emphatic
extension
suspect
staccato

1. obstinate   stubborn   firm   unkind   bullheaded
2. emphatic   mean   expressive   energetic   lively
3. extension   continuation   more time   prolongation termination
4. suspect   suspicious   pointless   questionable dubious
5. staccato   tapping   rhythmic   sharp sound   painful

Expressing Your Ideas

Writing Choices

Father Knows Best Tell the **story** from Papa's perspective. Why do you need an extension on your loan? What was it like to go to the bank this afternoon and ask for more time? How did you manage to convince the board to see things your way?

What Do You Mean? Helen said at the beginning of the story, "I have friends I'd just as soon not bring here," but later, at the end, she said she'd like to give a party. Have her write a **letter** to Maud Martha explaining why she changed her mind.

Losing Your Place Look at the list of ideas you brainstormed before reading for why a person might have to give up his or her home. Write a new **story** based on one of those ideas.

Other Options

A Game of Chance Design a **board game** based on the events of the story. You can work either by yourself or in a small group. First, decide what the goal of the game will be. Then decide what can happen to people as they move around the board.

Hello? What do you do if someone misses a mortgage payment? To find out, call a local bank and ask if you can **interview** someone who works there. Be sure to observe the following phone etiquette: introduce yourself; be polite; state your purpose clearly; be brief; thank him or her at the end.

Get Creative Use your imagination as well as information from the story to **draw** the house and its surroundings. To add an element of authenticity to your drawing, perhaps you could research *snake plant, Michigan fern,* and *poplar tree* to find out how to draw these parts of the landscape. Be creative when filling in details not covered in the story.

Before Reading

The Kid Nobody Could Handle

by Kurt Vonnegut, Jr.

Kurt Vonnegut, Jr.
born 1922

Kurt Vonnegut, Jr., has an intimate knowledge of adoption—he adopted his sister's children after her death. Vonnegut generally writes about serious subjects in a light way. When he talks about the problems of the world, such as bombs and people dying because no one cares, he says, "This has to be a joke. What else is there to do but laugh?" Although some of his books have been banned or burned because they have offended certain groups, they have always been widely read and appreciated by many people.

Building Background

Foster Care When children cannot live with their "real" parents, they are sometimes placed in foster care. Foster care is not the same as adoption. Children who are adopted into families usually no longer have connections to their biological parents. When a child is in foster care, usually everyone hopes that the child will be able to return to his or her own parents after some of the problems have been worked out. Whenever possible, social services try very hard to place a child with foster parents who are either related to or know the child. By doing so, the child maintains an important sense of not being abandoned.

Getting into the Story

Writer's Notebook   Most of us have activities we really enjoy or are even passionate about. Is there an activity for which *you* have a passion? Describe the activity in your notebook. Then write about a person (or the people) who helped you get started or who encouraged you to develop this interest. What sorts of things has this person done to encourage your interest?

Reading Tip

Compare/Contrast On a clean sheet of paper write *Helmholtz* on one side and *Quinn* on the other. As you read, make note of the information provided about each man.

Helmholtz	Quinn
married	bachelor
head full of music	humorless
bandmaster	

THE KID NOBODY COULD HANDLE

KURT VONNEGUT, JR.

It was seven-thirty in the morning. Waddling, clanking, muddy machines were tearing a hill to pieces behind a restaurant, and trucks were hauling the pieces away. Inside the restaurant, dishes rattled on their shelves. Tables quaked, and a very kind fat man with a headful of music looked down at the jiggling yolks of his breakfast eggs. His wife was visiting relatives out of town. He was on his own.

The kind fat man was George M. Helmholtz, a man of forty, head of the music department of Lincoln High School, and director of the band. Life had treated him well. Each year he dreamed the same big dream. He dreamed of leading as fine a band as there was on the face of the earth. And each year the dream came true.

▲ *Portrait of Scott* was painted by Robert Vickrey in 1968. How would you describe Scott's expression? What do you think is on his mind?

It came true because Helmholtz was sure that a man couldn't have a better dream than his. Faced by this unnerving[1] sureness, Kiwanians, Rotarians, and Lions[2] paid for band uniforms that cost twice as much as their best suits, school administrators let Helmholtz raid the budget for expensive props, and youngsters played their hearts out for him. When youngsters had no talent, Helmholtz made them play on guts alone.

Everything was good about Helmholtz's life save his finances. He was so dazzled by his big dream that he was a child in the marketplace. Ten years before, he had sold the hill behind the restaurant to Bert Quinn, the restaurant owner, for one thousand dollars. It was now apparent, even to Helmholtz, that Helmholtz had been had.

Quinn sat down in the booth with the bandmaster. He was a bachelor, a small, dark, humorless man. He wasn't a well man. He couldn't sleep, he couldn't stop working, he couldn't smile warmly. He had only two moods: one suspicious and self-pitying, the other arrogant and boastful. The first mood applied when he was losing money. The second mood applied when he was making it.

Quinn was in the arrogant and boastful mood when he sat down with Helmholtz. He sucked whistlingly on a toothpick, and talked of vision—his own.

"I wonder how many eyes saw the hill before I did?" said Quinn. "Thousands and thousands, I'll bet—and not one saw what I saw. How many eyes?"

"Mine, at least," said Helmholtz. All the hill had meant to him was a panting climb, free blackberries, taxes, and a place for band picnics.

"You inherit the hill from your old man, and it's nothing but a pain in the neck to you," said Quinn. "So you figure you'll stick me with it."

"I didn't figure to stick you," Helmholtz protested. "The good Lord knows the price was more than fair."

"You say that now," said Quinn gleefully. "Sure, Helmholtz, you say that now. Now you see the shopping district's got to grow. Now you see what I saw."

THOSE BOOTS, THE BLACK JACKET— AND HE WON'T TALK. HE WON'T RUN AROUND WITH THE OTHER KIDS.

"Yes," said Helmholtz. "Too late, too late." He looked around for some diversion,[3] and saw a fifteen-year-old boy coming toward him, mopping the aisle between booths.

The boy was small but with tough, stringy muscles standing out on his neck and forearms. Childhood lingered[4] in his features, but when he paused to rest, his fingers went hopefully to the silky beginnings of sideburns and a mustache. He mopped like a robot, jerkily, brainlessly, but took pains not to splash suds over the toes of his black boots.

"So what do I do when I get the hill?" said Quinn. "I tear it down, and it's like somebody pulled down a dam. All of a sudden, everybody wants to build a store where the hill was."

"Um," said Helmholtz. He smiled genially at the boy. The boy looked through him without a twitch of recognition.

"We all got something," said Quinn. "You got music; I got vision." And he smiled, for it was perfectly clear to both where the money lay. "Think big!" said Quinn. "Dream big!

1. **unnerving** (un nėrv′ing), *adj.* making someone lose his or her nerve or self-control.
2. **Kiwanians, Rotarians, and Lions,** members of the Kiwanis, Rotary, and Lions clubs, which are groups of professional and business people who do things for the community.
3. **diversion** (də vėr′zhən, dī vėr′zhən), *n.* distraction.
4. **linger** (ling′gər), *v.* be slow to pass away or disappear.

That's what vision is. Keep your eyes wider open than anybody else's."

"That boy," said Helmholtz, "I've seen him around school, but I never knew his name."

Quinn laughed cheerlessly. "Billy the Kid? The storm trooper? Rudolph Valentino? Flash Gordon?" He called the boy. . . . "Hey, Jim! Come here a minute."

Helmholtz was appalled[5] to see that the boy's eyes were as expressionless as oysters.

"This is my brother-in-law's kid by another marriage—before he married my sister," said Quinn. "His name's Jim Donnini, and he's from the south side of Chicago, and he's very tough."

Jim Donnini's hands tightened on the mop handle.

"How do you do?" said Helmholtz.

"Hi," said Jim emptily.

"He's living with me now," said Quinn. "He's my baby now."

"You want a lift to school, Jim?"

"Yeah, he wants a lift to school," said Quinn. "See what you make of him. He won't talk to me." He turned to Jim. "Go on, kid, wash up and shave."

Robotlike, Jim marched away.

"Where are his parents?"

"His mother's dead. His old man married my sister, walked out on her, and stuck her with him. Then the court didn't like the way she was raising him, and put him in foster homes for a while. Then they decided to get him clear out of Chicago, so they stuck me with him." He shook his head. "Life's a funny thing, Helmholtz."

"Not very funny, sometimes," said Helmholtz. He pushed his eggs away.

"Like some whole new race of people coming up," said Quinn wonderingly. "Nothing like the kids we got around here. Those boots, the black jacket—and he won't talk. He won't run around with the other kids. Won't study. I don't think he can even read and write very good."

"Does he like music at all? Or drawing? Or animals?" said Helmholtz. "Does he collect anything?"

"You know what he likes?" said Quinn. "He likes to polish those boots—get off by himself and polish those boots. And when he's really in heaven is when he can get off by himself, spread comic books all around him on the floor, polish his boots, and watch television." He smiled ruefully. "Yeah, he had a collection too. And I took it away from him and threw it in the river."

"Threw it in the river?" said Helmholtz.

"Yeah," said Quinn. "Eight knives—some with blades as long as your hand."

Helmholtz paled. "Oh." A prickling sensation spread over the back of his neck. "This is a new problem at Lincoln High. I hardly know what to think about it." He swept spilled salt together in a neat little pile, just as he would have liked to sweep together his scattered thoughts. "It's a kind of sickness, isn't it? That's the way to look at it?"

"Sick?" said Quinn. He slapped the table. "You can say that again!" He tapped his chest. "And Doctor Quinn is just the man to give him what's good for what ails[6] him."

"What's that?" said Helmholtz.

"No more talk about the poor little sick boy," said Quinn grimly. "That's all he's heard from the social workers and the juvenile court. From now on, he's the no-good bum of a man. I'll ride his tail till he straightens up and flies right or winds up in the can for life. One way or the other."

"I see," said Helmholtz.

"Like listening to music?" said Helmholtz to Jim brightly, as they rode to school in Helmholtz's car.

Jim said nothing. He was stroking his mustache and sideburns, which he had not shaved off.

---

5. **appalled** (ə pôld′), *adj.* filled with horror or alarm.
6. **ail** (āl), *v.* be the matter with; trouble.

"Ever drum with the fingers or keep time with your feet?" said Helmholtz. He had noticed that Jim's boots were decorated with chains that had no function but to jingle as he walked.

Jim sighed with ennui.[7]

"Or whistle?" said Helmholtz. "If you do any of those things, it's just like picking up the keys to a whole new world—a world as beautiful as any world can be."

Jim gave a soft Bronx cheer.

"There!" said Helmholtz. "You've illustrated the basic principle of the family of brass wind instruments. The glorious voice of every one of them starts with a buzz on the lips."

The seat springs of Helmholtz's old car creaked under Jim, as Jim shifted his weight. Helmholtz took this as a sign of interest, and he turned to smile in comradely fashion. But Jim had shifted his weight in order to get a cigarette from inside his tight leather jacket.

Helmholtz was too upset to comment at once. It was only at the end of the ride, as he turned into the teachers' parking lot, that he thought of something to say.

"Sometimes," said Helmholtz, "I get so lonely and disgusted, I don't see how I can stand it. I feel like doing all kinds of crazy things, just for the heck of it—things that might even be bad for me."

Jim blew a smoke ring expertly.

"And then!" said Helmholtz. He snapped his fingers and honked his horn. "And then, Jim, I remember I've got at least one tiny corner of the universe I can make just the way I want it! I can go to it and gloat over it until I'm brand-new and happy again."

"Aren't you the lucky one?" said Jim. He yawned.

"I am, for a fact," said Helmholtz. "My corner of the universe happens to be the air around my band. I can fill it with music. Mr. Beeler, in zoology, has his butterflies. Mr. Trottman, in physics, has his pendulum and tuning forks. Making sure everybody has a cor-

ner like that is about the biggest job we teachers have. I—"

The car door opened and slammed, and Jim was gone. Helmholtz stamped out Jim's cigarette and buried it under the gravel of the parking lot.

EVALUATE: Who do you think has a better chance of getting through to Jim, Quinn or Helmholtz?

Helmholtz's first class of the morning was C Band, where beginners thumped and wheezed and tooted as best they could, and looked down the long, long, long road through B Band to A Band, the Lincoln High School Ten Square Band, the finest band in the world.

Helmholtz stepped onto the podium and raised his baton. "You are better than you think," he said. "A-one, a-two, a-three." Down came the baton.

C Band set out in its quest for beauty—set out like a rusty switch engine, with valves stuck, pipes clogged, unions leaking, bearings dry.

Helmholtz was still smiling at the end of the hour, because he'd heard in his mind the music as it was going to be someday. His throat was raw, for he had been singing with the band for the whole hour. He stepped into the hall for a drink from the fountain.

As he drank, he heard the jingling of chains. He looked up at Jim Donnini. Rivers of students flowed between classrooms, pausing in friendly eddies, flowing on again. Jim was alone. When he paused, it wasn't to greet anyone, but to polish the toes of his boots on his trousers legs. He had the air of a spy in a melodrama, missing nothing, liking nothing, looking forward to the great day when everything would be turned upside down.

---

7. ennui (än′wē), *n.* boredom.

"Hello, Jim," said Helmholtz. "Say, I was just thinking about you. We've got a lot of clubs and teams that meet after school. And that's a good way to get to know a lot of people."

Jim measured Helmholtz carefully with his eyes. "Maybe I don't want to know a lot of people," he said "Ever think of that?" He set his feet down hard to make his chains jingle as he walked away.

When Helmholtz returned to the podium for the rehearsal of B Band, there was a note waiting for him, calling him to a special faculty meeting.

The meeting was about vandalism.

Someone had broken into the school and wrecked the office of Mr. Crane, head of the English Department. The poor man's treasures—books, diplomas, snapshots of England, the beginnings of eleven novels—had been ripped and crumpled, mixed, dumped and trampled, and drenched with ink.

Helmholtz was sickened. He couldn't believe it. He couldn't bring himself to think about it. It didn't become real to him until late that night, in a dream. In the dream Helmholtz saw a boy with barracuda teeth, with claws like baling hooks. The monster climbed into a window of the high school and dropped to the floor of the band rehearsal room. The monster clawed to shreds the heads of the biggest drum in the state. Helmholtz woke up howling. There was nothing to do but dress and go to the school.

At two in the morning, Helmholtz caressed the drum heads in the band rehearsal room, with the night watchman looking on. He rolled the drum back and forth on its cart, and he turned the light inside on and off, on and off. The drum was unharmed. The night watchman left to make his rounds.

The band's treasure house was safe. With the contentment of a miser counting his money, Helmholtz fondled the rest of the instruments, one by one. And then he began to polish the sousaphones. As he polished, he could hear the great horns roaring, could see them flashing in the sunlight, with the Stars and Stripes and the banner of Lincoln High going before.

"Yump-yump, tiddle-tiddle, yump-yump, tiddle-tiddle!" sang Helmholtz happily. "Yump-yump-yump, ra-a-a-a-a, yump-yump, yump-yump—boom!"

As he paused to choose the next number for his imaginary band to play, he heard a furtive[8] noise in the chemistry laboratory next door. Helmholtz sneaked into the hall, jerked open the laboratory door, and flashed on the lights. Jim Donnini had a bottle of acid in either hand. He was splashing acid over the periodic table of the elements, over the blackboards covered with formulas, over the bust of Lavoisier. The scene was the most repulsive thing Helmholtz could have looked upon.

Jim smiled with thin bravado.

"Get out," said Helmholtz.

"What're you gonna do?" said Jim.

"Clean up. Save what I can," said Helmholtz dazedly. He picked up a wad of cotton waste and began wiping up the acid.

"You gonna call the cops?" said Jim.

"I—I don't know," said Helmholtz. "No thoughts come. If I'd caught you hurting the bass drum, I think I would have killed you with a single blow. But I wouldn't have had any intelligent thoughts about what you were—what you thought you were doing."

"It's about time this place got set on its ear," said Jim.

"Is it?" said Helmholtz. "That must be so, if one of our students wants to murder it."

"What good is it?" said Jim.

"Not much good, I guess," said Helmholtz. "It's just the best thing human beings ever managed to do." He was helpless, talking to himself. He had a bag of tricks for making boys

---

8. **furtive** (fèr′tiv), *adj.* sly, secret.

behave like men—tricks that played on boyish fears and dreams and loves. But here was a boy without fear, without dreams, without love.

"If you smashed up all the schools," said Helmholtz, "we wouldn't have any hope left."

"What hope?" said Jim.

"The hope that everybody will be glad he's alive," said Helmholtz. "Even you."

"That's a laugh," said Jim. "All I ever got out of this dump was a hard time. So what're you gonna do?"

"I have to do something, don't I?" said Helmholtz.

"I don't care what you do," said Jim.

"I know," said Helmholtz. "I know." He marched Jim into his tiny office off the band rehearsal room. He dialed the telephone number of the principal's home. Numbly, he waited for the bell to get the old man from his bed.

Jim dusted his boots with a rag.

Helmholtz suddenly dropped the telephone into its cradle before the principal could answer. "Isn't there anything you care about but ripping, hacking, bending, rending, smashing, bashing?" he cried. "Anything? Anything but those boots?"

"Go on! Call up whoever you're gonna call," said Jim.

Helmholtz opened a locker and took a trumpet from it. He thrust the trumpet into Jim's arms. "There!" he said, puffing with emotion. "There's my treasure. It's the dearest thing I own. I give it to you to smash. I won't move a muscle to stop you. You can have the added pleasure of watching my heart break while you do it."

Jim looked at him oddly. He laid down the trumpet.

"Go on!" said Helmholtz. "If the world has treated you so badly, it deserves to have the trumpet smashed!"

"I—" said Jim. Helmholtz grabbed his belt, put a foot behind him, and dumped him on the floor.

Helmholtz pulled Jim's boots off and threw them into a corner. "There!" said Helmholtz savagely. He jerked the boy to his feet again and thrust the trumpet into his arms once more.

Jim Donnini was barefoot now. He had lost his socks with his boots. The boy looked down. The feet that had once seemed big black clubs were narrow as chicken wings now—bony and blue, and not quite clean.

The boy shivered, then quaked. Each quake seemed to shake something loose inside, until, at last, there was no boy left. No boy at all. Jim's head lolled, as though he waited only for death.

Helmholtz was overwhelmed by remorse. He threw his arms around the boy. "Jim! Jim—listen to me, boy!"

Jim stopped quaking.

"You know what you've got there—the trumpet?" said Helmholtz. "You know what's special about it?"

Jim only sighed.

"It belonged to John Philip Sousa!"[9] said Helmholtz. He rocked and shook Jim gently, trying to bring him back to life. "I'll trade it to you, Jim—for your boots. It's yours, Jim! John Philip Sousa's trumpet is yours! It's worth hundreds of dollars, Jim—thousands!"

Jim laid his head on Helmholtz's breast.

"It's better than boots, Jim," said Helmholtz. "You can learn to play it. You're somebody, Jim. You're the boy with John Philip Sousa's trumpet!"

Helmholtz released Jim slowly, sure the boy would topple. Jim didn't fall. He stood alone. The trumpet was still in his arms.

"I'll take you home, Jim," said Helmholtz. "Be a good boy and I won't say a word about tonight. Polish your trumpet, and learn to be a good boy."

"Can I have my boots?" said Jim dully.

---

9. **John Philip Sousa,** 1854–1932, an American conductor and composer of band music.

"No," said Helmholtz. "I don't think they're good for you."

He drove Jim home. He opened the car windows and the air seemed to refresh the boy. He let him out at Quinn's restaurant. The soft pats of Jim's bare feet on the sidewalk echoed down the empty street. He climbed through a window, and into his bedroom behind the kitchen. And all was still.

PREDICT: Given what you know about Helmholtz and Jim, what do you think will happen tomorrow?

The next morning the waddling clanking, muddy machines were making the vision of Bert Quinn come true. They were smoothing off the place where the hill had been behind the restaurant. They were making it as level as a billiard table.

Helmholtz sat in a booth again. Quinn joined him again. Jim mopped again. Jim kept his eyes down, refusing to notice Helmholtz. And he didn't seem to care when a surf of suds broke over the toes of his small and narrow brown Oxfords.

"Eating out two mornings in a row?" said Quinn. "Something wrong at home?"

"My wife's still out of town," said Helmholtz.

"While the cat's away—" said Quinn. He winked.

"When the cat's away," said Helmholtz, "this mouse gets lonesome."

Quinn leaned forward. "Is that what got you out of bed in the middle of the night, Helmholtz? Loneliness?" He jerked his head at Jim. "Kid! Go get Mr. Helmholtz his horn."

Jim raised his head, and Helmholtz saw that his eyes were oysterlike again. He marched away to get the trumpet.

Quinn now showed that he was excited and angry. "You take away his boots and give him a horn, and I'm not supposed to get curious?" he said. "I'm not supposed to start ask-

René Magritte was known for his style of painting ordinary objects in realistic but odd ways. What effect does he create in this 1935 painting, *Le Modèle Rouge*?

ing questions? I'm not supposed to find out you caught him taking the school apart? You'd make a lousy crook, Helmholtz. You'd leave your baton, sheet music, and your driver's license at the scene of the crime."

"I don't think about hiding clues," said Helmholtz. "I just do what I do. I was going to tell you."

Quinn's feet danced and his shoes squeaked like mice. "Yes?" he said. "Well, I've got some news for you too."

"What is that?" said Helmholtz uneasily.

"It's all over with Jim and me," said Quinn. "Last night was the payoff. I'm sending him back where he came from."

"To another string of foster homes?" said Helmholtz weakly.

"Whatever the experts figure out to do with a kid like that." Quinn sat back, exhaled noisily, and went limp with relief.

"You can't," said Helmholtz.

"I can," said Quinn.

"That will be the end of him," said Helmholtz. "He can't stand to be thrown away like that one more time."

"He can't feel anything," said Quinn. "I can't help him; I can't hurt him. Nobody can. There isn't a nerve in him."

"A bundle of scar tissue," said Helmholtz.

The bundle of scar tissue returned with the trumpet. Impassively,[10] he laid it on the table in front of Helmholtz.

Helmholtz forced a smile. "It's yours, Jim," he said. "I gave it to you."

"Take it while you got the chance, Helmholtz," said Quinn. "He doesn't want it. All he'll do is swap it for a knife or a pack of cigarettes."

"He doesn't know what it is, yet," said Helmholtz. "It takes a while to find out."

"Is it any good?" said Quinn.

"Any good?" said Helmholtz, not believing his ears. "Any good?" He didn't see how anyone could look at the instrument and not be warmed and dazzled by it. "Any good?" he murmured. "It belonged to John Philip Sousa."

Quinn blinked stupidly. "Who?"

Helmholtz's hands fluttered on the table top like the wings of a dying bird. "Who was John Philip Sousa?" he piped. No more words

came. The subject was too big for a tired man to cover. The dying bird expired and lay still.

After a long silence, Helmholtz picked up the trumpet. He kissed the cold mouthpiece and pumped the valves in a dream of a brilliant cadenza. Over the bell of the instrument, Helmholtz saw Jim Donnini's face, seemingly floating in space—all but deaf and blind. Now Helmholtz saw the futility[11] of men and their treasures. He had thought that his greatest treasure, the trumpet, could buy a soul for Jim. The trumpet was worthless.

Deliberately, Helmholtz hammered the trumpet against the table edge. He bent it around a coat tree. He handed the wreck to Quinn.

"Ya busted it," said Quinn, amazed. "Why'dja do that? What's that prove?"

"HE CAN'T FEEL ANYTHING," SAID QUINN. "I CAN'T HELP HIM; I CAN'T HURT HIM."

"I—I don't know," said Helmholtz. A terrible blasphemy[12] rumbled deep in him, like the warning of a volcano. And then, irresistibly, out it came. "Life is no damn good," said Helmholtz. His face twisted as he fought back tears and shame.

Helmholtz, the mountain that walked like a man, was falling apart. Jim Donnini's eyes filled with pity and alarm. They came alive. They became human. Helmholtz had got a message through. Quinn looked at Jim, and something like hope flickered for the first time in his bitterly lonely old face.

———————————

10. impassively (im pas′iv lē), *adj.* without feeling or emotion.
11. futility (fyü til′ə tē), *n.* uselessness.
12. blasphemy (blas′fə mē), *n.* contempt for a holy or sacred thing; profanity.

Two weeks later, a new semester began at Lincoln High.

In the band rehearsal room, the members of C Band were waiting for their leader—were waiting for their destinies as musicians to unfold.

Helmholtz stepped onto the podium, and rattled his baton against his music stand. "The Voices of Spring," he said. "Everybody hear that? The Voices of Spring?"

There were rustling sounds as the musicians put the music on their stands. In the pregnant silence that followed their readiness, Helmholtz glanced at Jim Donnini, who sat on the last seat of the worst trumpet section of the worst band in school.

His trumpet, John Philip Sousa's trumpet, George M. Helmholtz's trumpet, had been repaired.

"Think of it this way," said Helmholtz. "Our aim is to make the world more beautiful than it was when we came into it. It can be done. You can do it."

A small cry of despair came from Jim Donnini. It was meant to be private, but it pierced every ear with its poignancy.

"How?" said Jim.

"Love yourself," said Helmholtz, "and make your instrument sing about it. A-one, a-two, a-three." Down came his baton.

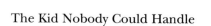

After Reading

Making Connections

1. If Helmholtz, Quinn, and Jim were musical instruments, what would each one be? What kind of vegetables would they be? Explain your answers.

2. Pick out a favorite passage from the story to read aloud. Explain why you like the passage.

3. Why do you think Helmholtz destroyed his trumpet at the end?

4. How is Jim different at the end of the story? What do you think makes him **change?**

5. What other ways do you think Helmholtz could have tried to reach Jim?

6. How would this story have been different if Helmholtz had been an art teacher? an English teacher? a baseball coach? Explain.

7. Music, art, and drama have been used as therapy for troubled people. How do you think the arts might help people overcome their emotional problems?

8. If you found someone destroying school property, what would you do? What are your choices?

Literary Focus: Symbolism

Writers make use of objects that **symbolize** certain things to the characters in the story. For example, in "Little Red Riding Hood," the basket of goodies for the grandmother could symbolize kindness and generosity. For many people, money symbolizes independence. Flowers symbolize innocence and simplicity. "The Kid Nobody Could Handle" also makes use of symbols. Locate some of the symbols, and decide what they mean to whom. A good example would be the black boots. What do you think they mean to Jim? Write a poem or a paragraph that explains the meaning of the boots in the story.

Vocabulary Study

unnerving
diversion
linger
appalled
ail
ennui
furtive
impassively
futility
blasphemy

A. On your paper, copy the blanks below and fill them in with words for the numbered definitions. Choose your answers from the list of words. The first one has been done for you.

1. unsettling U N (N) E R V I N G
2. go slowly __ __ __ __ __ (○)
3. lack of interest __ __ __ (○) __
4. profane language __ __ __ (○) __ __ __ __
5. as if feeling nothing __ (○) __ __ (○) __ __ __ __ __
6. done quickly to avoid being noticed __ __ __ (○) __ __ __
7. worthlessness __ __ (○) __ __ __ __
8. something that distracts you __ __ __ __ __ __ __ (○)
9. shocked __ __ __ __ __ __ (○) __
10. bother __ (○) __

B. Now, rearrange the letters in the circles to form a word that is instrumental to the story.

__ __ __ __ __ __ __ __ __ __ __ __

Expressing Your Ideas

Writing Choices

Sometime Down the Road Write an **epilogue** to the story. What happens to Jim a year later? When he grows up?

In His Own Words If Jim had kept a **journal,** what would he have written? Use the list of information about Helmholtz and Quinn that you kept during your reading, and write a description of each man in Jim's words.

Jim's Dream Helmholtz had a dream: to lead the finest band in the world. What was Jim's dream? Write a **poem** that expresses Jim's dream. Your poem might have two parts: what Jim would have said at the beginning and end of the story.

Other Options

Music, Maestro! Investigate the **music** of John Philip Sousa. Perhaps someone at a local record store, a music teacher, or your librarian could help you. If possible, tape Sousa's music and present it to the class, along with an explanation of his influence on music.

Paste It Up Create a **collage** that represents one of the characters in the story. Use magazine pictures, cut-out words, and little objects (for example, fabric or a key chain) to create a poster for Helmholtz, Quinn, or Jim. Present the collage to the class and explain your choice of materials and objects.

Why Is This Happening to Me?

High Jumpers

Sociology Connection

Ben Carson had a rough start in life. He used violence to solve his problems, but the problems only got worse. At this point, Ben did not start feeling sorry for himself and asking "Why is this happening to me?" Instead, he decided to change.

His are the hands that doodled and danced aimlessly on elementary school tests, threatened his mother with a hammer, and stabbed a friend whose belt buckle deflected the knife.

The same hands have since saved many lives. As one of the world's leading pediatric neurosurgeons, Carson has developed and performed several surgical procedures for children suffering from brain tumors and chronic seizures. In his most acclaimed operation, Carson, chief of pediatric neurosurgery at Johns Hopkins, led a team of 70 doctors, nurses, and technicians in the first successful separation of Siamese twins joined at the back of the head.

Ben Carson
A Man of Action

by Patricia Sellers

Says Carson: "People who know me now find it absolutely incredible that I ever got mad about things."

He often tells his life story to kids, hoping to inspire them to get an education and escape the ghetto as he has. Carson's father, a part-time preacher and factory worker, walked out when Ben was 8, leaving his mother, Sonya, to support Ben and his older brother, Curtis, now 42 and an engineer at Allied-Signal. To do so, she worked at a number of low-paying jobs simultaneously.

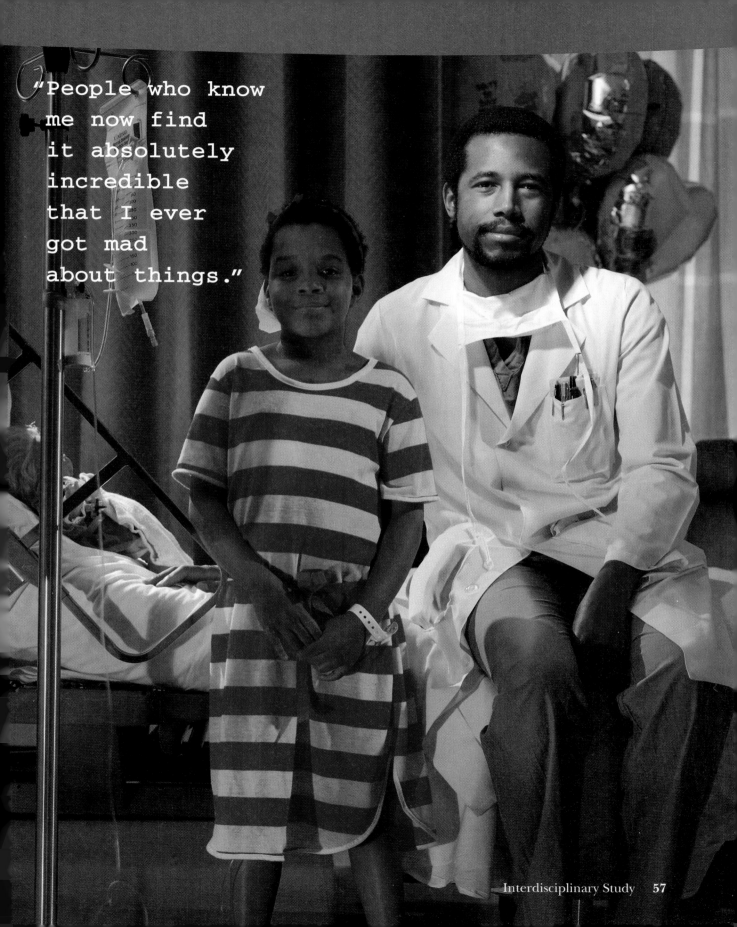

"People who know me now find it absolutely incredible that I ever got mad about things."

As a youngster in Detroit, Ben never cared about school and was known as the class dummy. So when he was 10, his mother reduced watching TV to three shows a week and made him read two books instead and write reports on them.

Only years later did Carson realize she did not know how to read herself, but her assignments saved him. "Reading was the transforming thing for me," he recalls. "I read about inventors and engineers and men like Booker T. Washington and Abraham Lincoln who took themselves from nowhere through reading, to become great men." In seventh grade he was winning spelling bees, and he became the top student in science.

He felt inspired, but Ben's temper blocked his progress. As a young teen, he says, "I'd hit people with bats and bricks. I was nuts." After he knifed a friend over an argument about changing a radio station, Carson locked himself in his bathroom for three hours and prayed. Reading from the Book of Proverbs, he came upon verses that warn about temper. For example, "He that hath no rule over his own spirit is like a city that is broken down." Says Carson: "I recognized that if I couldn't control that temper, I would never realize my dream of becoming a doctor." That dream harks back to age 8, when he heard stories at his Seventh-Day Adventist church about missionary doctors. To him, they seemed "the most noble people in the world."

Graduating third in his class at Detroit's Southwestern High, Carson had only $10 to spend on college application fees. He decided to apply to whichever school won that year's College Bowl, then a popular TV quiz show. Yale's ouster of Harvard determined his next move. Scholarships and grants helped pay the aspiring doctor's way through Yale and the University of Michigan School of Medicine. Carson now lives in a Baltimore suburb with his wife, Candy, their three sons, ages 5 through 8—and his mother. Inspired by her son, Sonya Carson earned a high school degree at 43 and went on to a two-year college to get an associate of the arts degree. At 64, she now works as an interior decorator.

"I recognized that if I couldn't control that temper, I would never realize my dream of becoming a doctor."

Responding

1. Ben Carson used men such as Booker T. Washington and Abraham Lincoln as role models. Who do you think makes a good role model for today's teens? Why?

2. Ben Carson is not the only person in this story who made a life change. What can you learn from Sonya, Ben's mother?

Mathematics Connection

Challenge wears a different mask for everyone. Depending on who you are, where you grow up, and how you relate to family and friends, you will face a few or many of the challenges represented in the following charts. Will you clear the hurdles?

Jumping the Hurdles

Junk Eating

In an average week, an American teenager consumes:

2.7 fast-food purchases
8.3 sticks of gum
3.6 salty snacks
2.3 candy bars
9.8 soft drinks

Source: Teenage Research Unlimited, Fall 1993

Top Concerns

The greatest problems facing the U.S. today, according to teenagers:

1 AIDS 21%
2 Economy 15%
3 Crime/gangs 13%
4 Education 10%
5 Intolerance/racism 6%

Source: Teenage Politics: Public and Personal, BKG Youth, Fall 1993

Post-Graduation Plans

What teenagers say they are likely to do after high school:

68% Attend college full time
18% Attend college part time
5% Join armed services
5% Work full time

Source: America's Youth in the 1990s, George H. Gallup International Institute, poll of 12- to 17-year-olds, Fall 1992

Lethal Weapon

POLICE LINE DO NOT CROSS POLICE LINE DO NOT CROSS

Source: FBI Crime Statistics, 1995

■ Number of homicide victims killed by guns, ages 10–19

■ Total number of U.S. homicide victims, ages 10–19

Responding

Study the chart of teens' top concerns. Then decide what *you* think the greatest problem facing the U.S. today is and write it on a small piece of paper. Everyone in the class should do the same thing. One student should collect the papers and write the total figures for each item on the board. As a class, determine the percentages for each concern. Discuss how your class statistics differ from those in the survey. Try to suggest reasons for the differences.

BE YOUR OWN

Check It Out

So how's *your* self-esteem? Check yourself out!

✔ Do you like who you are?

✔ Do you try new things even if they may seem hard?

✔ Do you think it's OK to make mistakes?

✔ Are you kind to others?

✔ Can you keep from getting angry if you are criticized?

✔ Can you do something different from what your friends do or say?

✔ Can you usually tell people how you feel and what you want?

Ken always works hard at school. He almost always gets A's and gets really upset if he gets anything else.

Brian's teachers say that he could do better if he would just try harder. But he doesn't. On the playground and in the halls, he bullies the other kids.

Who has high self-esteem, Ken or Brian? Neither one! You've probably heard about self-esteem, the way you feel about yourself and what you can do. Everybody has it, but whether your self-esteem is high or low depends on you—how *you* think about yourself.

Both Ken and Brian are showing low self-esteem in different ways. Brian feels as if he can't do new things, so he gives up easily. He also acts tough on the outside to make up for feeling weak on the inside. Ken may seem as if he is doing fine but thinks he is only good if he's always the best.

Good self-esteem is right in the middle: You aren't afraid to try new things, you treat others with respect, you do your best but let yourself make mistakes.

CHEER LEADER

If you answered *yes* to most of these questions, your self-esteem is in good shape. If you put yourself down a lot, feel shy, or are afraid to try new things, your self-esteem may need a boost. If you anger easily, feel jealous, or have a hard time telling people what you want or how you feel, you may want to work on liking yourself better.

Pump Yourself Up

If you decide your self-esteem could use some pumping up, here are some ways to start:

Think about your strengths.
So what are you good at? Write down a list of your strengths. Don't hold back.

Catch those negative thoughts.
"I can't." "They won't like me." What you say to yourself affects how you feel. Anytime you catch yourself saying something negative, stop and think it over. Try saying something positive instead: "I can."

Do something hard.
By trying something that seems hard and succeeding, your good feelings about yourself get stronger. It takes practice. You may have to try many times before you succeed; you may have to succeed many times before you really believe that you can do it.

Respect others and yourself.
If you treat others with kindness, it not only helps you feel good about yourself, it's easier to treat yourself the same way.

Let others know how you feel.
Being kind to others doesn't mean that you can't let people know what you want or when they hurt your feelings.

Make decisions.
You have to make decisions every day. Good self-esteem means making the best decision based on what you want, rather than following others.

Be responsible.
It's easy to feel good about yourself when you see yourself as responsible.

Ready to give it a try? This can be your best year ever. Work hard at school, make new friends, but most of all, be a best friend to yourself. After all, you're as good as you think you are.

Responding

1. Take the self-esteem test in this article. Decide whether your self-esteem needs a boost.

2. Now write down a plan. List at least three things you can do to boost your self-esteem. Concentrate on this plan until it becomes a part of you. If your self-esteem is in good shape, write a plan for helping someone you know feel better about him- or herself. Follow through with the plan.

Reading Mini-Lesson

Using Comparison and Contrast

Comparing is looking for similarities, and **contrasting** is pointing out differences. You rarely do one without doing the other. When you are shopping for a new bike, for example, you automatically compare and contrast when looking at prices, styles, and special features.

Some nonfiction articles and textbook sections are organized by comparison and contrast. A social studies article about the Civil War might compare and contrast the North and South with respect to population, industry, and agriculture. A science article about rocks might compare and contrast sedimentary and igneous rocks. A good way to see comparisons and contrasts is to use a chart or a Venn Diagram, such as the one in the margin.

Northern and Southern States During Civil War

North — industrial, pro-tariff, slavery illegal

sure of victory

South — agricultural, anti-tariff, slavery legal

Activity Options

1. Ben Carson, the surgeon described on pages 56–58, says that people who know him now would never believe what he was like in the past. Yet, in some ways, the young Ben was the same person he is today. Compare and contrast Ben's life as an adult with his life as a child and teenager. Make a chart to organize the details.

2. "Be Your Own Cheerleader" gives you suggestions for building self-esteem, but you could lower self-esteem by doing the opposite. Write a humorous article which tells people your age how to lower their self-esteem. Reverse each advice heading (start with "*Think about your weaknesses*") and explain the steps to follow. You will better understand any process if you understand its opposite.

3. Find a section of your social studies or science book that compares and contrasts something and make a Venn Diagram to show similarities and differences between the two events, cultures, or organisms discussed in the section. The overlapping part of the diagram will include characteristics shared by both items.

Part Two

The Many Faces of Change

Life is a story of change. Changes happen in our physical and emotional selves as well as in our perceptions of ourselves and others. The characters in these selections all must deal with change. Some are in control of the change, while others are controlled by it.

 Multicultural Focus **Perspective** involves seeing things from different points of view. At times your perspective is influenced by the ethnic group or community you belong to. Other times you may try to change the perspectives of others because of your unique experiences.

Literature

Ellen Conford	**Liverwurst and Roses** ◆ short story	.65
Russell Freedman	**A President's Wife** ◆ biography	.78
Eleanor Roosevelt	**from *The Autobiography of Eleanor Roosevelt*** ◆ autobiography	.82
	Language Mini-Lesson ◆ Commonly Misspelled Words	.86
May Swenson	**Fable for When There's No Way Out** ◆ poem	.88
Georgia Douglas Johnson	**Your World** ◆ poem	.89
Rod Serling	**Back There** ◆ play	93
Michael J. Caduto and Joseph Bruchac	**The Passing of the Buffalo** ◆ Kiowa folk tale	.107

Interdisciplinary Study Trailblazers

Survival of the Stronghearted by Anna Howard Shaw ◆ U.S. history . .109

A New Life on the Frontier ◆ U.S. history .112

    Reading Mini-Lesson ◆ Visualizing .114

Writing Workshop Narrative Writing

Traveling Through Time 115

Beyond Print Technology Skills

Electronic Research 121

Before Reading

Liverwurst and Roses

by Ellen Conford

Ellen Conford
born 1942

Ellen Conford writes realistic stories about typical problems of teenagers. Her stories have a humorous, lighthearted tone, and her titles are meant to make you curious. Here are two: *If This Is Love, I'll Take Spaghetti* and "Teacher from the Prehistoric Planet." She says this about her own writing: ". . . I write the kinds of books for children and teenagers that *I* liked to read at their age, books meant purely to entertain. . . ."

Building Background

Everything Has Changed! *Howie Freel didn't know the exact moment that he'd fallen in love with Bonnie Fitzgerald, but the thing was, he had. He didn't know why like had turned to love, how friendship had blossomed into romance. . . .* So begins the story you're about to read. Wow! What a change! When friendships change, it can be hard to know what to do or how to act. The **theme** of this group of selections is "The Many Faces of Change." The change in Howie's feelings is easy to see. Now, what is he going to do about it?

Getting into the Story

Writer's Notebook Do you find it hard to tell a person you care about just how you feel? Telling someone your true feelings can be difficult. What are the risks of revealing your feelings? What are the rewards? In your notebook, jot down your thoughts.

Reading Tip

Realistic Dialogue Ellen Conford is known for the realism in her stories. One way she gives her writing a sense of being real is by using **dialogue** that sounds the way people really talk. Here's an example from "Liverwurst and Roses":

> He cleared his throat. "I was —"
>
> "This stuff is awful!" She shoved her plate away.

An incomplete sentence such as "I was—" is unacceptable in formal writing, but it *is* the way people often speak, especially when they are interrupted. Exaggerations such as "This is awful!" or "I'm starving!" are also common in conversations. As you read the story, look for examples of realistic dialogue. Make notes in a chart something like this:

Humorous Exaggerations	Incomplete Sentences

Liverwurst and *Roses*

Ellen Conford

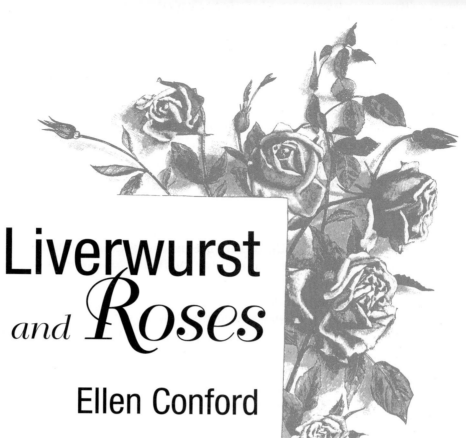

*H*owie Freel didn't know the exact moment that he'd fallen in love with Bonnie Fitzgerald, but the thing was, he had. He didn't know why like had turned to love, how friendship had blossomed into romance, or when the kid he'd known since they were first-grade babies had magically developed into a first-class babe.

And the other thing was, Bonnie didn't know it, either.

He was sure she had no idea that when she said, "Hi, Freel," as she always did, his knees turned to Jell-O. She didn't know what a struggle it was to keep his voice normal when he answered, "Hi, Fitz."

She didn't know the iron self-control it took to walk her home after school without throwing his arms around her and plastering her gorgeous face with kisses.

And she certainly showed no desire to plaster his face with kisses. She showed no desire for him whatsoever. He was just good old Howie, best buddy, great sense of humor, zero hunk quotient.[1]

---

1. **hunk quotient,** a boy's attractiveness to a girl.

Not knowing what to do with his turbulent[2] feelings, Howie kept them to himself. He suffered in silence, maintaining the relationship the way it had always been, afraid if he pushed for something closer, he might lose her entirely.

But the situation reached an intolerable level when Bonnie started to date. Other guys. Guys with considerable hunk quotient. Guys who probably weren't afraid to snuggle up to her in the movies, or plaster her face with kisses when they took her home.

Bonnie didn't tell him the gory details, but his imagination ran wild every time she went out with one of them.

At this point Howie could suffer in silence no longer.

"I can't stand it," he told Jon Kramer. They were shooting hoops in Jon's driveway. Howie blew six foul shots in a row. When Jon asked him what was wrong, he blurted out everything.

"Does she know you like her?" asked Jon.

"Like her?" Howie repeated. "*Like* her? I don't just 'like' her, Kramer. I *love* her. With a deep, burning, eternal flame of passion."

"That's pretty poetic," said Jon, impressed. "Why don't you tell her that?"

"I can't tell her that! I can hardly say hello to her without keeling over."

"Then write it," Jon said. "Girls really go for those flowery love letters."

"Write her a love letter?" Even thinking about it made Howie panicky. "That seems pretty drastic."

"Who's she going out with tonight?" asked Jon.

"Dexter Brevitch," Howie answered glumly.

"The wrestler?" Jon tossed the basketball at Howie's head. "Don't you think drastic steps are called for?"

The ball grazed Howie's ear. He hardly felt it. He thought of Dexter's meaty arm around Bonnie's slim waist, his broken nose nuzzling her delicate ear. He closed his eyes as if he could shut out the hideous image. But he couldn't switch off his imagination. His stomach churned, and prickles of sweat broke out on his upper lip.

"But what if she laughs in my face?" he asked.

"How can she laugh in your face?" Jon said. "You'll mail her the letter, she'll read it in private, and if she does laugh, you'll never know it."

"But what's the point?" Howie asked. "To her we're just friends. One mushy letter isn't going to change her mind."

"How do you know?" Jon demanded. "Maybe she feels the same way you do. Maybe she's just waiting for you to make the first move."

"Why would she wait?" said Howie. "Bonnie was never shy."

"Neither were you until you fell in love with her."

Howie sighed. "Well, I'll think about it." He headed down the driveway, shoulders slumping.

"Don't think about it too long," Jon called after him. "Those wrestlers know some pretty fancy holds."

Howie's stomach turned over again.

Dear Bonnie,
This is a hard letter to write . . .
(This is an impossible letter to write.)
For a long time, unbeknownst to you . . .
(Unbeknownst? *Unbeknownst?* Freel, are you nuts?)
You light up my life . . .
(Oh, puh-leeze!)

Howie ripped up the three sheets of paper and tossed the pieces into the air. They rained down on him like a shower of shattered hopes.

Howie could suffer in silence no longer.

---

2. **turbulent** (tėr′byə lənt), *adj.* disorderly; violent.

▲ *Together* was created by Diana Ong. What qualities of love do you think the artist meant to represent?

What made him think he could write a love letter? He'd never gotten higher than a C+ in English.

He picked up his guitar and began to strum a mournful series of chords. He wasn't a great musician, but he felt that he compensated for his lack of skill with an abundance of soul.

A song! Of course!

You could say anything you wanted in a song. As long as you made it rhyme and set it to music, you could talk about love and passion without making a fool of yourself.

He got his tape recorder and sat down cross-legged on the floor. He tuned his guitar and waited for the creative juices to flow.

It took him one afternoon to write the song and record it. But it took him three days to work up the courage to give the tape to Bonnie.

"What is it?" she asked as he thrust the tape at her abruptly Friday afternoon.

"It's a song I wrote." He wanted to add, "for you," but he couldn't bring himself to say it.

But she'd know, as soon as she heard it. He wouldn't have to spell out his feelings for her. They were all there, in melody, in lyrics, in the key of G.

> "I think of you in the morning
> when the sun begins to shine,
> "I think of you in the evening
> when the stars come out at nine,
> "I think of you the whole day through,
> how can I make you mine?
> "Ooh ooh. Ooh ooh. Ooh ooh."

"Hey, Freel!" Dexter Brevitch approached him in the locker room before gym class. He was wearing only his jockey shorts. Every muscle in his body rippled as he confronted Howie. And that was a lot of muscle.

Uh-oh. Howie was glad that he was still dressed. If Dexter wanted to kill him for putting a move on Bonnie, at least he wouldn't have to flee the locker room naked.

He cringed against his locker, trying to look as if he wasn't cringing.

"That was a nice song you wrote," Dexter said unexpectedly. "I liked it."

"Uh, thanks." Howie relaxed a little. Dexter didn't sound as if he were about to kill him. But then he realized something.

"You heard it?" he asked.

"Oh, yeah. Bonnie and me listened to it Friday night. It's real—you know—romantic." Dexter gave him a playful punch on the shoulder. Howie bounced off the locker and staggered sideways. "I think you got talent."

Howie was so outraged, he ignored the pain in his shoulder. Bonnie had taken his song and played it for Dexter. She'd used his soulful declaration of love to set the mood for a sordid smooching session with this overdeveloped, steroid-swilling troglodyte.[3]

"So, you gonna be a songwriter, or what?" Dexter asked.

I'll never write another song as long as I live, Howie vowed to himself.

But to Dexter he said, "I don't think so. I think I'll probably be a taxidermist."

PREDICT: How will Howie try to solve his problem?

"What a nightmare," he told Jon. "I pour out my heart in song and she uses it for make-out music with Dexter."

"I guess you have to be more direct," Jon said. "Apparently she didn't realize you were pouring out your heart."

"Oh, right," Howie retorted. "'I think of you the whole day through, how can I make you mine?' is too <u>subtle</u>."[4]

---

3. **troglodyte** (trog′lə dīt), cave man.
4. **subtle** (sut′l), *adj.* so fine or delicate as to be unnoticed.

"Well, you didn't say, 'I think of you the whole day through, how can I make you mine, *Bonnie*,'" Jon said.

"Nothing rhymes with Bonnie." Howie put his head in his hands.

"Look," said Jon. "this is ridiculous. How does any guy approach a girl? Take her to a romantic restaurant, send her flowers, buy her a bracelet."

"I have twenty-seven dollars in the bank," Howie said.

"Take her to McDonald's," Jon snapped. "Buy her a *small* bracelet. You don't need money to let a girl know you like her. Just do something to show her how much."

"That was a cute song you wrote," said Bonnie. "Dexter really liked it."

They were sitting at their usual table in the school cafeteria. Howie watched her poke at her chicken chow mein. It was, he realized, the perfect moment to reveal his feelings. She'd mentioned the song, so she must be curious about why he'd given it to her. And when he told her, she wouldn't laugh so hysterically that she'd choke on her food, because she wasn't eating any of it.

He took a deep breath. He cleared his throat. "I was—"

"This stuff is awful!" She shoved her plate away. "A liverwurst[5] sandwich would taste like caviar[6] compared to this."

"About my s—" he began again.

"I keep meaning to bring my own lunch," she grumbled. "But I never seem to have time in the morning."

Howie pushed half his sandwich toward her. He reached into his brown bag and took out an apple and two oatmeal cookies.

"Here. Listen, I wanted to tell—"

"Howie, I can't," she protested. "You'll be starving all day."

It was, he realized, the perfect moment . . .

"I don't mind." He swallowed hard. "See, I—"

"Well, maybe just one cookie." She bit into the oatmeal cookie and delicately licked the crumbs from her lips.

Such courage as Howie had mustered dissolved faster than a spoonful of sugar in a cup of scalding tea.

"Mmm, heavenly," said Bonnie. Her voice was deep and velvety.

Howie nearly passed out.

The idea hit him on the way home, as he was listening to his stomach rumble. Bonnie had eaten the cookie, the apple, and finally accepted part of his sandwich.

He could make her a special lunch, and surprise her with it the next day. He might even gift-wrap the sandwich, put everything in a bag, and tie a fancy bow to it, like a present.

Well, maybe the bow was too much.

A rose! he thought. One perfect rose. A liverwurst sandwich, a pickle, some cookies, and a rose. She would marvel at how thoughtful he was, how much he cared about her. She'd eat the lunch, smell the rose, and know that only someone who loved her very deeply would go to so much trouble.

He headed downtown. "Buds Я Us" wouldn't be open in time for him to buy the rose tomorrow morning. It would keep in the refrigerator overnight.

When he got to the flower shop, he was the only customer. A blonde girl behind the counter looked up from her paperback. She was tall and thin and wore earrings that looked like turkey bones, which hung down nearly to her shoulders.

---

5. **liverwurst** (liv′ər wėrst′, liv′ər wùrst), sausage made of liver.
6. **caviar** (kav′ē är, kä′vē är), fish eggs eaten as an appetizer.

"I want one perfect rose," he said.

"What color?" the girl asked.

"Red."

"Okey doke."[7] She went to a glass refrigerated case and picked out a red rose. She held it out to him. It *was* a perfect rose. It was a magnificent rose.

"That'll be four dollars."

"Four dollars!" For the second time that day Howie nearly passed out.

"They're cheaper if you buy them by the dozen," she said. "But for one perfect rose it's four bucks."

"What about one imperfect rose?" Howie asked desperately.

"They're all the same price," she said. "A rose is a rose is a rose." She grinned at him. "That's a florist joke."

Things were reaching a crisis point.

"Ha ha." Howie walked dejectedly out of "Buds Я Us." He couldn't spend four dollars on a rose.

Across the street, in Woolworth's window, he spotted a display of artificial flowers. Maybe a plastic rose would be okay. It was still a romantic gesture, even if it wasn't a real rose. It was the thought that counted.

Besides, he tried to convince himself, a real rose would be dead in a couple of days. This rose would live forever. Every time Bonnie looked at it, she would think of him.

After all, a rose is a rose is a rose, he told himself.

He crossed the street and went into Woolworth's.

*H*e didn't get to walk to school much with Bonnie anymore. Dexter drove her, and when he didn't have afternoon matches, he drove her home, too.

Things were reaching a crisis point. If this romantic lunch didn't work, he didn't know what he'd do. Maybe drop out of school and become a monk.

He got up half an hour early to prepare Bonnie's lunch. The plastic rose had cost eighty-nine cents. At the supermarket he'd bought liverwurst, a sourdough French baguette,[8] and a huge Comice pear. He'd never heard of Comice pears, but they were $2.19 a pound, so he figured they must be pretty special.

Fortunately there was a Pepperidge Farm carrot cake in his freezer. He hacked two slices from the cake, using a bread knife driven by a meat-tenderizing mallet. The slices were pretty ragged-looking, but they would still taste good when they thawed.

The rose was too long to fit in the bag. He could Scotch tape it to the outside, but he'd feel a little self-conscious carrying a lunch bag with a flower on it.

He hated to cut it—but he would have hated it more if he were cutting the four-dollar rose. So he lopped three inches off it and put it in the bag. It didn't look very elegant with its stem shortened, but then, it hadn't looked all that elegant to begin with.

At lunchtime Bonnie was already sitting at their table. He was sure that the only reason she still ate lunch with him was because Dexter had a different lunch period.

"Ms. Fitzgerald," he said, bowing low. Keep it light, Freel, he warned himself. "Your tragic plight moved me."

Bonnie looked at him curiously. "What tragic plight?"

"Your lunch plight. Therefore I have—"

"Oh." She grinned. "It moved me, too." She reached into her backpack and pulled out a brown paper bag. "It moved me to take your advice. I got up early and made my own lunch."

---

7. **okey doke,** okay.

8. **baguette** (ba get′), a long, narrow loaf of bread.

▲ The repetition of the hearts in *20 Hearts* by Jim Dine (1970) creates an abstract pattern of colors. How is this use of the heart shape different from the way the heart shape is used in the painting on page 67?

"You what?" Howie stood there stupidly, holding two lunch bags, unable to make his mouth form any more words. Hastily he tried to stick one of the bags behind his back. But he wasn't fast enough.

"Oh, Howie, did you make me lunch?"

He nodded.

"What a sweet thing to do."

"But obviously," he said, "pointless."

"Not at all," she protested. "I'll bet you made me a much nicer lunch than I brought. I just have a liverwurst sandwich. Howie, what's the matter?"

*H*ow could he have been so dumb? If he were going to make a gallant gesture, like preparing her lunch, why hadn't he made it something wonderful? Like smoked turkey with honey mustard? Or roast beef and Muenster cheese with horseradish dressing? Or—

Because liverwurst or bologna was all he could afford, and because she had told him that she'd rather have liverwurst than caviar. Well, she'd said something like that.

She reached for one of the bags.

"You've already got lunch," he said. "You don't want this."

"Yes I do," she insisted. "Come on, Howie, it was a lovely gesture. And I'm really hungry today."

He shoved the bag at her. "Fine. Now you have two liverwurst sandwiches."

"You made liverwurst, too?" She laughed delightedly. "What a funny coincidence."

"Hilarious," he said.

She opened the bag. "A rose! Howie, you put a rose in my lunch!" She pulled out the plastic flower and admired it. "What a sweet thing to do."

"Yeah. Sweet."

"Well, it is," she said. "And I certainly didn't bring myself a flower." She bent the rose and stuck it into her hair behind her ear. "I feel quite glamorous," she said.

I feel like a jerk, Howie thought.

"Hey, Howie, want to shoot some hoops?" Jon was on the phone.

"I want to shoot myself," Howie replied.

"Aww, you're not going to start this again, are you?"

"Listen carefully, Jon. I made a complete fool of myself. I don't ever want to eat lunch again."

"In our cafeteria that's the first rule of survival," Jon said.

"She was laughing at me."

"No, she wasn't," Jon argued. "She wore that rose in her hair all day. She told everyone that you gave it to her."

"So everyone could laugh at me."

"Wrong, wrong, wrong," Jon said. "She wore it because it made her feel happy. Now if you would just tell her—"

"I have to hang up," Howie cut in. "I'm going to jump out a second-story window and kill myself."

"Freel, you live in a ranch house."

"So I'll go next door."

CONNECT: What would you do next if you were Howie?

The following day Howie ate lunch in the locker room. On Thursday he took his lunch to the football field and ate in the bleachers.

Friday morning he opened his front door to find Bonnie standing on the steps. Her arms were folded across her chest, and the expression on her face was grim.

"Freel, why are you avoiding me?"

"I'm not avoiding you," he lied.

"Then why don't you eat lunch with me anymore? Why don't you talk to me anymore? Why don't I see you anymore?"

"Because you're always with Dexter," he said.

"Not at lunchtime. What's with you? You give a girl a sandwich and a rose and you never talk to her again? Do you always give girls flowers before you dump them?"

"Dump you?" he said. *"I dumped you?"*

"Well, what do you call it when you stop speaking to someone? When you look the other way when you see them coming?"

"Self-defense," Howie said miserably.

"What?" She searched his face. Her eyes were wide and her lips trembled. She looked very vulnerable.[9] "Don't you want to be friends anymore?" she whispered.

He finally lost it. "No!" he shouted. "No, I don't!"

Her eyes filled with tears. "But why? What did I do?"

He'd never seen her so hurt. He hated himself.

"Nothing!" he snapped. "Don't you understand? I *like* you."

She wiped her eyes with her fingers. "You like me? You sure have a funny way of showing it."

He dropped his books to the lawn. He put his hands on her shoulders. He took a deep breath. "I mean, I *like* you. Really like you. More than a friend."

"Oh." Her eyes widened in comprehension. *"Ohh."*

"But I know you don't feel the same way. And I made a fool of myself trying to show you. So for the sake of my mental health and emotional well-being—"

"Why didn't you tell me?" she demanded.

"I tried," he said. "I brought you lunch, I gave you a rose, I wrote you a song . . ."

"I didn't know you wrote that song for me," she said. "I just thought—well, I thought it was a joke."

"A *joke*?" Angrily he snatched his books from the lawn and stalked toward the street.

She hurried after him. "Howie, wait. I mean, I thought it was a sort of a parody.[10] You know, that ooh ooh part. I didn't realize—"

His face was hot with humiliation. There had been other moments in his life when he'd

thought, This is the worst thing that ever happened to me. But every one of them paled in comparison to this.

"Howie, please." She caught up to him and grabbed his arm. "If I knew you meant it for me, do you think I would have played it in front of Dexter?"

"Dexter loved it," Howie said bitterly. "He thought it was real romantic."

"Oh, Howie. Why didn't you just tell me?"

"How could I?" He stopped in the middle of the sidewalk. "What if you laughed at me? What if we had to stop being friends after I told you? Then I'd never get to see you. And I knew you didn't like me *that* way."

"How did you know I didn't?" Bonnie asked softly.

"Because you never told me you did."

"And you never told me," she replied.

Howie's heart lurched. He felt the blood rushing to his head so fast that he thought his corpuscles[11] might explode in his veins.

"You mean—are you saying—"

"I'm saying it's hard to change a relationship," Bonnie answered. "I'm saying that you've always been fun and I love your sense of humor."

"I'm a million laughs," Howie said.

"So how was I supposed to know you weren't just joking around?" she asked. "Like you always do? Like we always did?"

"Bonnie . . ." He wished she'd come right out and say whatever it was she was getting at. He didn't want to hope, and he couldn't bear not to.

"Why did you go out with Dexter?" he asked. It was the only thing he could think of to say. "And all those other guys?"

---

9. vulnerable (vul′nər ə bəl), *adj.* sensitive to criticism.
10. parody (par′ə dē), *n.* a humorous imitation of a serious writing.
11. **corpuscle** (kôr′pus′əl, kôr′pə səl), any of the cells that form the blood.

This is a detail from *Equestrian,* a 1931 painting of a couple on a horse by Marc Chagall. What details in the painting give it a feeling of romance?

"They asked me," she said simply. "And I thought maybe if I started going out, you'd look at me differently."

He could hardly see straight. The street disappeared, the houses disappeared, everything around him misted over like morning fog. Only Bonnie's face was clear. Bonnie's beautiful face.

"You should have told me," he said.

"Freel, you're the last person to criticize me for not telling you."

"You really like me?" he asked <u>incredulously</u>.[12] "Really, really like me?"

"I really like you," she said.

Stunned, Howie gazed down at her. Should he kiss her? Should he hug her? Should he throw his books in the air and shout, "YES!"?

Bonnie was his, at last, and he had no idea what his next move was supposed to be.

"What do we do now?" he asked finally.

"We walk to school," she said. She pressed her fingers against his palm. "Holding hands."

---

12. incredulously (in krej′ə ləs lē), *adv.* doubtfully; without being able to believe.

After Reading

Making Connections

1. Did you find this story believable? Explain why or why not.

2. Do you think Jon gives Howie good advice? Explain your answer.

3. As you might guess from the title, the story is intended to be humorous. Give two examples of humor from the story.

4. 👣 How might this story be different if it were told from Bonnie's **perspective?**

5. A story has a beginning, a middle, and an end, but these parts are not always clearly marked. Recall the **plot** of this story and divide it into these three parts. Explain where each part ends.

6. Authors choose **titles** very carefully, since titles usually create first impressions with readers. Do you think "Liverwurst and Roses" is a good title for this story? Tell why or why not.

7. Do you think the feelings and events in this story are typical of young adults, people around the ages of Howie and Bonnie? Why or why not?

Literary Focus: Hyperbole

"I don't ever want to eat lunch again."

The expression "hype" is a shortened form of the word **hyperbole** (hī pėr′bə lē), which means "exaggeration to create an effect on the reader or listener." We use hyperbole when simple description or explanation just won't make clear the emotional quality we want to express. Much of the humor in "Liverwurst and Roses" comes from the narrator's frequent exaggerations.

In this story, find two examples of hyperbole that show a character's feelings. For each example, tell what feeling the exaggeration expressed. If you kept a chart similar to the one suggested in the Reading Tip on page 64, use the notes you listed under *Humorous Exaggerations* as a starting point.

Vocabulary Study

On your paper, write the letter of the word or phrase that best completes each sentence.

vulnerable
parody
turbulent
incredulously
subtle

1. <u>Vulnerable</u> people are usually ____.

   a. weak and easily hurt   **b.** loud and obnoxious   **c.** tall and thin

2. A <u>parody</u> tells a story with ____.

   a. seriousness   **b.** humor   **c.** truthfulness

3. <u>Turbulent</u> feelings are ____.

   a. calm   **b.** sad   **c.** stormy

4. If you look at someone <u>incredulously</u>, you probably ____.

   a. are in love   **b.** are afraid   **c.** are doubtful

5. A <u>subtle</u> gesture would be ____.

   a. a wink   **b.** slamming a door   **c.** screaming hello across the street

Expressing Your Ideas

Writing Choices

Dear Bonnie *This is a hard letter to write.* Howie finds it impossible to write a love letter to Bonnie, but perhaps your writing abilities are up to the task. Write a **letter** for Howie to send Bonnie, declaring his love for her—the more flowery the language, the better! Howie will be eternally grateful.

That Kills Me This story uses hyperbole to express the feelings of characters. We use this technique often in conversation. "You missed it by a mile!" is one example. Make a **list** of five to ten expressions that use exaggeration for effect.

"Love/Hate/Lost" The title of the book in which the story about Howie is found is *I Love You, I Hate You, Get Lost.* Make up another story that could fit this title. Make an **outline** of the plot to show the story's action.

Other Options

Starring You as Narrator Select a part of the story to **read aloud.** As you prepare, think of what you will need to do with your voice to make each character clear to your listeners.

The Untold Story No story can tell everything. We find out about one special lunch in this story, but meals that were not as important are left out. Sometimes, however, the parts left out could make interesting stories in themselves. For example, how does Bonnie tell Dexter that it's over? Work with a classmate to brainstorm how that scene might take place, and then **act it out** for your class.

Ooh ooh. Ooh ooh. You know the lyrics to Howie's love song, but how does it sound? Put Howie's song to **music,** and perform it for an audience.

Before Reading

A President's Wife

by Russell Freedman

Russell Freedman
born 1929

Russell Freedman explains his interest in Eleanor Roosevelt in this way: "I think I'm attracted to subjects who had a strong sense of injustice and felt in a very deep personal sense that there were things that are wrong that have to be fixed. And because of that they're controversial; they're stepping on toes. . . ."

When he writes, he wants to convey his deep interest in his subject. The keys to this are being honest and making careful decisions about what to include and what to leave out. Instead of trying to tell everything about the person he writes about, he tries to focus on what is most important in the person's life.

Building Background

You Can't Do That! In the 1930s and 1940s, when Eleanor Roosevelt was First Lady, the roles of women were much more restricted than they are now. Women had only had the vote for a short time (since 1920), and they were not expected to take positions of authority in politics or the workforce. Eleanor Roosevelt directed much of her time and energy to removing restrictions on equal rights for all. In the process, she challenged stereotypes about women's roles—and set an example for future women.

Getting into the Selection

Writer's Notebook Other people's expectations can be a help. You might work hard, for example, to meet someone's high expectations for you. Expectations can also be limiting—obstacles in the way of your achievement. Our own expectations for ourselves can also be helpful or limiting. Think of a time when you did something others did not expect you to do, or that you yourself did not expect. In your notebook, tell what you did, why your action was unexpected, and what the result was.

Reading Tip

K-W-L Chart Prepare a K-W-L Chart similar to the one below. In a group, complete the first part of the K-W-L Chart by brainstorming what you already know (or think you know) about Eleanor Roosevelt, the wife of President Franklin Delano Roosevelt. Then complete the second part of the chart by listing what you want to know—the questions you want to have answered as you read. After you read the selection, you will add what you have learned to the chart.

What We **K** now	What We **W** ant to Know	What We **L** earned

A President's Wife

Russell Freedman

An expectant, windswept crowd of one hundred thousand had gathered in front of the capitol under gray skies to watch Franklin Delano Roosevelt take his oath as the nation's thirty-second president. Eleanor Roosevelt—wearing a blue coat and a bouquet of white orchids—stood among eighty dark-suited men on the inaugural[1] platform. She listened intently as her husband spoke.

On that raw winter day—March 4, 1933—the Great Depression was in its fourth destructive year. As many as fifteen million men and women—one-third of the available work force—had lost their jobs and could not find work. Thousands of banks had failed, wiping out the savings of their depositors. In America's great cities, hungry and homeless people stood in long lines at charity soup kitchens and foraged for food in garbage cans. Not since 1861, when Abraham Lincoln assumed leadership of a divided nation, had a new president faced such a crisis.

▲ Mrs. Roosevelt's White House press conferences gave women journalists a unique opportunity to report on political issues.

"This nation asks for action, and action now," Roosevelt declared. "I shall ask Congress for . . . broad Executive power to wage a war against the emergency, as great as the power that would be given to me if we were in fact invaded by a foreign foe."

Back at the White House, Lorena Hickok waited in the room that had once been Abraham Lincoln's bedroom and would now

---

1. inaugural (in ô′gyər əl), *adj.* of or for the ceremony of installing a person in office.

be Eleanor Roosevelt's sitting room and study. During the presidential campaign,[2] the two women had formed a close bond of friendship and mutual affection. Hick knew better than anyone Eleanor's private anguish as she faced the prospect of life in the White House.

Eleanor had promised her friend an exclusive interview following the inauguration. "It was very, very solemn and a little terrifying," she told Hick. "The crowds were so tremendous, and you felt that they would do *anything*—if only someone would tell them *what* to do."

As he had promised, President Roosevelt acted swiftly to meet the crisis and restore confidence. During his first hundred days in office he pushed through Congress the most far-reaching legislative program in American history. At the same time, Eleanor Roosevelt proved to herself and to an astonished nation of Roosevelt watchers that she did not intend to be a conventional White House hostess.

She broke with tradition when she announced that she would hold regular press conferences open to women reporters only—an idea suggested by Lorena Hickok. They would be the first press conferences ever given by a First Lady, on the record, in the White House. Other presidential wives, shielded from the press, had refused even to grant interviews. Eleanor believed that the nation's citizens had a right to know what the people in the White House were thinking and doing. She met with thirty-five "press girls" for the first time on March 6, just two days after FDR's inauguration.

The White House staff was flabbergasted[3] by the First Lady's easy informality. In her eagerness to get settled, Eleanor pitched in and helped move furniture around. She insisted on running the little wood-paneled elevator herself, without waiting for a porter to run it for her. And she refused to be shadowed by Secret Service agents whenever she went out. "No one's going to hurt me," she said. "I simply can't imagine being afraid of

going among [Americans] as I always have, as I always shall."

Rather than go everywhere in a limousine, she bought a light-blue Plymouth roadster—a sporty convertible with a rumble seat.[4] She would drive it herself, she announced, as she was accustomed to doing—without a chauffeur or police escort. That summer, she invited Hick to join her on a three-week motor tour of New England and Canada. Eleanor had not yet been photographed often enough to be recognized. The two friends traveled as "ordinary tourists" without anyone realizing who they were.

Early in her husband's administration, Mrs. Roosevelt made a surprise appearance that dramatized her resolve[5] to stay in touch with ordinary citizens. The year before, when Herbert Hoover was still president, thousands of unemployed war veterans had marched on Washington, demanding that bonuses promised them in the future be paid immediately. Hoover was so alarmed that he called out the Army. Troops commanded by General Douglas MacArthur routed the jobless veterans with tear gas and burned their encampment.[6]

Shortly after FDR took office, the bonus marchers returned to the capital. This time the government opened an old army camp to house the men and provided them with food and medical care. Even so, many people feared that violence would erupt again. Critics charged that the unemployed veterans were

---

2. campaign (kam pān′), *n.* series of connected activities to do or get something, such as to win an election.
3. **flabbergasted,** astonished greatly; amazed
4. **rumble seat,** an extra seat that opens out from the back of some automobiles.
5. resolve (ri zolv′), *n.* firmness in carrying out a purpose; determination.
6. encampment (en kamp′mənt), *n.* place where a group, such as soldiers, make a camp.

A President's Wife   **79**

led by Communist agitators who wanted to stir up trouble.

One afternoon, Eleanor took Louis Howe for a drive in her new roadster. He suggested that they stop by the veterans' encampment. When they arrived, he announced that he was going to sit in the car and wait while Eleanor toured the rows of tents. "Hesitatingly, I got out and walked over to where I saw a line-up of men waiting for food," she wrote later. "They looked at me curiously and one of them asked my name and what I wanted. When I said I just wanted to see how they were getting on, they asked me to join them."

Eleanor spent an hour chatting with the men. Before leaving, she joined in as everyone sang "There's a Long, Long Trail." "Then I got into the car and drove away," she recalled. "Everyone waved and I called, 'Good luck,' and they answered, 'Good-bye and good luck to you.'"

At her next press conference, Mrs. Roosevelt described the camp as "remarkably clean and orderly" and the veterans as "grand-looking boys with a fine spirit." Her unannounced visit and courteous reception helped calm the public's fears about the bonus marchers and created sympathy for their demands. She had discovered that a personal appearance by the First Lady could have a powerful impact on public opinion. As one of the veterans remarked: "Hoover sent the Army. Roosevelt sent his wife."

Never before had the American people seen a First Lady like Eleanor Roosevelt. Soon she was flying off all over the country, serving as her husband's personal investigative reporter and gathering material for her columns, articles, radio talks, and books. Reporters who covered the White House and traveled with Mrs. Roosevelt marveled at her energy and pace.

She was a frequent flier at a time when a trip in an airplane was considered a great adventure. Once, in order to impress the public with the ease and safety of air travel, Amelia Earhart invited the First Lady to join her on a flight from Washington to Baltimore. They both wore evening dresses. "How do you feel being piloted by a woman?" Eleanor was asked. "Absolutely safe," she replied. "I'd give a lot to do it myself!"

Eleanor seemed to go everywhere. Since she could travel more freely than Franklin, she again became his "eyes and ears." She dropped in on coal miners in Appalachia, slum-dwellers in Puerto Rico, and sharecroppers[7] in their tarpaper shacks in southern cotton fields. And she inspected government relief projects from one end of the country to the other, "often managing to arrive without advance notice so that they could not be polished up for my inspection." Her sympathetic visits created a feeling among millions of Americans that someone in the highest levels of government cared about their problems.

She had been writing for newspapers and magazines since the 1920s. As First Lady, she began a daily syndicated[8] newspaper column called "My Day," which reported on her travels and her life in the White House. She also wrote a monthly column, and turned out a steady flow of articles for magazines. And she wrote every word herself.

When critics complained that the First Lady's sentences were wordy and her topics trivial, magazine writer Bruce Bliven came to her defense: "I have a feeling that the New York sophisticates are all wrong and that the country as a whole likes the sort of person Mrs. Roosevelt has in her column demonstrated herself to be—friendly, unpretentious,[9] possessed of inexhaustible vitality, a broad interest in all

---

7. **sharecroppers,** people who farm land for an owner in return for part of the crops.
8. **syndicated,** distributed to many newspapers.
9. unpretentious (un'pri ten'shəs), *adj.* modest.

sorts of people and a human wish for their welfare."

Along with her writing, Eleanor spoke regularly on the radio and toured widely as a lecturer. She hired a voice coach who helped her modulate the high-pitched tones that sometimes marred her talks. When she rose to speak, she prayed silently that she would have something meaningful to say to the people in front of her. Then she focused on two or three faces in the audience. By speaking directly to those people, she was able to infuse her talk with warmth and spontaneity.[10] She became one of the most popular lecturers in America.

The first president's wife to fly, she earned the nickname "Eleanor Everywhere."

She was admired for the calm and authoritative manner with which she handled questions after a speech, including those meant to embarrass her. One hostile questioner asked: "Do you think your husband's illness has affected his mentality?" Without changing her expression, Eleanor replied: "I am glad that question was asked. The answer is Yes. Anyone who has gone through great suffering is bound to have a greater sympathy and understanding of the problems of mankind." The audience gave her a standing ovation.

Mrs. Roosevelt used her lectures, her radio talks, her columns and articles, her press conferences, and her endless travels through America to publicize her views on social justice, and to help bring the White House closer to the American people. The most outspoken of First Ladies, she became a powerful advocate[11] for the weak and disadvantaged in American society—for blacks and other minorities, for tenant farmers, the unemployed, the hungry and the homeless, for all those who had no platform[12] or spokesperson of their own.

10. **spontaneity** (spon′tə nē′ə tē), *n.* the quality of being natural, unplanned, and unforced.
11. **advocate** (ad′və kit, ad′və kāt), *n.* person who pleads or argues for; supporter.
12. **platform** (plat′fôrm), *n.* a plan of action or statement of principles for a political party or group.

from **The Autobiography of Eleanor Roosevelt**

In the beginning, because I felt, as only a young girl can feel it, all the pain of being an ugly duckling, I was not only timid, I was afraid. Afraid of almost everything, I think: of mice, of the dark, of imaginary dangers, of my own _inadequacy_.[1] My chief objective, as a girl, was to do my duty. This had been drilled into me as far back as I could remember. Not my duty as I saw it, but my duty as laid down for me by other people. It never occurred to me to revolt. Anyhow, my one overwhelming need in those days was to be approved, to be loved, and I did whatever was required of me, hoping it would bring me nearer to the approval and love I so much wanted.

As a young woman, my sense of duty remained as strict and rigid as it had been when I was a girl, but it had changed its focus. My husband and my children became the center of my life and their needs were my new duty. I am afraid now that I approached this new _obligation_[2] much as I had my childhood duties. I was still timid, still afraid of doing something wrong, of making mistakes, of not living up to the standards required by my mother-in-law, of failing to do what was expected of me.

As a result, I was so hidebound by duty that I became too critical, too much of a disciplinarian. I was so concerned with

---

1. inadequacy (in ad′ə kwə sē), _n._ a being not adequate, not as much as is needed.
2. obligation (ob′lə gā′shən), _n._ duty due to a promise, contract, or relationship; responsibility.

bringing up my children properly that I was not wise enough just to love them. Now, looking back, I think I would rather spoil a child a little and have more fun out of it.

It was not until I reached middle age that I had the courage to develop interests of my own, outside of my duties to my family. In the beginning, it seems to me now, I had no goal beyond the interests themselves, in learning about people and conditions and the world outside our own United States. Almost at once I began to discover that interest leads to interest, knowledge leads to more knowledge, the capacity for understanding grows with the effort to understand.

From that time on, though I have had many problems, though I have known the grief and the loneliness that are the lot of most human beings, though I have had to make and still have to make endless adjustments, I have never been bored, never found the days long enough for the range of activities with which I wanted to fill them. And, having learned to stare down fear, I long ago reached the point where there is no living person whom I fear, and few challenges that I am not willing to face.

Eleanor's wedding portrait (March 17, 1905) ➤

After Reading

Making Connections

1. Suppose you were one of the reporters invited to Mrs. Roosevelt's press conferences. What questions would you ask?

2. From your reading, what did you learn about Eleanor Roosevelt? Go back and complete the final column of the K-W-L Chart you started on page 77.

3. A **biography** is a life-picture, and an **autobiography** is a self-portrait. Make two lists of Mrs. Roosevelt's **character traits.** In the first column, list the traits revealed in "A President's Wife." In the second column, list the traits revealed in her autobiography. How do the lists differ?

4. How do you think the author of "A President's Wife" feels about Eleanor Roosevelt? Go back to the selection and find passages that support your answer.

5. ☝ Describe one important way in which Eleanor Roosevelt changed Americans' **perspective** on the role of a First Lady.

6. If she were First Lady today, what do you think Mrs. Roosevelt would try to accomplish?

7. How do you think people today would react to Mrs. Roosevelt if she tried to accomplish the goals you listed in your answer to the previous question?

Literary Focus: Characterization

Writers can show the personalities of people and characters in a number of ways:

- by what characters say
- by what characters do
- by what narrators or other characters say about them.

On your own paper, make a chart like the one below. Then, review the selection to find at least one example of each type of characterization. An example is given for you.

Method	Example	Personality
Her Words	"No one's going to hurt me."	She is confident and unafraid.
Her Actions		
Others' Words		

inaugural
campaign
resolve
encampment
unpretentious
spontaneity
advocate
platform
inadequacy
obligation

Vocabulary Study

A. Write the word that best completes the meaning of each sentence.

As a young woman, Eleanor Roosevelt had felt it was her __(1)__ to satisfy everyone. She had been afraid people would notice her __(2)__ if she didn't do everything right. As a result, she was afraid to do many things. By the time she stood watching the __(3)__ ceremonies in which her husband was sworn in as President, she had changed. People were impressed with her lively __(4)__ as she lectured and spoke on the radio. Whereas some First Ladies are formal and reserved, Eleanor seemed __(5)__ and down-to-earth.

B. Write the letter of the word that is not related in meaning to the other words in the set.

1. **a.** commitment   **b.** resolve   **c.** attempt   **d.** decision
2. **a.** defender   **b.** opponent   **c.** supporter   **d.** advocate
3. **a.** campaign   **b.** strategy   **c.** accident   **d.** plan
4. **a.** hill   **b.** encampment   **c.** shelter   **d.** housing
5. **a.** beliefs   **b.** position   **c.** platform   **d.** event

Expressing Your Ideas

Writing Choices

Dear Mrs. Roosevelt You've read about some of the goals Mrs. Roosevelt was trying to accomplish. Select one or two of these goals and write a **letter** to tell her what progress has been made toward those goals between her lifetime and the present.

Wanted . . . First Lady Eleanor Roosevelt was not an elected official, but she did have great power and influence while her husband was President. Write a **job description** for a First Lady. List the personality traits, skills, and knowledge needed, as well as some of the activities a First Lady might be expected to perform. Look back through the selection for ideas.

Another Option

First Ladies' Convention Working in a group, **research** the life of a former First Lady. Find out what activities she enjoyed and what she tried to do as First Lady. Then hold a convention of former First Ladies. One member of your group will play the part of your First Lady. Prepare an opening **speech** from the point of view of your First Lady. Talk about her goals, actions, and achievements. If you are chosen to play the part of a First Lady, use Mrs. Roosevelt's speaking tips:

- concentrate on what you want to say
- say it directly to one or two people in your audience

After the opening statements, be ready to continue the conversation.

Language Mini-Lesson

Commonly Misspelled Words

Recognizing Homophones When Mary wrote to say she was having fun at the youth hostile, her parents weren't sure whether she was at a lodging or with some unfriendly kids. Mary meant to say that she was at a *hostel.* Miscommunication can happen when homophones—words that sound alike but have different spellings and meanings—get confused. For example, what misunderstanding might come up if the wrong homophone were used in the sentence, *They reserved a suite at the hotel?* How is the meaning of the word *sweet* different?

Computer Tip

Only you can catch spelling errors due to confused homophones. That's because computers can't understand the meaning you're trying to get across. So, to the computer, these words seem to be spelled correctly.

Spelling Strategy To use homophones correctly, you first need to know what they mean. What is the difference in meaning between *allowed* and *aloud? overdue* and *overdo?* If you're not sure which homophone to use, look them both up in the dictionary.

Even if you know the meanings of the words, you might make careless errors if you don't think about the meanings as you write. For example, you probably know that *too* means "also," but if you're not careful you might use *to* or *two* instead. Other commonly confused homophones to watch for include *it's/its, they're/their/there,* and *you're/your.*

Activity Options

1. What crazy misunderstandings might come up if two people were having a conversation on the Internet and homophones got confused? Write an e-mail "dialogue" that features some funny miscommunications with homophones.

2. Memory tricks, such as the sentence *Use a cymbal as a symbol for noise,* can help you remember the meanings of homophones. Make up your own memory tricks for the homophones *hour-our, knew-new, assistants-assistance,* and *allowed-aloud.*

3. Write sentences that can be completed with each of the following homophones: *there-their-they're, whole-hole, to-too-two,* and *your-you're.* Trade with a partner and try to fill in each other's sentences.

Before Reading

Fable for When There's No Way Out by May Swenson
Your World by Georgia Douglas Johnson

May Swenson
1919–1989

May Swenson is one of America's most famous modern poets. In much of her poetry, Swenson played with language—putting words together in unusual combinations and creating puns. She believed that a good poem should leave something for the reader to do.

Georgia Douglas Johnson
1886–1966

Georgia Douglas Johnson was one of the first African American female poets to become widely known and read. She was a musician and a playwright, as well as a poet and a strong supporter of social and personal change.

Building Background

You're Getting Hot! Words can have more than one meaning. The literal meaning of *hot* is "very warm." However, in this phrase—*that hot new music group*—*hot* is used not in a literal or ordinary way, but in a figurative or unusual way. We use **figurative language** to add beauty or force to our expressions. Poetry is an especially rich source of figurative language.

Getting into the Poetry

Discussion Good readers tend to read with questions in mind. Often, the first questions come from looking at the title. In a small group or with a partner, discuss the titles of these two poems. Together, copy and complete the chart that follows by writing one or two questions to ask about each title.

"Fable for When There's No Way Out"

_____?
_____?

"Your World"

_____?
_____?

Reading Tip

Metaphors A **metaphor** is a kind of figurative language which makes an unusual comparison. The comparison is unusual because, at first glance, the two things compared don't appear to be similar. Comparing apples and oranges probably won't produce a metaphor, since the things being compared are both fruits. However, we can produce a metaphor by comparing someone's personality to an onion: To get to the center of each, you have to peel away many layers. As you read the poems, look for the unusual comparisons being made by each writer—the comparisons will probably be metaphors.

Fable for When There's No Way Out

May Swenson

Grown too big for his skin,
and it grown hard,

without a sea and atmosphere—
he's drunk it all up—

5 his strength's inside him now,
but there's no room to stretch.

He pecks at the top
but his beak's too soft;

though instinct or ambition shoves,
10 he can't get through.

Barely old enough to bleed
and already bruised!

In a case this tough
what's the use

15 if you break your head
instead of the lid?

Despair tempts him
to just go limp:

Maybe the cell's
20 already a tomb,

and beginning end
in this round room.

Still, stupidly he pecks
and pecks, as if from under

25 his own skull—
yet makes no crack . . .

No crack until
he finally cracks,

and kicks and stomps.
30 What a thrill

and shock to feel
his little gaff[1] poke

through the floor!
A way he hadn't known or meant.

35 Rage works if reason won't.
When locked up, bear down.

---

1. **gaff** (gaf), an iron hook with a handle for landing
fish; in this case it refers to the sharp spine on the
back of a bird's leg.

▶ *Soaring* was done by American painter Andrew Wyeth in 1950. Describe the unusual **perspective** of the painting. What do you think the perspective tells you about Wyeth's feelings for the American landscape?

Your World

Georgia Douglas Johnson

Your world is as big as you make it.
I know, for I used to abide[1]
In the narrowest nest in a corner,
My wings pressing close to my side.

5 But I sighted the distant horizon
Where the skyline encircled the sea
And I throbbed with a burning desire
To travel this immensity.[2]

I battered the cordons[3] around me
10 And cradled my wings on the breeze
Then soared to the uttermost reaches
With rapture,[4] with power, with ease!

---

1. abide (ə bīd′), *v.* continue to live (in a place); dwell.
2. immensity (i men′sə tē), *n.* very great size or extent.
3. **cordon** (kôrd′n), line or circle of soldiers, policemen, forts, etc., enclosing or guarding a place.
4. rapture (rap′chər), *n.* a strong feeling, especially of delight or joy.

After Reading

Making Connections

1. These two poems are quite different in style. Which poem do you prefer? Explain.

2. Look back at the questions you wrote about the titles of the two poems. Did the poems answer your questions? Explain.

3. 👣 Georgia Douglas Johnson writes from the **perspective** of an African American. How might that have influenced what she wrote in "Your World"?

4. How does "Your World" fit the **theme** of change? What do you think the poet is saying about personal change?

5. What words in the poems help to make the nest and the eggshell work as images of confinement and limitation?

6. At what point did you realize who "he" is in "Fable for When There's No Way Out"?

7. Where (at what line or lines) is the **turning point** in "Fable," the point when a solution is found to the problem? What is your evidence for thinking so?

8. What do you think each poet wants the reader to learn?

Literary Focus: Metaphors

Review the explanation of **metaphors** on page 87. Now look closely at "Fable for When There's No Way Out." The poem contains several metaphors for the eggshell. In your notebook, complete this word web by writing in each empty oval one of the things to which May Swenson compares the shell. Around the outside of each oval, write a few words about what the metaphor means. The first one has been done for you.

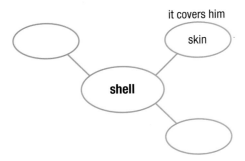

Vocabulary Study

Analogies Write the letter of the word pair that best expresses a relationship similar to that expressed in the first pair.

immensity
abide
rapture

1. **immensity : immense ::** (A) trivial : importance (B) intensity : intense
   (C) engineer : train (D) singing : songs (E) backward : forward

2. **abide : reside ::** (A) disobey : misbehave (B) yell : whisper
   (C) jog : walk (D) smile : frown (E) hide : seek

3. **abide : nest ::** (A) grow : child (B) escape : prison
   (C) fly : bird (D) sleep : bed (E) peck : beak

4. **immensity : smallness ::** (A) hot : warm (B) sad : upset
   (C) black : dark (D) sleepy : drowsy (E) tallest : shortest

5. **rapture : pleased ::** (A) thrill : empty (B) depression : unhappy
   (C) wealth : poor (D) skill : rehearsed (E) safety : protected

Expressing Your Ideas

Writing Choices

Show *and* Tell "Fable for When There's No Way Out" is a fable because it tells a story that ends with a *moral,* a statement that expresses a teaching or lesson. Working in a group, write your own **fable**. Begin by defining the moral you want to teach. Next, create a story that will *show* your moral. End with a few short sentences that tell the moral.

Expanding Your Horizons Can you think of a time when you dared to take a risk, even though it seemed too hard or dangerous? Write a **diary entry** for that day, beginning with the date and the words "Today I made my world a little bigger. . . ." If you can't think of an experience, write such a diary entry for an imaginary person.

To Rhyme or Not to Rhyme? Determine the rhyme scheme in "Your World" by noting which lines rhyme with each other. Then write a brief **poem** that follows the same rhyme scheme.

Other Options

Poetry-Cartoons Choose one of the poems and create a **cartoon strip** to show the action in it. Sketch pictures for three or four panels. Under each picture, write one or two lines from the poem that the picture illustrates.

Time Line for Chicks? We all have had experiences that broke old limits and brought new freedoms and horizons. Draw a **time line** and write in three or four such events that you think most people experience when they are young. (Don't forget the first day of school.)

birth 1 2 3 4 5 6 7 8 9 10 11 12

A Puzzling Poet Find a book of May Swenson's poetry, and choose a poem that you enjoy. Present it to the class in an **oral reading.**

Before Reading

Back There

by Rod Serling

Rod Serling
1924–1975

The Twilight Zone, a science fiction series for television which ran from 1959 to 1964, is probably the work for which Rod Serling is best known. In addition to writing TV scripts and hosting the show, he was also a producer, screenplay writer, and a teacher of drama at Ithaca College.

Rod Serling liked to explore the unknown—but not in outer space. His explorations took place within the human mind and heart. He once said, "I think you'll find that I have an awareness of human conflict—people fighting other people on many levels other than physical. I'm constantly aware—having lived to a certain extent in this kind of environment—of the combat that human beings enter into with themselves and others."

Building Background

Time and Again If you have read many science fiction stories, or seen movies and television programs of this kind, you know that traveling through space to strange places is a favorite topic for writers. Traveling through *time* is another popular topic of science fiction writers. Perhaps the best-known story of time travel is *The Time Machine,* written by H. G. Wells.

Getting into the Play

Writer's Notebook The word *regret* contains the prefix *re,* meaning "back" or "again." When we feel regret, it is usually about actions in the past—things we wish we had done, or things we wish we had not done. Wouldn't it be nice to be able to go back and live over again a day that you regret? As part of a unit on change, the play *Back There* explores a kind of change that boggles the mind—changing the past!

If you could go back in time and change one event in history, what would you change? In your notebook, describe the past event you would change and tell how you think that change would alter the course of history.

Reading Tip

Stage Directions *Back There* has no narrator, except at the very end. When a play is performed, live or on television, the setting, costumes, and action are all visible, so a narrator is not usually needed. However, when you read a play, setting, costumes, and action are shown through the **stage directions,** usually printed in italics. Stage directions are placed at the beginnings of scenes and also within the scenes. Many important things happen when no one is talking or when a character is alone on the stage, so you need to pay careful attention to these directions. As you read, focus on the stage directions for important information about setting, costumes, and action.

Rod Serling

Back There

CHARACTERS

PETER CORRIGAN, a young man
JACKSON, member of the Washington Club
MILLARD, member of the Washington Club
WHITAKER, member of the Washington Club
WILLIAM, attendant at the Washington Club
ATTENDANT ONE, at the Washington Club
ATTENDANT TWO, at the Washington Club
MRS. LANDERS, landlady of a rooming house
LIEUTENANT
LIEUTENANT'S WIFE
POLICE CAPTAIN
POLICEMAN
TURNKEY
POLICE OFFICER
JONATHAN WELLINGTON
LANDLADY
NARRATOR

Act One

SCENE ONE

Exterior of club at night. Near a large front entrance of double doors is a name plaque in brass which reads "The Washington Club, Founded 1858." In the main hall of the building is a large paneled foyer with rooms leading off on either side. An attendant, WILLIAM, *carrying a tray of drinks, crosses the hall and enters one of the rooms. There are four men sitting around in the aftermath of a card game.* PETER CORRIGAN *is the youngest, then two middle-aged men named* WHITAKER *and* MILLARD, *and* JACKSON, *the oldest, a white-haired man in his sixties, who motions the tray from the attendant over to the table.*

JACKSON. Just put it over here, William, would you?

WILLIAM. Yes, sir. (*He lays the tray down and walks away from the table.*)

CORRIGAN. Now what's your point? That if it were possible for a person to go back in time there'd be nothing in the world to prevent him from altering the course of history—is that it?

MILLARD. Let's say, Corrigan, that you go back in time. It's October, 1929. The day before the stock market crashed.[1] You know on the following morning that the securities are going to tumble into an abyss. Now using that prior knowledge, there's a hundred things you can do to protect yourself.

CORRIGAN. But I'm an anachronism[2] back there. I don't really belong back there.

MILLARD. You could sell out the day before the crash.

CORRIGAN. But what if I did and that started the crash earlier? Now history tells us that on October 24th, 1929, the bottom dropped out of the stock market. That's a fixed date. October 24th, 1929. It exists as an event in the history of our times. It *can't* be altered.

MILLARD. And I say it can. What's to prevent it? What's to prevent me, say, from going to a broker[3] on the morning of October 23rd?

---

1. **stock market crashed.** In October, 1929, stocks suddenly became greatly devalued, leading to a nationwide financial disaster and the ruin of many people.
2. anachronism (ə nak′rə niz′əm), *n.* anything out of keeping with a specified time.
3. **broker,** a person who buys and sells stocks and bonds for a client; stockbroker.

CORRIGAN. Gentlemen, I'm afraid I'll have to leave this time travel to H. G. Wells.[4] I'm much too tired to get into any more metaphysics[5] this evening. And since nobody has ever gone back in time, the whole blamed thing is much too theoretical. I'll probably see you over the weekend.

WHITAKER. Don't get lost back in time now, Corrigan.

CORRIGAN. I certainly shall not. Good night, everybody.

VOICES. Good night, Pete. Good night, Corrigan. See you tomorrow.

(CORRIGAN *walks out into the hall and heads toward the front door.*)

WILLIAM (*going by*). Good night, Mr. Corrigan.

CORRIGAN. Good night, William. (*Then he looks at the elderly man a little more closely.*) Everything all right with you, William? Looks like you've lost some weight.

WILLIAM (*with a deference built of a forty-year habit pattern*). Just the usual worries, sir. The stars and my salary are fixed. It's the cost of living that goes up. (CORRIGAN *smiles, reaches in his pocket, starts to hand him a bill.*)

WILLIAM. Oh no, sir, I couldn't.

CORRIGAN (*forcing it into his hand*). Yes, you can, William. Bless you and say hello to your wife for me.

WILLIAM. Thank you so much, sir. (*A pause*) Did you have a coat with you?

CORRIGAN. No. I'm rushing the season a little tonight, William. I felt spring in the air. Came out like this.

WILLIAM (*opening the door*). Well, April *is* spring, sir.

CORRIGAN. It's getting there. What is the date, William?

WILLIAM. April 14th, sir.

CORRIGAN. April 14th. (*Then he turns and grins at the attendant.*) 1965—right?

WILLIAM. I beg your pardon, sir? Oh, yes, sir. 1965.

CORRIGAN (*going out*). Good night, William. Take care of yourself. (*He goes out into the night.*)

SCENE TWO

Exterior of the club. The door closes behind CORRIGAN. *He stands there near the front entrance. The light from the street light illuminates the steps. There's the sound of chimes from the distant steeple clock.* CORRIGAN *looks at his wristwatch, holding it out toward the light so it can be seen more clearly. Suddenly his face takes on a strange look. He shuts his eyes and rubs his temple. Then he looks down at his wrist again. This time the light has changed. It's a wavery, moving light, different from what it had been.* CORRIGAN *looks across toward the light again. It's a gaslight[6] now. He reacts in amazement. The chimes begin to chime again, this time eight times. He once again looks at the watch, but instead of a wristwatch there is just a fringe of lace protruding from a coat. There is no wristwatch at all. He grabs his wrist, pulling at the lace and coat. He's dressed now in a nineteenth-century costume. He looks down at himself, looks again toward the gaslight that flickers, and then slowly backs down from the steps staring at the building from which he's just come. The plaque reads "Washington Club." He jumps the steps two at a time, slams against the front door, pounding on it. After a long moment the door opens. An attendant, half undressed, stands there peering out into the darkness.*

ATTENDANT ONE. Who is it? What do you want?

CORRIGAN. I left something in there.

(*He starts to push his way in and the* ATTENDANT *partially closes the door on him.*)

---

4. **H. G. Wells,** 1866–1946, an English writer known particularly for his prophetic science fiction. One of his best-known novels is *The Time Machine*, about traveling in time.

5. **metaphysics** (met′ə fiz′iks), the philosophical study of the nature of reality, including such concepts as time and space.

6. **gaslight.** Gas was used for lighting on streets and in buildings, chiefly during the nineteenth century.

ATTENDANT ONE. Now here you! The Club is closed this evening.

CORRIGAN. The devil it is. I just left here a minute ago.

ATTENDANT ONE *(peers at him)*. You did what? You drunk, young man? That it? You're drunk, huh?

CORRIGAN. I am not drunk. I want to see Mr. Jackson or Mr. Whitaker, or William. Let me talk to William. Where is he now?

ATTENDANT ONE. Who?

CORRIGAN. William. What's the matter with you? Where did *you* come from? *(Then he looks down at his clothes.)* What's the idea of this? *(He looks up. The door has been shut. He pounds on it again, shouting.)* Hey! Open up!

VOICE *(from inside)*. You best get away from here or I'll call the police. Go on. Get out of here.

(CORRIGAN backs away from the door, goes down to the sidewalk, stands there, looks up at the gaslight, then up and down the street, starts at the sound of noises. It's the clip-clop of horses' hooves and the rolling, squeaky sound of carriage wheels. He takes a few halting, running steps out into the street. He bites his lip, looks around.)

CORRIGAN *(under his breath)*. I'll go home. That's it. Go home. I'll go home. *(He turns and starts to walk and then run down the street, disappearing into the night.)*

SCENE THREE

Hallway of rooming house. There is the sound of a doorbell ringing. MRS. LANDERS, *the landlady, comes out from the dining room and goes toward the door.*

MRS. LANDERS. All right. All right. Have a bit of patience. I'm coming. *(Opening door)* Yes?

CORRIGAN. Is this 19 West 12th Street?

MRS. LANDERS. That's right. Whom did you wish to see?

CORRIGAN I'm just wondering if . . . *(He stands there trying to look over her shoulder.* MRS. LANDERS *turns to look behind her and then suspi-*ciously *back toward* CORRIGAN.*)*

MRS. LANDERS. Whom did you wish to see, young man?

CORRIGAN. I . . . I used to live here. It's the oldest building in this section of town.

MRS. LANDERS *(stares at him)*. How's that?

CORRIGAN *(wets his lips)*. What I mean is . . . as I remember it . . . it was the oldest—

MRS. LANDERS. Well now really, young man. I can't spend the whole evening standing here talking about silly things like which is the oldest building in the section. Now if there's nothing else—

CORRIGAN *(blurting it out)*. Do you have a room?

MRS. LANDERS *(opens the door just a little bit wider so that she can get a better look at him; looks him up and down and appears satisfied)*. I have a room for acceptable boarders. Do you come from around here?

CORRIGAN. Yes. Yes, I do.

MRS. LANDERS. Army veteran?

CORRIGAN. Yes. Yes, as a matter of fact I am.

MRS. LANDERS *(looks at him again up and down)*. Well, come in. I'll show you what I have.

(She opens the door wider and CORRIGAN *enters. She closes it behind him. She looks expectantly up toward his hat and* CORRIGAN *rather hurriedly and abruptly removes it. He grins, embarrassed.)*

CORRIGAN. I'm not used to it.

MRS. LANDERS. Used to what?

CORRIGAN *(points to the hat in his hand)*. The hat. I don't wear a hat very often.

MRS. LANDERS *(again gives him her inventory look, very unsure of him now)*. May I inquire as to what your business is?

CORRIGAN. I'm an engineer.

MRS. LANDERS. Really. A professional man. Hmmm. Well, come upstairs and I'll show you.

(She points to the stairs that lead off the hall and CORRIGAN *starts up as an army officer and his wife come down them.)*

MRS. LANDERS (*smiling*). Off to the play?

LIEUTENANT. That's right, Mrs. Landers. Dinner at The Willard and then off to the play.

MRS. LANDERS. Well, enjoy yourself. And applaud the President for me!

LIEUTENANT. We'll certainly do that.

LIEUTENANT'S WIFE. Good night, Mrs. Landers.

MRS. LANDERS. Good night, my dear. Have a good time. This way, Mr. Corrigan.

(*The* LIEUTENANT *and* CORRIGAN *exchange a nod as they pass on the stairs. As they go up the steps,* CORRIGAN *suddenly stops and* MRS. LANDERS *almost bangs into him.*)

MRS. LANDERS. Now what's the trouble?

CORRIGAN (*whirling around*). What did you say?

MRS. LANDERS. What did I say to whom? When?

CORRIGAN. To the lieutenant. To the officer. What did you just say to him?

(*The* LIEUTENANT *has turned. His wife tries to lead him out, but he holds out his hand to stop her so that he can listen to the conversation from the steps.*)

CORRIGAN. You just said something to him about the President.

LIEUTENANT (*walking toward the foot of the steps*). She told me to applaud him. Where might your sympathies lie?

MRS. LANDERS (*suspiciously*). Yes, young man. Which army *were* you in?

CORRIGAN (*wets his lips nervously*). The Army of the Republic,[7] of course.

LIEUTENANT (*nods, satisfied*). Then why make such a thing of applauding President Lincoln? That's his due, we figure.

MRS. LANDERS. That and everything else, may the good Lord bless him.

CORRIGAN (*takes a step down the stairs, staring at the* LIEUTENANT). You're going to a play tonight? (*The* LIEUTENANT *nods.*)

LIEUTENANT'S WIFE (*at the door*). We may or we may not, depending on when my husband makes up his mind to get a carriage in time to have dinner and get to the theater.

CORRIGAN. What theater? *What* play?

LIEUTENANT. Ford's Theater, of course.

CORRIGAN (*looking off, his voice intense*). Ford's Theater. Ford's Theater.

LIEUTENANT. Are you all right? I mean do you feel all right?

CORRIGAN (*whirls around to stare at him*). What's the name of the play?

LIEUTENANT (*exchanges a look with his wife*). I beg your pardon?

CORRIGAN. The play. The one you're going to tonight at Ford's Theater. What's the name of it?

LIEUTENANT'S WIFE. It's called "Our American Cousin."

CORRIGAN (*again looks off thoughtfully*). "Our American Cousin" and Lincoln's going to be there. (*He looks from one to the other, first toward the landlady on the steps, then down toward the soldier and his wife.*) And it's April 14th, 1865, isn't it? Isn't it April 14th, 1865? (*He starts down the steps without waiting for an answer. The* LIEUTENANT *stands in front of him.*)

LIEUTENANT. Really, sir, I'd call your actions most strange.

(CORRIGAN *stares at him briefly as he goes by, then goes out the door, looking purposeful and intent.*)

SCENE FOUR

Alley at night. On one side is the stage door with a sign over it reading "Ford's Theater." CORRIGAN *turns the corridor into the alley at a dead run. He stops directly under the light, looks left and right, then vaults over the railing and pounds on the stage door.*

CORRIGAN (*shouting*). Hey! Hey, let me in! President Lincoln is going to be shot tonight!

(*He continues to pound on the door and shout.*)

---

7. **Army of the Republic,** the northern army, or Federal Army, in the United States Civil War.

The photographs show Ford's Theater in 1865 (left) and today (right). What changes in the right-hand photo indicate that time has passed?

Act Two

SCENE ONE

Police station at night. It's a bare receiving room with a POLICE CAPTAIN *at a desk. A long bench on one side of the room is occupied by sad miscreants awaiting disposition. There is a line of three or four men standing in front of the desk with several policemen in evidence. One holds onto* CORRIGAN *who has a bruise over his eye and his coat is quite disheveled. The* POLICE CAPTAIN *looks up to him from a list.*

CAPTAIN. Now what's this one done? *(He peers up over his glasses and eyes* CORRIGAN *up and down.)* Fancy Dan with too much money in his pockets, huh?

CORRIGAN. While you idiots are sitting here, you're going to lose a President!

(The CAPTAIN *looks inquiringly toward the* POLICEMAN.*)*

POLICEMAN. That's what he's been yellin' all the way over to the station. And that's what the doorman at Ford's Theater popped him on the head for. *(He nods toward* COR-RIGAN.*)* Tried to pound his way right through the stage door. Yellin' some kind of crazy things about President Lincoln goin' to get shot.

CORRIGAN. President Lincoln *will* be shot! Tonight. In the theater. A man named Booth.

CAPTAIN. And how would you be knowin' this? I suppose you're clairvoyant[8] or something. Some kind of seer or wizard or something.

CORRIGAN. I only know what I know. If I told you *how* I knew, you wouldn't believe me. Look, keep me here if you like. Lock me up.

CAPTAIN *(motions toward a* TURNKEY,[9] *points to cell block door).* Let him sleep it off.

(The TURNKEY *grabs* CORRIGAN'*s arm and starts to lead him out of the room.)*

CORRIGAN *(shouting as he's led away).* Well, you

better hear me out. Somebody better get to the President's box at Ford's Theater. Either keep him out of there or put a cordon of men around him. A man named John Wilkes Booth is going to assassinate him tonight!

(He's pushed through the door leading to the cell block. A tall man in cape and black moustache stands near the open door at the other side. He closes it behind him, takes a step into the room, then with a kind of very precise authority, he walks directly over to the CAPTAIN'*s table, shoving a couple of people aside as he does so with a firm gentleness. When he reaches the* CAPTAIN'*s table he removes a card from his inside pocket, puts it on the table in front of the* CAPTAIN.*)*

WELLINGTON. Wellington, Captain. Jonathan Wellington.

(The CAPTAIN *looks at the card, peers at it over his glasses, then looks up toward the tall man in front of him. Obviously the man's manner and dress impresses him. His tone is respectful and quiet.)*

CAPTAIN. What can I do for you, Mr. Wellington?

WELLINGTON. That man you just had incarcerated.[10] Mr. Corrigan I believe he said his name was.

CAPTAIN. Drunk, sir. That's probably what he is.

WELLINGTON. Drunk or . . . *(He taps his head meaningfully.)* Or perhaps, ill. I wonder if he could be remanded in my custody. He might well be a war veteran, and I'd hate to see him placed in jail.

CAPTAIN. Well, that's real decent of you, Mr. Wellington. You say you want him remanded in *your* custody?

WELLINGTON. Precisely. I'll be fully responsible

---

8. **clairvoyant** (kler voi′ənt, klar voi′ənt), *adj.* supposedly having the power of seeing or knowing things that are out of sight.
9. **turnkey,** jailer.
10. **incarcerate** (in kär′sə rāt′), *v.* imprison, put in prison.

for him. I think perhaps I might be able to help him.

CAPTAIN. All right, sir. If that's what you'd like. But I'd be careful of this one if I was you! There's a mighty bunch of crackpots running the streets these days and many of them his like, and many of them dangerous too, sir. (*He turns toward* TURNKEY.) Have Corrigan brought back out here. This gentleman's going to look after him. (*Then he turns to* WELLINGTON.) It's real decent of you, sir. Real decent indeed.

WELLINGTON. I'll be outside. Have him brought out to me if you would.

CAPTAIN. I will indeed, sir.

(WELLINGTON *turns. He passes the various people who look at him and make room for him. His walk, his manner, his positiveness suggest a commanding figure and everyone reacts accordingly. The* CAPTAIN *once again busies himself with his list and is about to check in the next prisoner, when a young* POLICE OFFICER *alongside says.*)

POLICE OFFICER. Begging your pardon, Captain.

CAPTAIN. What is it?

POLICE OFFICER. About that Corrigan, sir.

CAPTAIN. What about him?

POLICE OFFICER. Wouldn't it be wise, sir, if—

CAPTAIN (*impatiently*). If what?

POLICE OFFICER. He seemed so positive, sir. So sure. About the President, I mean.

CAPTAIN (*slams on the desk with vast impatience*). What would you have us do? Send all available police to Ford's Theater? And on what authority? On the word of some demented fool who probably left his mind someplace in Gettysburg.[11] If I was you, mister, I'd be considerably more thoughtful at sizing up situations or you'll not advance one-half grade the next twenty years. Now be good enough to stand aside and let me get on with my work.

POLICE OFFICER (*very much deterred by all this, but pushed on by a gnawing sense of disquiet*). Captain, it wouldn't hurt.

CAPTAIN (*interrupting with a roar*). It wouldn't hurt if what?

POLICE OFFICER. I was going to suggest, sir, that if perhaps we place extra guards in the box with the President—

CAPTAIN. The President has all the guards he needs. He's got the whole Federal Army at his disposal and if they're satisfied with his security arrangements, then I am too and so should you. Next case!

(*The young* POLICE OFFICER *bites his lip and looks away, then stares across the room thoughtfully. The door opens and the* TURNKEY *leads* CORRIGAN *across the room and over to the door. He opens it and points out.* CORRIGAN *nods and walks outside. The door closes behind him. The young* POLICE OFFICER *looks briefly at the* CAPTAIN, *then puts his cap on and starts out toward the door.*)

SCENE TWO

Lodging-house, WELLINGTON *'s room.* WELLINGTON *is pouring wine into two glasses.* CORRIGAN *sits in a chair, his face in his hands. He looks up at the proffered drink and takes it.*

WELLINGTON. Take this. It'll make you feel better. (CORRIGAN *nods his thanks, takes a healthy swig of the wine, puts it down, then looks up at the other man.*) Better?

CORRIGAN (*studying the man*). Who are you, anyway?

WELLINGTON (*with a thin smile*). At the moment I'm your benefactor[12] and apparently your only friend. I'm in the Government ser-

---

11. **Gettysburg** (get′iz bėrg′), a town in Pennsylvania, the site of one of the major battles of the Civil War in July, 1863.
12. **benefactor** (ben′ə fak′tər, ben′ə fak′tŏr), *n.* person who has given money or kindly help.

vice, but as a young man in college I dabbled in medicine of a sort.

CORRIGAN. Medicine?

WELLINGTON. Medicine of the mind.

CORRIGAN (smiles grimly). Psychiatrist.

WELLINGTON (turning to him). I don't know the term.

CORRIGAN. What about the symptoms?

WELLINGTON. They *do* interest me. This story you were telling about the President being assassinated.

CORRIGAN (quickly). What time *is* it?

WELLINGTON. There's time. (Checks a pocket watch) A quarter to eight. The play won't start for another half hour. What gave you the idea that the President would be assassinated?

CORRIGAN. I happen to know, that's all.

WELLINGTON (again the thin smile). You have a premonition?

CORRIGAN. I've got a devil of a lot more than a premonition. Lincoln *will* be assassinated. (Then quickly) Unless somebody tries to prevent it.

WELLINGTON. *I* shall try to prevent it. If you can convince me that you're neither drunk nor insane.

CORRIGAN (on his feet). If I told you what I was, you'd be convinced I *was* insane. So all I'm *going* to tell you is that I happen to know for a fact that a man named John Wilkes Booth will assassinate President Lincoln in his box at Ford's Theater. I don't know what time it's going to happen . . . that's something I forgot—but—

WELLINGTON (softly). Something you forgot?

CORRIGAN (takes a step toward him). Listen, please—(He stops suddenly, and begins to waver. He reaches up to touch the bruise on his head.)

WELLINGTON (takes out a handkerchief and hands it to CORRIGAN). Here. That hasn't been treated properly. You'd best cover it.

CORRIGAN (very, very shaky, almost faint, takes the handkerchief, puts it to his head and sits back down weakly). That's . . . that's odd. (He looks up, still holding the handkerchief.)

WELLINGTON. What is?

CORRIGAN. I'm so . . . I'm so faint all of a sudden. So weak. It's almost as if I were—

WELLINGTON. As if you were what?

CORRIGAN (with a weak smile). As if I'd suddenly gotten drunk or some—(He looks up, desperately trying to focus now as his vision starts to become clouded.) I've never . . . I've never felt like this before. I've never—(His eyes turn to the wine glass on the table. As his eyes open wide, he struggles to his feet.) You . . . you devil! You drugged me, didn't you! (He reaches out to grab WELLINGTON, half struggling in the process.) You drugged me, didn't you!

WELLINGTON. I was forced to, my young friend. You're a very sick man and a sick man doesn't belong in jail. He belongs in a comfortable accommodation where he can sleep and rest and regain his . . . (He smiles a little apologetically.) his composure, his rationale. Rest, Mr. Corrigan. I'll be back soon. (He turns and starts toward the door. CORRIGAN starts to follow him, stumbles to his knees, supports himself on one hand, looks up as WELLINGTON opens the door.)

CORRIGAN. Please . . . please, you've got to believe me. Lincoln's going to be shot tonight.

WELLINGTON (smiling again). And *that's* odd! Because . . . perhaps I'm *beginning* to believe you! Good night, Mr. Corrigan. Rest well. (He turns and goes out of the room, closing the door behind him. We hear the sound of the key being inserted, the door locked.) (CORRIGAN tries desperately to rise and then weakly falls over on his side. He crawls toward the door. He scrabbles at it with a weak hand.)

CORRIGAN (almost in a whisper). Please . . . please . . . somebody . . . let me out. I wasn't kidding . . . I know . . . *the*

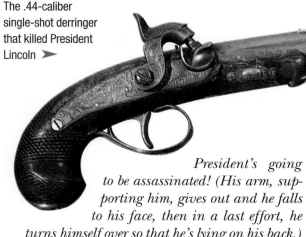

The .44-caliber single-shot derringer that killed President Lincoln ➤

President's going to be assassinated! (His arm, supporting him, gives out and he falls to his face, then in a last effort, he turns himself over so that he's lying on his back.)

(There is a sound of a heavy knocking on the door. Then a LANDLADY's *voice from outside.)*

LANDLADY. There's no need to break it open, Officer. I've got an extra key. Now if you don't mind, stand aside. *(There's the sound of the key inserted in the lock and the door opens. The young* POLICE OFFICER *from earlier is standing there with an angry-faced* LANDLADY *behind him. The* POLICE OFFICER *gets down on his knees, props up* CORRIGAN's *head.)*

POLICE OFFICER. Are you all right? What happened?

CORRIGAN. What time is it? *(He grabs the* OFFICER, *almost pulling him over.)* You've got to tell me what time it is.

POLICE OFFICER. It's ten-thirty-five. Come on, Corrigan. You've got to tell me what you know about this. You may be a madman or a drunk or I don't know what—but you've got me convinced and I've been everywhere from the Mayor's office to the Police Commissioner's home trying to get a special guard for the President.

CORRIGAN. Then go yourself. Find out where he's sitting and get right up alongside of him. He'll be shot from behind. That's the way it happened. Shot from behind. And then the assassin jumps from the box to the stage and he runs out of the wings.

POLICE OFFICER *(incredulous).* You're telling me

this as if, as if it has already happened.

CORRIGAN. It *has* happened. It happened a hundred years ago and I've come back to see that it *doesn't* happen. *(Looking beyond the* POLICE OFFICER) Where's the man who brought me in here? Where's Wellington?

LANDLADY *(peering into the room).* Wellington? There's no one here by that name.

CORRIGAN *(waves a clenched fist at her, still holding the handkerchief).* Don't tell me there's no one here by that name. He brought me in here. He lives in this room.

LANDLADY. There's no one here by that name.

CORRIGAN *(holds the handkerchief close to his face, again waving his fist).* I tell you the man who brought me here was named— *(He stops abruptly, suddenly caught by something he sees on the handkerchief. His eyes slowly turn to stare at it in his hand. On the border are the initials J. W. B.)*

CORRIGAN. J. W. B.?

LANDLADY. Of course! Mr. John Wilkes Booth who lives in the room and that's who brought you here.

CORRIGAN. He said his name was Wellington! And *that's* why he drugged me. *(He grabs the* POLICE OFFICER *again.)* He gave me wine and he drugged me. He didn't want me to stop him. He's the one who's going to do it. Listen, you've got to get to that theater. You've got to stop him. John Wilkes Booth! He's going to kill Lincoln. Look, get out of here now! Will you stop him? Will you—

(He stops abruptly, his eyes look up. All three people turn to look toward the window. There's the sound of crowd noises building, suggestive of excitement, and then almost a collective wail, a mournful, universal chant that comes from the streets, and as the sound builds we suddenly hear intelligible words that are part of the mob noise.)

VOICES. The President's been shot. President Lincoln's been assassinated. Lincoln is dying.

▲ This woodcut of John Wilkes Booth shooting President Lincoln was published in a newspaper in late April, 1865. What details match Peter Corrigan's account of the assassination?

(The LANDLADY *suddenly bursts into tears. The* POLICE OFFICER *rises to his feet, his face white.)*

POLICE OFFICER. Oh my dear God! You were right. You *did* know. Oh . . . my . . . dear . . . God!

(He turns almost trance-like and walks out of the room. The LANDLADY *follows him.* CORRIGAN *rises weakly and goes to the window, staring out at the night and listening to the sounds of a nation beginning its mourning. He closes his eyes and puts his head against the window pane and with fruitless, weakened smashes, hits the side of the window frame as he talks.)*

CORRIGAN. I tried to tell you. I tried to warn you. Why didn't anybody listen? Why? Why didn't anyone listen to me?

(His fist beats a steady staccato on the window frame.)

SCENE THREE

The Washington Club at night. CORRIGAN *is pounding on the front door of the Washington Club.* CORRIGAN *is standing there in modern dress once again. The door opens. An* ATTENDANT *we've not seen before appears.*

ATTENDANT TWO. Good evening. Mr. Corrigan. Did you forget something, sir?

(CORRIGAN *walks past the* ATTENDANT, *through the big double doors that lead to the card room as in Act One. His three friends are in the middle of a discussion. The fourth man at the table, sitting in his seat, has his back to the camera.*)

MILLARD (*looking up*). Hello, Pete. Come on over and join tonight's bull session. It has to do with the best ways of amassing a fortune. What are your tried-and-true methods?

CORRIGAN (*his voice intense and shaky*). We were talking about time travel, about going back in time.

JACKSON (*dismissing it*). Oh that's old stuff. We're on a new tack now. Money and the best ways to acquire it.

CORRIGAN. Listen . . . listen, I want to tell you something. This is true. If you go back into the past you can't change anything. (*He takes another step toward the table.*) Understand? You can't change anything. (*The men look at one another, disarmed by the intensity of* CORRIGAN*'s tone.*)

JACKSON (*rises, softly*). All right, old man, if you say so. (*Studying him intensely*) Are you all right?

CORRIGAN (*closing his eyes for a moment*). Yes . . . yes, I'm all right.

JACKSON. Then come on over and listen to a lot of palaver from self-made swindlers. William here has the best method.

CORRIGAN. William?

(*He sees the attendant from Act One but now meticulously dressed, a middle-aged millionaire obviously, with a totally different manner, who puts a cigarette in a holder with manicured hands in the manner of a man totally accustomed to wealth.* WILLIAM *looks up and smiles.*)

WILLIAM. Oh yes. My method for achieving security is by far the best. You simply inherit it. It comes to you in a beribboned box. I was telling the boys here, Corrigan. My great-grandfather was on the police force here in Washington on the night of Lincoln's assassination. He went all over town trying to warn people that something might happen. (*He holds up his hands in a gesture.*) How he figured it out, nobody seems to know. It's certainly not recorded any place. But because there was so much publicity, people never forgot him. He became a police chief, then a councilman, did some wheeling and dealing in land and became a millionaire. What do you say we get back to our bridge, gentlemen?

(JACKSON *takes the cards and starts to shuffle.* WILLIAM *turns in his seat once again.*)

WILLIAM. How about it, Corrigan? Take a hand?

CORRIGAN. Thank you, William, no. I think I'll . . . I think I'll just go home.

(*He turns very slowly and starts toward the exit. Over his walk we hear the whispered, hushed murmurings of the men at the table.*)

VOICES. Looks peaked, doesn't he? Acting so strangely. I wonder what's the matter with him.

(CORRIGAN *walks into the hall and toward the front door.*)

NARRATOR'S VOICE. Mr. Peter Corrigan, lately returned from the place "Back There"; a journey into time with highly questionable results. Proving, on one hand, that the threads of history are woven tightly and the skein of events cannot be undone; but, on the other hand, there are small fragments of tapestry that *can* be altered. Tonight's thesis,[13] to be taken as you will, in *The Twilight Zone!*[14]

---

13. **thesis** (thē′sis), *n.* statement to be proved or maintained against objections.

14. ***The Twilight Zone,*** the name of the television program on which "Back There" was originally produced.

After Reading

Making Connections

1. Are you satisfied with the ending of this play? Why or why not? If you are not satisfied, tell how you would like the play to end.

2. What words come to mind when you think of Peter Corrigan? What kind of actor should play his part?

3. Although a work of **science fiction** is not supposed to be real, the best ones are believable enough so that the reader can get into the story and live with the characters. What made this play seem realistic or true to life?

4. Why do you think the author chose Peter Corrigan as the character to be sent back in time?

5. What does the play suggest to you about attempting to alter the events of the past—to change the course of history?

6. Considering that things such as TV, cars, spaceships, and computers were once thought of as impossibilities, do you think there will ever be a true time machine that would allow people to move back and forth through the years? What time period would you travel to if there were such a machine? Explain why.

Scene	Date
Act One	
Scene One	____
Scene Two	____
Scene Three	____
Scene Four	____
Act Two	
Scene One	____
Scene Two	____
Scene Three	____

Literary Focus: Setting

The **setting** of a literary work refers to the time and place of the action. Some stories, such as "Liverwurst and Roses," have simple time settings. The story moves from beginning to end with the ordinary passage of time. *Back There,* however, has a more complex time setting. To see how this setting is constructed, copy the scene map at the left in your own notebook. Then review the play and complete the map by writing the date (month, day, and year) on which each scene is supposed to take place.

Vocabulary Study

For each word decide if the definition paired with it has the same or a different meaning. On your paper write *Same* or *Different.*

incarcerate
anachronism
clairvoyant
benefactor
thesis

1. incarcerate — release from jail
2. anachronism — placed in the correct time period
3. clairvoyant — able to see things most people cannot see
4. benefactor — someone who has been helped
5. thesis — a statement to be discussed and defended

Expressing Your Ideas

Writing Choices

Hatch Your Own Plot The play shows that our actions don't always produce the results that we want. Write a **plot outline** for a story about a person who set out to accomplish something and ended up with a different result, a result that was not expected.

Altering (Hi)story It might be difficult to alter the course of history, but it is easy to alter the course of a *story.* Take Mr. Serling's story into the Twilight Zone, where strange things happen, and alter the **perspective** by changing the main character. Replace Peter Corrigan with a female character about his age, or with a boy or girl about your age. Begin your **story** at the point where the character is taken back one hundred years, and tell what your character might have done in the situation.

Assassin! Find out more about John Wilkes Booth. Why did he assassinate President Lincoln? Did he act alone, or did others conspire with him? Was he caught? Write a **research report** detailing what you find out.

Other Options

But What If It Had Worked? Suppose Corrigan had been successful and had prevented Lincoln's assassination. How might history have been altered? Working in a group, brainstorm some possibilities and then complete two **time lines,** one for the actual events of history, and another for what might have been. You will probably want to use a social studies book or talk to your social studies teacher for help.

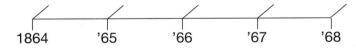

1864   '65   '66   '67   '68

In Theaters Now! Design and create your own **movie poster** for *Back There.* Think of an important scene to show on the poster, and then sketch it on paper. Be sure to feature the title in an attention-getting way. If you want to show who stars in the movie, just use the names of actors and actresses you think would fit the parts.

Center Stage In a small group, choose one scene to **act out.** Select parts, rehearse your lines, and present it for the rest of the class.

Before Reading

The Passing of the Buffalo

retold by Michael J. Caduto and Joseph Bruchac

Michael J. Caduto
born 1955

Michael J. Caduto is an author, ecologist, teacher, storyteller, and musician who promotes environmental awareness, appreciation, and stewardship.

Joseph Bruchac
born 1942

Joseph Bruchac has said, "Much of my writing and my life relates to the problem of being an American." He himself has both Native American and European ancestors. He is the author of over thirty published books of poetry and fiction.

Building Background

The Fate of the Buffalo The traditional way of life of the Plains Indians had centered on hunting the buffalo. Beginning in the 1860s, this way of life was destroyed by the coming of the railroads to the Great Plains. The railroads transported farmers, ranchers, and other settlers who entered tribal lands. The railroads also brought professional hunters who systematically destroyed the buffalo. In 1850 there were still twenty million buffalo on the Great Plains, but by the early 1880s the once vast herds had all but vanished. At that point people began to work to protect the remaining buffalo. Today the buffalo is no longer endangered.

Getting into the Story

Writer's Notebook Loss can be one result of change. The near loss of the buffalo is described above. What other loss can you think of that happened as a result of historical, social, or technological change? Describe that loss, and why it occurred, in your notebook.

Buffalo Dream was painted by the Kiowa artist Al Momaday.

Reading Tip

Fact and Myth Like many folk tales, "The Passing of the Buffalo" is a mixture of fact and myth. As you read, identify the details that could be verified as fact and the details that are imaginative and mythical. Use a chart like the one below to list the details you find.

Details Based on Fact	Details That Are Imaginative

The Passing of the Buffalo

Michael J. Caduto and Joseph Bruchac

Once, not long ago, the buffalo were everywhere. Wherever the people were, there were the buffalo. They loved the people, and the people loved the buffalo. When the people killed a buffalo, they did it with reverence. They gave thanks to the buffalo's spirit. They used every part of the buffalo they killed. The meat was their food. The skins were used for clothing and to cover their tipis. The hair stuffed their pillows and saddlebags. The sinews[1] became their bowstrings. From the hooves they made glue. They carried water in the bladders and stomachs. To give the buffalo honor, they painted the skull and placed it facing the rising sun.

Then the whites came. They were new people, as beautiful and as deadly as the black spider. The whites took the lands of the people. They built the railroad to cut the lands of the people in half. It made life hard for the people, and so the buffalo fought the railroad. The buffalo tore up the railroad tracks. They chased away the cattle of the whites. The buffalo loved the people and tried to protect their way of life. So the army was sent to kill the buffalo. But even the soldiers could not hold the buffalo back. Then the army hired hunters. The hunters came and killed and killed. Soon the bones of the buffalo covered the land to the height of a tall man. The buffalo saw they could fight no longer.

One morning, a Kiowa[2] woman whose family was running from the Army rose early one morning from their camp deep in the hills. She went down to the spring near the mountainside to get water. She went quietly, alert for enemies. The morning mist was thick, but as she bent to fill her bucket she saw something. It was something moving in the mist. As she watched, the mist parted and out of it came an old buffalo cow. It was one of the old buffalo women who always led the herds. Behind her came the last few young buffalo warriors, their horns scarred from fighting, some of them wounded. Among them were a few calves and young cows.

Straight toward the side of the mountain, the old buffalo cow led that last herd. As the Kiowa woman watched, the mountain opened up in front of them and the buffalo walked into the mountain. Within the mountain the earth was green and new. The sun shone and the meadowlarks were singing. It was as it had been before the whites came. Then the mountain closed behind them. The buffalo were gone.

▲ *King Thunder* is a bronze sculpture by Robert Deurloo. How does this image of a buffalo compare with the one on the facing page?

---

1. **sinew** (sin′yū), *n.* tendon; tough band of fibrous tissue that joins a muscle to a bone.
2. **Kiowa** (kī′ə wə), a member of a Plains Indian people.

After Reading

Making Connections

1. Look back at the loss you wrote about in your notebook (p. 106). How does the loss in this story compare with your loss?

2. Are you satisfied with the ending of this story? Why or why not?

3. "Then the whites came. They were a new people, as beautiful and deadly as the black spider." What is the effect of this unusual description?

4. Why do you think the author gave the buffalo human characteristics? Why are they called "warriors" and "women"?

5. 🐾 What aspects of this story reveal that it is told from the **perspective** of Native Americans?

6. The destruction of the vast buffalo herds on the Great Plains is not a unique tragedy. What human activities can you think of that are endangering animal and plant species today?

Literary Focus: The Author's Style

Although this is a written **folk tale,** earlier such tales were meant to be spoken to a listening audience. The **style** is simple and graceful. Sentences are short, and most of the words are familiar. Yet this story can have a powerful effect because of the rhythm of the language. Your ear will tell you things that your eye can't see. Take turns reading passages from the story aloud with a partner. Discuss what aspects of the style appeal to you as you listen.

Expressing Your Ideas

Your Own Folk Tale Choose an endangered or extinct animal, find out more about it, and write a **folk tale** that explains the loss of the animal. See if you can produce the style that you find in "The Passing of the Buffalo."

A Sound Track Music for movie sound tracks is chosen to create a mood that fits the action. For each of the four paragraphs of the story, select **music** that would help to create the effect of the story. Bring in recordings of the music or describe it to the class.

The Many Faces of Change

Trailblazers

U.S. History Connection

Some people, such as Anna, are able to accept even the greatest challenges that accompany change. Others, such as Anna's mother, are crushed by their weight.

SURVIVAL OF THE STRONGHEARTED

from the diary of Anna Howard Shaw

Writing letters and diary entries broke the tedium of daily chores for many pioneer women.

In 1859, when Anna Howard Shaw was twelve years old, her father became a homesteader in northern Michigan. Homesteading laws allowed a man to file a claim on a piece of land, paying a small sum per acre. The land became his if he cleared it, built a house on it, and farmed it for a certain number of years. The Federal Homestead Act of 1862 allowed single women over twenty-one, women who were heads of households, and women immigrants in the process of becoming citizens to acquire land too.

Anna Howard Shaw's father and her three oldest brothers cleared just enough land on their claim to put up the walls of a log cabin. James, the twenty-year-old son, stayed on; the others returned home to Lawrence, Massachusetts, to work in the textile mills. A few months later Mr. Shaw sent his wife and their four youngest children to Michigan. Anna Howard Shaw describes how shocked her mother was at what she found and how it affected her. Life in Michigan was as primitive as life had been in colonial America two hundred years before.

We all had an idea that we were going to a farm, and we expected some resemblance at least to the prosperous farms we had seen in New England. What we found awaiting us were the four walls and the roof of a good-sized log-house, standing in a small cleared strip of the wilderness, its doors and windows represented by square holes, its floor also a thing of the future, its whole effect achingly forlorn and desolate. It was late in the afternoon when we drove up to the opening that was its front entrance, and I shall never forget the look my mother turned upon the place. Without a word she crossed its threshold, and, standing very still, looked slowly around her. Then something within her seemed to give way, and she sank upon the ground. She could not realize even then, I think, that this was really the place father had prepared for us,

WESTWARD MIGRATION

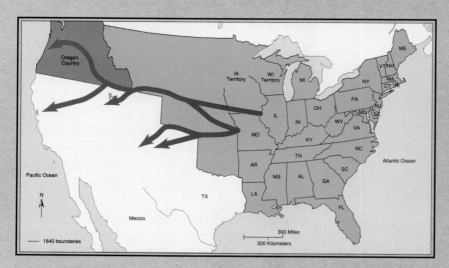

How many pioneers moved west?

Year	Estimate	Year	Estimate
1841	100	1854	10,000
1842	200	1855	5,000
1843	1,000	1856	5,000
1844	2,000	1857	5,000
1845	5,000	1858	10,000
1846	1,000	1859	30,000
1847	2,000	1860	15,000
1848	4,000	1861	5,000
1849	30,000	1862	5,000
1850	55,000	1863	10,000
1851	10,000	1864	20,000
1852	50,000	1865	25,000
1853	20,000	1866	25,000

Source: Nebraska State Historical Society, 1969.

Hundreds of thousands of pioneers crossed the plains to find a new life in the West. Their heavy, oxen-pulled covered wagons often traveled only two miles a day.

that here he expected us to live. When she finally took it in she buried her face in her hands, and in that way she sat for hours without moving or speaking. For the first time in her life she had forgotten us; and we, for our part, dared not speak to her. We stood around her in a frightened group, talking to one another in whispers. Our little world had crumbled under our feet. Never before had we seen our mother give way to despair.

Night began to fall. The woods became alive with night creatures, and the most harmless made the most noise. The owls began to hoot, and soon we heard the wildcat, whose cry—a screech like that of a lost and panic-stricken child—is one of the most appalling sounds of the forest. Later the wolves added their howls to the uproar, but though darkness came and we children whimpered around her, our mother still sat in her strange lethargy.

[While my brother] was picketing the horses and building his protecting fires my mother came to herself, but her face when she raised it was worse than her silence had been. She seemed to have died and returned to us from the grave, and I am sure she felt that she had done so. From that moment she took up again the burden of her life, a burden she did not lay down until she passed away; but her face never lost the deep lines those first hours of her pioneer life had cut upon it.

[That night what] I most feared was within, not outside of, the cabin. The one sure refuge in our new world had been taken from us. I hardly knew the silent woman who lay near me, tossing from side to side and staring into the darkness; I felt that we had lost our mother.

[When my father] took up his claim, and sent [us] to live there alone until he could join us eighteen months later, he gave no thought of the manner in which we were to make the struggle and survive the hardships before us. He had furnished us with land and the four walls of a log cabin. We were one hundred miles from a railroad, forty miles from the nearest post-office, and half a dozen miles from any neighbors; we were wholly unlearned in the ways of the woods as well as in the most primitive methods of farming; we lacked not only every comfort, but even the bare necessities of life.

We faced our situation with clear and unalarmed eyes the morning after our arrival. We had brought with us enough coffee, pork and flour to last for several weeks; and the one necessity father had put inside the cabin walls was a great fireplace, made of mud and stones, in which our food could be cooked. [We found] a creek a long distance from the house; and for months we carried from this creek, in pails, every drop of water we used, save that which we caught in troughs when the rain fell.

Obviously the first thing to do was to put doors and windows into the yawning holes father had left for them, and to lay a board flooring over the earth inside our cabin walls, and these duties we accomplished before we had occupied our new home a fortnight. [We made] three windows and two doors; then, inspired by these achievements, we ambitiously constructed an attic and divided the ground floor with partitions, which gave us four rooms.

The general effect was temperamental and sketchy. The boards which formed the floor were never even nailed down; they were fine, wide planks without a knot in them, and they looked so well that we merely fitted them together as closely as we could and lightheartedly let them go at that. Neither did we properly chink the house. Nothing is

He had furnished us with land and the four walls of a log cabin.

more comfortable than a log cabin which has been carefully built and finished; but for some reason—probably because there seemed always a more urgent duty calling to us around the corner—we never plastered our house at all. The result was that on many future winter mornings we awoke to find ourselves chastely blanketed by snow, while the only warm spot in our living-room was that directly in front of the fireplace, where great logs burned all day. Even there our faces scorched while our spines slowly congealed, until we learned to revolve before the fire like a bird upon a spit. No doubt we would have worked more thoroughly if my brother James, who was twenty years old and our tower of strength, had remained with us; but when we had been in our home only a few months he fell ill and was forced to go East for an operation. He was never able to return to us, and thus my mother, we three young girls, and my youngest brother—Harry, who was only eight years old—made our fight alone until father came to us, more than a year later.

Responding

1. How did the homestead in northern Michigan differ from what Anna expected?

2. Put yourself in Anna's place. Describe how you might have managed in your new home.

Change wears many faces. These pioneer women accepted countless changes and challenges that altered their entire lives when they became trailblazers to the West.

The Shores family proudly pose on their homestead near Westerville, Nebraska, in 1887.

A NEW LIFE ON THE FRONTIER

A Wyoming pioneer woman and her child stand in a vast ocean of wheat.

Shown here in 1899, the Quinn family made their home in San Diego, California.

In California, a homesteader receives the deed to her land.

Mrs. Smith displays the wildcat she shot near Glenrock, Wyoming.

Responding

1. What changes do you think the women pioneers in these photographs had to make when they left their homes in the East?

2. What qualities do you think are necessary to make a successful pioneer?

Reading Mini-Lesson

Visualizing

"A picture is worth a thousand words." If this expression is true, then **visualizing**, forming a mental picture from the descriptions you read, is a very important reading skill. If you've ever tried to assemble a toy or piece of equipment from written directions, you know how much a sketch or diagram can help. Whether you are constructing a mental picture or a sketch on paper, it is probably best to get "the big picture" first. Imagine or draw the outline or outside boundary of the object or scene, and then try to fill in the details.

"Survival of the Stronghearted" contains strong visual images both of the setting and the people. These images or word-pictures help you to see and feel a little of what the people in the selection experienced. A diagram such as the one in the margin might help you track details of the setting.

log cabin with no floor, doors, or windows

setting

40 miles from post office

small clearing in wilderness

Activity Options

1. Use Lincoln Logs or other building kit materials to construct a model of the log cabin Mrs. Shaw saw when she and the four children arrived in Michigan. Place the model on a large sheet of poster paper so you can show the landscape around the cabin. Leave off the roof so the interior can be seen.

2. One of the most striking images in the selection is the description of Mrs. Shaw's face after she recovered from her shock at seeing the cabin. Use your imagination and the details from the selection to help you draw a mask of Mrs. Shaw's face. Talk to your art teacher and see if your school has the materials for you to make the mask.

3. "Before and after" pictures are often used to help show a change that has taken place. Sketch a "before" picture of the inside of the cabin as Mrs. Shaw found it when she arrived. Next to it sketch an "after" picture to show the improvements made by the Shaws after they arrived.

Writing Workshop

Traveling Through Time

Assignment Peter Corrigan in *Back There* learns that through time travel he can alter past events and change the future. With two class-mates write a three-act play exploring this aspect of time travel.

WRITER'S BLUEPRINT

Product   Three-act play
Purpose   To explore the effects of time travel
Audience   The people who come to see your play performed
Specs   To write a successful play, your group should:

- ❏ In the first act establish the present setting, the characters, and the idea of time travel.
- ❏ In the second act show your characters' arrival in the past. Establish the setting and major historical events that will occur while your characters are there.
- ❏ Dramatize the interactions between characters from the present and the past.
- ❏ In the third act bring your characters back to the present. Show the effect of their time travel on the present.
- ❏ Make dialogue realistic through the use of idioms, dialect, sentence fragments, or slang.
- ❏ Follow the rules for grammar, usage, spelling, and mechanics. Use correct play format.

STEP  PREWRITING

Start with the literature. To see how a play is put together, your group should review *Back There* and complete a chart in which you explore the major historical event and the future impact of Peter Corrigan's time travel.

EVENT CHART

Historical Event	Future Impact
Event: President Lincoln's Assassination	**Event:** Corrigan tries to stop the assassination.
What happened?	**What happened?**
Who was involved?	**Who was involved?**
When did it happen?	**When did it happen?**
Where did it happen?	**Where did it happen?**
Impact on history:	**Impact on history:**

Brainstorm major events from history. Your play will feature a historical event as part of the setting and action. In your group, brainstorm events from American history that interest you. Choose one and develop a chart for it as you did in the previous step. Gather information from books, magazines, newspapers, museums, or videos.

Make a web of possible future impacts. Peter Corrigan learns that only minor events can be changed through time travel. Decide what future impact your character's time travel will have. How does this connect to the historical event? Spend a few minutes with your group making a web of ideas for this.

> **OR . . .**
> Instead of a web, you might want to make a chart similar to the one you created for your major historical event.

Create characters. Now that you have your events in order, you need characters. A successful play must have strong characters that react to events as real people would. Work together to develop an outline for each character in the play. Write down qualities such as age, physical features, clothes, personality, and way of speaking. If any of your characters change as a result of time travel, do a before and after chart for each.

Plan the acts and scenes. Each member of your group will write one act of the three-act play. Decide on a title and work together to plan a structure like this:

- **Act One** is set in the present. It introduces the setting and the characters, and sets up the theme of time travel.

- **Act Two** is set in the past at the site of the historical event you chose. It introduces the new setting and characters in the past. The main character from the present interacts with people in the past. The result will be a change in the future.

- **Act Three** returns to the present. The main character discovers the change that has resulted from the trip.

Each act should include at least one scene. Make a list of all the scenes and their settings. List the characters in each scene and what action occurs. When your plan is complete, decide which act each group member will write.

Make a storyboard. To keep everything straight, you may want to create a series of drawings of each of your scenes. Alongside each drawing or on the back of each, write a few lines of key dialogue or a brief description of what happens.

STEP 2 DRAFTING

Before you draft review the Writer's Blueprint and your materials from the prewriting steps. Check to see if you have left out important information. Also, look over *Back There* to review play format.

Realistic dialogue will give your play an authentic feel by making the characters' speech more natural. For ideas on writing realistic dialogue, see the Revising Strategy on page 118.

As you draft visualize the characters and setting for each scene. Don't worry about spelling, punctuation, or format at this point. Here are some tips that might help you get started.

- Write a description of the opening setting for your act.

- Speak the characters' lines aloud after you write them. Do they sound like ordinary speech?

- Think of how you'd react if you were in your characters' shoes. Then use your emotions to guide what you have them say.

STEP 3 REVISING

Ask your group members for comments on your draft before you revise it. Use these questions as a guide.

✔ Have I followed the specs in the Writer's Blueprint?

✔ Have I followed the group's plan for characters, setting, and plot?

✔ Have I created realistic dialogue using idioms, dialect, sentence fragments, and slang when appropriate?

Revising Strategy

Writing Realistic Dialogue

Realistic dialogue sounds like real people talking. Everyday speech rarely sounds like polished sentences in a book. To write dialogue that sounds realistic, try using some of the following.

- Use idioms (an expression that means something different from the usual meaning of the words in it), such as *Give me a ring* for *Call me on the telephone.*

- Use sentence fragments (incomplete sentences) to mimic actual speech, such as *Need a ride?* for *Do you need a ride?* Notice how Rod Serling does this in the Literary Source.

- Use slang, such as *cash* when *money* is the appropriate word.

- Insert shortened phrases, such as *gonna* for *going to.*

- Use interruptions and speech that overlaps to mimic dialogue between two people, as Rod Serling does in the Literary Source.

Notice how the writer of the dialogue below revised to include a sentence fragment.

STUDENT MODEL

Act Three
Scene One

(HERMAN *is sleeping in his bed. The room is dark. He snorts and wakes up. The calendar over his desk shows May 21, 1999.*)

HERMAN (*glancing at calendar*). Huh? That's funny. I thought it was May 21 yesterday. ~~I made a booboo.~~ *Only a minor mistake.* Oh, well.

(*He gets out of bed and stretches. He grabs his backpack and heads for the door.*)

4 EDITING

Ask a group member to review your revised draft before you edit. When you edit, watch for errors in grammar, usage, spelling, and mechanics. Make sure you've used the correct format for a play.

Editing Strategy

Correct Format for a Play

From your reading, you know that there's a special written format for plays. When editing your play, make sure you've used this format. Here are some guidelines to follow. You can also look back at Rod Serling's play to see how this format looks on the page.

COMPUTER TIP
If you're editing your play on a computer, format the speakers' names in boldface and the stage directions in italics.

- Write the correct heading for each section of the play, such as Act One, Scene One.

- Write the entire name of the character who is speaking before each section of dialogue. The name should be in upper case letters. Put a period or colon after the name.

- Indent each section of dialogue starting with the second line. The indent should be about one-half inch.

- Put stage directions in parentheses. If characters' names appear, write them in all capital letters. Italicize stage directions.

Notice how the writer of the draft below has edited to correct format.

STUDENT MODEL

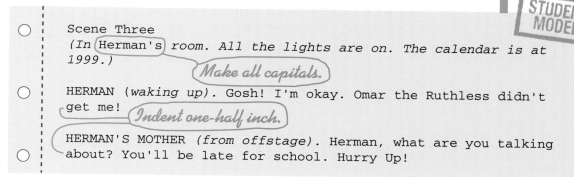

```
○   Scene Three
      (In Herman's room. All the lights are on. The calendar is at
      1999.)
                    Make all capitals.
○   HERMAN (waking up). Gosh! I'm okay. Omar the Ruthless didn't
     get me!    Indent one-half inch.
     HERMAN'S MOTHER (from offstage). Herman, what are you talking
○    about? You'll be late for school. Hurry Up!
```

5 PRESENTING

Here are two ideas for presenting your play.

- **Hold a classroom theater festival.** Work with your group to rehearse your play. If you need extra actors recruit other class-mates. Use simple props. Perform your play in front of the class as part of a festival of plays.

- **Read the play to your family.** Gather your family for a reading of your play. You can read all the parts yourself, or invite the other family members to join the performance.

6 LOOKING BACK

Self-evaluate. How would you grade your writing? Look back at the Writer's Blueprint and evaluate yourself on each point, from 6 (super-ior) to 1 (weak).

Reflect. Think about what you have learned from writing this play. Write answers to these questions.

✔ Did your dialogue sound like you thought it would when actors recited it? If not, how was it different?

✔ As you proofread, did you make any mistakes spelling homo-phones? What other spelling mistakes did you make? Keep a list of these in your working portfolio. Write the incorrect and correct spelling. Add to it all year.

For Your Working Portfolio: Add your finished play, self-evaluation, and reflection responses to your working portfolio.

Beyond Print

Computer Terms

CD-ROM, Compact Disc Read Only Memory. This disc, which looks similar to an audio CD, is only readable with a computer that has a CD-ROM player. The disc is used to store information such as text, sound, pictures, and movies.

database, an organized collection of information, especially one in electronic form that can be accessed by computer software.

Internet, a series of computer servers connected together around the world.

network, two or more computers connected together by cables, allowing them to communicate with each other.

server, a computer that operates a network.

Electronic Research

Computer searches are an invaluable aid to the researcher. What used to take hours, days, or even years to find now can often be tracked down in only seconds. In your school or local library, or even possibly your own home, you may find these resources for research projects:

Reference materials such as dictionaries, atlases, indexes to magazine and newspaper articles, and almanacs are available on CD-ROM. Entire encyclopedias can be put on a single CD-ROM!

Online services connect you with other computers across the country or even around the world, giving you access to magazines, reviews, interviews, and subject-specific databases. Using online services, librarians often can search other libraries for books, articles, or other material necessary for your research.

With so much information at your fingertips, the biggest challenge is narrowing down the search so that you get the facts you want. Keep in mind:

- The computer can't read your mind! If you are searching for an author, for example, be sure to spell the author's name correctly.

- If you are searching by subject, try several different key words. If you are looking for more information on the internment of Japanese Americans in the U.S. during World War II, the information you want may be filed under *Japanese Americans, relocation, internment, World War II,* or any number of other key words. Keep trying!

Activity Options

1. Ask your librarian for a tour of your library's electronic research resources. Prepare a guide that can be used by "computer shy" students to more effectively use the electronic tools in your library.

2. Create a list of key words on a topic. Then try using these key words to search for information on a computer. Print out your results.

Projects for Collaborative Study

Theme Connection

Growing Pains Customs vary around the world, yet growing up involves many of the same feelings and experiences no matter where you live. To find out what teens face in other lands, invite several guest speakers to come to your class and describe what it was like to grow up in their home countries.

■ To prepare, brainstorm the names of possible speakers and make a list of questions to ask. For example, you may be interested in when young people begin to date or what a day in school is like.

■ As a wrap-up, draw a chart that compares growing up in America to growing up in other countries.

Literature Connection

A New Place and Time In this unit, the **setting**—the time and place of the story—has a major influence on the actions and emotions of the **characters.** In "Viva New Jersey," for example, Lucinda responds to her urban environment in ways that show how much she misses the quiet countryside of her former home in Cuba. Choose two or three selections in the unit and, in a small group, discuss how the main character in each selection responds to the setting.

■ As a group, choose a character from this unit and together write a story in which you place that character in a new setting—a different place or time. Discuss: How would the character react? What would he or she say, do, and feel?

Life Skills Connection

Rewind, Then Fast Forward Think back to a moment in time five years ago. Freeze that thought and take a mental photograph. If you were describing yourself then, what would you say? Now . . . fast forward to the present. Chances are you look, think, and act differently. You and your classmates share many experiences of change. Some of these have brought you joy, while others may have been painful.

■ As a class, brainstorm changes that affect people's lives, such as moving, changing schools, dealing with a loss, learning a new skill, or developing a new friendship.

■ Determine the Top Ten Changes that affect the lives of your classmates. Discuss how these experiences will affect your ability to face changes in the future.

Multicultural Connection

Coming to America Through history, many people have come to the United States to make a **change** in their lives. With a group of your classmates, learn about immigrants in America and prepare a dramatization for sharing your information. To portray a fictional family, you'll first want to see things from their **perspective.**

■ Choose a home country and appropriate name for your family.

■ Learn about immigration patterns—why did your family come to America? What did they hope to find? In what part of America did they choose to locate their new home? How did the family members earn a living?

Read More About Change

Baseball in April (1990) by Gary Soto. The eleven short stories in this collection involve moments of triumph, feelings of insecurity, and, sometimes, embarrassment about something said or done.

I Love You, I Hate You, Get Lost (1994) by Ellen Conford. If you enjoyed "Liverwurst and Roses," you won't want to miss reading other stories in the same collection. In spite of the dilemmas faced by the teen characters, the author's humorous style makes for entertaining reading.

More Good Books

The Glory Field (1994) by Walter Dean Myers. This novel shows change through the lives and times experienced by one African American family.

People Who Make a Difference (1989) by Brent Ashabranner. A country doctor and a karate teacher are among the enterprising people who make changes to bring about a better world.

Children of the River (1989) by Linda Crew. Uprooted by a bloody civil war, Sundara flees Cambodia with members of her family and settles in America, where she finds it isn't easy balancing Cambodian and American ways.

Jacob Have I Loved (1980) by Katherine Paterson. From birth, Wheeze has been overshadowed by her beautiful twin sister, who gets the attention and the breaks in life.

April Morning (1961) by Howard Fast. Adam Cooper changes from a boy to a man in the Battle of Lexington during the American Revolutionary War.

Challenges

Searching for the Real You
Part One, pages 128–173

Outside Forces
Part Two, pages 174–237

Talking About
CHALLENGES

Not all challenges involve mountain climbing or daring rescues. It is a challenge just to be the best you can in a difficult world. Whether you battle against forces of evil or struggle to discover who you are, success depends on perseverance, hard work, and the assistance of others who care.

"It's a challenge to get good grades, get my homework done, and meet parents' and teachers' expectations."

Amy—Los Angeles, CA

She said, without turning her head, to me, "I hear you're doing very good schoolwork, Marguerite, but that it's all written. The teachers report that they have trouble getting you to talk in class."

from "I Know Why the Caged Bird Sings" by Maya Angelou, page 156

"To me the biggest challenges are becoming successful in your life and doing what you want to do."

Tom—Jacksonville, FL

Today Miss McIntyre, our guidance counselor, said, "You have to decide who you are and where you're going."

from "Who You Are" by Jean Little, page 130

". . . sports, money, battling a shark, living with my brother."

Albert—Durham, NC

He realized that it was no longer a mere matter of freezing his fingers and toes, or of losing his hands and feet, but that it was a matter of life and death with the chances against him.

from "To Build a Fire" by Jack London, page 187

"I like to read about true challenges that kids our age face."

Janine—Philadelphia, PA

He was a restless boy, and he kept moving all the time every summer. He was making mistakes and paying for them.

from "The Parsley Garden" by William Saroyan, page 146

"" There are many more challenges in the world today. ""

Gina—Seattle, WA

Part One

Searching for the Real You

Who are you? What do you want to do with your life? What are some of the things you do well? Such short little questions often have such complicated answers! It's not as if you wake up one morning and say, "Hey, I want to be the mayor of the town and only eat vegetables." This can happen to some people, but for most, learning about what and who you are is a slow process of quiet little discoveries.

Multicultural Connection **Choice** involves both drawing upon cultural experience and deciding to move into new situations. It may also involve learning to juggle different roles and conflicting cultural pressures. What cultural challenges do the people in these selections face, and what choices do they make?

Literature

Jean Little	**Who You Are** ◆ interior monologue	130
Gary Soto	**The Mechanical Mind** ◆ short story	135
William Saroyan	**The Parsley Garden** ◆ short story	142
	Writing Mini-Lesson ◆ Showing, Not Telling	150
Maya Angelou	**from *I Know Why the Caged Bird Sings*** ◆ autobiography	152
Diane Mei Lin Mark	**Rice and Rose Bowl Blues** ◆ poem	162
Lillian Morrison	**The Sidewalk Racer** ◆ poem	163
Julio Noboa Polanco	**Identity** ◆ poem	 164

Interdisciplinary Study **Brainstorms**

Corn Flake Kings: The Kellogg Brothers by Meredith Hooper ◆ history/health	167
19th-Century U.S. Inventions ◆ history	170
Now You Invent a Cereal! ◆ health	172
Reading Mini-Lesson ◆ Main Idea and Supporting Details	173

Who You Are

by Jean Little

Jean Little
born 1932

Jean Little is a teacher of children with physical handicaps. She herself is only partially sighted, and was teased by her classmates, who called her "cross eyes." She says that she never read a book with a cross-eyed heroine, so many of her books have heroes with physical challenges. It's not that handicapped children need books to help them adjust, she says, but they have "a right to find themselves represented in fiction."

Building Background

No Limitations All of us have to make decisions about our future. Some of us know what we want to do, and some of us are more like Henry David Thoreau (1817–1862), an American writer. He actually decided not to have a "real job," choosing instead to do odd jobs to earn just enough to buy what he needed. This arrangement permitted him time to observe nature, think, and write. When people laughed at him, he said, "If a man does not keep pace with his companions, perhaps it is because he hears a different drummer. Let him step to the music which he hears, however measured or far away." In small groups, discuss what you think Thoreau meant and whether or not you agree.

Getting into the Selection

Writer's Notebook In the center of a page in your notebook, write your name and draw a box around it. Then surround the box with labels that apply to you. Think of as many as you can. What labels could your parents apply? Your friends? The principal? What types of things go into defining who you are? Here's an example.

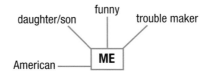

Reading Tip

Genre This selection takes the form of an **interior monologue.** A monologue is a long speech, and an interior monologue is a speech that is going on inside a person's head. In other words, this piece is a person's thoughts. Try this type of writing yourself. Suppose you are on your way to school and know you are going to be late. Write a quick interior monologue of your thoughts as you decide how to explain why you're late.

WhO yOu ARe

Jean Little

Today Miss McIntyre, our guidance counselor, said, "You have to decide who you are and where you're going."

Sounds simple. Just decide. I think it *is* simple for Emily. She's Emily Blair, daughter of the Manager of the Royal Bank, member of the Presbyterian Church, high achiever in school, sister of Louisa. And she knows where she's going—or she thinks she does. She wants to teach Grade One. She's out of her mind. Only . . . maybe not. . . .

I could do that about me too, of course. There are labels that partly fit. I too am the child of my parents, except I'm beginning to see that Mother and Dad are not just my parents, the way I used to think. They are separate people with thoughts of their own. Sometimes they seem like strangers. I don't belong to a church. I'm Jewish—but I don't know, yet, what being Jewish is going to mean to me.

That's not what I'm talking about though, or it's only one part of it. I want to find out how important it is, my being Jewish, but I'd like to be everything else too. And nothing else.

I'd like to teach Grade Five but I want to write a symphony and live in a lighthouse and fly an airplane. I'd like to own an orchard or keep bees. I'd like to be a policewoman and I've thought about being a nun. I think I'll write books . . . I sound like a little kid.

There are so many roads, though. I can't write a symphony, I know that. And I'm pretty sure I'd never make it as a nun. But I just might keep bees, if I really wanted to. Except . . . what about my lighthouse?

Right now I could be anybody, Miss McIntyre. Can't you understand that? I could be anybody at all.

I'm not ready to choose and besides, I'm choosing more than one road. I'm putting myself together, Miss McIntyre. But it is like a jigsaw puzzle. I keep on finding new pieces.

If you were once a puzzle, you soon found the edge pieces and fitted yourself inside. There is no edge to me yet. I hope the picture turns out to be worth the work. I hope I never discover an edge.

Self-Portrait was painted in 1995 by Sandra Arriazola, a Mexican American artist. How does the artist's **choice** of images reflect her cultural background? ➤

After Reading

Making Connections

1. In your opinion, at what age should someone be able to respond to the statement "You have to decide who you are and where you are going"? Explain your answer.

2. What are some of the advantages and disadvantages of knowing who you want to be?

3. How do you think Emily Blair would respond to the narrator's description of her?

4. What does the narrator mean when she says, "I hope I never discover an edge"?

5. 👣 What **choice** does the narrator still have to make about being Jewish?

6. Look at the labels you wrote at the beginning of the reading. How can they help you decide what you want for your future?

Literary Focus: Theme

A **theme** is the underlying meaning of a piece of literature. It is important to recognize the difference between the theme of a literary work and the subject of a literary work. The subject is the topic on which an author has chosen to write—for example, the topic of war. The theme, however, makes some statement about or expresses some opinion on that topic. For instance, a possible theme for a selection on the subject of war might be "the futility of war" or "the end never justifies the means."

In a small group, brainstorm possible themes for this selection. After coming up with about ten possible themes, review your list. Which of your ideas are really just a statement of the subject or of the plot? Look at the ideas you have left. Can any be combined? Then share the themes with the class.

Expressing Your Ideas

Writing Choices

A Little Guidance Create a list of questions to ask a guidance counselor about careers and interview him or her. Write up a brief **report** on the results of the interview.

Dear Me, How Are You? Write a **letter** to yourself to open ten years from now. What do you want to remember? What are your dreams for the future? How do you see yourself?

Mirror, Mirror This painting by Fran Beallor is called *Light Year's Returning.* What is happening in the painting? How many different people are portrayed? Do you think this is a self-portrait? Write an **interpretive essay** explaining this art.

Other Options

Make a Collage of Yourself Find pictures of how you see yourself in the future and paste them onto a cardboard backing. Then write captions that explain what "you" are doing in the pictures. Share your **collage** with a partner or a small group. Then cut it into pieces to make a jigsaw puzzle. Your puzzle does not need a straight edge.

Take a Poll How many people in your class know exactly what they want to be when they finish school? How many don't know at all? How many are somewhere in the middle? Take a **poll** to find out. Summarize the results of your poll in a graph, and convert the results into percentages.

I'm the One You Want for That Job With a partner, act out an **interview** for a job that you mutually decide upon. Use your imagination! The job can be a street sweeper or a brain surgeon. You decide! Take turns being the interviewer and the interviewee. Have the rest of the class evaluate your interviewing skills.

Before Reading

The Mechanical Mind

by Gary Soto

Gary Soto
born 1952

Gary Soto is from Fresno, California. He came from a family that did migrant farm work. He went on to become a college professor and a poet. Soto started studying geography in college but found literature to be more interesting. As a writer, he says, "It's sort of a silly act, writing itself." However, that doesn't stop him.

Building Background

Nature or Nurture? Some people are good with language, some excel at math, and some are very athletic. Some people are musical, some have a knack for working with people, and some are good at reflecting on what they see. Both nature—what you are born with—and nurture—how you cultivate what you are born with—play important roles in the development of skills. In your notebook, list your skills (don't be shy!) and tell whether they are based on nature or nurture or both.

Getting into the Story

Discussion How do people discover that they have particular skills or talents? Brainstorm different ways that people learn about their strengths as well as their weaknesses.

Ways to Learn About Yourself

school subjects

sports

trying out for play

Reading Tip

Generalizations When you make a broad statement or rule, based on several examples, you've made a **generalization**. A **valid** generalization is based on sufficient examples and good reasoning. For example, after reading many fairy tales over the years, you might make the valid generalization that "Most fairy tales include some kind of magic." However, if, after reading one fairy tale, you conclude that "all fairy tales include a magic lamp," you have made a **faulty** generalization based on insufficient evidence. In this story, Philip Quintana fixes something, and from that one success he makes a statement that he thinks will apply to him no matter what. As you read, look for that statement. Then decide how correct he is.

The Mechanical MIND

Gary Soto

Philip Quintana discovered that he was mechanical on a hot summer day when he took a pair of pliers, climbed to the roof of his house with a boost from his younger sister, Leticia, and straightened the kinked tubing that fed water to their evaporator cooler.[1] He opened the sides of the cooler and, peering in, studied the small greasy motor, its fan belt jumping violently as it turned the cagelike fan.

The pads were rotted, black as a diseased lung. They crumbled when he poked the pliers at them and gave off a musty smell from the years of water that had dribbled over them. Remembering the new pads stored in the garage, Philip tore the old ones out and, holding his breath, jumped off the roof. He landed with a groan but got up brushing grass from his palms. He fetched the new pads and, with the help once again of his sister, who complained that he was too heavy, Philip climbed to the roof.

"Higher, Leti," he yelled at his sister, who was trying to fling the new pads onto the roof. But Leticia was only seven and too weak to throw the pads high enough for Philip to catch them. Eventually a high school student riding by on his dirt bike stopped and flung the pads to the roof, and then Philip was able to get to work. And the work was easy. The pads were crisp as shredded wheat, and in a matter of minutes Philip, whistling away, was able to tuck them into the walls of the cooler.

"All right," he said, admiring his handiwork.[2] He slapped his hands clean and jumped off the roof with the old pads, one in each hand. He heaved the pads into the alley and paraded into the house with his sister in tow.

"Smells good," Philip said, breathing in the smell of new cooler pads.

"Smells funny," his sister said. She stood under the vent that threw out the cool air. "It smells like when you sharpen pencils."

"Mom and Dad are gonna be surprised."

Their parents were at work, and because Philip was twelve and going into the seventh grade, he was expected to take care of his sister.

"Let's have lunch," Philip suggested. He washed his hands at the kitchen sink and made bologna-and-cheese sandwiches for his sister and for himself. They took their sandwiches, along with an orange soda to share, and sat at the kitchen table. Philip fed off his sandwich and the discovery that he was

---

1. **evaporator cooler**, a cooling unit in which air passes through water-soaked pads, causing some of the water in the pads to evaporate, cooling and humidifying the air. Evaporator coolers only work in arid climates.
2. handiwork (han′dē wėrk′), *n.* work done by a person's hands.

mechanically minded. Right then, as he ate, Philip got it into his head that he would look inside the telephone hanging on the wall. He ate quickly and then used a screwdriver to pop off the plastic front of the telephone.

"You're gonna get in trouble," Leticia said, her mouth full and her face greasy from the sandwich.

"No, I'm not," Philip replied. "If it breaks, I'll just fix it. I have a mechanical mind." He strummed the bunched strands of red and yellow wires, then put his ear to the receiver. The telephone still worked.

"See," he said when he dialed his best friend, Ricky, and got Ricky's mother, who answered, *"Bueno."*[3] He hung up and said, "It ain't broke."

His curiosity satisfied, Philip replaced the face of the telephone and decided to open the back of the clock radio in his parents' bedroom. Ever since his father had knocked it over while putting a new light bulb in the lamp by the bed, the radio had hummed. Now Philip would see what was wrong. He unscrewed the back and lifted the top, discovering a simple network of circuits and wires. There were also clots of dust and a mysterious toothpick lodged inside. He blew away the dust and used the end of his T-shirt to clean the corners. He was surprised at the tiny puddles of solder[4] and the fishline device that changed the stations. The humming miraculously stopped. Philip stood, hands on hips, feeling proud.

"See, it don't buzz no more," he said to his sister.

Leticia lowered her ear to the radio. The buzzing had indeed stopped.

Perched on their parents' end table, along with the radio, was a bottle of moisturizing lotion with a pump. Philip pressed the pump, and a yellowish lotion oozed into his hand. He rubbed it into his face, some of it sticking to his eyelashes.

"The lotion works like this," Philip started. "You see the pump—it works like gravity, like when astronauts jump on the moon. You probably don't understand, Leti, because you're not mechanically minded."

Leticia looked at her brother with new respect. She had never heard talk like this. She pumped a dimple of lotion into one palm, pressed her hands together, and then rubbed it on her arms.

Next Philip unscrewed the hair dryer. He looked at the wires and the small motor encased in hard plastic. He explained to his awed[5] sister that an electric fire was created in the motor and then air was trapped in a chamber that exploded every two or three seconds. "That's how your head heats up," he reasoned. He flicked on the hair dryer, and Leticia ran from the bathroom, her hands covering her head, screaming, "Don't burn my hair!"

Feeling more ambitious, Philip decided he would take apart the microwave oven. First he microwaved an ice cube and explained to Leticia that the waves were radar that could zap water from a stone.

"Go ahead and drink it," Philip dared Leticia as he shoved a cup of melted ice at her. Steam was rising from the near-boiling water.

"No way!" Leticia yelled. "And you better not mess with the microwave. Mom'll kill you."

But it was too late. Philip's screwdriver slipped and scraped off a piece of the imitation-wood facing. He decided to leave the microwave oven alone.

"Well, it was getting too old," he said. "Some of the radar leaked out and hurt the paint."

"Radar?" Leticia asked. "You're making this up."

---

3. *Bueno* (bwe′nō), good, well (Spanish).
4. solder (sŏd′ər), *n.* metal that is melted and used to connect other metal parts.
5. awed (ôd), *adj.* filled with wonder and amazement.

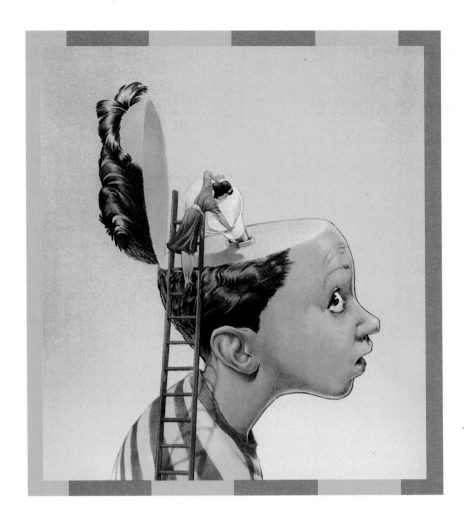

◄ What does this illustration by Dennis Auth suggest to you about how ideas are sometimes acquired?

"Radar heats the food," he said, feeling insulted that his mechanical mind was being doubted by a seven-year-old. "It's a proven fact. That's how astronauts heat up their grub in space."

Leticia looked up at her brother, again awed.

Then Philip remembered their television's lousy reception. He hurried to the living room with his screwdriver and studied the large, beastlike console,[6] a gift from his grand-mother, who had won it in a drawing at the bingo parlor. He turned it on and heard TV laughter as a clear picture came into view. A game show host was standing on his head.

"Is the TV upside down?" Leticia asked.

Her mouth was stuffed with an Oreo cookie that blackened her front teeth.

"He's being stupid," Philip answered. "Leti, I'm going to climb the roof and adjust the antenna. I think that's the problem."

"I'm not going to help you up. You're too heavy."

"Just tell me when the picture is clear, OK?" he asked as he walked out the front door.

The afternoon heat created a mirage[7] of water wavering on the street. On tiptoes, one hand cupped like a salute over his brow,

---

6. **console** (kon′sōl), *n.* a cabinet that stands on the floor and houses, in this case, a television.

7. **mirage** (mə razh′), *n.* an optical illusion.

Philip eyed the roof. The antenna, leaning slightly, stood right over the living room.

Using a ladder he had retrieved from behind the garage, Philip climbed onto the roof. He remembered his father saying that the television's reception could be adjusted by turning the antenna clockwise. Philip spit into his palms and turned the antenna, which bobbed softly as a tree branch.

"Is it better?" he yelled to Leticia.

"No," she yelled, her voice rising powerfully through the roof.

He turned it again and yelled, "How 'bout now?"

"No, it's really bad."

Sweating from the summer heat, Philip groaned and rotated the antenna, which began to shake and lean even more. "How 'bout now?"

"It's all weird."

Confused, Philip jumped off the roof. He was going to see for himself. He smashed a snail with the heel of one palm when he landed on the grass, but he didn't have time to get disgusted. It was time to put his mechanical mind to work. He went inside and saw that the television picture was a zigzag of colors. Philip watched the commercial. To him it looked like a woman was shampooing her hair with blue fire.

"It's makin' me sick," Leticia whined. She put her Oreo down on the coffee table and covered her mouth with both hands. She was getting ready to lose her sandwich and cookies—maybe even some of her breakfast.

Philip had to agree that the TV picture was

> # Philip rotated the antenna until a clamp snapped and the antenna fell like a tree....

sickening. He turned off the television, waited a few seconds, and then turned the set back on. The screen was still a zigzag of colors and long, frightful faces.

"Stupid thing," he scolded, pounding the television. The faces flickered but wouldn't fatten into regular human features. Philip wouldn't give up. He told Leticia, "I'm goin' to try again."

He climbed the ladder again but was having doubts. Maybe I'm not mechanically minded, he thought. He slipped on the roof and clutched at the grainy shingles so he wouldn't slide off. He got back to his feet, one knee bleeding, and leaned as he walked, as if he were trudging through a blizzard. He took the antenna in his hands and turned it clockwise, just as his father had explained.

"How is it now?" he yelled.

"I think the man is standing on his head again," Leticia yelled back.

"How 'bout now?"

"It's really bad."

"Now?"

"Everyone's orange."

Philip rotated the antenna until a clamp snapped and the antenna fell like a tree, striking the cooler and splitting the copper tubing he had repaired only an hour ago.

Philip's mouth fell open as he watched the water rush over the roof and off the eaves like a waterfall.

"It's working!" he heard his sister squeal. He could imagine her jumping up and down. "The TV is working. The guy is standing on his feet." His sister laughed and screamed through the roof, "Phil, you have a mechanical mind!"

After Reading

Making Connections

1. What did you think of the story? What parts did you particularly like or dislike?

2. Do you think Philip has a mechanical mind? Why or why not?

3. If you were one of Philip's parents, how would you have reacted when you came home and found that Philip had been taking apart all of the appliances?

4. Review the Reading Tip on **generalizations** on page 134. What role does a generalization play in the story?

5. Philip gets in over his head with the microwave and the TV antenna. How does this happen?

6. The **theme** of this group of selections concerns people who are trying to discover who they are. Has Philip made such a discovery? Why or why not?

7. Have you made **generalizations** that turned out to be wrong? What makes something a good or true generalization?

Literary Focus: Irony

Irony is a contrast between what is expected or hoped for and what actually happens. An example of irony might be when you clean up your room because your favorite uncle is coming over, and just as you finish he calls to say he can't make it. "How ironic," you think. "I spent all this time cleaning and now no one will see it." Or perhaps you never study for tests, but this time, you decide to really hit the books to ace the test. You walk into the class, all pumped up and ready to go—but the teacher is absent and the test is postponed. "How ironic," you think to yourself, "For the first time I'm ready for a test, and now I can't prove it!"

This story illustrates irony. In a small group, explain how the irony occurs. Then brainstorm other examples of irony. You could use sources from TV, other stories, music, or your own life.

Vocabulary Study

On your paper, write the word from the list at the left that best matches the definition.

handiwork
mirage
console
awed
solder

1. a cabinet that holds electronic equipment
2. something you think you see but really don't see
3. melted metal used to join things together
4. creation
5. feeling amazed by something of great beauty or power

Expressing Your Ideas

Writing Choices

For Those Who Know Better Is it wise to use a ladder when no one else is there? Make a **list** of the dangerous things that Philip did. Then explain what could have gone wrong.

To Whom It May Concern Pretend you are Philip. Write a **letter of introduction** summarizing your skills to a potential employer. For example, you might say "I'm very good at taking complicated things apart and putting them back together." As an alternative, write the same kind of letter about yourself.

You're the Expert Investigate how antennas or microwaves work and explain your findings to the rest of the class. As an alternative, write a **how-to paragraph** on how to fix something. If possible, bring the item to class and explain how it works or show how to fix it.

Other Options

A Connects to B Research how something works—a machine or perhaps a part of the body. Then make a **diagram** showing its function. Include clearly written labels.

Action Hero? Create a **comic strip** of Philip and his adventures. You could retell the story or make up new adventures for Philip.

Have Screwdriver, Will Travel Create a **brochure** advertising Philip's services as a mechanic or small-engine repair expert. Use a logo, illustrations, and wording that will assure him of plenty of customers. If you'd like, do the brochure for yourself, advertising your own skills and abilities. Post your brochure on the bulletin board.

Before Reading

The Parsley Garden

by William Saroyan

William Saroyan
1908–1981

William Saroyan was born Sirak Goryan. He left school at age fifteen and decided to become a writer. During his illustrious career, he wrote hundreds of stories and many plays and novels. Probably his best-known novel is *The Human Comedy,* which was later made into a movie. He won a Pulitzer Prize in 1940 for his play, *The Time of Your Life.* He refused the prize, however, because he thought that businessmen should not judge art. After he died, he was cremated. Half of his ashes are in Fresno, California, where he was born, and the other half are buried in Armenia.

Building Background

Another Holocaust Armenia and Turkey have long been at odds with each other. Between 1894 and 1896 many thousands of Armenians were massacred by the Turks. Then, in 1915, almost a million Armenians died of starvation when they were deported from their country by the Turks. William Saroyan's parents and three of their children immigrated to the United States seeking refuge from the violence. Many of Saroyan's stories, including this one, feature Armenian Americans.

Armenia became an independent nation in 1991, breaking away from the Soviet Union.

Getting into the Story

Writer's Notebook Imagine you are carrying a tray in the lunchroom when you trip. The result is soup on the floor, on you, and on your friend. *Humiliation* is probably a good word to describe your feelings. Humiliation, which is a lowering of pride, dignity, or self-respect, can be a terrible feeling. It damages a person's self-esteem, even if only temporarily. In your notebook, jot down ideas about humiliation, from how it happens and its effect on a person to how a person can get rid of the bad feeling.

Reading Tip

Author's Clues As you read, you will find clues that Al Condraj is poor—for example, he doesn't have a penny to spend. You will also discover that he has great pride in himself. As you read, note how the author provides these clues without actually telling you that "Al Condraj was poor" or "Al Condraj had great dignity." If you find any other traits worth noting, add them to your notes.

The Parsley Garden

William Saroyan

One day in August Al Condraj was wandering through Woolworth's without a penny to spend when he saw a small hammer that was not a toy but a real hammer and he was possessed with a longing to have it. He believed it was just what he needed by which to break the monotony[1] and with which to make something. He had gathered some first-class nails from Foley's Packing House where the boxmakers worked and where they had carelessly dropped at least fifteen cents' worth. He had gladly gone to the trouble of gathering them together because it had seemed to him that a nail, as such, was not something to be wasted. He had the nails, perhaps a half pound of them, at least two hundred of them, in a paper bag in the apple box in which he kept his junk at home.

The Art of Painting No.2 (detail) was painted in 1973 by Jim Dine. How do the tools in the painting symbolize the lives of Al and his mother?

---

1. **monotony** (mə not′n ē), *n.* lack of variety; sameness.

Now, with the ten-cent hammer he believed he could make something out of box wood and the nails, although he had no idea what. Some sort of a table perhaps, or a small bench.

At any rate he took the hammer and slipped it into the pocket of his overalls, but just as he did so a man took him firmly by the arm without a word and pushed him to the back of the store into a small office. Another man, an older one, was seated behind a desk in the office, working with papers. The younger man, the one who had captured him, was excited and his forehead was covered with sweat.

"Well," he said, "here's one more of them."

The man behind the desk got to his feet and looked Al Condraj up and down.

"What's *he* swiped?"

"A hammer." The young man looked at Al with hatred. "Hand it over," he said.

The boy brought the hammer out of his pocket and handed it to the young man, who said, "I ought to hit you over the head with it, that's what I ought to do."

He turned to the older man, the boss, the manager of the store, and he said, "What do you want me to do with him?"

"Leave him with me," the older man said.

The younger man stepped out of the office, and the older man sat down and went back to work. Al Condraj stood in the office fifteen minutes before the older man looked at him again.

"Well," he said.

Al didn't know what to say. The man wasn't looking at him, he was looking at the door.

Finally Al said, "I didn't mean to steal it. I just need it and I haven't got any money."

"Just because you haven't got any money doesn't mean you've got a right to steal things," the man said. "Now, does it?"

"No, sir."

"Well, what am I going to do with you? Turn you over to the police?"

Al didn't say anything, but he certainly didn't want to be turned over to the police. He hated the man, but at the same time he realized somebody else could be a lot tougher than he was being.

"If I let you go, will you promise never to steal from this store again?"

"Yes, sir."

"All right," the man said. "Go out this way and don't come back to this store until you've got some money to spend."

He opened a door to the hall that led to the alley, and Al Condraj hurried down the hall and out into the alley.

The first thing he did when he was free was laugh, but he knew he had been humiliated[2] and he was deeply ashamed.[3] It was not in his nature to take things that did not belong to him. He hated the young man who had caught him and he hated the manager of the store who had made him stand in silence in the office so long. He hadn't liked it at all when the young man had said he ought to hit him over the head with the hammer.

He should have had the courage to look him straight in the eye and say, "You and who else?"

Of course he *had* stolen the hammer and he had been caught, but it seemed to him he oughtn't to have been so humiliated.

After he had walked three blocks he decided he didn't want to go home just yet, so he turned around and started walking back to town. He almost believed he meant to go back and say something to the young man who had caught him. And then he wasn't sure he didn't mean to go back and steal the hammer again,

---

2. **humiliated** (hyü mil′ē āt id), *adj.* made to feel lowered and shamed in the eyes of others.
3. **ashamed** (ə shāmd′), *adj.* feeling shame; disturbed or uncomfortable because one has done something wrong, improper, or foolish.

and this time *not* get caught. As long as he had been made to feel like a thief anyway, the least he ought to get out of it was the hammer.

Outside the store he lost his nerve, though. He stood in the street, looking in, for at least ten minutes.

His humiliation was beginning to really hurt now.

Then, crushed and confused and now bitterly[4] ashamed of himself, first for having stolen something, then for having been caught, then for having been humiliated, then for not having guts enough to go back and do the job right, he began walking home again, his mind so troubled that he didn't greet his pal Pete Wawchek when they came face to face outside Graf's Hardware.

hen he got home he was too ashamed to go inside and examine his junk, so he had a long drink of water from the faucet in the back yard. The faucet was used by his mother to water the stuff she planted every year: okra, bell peppers, tomatoes, cucumbers, onions, garlic, mint, eggplants and parsley.

His mother called the whole business the parsley garden, and every night in the summer she would bring chairs out of the house and put them around the table she had had Ondro, the neighborhood handyman, make for her for fifteen cents, and she would sit at the table and enjoy the cool of the garden and the smell of the things she had planted and tended.

Sometimes she would even make a salad and moisten the flat old-country bread and slice some white cheese, and she and he would have supper in the parsley garden. After supper she would attach the water hose to the faucet and water her plants and the place would be cooler than ever and it would smell real good, real fresh and cool and green, all the different growing things making a green-garden smell out of themselves and the air and the water.

After the long drink of water he sat down where the parsley itself was growing and he pulled a handful of it out and slowly ate it. Then he went inside and told his mother what had happened. He even told her what he had *thought* of doing after he had been turned loose: to go back and steal the hammer again.

"I don't want you to steal," his mother said in broken English. "Here is ten cents. You go back to that man and you give him this money and you bring it home, that hammer."

"No," Al Condraj said. "I won't take your money for something I don't really need. I just thought I ought to have a hammer, so I could make something if I felt like it. I've got a lot of nails and some box wood, but I haven't got a hammer."

"Go buy it, that hammer," his mother said.

"No," Al said.

"All right," his mother said. "Shut up."

That's what she always said when she didn't know what else to say.

Al went out and sat on the steps. His humiliation was beginning to really hurt now. He decided to wander off along the railroad tracks to Foley's because he needed to think about it some more. At Foley's he watched Johnny Gale nailing boxes for ten minutes, but Johnny was too busy to notice him or talk to him, although one day at Sunday school, two or three years ago, Johnny had greeted him and said, "How's the boy?" Johnny worked with a boxmaker's hatchet and everybody in Fresno said he was the fastest boxmaker in town. He was the closest thing to a machine any packing house ever saw. Foley himself was proud of Johnny Gale.

---

4. **bitterly** (bit′ər lē), *adv.* painfully.

▲ *The Artist and His Mother* by Arshile Gorky was worked on from about 1926 to 1936. Gorky, an Armenian American, and his family suffered greatly when Turkish forces invaded their small Armenian village in 1915. How does this painting reflect the family's suffering?

Al Condraj finally set out for home because he didn't want to get in the way. He didn't want somebody working hard to notice that he was being watched and maybe say to him, "Go on, beat it." He didn't want Johnny Gale to do something like that. He didn't want to invite another humiliation.

On the way home he looked for money but all he found was the usual pieces of broken glass and rusty nails, the things that were always cutting his bare feet every summer.

When he got home his mother had made a salad and set the table, so he sat down to eat, but when he put the food in his mouth he just didn't care for it. He got up and went into the three-room house and got his apple box out of the corner of his room and went through his junk. It was all there, the same as yesterday.

He wandered off back to town and stood in front of the closed store, hating the young man who had caught him, and then he went along to the Hippodrome[5] and looked at the display photographs from the two movies that were being shown that day.

Then he went along to the public library to have a look at all the books again, but he didn't like any of them, so he wandered around town some more, and then around half-past eight he went home and went to bed.

His mother had already gone to bed because she had to be up at five to go to work at Inderrieden's, packing figs. Some days there would be work all day, some days there would be only half a day of it, but whatever his mother earned during the summer had to keep them the whole year.

He didn't sleep much that night because he couldn't get over what had happened, and he went over six or seven ways by which to adjust the matter. He went so far as to believe it would be necessary to kill the young man who had caught him. He also believed it would be necessary for him to steal systematically[6] and successfully the rest of his life. It was a hot night and he couldn't sleep.

Finally, his mother got up and walked barefooted to the kitchen for a drink of water and on the way back she said to him softly, "Shut up."

When she got up at five in the morning he was out of the house, but that had happened many times before. He was a restless boy, and he kept moving all the time every summer. He was making mistakes and paying for them, and he had just tried stealing and had been caught at it and he was troubled. She fixed her breakfast, packed her lunch and hurried off to work, hoping it would be a full day.

It was a full day, and then there was overtime, and although she had no more lunch she decided to work on for the extra money, anyway. Almost all the other packers were staying on, too, and her neighbor across the alley, Leeza Ahboot, who worked beside her, said, "Let us work until the work stops, then we'll go home and fix a supper between us and eat it in your parsley garden where it's so cool. It's a hot day and there's no sense not making an extra fifty or sixty cents."

When the two women reached the garden it was almost nine o'clock, but still daylight, and she saw her son nailing pieces of box wood together, making something with a hammer. It looked like a bench. He had already watered the garden and tidied up the rest of the yard, and the place seemed very nice, and her son seemed very serious and busy. She and Leeza

> "I just looked at them and picked up my hammer and walked out."

---

5. **Hippodrome,** in this case, the movie theater.
6. systematically (sis′tə mat′ik lē), *adv.* according to a method; in an organized way.

went straight to work for their supper, picking bell peppers and tomatoes and cucumbers and a great deal of parsley for the salad.

Then Leeza went to her house for some bread which she had baked the night before, and some white cheese, and in a few minutes they were having supper together and talking pleasantly about the successful day they had had. After supper, they made Turkish coffee[7] over an open fire in the yard. They drank the coffee and smoked a cigarette apiece, and told one another stories about their experiences in the old country and here in Fresno, and then they looked into their cups at the grounds[8] to see if any good fortune was indicated, and there was: health and work and supper out of doors in the summer and enough money for the rest of the year.

Al Condraj worked and overheard some of the things they said, and then Leeza went home to go to bed, and his mother said, "Where you get it, that hammer, Al?"

"I got it at the store."

"How you get it? You steal it?"

Al Condraj finished the bench and sat on it. "No," he said. "I didn't steal it."

"How you get it?"

"I worked at the store for it," Al said.

"The store where you steal it yesterday?"

"Yes."

"Who give you job?"

"The boss."

"What you do?"

"I carried different stuff to the different counters."

"Well, that's good," the woman said. "How long you work for that little hammer?"

"I worked all day," Al said. "Mr. Clemmer gave me the hammer after I'd worked one hour, but I went right on working. The fellow who caught me yesterday showed me what to do, and we worked together. We didn't talk, but at the end of the day he took me to Mr. Clemmer's office and he told Mr. Clemmer that I'd worked hard all day and ought to be paid at least a dollar."

"That's good," the woman said.

"So Mr. Clemmer put a silver dollar on his desk for me, and then the fellow who caught me yesterday told him the store needed a boy like me every day, for a dollar a day, and Mr. Clemmer said I could have the job."

"That's good," the woman said. "You can make it a little money for yourself."

"I left the dollar on Mr. Clemmer's desk," Al Condraj said, "and I told them both I didn't want the job."

"Why you say that?" the woman said. "Dollar a day for eleven-year-old boy good money. Why you not take job?"

"Because I hate the both of them," the boy said. "I would never work for people like that. I just looked at them and picked up my hammer and walked out. I came home and I made this bench."

"All right," his mother said. "Shut up."

His mother went inside and went to bed, but Al Condraj sat on the bench he had made and smelled the parsley garden and didn't feel humiliated any more.

But nothing could stop him from hating the two men, even though he knew they hadn't done anything they shouldn't have done.

---

7. **Turkish coffee:** very strong coffee.
8. **grounds:** Some people tell their fortunes by looking at tea leaves or coffee grounds left in the bottom of a cup.

After Reading

Making Connections

1. Why do you think Al still hates the two men at the end of the story?

2. What do you think of his way of getting the hammer?

3. ☺ What other **choices** did Al have for regaining his pride?

4. How would you describe the **character** of Al's mother?

5. How would you describe the relationship between Al and his mother? Does she really help Al? Does he trust her?

6. Why do you think the story is called "The Parsley Garden"? What other **titles** would you suggest?

7. In your opinion, what is the **theme** of this story?

8. Do you think this experience has helped Al learn who he is? Why or why not?

9. If you were a store manager or clerk who found someone stealing, what would you do?

Literary Focus: Characterization

An author uses a variety of methods to acquaint the reader with his or her **characters.** An author may describe the character's physical traits and personality, report the character's speech and behavior, give opinions and reactions of other characters toward this individual, or reveal the character's thoughts and feelings. What sort of person is Al? How do you know this? Look through the story for the clues the author gave you and list the character traits and clues you found. In small groups, answer the questions, "Why did Al steal the hammer?" and "Why did he go back to work for Mr. Clemmer?" Justify your answers with information from the story.

What Kind of Person is Al?

Clues in Story	My Conclusions
Gathered loose nails and saved them.	He places a high value on materials for making things.

Vocabulary Study

monotony
humiliated
ashamed
bitterly
systematically

Use the five vocabulary words in this selection plus five other words from the story to create a crossword puzzle. This means you will have to write short definitions or clues for all of the words. Use your Glossary and a dictionary if you need help. Exchange your puzzle with a partner for him or her to solve.

Expressing Your Ideas

Writing Choices

Say It in Writing Imagine you are Al. Write a **letter of resignation** to Mr. Clemmer explaining why you are quitting your job.

Presidential Material It is thirty years later, and Al Condraj is running for president. Some reporter finds the clerk in the store and discovers that, long ago, Al was caught stealing. At a press conference, the reporter asks Mr. Condraj about the incident. Write Al's **response.**

What Would They Say? Suppose Al's mother and her friend Mrs. Ahboot were sitting in the parsley garden discussing Al. Write the **dialogue** that might occur.

Other Options

Design the Garden Reread sections of the story to find descriptions of the garden. Then make a **model** of the garden showing such details as the table where Al and his mother eat and the kinds of things that are planted.

A Picture's Worth a Thousand Words Turn this story into a **picture book.** Think of an age group for which you might like to write, and draw pictures that are appropriate for the group. If possible, find a young audience to tell the story to in your own words.

That Night at the Dinner Table Assume the **role** of the clerk at Woolworth's. Have a partner play the role of your mother or wife or father or husband. That night at home, your partner asks, "Well, dear, did anything interesting happen today?" Tell her/him about the little thief you caught.

Writing mini-Lesson

Showing, Not Telling

Use examples. It is often more effective in writing to show readers what you want them to know through examples and anecdotes rather than tell them. Compare the following descriptions.

Telling
Joe was a miser.

Showing through examples
Very little changed after Joe got a big raise at work. His small apartment remained sparsely furnished with secondhand relics from garage sales. He walked to work in any weather to avoid paying bus fare, and he wore the same tattered shoes until they were falling off his feet.

Writing Strategy To write descriptions that show instead of tell, decide what you want to convey to readers. Then, rather than saying it directly, illustrate your point with concrete examples. Try to put your reader right into a situation so they can "see" things for themselves.

Activity Options

1. Skim a favorite book to find passages that show information rather than tell it. Choose one to share with the rest of the class. Discuss your reasons for choosing it.

2. With a partner, rewrite the following so each shows, not tells.

   • The fire burned out of control.

   • Gabby was the smartest kid in class.

   • Their house was in poor condition.

   • Mary is a great cook.

   • It was the most thrilling roller coaster I've been on.

3. The decision to show rather than tell depends on what you're writing. For example, in fiction it's usually best to show, whereas in a business letter it's usually best to tell. Work with a partner to list times that showing is better and times that telling is better.

Before Reading

from I Know Why the Caged Bird Sings

by Maya Angelou

Maya Angelou
born 1928

Maya Angelou was named Marguerite, but her brother called her "Maya," which was his way of saying "my sister." By the time she was in her twenties, she'd been a Creole cook, a streetcar conductor, a waitress, a dancer, and a mother. She then developed an interest in writing. Besides her autobiography, she has written plays, poems, and short stories. In 1993 Ms. Angelou recited one of her poems at President Clinton's inauguration.

Building Background

A Small Slice of Life This selection is from Maya Angelou's **autobiography.** The book recalls her life from the age of three, when her parents sent her and her four-year-old brother Bailey by themselves from California to Arkansas, to the age of sixteen. In the chapter you are about to read, Angelou is about eight years old. She lives with her grandmother, whom she calls Momma, in Stamps, Arkansas. She has just come back to Stamps from St. Louis, where she had been visiting her mother. She was abused there and has stopped talking as a result. Then she meets Mrs. Flowers.

Getting into the Selection

Discussion There are certain people who stand out in a crowd. Sometimes, it's their looks, or a way of speaking. Often, people like this are said to have **charisma,** which is a way of saying they have the power to attract. List traits that make someone stand out for you, and share this list with the class. Perhaps you might share the name of someone who you think is charismatic, and explain why.

Reading Tip

Context There are many uncommon words in this story, but most of them can be figured out by **context.** For example, in the first paragraph, Mrs. Flowers is described as "thin without the taut look of wiry people." Well, you know she's thin, and *wiry* comes from *wire*, so what does *taut* suggest to you? Further on in the story, the word *voile* is immediately followed by the word *dresses,* so you can guess that voile is a type of fabric. When you come to an unfamiliar word, look at the words around it, and usually you will find another word that will help you make sense of what you are reading. As you read, make a list of unfamiliar words and guess their meaning from context. Later, check a dictionary to see how close you were.

I Know Why the Caged Bird Sings

Maya Angelou

Mrs. Bertha Flowers was the aristocrat[1] of Black Stamps.[2] She had the grace of control to appear warm in the coldest weather, and on the Arkansas summer days it seemed she had a private breeze which swirled around, cooling her. She was thin without the taut look of wiry people, and her printed voile dresses and flowered hats were as right for her as denim overalls for a farmer. She was our side's answer to the richest white woman in town.

Her skin was a rich black that would have peeled like a plum if snagged, but then no one would have thought of getting close enough to Mrs. Flowers to ruffle her dress, let alone snag her skin. She didn't encourage familiarity. She wore gloves too.

I don't think I ever saw Mrs. Flowers laugh, but she smiled often. A slow widening of her thin black lips to show even, small white teeth, then the slow effortless closing. When she chose to smile on me, I always wanted to thank her. The action was so graceful and inclusively[3] benign.[4]

She was one of the few gentlewomen I have ever known, and has remained throughout my life the measure of what a human being can be.

---

1. aristocrat (ə ris′tə krat), n. a person who holds a high position in society.
2. **Stamps,** a town in Arkansas.
3. inclusively (in klü′siv lē), adv. including everyone.
4. benign (bi nīn′), adj. kindly and gentle.

Before Dawn is a glass tile mural created in 1989 from a collage by Romare Bearden. Study the details in this mural. Does it look like the place you imagined Mrs. Flowers might live? Why?

Momma[5] had a strange relationship with her. Most often when she passed on the road in front of the Store, she spoke to Momma in that soft yet carrying voice, "Good day, Mrs. Henderson." Momma responded with "How you, Sister Flowers?"

Mrs. Flowers didn't belong to our church, nor was she Momma's familiar.[6] Why on earth did she insist on calling her Sister Flowers? Shame made me want to hide my face. Mrs. Flowers deserved better than to be called Sister. Then, Momma left out the verb. Why not ask, "How *are* you, *Mrs.* Flowers?" With the unbalanced passion of the young, I hated her for showing her ignorance to Mrs. Flowers. It didn't occur to me for many years that they were as alike as sisters, separated only by formal education.

Although I was upset, neither of the women was in the least shaken by what I thought an unceremonious[7] greeting. Mrs. Flowers would continue her easy gait up the hill to her little bungalow,[8] and Momma kept on shelling peas or doing whatever had brought her to the front porch.

Occasionally, though, Mrs. Flowers would drift off the road and down to the Store and Momma would say to me, "Sister, you go on and play." As I left I would hear the beginning

---

5. **Momma,** Maya Angelou's grandmother.
6. familiar (fə mil′yər), *n.* intimate friend.
7. unceremonious (un′ser ə mō′nē əs), *adj.* informal; not as polite as would be expected.
8. bungalow (bung′gə lō), *n.* a small house, usually of one story.

of an intimate conversation, Momma persistently using the wrong verb, or none at all.

"Brother and Sister Wilcox is sho'ly the meanest—" "Is," Momma? "Is"? Oh, please, not "is," Momma, for two or more. But they talked, and from the side of the building where I waited for the ground to open up and swallow me, I heard the soft-voiced Mrs. Flowers and the textured voice of my grandmother merging and melting. They were interrupted from time to time by giggles that must have come from Mrs. Flowers (Momma never giggled in her life). Then she was gone.

She appealed to me because she was like people I had never met personally. Like women in English novels who walked the moors (whatever they were) with their loyal dogs racing at a respectful distance. Like the women who sat in front of roaring fireplaces, drinking tea incessantly[9] from silver trays full of scones[10] and crumpets.[11] Women who walked over the "heath" and read morocco-bound books[12] and had two last names divided by a hyphen. It would be safe to say that she made me proud to be Negro, just by being herself.

She acted just as refined[13] as whitefolks in the movies and books and she was more beautiful, for none of them could have come near that warm color without looking gray by comparison.

CONNECT: Do you know anyone like Mrs. Flowers?

It was fortunate that I never saw her in the company of powhitefolks. For since they tend to think of their whiteness as an evenizer, I'm certain that I would have had to hear her spoken to commonly as Bertha, and my image of her would have been shattered like the unmendable Humpty-Dumpty.

One summer afternoon, sweet-milk fresh

in my memory, she stopped at the Store to buy provisions. Another Negro woman of her health and age would have been expected to carry the paper sacks home in one hand, but Momma said, "Sister Flowers, I'll send Bailey up to your house with these things."

She smiled that slow dragging smile, "Thank you, Mrs. Henderson. I'd prefer Marguerite, though." My name was beautiful when she said it. "I've been meaning to talk to her, anyway." They gave each other age-group looks.

Momma said, "Well, that's all right then. Sister, go and change your dress. You going to Sister Flowers's."

The chifforobe[14] was a maze. What on earth did one put on to go to Mrs. Flowers's house? I knew I shouldn't put on a Sunday dress. It might be sacrilegious. Certainly not a house dress, since I was already wearing a fresh one. I chose a school dress, naturally. It was formal without suggesting that going to Mrs. Flowers's house was equivalent to attending church.

I trusted myself back into the Store.

"Now, don't you look nice." I had chosen the right thing, for once.

"Mrs. Henderson, you make most of the children's clothes, don't you?"

"Yes, ma'am. Sure do. Store-bought clothes ain't hardly worth the thread it take to stitch them."

"I'll say you do a lovely job, though, so neat. That dress looks professional."

Momma was enjoying the seldom-received compliments. Since everyone we knew (except Mrs. Flowers, of course) could sew competently,

---

9. **incessantly** (in ses′nt lē), *adv.* always; without stopping.
10. **scone,** a thick, flat, round cake.
11. **crumpet,** a round, flat cake that is usually toasted.
12. **morocco-bound books,** books bound in fine leather.
13. **refined** (ri find′), *adj.* well-bred.
14. **chifforobe:** a piece of furniture that is used as a closet, having both drawers and space for hanging clothes.

▲ *Easter Bonnet* was painted by Stephen Scott Young in 1995. What qualities does the girl in this portrait share with Marguerite?

praise was rarely handed out for the commonly practiced craft.

"I try, with the help of the Lord, Sister Flowers, to finish the inside just like I does the outside. Come here, Sister."

I had buttoned up the collar and tied the belt, apronlike, in back. Momma told me to turn around. With one hand she pulled the strings and the belt fell free at both sides of my waist. Then her large hands were at my neck, opening the button loops. I was terrified. What was happening?

"Take it off, Sister." She had her hands on the hem of the dress.

"I don't need to see the inside, Mrs. Henderson, I can tell . . ." But the dress was over my head and my arms were stuck in the sleeves. Momma said, "That'll do. See here, Sister Flowers, I French-seams around the armholes." Through the cloth film, I saw the shadow approach. "That makes it last longer. Children these days would bust out of sheet-metal clothes. They so rough."

"That is a very good job, Mrs. Henderson. You should be proud. You can put your dress back on, Marguerite."

"No, ma'am. Pride is a sin. And 'cording to the Good Book, it goeth before a fall."

"That's right. So the Bible says. It's a good thing to keep in mind."

I wouldn't look at either of them. Momma hadn't thought that taking off my dress in front of Mrs. Flowers would kill me stone dead. If I had refused, she would have thought I was trying to be "womanish" and might have remembered St. Louis. Mrs. Flowers had known that I would be embarrassed and that was even worse. I picked up the groceries and went out to wait in the hot sunshine. It would be fitting if I got a sunstroke and died before they came outside. Just dropped dead on the slanting porch.

There was a little path beside the rocky road, and Mrs. Flowers walked in front swinging her arms and picking her way over the stones.

She said, without turning her head, to me, "I hear you're doing very good schoolwork, Marguerite, but that it's all written. The teachers report that they have trouble getting you to talk in class." We passed the triangular farm on our left and the path widened to allow us to walk together. I hung back in the separate unasked and unanswerable questions.

QUESTION: What do you think the "unasked and unanswerable questions" might be?

"Come and walk along with me, Marguerite." I couldn't have refused even if I wanted to. She pronounced my name so nicely. Or more correctly, she spoke each word with such clarity that I was certain a foreigner who didn't understand English could have understood her.

"Now no one is going to make you talk—possibly no one can. But bear in mind, language is man's way of communicating with his fellow man and it is language alone which separates him from the lower animals." That was a totally new idea to me, and I would need time to think about it.

"Your grandmother says you read a lot. Every chance you get. That's good, but not good enough. Words mean more than what is set down on paper. It takes the human voice to infuse them with the shades of deeper meaning."

I memorized the part about the human voice infusing words. It seemed so valid and poetic.

She said she was going to give me some books and that I not only must read them, I must read them aloud. She suggested that I try to make a sentence sound in as many different ways as possible.

"I'll accept no excuse if you return a book to me that has been badly handled." My imagination boggled at the punishment I would deserve if in fact I did abuse a book of Mrs. Flowers's. Death would be too kind and brief.

The odors in the house surprised me. Somehow I had never connected Mrs. Flowers with food or eating or any other common experience of common people. There must have been an outhouse, too, but my mind never recorded it.

The sweet scent of vanilla had met us as she opened the door.

"I made tea cookies this morning. You see, I had planned to invite you for cookies and lemonade so we could have this little chat. The lemonade is in the icebox."

It followed that Mrs. Flowers would have ice on an ordinary day, when most families in our town bought ice late on Saturdays only a few times during the summer to be used in the wooden ice-cream freezers.

She took the bags from me and disappeared through the kitchen door. I looked around the room that I had never in my wildest fantasies imagined I would see. Browned photographs leered or threatened from the walls and the white, freshly done curtains pushed against themselves and against the wind. I wanted to gobble up the room entire and take it to Bailey, who would help me analyze and enjoy it.

"Have a seat, Marguerite. Over there by the table." She carried a platter covered with a tea towel. Although she warned that she hadn't tried her hand at baking sweets for some time, I was certain that like everything else about her the cookies would be perfect.

They were flat round wafers, slightly browned on the edges and butter-yellow in the center. With the cold lemonade they were sufficient for childhood's lifelong diet. Remembering my manners, I took nice little lady-like bites off the edges. She said she had made them expressly for me and that she had a few in the kitchen that I could take home to my brother. So I jammed one whole cake in my mouth and the rough crumbs scratched the insides of my jaws, and if I hadn't had to swallow, it would have been a dream come true.

As I ate she began the first of what we later called "my lessons in living." She said that I must always be intolerant of ignorance but understanding of illiteracy. That some people, unable to go to school, were more educated and even more intelligent than college professors. She encouraged me to listen carefully to what country people called mother wit. That in those homely sayings was couched the collective wisdom of generations.

When I finished the cookies she brushed off the table and brought a thick, small book from the bookcase. I had read *A Tale of Two Cities* and found it up to my standards as a romantic novel. She opened the first page and I heard poetry for the first time in my life.

She opened the first page and I heard poetry for the first time in my life.

"It was the best of times and the worst of times . . ." Her voice slid in and curved down through and over the words. She was nearly singing. I wanted to look at the pages. Were they the same that I had read? Or were there notes, music, lined on the pages, as in a hymn book? Her sounds began cascading gently. I knew from listening to a thousand preachers that she was nearing the end of her reading, and I hadn't really heard, heard to understand, a single word.

"How do you like that?"

It occurred to me that she expected a response. The sweet vanilla flavor was still on my tongue and her reading was a wonder in my ears. I had to speak.

I said, "Yes, ma'am." It was the least I could do, but it was the most also.

"There's one more thing. Take this book of poems and memorize one for me. Next time you pay me a visit, I want you to recite."

I have tried often to search behind the sophistication[15] of years for the enchantment I so easily found in those gifts. The essence escapes but its aura[16] remains. To be allowed, no, invited, into the private lives of strangers, and to share their joys and fears, was a chance to exchange the Southern bitter wormwood[17] for a cup of mead[18] with Beowulf or a hot cup of tea and milk with Oliver Twist. When I said aloud, "It is a far, far better thing that I do, than I have ever done . . ." tears of love filled my eyes at my selflessness.

On that first day, I ran down the hill and into the road (few cars ever came along it) and had the good sense to stop running before I reached the Store.

I was liked, and what a difference it made.

I was liked, and what a difference it made. I was respected not as Mrs. Henderson's grandchild or Bailey's sister but for just being Marguerite Johnson.

Childhood's logic never asks to be proved (all conclusions are absolute). I didn't question why Mrs. Flowers had singled me out for attention, nor did it occur to me that Momma might have asked her to give me a little talking to. All I cared about was that she had made tea cookies for *me* and read to *me* from her favorite book. It was enough to prove that she liked me.

---

15. **sophistication** (sə fis′tə kā′shən), *n.* worldly experience.
16. **aura** (ôr′ə), *n.* an atmosphere that surrounds something or someone.
17. **wormwood,** something very bitter and unpleasant.
18. **mead,** drink made from fermented honey and water.

After Reading

Making Connections

1. What is your very first reaction to this story?

2. What techniques does the writer use to create the **character** of Mrs. Flowers?

3. Why does it bother Marguerite when Momma uses the wrong verbs in speaking to Mrs. Flowers?

4. 🐾 What influence do you think Mrs. Flowers had on Maya Angelou's **choice** to become a writer?

5. Why do you think Marguerite wrote an **autobiography?** Come up with as many reasons as you can.

6. Do you agree with Mrs. Flowers that language is the only thing that separates humans from other animals? Why?

Literary Focus: Descriptive Style

Mrs. Flowers is described as the "aristocrat of Black Stamps." If you were to look up the word *aristocrat* in a dictionary, you would find its standard definition—"a noble or someone belonging to the aristocracy." Aside from the dictionary definition, or **denotation,** however, the word *aristocrat* has other meanings, or connotations. The feelings, images, and memories that surround a word make up its **connotation.** Reread sections of the selection and choose several descriptions of Mrs. Flowers. Copy them onto the lines of a diagram such as the one below. Then, in the boxes, write the connotations that are suggested by the words.

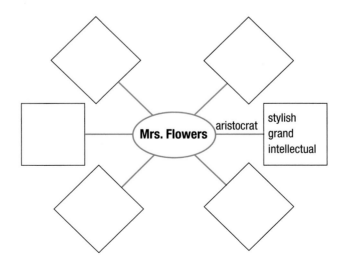

Vocabulary Study

incessantly
unceremonious
familiar
inclusively
aristocrat
refined
aura
bungalow
sophistication
benign

A. Antonyms Write the vocabulary word from the list at the left that is the *opposite* of each numbered word below.

1. stranger

2. exclusively

3. never

4. formal

5. servant

B. Synonyms In small groups, see how many synonyms you can provide for *refined, aura, bungalow, sophistication*, and *benign* in one minute.

Expressing Your Ideas

Writing Choices

You'd Like Her, Too Write a **descriptive paragraph** about a person who has a charismatic personality. Choose words that are descriptive on many levels. For example, instead of saying, "She's pretty," you could say, "Her eyes are large and sparkle with fun, and you forget to look at the rest of her face." You may wish to refer to the discussion you had about charisma before reading. If possible, use some vocabulary words in your description.

Switching Roles How do you think Al Condraj would have acted at Mrs. Flowers' house? Rewrite a **story scene** replacing the character of Marguerite with Al.

"They Were As Alike As Sisters . . ." Write an essay **comparing and contrasting** Momma and Mrs. Flowers. How are they alike? How are they different? Conclude by stating whether you agree or disagree with Maya Angelou's statement that the two women really were very much alike.

Other Options

Her Voice Slid In and Curved Read aloud a passage from your favorite book to make it come alive. As an alternative, find a copy of Charles Dickens' book, *A Tale of Two Cities.* Practice reading the first paragraph, the one Mrs. Flowers read to Marguerite, or your own selection, until you are comfortable doing an **oral reading** for the class.

Outside the Store Compare and contrast Mrs. Flowers and Momma by acting out with a partner a **conversation** between them. Then discuss what aspects of their characters you were trying to convey through the conversation.

Lessons for Living Write your own lessons for living. Try to think of four rules that you use to guide your actions. Make a **poster** of these sayings.

Before Reading

Rice and Rose Bowl Blues by Diane Mei Lin Mark
The Sidewalk Racer by Lillian Morrison
Identity by Julio Noboa Polanco

Diane Mei Lin Mark
Diane Mei Lin Mark divides her time between Hawaii and New York. She is a writer and a filmmaker.

Lillian Morrison
born 1917

Of "Sidewalk Racer," Lillian Morrison says, "I love rhythms, the body movement implicit in poetry, explicit in sports."

Julio Noboa Polanco
born 1949

Julio Noboa Polanco is a bilingual poet who wrote "Identity" when he was in the eighth grade.

Building Background

Individualism Our nation has a rich heritage of respect for individualism. In the early 1700s, a movement known as the Great Awakening burst upon the American scene. Perhaps the most dramatic effect of the Great Awakening was the sense of democracy and equality it inspired among its followers. A celebration of the individual had begun. This celebration helped spur the colonists to adopt the Declaration of Independence in 1776. In the Declaration, the colonists resolved to fight for their right "to assume among the powers of the earth, the separate and equal station to which the Laws of Nature . . . entitle them." With such a heritage, it should come as no surprise that American literature is full of poems that celebrate individuality in a variety of ways. You are about to read three of them.

Getting into the Poetry

Writer's Notebook All of these poems include motion. Words like "wind-wavering," "swayed," "pour some water," and—well, you'll read Lillian Morrison's poem and see for yourself. In your notebook, write down some of your own favorite "motion words." As you read, add any new ones that you find.

Reading Tip

Visualizing The movement in these poems helps bring some vivid images to mind. After you read each poem, stop for a second. Close your eyes. What do you see? Then jot down the image you see.

Rice and Rose Bowl Blues

Diane Mei Lin Mark

▲ This illustration of a Japanese rice bowl and rising origami bird was painted by Kam Mak. What is the significance of the two pictures on the bowl? What do you think the bird symbolizes?

I remember the day
Mama called me in from
the football game with brothers
and neighbor boys
5 in our front yard

said it was time
I learned to
wash rice for dinner

glancing out the window
10 I watched a pass interception
setting the other team up
on our 20
    Pour some water
    into the pot,
15 *she said pleasantly,*
    turning on the tap
    Rub the rice
    between your hands,
    pour out the clouds,
20 *fill it again*
    (I secretly traced
    an end run through
    the grains in
    between pourings)

25 with the rice
settled into a simmer[1]
I started out the door
but was called back

the next day
30 Roland from across the street
sneeringly said he heard
I couldn't play football
anymore

I laughed loudly,
35 asking him
where
he'd heard
such a thing

---

1. simmer (sim′ər), *n.* process of cooking at or just below boiling point.

The Sidewalk Racer or On the Skateboard

Lillian Morrison

> Skimming
> an asphalt[1] sea
> I swerve, I curve, I
> sway; I speed to whirring
> 5   sound an inch above the
> ground; I'm the sailor
> and the sail, I'm the
> driver and the wheel
> I'm the one and only
> 10   single engine
> human auto
> mobile.

---

1. asphalt (as′fôlt), *n.* a mix of tar and stones that is used for road surfaces; blacktop.

A boy seemingly defies gravity as he maneuvers his skateboard over a ramp on a playground in the Bronx, New York.

IDENTITY

JULIO NOBOA POLANCO

Let them be as flowers,
always watered, fed, guarded, admired,
but harnessed[1] to a pot of dirt.

I'd rather be a tall, ugly weed,
5 clinging on cliffs, like an eagle
wind-wavering above high, jagged rocks.

To have broken through the surface of stone,
to live, to feel exposed to the madness
of the vast, eternal sky.
10 To be swayed by the breezes of an ancient sea,
carrying my soul, my seed, beyond the mountains of time
or into the abyss[2] of the bizarre.

I'd rather be unseen, and if
then shunned by everyone,
15 than to be a pleasant-smelling flower,
growing in clusters in the fertile[3] valley,
where they're praised, handled, and plucked
by greedy, human hands.

I'd rather smell of musty, green stench
20 than of sweet, fragrant lilac.
If I could stand alone, strong and free,
I'd rather be a tall, ugly weed.

---

1. harness (här′nis), v. tie or strap to
   something.
2. abyss (ə bis′), n. a very great bottomless depth.
3. fertile (fėr′tl), adj. soil that is rich and productive.

After Reading

Making Connections

1. With which poem did you most identify? Why?

2. Draw some of the **images** that the poems brought to mind. Explain how they connect to the text.

3. How do each of the authors use motion words in their poems?

4. Why would the narrator of "Identity" rather be a "tall, ugly weed"? What are some of the advantages to this? What are some of the disadvantages?

5. What is the **conflict** in "Rice and Rose Bowl Blues"?

6. 👣 What **choice** does it seem that the narrator in "Rice and Rose Bowl Blues" must make? How is that choice related to cultural expectations for girls? Is compromise possible?

7. How are the poems "Identity" and "Rice and Rose Bowl Blues" similar? How are they different?

8. How does each poem fit the **theme** "Searching for the Real You"?

Literary Focus: Alliteration

The poem "Sidewalk Racer" contains much **alliteration,** which is the repetition of consonant sounds. This can occur at the beginning of words, as in "Big bad Bob bops beautifully," or it can occur within words, as in, "It's a little late to alliterate," lamented Allison Kate. In the first sentence, the /b/ sound is alliterated. In the second, both the /l/ and the /t/ sounds provide the alliteration.

Look at the poem "The Sidewalk Racer." What are some of the repeated sounds? Make a chart like the one below and fill it in. Discuss: What does the use of alliteration add to the poem?

Repeated Sound	Words with That Sound
v	swerve, curve

Vocabulary Study

harness
simmer
fertile
asphalt
abyss

On your paper, write the vocabulary word that completes each numbered group.

1. tie, strap, ___
2. blacktop, tar, ___
3. bottomless, pit, ___
4. boil gently, cook evenly, ___
5. rich soil that grows things, productive, ___

Expressing Your Ideas

Writing Choices

You're a Poet and You Don't Know It Try your own hand at writing a **poem** that uses motion and alliteration. The subject should be some aspect of individuality (especially yours!) such as a particular activity that some people like to do, or a place where a person feels either very free or very confined.

Like a What? The author of "Identity" uses the metaphor of plants. He says that people are flowers, and that he would rather be "a tall, ugly weed." To what other things can people be compared? Make a list of **metaphors** that describe people. It might be easier to complete the phrase, "I am a _____" in order to make the list. If there's one metaphor you really like, why not use it in a poem?

Call It As You See It Write a short **play-by-play description** of a skateboarder maneuvering a challenging course.

Other Options

Move It How about **dancing out** who you are or what you are feeling? You could even dance out a story about something that is significant to you, or allow the music to tell the story while you interpret the story through movement. An alternative to dance, if you wish to try something a little different, is pantomime.

May I Have a Taste? Rice is important to the characters in "Rice and Rose Bowl Blues." A certain food or foods probably plays or has played a significant role in your life too. Perhaps you remember the day you learned to cook a particular dish, or maybe the food is important because another person made it or brought it to family gatherings. If possible, bring in one of those food items and share both the **food** and the memory with the class. If this isn't possible, find or draw a picture of the food, and write, draw, or paste pictures of the memories around the food.

Freestyle Paste-Up Using pictures clipped from newspapers and sports magazines, create a **collage** of skateboarders or other athletes. Make your collage work like a poem to show the action of the sport.

Searching for the Real You

Brainstorms

History/Health Connection

For some people, finding who they are and what they want in life seems obvious. To most, searching for the real you is a challenge. Like the Kellogg brothers, you may travel many roads before you find the one that takes you in the right direction.

Corn Flake Kings: The Kellogg Brothers

by Meredith Hooper

Her secret

Don't you tell—this is my third dish

Kellogg's
TOASTED CORN FLAKES
W.K. Kellogg
TOASTED CORN FLAKE MFG.
BATTLE CREEK MICH

Kellogg's
TOASTED CORN FLAKES

If you want to see the children eat—grow—thrive—give them Kellogg's Toasted Corn Flakes. If you want to know the reason why—taste it yourself. Then you'll understand its wonderful popularity. You'll know why you should always look for the signature on the package. This is the sign of the genuine. The kind with the flavor so delicious, that it can't be duplicated by any other food, by any other grain, by any other make.
Your Grocer has it, in large packages. Get it and remember the signature.

W.K. Kellogg

John Harvey Kellogg, his brother Will Keith, and all their fourteen other brothers and sisters ate hot pancakes with bacon fat and molasses most days for breakfast. Mrs. Kellogg got up early, stoked the fire, and had the pancakes cooking before anyone came down to eat. The Kelloggs lived in a log cabin in the Michigan forest, then in the small town of Battle Creek, Michigan.

Mr. and Mrs. Kellogg belonged to a strict religious group called the Seventh Day Adventists, who believed in health reform and eating a simple diet with no tea, coffee, alcohol, tobacco, spices, and also, they eventually decided, no meat. Battle Creek was the Adventist headquarters; here the group set up a medical boarding-house where people could be treated for their illnesses by following Adventist teaching on diet and behavior. But the Health Reform Institute was still very small when, in 1876, John Harvey Kellogg, now a young doctor, took over. He ran it for the next sixty-five years.

The Battle Creek Sanitarium, as the institute was renamed, became very popular, even world-famous. Overweight ladies and their overworried businessmen husbands came to rest, exercise, diet, and breathe fresh air.

People a hundred years ago ate very badly by today's standards. Out west, the diet was far too monotonous: coffee, hog, and hominy (a maize porridge) for every meal. In big cities the rich overate. A meal included two or three kinds of meat, fish and game, plus spices and pickles.

A stay at the Battle Creek Sanitarium made patients think about the importance of a good diet, probably for the first time in their lives. Dr. John Kellogg believed in a proper diet, not drugs, to cure illness. Meat, alcohol, and smoking were strictly forbidden at Battle Creek Sanitarium, because of Adventist teaching. But the vegetarian meals served in the dining-room were very monotonous, and some patients left because they did not like the food.

From the beginning Dr. John Kellogg experimented in the kitchens with new, appetizing ways of preparing vegetarian foods. He invented Granola, which looked like toasted breadcrumbs, and he also invented peanut butter. He used the things vegetarians are allowed to eat, such as nuts, grain, and vegetables, to invent foods that tasted like the things they were not allowed to eat. Ex-patients began to ask for supplies of the Sanitarium health foods, so Dr. Kellogg set up small companies to manufacture his inventions, and sent his foods to his customers by mail order.

In the middle of Dr. John's experimenting, an inventor called Henry D. Perky made a machine for shredding wheat, and sold the resulting little pillow-shaped product as Shredded Wheat. People liked it. Then a business man called Charles W. Post came to the Sanitarium for a cure, but spent most of his time in the kitchens and laboratories. He soon set up a factory in Battle Creek and started to manufacture his own cereal substitute for coffee, called Postum. Post advertised heavily and cleverly. "Do you suffer from coffee headaches? Take Postum." "POSTUM MAKES RED BLOOD." Soon he invented Grape-Nuts, a hard, chewy cereal food. Grape-Nuts was advertised as being beneficial for the appendix, malaria, loose teeth, and the brain. Post's profits went up so fast he was a multi-millionaire within seven years.

Dr. John and Will Keith Kellogg made the first pre-cooked flaked cereal in 1894. Dr. John was experimenting with wheat, which he

John Harvey Kellogg

The packets of corn flakes rolled out of Will Keith's factory in Battle Creek in ever increasing numbers.

boiled for varying lengths of time, and then pushed through rollers. Will scraped the sticky dough off the rollers with a knife. Nothing useful could be done with this mess. One batch of boiled wheat got left for several days; no one had time to do anything with it. In the end the brothers decided to put it through the rollers, although it was very moldy, to see what would happen. Out came large thin flakes, each grain of wheat forming one flake. The flakes were baked in the oven and emerged crisp and tasty. After more experimenting, the Kelloggs found out how to leave the boiled wheat long enough to produce flakes, without the wheat becoming moldy.

Even though they were tough and rather tasteless, the wheat flakes were instantly popular with the Sanitarium patients. The secret of how to make them leaked out; soon there were dozens of manufacturers copying the recipe.

Battle Creek suffered a breakfast-food rush. Post's success and the various Kellogg inventions brought hundreds of hopeful money-makers into the town to try their luck at making a breakfast food in a box.

Will Keith could see all the Sanitarium food inventions being taken over and developed by other people. He was determined not to let this happen to the best invention of them all, corn flakes. Will Keith Kellogg set up in Battle Creek the Toasted Corn Flake Company.

The packets of corn flakes rolled out of Will Keith's factory in Battle Creek in ever increasing numbers. The taste of corn flakes had been improved by adding malt, sugar, and salt for flavor. Like Post, with Postum, he spent huge amounts on advertising, using especially the new invention, radio. Free samples of Toasted Corn Flakes were given away to millions of housewives. Breakfast-food manufacturers were some of the first to concentrate on *children:* if children wanted Kellogg's Corn Flakes, then their mothers would probably buy them. Give-away presents were included in each packet: cut-outs, sets of cards, models. W.K. became known as the "Cornflake King," and his products were made and sold around the world. Fifty years after the company began, the factories at Battle Creek alone produced six million packets of cereals a day, and a million of these were corn flakes.

Responding

1. Many people ate unhealthy diets one hundred years ago. Fresh fruits and vegetables and other nutritious foods were often not available. What about your diet? Make a food diary. Write down everything you eat for three days.

2. Discuss some of your diary entries with a small group of classmates. How might you make your diet healthier?

U.S. History Connection

Some of the best ideas come as the result of brainstorming. Inventors don't know the meaning of the word *impossible*. Those who are willing to experiment can make almost anything possible. The proof is in the inventions on these pages.

I 19th-Century U.S. INVENTIONS

1870
Square Bottomed Paper Bag invented by Margaret Knight.

1872
Baby Jumper invented by Jane Wills.

1873
Barbed Wire invented by Joseph E. Glidden.

Canvas Athletic Shoes

Dr. W. E. Meanwell's "Athlete" Shoes
Designed by the famous coach, Dr. W. E. Meanwell. Khaki color canvas uppers, treated with a preparation which makes them waterproof and decay-proof. Equipped with pure crepe rubber soles. Scientifically designed last which supports instep and foot muscles. Stubber toe guards give protection against toe knocks. **State size.** Shpg. wt., 2 lbs.
6H1986—Boys'. Regular $2.50 retail value. Sizes and half sizes, 2½ to 6. **$1.98**
6H1987—Men's. Regular $2.75 retail value. Sizes and half sizes, 6½ to 11. **$2.23**
6H1989—Women's. Regular $2.50 retail value. Sizes and half sizes, 3 to 7. **$1.98**
6H1988—Youths'. Regular $2.25 retail value. Sizes and half sizes, 11 to 2. **$1.79**

Low Priced Canvas Shoes
A good quality trimmed canvas shoe at a moderately low price. White duck uppers with rubber trimmings and imitation crepe sole; laced to toe pattern. Adaptable for all kinds of wear. **State size.** Shipping weight, 2 pounds.
6H1981—Boys'. Sizes and half sizes, 1 to 5½. **$0.95**
6H1982—Men's. Sizes and half sizes, 6 to 11. **1.00**
6H1983—Women's. Sizes and half sizes, 3 to 7. **.98**

Ralph Jones Professional Basketball Shoes
Heavy white canvas uppers. Equipped with long wearing molded rubber suction soles that hold on smoothest floor. Extra heavy toe cap, double foxing joins sole to upper. Leather trimmed. Non-heat insole. **State size.** Shpg. wt., 2½ lbs.
6H1972—Boys'. Regular $3.75 retail value. Sizes and half sizes, 4 to 6. **$2.98**
Team lots of five pairs or more. Per pair. **2.85**
6H1973—Men's. Regular $4.00 retail value. Sizes and half sizes, 6½ to 11. **$3.29**
Team lots of five pairs or more. Per pair. **3.10**

1868
First Sneaker invented by Candee Manufacturing Company.

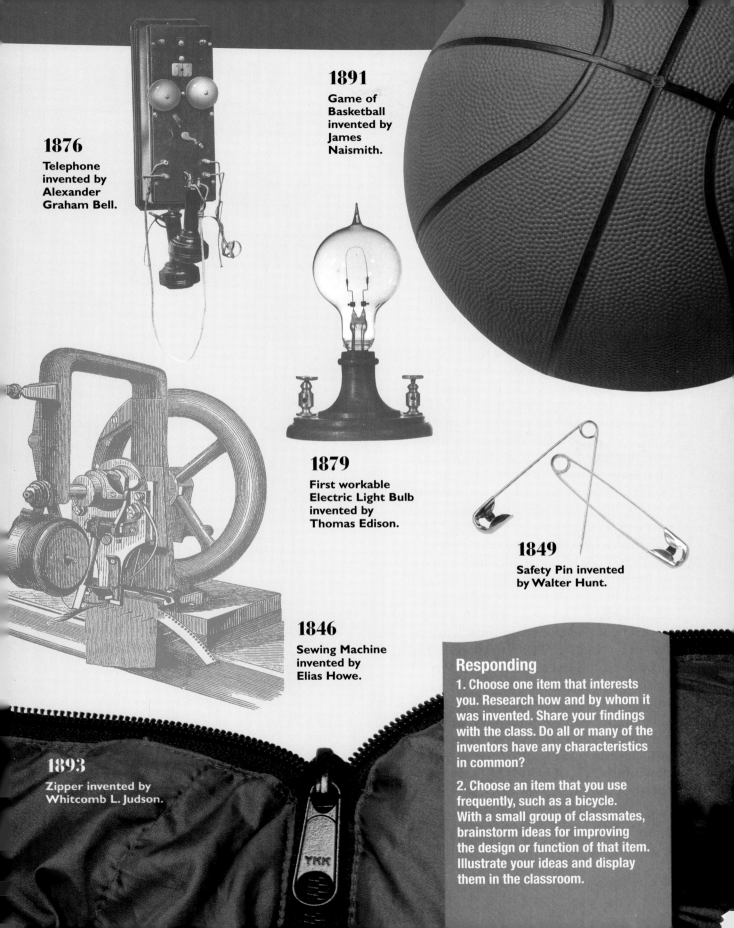

1876
Telephone invented by Alexander Graham Bell.

1891
Game of Basketball invented by James Naismith.

1879
First workable Electric Light Bulb invented by Thomas Edison.

1849
Safety Pin invented by Walter Hunt.

1846
Sewing Machine invented by Elias Howe.

1893
Zipper invented by Whitcomb L. Judson.

Responding

1. Choose one item that interests you. Research how and by whom it was invented. Share your findings with the class. Do all or many of the inventors have any characteristics in common?

2. Choose an item that you use frequently, such as a bicycle. With a small group of classmates, brainstorm ideas for improving the design or function of that item. Illustrate your ideas and display them in the classroom.

Now you invent a cereal!

by Steven Carney

Fantasy Inventions

Food is something so basic to everyday life that we often take it for granted, but, like Will Kellogg, the inventor who can produce or package differently new kinds of food is bound to tap a market as big as the world itself.

Look at the following list of fantasy inventions. Which ones do you think people might actually buy?

Vitamin Chewing Gum

Enjoy the flavor and the fun of chewing while getting the daily vitamins and minerals you need.

Leftover Foods Reprocessor

Converts leftover table and cooking scraps into healthful foods—such as roasted beef puffs or chewy dried fruit.

Dinner Table Condiment Bar

Handily dispenses ketchup, mustard, steak sauce, and other condiments through a controlled-flow tube nozzle.

Anyone can be an inventor! All inventions start as someone's idea—and nearly everyone has plenty of ideas about ways things could be improved. Some ideas are for things that do what no one has ever done before; others make old inventions better or just make jobs easier or more fun to do. Some people's ideas are futuristic and may even depend on technologies that haven't been created yet. And some, although they might seem silly to others, offer solutions that are practical answers to the inventor's needs—like eyeglasses for chickens so their eyes won't get poked, or seat belts for dogs and cats. Even though anyone can have a good idea, that does not make him an inventor.

To be an inventor you must learn to let your mind search, to think of many possible solutions to each invention problem you encounter. Even if many of your ideas seem foolish or impractical, they might lead you to a truly unique solution and a successful invention. If you can train yourself to look at every-day things in a new and different way, then your mind will always be inventing.

Responding
Now it's your turn. Invent a food or machine for making a new food. Write a brief description of your invention. Then illustrate it. Share your invention with your classmates.

Reading Mini-Lesson

Finding the Main Idea and Supporting Details

Main ideas and details are the building blocks of textbooks, informational articles, and other types of writing. The **main idea** gives the most important point of the whole passage and can usually be summed up in one sentence. **Details** support the main idea and paint a clearer picture by providing specifics.

When trying to explain an event, people often say, "Do you want the short version or the long version?" The difference between the two versions is the degree of supporting details included in the telling. The short version gives you just the basic idea or story line. The long version gives you the details you need to let you visualize and better understand the information.

One way to organize information in your notes is to use a **pie chart.** Below the pie chart state the main idea. Each "slice" of the pie can contain a subtopic or group of details. You will have to decide how many slices the pie will have. The example at the left is a way to organize the information from the second paragraph of "Corn Flake Kings" on page 167.

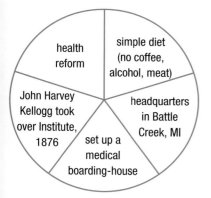

The Seventh Day Adventists were a strict religious group.

Activity Options

1. In one or two sentences, summarize the main idea of the entire article "Corn Flake Kings." Then find four or five details (or groups of details) that support the main idea. Organize the information into a pie chart similar to the one on this page.

2. Make a pie chart about a recent event in the news. Write the short version of the event below the pie, telling what happened in one sentence. Fill in the slices of the pie with the details that provide the long version of when, where, how, and why the event happened.

3. Research the development of one of the inventions pictured on pages 170–171. Write down at least three main ideas you discovered from your research, and list two or three supporting details for each main idea.

Part Two

Outside Forces

Powerful forces outside of characters' control can present them with challenges they did not ask for or expect. Can the character solve the problem? Does the character have the will to go on? Some people overcome nearly impossible challenges in surprising ways, while others underestimate forces beyond their control.

✿ Multicultural Connection **Change** can create challenges because it sets up conditions which go beyond a person's past cultural experiences. Compare and contrast how the characters in these selections react to change.

Literature

Jack London	**To Build a Fire** ◆ short story	.176
	Language Mini-Lesson ◆ Placement of Modifiers	.192
James Berry	**The Banana Tree** ◆ short story	.194
Dionne Brand	**Hurricane** ◆ poem	.201
Ann Petry	**from *Harriet Tubman*** ◆ biography	.205
Anonymous	**Go Down, Moses** ◆ traditional song	.213
Irwin Shapiro	**Strong but Quirky: The Birth of Davy Crockett**	
	◆ North American tall tale	.217
Judith Ortiz Cofer	**Aunty Misery** ◆ Puerto Rican folk tale	.220

Interdisciplinary Study **Forces of Destruction**

How Does a Hurricane Develop? by Howard Smith ◆ earth science ..224
Hurricanes ◆ earth science 226
    Reading Mini-Lesson ◆ Taking Notes and Outlining 228

Writing Workshop **Expository Writing**

Characters Inside and Out 229

Beyond Print **Visual Literacy**

Images of You 235

Before Reading

To Build a Fire

by Jack London

Jack London
1876–1916

By the time Jack London was eighteen years old, he had worked at jobs in factories and mills, gone "on the road" as a tramp, crisscrossed the United States by hopping rides on freight trains, and worked as an oyster pirate and a sailor on a sealing vessel. At age twenty-one, he caught "gold fever" and went to the Klondike area in Alaska. He returned not with gold, but with a wealth of experiences that he turned into stories such as "To Build a Fire." Like many of his stories, this one takes place in a setting where adventure and danger are always possibilities.

Building Background

Freezing to Death The literature in this part of the book is about challenges from outside forces. In "To Build a Fire," the outside force is extreme cold. Facing the cold can be a life-or-death challenge. Without protective clothing, your body cannot withstand extreme cold for long. The colder your surroundings, the faster and more severe the effects on your body. Exposure to the cold can cause *hypothermia,* a decrease in body temperature that can lead to loss of coordination and speech, confusion, unconsciousness, and death.

Getting into the Story

Discussion "You ought to . . . you should . . . don't forget to . . ." As you grow up, you get lots of advice from people older than you. Sometimes you can't tell how good the advice is until after you ignore it and find yourself with a problem or in a dangerous spot. In a small group, discuss the following questions: Why do people sometimes ignore good advice? How can you decide whether the advice you get is good?

Reading Tip

Foreshadowing Just as good drivers anticipate the road ahead, good readers think ahead about likely outcomes of stories. **Foreshadowing,** as the "fore" in the word suggests, involves giving clues about events before they happen. This writing technique helps create tension. You get a feeling about what will happen, but you have to read on to see if it does. The clues may be subtle. For example, at the beginning of "To Build a Fire," the author says, "It was a clear day, and yet there seemed an intangible pall over the face of things. . . ." Taken at face value, this says it was a dark day because the sun was low on the horizon. But the word *pall* has an ominous tone, suggesting the cloth spread over a coffin. It is your first hint that things may not go well for the character in this story! As you read "To Build a Fire," be alert to suggestions about how the story will turn out. Keep a record of your predictions at various points in the story.

TO BUILD A FIRE

Jack London

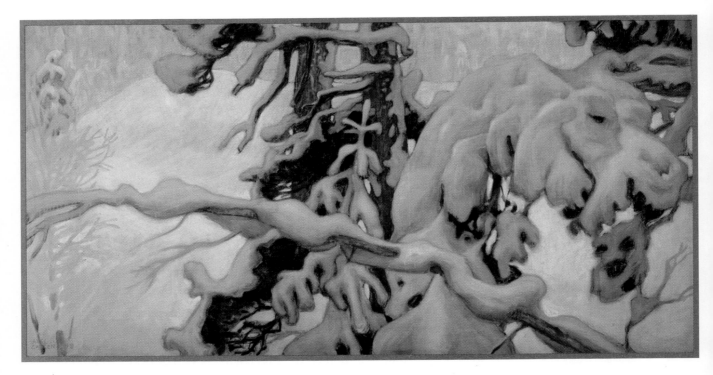

▲ *Landscape Under Snow* was painted in 1902 by Akseli Gallen-Kallela. The artist included this painting in a series on the victory of death over life. How does the painting express that theme?

Day had broken cold and gray, exceedingly cold and gray, when the man turned aside from the main Yukon trail[1] and climbed the high earth bank, where a dim and little-traveled trail led eastward through the fat spruce timberland. It was a steep bank, and he paused for breath at the top, excusing the act to himself by looking at his watch. It was nine o'clock. There was no sun nor hint of sun, though there was not a cloud in the sky. It was a clear day, and yet there seemed an intangible pall over the face of things, a subtle gloom that made the day dark and that was due to the absence of sun. This fact did not worry the man. He was used to the lack of sun. It had been days since he had seen the sun, and he knew that a few more days must pass before that cheerful orb, due south, would just peep above the skyline and dip immediately from view.

The man flung a look back along the way he had come. The Yukon lay a mile wide and hidden under three feet of ice. On top of this ice were as many feet of snow. It was all pure white, rolling in gentle undulations where the ice jams of the freeze-up had formed. North and south, as far as his eye could see, it was unbroken white, save for a dark hairline that curved and twisted from around the spruce-covered island to the south and that curved and twisted away into the north, where it disappeared behind another spruce-covered island. This dark hairline was the trail—the main trail—that led south five hundred miles to the Chilcoot Pass, Dyea,[2] and salt water, and that led north seventy miles to Dawson, and still on to the north a thousand miles to Nulato, and finally to St. Michael on the Bering Sea,[3] a thousand miles and half a thousand more.

But all this—the mysterious, far-reaching hairline trail, the absence of sun from the sky, the tremendous cold, and the strangeness and weirdness of it all—made no impression on the man. It was not because he was long used to it. He was a newcomer in the land, a *chechaquo*,[4] and this was his first winter. The trouble with him was that he was without imagination. He was quick and alert in the things of life, but only in the things, and not in the significances. Fifty degrees below zero meant eighty-odd degrees of frost. Such fact impressed him as being cold and uncomfortable, and that was all. It did not lead him to meditate upon his frailty as a creature of temperature, and upon man's frailty in general, able only to live within certain narrow limits of heat and cold; and, from there on, it did not lead him to the conjectural field of immortality and man's place in the universe. Fifty degrees below zero stood for a bite of frost that hurt and that must be guarded against by the use of mittens, ear flaps, warm moccasins, and thick socks. Fifty degrees below zero was to him just precisely fifty degrees below zero. That there should be anything more to it than that was a thought that never entered his head.

PREDICT: How could his lack of imagination turn out to be important?

As he turned to go on, he spat speculatively. There was a sharp, explosive crackle that startled him. He spat again. And again, in the air, before it could fall to the snow, the

---

1. **Yukon** (yū′kon) **trail,** a trail which runs through the Yukon, a territory in northwestern Canada.
2. **Chilcoot** (chil′kŭt) **Pass, Dyea** (dī′ā). Chilcoot Pass is a mountain pass in British Columbia, the territory just south of the Yukon. At the time of the story, Dyea was a town in western British Columbia, south of Chilcoot Pass.
3. **Dawson . . . Bering Sea.** Dawson is a city in the western part of the Yukon. Nulato (nū lä′tō) is a city in western Alaska. St. Michael is a port city on the western coast of Alaska.
4. **chechaquo** (chē chä′kō), a greenhorn; tenderfoot in Alaska or the Pacific northwest. [Chinook jargon]

spittle crackled. He knew that at fifty below spittle crackled on the snow, but this spittle had crackled in the air. Undoubtedly it was colder than fifty below—how much colder he did not know. But the temperature did not matter. He was bound for the old claim on the left fork of Henderson Creek, where the boys were already. They had come over across the

It was seventy-five below zero.

divide from the Indian Creek country, while he had come the roundabout way to take a look at the possibilities of getting out logs in the spring from the islands in the Yukon. He would be in to camp by six o'clock; a bit after dark, it was true, but the boys would be there, a fire would be going, and a hot supper would be ready. As for lunch, he pressed his hand against the protruding bundle under his jacket. It was also under his shirt, wrapped up in a handkerchief and lying against the naked skin. It was the only way to keep the biscuits from freezing. He smiled agreeably to himself as he thought of those biscuits, each cut open and sopped in bacon grease, and each enclosing a generous slice of fried bacon.

He plunged in among the big spruce trees. The trail was faint. A foot of snow had fallen since the last sled had passed over, and he was glad he was without a sled, traveling light. In fact, he carried nothing but the lunch wrapped in the handkerchief. He was surprised, however, at the cold. It certainly was cold, he concluded, as he rubbed his numb nose and cheekbones with his mittened hand. He was a warm-whiskered man, but the hair on his face did not protect the high cheekbones and the eager nose that thrust itself aggressively into the frosty air.

At the man's heels trotted a dog, a big native husky, the proper wolf dog, gray-coated and without any visible or temperamental difference from its brother, the wild wolf. The ani-mal was depressed by the tremendous cold. It knew that it was no time for traveling. Its instinct told it a truer tale than was told to the man by the man's judgment. In reality, it was not merely colder than fifty below zero; it was colder than sixty below, than seventy below. It was seventy-five below zero. Since the freezing point is thirty-two above zero, it meant that one hundred and seven degrees of frost obtained. The dog did not know anything about thermometers. Possibly in its brain there was no sharp consciousness of a condition of very cold such as was in the man's brain. But the brute had its instinct. It experienced a vague but menacing apprehension[5] that subdued it and made it slink along at the man's heels, and that made it question eagerly every unwonted movement of the man as if expecting him to go into camp or to seek shelter somewhere and build a fire. The dog had learned fire, and it wanted fire, or else to burrow under the snow and cuddle its warmth away from the air.

The frozen moisture of its breathing had settled on its fur in a fine powder of frost, and especially were its jowls, muzzle,[6] and eyelashes whitened by its crystalled breath. The man's red beard and mustache were likewise frosted, but more solidly, the deposit taking the form of ice and increasing with every warm, moist breath he exhaled. Also, the man was chewing tobacco, and the muzzle[7] of ice held his lips so rigidly that he was unable to clear his chin when he expelled the juice. The result was that a crystal beard of the color and

---

5. **apprehension** (ap′ri hen′shən), *n.* expectation of misfortune; dread of impending danger.
6. **muzzle** (muz′əl), *n.* the projecting part of the head of an animal, including the nose, mouth, and jaws.
7. **muzzle** (muz′əl), *n.* literally, a cover or cage of straps or wires to put over an animal's head or mouth to keep it from biting or eating; here, used figuratively to describe the covering of ice over the man's mouth and chin.

solidity of amber was increasing its length on his chin. If he fell down it would shatter itself, like glass, into brittle fragments. But he did not mind the appendage. It was the penalty all tobacco chewers paid in that country, and he had been out before in two cold snaps. They had not been so cold as this, he knew, but by the spirit thermometer at Sixty Mile[8] he knew they had been registered at fifty below and at fifty-five.

He held on through the level stretch of woods for several miles, crossed a wide flat, and dropped down a bank to the frozen bed of a small stream. This was Henderson Creek, and he knew he was ten miles from the forks. He looked at his watch. It was ten o'clock. He was making four miles an hour, and he calculated that he would arrive at the forks at half-past twelve. He decided to celebrate that event by eating his lunch there.

The dog dropped in again at his heels, with a tail drooping discouragement, as the man swung along the creek bed. The furrow of the old sled trail was plainly visible, but a dozen inches of snow covered the marks of the last runners. In a month no man had come up or down that silent creek. The man held steadily on. He was not much given to thinking, and just then, particularly, he had nothing to think about save that he would eat lunch at the forks and that at six o'clock he would be in camp with the boys. There was nobody to talk to, and, had there been, speech would have been impossible because of the ice muzzle on his mouth. So he continued monotonously to chew tobacco and to increase the length of his amber beard.

Once in a while the thought reiterated itself that it was very cold and that he had never experienced such cold. As he walked along he rubbed his cheekbones and nose with the back of his mittened hand. He did this automatically, now and again changing hands. But, rub as he would, the instant he stopped his cheekbones went numb, and the following instant the end of his nose went numb. He was sure to frost his cheeks; he knew that, and experienced a pang of regret that he had not devised a nose strap of the sort Bud wore in cold snaps. Such a strap passed across the cheeks as well and saved them. But it didn't matter much, after all. What were frosted cheeks? A bit painful, that was all; they were never serious.

Empty as the man's mind was of thoughts, he was keenly observant, and he noticed the changes in the creek, the curves and bends and timber jams, and always he sharply noted where he placed his feet. Once, coming around a bend, he shied abruptly, like a startled horse, curved away from the place where he had been walking, and retreated several paces back along the trail. The creek he knew was frozen clear to the bottom—no creek could contain water in that arctic winter—but he knew also that there were springs that bubbled out from the hillsides and ran along under the snow and on top the ice of the creek. He knew that the coldest snaps never froze these springs, and he knew likewise their danger. They were traps. They hid pools of water under the snow that might be three inches deep, or three feet. Sometimes a skin of ice half an inch thick covered them, and in turn was covered by the snow. Sometimes there were alternate layers of water and ice skin, so that when one broke through, he kept on breaking through for a while, sometimes wetting himself to the waist.

That was why he had shied in such panic. He had felt the give under his feet and heard the crackle of a snow-hidden ice skin. And to get his feet wet in such a temperature meant trouble and danger. At the very least it meant delay, for he would be forced to stop and build a fire, and, under its protection, to bare

---

8. **Sixty Mile,** a village in the western part of the Yukon near the Alaskan border.

his feet while he dried his socks and moccasins. He stood and studied the creek bed and its banks and decided that the flow of water came from the right. He reflected awhile, rubbing his nose and cheeks, then skirted to the left, stepping gingerly and testing the footing for each step. Once clear of the danger, he took a fresh chew of tobacco and swung along at his four-mile gait.

In the course of the next two hours he came upon several similar traps. Usually the snow above the hidden pools had a sunken, candied appearance that advertised the danger. Once again, however, he had a close call, and once, suspecting danger, he compelled the dog to go on in front. The dog did not want to go. It hung back until the man shoved it forward, and then it went quickly across the white, unbroken surface. Suddenly it broke through, floundered[9] to one side, and got away to firmer footing. It had wet its forefeet and legs, and almost immediately the water that clung to it turned to ice. It made quick efforts to lick the ice off its legs, then dropped down in the snow and began to bite out the ice that had formed between the toes. This was a matter of instinct. To permit the ice to remain would mean sore feet. It did not know this. It merely obeyed the mysterious prompting that arose from the deep crypts of its being. But the man knew, having achieved a judgment on the subject, and he removed the mitten from his right hand and helped tear out the ice particles. He did not expose his fingers more than a minute, and was astonished at the swift numbness that smote them. It certainly was cold. He pulled on the mitten hastily and beat the hand savagely across his chest.

At twelve o'clock the day was at its brightest. Yet the sun was too far south on its winter journey to clear the horizon. The bulge of the earth intervened between it and Henderson Creek, where the man walked under a clear sky

at noon and cast no shadow. At half-past twelve, to the minute, he arrived at the forks of the creek. He was pleased at the speed he had made. If he kept it up, he would certainly be with the boys by six. He unbuttoned his jacket and shirt and drew forth his lunch. The action consumed no more than a quarter of a minute, yet in that brief moment the numbness laid hold of the exposed fingers. He did not put the mitten on, but, instead, struck the fingers a dozen sharp smashes against his leg. Then he sat down on a snow-covered log to eat. The sting that followed upon the striking of his fingers against his leg ceased so quickly that he was startled. He had had no chance to take a bite of biscuit. He struck the fingers repeatedly and returned them to the mitten, baring the other hand for the purpose of eating. He tried to take a mouthful, but the ice muzzle prevented. He had forgotten to build a fire and thaw out. He chuckled at his foolishness, and as he chuckled he noted the numbness creeping into the exposed fingers. Also, he noted that the stinging which had first come to his toes when he sat down was already passing away. He wondered whether the toes were warm or numb. He moved them inside the moccasins and decided that they were numb.

CLARIFY: What signs indicate that the man may be in trouble?

He pulled the mitten on hurriedly and stood up. He was a bit frightened. He stamped up and down until the stinging returned into the feet. It certainly was cold, was his thought. That man from Sulphur Creek had spoken the truth when telling how cold it sometimes got in the country. And he had laughed at him at the time! That showed one must not be too sure of things. There was no mistake about it,

---

9. flounder (floun′dər), v. struggle awkwardly without making much progress.

it *was* cold. He strode up and down, stamping his feet and threshing his arms, until reassured by the returning warmth. Then he got out matches and proceeded to make a fire. From the undergrowth, where high water

When it is seventy-five below zero, a man must not fail in his first attempt to build a fire . . .

of the previous spring had lodged a supply of seasoned twigs, he got his firewood. Working carefully from a small beginning, he soon had a roaring fire, over which he thawed the ice from his face and in the protection of which he ate his biscuits. For the moment the cold of space was outwitted. The dog took satisfaction in the fire, stretching out close enough for warmth and far enough away to escape being singed.

When the man had finished, he filled his pipe and took his comfortable time over a smoke. Then he pulled on his mittens, settled the ear flaps of his cap firmly about his ears, and took the creek trail up the left fork. The dog was disappointed and yearned back toward the fire. This man did not know cold. Possibly all the generations of his ancestry had been ignorant of cold, of real cold, of cold one hundred and seven degrees below freezing point. But the dog knew; all its ancestry knew, and it had inherited the knowledge. And it knew that it was not good to walk abroad in such fearful cold. It was the time to lie snug in a hole in the snow and wait for a curtain of cloud to be drawn across the face of outer space whence this cold came. On the other hand, there was no keen intimacy between the dog and the man. The one was the toil slave of the other, and the only caresses it had ever received were the caresses of the whip lash and of harsh and menacing throat sounds that threatened the whip lash. So the dog made no effort to communicate its apprehension to the man. It was not concerned in the welfare of the man; it was for its own sake that it yearned back toward the fire. But the man whistled and spoke to it with the sound of whip lashes, and the dog swung in at the man's heels and followed after.

The man took a chew of tobacco and proceeded to start a new amber beard. Also, his moist breath quickly powdered with white his mustache, eyebrows, and lashes. There did not seem to be so many springs on the left fork of the Henderson, and for half an hour the man saw no signs of any. And then it happened. At a place where there were no signs, where the soft, unbroken snow seemed to advertise solidity beneath, the man broke through. It was not deep. He wet himself halfway to the knees before he floundered out to the firm crust.

He was angry and cursed his luck aloud. He had hoped to get into camp with the boys at six o'clock, and this would delay him an hour, for he would have to build a fire and dry out his footgear. This was imperative[10] at that low temperature—he knew that much; and he turned aside to the bank, which he climbed. On top, tangled in the underbrush about the trunks of several small spruce trees, was a high-water deposit of dry firewood—sticks and twigs, principally, but also larger portions of seasoned branches and fine, dry, last year's grasses. He threw down several large pieces on top of the snow. This served for a foundation and prevented the young flame from drowning itself in the snow it otherwise would melt. The flame he got by touching a match to a small shred of birch bark that he took from his pocket. This burned even more readily than paper. Placing it on the founda-

---

10. **imperative** (im/pər/ə tiv), *adj.* necessary; urgent.

tion, he fed the young flame with wisps of dry grass and with the tiniest dry twigs.

He worked slowly and carefully, keenly aware of his danger. Gradually, as the flame grew stronger, he increased the size of the twigs with which he fed it. He squatted in the snow, pulling the twigs out from their entanglement in the brush and feeding directly to the flame. He knew there must be no failure. When it is seventy-five below zero, a man must not fail in his first attempt to build a fire—that is, if his feet are wet. If his feet are dry, and he fails, he can run along the trail for half a mile and restore his circulation. But the circulation of wet and freezing feet cannot be restored by running when it is seventy-five below. No matter how fast he runs, the wet feet will freeze the harder.

All this the man knew. The old-timer on Sulphur Creek had told him about it the previous fall, and now he was appreciating the advice. Already all sensation had gone out of his feet. To build the fire he had been forced to remove his mittens, and the fingers had quickly gone numb. His pace of four miles an hour had kept his heart pumping blood to the surface of his body and to all the extremities.[11] But the instant he stopped, the action of the pump eased down. The cold of space smote the unprotected tip of the planet, and he, being on that unprotected tip, received the full force of the blow. The blood of his body recoiled before it. The blood was alive, like the dog, and like the dog it wanted to hide away and cover itself up from the fearful cold. So long as he walked four miles an hour, he pumped that blood, willy-nilly, to the surface, but now it ebbed away and sank down into the recesses of his body. The extremities were the first to feel its absence. His wet feet froze the faster, and his exposed fingers numbed the faster, though they had not yet begun to freeze. Nose and cheeks were already freezing, while the skin of all his body chilled as it lost its blood.

But he was safe. Toes and nose and cheeks would be only touched by the frost, for the fire was beginning to burn with strength. He was feeding it with twigs the size of his finger. In another minute he would be able to feed it with branches the size of his wrist, and then he

_____

11. **extremities** (ek strem′ə tēz), *n.* the hands and feet.

could remove his wet footgear, and, while it dried, he could keep his naked feet warm by the fire, rubbing them at first, of course, with snow. The fire was a success. He was safe. He remembered the advice of the old-timer on Sulphur Creek and smiled. The old-timer had been very serious in laying down the law that no man must travel alone in the Klondike[12]

This 1913 painting by J.C. Dollman is a tribute to Captain Oates, a South Pole explorer who courageously walked out into a blizzard to die, rather than burden the other members of the exploration as gangrene from frostbite overcame him. What is the mood of this painting?

12. **Klondike** (klon′dīk), a region in the western part of the Yukon territory.

after fifty below. Well, here he was; he had had the accident; he was alone; and he had saved himself. Those old-timers were rather womanish, some of them, he thought. All a man had to do was to keep his head, and he was all right. Any man who was a man could travel alone. But it was surprising, the rapidity with which his cheeks and nose were freezing. And he had not thought his fingers could go lifeless in so short a time. Lifeless they were, for he could scarcely make them move together to grip a twig, and they seemed remote from his body and from him. When he touched a twig, he had to look and see whether or not he had hold of it. The wires were pretty well down between him and his finger ends.

All of which counted for little. There was the fire, snapping and crackling and promising life with every dancing flame. He started to untie his moccasins. They were coated with ice; the thick German socks were like sheaths of iron halfway to the knees; and the moccasin strings were like rods of steel all twisted and knotted as by some conflagration. For a moment he tugged with his numb fingers; then, realizing the folly of it, he drew his sheath knife.

But before he could cut the strings, it happened. It was his own fault or, rather, his mistake. He should not have built the fire under the spruce tree. He should have built it in the open. But it had been easier to pull the twigs from the brush and drop them directly on the fire. Now the tree under which he had done this carried a weight of snow on its boughs. No wind had blown for weeks, and each bough was fully freighted. Each time he had pulled a twig he had communicated a slight agitation to the tree—an imperceptible agitation, so far as he was concerned, but an agitation sufficient to bring about the disaster. High up in the tree one bough capsized its load of snow. This fell on the boughs beneath, capsizing them. This process continued, spreading out and involving the whole tree. It grew like an avalanche, and it descended without warning upon the man and the fire, and the fire was blotted out! Where it had burned was a mantle of fresh and disordered snow.

EVALUATE: Why do you think the man made this mistake?

The man was shocked. It was as though he had just heard his own sentence of death. For a moment he sat and stared at the spot where the fire had been. Then he grew very calm. Perhaps the old-timer on Sulphur Creek was right. If he had only had a trail mate he would have been in no danger now. The trail mate could have built the fire. Well, it was up to him to build the fire over again, and this second time there must be no failure. Even if he succeeded, he would most likely lose some toes. His feet must be badly frozen by now, and there would be some time before the second fire was ready.

Such were his thoughts, but he did not sit and think them. He was busy all the time they were passing through his mind. He made a new foundation for a fire, this time in the open, where no treacherous[13] tree could blot it out. Next he gathered dry grasses and tiny twigs from the high-water flotsam. He could not bring his fingers together to pull them out, but he was able to gather them by the handful. In this way he got many rotten twigs and bits of green moss that were undesirable, but it was the best he could do. He worked methodically, even collecting an armful of the larger branches to be used later when the fire gathered strength. And all the while the dog sat and watched him, a certain yearning wistfulness in its eyes, for it looked upon him as the fire provider, and the fire was slow in coming.

---

13. **treacherous** (trech′ər əs), *adj.* having a false appearance of strength, security, etc.; not reliable; deceiving.

When all was ready, the man reached in his pocket for a second piece of birch bark. He knew the bark was there, and, though he could not feel it with his fingers, he could hear its crisp rustling as he fumbled for it. Try as he would, he could not clutch hold of it. And all the time, in his consciousness, was the knowledge that each instant his feet were freezing. This thought tended to put him in a panic, but he fought against it and kept calm. He pulled on his mittens with his teeth, and threshed his arms back and forth, beating his hands with all his might against his sides. He did this sitting down, and he stood up to do it; and all the while the dog sat in the snow, its wolf brush of a tail curled around warmly over its forefeet, its sharp wolf ears pricked forward intently as it watched the man. And the man, as he beat and threshed with his arms and hands, felt a great surge of envy as he regarded the creature that was warm and secure in its natural covering.

After a time he was aware of the first faraway signals of sensation in his beaten fingers. The faint tingling grew stronger till it evolved into a stinging ache that was excruciating[14] but which the man hailed with satisfaction. He stripped the mitten from his right hand and fetched forth the birch bark. The exposed fingers were quickly going numb again. Next he brought out his bunch of sulphur matches. But the tremendous cold had already driven the life out of his fingers. In his effort to separate one match from the others, the whole bunch fell in the snow. He tried to pick it out of the snow, but failed. The dead fingers could neither touch nor clutch. He was very careful. He drove the thought of his freezing feet, and nose, and cheeks, out of his mind, devoting his whole soul to the matches. He watched, using the sense of vision in place of that of touch, and when he saw his fingers on each side of the bunch, he closed them—that is, he willed to close them, for the wires were down, and the fingers did not

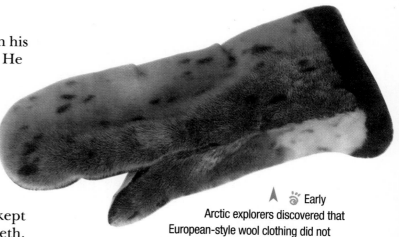

▲ ◉ Early Arctic explorers discovered that European-style wool clothing did not adequately protect them from the Arctic cold. The most successful explorers met this **change** in climate by learning from the local Inuit people to wear sealskin hoods and mittens, such as the mitten pictured here, to keep out the cold.

obey. He pulled the mitten on the right hand, and beat it fiercely against his knee. Then, with both mittened hands, he scooped the bunch of matches, along with much snow, into his lap. Yet he was no better off.

After some manipulation he managed to get the bunch between the heels of his mittened hands. In this fashion he carried it to his mouth. The ice crackled and snapped when, by a violent effort, he opened his mouth. He drew the lower jaw in, curled the upper lip out of the way, and scraped the bunch with his upper teeth in order to separate a match. He succeeded in getting one, which he dropped on his lap. He was no better off. He could not pick it up. Then he devised a way. He picked it up in his teeth and scratched it on his leg. Twenty times he scratched before he succeeded in lighting it. As it flamed he held it with his teeth to the birch bark. But the burning brimstone went up his nostrils and into his lungs, causing him to cough spasmodically. The match fell into the snow and went out.

---

14. **excruciating** (ek skrü′shē ā′ting), *adj.* causing great suffering; very painful.

The old-timer on Sulphur Creek was right, he thought in the moment of controlled despair that ensued: after fifty below, a man should travel with a partner. He beat his hands but failed in exciting any sensation. Suddenly he bared both hands, removing the mittens with his teeth. He caught the whole bunch between his heels of his hands. His arm muscles not being frozen enabled him to press the hand heels tightly against the matches. Then he scratched the bunch along his leg. It flared into flame, seventy sulphur matches at once! There was no wind to blow them out. He kept his head to one side to escape the strangling fumes, and held the blazing bunch to the birch bark. As he so held it, he became aware of sensation in his hand. His flesh was burning. He could smell it. Deep down below the surface he could feel it. The sensation developed into pain that grew acute. And still he endured it, holding the flame of the matches clumsily to the bark that would not light readily because his own burning hands were in the way, absorbing most of the flame.

At last, when he could endure no more, he jerked his hands apart. The blazing matches fell sizzling into the snow, but the birch bark was alight. He began laying dry grasses and the tiniest twigs on the flame. He could not pick and choose, for he had to lift the fuel between the heels of his hands. Small pieces of rotten wood and green moss clung to the twigs, and he bit them off as well as he could with his teeth. He cherished the flame carefully and awkwardly. It meant life, and it must not perish. The withdrawal of blood from the surface of his body now made him begin to shiver, and he grew more awkward. A large piece of green moss fell squarely on the little fire. He tried to poke it out with his fingers, but his shivering frame made him poke too far, and he disrupted the nucleus of the little fire, the burning grasses and tiny twigs separating and scattering. He tried to poke them together again, but in spite of the tenseness of the effort, his shivering got away with him, and the twigs were hopelessly scattered. Each twig gushed a puff of smoke and went out. The fire provider had failed. As he looked apathetically about him, his eyes chanced on the dog, sitting across the ruins of the fire from him, in the snow, making restless, hunching movements, slightly lifting one forefoot and then the other, shifting its weight back and forth on them with wistful eagerness.

It struck him as curious that one should have to use his eyes in order to find out where his hands were.

The sight of the dog put a wild idea into his head. He remembered the tale of the man, caught in a blizzard, who killed a steer and crawled inside the carcass and so was saved. He would kill the dog and bury his hands in the warm body until the numbness went out of them. Then he could build another fire. He spoke to the dog, calling it to him, but in his voice was a strange note of fear that frightened the animal, who had never known the man to speak in such a way before. Something was the matter, and its suspicious nature sensed danger—it knew not what danger, but somewhere, somehow, in its brain arose an apprehension of the man. It flattened its ears down at the sound of the man's voice, and its restless, hunching movements and the liftings and shiftings of its forefeet became more pronounced; but it would not come to the man. He got on his hands and knees and crawled toward the dog. This unusual posture again excited suspicion, and the animal sidled mincingly away.

The man sat up in the snow for a moment

and struggled for calmness. Then he pulled on his mittens, by means of his teeth, and got upon his feet. He glanced down at first in order to assure himself that he was really standing up, for the absence of sensation in his feet left him unrelated to the earth. His erect position in itself started to drive the webs of suspicion from the dog's mind, and when he spoke peremptorily, with the sound of whip lashes in his voice, the dog rendered its customary allegiance[15] and came to him. As it came within reaching distance, the man lost his control. His arms flashed out to the dog, and he experienced genuine surprise when he discovered that his hands could not clutch, that there was neither bend nor feeling in the fingers. He had forgotten for the moment that they were frozen and that they were freezing more and more. All this happened quickly, and before the animal could get away, he encircled its body with his arms. He sat down in the snow and in this fashion held the dog, while it snarled and whined and struggled.

But it was all he could do, hold its body encircled in his arms and sit there. He realized that he could not kill the dog. There was no way to do it. With his helpless hands he could neither draw nor hold his sheath knife nor throttle the animal. He released it, and it plunged wildly away, with tail between its legs and still snarling. It halted forty feet away and surveyed him curiously, with ears sharply pricked forward. The man looked down at his hands in order to locate them, and found them hanging on the ends of his arms. It struck him as curious that one should have to use his eyes in order to find out where his hands were. He began threshing his arms back and forth, beating the mittened hands against his sides. He did this for five minutes, violently, and his heart pumped enough blood up to the surface to put a stop to his shivering. But no sensation was aroused in the hands. He had an impression that they hung like weights on the ends of his arms, but when he tried to run the impression down, he could not find it.

PREDICT: What do you think will happen to the man?

A certain fear of death, dull and oppressive, came to him. This fear quickly became poignant[16] as he realized that it was no longer a mere matter of freezing his fingers and toes, or of losing his hands and feet, but that it was a matter of life and death with the chances against him. This threw him into a panic, and he turned and ran up the creek bed along the old, dim trail. The dog joined in behind and kept up with him. He ran blindly, without intention, in fear such as he had never known in his life. Slowly, as he plowed and floundered through the snow, he began to see things again—the banks of the creek, the old timber jams, the leafless aspens, and the sky. The running made him feel better. He did not shiver. Maybe, if he ran on, his feet would thaw out; and, anyway, if he ran far enough, he would reach camp and the boys. Without doubt he would lose some fingers and toes and some of his face, but the boys would take care of him, and save the rest of him when he got there. And at the same time there was another thought in his mind that said he would never get to the camp and the boys; that it was too many miles away, that the freezing had too great a start on him, and that he would soon be stiff and dead. This thought he kept in the background and refused to consider. Sometimes it pushed itself forward and

---

15. **allegiance** (ə lē′jəns), *n.* faithfulness to a person or thing.
16. **poignant** (poi′nyənt), *adj.* stimulating to the mind, feelings, or passions; intense.

demanded to be heard, but he thrust it back and strove to think of other things.

It struck him as curious that he could run at all on feet so frozen that he could not feel them when they struck the earth and took the weight of his body. He seemed to himself to skim along above the surface and to have no connection with the earth. Somewhere he had once seen a winged Mercury,[17] and he wondered if Mercury felt as he felt when skimming over the earth.

His theory of running until he reached camp and the boys had one flaw in it: he lacked the endurance.[18] Several times he stumbled, and finally he tottered, crumpled up, and fell. When he tried to rise, he failed.

He must sit and rest, he decided, and next time he would merely walk and keep on going. As he sat and regained his breath, he noted that he was feeling quite warm and comfortable. He was not shivering, and it even seemed that a warm glow had come to his chest and trunk. And yet, when he touched his nose or cheeks, there was no sensation. Running would not thaw them out. Nor would it thaw out his hands and feet.

---

17. **Mercury,** in Roman mythology, the messenger of the gods. He is usually depicted as having wings on his sandals.

18. endurance (en dùr′əns), *n.* power to last and to withstand hard wear.

Then the thought came to him that the frozen portions of his body must be extending. He tried to keep this thought down, to forget it, to think of something else; he was aware of the panicky feeling that it caused, and he was afraid of the panic. But the thought asserted itself and persisted, until it produced a vision of his body totally frozen. This was too much, and he made another wild run along the trail. Once he slowed down to a walk, but the thought of the freezing extending itself made him run again.

And all the time the dog ran with him, at his heels. When he fell down a second time, it curled its tail over its forefeet and sat in front of him, facing him, curiously eager and intent. The warmth and security of the animal angered him, and he cursed it till it flattened down its ears appeasingly. This time the shivering came more quickly upon the man. He was losing in his battle with the frost. It was creeping into his body from all sides. The thought of it drove him on, but he ran no more than a hundred feet when he staggered and pitched headlong. It was his last panic. When he had recovered his breath and control, he sat up and entertained in his mind the conception of meeting death with dignity. However, the conception did not come to him in such terms. His idea of it was that he had been making a fool of himself, running around like a chicken with its head cut off—such was the simile that occurred to him. Well, he was bound to freeze anyway, and he might as well take it decently. With this newfound peace of mind came the first glimmerings of drowsiness. A good idea, he thought, to sleep off to death. It was like taking an anesthetic. Freezing was not so bad as people thought. There were lots worse ways to die.

He tried to keep this thought down, to forget it. . . .

He pictured the boys finding his body next day. Suddenly he found himself with them, coming along the trail and looking for himself. And, still with them, he came around a turn in the trail and found himself lying in the snow. He did not belong with himself any more, for even then he was out of himself, standing with the boys and looking at himself in the snow. It certainly was cold, was his thought. When he got back to the States he could tell the folks what real cold was. He drifted on from this to a vision of the old-timer on Sulphur Creek. He could see him quite clearly, warm and comfortable, and smoking a pipe.

"You were right, old hoss; you were right," the man mumbled to the old-timer of Sulphur Creek.

Then the man drowsed off into what seemed to him the most comfortable and satisfying sleep he had ever known. The dog sat facing him and waiting. The brief day drew to a close in a long, slow twilight. There were no signs of a fire to be made, and, besides, never in the dog's experience had it known a man to sit like that in the snow and make no fire. As the twilight drew on, its eager yearning for the fire mastered it, and with a great lifting and shifting of forefeet, it whined softly, then flattened its ears down in anticipation of being chidden by the man. But the man remained silent. Later the dog whined loudly. And still later it crept close to the man and caught the scent of death. This made the animal bristle and back away. A little longer it delayed, howling under the stars that leaped and danced and shone brightly in the cold sky. Then it turned and trotted up the trail in the direction of the camp it knew, where were the other food providers and fire providers.

After Reading

Making Connections

1. Who is to blame for the man's death? On a scale of 1 to 10 (with 10 showing him completely responsible), give a rating which shows how responsible you think he is for his own death.

1   2   3   4   5   6   7   8   9   10

2. What purpose does the description of the dog's reactions serve in the story?

3. In addition to the coldness, what other elements of the **setting** does the author emphasize? Give some examples.

4. Give three examples of **foreshadowing** in the story—hints or clues about the eventual outcome.

5. What could the man have done differently to save his life?

6. The author says of the main character, "He was quick and alert in the things of life, but only in the things, and not in the significances." Is this a good description of any other character or person you've known or read about?

Literary Focus: Setting

In a story like this one, the **setting** is as important as a character. This is not a story that could happen anywhere; the location is vital to the narrative. Therefore, it was important to the author to fully develop the setting in a very specific and detailed way. One way to develop a setting is to use **imagery,** or descriptive details that make it easy to see, hear, smell, taste, or feel the setting. Review the story and find examples of images related to the setting. On your own paper, cluster the images you find around several senses, as shown in the examples below.

Vocabulary Study

Choose a word from the list that best completes each sentence.

apprehension
muzzle
flounder
imperative
extremities
treacherous
allegiance
poignant
excruciating
endurance

1. The man went through intense, _____ pain in the cold.
2. His fingers were numb; he was losing feeling in his _____ .
3. When he thought of the warmth and safety of camp, he was filled with _____ longing.
4. Dangerous hidden springs made travel _____ .
5. As it got colder, even the dog had a feeling of _____ .
6. The _____ of the dog looked ferocious because of its big teeth.
7. It was _____ for the man to build a fire or he would freeze.
8. He began to _____ through the thick brush trying to find dry wood.
9. He ran for as long as he could, but he had little _____ left.
10. The dog felt some _____ toward his master and stayed by his side.

Expressing Your Ideas

Writing Choices

Lost and Found Work in a small group to create a **found poem** describing how cold it was. Skim through the story and find five to ten descriptions of the cold. Rearrange them until you find an order you like. Decide how many words should go on each line. Finally, read your poem to the class.

Found Frozen in Yukon Write a **newspaper article** about finding the man's body. Skim the story for authentic details to answer the news questions of *who, what, when, where, why,* and *how.*

"I Told Him So!" Imagine that you are the old-timer who gave the man advice. You have just learned how the man died, and you write a **letter** about the man to a friend. First, briefly describe your advice and the man's reaction to it. Then tell what happened to the man. Conclude your letter by expressing your own feelings.

Other Options

Let Me Tell You About It Suppose he had made it? Wouldn't the man have an exciting story to tell? First, think of a way to change the ending of the story so that the man survives. Then, **act out** the role of the man on a talk show or at a press conference. Skim the story for details about your experience, and be ready to answer questions about your dangerous adventure and rescue or escape.

Missing! Create a "missing person" **poster** for the man. Give him a name and describe where he was last seen, where he was going, what he was wearing, and any other helpful information. Use details from the story to draw the man's face and describe any characteristics that might help searchers identify him.

Language Mini-Lesson

Placement of Modifiers

Misplaced Modifiers What's wrong with these sentences?

> They watched the whale dive through their binoculars.

> Jim returned the shoes to the store that he bought yesterday.

Did a whale dive through a pair of binoculars? Did Jim buy a store? Of course not, but the placement of the modifiers in the sentences makes what really happened unclear. These **misplaced modifiers** can result in sentences that are awkward, confusing, or even funny. How would you rewrite those examples to make what happened clear?

Writing Strategy A modifier should be placed in a sentence where it will clearly show what word it modifies. A modifier not placed close to the word it modifies is called a **misplaced modifier.**

Activity Options

1. Write sentences in which you use the following phrases as modifiers. Intentionally misplace each modifier. Exchange papers with a partner and correct each other's sentences.

   tied to a lamppost   climbing a telephone pole
   waving to the crowds   guarded by a watchdog

2. Work with a partner to write a television news report that's full of misplaced modifiers. Some possible topics might include an election or other political report, a sports report, a report of a fashion event, or a weather report.

3. Review the writing in your portfolio or your writing from other classes for misplaced modifiers. Correct any you find. If you don't find any, give yourself a star.

The Banana Tree

by James Berry

James Berry
born 1925

"In the Caribbean, we were the last outpost of the [British] Empire. No one has reported our stories, or the way we saw things. It's the function of writers and poets to bring in the left-out side of the human family." So says author James Berry, who has made it a point to bring in the left-out side.

Berry was born in Jamaica and moved to England when he was twenty-three years old. He now divides his time between the two countries. He is a distinguished writer and poet, who often writes directly from his childhood experiences growing up in Jamaica. For example, the highly acclaimed *A Thief in the Village and Other Stories* is a collection of short stories told from the point of view of Jamaican children.

Building Background

A Jamaican Custom In Jamaica and some African cultures, the birth of a child is marked by the planting of a tree near the household. When the baby's umbilical cord (or *navel string*) drops off a few weeks after birth, the cord is then buried under the plant, joining together the fate of the child and the tree. The family takes special care of the tree, thus helping to ensure the health of the child. This custom plays a special role in "The Banana Tree."

Getting into the Story

Discussion What do you and your classmates know about hurricanes? Discuss your ideas and record your knowledge in a semantic map like the one shown here.

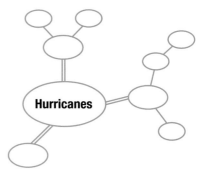

Reading Tip

Spoken Language When James Berry writes conversation, he writes it the way the people in his stories really speak. Mr. Berry believes that the language he records in his stories is an important part of Caribbean culture. "People should not be alienated or put down for their root languages," he says. "Sounds are community. . . . And if we celebrate one language over the many, we are deprived. When people share, they are joyful and enriched."

When characters are speaking, words are spelled to show how they would sound. Some spellings are unusual: the word *boy* is spelled *bwoy*. Missing letters in words are marked by apostrophes: "I'm harboring nothing" is written as "I'm harborin' nothin'." When you read the dialogue in this story, it helps to think of how the words would sound.

The BANANA Tree

James Berry

In the hours the hurricane stayed, its presence made everybody older. It made Mr. Bass see that not only people and animals and certain valuables were of most importance to be saved.

From its very buildup the hurricane meant to show it was merciless, unstoppable, and, with its might, changed landscapes.

All day the Jamaican sun didn't come out. Then, ten minutes before, there was a swift shower of rain that raced by and was gone like some urgent messenger-rush of wind. And again everything went back to that quiet, that unnatural quiet. It was as if trees crouched quietly in fear. As if, too, birds knew they should shut up. A thick and low black cloud had covered the sky and shadowed everywhere, and made it seem like night was coming on. And the cloud deepened. Its deepening spread more and more over the full stretch of the sea.

The doom-laden afternoon had the atmosphere of Judgment Day for everybody in all the districts about. Everybody knew the hour of disaster was near. Warnings printed in bold lettering had been put up at post offices, police stations, and schoolyard entrances and in clear view on shop walls in village squares.

Carrying children and belongings, people hurried in files and in scattered groups, headed for the big, strong, and safe community buildings. In Canerise Village, we headed for the schoolroom. Loaded with bags and cases, with bundles and lidded baskets, individuals carrying or leading an animal, parents shrieking for children to stay at their heels, we arrived there. And, looking around, anyone would think the whole of Canerise was here in this vast super-barn of a noisy chattering schoolroom.

With violent gusts and squalls the storm broke. Great rushes, huge bulky rushes, of wind struck the building in heavy repeated thuds, shaking it over and over, and carrying on.

CONNECT: Have you ever been in a storm or other situation as dangerous as this one?

Families were huddled together on the floor. People sang, sitting on benches, desks, anywhere there was room. Some people knelt in loud prayer. Among the refugees' noises a goat bleated, a hen fluttered or cackled, a dog whined.

Mr. Jetro Bass was sitting on a soap box. His broad back leaned on the blackboard against the wall. Mrs. Imogene Bass, largely pregnant, looked a midget beside him. Their children were sitting on the floor. The eldest boy, Gustus, sat farthest from his father. Altogether, the children's heads made seven different levels of height around the parents. Mr. Bass forced a reassuring smile. His toothbrush mustache moved about a little as he said, "The storm's bad, chil'run. Really bad. But it'll blow off. It'll spen' itself out. It'll kill itself."

Except for Gustus's, all the faces of the children turned up with subdued fear and looked at their father as he spoke.

"Das true wha' Pappy say," Mrs. Bass said. "The good Lord won' gi' we more than we can bear."

Mr. Bass looked at Gustus. He stretched fully through the sitting children and put a lumpy, blistery hand—though a huge hand—on the boy's head, almost covering it. The boy's clear brown eyes looked straight and unblinkingly into his father's face. "Wha's the matter, bwoy?" his dad asked.

He shook his head. "Nothin', Pappy."

"Wha' mek you say nothin'? I sure somet'ing bodder you, Gustus. You not a bwoy who frighten easy. Is not the hurricane wha' bodder you? Tell Pappy."

"Is nothin'."

"You're a big bwoy now. Gustus—you nearly thirteen. You strong. You very useful fo' you age. You good as mi right han'. I depen' on you. But this afternoon—earlier—in the rush, when we so well push to move befo' storm broke, you couldn' rememba a t'ing! Not one t'ing! Why so? Wha' on you mind? You harborin' t'ings[1] from me, Gustus?"

Gustus opened his mouth to speak, but

---

1. **harborin' t'ings,** *harboring things,* having and keeping things in the mind.

The painting *Runaway Beach,* by Shakito, depicts a scene in Antigua. Both Antigua and Jamaica are Caribbean islands. What does the painting tell you about the way of life of people who live in the Caribbean?

closed it again. He knew his father was proud of how well he had grown. To strengthen him, he had always given him "last milk" straight from the cow in the mornings. He was thankful. But to him his strength was only proven in the number of innings he could pitch for his cricket[2] team. The boy's lips trembled. What's the good of tellin' when Pappy don' like cricket. He only get vex an' say it's Satan's game for idle hands! He twisted his head and looked away. "I'm harborin' nothin', Pappy."

"Gustus . . ."

At that moment a man called, "Mr. Bass!" He came up quickly. "Got a hymnbook, Mr. Bass? We want you to lead us singing."

The people were sitting with bowed heads, humming a song. As the repressed singing grew louder and louder, it sounded mournful in the room. Mr. Bass shuffled, looking around as if he wished to back out of the suggestion. But his rich voice and singing leadership were too famous. Mrs. Bass already had the hymnbook in her hand, and she pushed it at her husband. He took it and began turning the leaves as he moved toward the center of the room.

Immediately Mr. Bass was surrounded. He started with a resounding[3] chant over the heads of everybody. "Abide wid me; fast fall the eventide. . . ." He joined the singing, but broke off to recite the next line. "The darkness deepen; Lord, wid me, abide. . . ." Again, before the last long-drawn note faded from the deeply stirred voices, Mr. Bass intoned musically, "When odder helpers fail, and comfo'ts flee. . . ."

In this manner he fired inspiration into the singing of hymn after hymn. The congregation swelled their throats, and their mixed voices filled the room, pleading to heaven from the depths of their hearts. But the wind outside mocked viciously. It screamed. It whistled. It smashed everywhere up.

Mrs. Bass had tightly closed her eyes, singing and swaying in the center of the children who nestled around her. But Gustus was by himself. He had his elbows on his knees and his hands blocking his ears. He had his own worries.

What's the good of Pappy asking all those questions when he treat him so bad? He's the only one in the family without a pair of shoes! Because he's a big boy, he don't need anyt'ing an' must do all the work. He can't stay at school in the evenings an' play cricket because there's work to do at home. He can't have no outings with the other children because he has no shoes. An' now when he was to sell his bunch of bananas an' buy shoes so he can go out with his cricket team, the hurricane is going to blow it down.

It was true; the root of the banana was his "navel string." After his birth the umbilical cord was dressed with castor oil and sprinkled with nutmeg and buried, with the banana tree planted over it for him. When he was nine days old, the nana midwife[4] had taken him out into the open for the first time. She had held the infant proudly, and walked the twenty-five yards that separated the house from the kitchen, and at the back showed him his tree. "Memba when you grow up," her toothless mouth had said, "it's you nable strings feedin' you tree, the same way it feed you from you mudder."

Refuse[5] from the kitchen made the plant flourish out of all proportion. But the rich soil around it was loose. Each time the tree gave a shoot, the bunch would be too heavy for the soil

---

2. **cricket,** an outdoor game played by two teams of eleven players each, with a ball, a bat, and a pair of wickets.
3. resounding (ri zoun′ding), *adj.* sounding loudly.
4. **midwife,** person who helps women in childbirth.
5. refuse (ref′yüs), *n.* waste; rubbish; trash.

to support; so it crashed to the ground, crushing the tender fruit. This time, determined that his banana must reach the market, Gustus had supported his tree with eight props. And as he watched it night and morning, it had become very close to him. Often he had seriously thought of moving his bed to its root.

Muffled cries, and the sound of blowing noses, now mixed with the singing. Delayed impact of the disaster was happening. Sobbing was everywhere. Quickly the atmosphere became sodden with the wave of weeping outbursts. Mrs. Bass's pregnant belly heaved. Her younger children were upset and cried, "Mammy, Mammy, Mammy. . . ."

Realizing that his family, too, was overwhelmed by the surrounding calamity,[6] Mr. Bass bustled over to them. Because their respect for him bordered on fear, his presence quieted all immediately. He looked around. "Where's Gustus! Imogene . . . where's Gustus!"

"He was 'ere, Pappy," she replied, drying her eyes. "I dohn know when he get up."

Briskly Mr. Bass began combing the schoolroom to find his boy. He asked; no one had seen Gustus. He called. There was no answer. He tottered, lifting his heavy boots over heads, fighting his way to the jalousie.[7] He opened it and his eyes gleamed up and down the road, but saw nothing of the boy. In despair, Mr. Bass gave one last thunderous shout: "Gustus!" Only the wind sneered.

By this time Gustus was halfway on the mile journey to their house. The lone figure in the raging wind and shin-deep road flood was tugging, snapping, and pitching branches out of his path. His shirt was fluttering from his back like a boat sail. And a leaf was fastened to his cheek. But the belligerent[8] wind was merciless. It bellowed into his ears and drummed a deafening commotion. As he grimaced and covered his ears, he was forcefully slapped against a coconut tree trunk that lay across the road.

When his eyes opened, his round face was turned up to a festered sky. Above the tormented[9] trees a zinc sheet writhed, twisted, and somersaulted in the tempestuous[10] flurry. Leaves of all shapes and sizes were whirling and diving like attackers around the zinc sheet. As Gustus turned to get up, a bullet drop of rain struck his temple. He shook his head, held grimly to the tree trunk, and struggled to his feet.

Where the road was clear, he edged along the bank. Once, when the wind staggered him, he recovered with his legs wide apart. Angrily he stretched out his hands with clenched fists and shouted, "I almos' hol' you that time . . . come solid like that again an' we fight like man an' man!"

When Gustus approached the river he had to cross, it was flooded and blocked beyond recognition. Pressing his chest against the gritty road bank, the boy closed his weary eyes on the brink of the spating[11] river. The wrecked footbridge had become the harboring fort for all the debris, branches, and monstrous tree trunks which the river swept along its course. The river was still swelling. More accumulation arrived each moment, ramming and pressing the bridge. Under pressure it was cracking and shifting minutely toward a turbulent forty-foot fall.

CLARIFY: What is happening to the bridge?

---

6. **calamity** (kə lam′ə tē), *n.* a great misfortune.
7. **jalousie,** shade or shutter made of horizontal slats which may be tilted to let in light and air but keep out sun and rain.
8. **belligerent** (bə lij′ər ənt), *adj.* fond of fighting; warlike.
9. **tormented** (tôr ment′əd), *adj.* tortured.
10. **tempestuous** (tem pes′chü əs), *adj.* stormy.
11. **spating,** suddenly flooding.

The Banana Tree   **197**

Gustus had seen it! A feeling of dismay paralyzed him, reminding him of his foolish venture. He scraped his cheek on the bank looking back. But how can he go back? He has no strength to go back. His house is nearer than the school. An' Pappy will only strap him for nothin' . . . for nothin' . . . no shoes, nothin' when the hurricane is gone.

With trembling fingers he tied up the remnants[12] of his shirt. He made a bold step and the wind half lifted him, ducking him in the muddy flood. He sank to his neck. Floating leaves, sticks, coconut husks, dead ratbats, and all manner of feathered creatures and refuse surrounded him. Forest vines under the water entangled him. But he struggled desperately until he clung to the laden bridge and climbed up among leafless branches.

His legs were bruised and bore deep scratches, but steadily he moved up on the slimy pile. He felt like a man at sea, in the heart of a storm, going up the mast of a ship. He rested his feet on a smooth log that stuck to the water-splashed heap like a black torso. As he strained up for another grip, the torso came to life and leaped from under his feet. Swiftly sliding down, he grimly clutched some brambles.

The urgency of getting across became more frightening, and he gritted his teeth and dug his toes into the debris, climbing with maddened determination. But a hard gust of wind slammed the wreck, pinning him like a motionless lizard. For a minute the boy was stuck there, panting, swelling his naked ribs.

He stirred again and reached the top. He was sliding over a breadfruit limb when a flutter startled him. As he looked and saw the clean-head crow and glassy-eyed owl close together, there was a powerful jolt. Gustus flung himself into the air and fell in the expanding water on the other side. When he surfaced, the river had dumped the entire wreckage into the gurgling gully. For once the wind helped. It blew him to land.

Gustus was in a daze when he reached his house. Mud and rotten leaves covered his head and face, and blood caked around a gash on his chin. He bent down, shielding himself behind a tree stump whose white heart was a needly splinter, murdered by the wind.

He could hardly recognize his yard. The terrorized trees that stood were writhing in turmoil. Their thatched house had collapsed like an open umbrella that was given a heavy blow. He looked the other way and whispered, "Is still there! That's a miracle. . . . That's a miracle."

Dodging the wind, he staggered from tree to tree until he got to his own tormented banana tree. Gustus hugged the tree. "My nable string!" he cried. "My nable string! I know you would stan' up to it, I know you would."

The bones of the tree's stalky leaves were broken, and the wind lifted them and harassed[13] them. And over Gustus's head the heavy fruit swayed and swayed. The props held the tree, but they were squeaking and slipping. And around the plant the roots stretched and trembled, gradually surfacing under loose earth.

With the rags of his wet shirt flying off his back, Gustus was down busily on his knees, bracing, pushing, tightening the props. One by one he was adjusting them until a heavy rush of wind knocked him to the ground. A prop fell on him, but he scrambled to his feet and looked up at the thirteen-hand[14] bunch of bananas. "My good tree," he bawled, "hol'

---

12. **remnant** (rem′nənt), *n.* small part left; fragment.
13. **harass** (har′əs, hə ras′), *v.* trouble by repeated attacks.
14. **thirteen-hand.** The hand is a unit of measure equal to four inches.

Fruit Stand Vendor was painted by Hyacinth Manning-Carner. How do you think this vendor feels about his fruit?

you fruit. . . . Keep it to you heart like a mudder savin' her baby! Don't let the wicked wind t'row you to the groun' . . . even if it t'row me to the groun'. I will not leave you."

But several attempts to replace the prop were futile. The force of the wind against his weight was too much for him. He thought of a rope to lash the tree to anything, but it was difficult to make his way into the kitchen, which, separate from the house, was still standing. The invisible hand of the wind tugged, pushed, and forcefully restrained him. He got down and crawled on his belly into the earth-floor kitchen. As he showed himself with the rope, the wind tossed him, like washing on the line, against his tree.

The boy was hurt! He looked crucified against the tree. The spike of the wind was slightly withdrawn. He fell, folded on the ground. He lay there unconscious. And the wind had no mercy for him. It shoved him, poked him, and molested his clothes like muddy newspaper against the tree.

As darkness began to move in rapidly, the wind grew more vicious and surged a mighty gust that struck the resisting kitchen. It was heaved to the ground in a rubbled pile. The brave wooden hut had been shielding the banana tree, but in its death fall missed it by inches. The wind charged again and the soft tree gurgled—the fruit was torn from it and plunged to the ground.

QUESTION: What do you want to know next?

The wind was less fierce when Mr. Bass and a searching party arrived with lanterns. Because the bridge was washed away, the hazardous roundabout journey had badly impeded[15] them.

Talks about safety were mockery to the anxious father. Relentlessly he searched. In the darkness his great voice echoed everywhere, calling for his boy. He was wrenching and ripping through the house wreckage when suddenly he vaguely remembered how the boy had been fussing with the banana tree. Desperate, the man struggled from the ruins, flagging the lantern he carried.

The flickering light above his head showed Mr. Bass the forlorn and pitiful banana tree. There it stood, shivering and twitching like a propped-up man with lacerated[16] throat and dismembered head. Half of the damaged fruit rested on Gustus. The father hesitated. But when he saw a feeble wink of the boy's eyelids, he flung himself to the ground. His bristly chin rubbed the child's face while his unsteady hand ran all over his body. "Mi bwoy!" he murmured. "Mi hurricane bwoy! The Good Lord save you. . . . Why you do this? Why you do this?"

"I did want buy mi shoes, Pappy. I . . . I can't go anywhere 'cause I have no shoes. . . . I didn' go to school outing at the factory. I didn' go to Government House. I didn' go to Ol' Fort in town."

Mr. Bass sank into the dirt and stripped himself of his heavy boots. He was about to lace them to the boy's feet when the onlooking men prevented him. He tied the boots together and threw them over his shoulder.

Gustus's broken arm was strapped to his side as they carried him away. Mr. Bass stroked his head and asked how he felt. Only then grief swelled inside him and he wept.

---

15. **impede** (im pēd′), *v.* stand in the way of; hinder.
16. **lacerated** (las′ə rāt′əd), *adj.* torn roughly; mangled.

▲ *Wind and Geometry* was painted by David True in 1978. What details of the painting suggest the power of the wind?

HURRICANE
DIONNE BRAND

Shut the windows
Bolt the doors
Big rain coming
Climbing up the mountain

5 Neighbors whisper
Dark clouds gather
Big rain coming
Climbing up the mountain

Gather in the clotheslines
10 Pull down the blinds
Big wind rising
Coming up the mountain

Branches falling
Raindrops flying
15 Treetops swaying
People running
Big wind blowing
Hurricane! on the mountain.

After Reading

Making Connections

1. What is the most important moment or scene in the story? Why do you think so?

2. Was Gustus courageous or foolish in his attempt to save the tree? Explain.

3. Give examples of how the author shows the hurricane to be a hostile force.

4. ☞ What does Gustus want to **change** in his relationship with his father? Is he successful?

5. Why do you think the father tries to lace his boots to his son's feet at the end of the story?

6. Why do you think a crisis often pulls people together in a community? Do you personally know of an example of this happening?

7. Mr. Bass doesn't understand the importance of shoes to Gustus. Tell of another situation, real or imaginary, in which one person in a family doesn't know the importance of something to another family member.

Literary Focus: Personification

As you might guess from the root of the word, the literary term **personification** means "making into a person" or "giving human qualities to something not human." In other words, an author personifies by giving something, often a natural force, a personality. In the second paragraph of "The Banana Tree," James Berry says this about the hurricane: "From its very buildup the hurricane meant to show it was merciless, unstoppable. . . ." The hurricane in this story is nearly one of the characters, with a personality all its own: angry, fierce, and out to destroy everything in its path!

Choose a natural force or feature you have experienced and write a poem or a paragraph in which you personify it. You might choose a mountain, a river, a storm, a wave, the sun, or anything else you have experienced first-hand. Before you write, consider these questions:

- Is the force harmful, helpful, both, or neither?

- What human thoughts and feelings might this force have? What words or descriptions will show them?

- What characteristics (size, speed, sound) stand out most?

Vocabulary Study

Write the letter of the word that is not related in meaning to the other words in the set. Read across.

resounding
refuse
calamity
belligerent
tormented
tempestuous
remnant
harass
impede
lacerated

1. **a.** calamity   **b.** catastrophe   **c.** disaster   **d.** victory
2. **a.** angry   **b.** belligerent   **c.** friendly   **d.** hostile
3. **a.** treasure   **b.** garbage   **c.** refuse   **d.** litter
4. **a.** hurt   **b.** tormented   **c.** tortured   **d.** excited
5. **a.** calm   **b.** turbulent   **c.** perilous   **d.** tempestuous
6. **a.** harass   **b.** bother   **c.** soothe   **d.** disturb
7. **a.** remnant   **b.** whole   **c.** piece   **d.** remainder
8. **a.** silent   **b.** ringing   **c.** resounding   **d.** sonorous
9. **a.** impede   **b.** hinder   **c.** help   **d.** obstruct
10. **a.** healed   **b.** lacerated   **c.** injured   **d.** wounded

Expressing Your Ideas

Writing Choices

Gustus and the Tree The custom of burying the navel string suggests that the futures of the child and the plant are linked. Does "The Banana Tree" show this same connection? Write a paper in which you **compare and contrast** Gustus and his tree with respect to age and appearance, treatment by the storm, and condition at the end of the story.

The Next Day . . . What happened next to Gustus? Write an **epilogue** to "The Banana Tree," wrapping up any loose ends, getting everyone back home, and showing how Gustus and his father behave toward each other after the storm has ended.

Dear Diary Imagine that Gustus was keeping a diary. What would he have written in it about the day described in the story? Write a **diary entry** that Gustus might write at the end of the day.

Other Options

Create a Scene Select an important scene in the story and draw a **sketch** of it. Add notes for a sound track: What words from the story go with this picture? Besides the words, what other sounds might be heard? What music could accompany this scene?

Here Comes Another Hurricane Working in a group, **discuss** the different roles the hurricanes play in the poem "Hurricane" and in "The Banana Tree." For each selection, think about the way the word *hurricane* is used, the way the storm is described or characterized, and the main subject of the work.

Dramatic Moments Gustus's challenging journey home through the hurricane to save his tree is full of drama! **Pantomime** his actions as he battles the force of the wind to reach the tree. You might want to add music to your pantomime to increase the drama.

Before Reading

from Harriet Tubman

by Ann Petry

Ann Petry
born 1908

When she was a child, Ann Petry was so strongly influenced by some books that she used to act out her favorite scenes. She would like the books she writes to have such an impact on young readers.

Of the characters she writes about, she says, "These are people. Look at them, listen to them; watch Harriet Tubman in the nineteenth century, a heroic woman, a rescuer of other slaves." One point she wants to make in these books is that African Americans are an important part of the history of America. "Remember for what a long, long time black people have been in this country, have been a part of America: a sturdy, indestructible, wonderful part of America, woven into its heart and into its soul."

Building Background

Escape from Slavery The Underground Railroad was not under the ground, nor was it a railroad. It was a secret network of escape routes used by runaway slaves during the mid-1800s. A "conductor" helped slaves move from one "station" to another. Runaway slaves usually worked their way to free states and then northward. The map shows the major escape routes.

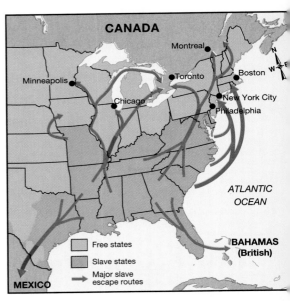

Getting into the Selection

Writer's Notebook Until it is lost, freedom is easy to take for granted. Think of a time when you experienced a loss of freedom:

* freedom of movement, as in an injury
* freedom of privilege, as in being grounded or restricted
* freedom of choice, as in having no say in a decision

In your notebook, describe how you felt during the time your freedom was limited. Explain how your freedom was regained.

Reading Tip

Sequence When you read a story, it is important to keep straight the **sequence** of events. In effect, you make a time line in your head as you read. If you are alert to time markers, words and phrases such as *later* and *the next day,* you will keep track of events on that internal time line. When you read this narrative about Harriet Tubman and the Underground Railroad, watch for the time markers. Keep a time line—in your head or on paper—to help you keep track of the sequence.

Harriet Tubman

ANN PETRY

Along the eastern shore of Maryland, in Dorchester County, in Caroline County, the masters kept hearing whispers about the man named Moses, who was running off slaves. At first they did not believe in his existence. The stories about him were fantastic, unbelievable. Yet they watched for him. They offered rewards for his capture.

They never saw him. Now and then they heard whispered rumors to the effect that he was in the neighborhood. The woods were searched. The roads were watched. There was never anything to indicate his whereabouts. But a few days afterward, a goodly number of slaves would be gone from the plantation. Neither the master nor the overseer had heard or seen anything unusual in the quarter. Sometimes one or the other would vaguely remember having heard a whippoorwill call somewhere in the woods, close by, late at night. Though it was the wrong season for whippoorwills.

Sometimes the masters thought they had heard the cry of a hoot owl, repeated, and would remember having thought that the intervals between the low moaning cry were wrong, that it had been repeated four times in succession instead of three. There was never anything more than that to suggest that all was not well in the quarter. Yet when morning came, they invariably discovered that a group of the finest slaves had taken to their heels.

Unfortunately, the discovery was almost always made on a Sunday. Thus a whole day was lost before the machinery of pursuit could be set in motion. The posters offering rewards for the fugitives[1] could not be printed until Monday. The men who made a living hunting for runaway slaves were out of reach, off in the woods with their dogs and their guns, in pursuit of four-footed game, or they were in camp meetings saying their prayers with their wives and families beside them.

Harriet Tubman could have told them that there was far more involved in this matter of running off slaves than signaling the would-be runaways by imitating the call of a whippoorwill, or a hoot owl, far more involved than a matter of waiting for a clear night when the North Star was visible.

In December, 1851, when she started out with the band of fugitives that she planned to take to Canada, she had been in the vicinity of the plantation for days, planning the trip,

---

1. fugitive (fyü′jə tiv), *n.* person who runs away or attempts to escape.

carefully selecting the slaves that she would take with her.

She had announced her arrival in the quarter by singing the forbidden spiritual—"Go down, Moses, 'way down to Egypt Land"—singing it softly outside the door of a slave cabin, late at night. The husky voice was beautiful even when it was barely more than a murmur borne on the wind.

Once she had made her presence known, word of her coming spread from cabin to cabin. The slaves whispered to each other, ear to mouth, mouth to ear, "Moses is here." "Moses has come." "Get ready. Moses is back again." The ones who had agreed to go North with her put ashcake and salt herring in an old bandanna, hastily tied it into a bundle, and then waited patiently for the signal that meant it was time to start.

There were eleven in this party, including one of her brothers and his wife. It was the largest group that she had ever conducted, but she was determined that more and more slaves should know what freedom was like.

She had to take them all the way to Canada. The Fugitive Slave Law[2] was no longer a great many incomprehensible words written down on the country's lawbooks. The new law had become a reality. It was Thomas Sims, a boy, picked up on the streets of Boston at night and shipped back to Georgia. It was Jerry and Shadrach, arrested and jailed with no warning.

She had never been in Canada. The route beyond Philadelphia was strange to her. But she could not let the runaways who accompanied her know this. As they walked along she told them stories of her own first flight; she kept painting vivid word pictures of what it would be like to be free.

But there were so many of them this time. She knew moments of doubt when she was half-afraid, and kept looking back over her shoulder, imagining that she heard the sound of pursuit. They would certainly be pursued. Eleven of them. Eleven thousand dollars' worth of flesh and bone and muscle that belonged to Maryland planters. If they were caught, the eleven runaways would be whipped and sold South, but she—she would probably be hanged.

They tried to sleep during the day but they never could wholly relax into sleep. She could tell by the positions they assumed, by their restless movements. And they walked at night. Their progress was slow. It took them three nights of walking to reach the first stop. She had told them about the place where they would stay, promising warmth and good food, holding these things out to them as an incentive[3] to keep going.

When she knocked on the door of a farmhouse, a place where she and her parties of runaways had always been welcome, always been given shelter and plenty to eat, there was no answer. She knocked again, softly. A voice from within said, "Who is it?" There was fear in the voice.

She knew instantly from the sound of the voice that there was something wrong. She said, "A friend with friends," the password on the Underground Railroad.

The door opened, slowly. The man who stood in the doorway looked at her coldly, looked with unconcealed astonishment and fear at the eleven disheveled runaways who were standing near her. Then he shouted, "Too many, too many. It's not safe. My place was searched last week. It's not safe!" and slammed the door in her face.

---

2. **Fugitive Slave Law.** In 1793 and 1850, Congress enacted severe laws to provide for the return of escaped slaves. The Underground Railroad was largely a result of public distaste for these laws. Among other harsh measures, the law of 1850 imposed severe penalties upon anyone who helped a slave in his or her escape.

3. incentive (in sen′tiv), *n.* thing that urges a person on.

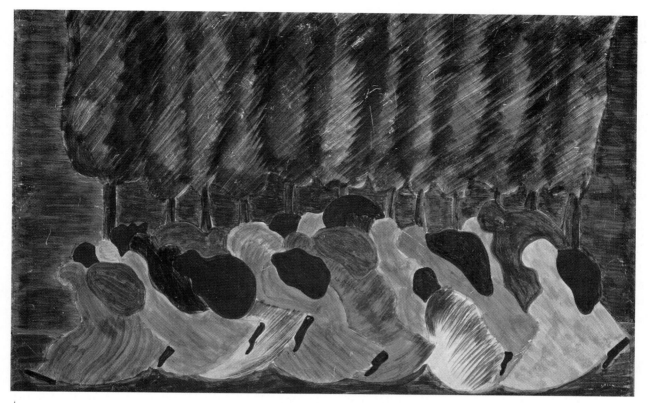

Plate 16 of the *Harriet Tubman* series was painted by Jacob Lawrence in 1939–40. Jacob Lawrence, one of America's most important artists, painted a series of thirty-one paintings of Harriet Tubman's life early in his career. How has Lawrence created a sense of the fear, speed, and secrecy of the runaway slaves in this painting?

She turned away from the house, frowning. She had promised her passengers food and rest and warmth, and instead of that, there would be hunger and cold and more walking over the frozen ground. Somehow she would have to instill courage into these eleven people, most of them strangers, would have to feed them on hope and bright dreams of freedom instead of the fried pork and corn bread and milk she had promised them.

They stumbled along behind her, half-dead for sleep, and she urged them on, though she was as tired and as discouraged as they were. She had never been in Canada, but she kept painting wondrous word pictures of what it would be like. She managed to dispel[4] their fear of pursuit, so that they would not become hysterical, panic-stricken. Then she had to bring some of the fear back, so that they would stay awake and keep walking though they drooped with sleep.

Yet during the day, when they lay down deep in a thicket, they never really slept, because if a twig snapped or the wind sighed in the branches of a pine tree, they jumped to their feet, afraid of their own shadows, shivering and shaking. It was very cold, but they dared not make fires because someone would see the smoke and wonder about it.

---

4. **dispel** (dis pel′), *v.* drive away and scatter.

Harriet Tubman　**207**

She kept thinking, eleven of them. Eleven thousand dollars' worth of slaves. And she had to take them all the way to Canada. Sometimes she told them about Thomas Garrett, in Wilmington. She said he was their friend even though he did not know them. He was the friend of all fugitives. He called them God's poor. He was a Quaker[5] and his speech was a little different from that of other people. His clothing was different, too. He wore the wide-brimmed hat that the Quakers wear.

She said that he had thick white hair, soft, almost like a baby's, and the kindest eyes she had ever seen. He was a big man and strong, but he had never used his strength to harm anyone, always to help people. He would give all of them a new pair of shoes. Everybody. He always did. Once they reached his house in Wilmington, they would be safe. He would see to it that they were.

She described the house where he lived, told them about the store where he sold shoes. She said he kept a pail of milk and a loaf of bread in the drawer of his desk so that he would have food ready at hand for any of God's poor who should suddenly appear before him, fainting with hunger. There was a hidden room in the store. A whole wall swung open, and behind it was a room where he could hide fugitives. On the wall there were shelves filled with small boxes—boxes of shoes—so that you would never guess that the wall actually opened.

While she talked, she kept watching them. They did not believe her. She could tell by their expressions. They were thinking, New shoes, Thomas Garrett, Quaker, Wilmington—what foolishness was this? Who knew if she told the truth? Where was she taking them anyway?

That night they reached the next stop—a farm that belonged to a German. She made the runaways take shelter behind the trees at the edge of the fields before she knocked at the door. She hesitated before she approached the door, thinking, suppose that he, too, should refuse shelter, suppose—Then she thought, Lord, I'm going to hold steady on to You and You've got to see me through—and knocked softly.

She heard the familiar guttural voice say, "Who's there?"

She answered quickly, "A friend with friends."

He opened the door and greeted her warmly. "How many this time?" he asked.

"Eleven," she said and waited, doubting, wondering.

He said, "Good. Bring them in."

He and his wife fed them in the lamplit kitchen, their faces glowing, as they offered food and more food, urging them to eat, saying there was plenty for everybody, have more milk, have more bread, have more meat.

They spent the night in the warm kitchen. They really slept, all that night and until dusk the next day. When they left, it was with reluctance. They had all been warm and safe and well-fed. It was hard to exchange the security offered by that clean warm kitchen for the darkness and the cold of a December night. . . .

Harriet had found it hard to leave the warmth and friendliness, too. But she urged them on. For a while, as they walked, they seemed to carry in them a measure of contentment; some of the serenity[6] and the cleanliness of that big warm kitchen lingered on inside them. But as they walked farther and farther away from the warmth and the light, the cold and the darkness entered into them. They fell silent, sullen, suspicious. She waited for the moment when some one of them would turn mutinous.[7] It did not happen that night.

---

5. **Quaker,** a member of a Christian group called the Society of Friends. The Quakers participated actively in the antislavery effort.
6. serenity (sə ren′ə tē), *n.* peace and quiet.
7. mutinous (myüt′n əs), *adj.* rebellious; uncontrollable.

Two nights later she was aware that the feet behind her were moving slower and slower. She heard the irritability[8] in their voices, knew that soon someone would refuse to go on.

She started talking about William Still and the Philadelphia Vigilance Committee.[9] No one commented. No one asked any questions. She told them the story of William and Ellen Craft and how they escaped from Georgia. Ellen was so fair that she looked as though she were white, and so she dressed up in a man's clothing and she looked like a wealthy young planter. Her husband, William, who was dark, played the role of her slave. Thus they traveled from Macon, Georgia, to Philadelphia, riding on the trains, staying at the finest hotels. Ellen pretended to be very ill—her right arm was in a sling, and her right hand was bandaged, because she was supposed to have rheumatism. Thus she avoided having to sign the register at the hotels, for she could not read or write. They finally arrived safely in Philadelphia, and then went on to Boston.

No one said anything. Not one of them seemed to have heard her.

She told them about Frederick Douglass,[10] the most famous of the escaped slaves, of his eloquence,[11] of his magnificent appearance. Then she told them of her own first vain effort at running away, evoking[12] the memory of that miserable life she had led as a child, reliving it for a moment in the telling.

But they had been tired too long, hungry too long, afraid too long, foot-sore too long. One of them suddenly cried out in despair, "Let me go back. It is better to be a slave than to suffer like this in order to be free."

She carried a gun with her on these trips. She had never used it—except as a threat. Now as she aimed it, she experienced a feeling of guilt, remembering that time, years ago, when she had prayed for the death of Edward Brodas, the Master, and then not too long afterward had heard that great wailing cry that came from the throats of the field hands, and knew from the sound that the Master was dead.

One of the runaways said, again, "Let me go back. Let me go back," and stood still, and then turned around and said, over his shoulder, "I am going back."

She lifted the gun, aimed it at the despairing slave. She said, "Go on with us or die." The husky low-pitched voice was grim.

He hesitated for a moment, and then he joined the others. They started walking again. She tried to explain to them why none of them could go back to the plantation. If a runaway returned, he would turn traitor, the master and the overseer would force him to turn traitor. The returned slave would disclose the stopping places, the hiding places, the cornstacks they had used with the full knowledge of the owner of the farm, the name of the German farmer who had fed them and sheltered them. These people who had risked their own security to help runaways would be ruined, fined, imprisoned.

She said, "We got to go free or die. And freedom's not bought with dust."

This time she told them about the long agony of the Middle Passage[13] on the old slave

We got to go free or die. And freedom's not bought with dust.

---

8. irritability (ir/ə tə bil/ə tē), *n.* impatience; unnatural sensitivity; annoyance.
9. **Philadelphia Vigilance Committee,** a group of citizens who guided slaves and helped pay their way North.
10. **Frederick Douglass** (1817–1895), an ex-slave who became a leading figure in the antislavery movement through his eloquent lectures and abolitionist newspaper, *The North Star.*
11. eloquence (el/ə kwəns), *n.* flow of forceful speech.
12. evoke (i vōk/), *v.* call forth; bring out.
13. **Middle Passage,** the slaves' journey from Africa to the New World across the Atlantic Ocean.

ships, about the black horror of the holds, about the chains and the whips. They too knew these stories. But she wanted to remind them of the long hard way they had come, about the long hard way they had yet to go. She told them about Thomas Sims, the boy picked up on the streets of Boston and sent back to Georgia. She said when they got him back to Savannah, got him in prison there, they whipped him until a doctor who was standing by watching said, "You will kill him if you strike him again!" His master said, "Let him die!"

T hus she forced them to go on. Sometimes she thought she had become nothing but a voice speaking in the darkness, cajoling,[14] urging, threatening. Sometimes she told them things to make them laugh, sometimes she sang to them, and heard the eleven voices behind her blending softly with hers, and then she knew that for the moment all was well with them.

She gave the impression of being a short, muscular, indomitable[15] woman who could never be defeated. Yet at any moment she was liable to be seized by one of those curious fits of sleep, which might last for a few minutes or for hours.[16]

Even on this trip, she suddenly fell asleep in the woods. The runaways, ragged, dirty, hungry, cold, did not steal the gun as they might have, and set off by themselves, or turn back. They sat on the ground near her and waited patiently until she awakened. They had come to trust her implicitly, totally. They, too, had come to believe her repeated statement, "We got to go free or die." She was leading them into freedom, and so they waited until she was ready to go on.

Finally, they reached Thomas Garrett's house in Wilmington, Delaware. Just as Harriet had promised, Garrett gave them all new shoes, and provided carriages to take them on to the next stop.

By slow stages they reached Philadelphia, where William Still hastily recorded their names, and the plantations whence they had come, and something of the life they had led in slavery. Then he carefully hid what he had written, for fear it might be discovered. In 1872 he published this record in book form and called it *The Underground Railroad*. In the foreword to his book he said: "While I knew the danger of keeping strict records, and while I did not then dream that in my day slavery would be blotted out, or that the time would come when I could publish these records, it used to afford me great satisfaction to take them down, fresh from the lips of fugitives on the way to freedom, and to preserve them as they had given them."

William Still, who was familiar with all the station stops on the Underground Railroad, supplied Harriet with money and sent her and her eleven fugitives on to Burlington, New Jersey.

Harriet felt safer now, though there were danger spots ahead. But the biggest part of her job was over. As they went farther and farther north, it grew colder; she was aware of the wind on the Jersey ferry and aware of the cold damp in New York. From New York they went on to Syracuse, where the temperature was even lower.

In Syracuse she met the Reverend J. W. Loguen, known as "Jarm" Loguen. This was the beginning of a lifelong friendship. Both Harriet and Jarm Loguen were to become friends and supporters of Old John Brown.[17]

---

14. **cajole** (kə jōl′), *v.* persuade by pleasant words or flattery; coax.
15. **indomitable** (in dom′ə tə bəl), *adj.* unbeatable; unconquerable.
16. **curious . . . hours.** At thirteen, Harriet Tubman nearly died from a blow on her head. The heavy blow caused periodic sleep seizures that troubled her throughout her life.
17. **Old John Brown** (1800–1859), a devoted American abolitionist who tried to stir up a rebellion among the slaves. When he attempted to raid a government arsenal at Harpers Ferry in 1859, he was captured and executed.

In plate 20 of the *Harriet Tubman* series by Jacob Lawrence (1939–40), Harriet Tubman leads the escaped slaves into Canada. How is this painting similar to plate 16 (page 207)? How is it different?

From Syracuse they went north again, into a colder, snowier city—Rochester. Here they almost certainly stayed with Frederick Douglass, for he wrote in his autobiography:

"On one occasion I had eleven fugitives at the same time under my roof, and it was necessary for them to remain with me until I could collect sufficient money to get them to Canada. It was the largest number I ever had at any one time, and I had some difficulty in providing so many with food and shelter, but, as may well be imagined, they were not very fastidious in either direction, and were well content with very plain food, and a strip of carpet on the floor for a bed, or a place on the straw in the barn-loft."

Late in December, 1851, Harriet arrived in St. Catharines, Canada West (now Ontario), with the eleven fugitives. It had taken almost a month to complete this journey; most of the time had been spent getting out of Maryland.

That first winter in St. Catharines was a terrible one. Canada was a strange frozen land, snow everywhere, ice everywhere, and a bone-biting cold the like of which none of them had ever experienced before. Harriet rented a small frame house in the town and set to work to make a home. The fugitives boarded with her. They worked in the forests, felling trees, and so did she. Sometimes she took other jobs, cooking or cleaning house for people in the town. She cheered on these newly arrived fugitives, working herself, finding work for them, finding food for them, praying for them, sometimes begging for them.

Often she found herself thinking of the beauty of Maryland, the mellowness of the soil, the richness of the plant life there. The climate itself made for an ease of living that could never be duplicated in this bleak, barren countryside.

In spite of the severe cold, the hard work, she came to love St. Catharines, and the other towns and cities in Canada where black men lived. She discovered that freedom meant more than the right to change jobs at will, more than the right to keep the money that one earned. It was the right to vote and to sit on juries. It was the right to be elected to office. In Canada there were black men who were county officials and members of school boards. St. Catharines had a large colony of ex-slaves, and they owned their own homes, kept them neat and clean and in good repair. They lived in whatever part of town they chose and sent their children to the schools.

When spring came she decided that she would make this small Canadian city her home—as much as any place could be said to be home to a woman who traveled from Canada to the eastern shore of Maryland as often as she did.

In the spring of 1852, she went back to Cape May, New Jersey. She spent the summer there, cooking in a hotel. That fall she returned, as usual, to Dorchester County, and brought out nine more slaves, conducting them all the way to St. Catharines, in Canada West, to the bone-biting cold, the snow-covered forests—and freedom.

She continued to live in this fashion, spending the winter in Canada, and the spring and summer working in Cape May, New Jersey, or in Philadelphia. She made two trips a year into slave territory, one in the fall and another in the spring. She now had a definite crystallized purpose, and in carrying it out, her life fell into a pattern which remained unchanged for the next six years.

Go Down, Moses

When Israel was in Egypt's land,
    Let my people go!
Oppress'd so hard dey could not stand,
    Let my people go!

Chorus
5 Go down, Moses,
    Way down in Egypt's land.
Tell ole Pha-raoh,
    Let my people go!

Thus say de Lord, bold Moses said,
10   Let my people go!
If not I'll smite your first-born dead,
    Let my people go!

No more shall dey in bondage toil,
    Let my people go!
15 Let dem come out wid Egypt's spoil,
    Let my people go!

Plate 10 of the *Harriet Tubman* series by Jacob Lawrence (1939–40) portrays Harriet Tubman's escape from slavery when she was between twenty and twenty-five years old. What symbols do you see in the painting?

After Reading

Making Connections

1. What part of this selection stands out the most for you? Why?

2. What did Harriet Tubman mean by the words, ". . . freedom's not bought with dust"?

3. The author is writing over one hundred years after these events. What evidence does she give that her information is accurate?

4. Some slaves wanted to turn back at various points. What methods did Harriet use to persuade them to continue?

5. What **character traits** does Harriet Tubman show on the trip from Maryland to Canada? Give an example for each trait you list.

6. 🐾 How was life in Canada different from life in Maryland for Harriet? How did her past prepare her to cope with the **changes?**

7. 🐾 What injustices are you aware of in the world today? Are leaders working to **change** these injustices? Support your answer.

Literary Focus: Mood

As Harriet Tubman leads her party of runaways to Canada, the mood is fearful and full of suspense. The runaways move only at night. They constantly look over their shoulders, afraid of being followed. They keep quiet, jumping at every sound. The **mood,** the atmosphere or feeling of a work, is created by the author through her choice of the setting, details, images, events, and words.

Review the selection to see how Ann Petry created a suspenseful mood. Find what you think to be the two most suspenseful moments in the narrative. In your writer's notebook, list specific words and details that help create the mood.

Vocabulary Study

Write the word from the list at the top of the next page that best completes each sentence.

1. Once he had escaped, each _____ had a price on his head.

2. The reward money was a strong _____ to find the missing people.

3. Once they began the long journey, there was no peace or _____ for the slaves until they reached Canada.

cajole
indomitable
eloquence
dispel
evoke
irritability
fugitive
mutinous
incentive
serenity

4. At times the runaways became ____ and began to rebel.

5. Fear and harsh conditions increased the ____ of the fugitives.

6. Harriet Tubman's ____ as a speaker helped to convince the slaves to continue the journey.

7. Harriet often had to tease and ____ the runaways, trying to convince them to go on.

8. She often told stories that made word-paintings, stories to ____ images of what freedom would be like.

9. Harriet described the people who would help them along the way, hoping to ____ the fears of the runaways.

10. Her ____ spirit made her always push on, in spite of dangers.

Expressing Your Ideas

Writing Choices

Making a Reference Write a brief **encyclopedia entry** on Harriet Tubman's role in the Underground Railroad. Review the story for the information you will need, noting time markers to help you with the sequence.

For Her Great Valor . . . Assume that Harriet Tubman has been chosen to receive a "Show of Courage" award for her service to others. Write a **commendation** or tribute in which you explain why she deserves the award.

Civil Disobedience Harriet Tubman broke the law in helping slaves escape. The theory of "civil disobedience," or refusing to obey a law that you consider unjust, is one with deep roots in religious and political thought. Research the views of one of the great leaders in civil disobedience—Henry David Thoreau, Mohandas Gandhi, or Martin Luther King, Jr.—and write a **research paper** explaining this person's views on civil disobedience.

Other Options

The Great Escape Prepare a **map** that covers the area from eastern Maryland to St. Catharines, Canada West (now Ontario). Trace the route to Canada taken by Harriet Tubman and the eleven runaways. You will need to reread the selection and note the stops that are mentioned. You might find the map on page 204 helpful.

Now You See It. . . . Sketch or build a **model** of the inside of Thomas Garrett's store. Show how the entire wall could swing open to reveal the hidden room behind it, the room where he hid runaway slaves.

Interview with a Runaway Harriet Tubman is the focus of the events in this selection. Change that focus by developing the character of one of the eleven slaves who made the journey with her. Working with a classmate, prepare **interview questions** for the runaway and then prepare the answers. Conduct the interview as if you were at a meeting in Canada.

Before Reading

Strong but Quirky: The Birth of Davy Crockett retold by Irwin Shapiro

Aunty Misery by Judith Ortiz Cofer

Irwin Shapiro
1911–1981

Although he was first interested in painting, Irwin Shapiro's interest in American folklore led him instead to retelling and writing. He even adapted *The Adventures of Tom Sawyer* and *The Red Badge of Courage* for Marvel comic books. Some of his favorite figures from American folk tales are Paul Bunyan, John Henry, Daniel Boone, and Davy Crockett.

Judith Ortiz Cofer
born 1952

Of Puerto Rican descent, Judith Ortiz Cofer reveals a strong sense of family in her play, novels, and poems. She believes her family is her most important subject, and that by discovering more about their lives, she better understands her own.

Building Background

A Man Who Created His Own Legend Davy Crockett was a famous hunter, scout, soldier, and legislator to the U.S. Congress. Partly because of his speaking ability, he was elected to Congress not just once, but three times. He was a famous storyteller, mostly of tall tales about his adventures. One of his favorites was of the raccoon who climbed down from a tree and surrendered when he discovered the identity of the great hunter pursuing him—Davy Crockett.

Getting into the Stories

Writer's Notebook A **folk tale** is a tale that is passed on by word of mouth for a long time before being written down. As each story-teller tells the story to a new audience, the story gradually changes. Often a folk tale exists in many different versions around the world. "Aunty Misery" is a Puerto Rican tale, but you may know some other version of it, from Puerto Rico or another culture.

Some folk tales, such as "Strong but Quirky," began as stories about a real person. Over the years, the characters got bigger than life and their adventures were exaggerated to the point of being impossible. In your notebook, write about a situation you remember in which the speaker (perhaps it was you!) stretched things a little to try to make a story a little more funny, scary, or exciting. In that story is the germ of a tall tale!

Reading Tip

Informal Speech Another characteristic of tall tales is that the language is usually informal and conversational, and characters such as Davy Crockett speak the language of the American frontier. Slang expressions are common:

"'That'll be enough o' your sass,' says she, kind of sharplike."

As you can see, this frontier speech, like the Jamaican speech in "The Banana Tree," tends to leave out letters from some words. As you read this tall tale, mentally listen to what the language would sound like if you read it aloud.

Strong but Quirky: The Birth of Davy Crockett

Irwin Shapiro

The morning Davy Crockett was born Davy's pa came busting out of his cabin in Tennessee alongside the Nolachucky River. He fired three shots into the air, gave a whoop, and said, "I've got me a son. His name is Davy Crockett, and he'll be the greatest hunter in all creation."

When he said that, the sun rose up in the sky like a ball of fire. The wind howled riproariously. Thunder boomed, and all the critters and varmints[1] of the forest let out a moan.

Then Davy's pa went back into the cabin. Little Davy was stretched out in a cradle made of a snapping turtle's shell. There was a pair of elk horns over the top, and over the elk horns was the skin of a wildcat. The cradle was run by water power, and it was rocking away—*rockety-whump, rockety-whump.*

Now all the Crocketts were big, but Davy was big even for a Crockett. He weighed two hundred pounds, fourteen ounces, and he was as frisky as a wildcat. His ma and his aunt Ketinah stood over Davy, trying to get him to sleep.

"Sing somethin' to quiet the boy," said Aunt Ketinah to his uncle Roarious, who was standing in a corner combing his hair with a rake.

Uncle Roarious opened his mouth and sang a bit of "Over the River to Charley." That is, it was meant for singing. It sounded worse than a nor'easter[2] howling around a country barn at midnight.

"Hmmm," said Uncle Roarious. He reached for a jug and took a sip of kerosene oil to loosen up his pipes.

Davy was sitting up in his cradle. He kept his peepers on his uncle, watching him pull at the jug.

"I'll have a sip o' the same," said Davy, as loud as you please.

That kerosene jug slipped right out of Uncle Roarious's hand. Davy's ma and his aunt Ketinah let out a shriek.

"Why, the little shaver can talk!" said Davy's pa.

"We-ell," said Davy, talking slow and easy-like, "maybe I don't jabber good enough to make a speech in Congress, but I reckon I got the hang of 'er. It's nothin' to Davy Crockett."

---

1. **varmint** (vär'mənt), *n.* unliked animal or person (dialect).
2. **nor'easter** (nôr ē'stər), violent storm coming from the northeast.

"That's mighty big talk, son," said Davy's pa.

"It ought to be," said Davy. "It's comin' from a big man."

And with that he leapt out of his cradle, kicked his heels together, and crowed like a rooster. He flapped his arms and he bellowed, "I'm Davy Crockett, fresh from the backwoods! I'm half horse, half alligator, with a little touch o' snappin' turtle! I can wade the Mississippi, ride a streak o' lightnin', hug a bear too close for comfort, and whip my weight in wildcats! I can outeat, outsleep, outfight, outshoot, outrun, outjump, and outsquat any man in these here United States! And I will!"

Aunt Ketinah eyed him as if he was a little bit of a mosquito making a buzz.

"That'll be enough o' your sass," said she, kind of sharplike. "Now get back into your cradle and behave."

"Yes, ma'am," said Davy. He was always polite to the ladies.

"No such thing!" said Uncle Roarious. "Settin' in the cradle won't grow him none! We've got to plant him in the earth and water him with wild buffalo's milk, with boiled corncobs and tobacco leaves mixed in."

"Can't do any harm," said Davy's ma.

"Might do good," said Davy's pa.

"Suits me," said Davy. "Let's give 'er a try."

So they took Davy out to Thunder Shower Hill and planted him in the earth. They watered him with wild buffalo's milk, with boiled corncobs and tobacco leaves mixed in. The sun shone on him by day, and the moon beamed down on him by night. The wind cooled him and the rain freshened him. And Davy Crockett began to grow proper.

One morning Davy's pa got up as usual and looked out the window. Instead of the sun shining, it was like a cloudy night with fog and no moon. Davy's pa had never seen it so dark in all his born days.

"Hurricane's comin' up," he said to Uncle Roarious, who was standing in a corner buttoning up his cast-iron shirt.

"We'd better water Davy before she breaks," said Uncle Roarious.

Davy's pa and Uncle Roarious each picked up a barrel of wild buffalo's milk, with boiled corncobs and tobacco leaves mixed in. Davy's ma and Aunt Ketinah followed along, carrying another barrel between them.

But when they got outside there wasn't a sign of a hurricane. There wasn't a hurricane coming up, going down, or standing still. There wasn't any hurricane at all. The sky was blue with little white clouds, and the sun was shining just as pretty. Only reason it was so dark was that Davy's shadow was falling over the cabin.

"Davy must have growed some," said Davy's ma, and they all hurried over to Thunder Shower Hill. Davy was standing on tiptoe with his head poked through a cloud. He was taller than the tallest tree, and a sight friskier.

Uncle Roarious let out a yip and Davy leaned down. Davy wiped a bit of cloud out of his eye and said, "I've been lookin' over the country. She's right pretty, and I think I'm goin' to like 'er."

"You'd better," said Aunt Ketinah, kind of snappylike. "She's the only one you've got."

"Yes, ma'am!" roared out Davy. His voice was so loud it started an avalanche[3] at Whangdoodle Knob, thirty miles away. The trees all around flattened out, and Aunt Ketinah, Uncle Roarious, and Davy's ma and pa fell over from the force of it.

Davy's pa picked himself up and shook his head.

"He's too big," he said.

"Oh, I don't know," said Uncle Roarious. "He'll settle some."

---

3. avalanche (av′ə lanch), n. a large mass of snow and ice, or dirt and rocks, loosened from a mountainside and descending swiftly into the valley below.

Davy Crockett was identified by his coonskin cap and rugged, outdoorsman appearance. Do you know why Robert Lindneux, the artist, showed the Alamo in the background of this portrait? ➤

"No," said Davy's pa, "he's too big for a hunter. It wouldn't be fair and square."

"What are we goin' to do?" asked Uncle Roarious.

"Only one thing *to* do," said Davy's pa. "We've got to uproot him and let him grow down to man-size."

So Davy's ma and pa, his aunt Ketinah and his uncle Roarious uprooted Davy. Soon as his feet were free, Davy leapt high into the air. He kicked his heels together, flapped his arms, and he bellowed, "Look out, all you critters and varmints o' the forest! For here comes Davy Crockett, fresh from the backwoods! I'm half horse, half alligator, with a little touch o' snappin' turtle! I can run faster, jump higher,

squat lower, dive deeper, stay under water longer, and come up drier than any man in these here United States! *Who-o-o-o-p!*"

Uncle Roarious listened to Davy and he looked at Davy. Then he said, "He's strong, but he's quirky."[4]

Davy's pa looked at Davy and he listened to Davy.

"He'll do," he said. "He'll do for a Crockett till a better one comes along."

And when Davy's pa said that, lightning flashed and thunder boomed. The wind howled riproariously, and all the critters and varmints of the forest let out a moan.

---

4. **quirky** (kwėr′kē), *adj.* peculiar or odd.

Strong but Quirky: The Birth of Davy Crockett   **219**

Judith Ortiz Cofer

This is a story about an old, very old woman who lived alone in her little hut with no other company than a beautiful pear tree that grew at her door. She spent all her time taking care of her pear tree. But the neighborhood children drove the old woman crazy by stealing her fruit. They would climb her tree, shake its delicate limbs, and run away with armloads of golden pears, yelling insults at "Aunty Misery," as they called her.

One day a pilgrim stopped at the old woman's hut and asked her permission to spend the night under her roof. Aunty Misery saw that he had an honest face and bade the traveler come in. She fed him and made a bed for him in front of her hearth. In the morning, while he was getting ready to leave, the stranger told her that he would show his gratitude for her hospitality by granting her one wish.

"There is only one thing that I desire," said Aunty Misery.

"Ask, and it shall be yours," replied the stranger, who was a sorcerer[1] in disguise.

"I wish that anyone who climbs up my pear tree should not be able to come back down until I permit it."

"Your wish is granted," said the stranger, touching the pear tree as he left Aunty Misery's house.

And so it happened that when the children came back to taunt[2] the old woman and to steal her fruit, she stood at her window watching them. Several of them shimmied up the trunk of the pear tree and immediately got stuck to it as if with glue. She let them cry and beg her for a long time before she gave the tree permission to let them go, on the condition that they never again steal her fruit or bother her.

Time passed, and both Aunty Misery and her tree grew bent and gnarled[3] with age. One day another traveler stopped at her door.

---

1. **sorcerer** (sôr′sər ər), wizard or magician.
2. **taunt** (tônt), *v.* jeer at; mock.
3. **gnarled** (närld), *adj.* twisted; knotted.

Misery

This one looked suffocated and exhausted, so the old woman asked him what he wanted in her village. He answered her in a voice that was dry and hoarse, as if he had swallowed a desert: "I am Death, and I have come to take you with me."

Thinking fast, Aunty Misery said, "All right, but before I go, I would like to pluck some pears from my beloved pear tree, to remember how much pleasure it brought me in this life. But, I am a very old woman and cannot climb to the tallest branches where the best fruit is; will you be so kind as to do it for me?"

With a heavy sigh like wind through a catacomb,[4] Death climbed the pear tree. Immediately he became stuck to it as if with glue. And no matter how much he cursed and threatened, Aunty Misery would not give the tree permission to release Death.

Many years passed, and there were no deaths in the world. The people who make their living from death began to protest loudly. The doctors claimed no one bothered to come in for examinations or treatments anymore because they did not fear dying; the pharmacists' business suffered, too, because medicines are, like magic potions, bought to prevent or postpone the inevitable;[5] the priests and undertakers were unhappy with the situation also, for obvious reasons. There were also many old folks tired of life who wanted to pass on to the next world to rest from the miseries of this one.

Aunty Misery realized all this, and not wishing to be unfair, she made a deal with her prisoner, Death: if he promised not ever to come for her again, she would give him his freedom. He agreed. And that is why so long as the world is the world, Aunty Misery will always live.

---

4. **catacomb** (kat′ə kōm), underground burial place.
5. inevitable (in ev′ə tə bəl), *n.* not to be avoided.

After Reading

Making Connections

1. Which **character** would you rather talk to, Aunty Misery or Davy Crockett? Explain your choice.

2. How did the author make the Davy Crockett story fun to read?

3. ☼ The elements that are exaggerated in a tall tale often tell you what the teller of the tale thought was important and valuable. Based on the Davy Crockett story, what can you infer about the values of American frontier culture?

4. Do you think Aunty Misery's decisions about Death—to send him up the tree, and then to call him back down—were wise ones? Explain.

5. What message do you think "Aunty Misery" communicates about the force of death?

6. If you were granted a wish by the sorcerer, what would your wish be?

7. What other stories can you think of that involve wishes being granted? Do any of them have unexpected results when the wishes are granted?

Literary Focus: Tone

Look at this title: "Aunty Misery." What would you expect the **tone** of a story to be if it had this title? How would your expectations differ for a story called "Strong but Quirky: The Birth of Davy Crockett"? If you told the Davy Crockett tale, you would probably tell it with a little smile, since it has a humorous tone. This humorous tone would not be appropriate for "Aunty Misery," which calls for a more serious and straightforward tone.

Contrast the tones of the two works by finding two short quotes from each tale to represent its tone. In small groups, read your quotes aloud, showing the difference in tone by your tone of voice. For each tale, choose the best two quotes your group found to read to the rest of the class.

Vocabulary Study

Write the vocabulary word that is associated with each word below. Some words will be used twice.

varmint
quirky
gnarled
avalanche
taunt
inevitable

1. tree
2. snow
3. tease
4. oddball
5. rat

6. mountain
7. twisted
8. bully
9. exterminator
10. fate

Expressing Your Ideas

Writing Choices

Up a Tree, Again Write your own **folk tale** based on the story of "Aunty Misery," but send a different character up the tree. Choose a character to represent a human quality or condition, such as greed, poverty, war, ignorance, illness, prejudice, or something else of your choice. Explain what would happen after your character was stuck up in the tree. Be sure to tell if you would have to ask the character to come back down.

Well, It Happened Like This . . . Make up a **tall tale** about an experience in your own life. Davy Crockett tells how he was born, but you can write about any event, as long as you turn it into an impossible happening. (You might want to start with the ideas you wrote in your notebook for the activity on page 216.) Be sure to exaggerate, use lots of detail, and keep the language informal. If you tell the tale, try to keep a straight face.

Who Was He Really? Research one aspect of Davy Crockett's real life: for example, his life as a frontiersman, his career as a Congressman, or his role at the Alamo. Write a brief **report** on what you learn.

Other Options

You Tell the Tale Pick a section of the Davy Crockett tale to **read aloud** to your classmates or another group. Read it carefully to see at what points you need to speed up or slow down, increase or decrease the loudness of your voice, and pause for effect. Rehearse aloud to be sure you can pronounce all the words comfortably, and then present the tale.

T-Shirts 'R' Us Design a T-shirt that represents either Davy Crockett or the character Death from "Aunty Misery." (If you do not have an old T-shirt to use for this project, just draw the shape of a shirt on a large piece of paper.) Before you start to plan your **design,** review the tale to find specific information to help you get ideas. Be ready to display your T-shirt and explain why you created that design.

Picture It Turn "Aunty Misery" or "Strong but Quirky" into a **picture book** or comic strip for younger children. Decide which events to picture, draw the scenes, and then write a simplified version of the tale beneath the pictures. Share your book with a younger child if possible.

Outside Forces

Forces of Destruction

Earth Science Connection

Outside forces of destruction, such as hurricanes, are all around us. Although unable to control when or where a hurricane will strike, scientists have met the challenge of hurricane survival. They can now predict where a hurricane will hit and how dangerous it will be.

How Does a HURRICANE Develop?

by Howard E. Smith

In spite of great efforts and millions of dollars spent on research, no one knows exactly how a hurricane gets started. But we do know that during the summer and early autumn months, the constantly flowing warm trade winds, blowing from the northeast in the South Atlantic, become disturbed when cold air masses from the north pass them. The crosswinds often form tropical storms.

If you could see all of such a storm, it would resemble an enormous doughnut up to hundreds of miles wide. Clouds might at times rise 60,000 feet high. The storm would have a small hollow place in its center, which is called the eye of the storm.

Winds of tropical storms move in a typical pattern. Warm, damp air from the sun-heated tropical ocean water rises up inside of the eye several miles high. As it does, it cools; raindrops form and then fall. This newly cooled air rides up over the top and outside surface of the doughnut-shaped storm and falls down its sides. This falling cool air puts pressure on the warm sea air, forcing it back up inside the eye of the storm. This cycle continues, and the storm soon resembles a tremendously large and powerful heat engine, which continually pumps up warm air.

Not all tropical storms keep going. Cool air over land or cool ocean currents can break them up. If, however, a storm continues, it becomes larger. Some grow to be hundreds of miles in diameter. Wind speeds increase. Once winds hit 74 miles per hour or higher, the storm is called a hurricane. In some hurricanes, winds have reached 200 miles per hour. The winds are strongest near the eye. Oddly enough, the air inside the eye is calm, with nothing more than gentle breezes.

Many rain clouds appear in a hurricane. They form arc-shaped concentric bands around the center of the storm. Torrents of rain fall from them. Fierce thunderstorms appear. Hail often falls. Tornadoes or waterspouts, or both, may appear. Waterspouts are actually tornadoes that appear over open water. Tons of water are sucked up into them. Though not as dangerous as tornadoes, waterspouts can sink small ships.

A hurricane not only rotates around the eye, it also moves along a storm path. No one ever knows where a hurricane will go—Bermuda, the Caribbean islands, Mexico, the Atlantic or Gulf coast of the United States.

Many methods are used to track hurricanes. Sensors on satellites circling the earth, hundreds of miles above the oceans, detect cloud formations that could develop into hurricanes. Radar follows the storms. To keep track of them, airplanes fly above them.

Once a dangerous tropical storm is found, the U.S. National Weather Service will broadcast its location. When it heads for a shoreline area, warnings will be issued. If it turns into a hurricane, then hurricane warnings will be issued. Hurricane flags will be flown at Coast Guard stations. This international signal is two square red flags with black squares in the middle, flying one above the other.

To be safe, listen to warnings. These warnings are always broadcast hours, or sometimes even days, before a hurricane strikes. Follow the directions of authorities. Take in lawn furniture, trash cans, and other objects that might blow around and hit or cut people. Also board up or tape windows to keep them from shattering. If you are caught in the high winds, beware of objects flying in the air and seek shelter in a strong building on high land. Stay away from windows. Watch for falling trees. Beware of broken power lines which can electrocute you.

Only the tropical storms of the Atlantic Ocean are called hurricanes. In the Pacific they are called "typhoons," "cyclones," or "willy-willies."

In spite of their terrible power for destruction, hurricanes are not all bad. They bring much-needed rains from the tropics to the temperate zones.

HURRICANES

The Beaufort Scale

Wind is caused by the uneven heating of the earth by the sun. Cold air is heavier and more dense than warm air. Cold, dry air is the heaviest of all. Warm, humid air is least dense, and so it will rise above cold air. When it does, cold air moves in under it. When this happens, a wind blows.

You can tell how fast the wind is blowing by the Beaufort Scale.

On Land	Miles Per Hour
Smoke rises vertically	0–1
Smoke drifts slowly	1–3
Leaves rustle	4–7
Twigs are in motion	8–12
Small branches move	13–18
Small trees sway	19–24
Large branches sway	25–31
Whole trees are in motion	32–38
Twigs break off	39–46
Branches break	47–54
Trees snap or bow down	55–63
Widespread damage	64–72
Extreme damage	73–plus

On the Sea	Miles Per Hour
Sea calm	0–3
Parts of surface wind-ruffled	8
All the surface ruffled	13
A few whitecaps	18
About half of wave tops have whitecaps	23
All wave tops have whitecaps	28
Spray blows off whitecaps	34–48
High waves, breaking at crests	48–56
Wave tops blown away	56 and up

Names of Atlantic Storms

Source: National Weather Service

1997	1998	1999	2000	2001	2002
Ana	Alex	Arlene	Alberto	Allison	Arthur
Bill	Bonnie	Bret	Beryl	Barry	Bertha
Claudette	Charley	Cindy	Chris	Chantal	Cesar
Danny	Danielle	Dennis	Debby	Dean	Dolly
Erika	Earl	Emily	Ernesto	Erin	Edouard
Fabian	Frances	Floyd	Florence	Felix	Fran
Grace	Georges	Gert	Gordon	Gabrielle	Gustav
Henri	Hermine	Harvey	Helene	Humberto	Hortense
Isabel	Ivan	Irene	Isaac	Iris	Isidore
Juan	Jeanne	Jose	Joyce	Jerry	Josephina
Kate	Karl	Katrina	Keith	Kare	
Larry	Lisa	Lenny	Leslie	Luis	
Mindy	Mitch	Maria		Ma	
Nicholas	Nicole	Nate			
Odette	Otto	Ophelia			
Peter	Paul				
Rose					

Responding

1. Look at the Beaufort Scale. Based on this scale, what is the highest wind you have experienced?

2. Research the most recent hurricane to hit the United States. What was its highest on-land wind velocity? What was its highest velocity over water?

Reading Mini-Lesson

Hurricanes

1. **How They Form**
   - **a.** happen during summer and early fall
   - **b.** warm trade winds in South Atlantic disturbed by cold air from north
   - **c.** resulting crosswinds form tropical storms
2. **Appearance**
   - **a.** doughnut shape
   - **b.** _____
   - **c.** _____
3. **Patterns of Movement**
   - **a.** _____
   - **b.** _____
4. **Rain and Storms**
   - **a.** _____
   - **b.** _____
5. _____
6. _____
7. _____
8. _____

Taking Notes and Outlining

Taking notes on what you read involves some thought. It would do you little good to copy everything you read into a notebook. When you take notes, you have to decide what is important to know, and you have to decide how to organize your notes for later use. It's really a complicated process!

To take notes, you might write a summary, make an outline, jot down key words, make a semantic web, draw a sketch or diagram, make a map, build a model, or do something else that helps you organize and remember the information. The form you choose will depend on your reading purpose, the nature of the selection, and the eventual use you have for the notes. In the margin is an example of how you could begin to **outline** the first half of the article "How Does a Hurricane Develop?"

The activities that follow suggest three different methods for taking notes on the information in the same article.

Activity Options

1. Complete the **outline** for "How Does a Hurricane Develop?" Copy the subtopics (with spaces between them) on your own paper. Add more subtopics to outline the rest of the article (you should end up with about eight parts). Then fill in some of the more important details below each subtopic on your outline.

2. To show the relative size of a hurricane, make a **map** of the southeastern United States and Mexico, with the Gulf of Mexico in the center. You can trace this from a book or atlas. Place a hurricane in the middle of the Gulf. Use details from the article to draw the hurricane to scale. Draw arrows to show possible routes the hurricane might take.

3. To show the formation of a hurricane, draw a **diagram** that shows wind patterns and air movements. Use labels and arrows to show temperature and motion. Like many diagrams in a science book, this one shows how elements work together to form a system.

Writing Workshop

Characters Inside and Out

Assignment You've read about characters who struggled with outside forces such as nature and society. Explore how inside forces, such as ideas, emotions, and desires, affect the outcome of these struggles for two characters. See the Writer's Blueprint for details.

WRITER'S BLUEPRINT

Product	Analytical essay
Purpose	To explore the role of inside forces as two characters struggle with outside forces
Audience	Your classmates and teacher
Specs	As the writer of a successful essay, you should:

❑ Begin by introducing the characters, describing their situations, and explaining the outside forces they face.

❑ Go on to identify inside forces that determine how the characters respond to outside forces.

❑ Include specific examples that illustrate each of these inside forces and their effects on the characters' struggles.

❑ Conclude by summarizing how inside forces affect the two characters' abilities to handle outside forces.

❑ Write focused paragraphs that each include a main idea and supporting details.

❑ Follow the rules for grammar, usage, spelling, and mechanics, including clear pronoun reference.

The instructions that follow will help you to write a successful essay.

---

1 PREWRITING

Diagram inside and outside forces from the literature. Choose two characters from the literature who face challenges from outside forces. Then, draw open mind diagrams, silhouettes of a person's head, for each of the characters. Inside, draw things that represent the character's inside forces, such as beliefs, emotions, desires, motivations, or ideas. Outside, draw things that represent outside forces, such as the obstacles or challenges facing each character. Insert words or phrases if necessary.

Do a quickwrite. Beneath each open mind diagram, write for a few minutes about the outside forces that each character faces. Then, explain how the inside forces you have drawn influence the character's response to these outside forces. Here is part of one student's quickwrite.

> One of the outside forces Davy Crockett faced was his own size. He was too big for this world. It was hard for him to get along with other people because of his size. His size also brought about inside forces. It made him kind of boastful about being the biggest, strongest, and best.

STUDENT
MODEL

Write a thesis statement that summarizes the focus of your essay. The thesis statement makes clear what the subject of your essay will be and what you want to say about the subject. You can use this statement as a guide to writing your essay. The frame below will help you write your thesis statement.

> In (first story name) by (first author name) and (second story name) by (second author name), both main characters, (characters' names), struggle with outside forces. (First character name) is (successful/somewhat successful/not successful) in struggling with (outside force) because (inside force and its affect). (Second character name) is (successful/somewhat successful/not successful) in struggling with (outside force) because (inside force and its affect).

Briefly outline your essay. Include specific examples from the literature to support your thesis statement. You might use a plan like the following.

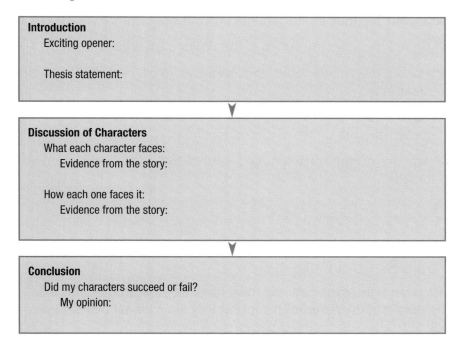

Introduction
   Exciting opener:

   Thesis statement:

Discussion of Characters
   What each character faces:
      Evidence from the story:

   How each one faces it:
      Evidence from the story:

Conclusion
   Did my characters succeed or fail?
      My opinion:

 DRAFTING

Before you write, make sure your assignment is clear in your mind. Remember that you want to develop the main idea of each paragraph with appropriate details. You might want to skip ahead to the Revising Strategy on writing focused paragraphs on page 232.

As you draft, use the following ideas to help you get started.

- Describe one of the characters as you would in a story. Tell about his or her situation and the outside forces involved.

- Explain the outside forces the characters face—the cold, the hurricane, Fugitive Slave Laws—and then introduce the characters in their own situations.

- Start with a quote from the literature about one of the characters. Use the quote as a lead-in to describe the character.

Ask your partner for comments on your draft before you revise it.

✔ Have I followed the specs in the Writer's Blueprint?

✔ Have I described the characters and explained their situations clearly?

✔ Have I used specific examples to explain the inside and outside forces at work on these characters?

✔ Are my paragraphs focused with a main idea and supporting details?

Revising Strategy

Writing Focused Paragraphs

A focused paragraph has one main idea, either stated or implied. The details in the paragraph support that main idea. Follow these points to develop focused paragraphs.

* Determine the main idea of the paragraph.

* List details about this main idea. Develop these details into sentences that support the main idea.

In the Literary Source, notice the details author James Berry uses to support the main idea that the hurricane has transformed the boy's familiar yard. Also, notice how the writer below deleted an unneccessary detail.

LITERARY SOURCE
"He could hardly recognize his yard. The terrorized trees that stood were writhing in turmoil. Their thatched house had collapsed like an open umbrella that was given a heavy blow."
    from "The Banana Tree" by James Berry

STUDENT MODEL

Davy Crockett was huge from the very beginning. He weighed two-hundred pounds at birth. He said he was half-horse and half-alligator. That's a pretty big baby. ~~The forces he faces are nature and society.~~

4 EDITING

Ask a partner to review your revised draft before you edit. When you edit, watch for errors in grammar, usage, spelling, and mechanics. Make sure your pronoun reference is clear.

Editing Strategy

FOR REFERENCE . . .
More rules for pronoun-antecedent agreement are listed under *agreement* in the Language and Grammar Handbook.

Clear Pronoun Reference

When you use pronouns in writing, make sure that the reference to the antecedent is clear.

- Keeping pronouns close to their antecedents will result in clear reference.

  Unclear: Gustus struggled across the bridge *who* was more frightened to face his father than to face the hurricane.
  Clear: Gustus, *who* was more frightened to face his father than to face the hurricane, struggled across the bridge.

- Make sure that your pronouns refer clearly to only one antecedent.

  Unclear: The man in "To Build a Fire" is like Gustus because *he* faces a natural disaster.
  Clear: The man in "To Build a Fire" and Gustus are similar because *they* both face forces of nature.

Notice how the writer below paid attention to clear pronoun reference.

> Davy was planted in Thunder Shower Hill and grew so tall he
> *His pa*
> shadowed his pa's house. ~~He~~ responded to this by uprooting ~~him~~ *Davy* to grow
>
> down to man size.
>
> STUDENT MODEL

STEP 5 PRESENTING

Here are two ideas for presenting your essay.

- Meet in small groups to read your essays aloud. Discuss the insights that different group members have about the role of inside and outside forces in each of the stories. Share your group's conclusions and most interesting ideas with the rest of the class.

- Begin an ongoing class literary magazine that focuses on elements of the short story. This issue will focus on forces that affect characters. Assemble the class essays into a magazine, complete with a title page and table of contents. Make copies and give one to each student in class. In later essays, you may focus on literary elements to use in additional issues of your literary magazine.

STEP 6 LOOKING BACK

Self-evaluate. What grade would you give your paper? Review the items in the Writer's Blueprint. Evaluate yourself on each point, from 6 (superior) to 1 (weak).

Reflect. As you write answers to these questions, think about what you learned from writing your essay.

✔ Review some of your earlier writing. Are your paragraphs more focused now? What are you doing to keep your writing focused?

✔ Can you recall a time in your own life when inside forces affected your ability to deal with outside forces? Write a paragraph about it.

For Your Working Portfolio: Add your essay and reflection responses to your working portfolio.

Beyond Print

Images of You

Part of this unit was about "searching for the real you." Although you probably have been asked to show who you are through writing, have you ever been asked to show yourself through pictures? What pictures would you select?

Activity

Your goal is to tell your story primarily using pictures and images from newspapers and magazines. You might look for pictures that show

- what you like to do: sports, hobbies, music, movies, TV;

- things you own: clothes, computers, stuffed animals;

- what you value: friendship, peace, leisure time, family;

- what you want to do: education, career, lifestyle;

- how you'd like the world to be: environment, technology, health.

Possible Formats

Collage Place all of your pictures on a single piece of posterboard. Consider how to overlap them and in what order to place them on the poster. You may want to cut out words to go with the images.

Montage Group your pictures on posterboard around topics, themes, or ages and stages of your life.

Picture Book Create a book of pictures. This book is organized like a montage, except that you place pictures on pages of colored paper. Make a cover, have chapters, and create picture headings. The book should be arranged either chronologically or thematically.

Materials You'll Need:

✓ magazines and newspapers

✓ family photographs

✓ glue or tape

✓ scissors

✓ posterboard or cardboard

✓ colored paper

Presentation

Display your picture essays for the class. Have a class party during the display session. After you have had a chance to look at all the essays, you will have the opportunity to present your essay to the class. See if your class can figure out why you selected the pictures that you did. Then tell your story using the pictures in your essay.

Projects for Collaborative Study

Theme Connection

Community Challenges Working in a group, find out what local organizations are doing to meet the challenges of life in your community.

■ Interview representatives of your local Red Cross or United Way. Ask: *What are the most important challenges facing people in our community? How are local organizations helping people meet those challenges? What opportunities are there for teenagers to help?*

■ Prepare a brochure on volunteer opportunities for teenagers in your area. Divide the work among members of your group: locating addresses and phone numbers, writing the brochure, designing a cover, and publishing and distributing it.

Literature Connection

Themes in Literature The theme of a piece of literature is its central meaning or message. In "To Build a Fire," for example, a man traveled alone across the Yukon on a bitter cold day, ignoring the advice of an old-timer. When he died, you probably decided a theme of the story was "Don't be too sure of yourself in new situations; listen to the advice of people with more experience."

Work in a small group to create a new story that has the same theme as "To Build a Fire." Change the setting and characters to ones *you* are familiar with: your school or your town, people your age. Make the challenge one *you* know how to deal with. Of course, you must have an "old-timer" who gives good advice that is ignored. Together, write your story, dramatize it, or tell it aloud to the class.

Life Skills Connection

The Ultimate Trade Over the years, you have collected many material items that you enjoy. In this activity, you will explore the value of your possessions.

■ Make a list of the Top Five Things you own. What is important to you about each?

■ What is the most important thing on your list? What makes it so valuable to you?

■ As a class, make a collage or drawing of your group's Most Important Things.
  After you have completed the class activity, discuss the following:

■ For what would you be willing to trade your Most Valuable Thing? What makes this other thing worth the trade for you?

■ What does your trade say about what's important to you in your life?

Multicultural Connection

Cultural Challenges Choose a time in U.S. history when a group faced a major challenge: for example, Native Americans were challenged by white pioneers moving into their territories out West, and African Americans were challenged by **change** in the country after slavery was abolished. What **choices** did members of the group you chose have in meeting the challenge?

Find at least two points of view among members of the group you chose. For example, some Native Americans argued for resisting white invasion into their territory while others argued for cooperation. Stage a debate in which members of your group represent the two points of view.

Read More About Challenges

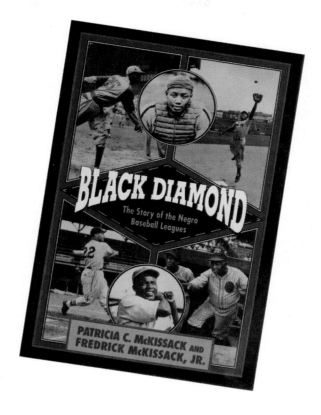

Dragonwings (1975) by Laurence Yep. This novel explores a young Chinese boy's trek to San Francisco, where he meets his father and both try to realize their dream to fly.

Black Diamond: The Story of the Negro Baseball Leagues (1994) by Patricia C. and Fredrick McKissack. Oral histories from surviving players add depth to this inspiring account of the Negro Baseball Leagues.

More Good Books

Better Mousetraps: Product Improvements That Led to Success (1989) by Nathan Aaseng. Did you ever think you could build a better mousetrap? The eight people in this book thought they could and, as a result, became famous for improving existing products.

The True Confessions of Charlotte Doyle (1990) by Avi. This historical novel follows the adventures of a thirteen-year-old who travels from England to America in 1832.

Woodsong (1990) by Gary Paulsen. In this autobiographical work, the author celebrates his love of dog sledding, including his participation in the Iditarod, a grueling race across the Alaskan wilderness.

White Fang (1906) by Jack London. In this fictional classic, a cross-bred dog trained to fight becomes domesticated by a kindly man.

American Women: Their Lives in Their Words (1990) by Doreen Rappaport. Through letters and diaries, women from all walks of life share their roles in the making of American history.

Conflict

Moments of Truth
Part One, pages 242–289

Things Are Not As They Seem
Part Two, pages 290–339

Talking About
CONFLICT

Conflict comes in many shapes and forms. You might have a minor disagreement with a brother or sister over what to watch on TV or a serious dispute with a parent or other adult. We all experience a wide variety of conflicts in our lives. Solving them is a challenge, but one that can be met if we work at it.

"I'm always worried about the way I look."

Jennifer—New York, NY

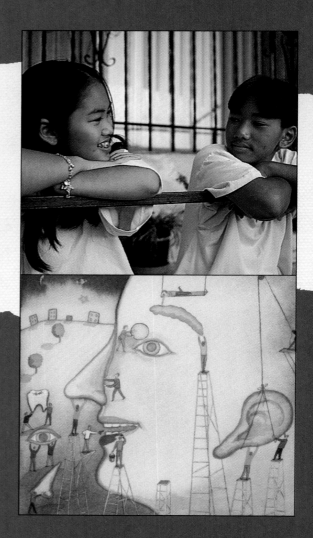

Stop trimming / your nose. . . . Better you should / have a nose / impertinent / as a flower, / sensitive / as a root; . . .

from "Without Commercials" by Alice Walker, page 311

"I like to read about how teenagers solve conflicts with their parents."

Aaron—Chicago, IL

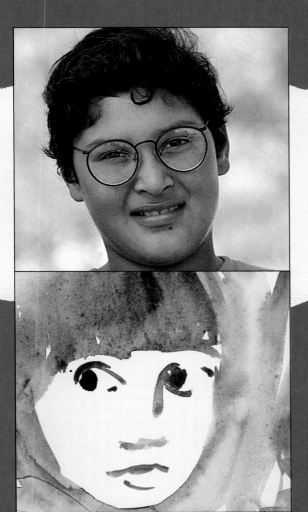

"We need to learn more about conflicts and violence in our cities."

Victor—San Diego, CA

It was about eleven o'clock at night, and she was walking alone, when a boy ran up behind her and tried to snatch her purse.

from "Thank You, Ma'am"
by Langston Hughes, page 254

When my mother began coming home late, I didn't say anything, and tried to keep Mona from saying anything either.

from "The White Umbrella" by Gish Jen, page 245

Moments of Truth

Conflict causes tension, and when things get tense, people do surprising things. Some of these acts can be heroic, some can be shameful, and others, simply unexpected. In many cases, conflict brings about a moment when the truth becomes clear. These moments of truth are like breaths of fresh air—they revitalize and invigorate us, setting us on new and exciting paths.

Multicultural Connection **Groups** create cultural hopes, expectations, and pressures on the individual. These may come from family relationships, ethnic traditions, national customs, religious beliefs, or membership in a certain generation. How do the individuals in these selections react to group pressures?

Literature

Gish Jen	**The White Umbrella** ◆ short story	.244
Langston Hughes	**Thank You, Ma'am** ◆ short story	.254
	Writing Mini-Lesson ◆ Point of View	.260
Edgar Allan Poe	**The Tell-Tale Heart** ◆ short story	.262
James D. Houston	**Elegy Written at the County Junkyard** ◆ essay	.270
Julia Alvarez	**Dusting** ◆ poem	.274
Virginia Hamilton	**He Lion, Bruh Bear, and Bruh Rabbit** ◆ American folk tale	.278

Interdisciplinary Study Reformers

Jacob Riis: Exposing the Truth ◆ photography	.284
Jane Addams by Deborah Gore Ohrn ◆ U.S. history	.286
Reading Mini-Lesson ◆ Varying Your Reading Rate	.289

Before Reading

The White Umbrella

by Gish Jen

Gish Jen
born 1956

The daughter of Chinese immigrants, Gish Jen grew up in a town where hers was the only Asian American family. She says, "Here's the most telling thing I could tell you about myself: My name's not Gish. Actually, it's Lillian, a name I now like but hated every minute of my growing up. I associated it with the type of librarian who wears orange support hose—you know, the kind who blinks more than she talks . . . ." Friends in high school nicknamed her Gish, after the actress Lillian Gish, and she kept the new name as her own. Jen currently lives in Massachusetts. She has won several prizes for her writing.

Building Background

In the Minority Most of us have had experiences of being in the minority. Perhaps you were the only girl on a boys' softball team, or the only young person in a room full of adults, or the only representative of your ethnic group at a school event. People who find themselves in the minority tend to respond in similar ways. They may feel self-conscious, as if others are watching them. They may feel they have to do better than others, because they are representing their group. They may try to conform. It can be hard to relax and just be yourself. As you read, look for ways the characters in this story react to being in the minority.

Getting into the Story

Writer's Notebook Think about a time when you really wanted something that your family could not give you. In your notebook, complete the sentences below, or, if you find that the incomplete sentences don't really capture your experience of wanting something, then write a paragraph of your own.

> I was _____ years old when I wanted this _____.
> I really wanted it because _____ and I thought it would _____.
> Wanting something so badly is like _____.
> While we're on the subject, I'd like to add that _____.

Reading Tip

Point of View Until recently, it was expected that middle-class and upper-class mothers would stay home and raise the family while fathers went off to work. Women who worked were often looked upon with curiosity or even scorn. However, times have changed, and today 75 percent of married mothers of school-age children are employed. In the story you are about to read, which takes place several years ago, the children are embarrassed by the fact that their mother works. As you read, try to understand their point of view as well as the points of view of the other characters in the story.

The White Umbrella

Gish Jen

◄ *Portrait 3,* by Diana Ong, is of a young Chinese American girl. How would you describe this water-color?

When I was twelve, my mother went to work without telling me or my little sister.

"Not that we need the second income." The lilt[1] of her accent drifted from the kitchen up to the top of the stairs, where Mona and I were listening.

"No," said my father, in a barely audible[2] voice. "Not like the Lee family."

The Lees were the only other Chinese family in town. I remembered how sorry my parents had felt for Mrs. Lee when she started waitressing downtown the year before; and so when my mother began coming home late, I didn't say anything, and tried to keep Mona from saying anything either.

"But why shouldn't I?" she argued. "Lots of people's mothers work."

"'Those are American people," I said.

"So what do you think we are? I can do the Pledge of Allegiance with my eyes closed."

Nevertheless, she tried to be discreet;[3] and if my mother wasn't home by 5:30, we would start cooking by ourselves, to make sure dinner would be on time. Mona would wash the vegetables and put on the rice; I would chop.

For weeks we wondered what kind of work she was doing. I imagined that she was selling perfume, testing dessert recipes for the local newspaper. Or maybe she was working for the florist. Now that she had learned to drive, she might be delivering boxes of roses to people.

"I don't think so," said Mona as we walked to our piano lesson after school. "She would've hit something by now."

A gust of wind littered the street with leaves.

"Maybe we better hurry up," she went on, looking at the sky. "It's going to pour."

"But we're too early." Her lesson didn't begin until 4:00, mine until 4:30, so we usually tried to walk as slowly as we could. "And anyway, those aren't the kind of clouds that rain. Those are cumulus clouds."

We arrived out of breath and wet.

"Oh, you poor, poor dears," said old Miss Crosman. "Why don't you call me the next time it's like this out? If your mother won't drive you, I can come pick you up."

"No, that's okay," I answered. Mona wrung her hair out on Miss Crosman's rug. "We just couldn't get the roof of our car to close, is all. We took it to the beach last summer and got sand in the mechanism." I pronounced this last word carefully, as if the credibility of my lie depended on its middle syllable. "It's never been the same." I thought for a second. "It's a convertible."

"Well then make yourselves at home." She exchanged looks with Eugenie Roberts, whose lesson we were interrupting. Eugenie smiled good-naturedly. "The towels are in the closet across from the bathroom."

Huddling at the end of Miss Crosman's nine-foot leatherette couch Mona and I watched Eugenie play. She was a grade ahead of me and, according to school rumor, had a boyfriend in high school. I believed it. Aside from her ballooning breasts—which threatened to collide with the keyboard as she played—she had auburn hair, blue eyes, and, I noted with a particular pang, a pure white, folding umbrella.

"I can't see," whispered Mona.

"So clean your glasses."

"My glasses *are* clean. You're in the way."

I looked at her. "They look dirty to me."

"That's because *your* glasses are dirty."

Eugenie came bouncing to the end of her piece.

"Oh! Just stupendous!" Miss Crosman hugged her, then looked up as Eugenie's mother walked in. "Stupendous!" she said again. "Oh! Mrs. Roberts! Your daughter has a gift, a real gift. It's an honor to teach her."

---

1. **lilt** (lilt), *n.,* a light, graceful rhythm.
2. **audible** (ô′də bəl), *adj.,* loud enough to be heard.
3. **discreet** (dis krēt′), *adj.,* very careful and sensible in speech and action.

Mrs. Roberts, radiant[4] with pride, swept her daughter out of the room as if she were royalty, born to the piano bench. Watching the way Eugenie carried herself, I sat up, and concentrated so hard on sucking in my stomach that I did not realize until the Robertses were gone that Eugenie had left her umbrella. As Mona began to play, I jumped up and ran to the window, meaning to call to them—only to see their brake lights flash then fade at the stop sign at the corner. As if to allow them passage, the rain had let up; a quivering[5] sun lit their way.

The umbrella glowed like a scepter[6] on the blue carpet while Mona, slumping over the keyboard, managed to eke out a fair rendition[7] of a catfight. At the end of the piece, Miss Crosman asked her to stand up.

"Stay right there," she said, then came back a minute later with a towel to cover the bench. "You must be cold," she continued. "Shall I call your mother and have her bring over some dry clothes?"

"No," answered Mona. "She won't come because she . . ."

"She's too busy," I broke in from the back of the room.

"I see." Miss Crosman sighed and shook her head a little.

"Your glasses are filthy, honey," she said to Mona. "Shall I clean them for you?"

Sisterly embarrassment seized me. Why hadn't Mona wiped her lenses when I told her to? As she resumed abuse of the piano, I stared at the umbrella. I wanted to open it, twirl it around by its slender silver handle; I wanted to dangle it from my wrist on the way to school the way the other girls did. I wondered what Miss Crosman would say if I offered to bring it to Eugenie at school tomorrow. She would be impressed with my consideration for others; Eugenie would be pleased to have it back; and I would have possession of the umbrella for an entire night. I looked at it

again, toying with the idea of asking for one for Christmas. I knew, however, how my mother would react.

"Things," she would say. "What's the matter with a raincoat? All you want is things, just like an American."

Sitting down for my lesson, I was careful to keep the towel under me and sit up straight.

"I'll bet you can't see a thing either," said Miss Crosman, reaching for my glasses. "And you can relax, you poor dear." She touched my chest, in an area where she never would have touched Eugenie Roberts. "This isn't a boot camp."

When Miss Crosman finally allowed me to start playing I played extra well, as well as I possibly could. See, I told her with my fingers. You don't have to feel sorry for me.

"That was wonderful," said Miss Crosman. "Oh! Just wonderful."

An entire constellation rose in my heart.

"And guess what," I announced proudly. "I have a surprise for you."

Then I played a second piece for her, a much more difficult one that she had not assigned.

"Oh! That was stupendous," she said without hugging me. "Stupendous! You are a genius, young lady. If your mother had started you younger, you'd be playing like Eugenie Roberts by now!"

I looked at the keyboard, wishing that I had still a third, even more difficult piece to play for her. I wanted to tell her that I was the school spelling bee champion, that I wasn't ticklish, that I could do karate.

"My mother is a concert pianist," I said.

She looked at me for a long moment, then

---

4. **radiant** (rā′dē ənt), *adj.*, shining; beaming.
5. **quivering** (kwiv′ər ing), *adj.*, trembling, shaking.
6. **scepter** (sep′tər), *n.*, the rod carried by a ruler as a symbol of royal power.
7. **rendition** (ren dish′ən), *n.*, the performance or interpretation of a piece of music.

finally, without saying anything, hugged me. I didn't say anything about bringing the umbrella to Eugenie at school.

The steps were dry when Mona and I sat down to wait for my mother.

The umbrella glowed like a scepter on the blue carpet...

"Do you want to wait inside?'" Miss Crosman looked anxiously at the sky.

"No," I said. "Our mother will be here any minute."

"In a while," said Mona.

"Any minute," I said again, even though my mother had been at least twenty minutes late every week since she started working.

According to the church clock across the street we had been waiting twenty-five minutes when Miss Crosman came out again.

"Shall I give you ladies a ride home?"

"No," I said. "Our mother is coming any minute."

"Shall I at least give her a call and remind her you're here? Maybe she forgot about you."

"I don't think she *forgot*," said Mona.

"Shall I give her a call anyway? Just to be safe?"

"I bet she already left," I said. "How could she forget about us?"

Miss Crosman went in to call.

"There's no answer," she said, coming back out.

"See, she's on her way," I said.

"Are you sure you wouldn't like to come in?"

"No," said Mona.

"Yes," I said. I pointed at my sister. "She meant yes, too. She meant no, she wouldn't like to go in."

Miss Crosman looked at her watch. "It's 5:30 now, ladies. My pot roast will be coming

out in fifteen minutes. Maybe you'd like to come in and have some then?"

"My mother's almost here," I said. "She's on her way."

We watched and watched the street. I tried to imagine what my mother was doing; I tried to imagine her writing messages in the sky, even though I knew she was afraid of planes. I watched as the branches of Miss Crosman's big willow tree started to sway; they had all been trimmed to exactly the same height off the ground, so that they looked beautiful, like hair in the wind.

It started to rain.

"Miss Crosman is coming out again," said Mona.

"Don't let her talk you into going inside," I whispered.

"Why not?"

"Because that would mean Mom isn't really coming any minute."

"But she isn't," said Mona. "She's *working*."

"Shhh! Miss Crosman is going to hear you."

"She's working! She's working! She's working!"

I put my hand over her mouth, but she licked it, and so I was wiping my hand on my wet dress when the front door opened.

"We're getting even *wetter*," said Mona right away. "Wetter and wetter."

"Shall we all go in?" Miss Crosman pulled Mona to her feet. "Before you young ladies catch pneumonia? You've been out here an hour already."

"We're *freezing*." Mona looked up at Miss Crosman. "Do you have any hot chocolate? We're going to catch *pneumonia*."

"I'm not going in," I said. "My mother's coming any minute."

"Come on," said Mona. "Use your *noggin*."

"Any minute."

"Come on, Mona," Miss Crosman opened the door. "Shall we get you inside first?"

"See you in the hospital," said Mona as she went in. "See you in the hospital with *pneumonia.*"

I stared out into the empty street. The rain was pricking me all over; I was cold; I wanted to go inside. I wanted to be able to let myself go inside. If Miss Crosman came out again, I decided, I would go in.

She came out with a blanket and the white umbrella.

I could not believe that I was actually holding the umbrella, opening it. It sprang up by itself as if it were alive, as if that were what it wanted to do—as if it belonged in my hands, above my head. I stared up at the network of silver spokes, then spun the umbrella around and around and around. It was so clean and white that it seemed to glow, to illuminate everything around it.

"It's beautiful," I said.

Miss Crosman sat down next to me, on one end of the blanket. I moved the umbrella over so that it covered that too. I could feel the rain on my left shoulder and shivered. She put her arm around me.

"You poor, poor dear."

I knew that I was in store for another bolt of sympathy, and braced myself by staring up into the umbrella.

"You know, I very much wanted to have children when I was younger," she continued.

"You did?"

She stared at me a minute. Her face looked dry and crusty, like day-old frosting.

"I did. But then I never got married."

I twirled the umbrella around again.

"This is the most beautiful umbrella I have ever seen," I said. "Ever, in my whole life."

"Do you have an umbrella?"

"No. But my mother's going to get me one just like this for Christmas."

"Is she? I tell you what. You don't have to wait until Christmas. You can have this one."

"But this one belongs to Eugenie Roberts,"

I protested. "I have to give it back to her tomorrow in school."

"Who told you it belongs to Eugenie? It's not Eugenie's. It's mine. And now I'm giving it to you, so it's yours."

"It is?"

She hugged me tighter. "That's right. It's all yours."

"It's mine?" I didn't know what to say. "Mine?" Suddenly I was jumping up and down in the rain. "It's beautiful! Oh! It's beautiful!" I laughed.

Miss Crosman laughed, too, even though she was getting all wet.

"Thank you, Miss Crosman. Thank you very much. Thanks a zillion. It's beautiful. It's *stupendous!*"

"You're quite welcome," she said.

"Thank you," I said again, but that didn't seem like enough. Suddenly I knew just what she wanted to hear. "I wish you were my mother."

Right away I felt bad.

"You shouldn't say that," she said, but her face was opening into a huge smile as the lights of my mother's car cautiously turned the corner. I quickly collapsed the umbrella and put it up my skirt, holding onto it from the outside, through the material.

"Mona!" I shouted into the house. "Mona! Hurry up! Mom's here! I told you she was coming!"

Then I ran away from Miss Crosman, down to the curb. Mona came tearing up to my side as my mother neared the house. We both backed up a few feet, so that in case she went onto the curb, she wouldn't run us over.

"But why didn't you go inside with Mona!" my mother asked on the way home. She had taken off her own coat to put over me and had the heat on high.

"She wasn't using her noggin," said Mona, next to me in the back seat.

"I should call next time," said my mother. "I just don't like to say where I am."

◄ *The Piano Lesson* by Diana Ong. What words and phrases from the story could you use to describe this painting?

That was when she finally told us that she was working as a check-out clerk in the A&P. She was supposed to be on the day shift, but the other employees were unreliable,[8] and her boss had promised her a promotion if she would stay until the evening shift filled in.

For a moment no one said anything. Even Mona seemed to find the revelation[9] disappointing.

"A promotion already!" she said, finally.

I listened to the windshield wipers.

"You're so quiet." My mother looked at me in the rear-view mirror. "What's the matter?"

"I wish you would quit," I said after a moment.

She sighed. "The Chinese have a saying: one beam cannot hold the roof up."

"But Eugenie Roberts's father supports their family."

She sighed once more. "Eugenie Roberts's father is Eugenie Roberts's father," she said.

---

8. **unreliable** (un′ri lī′ə bəl), *adj.*, not to be depended on.

9. **revelation** (rev′ə lā′shən), *n.*, the act of making known.

The White Umbrella   **249**

As we entered the downtown area, Mona started leaning hard against me every time the car turned right, trying to push me over. Remembering what I had said to Miss Crosman, I tried to maneuver[10] the umbrella under my leg so she wouldn't feel it.

"What's under your skirt?" Mona wanted to know as we came to a traffic light. My mother, watching us in the rear-view mirror again, rolled slowly to a stop.

"What's the matter?" she asked.

"There's something under her skirt," said Mona, pulling at me. "Under her skirt."

Meanwhile, a man crossing the street started to yell at us. "Who do you think you are, lady?" he said. "You're blocking the whole damn crosswalk."

We all froze. Other people walking by stopped to watch.

"Didn't you hear me?" he went on, starting to thump on the hood with his fist. "Don't you speak English?"

My mother began to back up, but the car behind us honked. Luckily, the light turned green right after that. She sighed in relief.

"What were you saying, Mona?" she asked.

We wouldn't have hit the car behind us that hard if he hadn't been moving, too, but as it was our car bucked violently, throwing us all first back and then forward.

"Uh oh," said Mona when we stopped. "*Another* accident."

I was relieved to have attention diverted from the umbrella. Then I noticed my mother's head, tilted back onto the seat. Her eyes were closed.

"Mom!" I screamed. "Mom! Wake up!"

She opened her eyes. "Please don't yell," she said. "Enough people are going to yell already."

"I thought you were dead," I said, starting to cry. "I thought you were dead."

She turned around, looked at me intently, then put her hand to my forehead.

"Sick," she confirmed. "Some kind of sick is giving you crazy ideas."

As the man from the car behind us started tapping on the window, I moved the umbrella away from my leg. Then Mona and my mother were getting out of the car. I got out after them; and while everyone else was inspecting the damage we'd done, I threw the umbrella down a sewer.

---

10. **maneuver** (mə nü′vər), *v.*, to move with great skill.

After Reading

Making Connections

1. What is your opinion of the narrator?
2. 👣 What problems is this family having adjusting to American life?
3. In your opinion, what is the importance of the umbrella?
4. Why do you think the narrator throws the umbrella down the sewer?
5. When did the narrator experience a **moment of truth?**
6. Does the weather play a role in this story? Why or why not?
7. How would this story have been different if it were told from the **point of view** of the mother?
8. 👣 How did the characters in this story react to being in a minority **group?**

Literary Focus: Symbolism

The American flag symbolizes freedom to many people. A white dove universally means peace. The white umbrella can also be considered a **symbol,** which is an object that has meaning in itself but suggests other meanings as well. What does the white umbrella mean to the narrator? To help answer this question, find all the references to the umbrella and explain what the narrator's choice of words or her reactions reveal about what the umbrella symbolizes. Use a chart like the one below.

Description	What This Says About the Umbrella
a pure, white folding umbrella	The word "pure" suggests perfection. White is a symbol of . . .
The umbrella glowed like a scepter.	"Glowed" suggests that . . . The word "scepter" suggests . . .

Vocabulary Study

On a sheet of paper, write the word from the list that best completes each **analogy.**

lilt
audible
discreet
radiant
quivering
scepter
rendition
unreliable
revelation
maneuver

1. *Silent* is to *soundless* as _____ is to *sound.*
2. _____ is to *voice* as *rhythm* is to *music.*
3. _____ is to *royalty* as *wand* is to *magician.*
4. *Dependable* is to *steady* as _____ is to *changeable.*
5. *Careful* is to _____ as *careless* is to *unthinking.*
6. _____ is to *gelatin* as *rippling* is to *water.*
7. *Version* is to *story* as _____ is to *music.*
8. An *object* is to *daylight* as *truth* is to _____.
9. _____ is to *skillful* as *fumble* is to *clumsy.*
10. *Beaming* is to _____ as *gloomy* is to *depressing.*

Expressing Your Ideas

Writing Choices

Well, Thanks! Even though you have thrown away the umbrella, you still should thank Miss Crosman for her gift. Write a **thank-you letter** to Miss Crosman.

Confucius Says Confucius (551–479 B.C.) was a Chinese philosopher and moral teacher. Today Confucianism is the main philosophy of China. Confucius was concerned with good conduct and the attainment of wisdom. One of his most famous ideas is that children must both honor and obey their parents. Find out more about Confucius and his ideas and write a **report** on your findings.

Other Options

What's the Symbol? The white umbrella seems to symbolize something about Eugenie to the narrator. Choose an object that you think symbolizes the narrator. **Draw or paint** the object and explain why it is a good symbol for the narrator.

Helpful Hints In small groups, create a **guidebook** for students in families where both parents work. Interview friends and family members for ideas.

Actions Speak Louder Than Words Create a **scene** in which the narrator discusses the guilt she felt at accepting the umbrella and then throwing it away with someone— maybe a friend or a school psychologist. Have the other person react and offer the narrator some advice.

Before Reading

Thank You, Ma'am

by Langston Hughes

Langston Hughes
1902–1967

Langston Hughes lived, at various times, in the U.S., Mexico, France, Italy, Spain, and the former Soviet Union. During the Harlem Renaissance of the 1920s, Hughes became the first known African American to earn a living solely from his writing and by giving speeches. Critics rejected his first book of poems; one newspaper headline screamed "LANGSTON HUGHES'S BOOK OF POEMS TRASH." Another scolded "LANGSTON HUGHES—THE SEWER DWELLER." One objection focused on the fact that he wrote about common people who weren't heroes or angels. He said, in response, "I personally knew very few good people who were wholly beautiful and wholly good. . . . I only knew the people I had grown up with . . . but they seemed to me good people, too."

Building Background

Juvenile Crime Major crimes committed by people under eighteen are increasing, statistics show. In 1965, for example, 21.3 percent of all arrests were from this age group. In the pie chart below are 1992 arrest statistics for all age groups. How did the under-eighteen age group do in that year? Why do you think that more than one-fourth of all arrests were in this age group? In your opinion, what is it about being young that makes people more likely than other groups to commit a crime?

Getting into the Story

Discussion We need to be trusted. But what really is trust? As a class, first brainstorm what trust is, then describe why people need to feel trusted. What happens to a person such as a criminal, whom no one trusts? What can make a person appear untrustworthy? Can trust be regained once it is lost?

U.S. Arrests for Serious Crimes (by age, 1992)

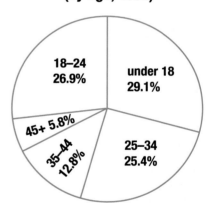

Reading Tip

Predictions Read the first paragraph of the story that follows. Then, in your notebook, jot down what you think will happen in this story. As you read, try to picture the "large woman with a large purse" and the boy who, even though he has just committed a crime, is still so polite that he can't stop saying "yes'm" (yes ma'am) and "no'm" (no ma'am). Try to imagine what each of these people might do or say next.

Thank You, Ma'am

LANGSTON HUGHES

She was a large woman with a large purse that had everything in it but a hammer and nails. It had a long strap, and she carried it slung across her shoulder. It was about eleven o'clock at night, and she was walking alone, when a boy ran up behind her and tried to snatch her purse. The strap broke with the tug the boy gave it from behind. But the boy's weight and the weight of the purse caused him to lose balance. Instead of taking off full blast, the boy fell on his back on the sidewalk, and his legs flew up. The large woman simply turned around and kicked him right square in his blue-jeaned sitter. She shook him until his teeth rattled. Then she reached down and picked the boy up by his shirt.

After that the woman said, "Pick up my pocketbook, boy, and give it here."

She still held him tightly. But she bent down enough to let him pick up her purse. Then she said, "Now ain't you ashamed of yourself?"

Firmly gripped by his shirt front, the boy said, "Yes'm."

The woman said, "What did you want to do it for?"

The boy said, "I didn't aim to."

She said, "You lie!"

By that time two or three people passed, turned to look, and some stood watching.

"If I turn you loose, will you run?" asked the woman.

"Yes'm," said the boy.

"Then I won't turn you loose," said the woman. She did not release him.

"Lady, I'm sorry," whispered the boy.

"Um-hum! Your face is dirty. I got a great mind to wash your face for you. Ain't you got nobody home to tell you to wash your face?"

"No'm," said the boy.

"Then it will get washed this evening," said the large woman, starting up the street, dragging the frightened boy behind her.

He looked as if he were fourteen or

▲ *My Brother* was painted by John Wilson in 1942. This contemplative portrait is a prime example of a picture being worth a thousand words. What are some of the words that come to mind as you study this painting? Would some of these words apply to Roger?

fifteen, thin and wild, in tennis shoes and blue jeans.

The woman said, "You ought to be my son. I would teach you right from wrong. Least I can do right now is to wash your face. Are you hungry?"

"No'm," said the boy. "I just want you to turn me loose."

"Was I bothering you when I turned that corner?" asked the woman.

"No'm."

"But you put yourself in contact with *me*," said the woman. "If you think that contact is not going to last a while, you got another thought coming. When I get through with you, sir, you are going to remember Mrs. Luella Bates Washington Jones."

weat popped out on the boy's face, and he began to struggle. Mrs. Jones stopped, jerked him around in front of her, put a half nelson[1] about his neck, and continued to drag him up the street. When she got to her door, she dragged the boy inside, down a hall, and into a large room at the rear of the house. She switched on the light and left the door open. The boy could hear other roomers laughing and talking. Some of their doors were open, too; so he knew he and the woman were not alone. The woman still had him by the neck in the middle of her room.

She said, "What is your name?"

"Roger," answered the boy.

"Then, Roger, you go to that sink and wash your face," said the woman. She turned him loose—at last. Roger looked at the door—and went to the sink.

"Let the water run until it gets warm," she said. "Here's a clean towel."

"You gonna take me to jail?" asked the boy, bending over the sink.

"Not with that face. I would not take you nowhere," said the woman. "Here I am trying to get home to cook me a bite to eat, and you snatch my pocketbook! Maybe you ain't been to your supper, either, late as it be. Have you?"

"There's nobody home at my house," said the boy.

The door was open. He would make a dash for it down the hall.

"Then we'll eat," said the woman. "I believe you're hungry—or been hungry—to try to snatch my pocketbook!"

"I want a pair of suede shoes," said the boy.

"Well, you didn't have to snatch *my* pocketbook to get some suede shoes," said Mrs. Luella Bates Washington Jones. "You could of asked me."

"Ma'am?"

The water dripping from his face, the boy looked at her. There was a long pause. A very long pause. After drying his face and not knowing what else to do, the boy dried it again. Then he turned around. The door was open. He would make a dash for it down the hall. He would run, run, run, *run!*

The woman was sitting on the day bed. After a while she said, "I were young once and I wanted things I could not get."

There was another long pause. The boy's mouth opened. Then he frowned, not knowing he frowned.

The woman said, "Um-hum! You thought I was going to say, *but I didn't snatch people's pocketbooks*. Well, I wasn't going to say that." Pause. Silence. "I have done things, too, which I would not tell you, son—neither tell God, if He didn't already know. Everybody's got something in common. Sit you down while I

---

1. **half nelson,** in wrestling, a hold in which one arm is hooked around the opponent's arm from behind and the hand is pressed against the back of the opponent's neck.

fix us something to eat. You might run that comb through your hair so you will look presentable."

In another corner of the room behind a screen was a gas plate and an icebox. Mrs. Jones got up and went behind the screen. The woman did not watch the boy to see if he was going to run now. She didn't watch her purse, which she left behind her on the day bed. But the boy took care to sit on the far side of the room, away from the purse. He thought she could easily see him out of the corner of her eye if she wanted to. He did not trust the woman *not* to trust him. And he did not want to be mistrusted now.

"Do you need somebody to go to the store," asked the boy, "to get some milk or something?"

"Don't believe I do," said the woman, "unless you want sweet milk yourself. I was going to make cocoa out of this canned milk I got here."

"That will be fine," said the boy.

She heated some lima beans and ham, made the cocoa, and set the table. The woman did not ask the boy anything about where he lived, or his folks, or anything else that would embarrass him. Instead, as they ate, she told him about her job in a hotel beauty shop, what the work was like, and how all kinds of women came in and out. Then she cut him half of her ten-cent cake.

"Eat some more, son," she said.

When they finished eating, she got up and said, "Now here, take this ten dollars and buy yourself some suede shoes. And, next time, do not make the mistake of latching onto my pocketbook nor nobody *else's*—because shoes got by devilish ways will burn your feet. I got to get my rest now. But from here on in, son, I hope you will behave yourself."

She led him down the hall to the front door and opened it. "Good night! Behave yourself, boy!" she said as he went down the steps.

The boy wanted to say something more than "Thank you, ma'am," to Mrs. Luella Bates Washington Jones. Although his lips moved, he couldn't even say that as he turned at the foot of the stairs and looked up at the large woman in the door. Then she shut the door.

After Reading

Making Connections

1. Were you surprised by anything that happened in this story? What happened that you would not have predicted from reading the first paragraph?

2. What are some words you would use to describe Mrs. Luella Bates Washington Jones?

3. 👣 Do you think Roger's membership in a **group,** specifically his possible relationship with his peers, might have had anything to do with his decision to steal Mrs. Jones's purse? Why?

4. What actors would you choose to play these two characters? Explain your answer.

5. In your view, what is the **motivation** behind, or reason for, Mrs. Jones's actions?

6. Do you think Roger experiences a **moment of truth** in the story? If so, what is it?

7. Explain your interpretation of the **title** of the story. What are some other possible titles?

8. What would happen if the purse snatching occurred today? How would the characters react? What would be the same? What would be different?

Literary Focus: Theme

A **theme** is the main idea or underlying meaning of a literary work. Theme differs from the subject of a literary work in that it involves a statement or opinion about the subject. For example, in the story "The White Umbrella," which comes just before "Thank You, Ma'am" in this book, the subject is "mother gets a job." The theme is a statement about the subject. It might be "changes in families can be hard to accept." In a chart similar to the one below, write what you consider to be the subject and the theme of the story "Thank You, Ma'am." Then, in a few short sentences, explain how the theme is different from the subject.

Subject:

Theme:

Differences:

Expressing Your Ideas

Writing Choices

Digging Up the Past What could be some of the things that Mrs. Luella Bates Washington Jones has done that she won't talk about? Use your imagination to write a brief **biography** of her with key details that explain how she became who she is now.

What's Your Interpretation? *The Moment I Saw the Man with a Rifle* was painted by A. Robert Birmelin in 1985. Write a short **critique** of the painting, telling how it does or does not fit the mood of the story.

Where's Roger? Place Roger in the painting above. Maybe he's one of the people whose hands we see, or perhaps he's just around the corner, out of sight. Use your imagination to write a short **narrative** in Roger's words and voice that explains what he's doing on this street.

Other Options

Reaching Out There are many organizations that match older people with younger people. One organization is Big Brothers–Big Sisters. Another is Everybody Wins, a group that arranges for adults to go into schools to read to children. Your local library or Yellow Pages will have listings of other such organizations. Find one and ask if you can **interview** someone about what that person does and how that person's work affects others. Report your findings to the class.

Everything But the Kitchen Sink Find a purse and fill it with "everything but a hammer and nails." Make sure each item is something that you think Mrs. Jones would use. Give the class a **demonstration** of the items in the purse and explain their significance.

Safety First Do an **oral report** on street safety—how to carry your purse or wallet, how to walk, what to do if you suspect someone is following you. Get information from the police or a public safety organization.

Writing Mini-Lesson

Point of View: First Person As a Story Character

Recognize first-person point of view. In "The White Umbrella," Gish Jen uses the first-person, or "I," point of view. In this point of view, the narrator is a character in the story. Look at the passage below that is written from the first-person and third-person points of view. What is the effect of each?

First Person: I hurried over to the window. My hand trembled as I pulled the curtain aside and looked down to the street. A taxi pulled up across the street. My stomach lurched as I watched a figure climb out of the cab and walk toward my building. He was back.

Third Person: He walked over to the window. He pulled the curtain aside and looked down to the street. He frowned as he saw a taxi pull up. A figure climbed out and walked toward his building.

Writing Strategy Writers use first-person point of view to pull a reader into the story and make the events seem as if they are happening right then. When something is written in the first person, the reader knows only what the narrator knows.

Activity Options

1. Write a short description using third-person point of view of what is happening in the classroom right now. Then get together with a partner and exchange descriptions. Rewrite each other's descriptions using first-person point of view. How does this change what you've written?

2. Locate a collection of short stories by Edgar Allen Poe. Work with a group to select stories that are written in first person. Ask each group member to read a specific story. Then discuss how the first-person point of view helps to make the story more chilling than if it had been written in third person.

3. Choose two cartoons from the newspaper, one written in first-person point of view and one written in the third-person point of view. Rewrite the text of each cartoon, changing the point of view. Share your rewrites. What is the effect of changing the point of view?

The Tell-Tale Heart

by Edgar Allan Poe

Edgar Allan Poe
1809–1849

Poe was orphaned at an early age and taken in by the John Allan family of Richmond, Virginia. He published his first book of poetry in 1827, and soon opted for a writing career. In 1841, with the publication of "Murders in the Rue Morgue," Poe created the first recognized detective story. He wrote a number of similar short stories in the next few years and published a collection in 1845. In the late 1840s Poe was in poor health from alcohol and drug abuse, and he died in Baltimore in 1849. Poe's personal life tarnished his reputation, but his obvious literary talents continue to attract new readers, and his writings have stayed in print for nearly one hundred years.

Building Background

Sheer Madness During the 1800s, when Poe wrote this story featuring an insane narrator, madness was considered to be a problem of the body, not of the mind. Because madness was considered a physical problem, it was treated with physical "therapy" such as being beaten or chained. There were many useless machines that were said to "cure" a person's madness. One was a rotary swing that was said to bring a person back into balance. Another was a chair called the "Tranquilizer." Basically, one was strapped to a chair and a box was placed over his or her head so that cold water or ice could be applied. According to the inventor, the device seemed to work. "Its effects have been truly delightful to me," he exclaimed.

Getting into the Story

Discussion What does it mean when someone says to you, "She's insane"? How does the person act? Compare your image of an insane person with the ideas of your classmates. You'll probably find a variety of behaviors described. Are there any common threads?

Reading Tip

Context Poe wrote a long time ago. Consequently, some of the vocabulary he uses to describe the insanity of this story may seem difficult and old-fashioned. Many words, however, can be figured out through **context,** that is, by where they appear in the sentence and by the words around them. As you read, keep a list of any unknown words. If possible, try to guess their meanings from their context. When you have finished reading, check the words in a dictionary to see how close you came to the correct definition.

THE TELL-TALE HEART

Edgar Allan Poe

True!—nervous—very, very dreadfully nervous I had been and am; but why *will* you say that I am mad? The disease had sharpened my senses—not destroyed—not dulled them. Above all was the sense of hearing acute.[1] I heard all things in the heavens and in the earth. I heard many things in hell. How, then, am I mad? Hearken! and observe how healthily—how calmly I can tell you the whole story.

It is impossible to say how first the idea entered my brain; but once conceived, it haunted me day and night. Object there was none. Passion there was none. I loved the old man. He had never wronged me. He had never given me insult. For his gold I had no desire. I think it was his eye! Yes, it was this! One of his eyes resembled that of a vulture—a pale blue eye, with a film over it. Whenever it fell upon me, my blood ran cold; and so by degrees—very gradually—I made up my mind to take the life of the old man, and thus rid myself of the eye forever.

Now this is the point. You fancy me mad. Madmen know nothing. But you should have seen *me*. You should have seen how wisely I proceeded—with what caution—

---

1. acute (ə kyüt′), *adj.*, sharp, keen.

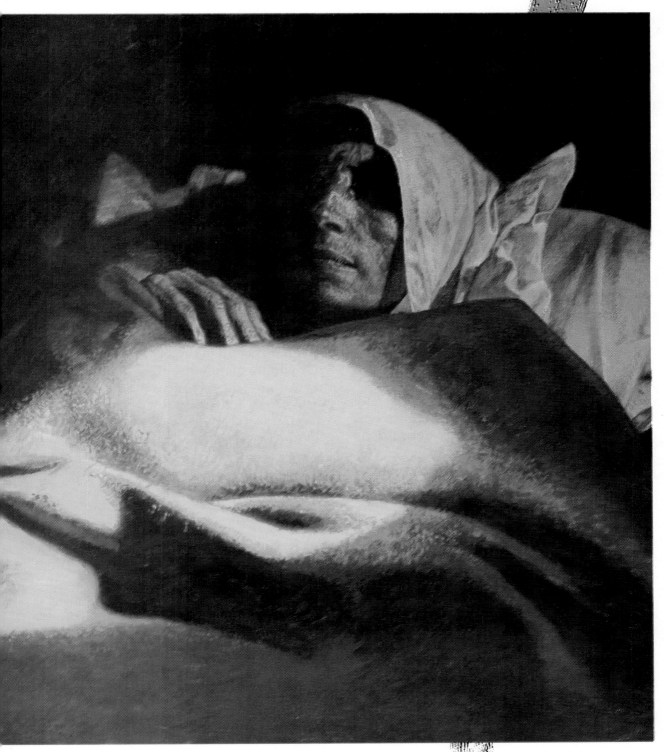

▲ The narrator of the story grew "furious" as he gazed upon the "vulture eye." It
"chilled the very marrow" in his bones. What emotions or feelings does this
illustration by John Thompson evoke?

with what foresight—with what dissimulation I went to work! I was never kinder to the old man than during the whole week before I killed him. And every night, about midnight, I turned the latch of his door and opened it— oh, so gently! And then, when I had made an opening sufficient for my head, I put in a dark lantern,[2] all closed, closed, so that no light shone out, and then I thrust in my head. Oh, you would have laughed to see how cunningly I thrust it in! I moved it slowly—very, very slowly, so that I might not disturb the old man's sleep. It took me an hour to place my whole head within the opening so far that I could see him as he lay upon his bed. Ha!— would a madman have been so wise as this? And then, when my head was well in the room, I undid the lantern cautiously—oh, so cautiously—cautiously (for the hinges creaked)— I undid it just so much that a single thin ray fell upon the vulture eye. And this I did for seven long nights—every night just at midnight—but I found the eye always closed; and so it was impossible to do the work; for it was not the old man who vexed me, but his Evil Eye. And every morning, when the day broke, I went boldly into the chamber, and spoke courageously to him, calling him by name in a hearty tone, and inquiring how he had passed the night. So you see he would have been a very profound[3] old man, indeed, to suspect that every night, just at twelve, I looked in upon him while he slept.

Upon the eighth night I was more than usually cautious in opening the door. A watch's minute hand moves more quickly than did mine. Never before that night had I *felt* the extent of my own powers— of my sagacity.[4] I could scarcely contain my feelings of triumph. To think that there I was, opening the door, little by little, and he not even to dream of my secret deeds or thoughts. I fairly chuckled at the idea; and perhaps he heard me; for he moved on the bed suddenly, as if startled. Now you may think that I drew back—but no. His room was as black as pitch with the thick darkness (for the shutters were close fastened, through fear of robbers), and so I knew that he could not see the opening of the door, and I kept pushing it on steadily, steadily.

PREDICT: What do you think will happen next?

I had my head in, and was about to open the lantern, when my thumb slipped upon the tin fastening, and the old man sprang up in the bed, crying out—"Who's there?"

I kept quite still and said nothing. For a whole hour I did not move a muscle, and in the meantime I did not hear him lie down. He was still sitting up in the bed listening—just as I have done, night after night, hearkening to the death watches[5] in the wall.

Presently I heard a slight groan, and I knew it was the groan of mortal terror. It was not a groan of pain or of grief—oh, no!—it was the low stifled sound that arises from the bottom of the soul when overcharged with awe. I knew the sound well. Many a night, just at midnight, when all the world slept, it has welled up from my own bosom, deepening, with its dreadful echo, the terrors that distracted me. I say I knew it well. I knew what the old man felt, and pitied him, although I chuckled at heart. I knew that he had been lying awake ever since the first slight noise, when he had turned in the bed. His fears had been ever since growing upon him. He had

---

2. **dark lantern,** lantern whose light can be hidden by a cover over the opening.
3. profound (prə found′), *adj.,* capable of having great knowledge or understanding.
4. sagacity (sə gas′ə tē), *n.,* sharp mental ability; shrewdness.
5. **death watches,** small beetles that live in wood and make a ticking sound.

been trying to fancy them causeless, but could not. He had been saying to himself: "It is nothing but the wind in the chimney—it is only a mouse crossing the floor," or "It is merely a cricket which has made a single chirp." Yes, he had been trying to comfort himself with these suppositions;[6] but he had found all in vain. *All in vain;* because Death, in approaching him, had stalked with his black shadow before him, and enveloped the victim. And it was the mournful influence of the unperceived shadow that caused him to feel—although he neither saw nor heard—to *feel* the presence of my head within the room.

When I had waited a long time, very patiently, without hearing him lie down, I resolved to open a little—a very, very little crevice in the lantern. So I opened it—you cannot imagine how stealthily, stealthily—until, at length, a single dim ray, like the thread of the spider, shot from out the crevice and full upon the vulture eye.

It was open—wide, wide open—and I grew furious as I gazed upon it. I saw it with perfect distinctness—all a dull blue, with a hideous veil over it that chilled the very marrow in my bones; but I could see nothing else of the old man's face or person, for I had directed the ray as if by instinct, precisely upon the spot.

And now have I not told you that what you mistake for madness is but overacuteness of the senses?—now, I say, there came to my ears a low, dull, quick sound, such as a watch makes when enveloped in cotton. I knew *that* sound well too. It was the beating of the old man's heart. It increased my fury, as the beating of a drum stimulates the soldier into courage.

But even yet I refrained and kept still. I scarcely breathed. I held the lantern motionless. I tried how steadily I could maintain the ray upon the eye. Meantime the hellish tattoo of the heart increased. It grew quicker and quicker, and louder and louder every instant.

The old man's terror *must* have been extreme! It grew louder, I say, louder every moment!—do you mark me well? I have told you that I am nervous: so I am. And now at the dead hour of the night, amid the dreadful silence of that old house, so strange a noise as this excited me to uncontrollable terror. Yet, for some minutes longer I refrained and stood still. But the beating grew louder, louder! I thought the heart must burst. And now a new anxiety[7] seized me—the sound would be heard by a neighbor! The old man's hour had come! With a loud yell, I threw open the lantern and leaped into the room. He shrieked once—once only. In an instant I dragged him to the floor, and pulled the heavy bed over him. I then smiled gaily, to find the deed so far done. But, for many minutes, the heart beat on with a muffled sound. This, however, did not vex me; it would not be heard through the wall. At length it ceased. The old man was dead. I removed the bed and examined the corpse. Yes, he was stone, stone dead. I placed my hand upon the heart and held it there many minutes. There was no pulsation. He was stone dead. His eye would trouble me no more.

QUESTION: Does the man's plan prove that he was sane? Why or why not?

If still you think me mad, you will think so no longer when I describe the wise precautions I took for the concealment of the body. The night waned, and I worked hastily, but in silence. First of all I dismembered the corpse. I cut off the head and the arms and the legs.

I then took up three planks from the flooring of the chamber, and deposited all between the scantlings. I then replaced the

6. supposition (sup′ə zish′ən), *n.*, belief or opinion.
7. anxiety (ang zī′ə tē), *n.*, uneasy thoughts or fears over the possibility of coming misfortune.

boards so cleverly, so cunningly, that no human eye—not even *his*—could have detected anything wrong. There was nothing to wash out—no stain of any kind—no bloodspot whatever. I had been too wary for that. A tub had caught all—ha! ha!

When I had made an end of these labors, it was four o'clock—still dark as midnight. As the bell sounded the hour, there came a knocking at the street door. I went down to open it with a light heart—for what had I *now* to fear? There entered three men, who introduced themselves, with perfect suavity, as officers of the police. A shriek had been heard by a neighbor during the night; suspicion of foul play had been aroused; information had been lodged at the police office, and they (the officers) had been deputed to search the premises.

I smiled—for *what* had I to fear? I bade the gentlemen welcome. The shriek, I said, was my own in a dream. The old man, I mentioned, was absent in the country. I took my visitors all over the house. I bade them search—search *well*. I led them, at length, to *his* chamber. I showed them his treasures, secure, undisturbed. In the enthusiasm of my confidence, I brought chairs into the room, and desired them *here* to rest from their fatigues, while I myself, in the wild audacity[8] of my perfect triumph, placed my own seat upon the very spot beneath which reposed the corpse of the victim.

The officers were satisfied. My *manner* had convinced them. I was singularly at ease. They sat, and while I answered cheerily, they chatted of familiar things. But, ere long, I felt myself getting pale and wished them gone. My head ached, and I fancied a ringing in my ears: but still they sat and still chatted. The ringing became more distinct; it continued and became more distinct; I talked more freely to

They were making a mockery of my horror!

get rid of the feeling; but it continued and gained definiteness—until, at length, I found that the noise was *not* within my ears.

No doubt I now grew *very* pale—but I talked more fluently, and with a heightened voice. Yet the sound increased—and what could I do? It was *a low, dull, quick sound—much such a sound as a watch makes when enveloped in cotton.* I gasped for breath—and yet the officers heard it not. I talked more quickly—more vehemently;[9] but the noise steadily increased. I arose and argued about trifles, in a high key and with violent gesticulations,[10] but the noise steadily increased. Why *would* they not be gone? I paced the floor to and fro with heavy strides, as if excited to fury by the observation of the men—but the noise steadily increased. Oh, what *could* I do? I foamed—I raved—I swore! I swung the chair upon which I had been sitting, and grated it upon the boards, but the noise arose over all and continually increased. It grew louder—louder—*louder!* And still the men chatted pleasantly, and smiled. Was it possible they heard not? No, no! They heard!—they suspected!—they *knew!*—they were making a mockery of my horror!—this I thought, and this I think. But anything was better than this agony! Anything was more tolerable than this derision![11] I could bear those hypocritical[12] smiles no longer! I felt that I must scream or die!—and now—again!—hark! louder! louder! louder! louder! *louder!*—

"Villains!" I shrieked, "dissemble no more! I admit the deed!—tear up the planks!—here, here!—it is the beating of his hideous heart!"

---

8. **audacity** (ô das′ə tē), *n.,* reckless daring; boldness.
9. **vehemently** (vē′ə mənt lē), *adv.,* forcefully, with strong feeling
10. **gesticulation** (je stik′yə lā′shən), *n.,* excited gesture.
11. **derision** (di rizh′ən), *n.,* ridicule.
12. **hypocritical** (hip′ə krit′ə kəl), *adj.,* insincere.

After Reading

Making Connections

1. What were some of the images that came to mind as you read? How were they developed?

2. Why do you think the narrator kills the old man?

3. In your opinion, is the narrator mad? Why or why not?

4. Poe uses several writer's "tricks" to create and increase **suspense.** For example, he uses active voice and writes in the first person. What are some additional tricks?

5. How would this story be different if it had been told from the **third-person point of view** rather than the first person? (In a third-person point of view story, the narrator is an outsider and not a character in the story.)

6. If this crime were tried today, the narrator would no doubt plead insanity. Do you think he should be held responsible for his actions? Why or why not?

Literary Focus: Mood

The total feeling in a literary work is the **mood.** The choice of setting, objects, details, images, and words all contribute to create a special mood. A mood might be suspenseful, melancholy, hopeful, among many others. Copy the diagram below in your notebook. In the center, write what you consider the mood of the story to be. Then on the rays surrounding the center, write down details from the story that help create this mood. You can use both quotes from the text and your own words.

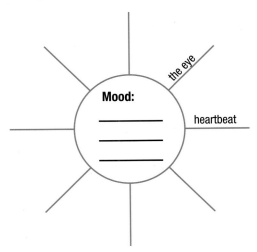

Vocabulary Study

acute
profound
sagacity
supposition
anxiety
audacity
vehemently
gesticulation
derision
hypocritical

A. For each vocabulary word numbered below, write down its **antonym,** or opposite, from the lettered words on the right.

1. sagacity
2. derision
3. acute
4. vehemently
5. hypocritical

a. stupidity
b. sincere
c. praise
d. gently
e. dull

B. Use all of the vocabulary words below in a paragraph that explains why you liked or did not like the selection.

profound   supposition   anxiety   audacity   gesticulation

Expressing Your Ideas

Writing Choices

Create a Mood Write a **mood piece,** either an entire story or just an opening for one. First, decide on what mood you wish to create—sad, tense, serene? Make a diagram like the one on page 267 and think of words or events that you associate with that mood. Use your diagram to help you write.

Read All About It! Write a **newspaper report** of the crime. The report can be strictly objective, such as the news stories in most reputable newspapers, or it can be sensational, such as the stories in some of the tabloids found at supermarket check-outs. Remember to answer the questions *who, what, when, where, why,* and *how.*

It Was a Hard Life Research Poe's life and write a **biographical sketch** that provides information not found in the biography on page 261.

Other Options

Thrill Your Listeners Work with other students to present a **dramatic reading** of this story, complete with sound effects and background music.

Excuse Me, Your Honor Work with a partner and examine the story for clues to the narrator's sanity or insanity. Prepare a **speech** defending your position on the man's mental state, using the evidence from the story.

Well, Sarge, It Was Like This Take on the character of one of the policemen and, in an **explanation** to your commander, describe what happened at the old man's house.

Before Reading

Elegy Written at the County Junkyard

by James D. Houston

James D. Houston
born 1933

The California author has written stories from both male and female perspectives. His wife, Jeanne Wakatsuki, is a Japanese American who, like Yoshiko Uchida, was also interned during World War II. Houston and his wife jointly wrote *Farewell to Manzanar* (1973), which was one of the first stories published about the Japanese internment. Houston has also written several novels, including *Continental Drift,* short stories, a biography, and a textbook, *Writing from the Inside.* In addition to writing, the author has been an instructor of writing, English, and guitar.

Building Background

Remembering . . . An **elegy** is a poem or song expressing a writer's serious reflections on some aspect of death. Several famous elegies include Thomas Gray's "Elegy Written in a Country Churchyard," which ponders death in general; A. E. Housman's "To an Athlete Dying Young," about the untimely death of a runner; and Mathew Arnold's "Rugby Chapel," in which the poet laments his father's untimely death. Although the piece by James Houston is not a poem or a song, it has all the elements of an elegy for his father.

Getting into the Selection

Discussion James Houston's father was one of those people who couldn't throw anything away. Why do people save things? And what sorts of things do people save? With your class, brainstorm the reasons that people save things and the things they save.

Reading Tip

Point of View In this selection, the narrator writes about his father. He talks about him from two perspectives—as a young man and as a thirteen-year-old boy. In effect, you have two people looking at the same person. Copy the diagram below into your notebook. As you read, or after you read, fill in the line from the man to his father with words or phrases that describe how the man feels about his father. Do the same for the boy.

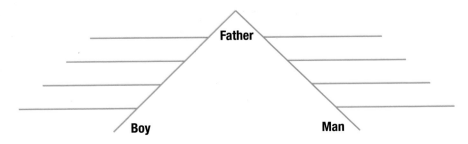

Elegy Written at the County Junkyard

James D. Houston

At the county dump I am throwing away my father. His old paint rags, and stumps of brushes. Color catalogues. The caked leather suitcase he used for so many years carrying small tools and tiny jars of his trade, suitcase so cracked and bent and buckle-ripped it's no good for anything now, not even what he used it for. I start to toss it on top of the brushes and the rags, but hesitate, toss instead the five-gallon drums that once held primer.[1] He stacked them against one wall of his shop, for nothing, kept dozens more than he'd ever use. Around these fall the ointments from his medicine chest. And cracked galoshes, filled with dust, as if in his closet it's been raining dust for years. And magazines. His fishing hat. Notes to himself.

Fix window
Grease car
Call Ed
Call Harlow about job

Bent nails in a jar, rolls of old wire, pipe sections, fiddle he always intended to mend, embossed[2] cards some salesman left, old paid bills, check stubs, pencils his teeth chewed.

Ragtaggle bits of this and that he touched, stacked, stored, useless to anyone but him, and he's gone now, so toss it all out there among the refrigerators and lettuce leaves and seven hundred truck tires, busted sofas, flower pots, and grass from the overgrown gardens of every household. Into it I throw my father, saving for last that suitcase of his, first seen twenty years back, and old then, the first day he took me out on a job, pair of his spattered overalls

---

1. **primer** (prī′mər), *n.,* paint that is used for the first coat of paint as a sealer or base.
2. **embossed** (em bôst′), *adj.,* decorated with a design that stands out from the surface.

Metropolis II was painted in 1986 by Jacek Yerka. The objects that make up this fanciful town each represent a memory from his youth. If you were to paint a picture of memories, what objects might you include?

to wear, rolled thick at the cuff, and Sherwin-Williams white billcap, and us two squatting while he unbuckles the case and touches dark labels of pigment[3] tubes, deciding something.

Crusted with splats of seventy colors now, lid corners split as if somebody sat on it. The ragged straps dangle. One shred of leather holds the chromium buckle, yet the buckle itself hasn't worn much at all, still catches the sun, where paint doesn't cover it, relic from those days before things tarnished in a week.

One last glance. By five tonight it'll be gone for good, when the bulldozer comes around to shove it over the side with the rest of today's arms and toes and parts of hearts.

"What're ya gonna do, dad?"

He doesn't answer. He never answers, as if it offends him to be interrupted. And I always wait, as if all those previous silences were exceptions, and this time he will turn and speak. It's a big reason for coming along this morning, the chance that out here on the job something might pass between us. I would never have been able to describe it ahead of time, but . . . something.

I wait and watch two minutes of puckering lips and long slow blinks while he studies the labels, then selects one tube, smudged and wrinkled, unscrews its top and squeezes out a little on his fingertips.

Five feet away a canvas dropcloth covers a few square yards of hardwood floor. I follow him to a five-gallon drum he's mixing paint in. A narrow stick of plywood holds the color he's shooting for—pale pale green. He's proud of his eye, his knack for figuring just how pale this green will be when it's dry. Squeeze a green strip from the tube and stir it in, wide easy stirs while the green spreads out like taffy strips. Stir and stir. Then test: dip another stick in. Pair it. Stir.

> ## I do not yet know that this wall is the beginning of the end.

"Okay, Jim. Take half this green paint and git that wall there covered."

He hands me a clean brush, black bristles glistening with yesterday's thinner. He pours a gallon bucket full, deft[4] tilt, and cuts the fall off clean.

"I'll be back in a minute," he says.

It's the first time I've painted anything away from home. I do not yet know that this wall is the beginning of the end, that before the summer is out I will dread the look of yet another long, unpainted wall and wince[5] at the smell of thinner. I want this one to be a good job. I want to live up to the paint he's just mixed. I start by the living room door, taking my time, keeping the molding[6] clear for a white trim later.

Ten minutes pass, and this first wall becomes my world, each piece I cover is a quadrant[7] on my map of it. I am moving across the wide-open middle country—working my brush like dad told me to the time we painted the back side of our house, using the wrist, lapping strokes over—when I feel compelled to turn around.

In the far doorway the lady of the house stands glaring at me, her eyes a blend of terror and hate. I realize how dangerous I must look to her: next to the wall of her priceless living room she finds Tom Sawyer with his cuffs rolled thick, whitewashing away an afternoon.

Under green freckles my face turns scarlet.

---

3. **pigment** (pig′mənt), *n.*, a coloring matter that is used to dye paint.
4. **deft** (deft), *adj.*, quick and skillful in action.
5. **wince** (wins), *v.*, draw back suddenly; flinch.
6. **molding** (mōl′ding), *n.*, decorative wood used along the walls of a room.
7. **quadrant** (kwod′rənt), *n.*, when you divide an area into four equal parts by using two lines, you get four quadrants.

She disappears.

From the hallway comes her loud whisper. "Mr. *Hous*ton! That boy painting my living room wall couldn't be over fifteen!"

"He's thirteen, ma'am."

"He's what?"

"It's my boy, Jim. He's giving me a hand this summer."

"I just wonder if he knows what he's *doing* in there."

"I painted my first house when I was ten."

"Well . . . I . . . if . . . I'd certainly be keeping an eye on him if I were you."

"Don't worry, ma'am, he knows what to do."

Behind me I hear her walking slowly across the room. I keep painting, don't look at her this time. Plenty of paint on the brush. But don't let it run. Feather it at the overlap. Cover. Cover.

Dad comes in and fills up another gallon bucket and helps me finish the wall. He catches my eye once and winks at the fast one we have pulled on Mrs. So-and-so. Then we are covering the middle country together, in a curiously enclosed stillness, broken only by the whish of bristles and cluck of brush handle against the can. Somewhere in the back of the house a radio is playing, but its faraway music doesn't penetrate our territory.

We finish the room by quitting time. Dad looks over the sections I've painted, finds a couple of holidays[8] along the baseboard and has me fill these in before we clean the brushes, saying only, "Keep an eye out for them holidays," and then a little later, when the sash tools are thinned, and the pigment tubes lined up the way he wants them, next to the knives he uses for cutting linoleum and spreading putty and spackling cracks, he drops the lid shut on his kit of a suitcase, snaps the buckle to, straps it, says, "Might as well take that on out to the truck."

I have never paid much attention to his kit.

Now I know just enough about what's inside for its contents to be mysteries. A year from now I will know too much about what's inside, and I will be able to read his half smile, already on the verge of apologizing for having only this to reward me with. But today it is an honor. No one has ever carried that kit but him. It has mysterious weight, with gypsy daubs of ivory, burnt umber, and vermilion all across the ancient leather. A fine weight for carrying from the house downstairs to the curb.

At the county dump I am throwing away my father, hefting this suitcase to toss the last of him onto the smoking heap, when that shred of leather gives and the buckle breaks. The kit flies open. As if compressed[9] inside, waiting to escape, the pungent[10] smell of oil and rare pigments cuts through smoke and rot and fills the air around me. The few tubes still in there begin to topple. My throwing arm stays. My other hand reaches. I'm holding the suitcase, inhaling the smell that always surrounded him, even after he had scrubbed. It rose from the creases in his hands, from permanent white liners rimming his fingernails, from the paint-motes he sometimes missed with thinner, at the corners of his eyes.

I breathe deep. Close the suitcase slowly. Prepare to heave it once and for all. This time with both hands. Out among all those things you only find by losing them. Out and up. And onto the truck bed. Where it lands with a thunk. And sits solid. Those aromatic tubes give it density. I wait for him to tie his ladder on the overhead rack, and we climb into the cab. He winks once more, as we prepare to leave Mrs. So-and-so behind. Reeking of paint and turpentine, billcaps shoved back, we are

---

8. **holidays,** places a painter carelessly missed and left unpainted.

9. compressed (kəm prest′), *adj.,* squeezed together.

10. pungent (pun′jənt), *adj.,* a taste or smell that is very sharp.

Sherwin and Williams calling it a day, with no way to talk much over the stuttering engine of this metal-floored Chevy, and no need to talk. The sticky clutch leaps. Wind rushes in, mixing paint and gasoline fumes, and all you need to do is stay loose for the jolts and the whole long rumble ride home.

Another Voice

Dusting

Julia Alvarez

Each morning I wrote my name
on the dusty cabinet, then crossed
the dining table in script, scrawled
in capitals on the backs of chairs,
5 practicing signatures like scales
while Mother followed, squirting
linseed from a burping can
into a crumpled-up flannel.

She erased my fingerprints
10 from the bookshelf and rocker,
polished mirrors on the desk
scribbled with my alphabets.
My name was swallowed in the towel
with which she jeweled the table tops.
15 The grain surfaced in the oak
and the pine grew <u>luminous</u>.[1]
But I refused with every mark
to be like her, anonymous.

---

1. luminous (lü′mə nəs), *adj.*, full of light; shining.

After Reading

Making Connections

1. Describe how you pictured the father in "Elegy."

2. Look over your reasons for why people save things. Why do you think the author's father kept his paints and equipment for so long?

3. Look back over the diagram that describes how the father is viewed by both the man and the boy. How has time changed the author's perspective of his father?

4. How does the author use words to create **sensory images?**

5. Why do you think the author wanted to write this selection about his father?

6. Describe the **character qualities** of the girl in "Dusting."

7. What do you think was the **author's purpose** for writing the poem? How does it compare to Houston's purpose for writing?

8. What are other reasons for writing elegies or poems about one's parents or other loved ones?

Literary Focus: Flashback

A **flashback** is an interruption in a story that describes an episode that happened before the story took place. A flashback allows an author to include events or memories from the past that help you better understand what is happening in the present. In this story, the suitcase triggers the author's memories of painting with his father. Flashbacks are used in stories, movies, songs, and TV shows. Work with a small group and outline how you would illustrate the author's use of flashback for a movie. In other words, how would the suitcase bring the man back to the past, to when he was thirteen years old? And how will the suitcase bring him back to the present?

Vocabulary Study

primer
embossed
pigment
deft
wince
molding
quadrant
compressed
pungent
luminous

Write the word that best completes each sentence.

1. Poking Tom with a paintbrush will make him ____.
2. Be sure to mix paint well, because the ____ can separate from the base color.
3. The painter added one more quick, ____ stroke to the portrait.
4. The smell of the paint thinner was so ____ that my eyes watered.
5. Before you paint your room pink, use a ____ to seal the walls.
6. In Victorian times, walls were made of plaster and you couldn't nail into them. People put ____ around the walls and hung pictures from that.
7. As I pulled into the driveway my heart lifted at the sight of the house, with the windows ____ and inviting.
8. The painter handed me a business card with his name ____ in gold.
9. Before we began the mural, we divided the wall into four equal sections. It was my job to paint a rose in the lower right ____.
10. The paints were so tightly ____ into the suitcase that when I unlocked it the top flew open and all the little tubes fell out.

Expressing Your Ideas ——————————

Writing Choices

Poetry in Motion Write a **poem** about one of your parents or a person you admire, in which you watch something that they do often. Make the poem a reflection on what this action says about this person.

I Remember When Write a brief **memoir** about a time when one of your parents or another family member taught you to do a particular job. Add details such as: Did this person teach you by showing you how to do the job or by describing it in words? Was the experience pleasant or frustrating? Have you taught this job to someone else?

Other Options

Color Swatches Mixing paint colors can be difficult. Prepare a **visual report** on paint colors and pigments. Ask an art teacher or someone who mixes paint at a hardware store for information. Demonstrate to the class how the mix of certain pigments can bring unexpected results.

Tools of the Trade **Interview** someone whom you admire—a cook, a writer, a carpenter, a teacher. Ask this person what tools are necessary for his or her job, and find out how this person feels about the tools. Then make a **poster** of those tools, with captions explaining how to use and take care of them.

Before Reading

He Lion, Bruh Bear, and Bruh Rabbit

by Virginia Hamilton

Virginia Hamilton
born 1936

Virginia Hamilton is descended from a fugitive (runaway) slave, farmers, and storytellers. She has done all types of jobs, from singing to bookkeeping, but now she spends her time writing. She usually writes stories for children and has won many prizes. She says that it was a good thing her first novel was rejected, because otherwise "I might not have become a writer of children's books." About her collection of folk tales, from which this story is taken, she says, "Remember also that these tales, like all folk tales, belong to all of us. They are part of our American tradition and part of the history of our country. They show you how I tell black folk tales. For they are told in my own voice, echoing the voices of slaves and fugitives, some of whom are my ancestors."

Building Background

Pleasingly Personified This story comes from *The People Could Fly: American Black Folktales.* In the introduction, Virginia Hamilton writes that African American slaves created stories that combined memories of Africa with the experiences of their new world. Most of the stories involved animals who took on characteristics of the people found on the plantation. Hamilton writes, "The rabbit, known as B'rabby and later called Brer, Buh, or Bruh Rabbit, became a particular favorite of the slave tellers. Rabbit was small and apparently helpless compared to the powerful bear, the wily fox, and the ferocious wolf. But the slave teller made the rabbit smart, tricky, and clever, the winner over larger and stronger animals."

Getting into the Story

Writer's Notebook Make a list of common human traits in your notebook. Assign an animal to each trait. Discuss your choices with the class.

Human Trait	Animal Standing for Trait
1. greedy	shark
2. cheerful	

Reading Tip

Style Most slaves were not allowed to learn to read and write. As a result, stories had to be passed along orally. People who collect these stories today have tried to keep their "out loud" qualities of **language** and **rhythm,** so they don't sound like other stories. Often, stories just tell you "First this happened and then this happened," but with folk tales, part of the appeal is in the rhythm of the story. So read the following story slowly. In fact, practice reading it aloud—complete with hand gestures—so that you can get a feel for the language.

Virginia Hamilton

He Lion, Bruh Bear, and Bruh Rabbit

Say that he Lion would get up each and every morning. Stretch and walk around. He'd roar, "ME AND MYSELF. ME AND MYSELF," like that. Scare all the little animals so they were afraid to come outside in the sunshine. Afraid to go huntin or fishin or whatever the little animals wanted to do.

"What we gone do about it?" they asked one another. Squirrel leapin from branch to branch, just scared. Possum playin dead, couldn't hardly move him.

He Lion just went on, stickin out his chest and roarin, "ME AND MYSELF. ME AND MYSELF."

The little animals held a sit-down talk, and one by one and two by two and all by all, they decide to go see Bruh Bear and Bruh Rabbit. For they know that Bruh Bear been around. And Bruh Rabbit say he has, too.

So they went to Bruh Bear and Bruh Rabbit. Said, "We have some trouble. Old he Lion, him scarin everybody, roarin every mornin and all day, 'ME AND MYSELF. ME AND MYSELF,' like that."

"Why he Lion want to do that?" Bruh Bear said.

"Is that all he Lion have to say?" Bruh Rabbit asked.

"We don't know why, but that's all he Lion can tell us and we didn't ask him to tell us that," said the little animals. "And him scarin the children with it. And we wish him to stop it."

"Well, I'll go see him, talk to him. I've known he Lion a long kind of time," Bruh Bear said.

"I'll go with you," said Bruh Rabbit. "I've known he Lion most long as you."

That bear and that rabbit went off through the forest. They kept hearin somethin. Mumble, mumble. Couldn't make it out. They got farther in the forest. They heard it plain now. "ME AND MYSELF. ME AND MYSELF."

"Well, well, well," said Bruh Bear. He wasn't scared. He'd been around the whole forest, seen a lot.

"My, my, my," said Bruh Rabbit. He'd seen enough to know not to be afraid of an old he lion. Now old he lions could be dangerous, but you had to know how to handle them.

The bear and the rabbit climbed up and up the cliff where he Lion had his lair.[1] They found him. Kept their distance. He watchin

---

1. lair (ler), *n.*, den or resting place of a wild animal.

them and they watchin him. Everybody actin cordial.[2]

"Hear tell you are scarin everybody, all the little animals, with your roarin all the time," Bruh Rabbit said.

"I roars when I pleases," he Lion said.

"Well, might could you leave off the noise first thing in the mornin, so the little animals can get what they want to eat and drink?" asked Bruh Bear.

"Listen," said he Lion, and then he roared:

"ME AND MYSELF. ME AND MYSELF. Nobody tell me what not to do," he said. "I'm the king of the forest, *me and myself.*"

"Better had let me tell you somethin," Bruh Rabbit said, "for I've seen Man, and I know him the real king of the forest."

He Lion was quiet awhile. He looked straight through that scrawny lil Rabbit like he

---

2. **cordial** (kôr′jəl), *adj.*, warm and friendly in manner.

▲ *Emma's Lion* by Christian Pierre. Is this the way you picture he Lion?

was nothin atall. He looked at Bruh Bear and figured he'd talk to him.

"You, Bear, you been around," he Lion said.

"That's true," said old Bruh Bear. "I been about everywhere. I've been around the whole forest."

"Then you must know somethin," he Lion said.

"I know lots," said Bruh Bear, slow and quiet-like.

"Tell me what you know about Man," he Lion said. "He think him the king of the forest?"

"Well, now, I'll tell you," said Bruh Bear, "I been around, but I haven't ever come across Man that I know of. Couldn't tell you nothin about him."

So he Lion had to turn back to Bruh Rabbit. He didn't want to but he had to. "So what?" he said to that lil scrawny hare.

"Well, you got to come down from there if you want to see Man," Bruh Rabbit said. "Come down from there and I'll show you him."

He Lion thought a minute, an hour, and a whole day. Then, the next day, he came on down.

He roared just once, "ME AND MYSELF. ME AND MYSELF. Now," he said, "come show me Man."

So they set out. He Lion, Bruh Bear, and Bruh Rabbit. They go along and they go along, rangin the forest. Pretty soon, they come to a clearin. And playin in it is a little fellow about nine years old.

"Is that there Man?" asked he Lion.

"Why no, that one is called Will Be, but it sure is not Man," said Bruh Rabbit.

So they went along and they went along. Pretty soon, they come upon a shade tree.

Awhile after he Lion met Man, things were some better in the forest.

And sleepin under it is an old, olden fellow, about ninety years olden.

"There must lie Man," spoke he Lion. "I knew him wasn't gone be much."

"That's not Man," said Bruh Rabbit. "That fellow is Was Once. You'll know it when you see Man."

So they went on along. He Lion is gettin tired of strollin. So he roars, "ME AND MYSELF. ME AND MYSELF." Upsets Bear so that Bear doubles over and runs and climbs a tree.

"Come down from there," Bruh Rabbit tellin him. So after a while Bear comes down. He keepin his distance from he Lion, anyhow. And they set out some more. Goin along quiet and slow.

In a little while they come to a road. And comin on way down the road, Bruh Rabbit sees Man comin. Man about twenty-one years old. Big and strong, with a big gun over his shoulder.

"There!" Bruh Rabbit says. "See there, he Lion? There's Man. You better go meet him."

"I will," says he Lion. And he sticks out his chest and he roars, "ME AND MYSELF. ME AND MYSELF." All the way to Man he's roarin proud, "ME AND MYSELF, ME AND MYSELF!"

"Come on, Bruh Bear, let's go!" Bruh Rabbit says.

"What for?" Bruh Bear wants to know.

"You better come on!" And Bruh Rabbit takes ahold of Bruh Bear and half drags him to a thicket.[3] And there he makin the Bear hide with him.

For here comes Man. He sees old he Lion real good now. He drops to one knee and he takes aim with his big gun.

---

3. **thicket** (thik′it), *n.*, shrubs and small trees growing close together

Old he Lion is roarin his head off: "ME AND MYSELF! ME AND MYSELF!"

The big gun goes off: PA-LOOOM!

He Lion falls back hard on his tail.

The gun goes off again. PA-LOOOM!

He Lion is flyin through the air. He lands in the thicket.

"Well, did you see Man?" asked Bruh Bear.

"I seen him," said he Lion. "Man spoken to me unkind, and got a great long stick him keepin on his shoulder. Then Man taken that stick down and him speakin real mean. Thunderin at me and lightnin comin from that stick, awful bad. Made me sick. I had to turn around. And Man pointin that stick again and thunderin at me some more. So I come in here, cause it seem like him throwed some stickers at me each time it thunder, too."

"So you've met Man, and you know zactly what that kind of him is," says Bruh Rabbit.

"I surely do know that," he Lion said back.

Awhile after he Lion met Man, things were some better in the forest. Bruh Bear knew what Man looked like so he could keep out of his way. That rabbit always did know to keep out of Man's way. The little animals could go out in the mornin because he Lion was more peaceable. He didn't walk around roarin at the top of his voice all the time. And when he Lion did lift that voice of his, it was like, "Me and Myself and Man. Me and Myself and Man." Like that.

Wasn't too loud atall.

Animal tales are the most widely known black folktales. Because of the menial[4] labor slaves were made to do, they observed and came to know many kinds of animals throughout their daily lives. They developed a keen interest in these lowly creatures. Because they had so little knowledge about the fauna[5] they found here, they made up tales that to some extent explained and fit their observations of animal behavior. Furthermore, the tales satisfied the slaves' need to explain symbolically and secretly the ruling behavior of the slaveowners in relation to themselves. As time passed, the tales were told more for entertainment and instruction.

"He Lion, Bruh Bear, and Bruh Rabbit" is a typical tale of an animal, whether it is wolf, lion, bear, rabbit, goat, tiger, etc., that learns through experience to fear man. It is the rabbit that shows man to the lion. And the rabbit, representing the slave in the animal tales, knows from experience to fear man. The tale ranges throughout North and South America, Europe, and Africa.

---

4. menial (mē′nē əl), *adj.,* low, humble.
5. fauna (fô′nə), *n. pl.,* the animals of a particular region or period.

After Reading

Making Connections

1. Which character did you like the best? Explain.

2. Why do you think Bruh Bear and Bruh Rabbit were chosen to help solve the problem?

3. What does he Lion seem to learn about himself?

4. What might be a good **moral** (lesson or teaching) for this story?

5. 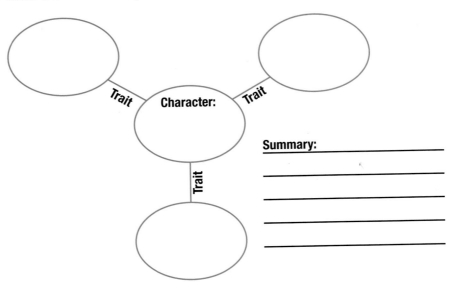 How does the author's identification with a cultural **group** affect her telling of the folk tale? (You may want to refer to the author's biography.)

6. Does knowing that this is a slave folk tale affect how you read it? Why or why not?

7. What other animal stories do you know that are similar to this one? How are they similar?

Literary Focus: Personification

Personification is a technique used by authors in which human characteristics are given to nonhuman things and events. Each of the animals in this story is the personification of a particular type of person. For the rabbit, bear, and lion, make a character trait web similar to the one below. In the connecting circles, write some of the animals' traits as described by the text. Then, under each web, write a summary sentence that describes each animal, or write the name of a person who is like the animal.

Trait

Trait

Character:

Trait

Summary: _____

_____

_____

_____

Vocabulary Study

lair
cordial
thicket
menial
fauna

On a separate sheet of paper, fill in the blanks with the vocabulary word that best completes each sentence.

Surprisingly, the lion was very __(1)__ to the rabbit. He even invited him into his __(2)__ for some tea.

"Where do you live?" asked the lion.

"Oh, just down the trail a piece, right behind the thorny __(3)__. We have quite a good variety of __(4)__ in my neighborhood— raccoons, skunks, squirrels, even a few possums."

"What do they do for a living?" the lion wondered.

"One of the raccoons is a rocket scientist. But most of the others work as ditch diggers or perform other __(5)__ labor."

Expressing Your Ideas

Writing Choices

Now You Tell a Tale Write your own **animal fable** or **folk tale** using the list that you generated in your notebook. Because you already have your cast of characters, all you need is a moral or point about human nature that you'd like to make. Decide on this before you write.

Animal Characteristics Our literature is full of animal stories. Brainstorm with a partner to come up with a **list** of stories that have animals as central characters. Beside each entry on the list, write down the name of the central character, the type of animal, and why you think this particular type of animal was chosen for the story.

Getting Back to the Story **Rewrite** the story using humans instead of animals. Change the setting if you wish, and anything else, except the actual point that you think this story is making.

Other Options

More Slave Stories Look up some of Aesop's fables. Create a **dramatization** of them for your class. Or find out about Aesop himself. He was a slave over two thousand years ago.

Hand Play Make puppets and put on a **puppet-show** version of this story. If possible, perform for a younger audience.

Animation Make a **comic book** or a **cartoon** of this story. Share it with a younger family member or a student in another class. Is it readable and entertaining? Revise your cartoons based on the audience feedback you get.

Moments of Truth

Reformers

Photography Connection

What makes a reformer? What makes someone want to help others? Someone might face a personal moment of truth—answer an aching conscience. Sometimes the problems are so great that there seems to be no choice but to take action.

Jacob Riis fought poverty with two powerful weapons—the pen and the camera. A Danish immigrant who arrived in the United States in 1870, Riis lived in poverty for many years until he found a job as a reporter for the *New York Tribune* newspaper. He first covered police beat stories. Night after night he witnessed the poverty, pain, and despair of the ghetto immigrants. Through hundreds of stories and photographs he brought the plight of these impoverished people to the attention of the American public. Riis then began his lifelong battle against the horrors of the slum tenements of New York and other large cities. The photographs you see on these pages are by Jacob Riis.

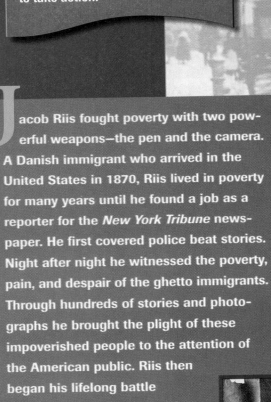

JACOB RIIS

Exposing the Truth

Photos clockwise from top left:

Baxter Street Alley in Mulberry Bend, c. 1888–1889. Crowded tenements gave children little room to play.

Scotty in His Lair, c. 1890. A young boy makes his bed in a pile of abandoned lumber and debris near Harlem River.

Five Cents a Spot. Each lodger stakes out his own small sleeping space in a Bayard Street tenement.

Tenement Interior in Poverty Gap. The faces of this immigrant family show the strain of living with too little money and scant space.

Washing Up, c. 1890. Several boys share their morning routine in a newsboys' lodging house.

Background:

Fifth Street, c. 1894. Mud, rotting garbage, and other debris made this and other New York streets almost impassable in the late nineteenth century.

Responding

1. Describe in your own words the social problems you see represented in these photographs.

2. Think about a problem you have witnessed in your neighborhood or city. What might you do to make a difference?

285

INTERDISCIPLINARY STUDY

U.S. History Connection
People deal with conflict, suffering, and injustice in many different ways. Some ignore it; others fear it. A reformer at heart, Jane Addams took action to eliminate suffering.

"A city is in many respects . . . enlarged housekeeping. . . . May we not say that city housekeeping has failed partly because women, the traditional housekeepers, have not been consulted as to its multiform activities?"

—*Newer Ideals of Peace*, 1907

JANE ADDAMS

(1860-1935)

by Deborah Gore Ohrn

Jane Addams and her staff at Hull House made some of the first studies of slums.

Jane Addams felt that women had a special mission to improve the conditions of everyday life—whether in the home, the city, or the world. The most admired American woman of her time, she was a pioneer social reformer who promoted social work in the United States.

Jane was born in Cedarville, Illinois, the eighth of nine children of Sara Weber Addams and John Addams, a prosperous timber merchant and banker. Her mother died when she was only two, and Jane was raised by her stepmother and older sister. Her father encouraged his intelligent daughter to work hard and excel.

A member of the first generation of college women, Addams attended the Rockford (Illinois) Female Seminary from 1877 to 1881. After graduation, she found herself restless and unfocused. She enrolled in medical school but was unable to continue due to a spinal illness.

On a second trip to Europe in 1888, Addams caught a glimpse of her life's work. While in London, she visited Toynbee Hall, a "settlement house" where educated young men lived in a poor neighborhood and sponsored lectures, classes, and other activities for the neighborhood residents.

In 1889, Addams and her friend Ellen Gates Starr decided to start a settlement house modeled after Toynbee Hall. They moved into an old mansion in one of Chicago's slums and named the mansion "Hull House" after the Chicago businessman who donated the land. It became America's best-known settlement house, offering academic and job-oriented classes as well as cultural, recreational, and day-care programs for the culturally diverse immigrants who lived in the neighborhood. Within four years, some two thousand people a week were coming to Hull House.

With three other women, Julia Lathrop, Florence Kelley, and Dr. Alice Hamilton, Addams also made Hull House a center for social reform. These women and some of the residents worked to improve the condition of the neighbor-hood and to change city and state laws on housing, public welfare, women's rights, and child labor.

Addams worked for women's rights on a national level too, becoming a vice president of the National American Woman Suffrage Association in 1911. She even got into politics, in 1912 serving as a delegate to the first national convention of the Progressive Party, which supported female suffrage.

SHE BECAME THE FIRST AMERICAN WOMAN TO WIN THE NOBEL PEACE PRIZE.

Located near Chicago's stockyards and a shipyard, Hull House served many neighboring immigrant groups.

In the early 1930s, Jane Addams reads to a few of the thousands of children she helped.

Hull House Today

by Stephanie Sammartino McPherson

Hull House still stands on Halsted Street, but the old neighborhood is gone. The original house has become part of the campus of the University of Illinois at Chicago. A museum now, it is restored to the way it looked when Jane Addams lived there. Crowds of students pass its doors every day just as crowds of immigrants once passed down the street.

Through the Hull House Association and the Women's International League for Peace and Freedom, Jane Addams was a good neighbor to those who lived on her block and to those who lived halfway across the world. The Women's International League continues to work for human rights and peace. The Hull House Association also continues its work with programs, organizations, and community centers all over the Chicago area.

Much more controversial was Addams's stand as a pacifist. When World War I (1914–1918) broke out, she joined an international group of women on a peace mission to Europe. On her return, she was labeled unpatriotic when she announced that soldiers had to be given intoxicants to lead a bayonet charge. After the war, her pacifism became associated in the public mind with Communism, and she was denounced as the "most dangerous woman in America." She was even expelled from the Daughters of the American Revolution.

Her international reputation thrived, however, and in 1931, she became the first American woman to win the Nobel Peace Prize. Addams turned her prize money over to the Women's International League for Peace and Freedom, of which she was president, and to Hull House, to help the unemployed.

On May 21, 1935, she died of cancer in Chicago. Columnist Walter Lippmann wrote in her obituary: "She had compassion without condescension. She had pity without retreat into vulgarity. She had infinite sympathy for common things without forgetfulness of those that are uncommon. That, I think, is why those who have known her say she was not only good, but great."

Responding

1. Jane Addams came from a wealthy family. She did not have to spend her adult life helping the poor. Why do you think she did it?

2. What are some reasons a person might want to help others?

3. What can you, a young person, do to make the world a better place?

Reading Mini-Lesson

Varying Your Reading Rate

The gear system of a bicycle is designed to let the bike work smoothly in varying conditions. High gears are for easy traveling at high speeds. Lower gears are for getting started or going uphill. You can think of reading as traveling through a text. To travel efficiently, you have to be able to change gears. To increase speed, however, you don't just move your eyes faster. Instead, you read selectively. Skimming and scanning are two gears you can use for high speed.

Skimming is reading quickly to get an overall impression of an article's subject and organization. The title tells you the article on page 286 is about Jane Addams. Try skimming: Quickly read the first paragraph, the last paragraph, and the first sentence of each paragraph between. You will have an overview of the article.

Scanning is another rapid reading technique, but it is used for a more specific purpose. You scan to find a specific piece or kind of information. Try scanning: Quickly read the same article to find important dates. Make a list of dates mentioned and the events that took place on those dates. Each of these years marks an important event in Jane Addams's life. Such a list has been started in the margin.

1860	birth
1877–81	college
1888	trip to Europe
1889	opened Hull House

Activity Options

1. Dates tell you the "when's" of an article. Now do something similar with the "where's" from the article. Scan "Jane Addams" for the places mentioned. List each place and note what happened at each.

2. Find an informational article in a magazine or book and skim through it to get an overview of the subject. Read the first paragraph, the last paragraph, and the first sentence of each remaining paragraph. Jot down brief notes as you skim. After, write an overview of the article. Then read the whole article and see how well your overview matches the article.

Part Two

Things Are Not As They Seem

Characters in these selections discover that things are not always what they seem to be. Inaccurate conclusions about people and circumstances can result from looking at things from only one point of view. Even after considering different viewpoints, we may still not be sure of the meaning of what we have seen.

🐚 **Multicultural Connection** Your **perspective** is influenced by emotions, needs, expectations, and training. Someone with a different background might look at the same situation from a very different point of view. In each selection in this part, ask yourself: Is there more than one way to look at this situation?

Literature
Gayle Pearson   **At the Avenue Eatery** ◆ short story 292
    Language Mini-Lesson ◆ Subject-Verb Agreement 300
Bruce Brooks   **Animal Craftsmen** ◆ essay 302
Deloras Lane   **Keepsakes** ◆ poem 309
Alice Walker   **Without Commercials** ◆ poem 310
Jacqueline Balcells   **The Enchanted Raisin** ◆ short story 315

Interdisciplinary Study   Deceiving to the Eye
Camouflage: The Big Cover-Up by Mary Batten ◆ life science 324
Patterns in Nature ◆ life science 326
What Is a Tessellation? ◆ mathematics 328
    Reading Mini-Lesson ◆ Classifying Ideas .330

Writing Workshop   Narrative Writing
Examining Points of View 331

Beyond Print   Critical Thinking
Living with Commercials 337

Before Reading

At the Avenue Eatery

by Gayle Pearson

Gayle Pearson
born 1947

Perhaps her experiences as a news writer, a social worker, and a child-care worker gave Gayle Pearson her eye for people and their personal problems. Why does she write? "I write because it affords me great power. I can *change* things. I can manipulate, until a character puts her foot down and says to me, No, I won't do that!"

As you can see from this statement, Ms. Pearson feels it is a great challenge to remain honest in her writing. Even though her stories are made up, she insists on keeping the characters realistic. This effort takes some digging. She has to get beneath the surface of the characters to discover the feelings that lie behind their actions.

Building Background

It's Not How It Looks! Journalists observe people and events, report those observations, and **draw conclusions**, which are interpretations of their observations. This is something like a scientist working in a laboratory, noting observations and also drawing conclusions. Although a journalist is supposed to be *objective*, that is, show no personal bias in the reporting, every journalist must see things through human eyes and hear them through human ears. In this story, a journalist takes his daughter to dinner and shows her that there is more than one way to interpret what she sees.

Getting into the Story

Writer's Notebook Our first impressions are not always confirmed by later events. A place that looks dull can turn out to be fun. A person who at first seems friendly can turn out to be someone you don't want for a friend. Can you think of a situation in which a person, place, or event turned out to be misleading? In your notebook, write about that mistaken first impression. Explain the situation, the first impression you had, and then how later information or experience changed your mind.

Reading Tip

Drawing Conclusions Drawing conclusions is an important part of reading. It is also an important part of living. If you could not draw conclusions, if you had to rely entirely on observations, you would never get through the day. For example, you'd have to go to school each day to see if school was in session.

Drawing a conclusion is not a sure thing. A number of conclusions can be drawn from any one observation, and some of them are likely to be incorrect or inaccurate. As you read this story, pay special attention to the conclusions Lindsey draws during the story—and to the conclusions you draw about the soundness of Lindsey's conclusions.

GAYLE PEARSON

indsey scanned the menu at the Avenue Eatery. Every so often her father took her out to dinner alone. They'd been to some good places, like Betty's Ocean View Diner, Soul Brother's Kitchen, and Little Joe's for spaghetti in San Francisco. The Avenue Eatery was the place they came to most often. It was close by and the pies were six inches high in the center.

She readjusted her jacket on the back of her chair so that the zipper was not digging into her back. Then she picked up the menu again. She might order a burger, fries, a salad, and dessert because she'd had soccer practice and was awfully hungry. Plus, she liked to order red meat when her mother wasn't along. Her mom often said, "If it's red and dead it's not to be fed."

Every time the door opened the wind gusted across the room, making the little yellow flames shiver inside their red candle holders. Lindsey wished it would snow. It seemed cold enough. She remembered it snowing once when she was back in the fifth grade, and school was canceled for the day.

Magnolia, the waitress, flashed them a warm, lingering smile. Then she came by to wipe down the table.

Lindsey's mother called her Sweet Magnolia. She claimed that the clay figure Lindsey's father, Jeff, was sculpting in his workroom looked suspiciously like Magnolia the waitress. Curves and bumps in all the same places—stuff like that. She liked to tease him about it.

"Hi, you two." Sweet Magnolia stood right over them, curves and bumps and all, and she gave Lindsey's father an extrasugary smile and winked.

Jeff blushed when he said, "Hey there, Magnolia," so cool-like back to her. Lindsey knew he'd die if Magnolia found out her name was associated with a slab of clay in his workroom, and how he hammered and chiseled away at all her parts.

"I guess we need another minute," said Jeff. "I think the kid here is still undecided."

"Sure enough, hon." Magnolia slipped the ticket into her uniform pocket and waltzed away to another table.

Lindsey leaned across the table. "Dad, she called you 'hon.'" Her father had on his teal blue sweater, and it brought out the blue in his eyes. She understood why a woman would call him "hon."

"Oh," said Jeff, shrugging. "I think she said 'hum.'"

"Hum? You think she said 'Sure enough, *hum?*' Right, Dad." She laughed.

"Well, don't tell your mother. Okay?" He winked at her over the top of his menu.

"Mm mmm."

"No, I mean it. Be sure not to tell your mom."

"Oh, all right."

"No, *really*, no matter *what*, don't tell your mother!" He winked again and grinned.

"Oh, Dad. You're goofy," she laughed.

She didn't always get along with him. He had a strong streak of obstinacy. Last week, for example, they were shopping for ingredients for a mocha bundt cake. He said the recipe called for whole wheat flour only and she said she was sure the recipe said half whole wheat and half unbleached white flour. He bought whole wheat. He was wrong. He made it with all whole wheat anyway. The cake weighed about sixteen tons after baking. Each bite sank to the pit of their stomachs like a large

This watercolor painting, *Country Girl Diner*, was painted by Ralph Goings in 1985. How is it similar to the watercolor by the same artist shown on page 297? ▼

stone. He didn't give up. He said it was delicious and ate it until he was sick.

Sweet Magnolia whizzed by in her very short skirt with two platters of chicken and french fries. Lindsey wondered how someone got to be a waitress. Was it possible she'd grown up wanting to be one? She supposed not. It looked like a hard job, and boring at the same time. She liked Magnolia and hoped she had someone at home who would wait on her.

Cold sandwiches, hot sandwiches, dinner entrees with salad and potatoes. . . . She cupped her hands over the red candle holder to warm them. Magnolia brought her father some coffee.

"Great. Thanks," he said, and laid down his menu.

Jammed into one of the booths against the wall, a crowd of teenage girls screeched and chattered. Everything seemed hilarious to them. Though Lindsey enjoyed going out with her dad, she couldn't wait to be old enough to do that herself.

> ... she raised her menu a little higher and peered over it at the lone woman.

If I'd gone shopping with Lorry and her mother, Lindsey thought, we might have stopped for pizza. These choices were sometimes hard to make. She would have gone with them if she hadn't gone out with her dad. Her mother hated shopping, so they only went when it was absolutely necessary, and by her mother's standards those times were rare. She didn't much like it herself. She'd never be one of the "mall dolls."

Her father was dumping NutraSweet into his coffee. She should bring up something interesting to talk about, but it wasn't always so easy. Sometimes you had to give them a topic or they just sat there, dumping NutraSweet into their coffee, and stirring, stirring, stirring. Surely the coffee was all stirred up by now. I mean, it's not *cement,* she said to herself. She wondered if most fathers were

like that, say in places like Florida and Alaska, France and China. He could tell a good story on paper, though. She had to admit that. Almost any evening she could pick up the *Tribune* and read a story with his byline.[1]

EVALUATE: What kind of father is Jeff?

"So what'll it be, Linny? You won't have to pass a quiz on the menu."

"Very funny, Father." She fingered the menu's tattered[2] edge, suddenly feeling dizzy with hunger. Everyone around them was eating. Ketchup drizzled down a little boy's chin at the next table. His mother twirled pasta around a fork, and his baby sister blew an arc of peas across the table.

Lindsey glanced again at the table of girls, where hilarity still reigned.[3] Every single one had her hand on a burger or french fry. "A burger," she said aloud, "and . . ." She was about to say "salad," because she felt the presence of her mother somewhere close to her left shoulder. But she turned to her right and said "fries" instead.

"Burger it is," said Jeff.

At that moment Lindsey spied a solitary[4] figure stuck away at a corner table just off to the right. Her stomach did a little flip-flop. She did not like to see people eating alone. It made her feel sad, blue.

"I wish Magnolia would hurry," she said. "I'm starved."

---

1. **byline,** the line giving the writer's name at the beginning of a newspaper article.
2. tattered (tat'ərd), *adj.* ragged.
3. **reign** (rān), exist everywhere; prevail.
4. solitary (sol'ə ter'ē), *adj.* alone or single.

"Well, I guess she's pretty busy. I'll try to catch her eye, though."

She didn't want to be caught staring, so she raised her menu a little higher and peered over it at the lone woman. The woman raised the spoon to her lips and blew on it. She put the spoon down and pushed up the sleeves of a heavy dark coat.

"It's a funny way to get someone's attention," said her father, clearing his throat.

"What?"

"To say that you 'catch someone's eye.' You know, like she was just walking by, I stuck out my hand, and bingo!"

Lindsey smiled. "Dad, you have a sick sense of humor."

"Here she comes. Let's be ready so we don't seem like nit-brains."

Lindsey tried to get a better look at the woman alone. Her coat seemed shabby.[5] Her gray hair looked as though it hadn't been combed. Lindsey had a sudden horrible thought, that that could be her mom someday, or her dad. Now she didn't feel hungry at all.

"Maybe I'll just have some tea," she said with a sigh.

"Tea? *Tea?*" Her father looked puzzled and surprised. "I thought you were hungry. What's the matter?"

"I—I was hungry."

"So?"

Lindsey shrugged. "I guess I'm not as hungry as I was. Dad, it just bothers me to see someone eating alone like that." She nodded in the woman's direction.

Jeff turned to look over his shoulder. He scratched the back of his neck and drew his eyebrows together. "Gee, I didn't know she was here. That's Mrs. Glass."

"You know her?"

"Su-u-ure." He sipped from his water glass, taking his time. "I'm surprised to see her here alone. Really surprised."

"Yeah? Why?" She watched the woman break a cracker in two and drop it into her bowl.

"Well, she usually looks like a barnacle, thirty-four grandchildren clinging to her arms and legs. Get the picture? She lives with one of her daughters not far from the lake in a house that's not very big. I doubt she has much privacy."

indsey studied her father's face. He knew a lot of people from the newspaper. They were always bumping into someone he'd written about—a pet psychologist,[6] a woman who'd had a lung transplant, a man who'd written a book about the art of flirting. . . .

"I'll bet she doesn't have her own room," continued Jeff. "Bet she shares a bed with one of those grandkids, and the kid's still in diapers and when she wakes up in the morning she's lying on a big wet spot."

Lindsey laughed. "Oh, Father, you don't really know her."

"O-o-oh, yes," he insisted, stretching and yawning. "I don't remember the exact story. Maybe she was the one who won the half-marathon in the senior division last month."

"She doesn't look like a runner to me."

"You've got a point there. I don't remember that coat in the photo. But I wouldn't worry about her, Lindsey, she's getting a well-deserved rest. When she eats at home the kids drool on her spaghetti. Now what's happened to Magnolia? I've got to concentrate on catching that eye."

Lindsey pulled a wisp of hair away from her face and smiled at her father. She knew he loved her a lot and didn't want her to feel bad about anything.

When she looked at the woman alone now she saw an entirely different person, someone

---

5. **shabby** (shab′ē), *adj.* much worn.

6. **psychologist,** an expert in the science or study of the mind.

enjoying the luxury of time to herself. Her coat was ragged from being pulled on by so many kids. Her hair was messy because she was so busy combing everyone else's. She was only eating a bowl of soup because she loved soup and none of her grandchildren would eat it.

"Bingo," said Jeff.

Magnolia retrieved a pencil and pad from her uniform pocket.

"I'll have turkey on rye, no mustard. Lindsey, you want a burger?"

Lindsey was about to say yes when she noticed the table where the high school girls had been sitting. It was littered with plates smeared with ketchup and bits of food.

"A banana walnut waffle and a cream soda without ice."

"Very creative," said Magnolia. She made a few marks on her pad and hurried away.

CLARIFY: Why do you think Lindsey changes her order?

Lindsey mused[7] over the fact that her father almost always ordered turkey sandwiches, breaking his routine with tuna or chicken. His tastes were plain. She liked that. She liked that he wasn't the type of person who wanted to impress people by ordering steaks and fancy wines. She didn't know why she liked that, but she did. She hoped when he finished the sculpture it would make him famous, even if he didn't care about things like that.

". . . starved," her dad was saying, drumming his fingers on the table.

As Lindsey twisted her bracelet around and around her wrist, she spied another person alone, a man sitting at a small table near the center of the room. She had not seen him come in. He was a homely[8] sort of person, with a long thin neck and a small head fringed with gray hair, and she hoped that wasn't why he was eating alone. He picked at a salad, absorbed in a paperback book.

"Here, hons." Magnolia set the two plates down on the table. Lindsey looked at the man and then down at her waffle, piled high with sliced bananas, chopped walnuts, and a dab of whipped cream.

"Empire State Building," said her dad. He scraped excess mayonnaise off a slice of rye bread.

The syrup smelled rich and sweet, but she was not sure she could eat it. "Right," she replied. She broke off a piece of the waffle with her fork and then made a face. She couldn't seem to help it.

"What's wrong, Lindsey?"

She detected just the slightest hint of impatience in his tone of voice. "Hmm? I don't know, dad. Maybe I'm coming down with something. I'm just not that hungry after all." She would try to eat, she knew she'd be hungry later on if she didn't, but her stomach had lurched once again at the sight of the old man alone.

Her father studied her for a moment. Then he said, "Well, perhaps you should've ordered something easier on the stomach, soup or some salad, like Art over there." He nodded in the homely man's direction.

Lindsey sighed. She sliced a piece of banana in half and ate it, then a small bite of waffle. She did not look over at the man. "Art?" she repeated. "Don't tell me you know him too?"

"Well, I don't really know him. But someone that I know knows him. She was just saying that she'd heard that Art's wife was out of

---

7. **muse** (myüz), v. be completely absorbed in thought.
8. **homely** (hōm′lē), adj. not good looking; having an ordinary appearance; plain.

town visiting relatives and he'd been pretty lonely."

"Oh," said Lindsey. So she was right this time. She kept her head down and tried to focus on her food.

Her dad hurried on. "So my friend said that Art's wife just called him, yesterday I think, just to tell him how much she missed him, and that she was coming home a few days early. I bet that he was so happy he decided to take himself out to dinner, and he looks like he's really enjoying it, doesn't he?"

Lindsey gave in to her curiosity and lifted her head. Art turned a page, sipping coffee or tea. She supposed you could be happy in a quiet sort of way, even if you were alone. You didn't have to be jumping up and down or near delirious with laughter, like the crowd of girls, to be happy.

"Think you can handle that waffle or what?" asked her dad.

"Oh, I'm doing all right," she said. "It's good. Want some?"

he wind battered a cold sheet of rain into their faces as they emerged from the Avenue Eatery. They hurried huddled together down Telegraph Avenue, passing an old woman crouched in an alcove, half buried under a pile of filthy rags. A gray kitten slept curled on her lap. Lindsey gaped at the woman as they passed and then turned her face up to her father's.

"Dad . . ." she said.

He clutched her hand and squeezed it, but he didn't say a word.

Diner Still Life was painted by Ralph Goings in 1977. A still life is a painting of inanimate objects—traditionally, a vase of flowers or a bowl of fruit. What is the subject of this still life? What do you think the artist is saying about the everyday objects of modern life? ➤

After Reading

Making Connections

1. On a scale of 1 to 10, how truthful do you think Lindsey's father is? Explain the reasons for your ranking. Cite specific evidence from the story to support your opinion.

2. At times in the story, Lindsey and her father draw opposite conclusions about what they observe. Describe a scene in which this happens. What conclusion do you draw from that scene?

3. What do you think causes the changes in Lindsey's hunger at various places in the story?

4. Why do you think the author included the teenage girls in this story?

5. How does the **point of view** from which the story is told affect you as a reader?

6. Why does Lindsey's father clutch her hand at the end of the story?

7. ☺ Do you think there is something about teen culture that makes it seem especially awful to be alone? How might Lindsey's **perspective** on diners eating alone be influenced by the fact that she is a teenager?

Literary Focus: Characterization

In an earlier lesson you saw that authors can **develop characters** through direct description, through characters' thoughts and speeches, and through their actions. In this story, you get to know a character, Lindsey's mother, even though she does not even appear in the story. Review the story and make a list of the references to Lindsey's mom. When you finish your list, write a summary statement that gives your impression of this character.

Vocabulary Study

tattered
solitary
shabby
muse
homely

Decide if the underlined words are used correctly in the sentences below. Write *Correct* or *Incorrect*, and if it's incorrect, explain why.

1. The menu's <u>tattered</u> edge showed that the restaurant was fancy.

2. Lindsey liked the <u>solitary</u> feeling of eating with other people.

3. She felt bad for Mrs. Glass, who was wearing <u>shabby</u> clothes.

4. Lindsey began to <u>muse</u> over the possibility that her parents might someday look like Mrs. Glass.

5. She thought the man with the stringy hair and thin neck was <u>homely</u>.

Expressing Your Ideas

Writing Choices

"But Dad . . . " Suppose Lindsey had insisted that her father discuss the woman she saw at the end of the story. **Continue the story** by writing what you think her dad would say in response to her questions.

To Be, or Not to Be . . . Alone. Being alone is not necessarily good or bad. Make two **lists,** giving at least three situations in which you would rather be alone and at least three in which you'd rather be with other people.

Who Is This Person? Work with a partner and write two different **personality profiles** to go with this painting, *Girl with Flowers in Her Hair* by Isador Kaufmann. Be sure to explain what features of the painting led you to draw your conclusions.

Other Options

Bring Your Own Find your own picture to talk about. Bring one to class and **tell a story** about the person in the picture. Tell about the life and circumstances of the person. In effect, you will be creating a biography for this person. Be sure to include in your story two or three significant experiences that had an impact on the life of the person.

Good Eating Create a **menu** for the Avenue Eatery. Review the story to find items to list on your menu, and then add other items you think would be offered at this type of restaurant. List prices for the items that are in line with prices at similar restaurants in your town or neighborhood.

Language Mini-Lesson

Subject and Verb Agreement

Recognize agreement problems. Good writers make sure that the subjects of sentences agree in number with the verbs. Subject-verb agreement can be tricky when indefinite pronouns are the subjects. Look over the list of singular and plural indefinite pronouns.

Singular Indefinite Pronouns	Plural Indefinite Pronouns
anybody, anyone, each, everyone, everybody, nobody, no one, nothing, somebody, someone	several, few, both, many

Can you identify the agreement problems in these sentences?

- Several of them has already changed color.

- Everyone in our class are going to the ball game on Friday.

- No one in this room want to turn the heat up.

Writing Strategy To check for agreement problems, first isolate the subject and verb in the sentence. Then check to see whether the subject is singular or plural. Make the verb agree in number. Look at the following sentence. Can you spot the agreement problem more easily? How would you correct it?
  Several [of them] **has** [already] **changed** [color.]

Activity Options

1. Write five sentences with indefinite pronouns as subjects. Make sure the subjects and verbs don't agree. Trade papers with a partner and correct each other's sentences.

2. Work with a partner to write a conversation between two people that includes at least four indefinite pronouns used incorrectly. Share your conversation with a small group whose task is to correct the problems.

3. Go through your working portfolio and locate any errors in agreement that you may have made. Mark the errors and correct them.

Before Reading

Animal Craftsmen

by Bruce Brooks

Bruce Brooks
born 1950

Bruce Brooks first received attention for his award-winning young adult novel, *The Moves Make the Man*. In recent years he has written more critically acclaimed novels for young people, as well as several nonfiction books that focus on nature. As a writer, he finds that the biggest challenge is that "you're always going to be a beginner as soon as you finish something. You wrap up one book and immediately you are a rookie again because you've never written your next book." He likes to write about nature because, by studying animals, we can understand them better and yet still enjoy "that wonderful sense of difference."

Building Background

Wasp Nests The familiar wasps you're likely to see all summer—the ones that fascinate author Bruce Brooks—are social wasps that live in groups. Their activity during the summer revolves around their nest. In the spring, a female wasp creates a nest out of paper-like material. The wasp chews on plant fibers from grass, pieces of board, and so on, making a pulp that she uses to build the cells of the nest. All summer long the queen wasp lays eggs, placing one egg in each cell of the nest. The eggs quickly develop into larvae, then pupae, and finally adult wasps. Most of the wasps born are female workers, who care for and feed the new young and defend the nest.

Getting into the Essay

Writer's Notebook In social studies you read about the adventures of famous explorers, out discovering the unknown. You may not have discovered a continent, but you must have done some exploring of your own—in an attic, a cellar, a barn, the woods, or some other place where such adventures lie. In your notebook, write about a fascinating discovery that was also a mystery. Tell about a time when you found something and didn't know what it was, or where it came from, or what its use was. If you can't recall such an event, use your imagination and invent a mystery discovery for a person about your age.

Reading Tip

Parent: Where did you go?   Child: Out.

Parent: Who did you go with?   Child: Friends.

Parent: What did you do?   Child: Nothing.

Descriptive Detail There's not much detail in this conversation. In contrast, Bruce Brooks uses hundreds of details in the essay that follows. In his first sentence, the ladder isn't just outside a barn; it's outside a "rickety old tobacco barn." Even if you don't know what a tobacco barn is, you can still get a picture of the building from the author's use of **descriptive detail.** As you read, look for other examples of details that create pictures in your mind's eye.

Animal Craftsmen

Bruce Brooks

One evening, when I was about five, I climbed up a ladder on the outside of a rickety old tobacco barn at sunset. The barn was part of a small farm near the home of a country relative my mother and I visited periodically; though we did not really know the farm's family, I was allowed to roam, poke around, and conduct sudden studies of anything small and harmless. On this evening, as on most of my jaunts, I was not looking for anything; I was simply climbing with an open mind. But as I balanced on the next-to-the-top rung and inhaled the spicy stink of the tobacco drying inside, I *did* find something under the eaves—something very strange.

It appeared to be a kind of gray paper sphere, suspended from the dark planks by a thin stalk, like an apple made of ashes hanging on its stem. I studied it closely in the clear light. I saw that the bottom was a little ragged, and open. I could not tell if it had been torn, or if it had been made that way on purpose—for it was clear to me, as I studied it, that this thing had been *made*. This was no fruit or fungus. Its shape, rough but trim; its intricately[1]

colored surface with subtle swirls of gray and tan; and most of all the uncanny[2] adhesiveness with which the perfectly tapered stem stuck against the rotten old pine boards—all of these features gave evidence of some intentional design. The troubling thing was figuring out who had designed it, and why.

I assumed the designer was a human being: someone from the farm, someone wise and skilled in a craft that had so far escaped my curiosity. Even when I saw wasps entering and leaving the thing (during a vigil[3] I kept every evening for two weeks), it did not occur to me that the wasps might have fashioned it for themselves. I assumed it was a man-made "wasp house" placed there expressly for the purpose of attracting a family of wasps, much as the "martin hotel," a giant birdhouse on a pole near the farmhouse, was maintained to shelter migrant purple martins who returned

---

1. **intricately** (in′trə kit lē), *adv.* in a complex or complicated way.
2. **uncanny** (un kan′ē), *adj.* strange and mysterious.
3. **vigil** (vij′əl), *n.* a staying awake for some purpose; a watch.

every spring. I didn't ask myself why anyone would want to give wasps a bivouac;[4] it seemed no more odd than attracting birds.

As I grew less wary of the wasps (and they grew less wary of me), and as my confidence on the ladder improved, I moved to the upper rung and peered through the sphere's bottom. I could see that the paper swirled in layers around some secret center the wasps inhabited, and I marveled at the delicate hands of the craftsman who had devised[5] such tiny apertures[6] for their protection.

I left the area in the late summer, and in my imagination I took the strange structure with me. I envisioned unwrapping it, and in the middle finding—what? A tiny room full of bits of wool for sleeping, and countless manufactured pellets of scientifically determined wasp food? A glowing blue jewel that drew the wasps at twilight, and gave them a cool infusion of energy as they clung to it overnight? My most definite idea was that the wasps lived in a small block of fine cedar the craftsman had drilled full of holes, into which they slipped snugly, rather like the bunks aboard submarines in World War II movies.

As it turned out, I got the chance to discover that my idea of the cedar block had not been wrong by much. We visited our relative again in the winter. We arrived at night, but first thing in the morning I made straight for the farm and its barn. The shadows under the eaves were too dense to let me spot the sphere from far off. I stepped on the bottom rung of the ladder—slick with frost—and climbed carefully up. My hands and feet kept slipping, so my eyes stayed on the rung ahead, and it was not until I was secure at the top that I could look up. The sphere was gone.

I was crushed. That object had fascinated me like nothing I had come across in my life; I had even grown to love wasps because of it.

I sagged on the ladder and watched my breath eddy[7] around the blank eaves. I'm afraid I pitied myself more than the apparently homeless wasps.

But then something snapped me out of my sense of loss: I recalled that I had watched the farmer taking in the purple martin hotel every November, after the birds left. From its spruce appearance when he brought it out in March, it was clear he had cleaned it and repainted it and kept it out of the weather. Of course he would do the same thing for *this* house, which was even more fragile. I had never mentioned the wasp dwelling to anyone, but now I decided I would go to the farm, introduce myself, and inquire about it. Perhaps I would even be permitted to handle it, or, best of all, learn how to make one myself.

I scrambled down the ladder, leaping from the third rung and landing in the frosty salad of tobacco leaves and windswept grass that collected at the foot of the barn wall. I looked down and saw that my left boot had, by no more than an inch, just missed crushing the very thing I was rushing off to seek. There, lying dry and separate on the leaves, was the wasp house.

I looked up. Yes, I was standing directly beneath the spot where the sphere had hung—it was a straight fall. I picked up the wasp house, gave it a shake to see if any insects were inside, and, discovering none, took it home.

My awe of the craftsman grew as I unwrapped the layers of the nest. Such beautiful paper! It was much tougher than any I

---

4. **bivouac** (biv′wak, biv′ü ak), temporary outdoor camp of soldiers, hikers, etc.
5. devise (di vīz′), *v.* think out, plan, or invent.
6. aperture (ap′ər chər, ap′ər chůr), *n.* opening or hole.
7. **eddy,** move in circles.

A field wasp on a comb. A pattern of repeating cells is a common design in nature. ➤

had encountered, and it held a curve (something my experimental paper airplanes never did), but it was very light, too. The secret at the center of the swirl turned out to be a neatly made fan of tiny cells, all of the same size and shape, reminding me of the heart of a sunflower that had lost its seeds to birds. The fan hung from the sphere's ceiling by a stem the thickness of a pencil lead.

The rest of the story is a little embarrassing. More impressed than ever, I decided to pay homage[8] to the creator of this habitable[9] sculpture. I went boldly to the farmhouse. The farmer's wife answered my knock. I showed her the nest and asked to speak with the person in the house who had made it. She blinked and frowned. I had to repeat my question twice before she understood what I believed my mission to be; then, with a gentle laugh, she dispelled my illusion about an ingenious[10] old papersmith fond of wasps. The nest, she explained, had been made entirely by the insects themselves, and wasn't that amazing?

Well, of course it was. It still is. I needn't have been so embarrassed—the structures that animals build, and the sense of design they display, *should* always astound us. On my way home from the farmhouse, in my own defense I kept thinking, "But *I* couldn't build anything like this! Nobody could!"

The most natural thing in the world for us to do, when we are confronted with a piece of animal architecture, is to figure out if we could possibly make it or live in it. Who hasn't peered into the dark end of a mysterious hole in the woods and thought, "It must be pretty weird to live in there!" or looked up at a hawk's nest atop a huge sycamore and shuddered at the thought of waking up every morning with nothing but a few twigs preventing a hundred-foot fall. How, we wonder, do these twigs stay together, and withstand the wind so high?

It is a human tendency always to regard animals first in terms of ourselves. Seeing the defensive courage of a mother bear whose cubs are threatened, or the cooperative determination of a string of ants dismantling a stray chunk of cake, we naturally use our own behavior as reference for our empathy.[11] We put ourselves in the same situation and express the animal's action in feelings—and words—that apply to the way people do things.

---

8. homage (hom′ij, om′ij), *n.* respect.
9. habitable (hab′ə tə bəl), *adj.* fit to live in.
10. ingenious (in jē′nyəs), *adj.* skillful in making; clever.
11. empathy (em′pə thē), *n.* quality of entering into another's feelings.

Sometimes this is useful. But sometimes it is misleading. Attributing human-like intentions to an animal can keep us from looking at the *animal's* sense of itself in its surroundings—its immediate and future needs, its physical and mental capabilities, its genetic instincts. Most animals, for example, use their five senses in ways that human beings cannot possibly understand or express. How can a forty-two-year-old nearsighted biologist have any real idea what a two-week-old barn owl sees in the dark? How can a sixteen-year-old who lives in the Arizona desert identify with the muscular jumps improvised by a waterfall-leaping salmon in Alaska? There's nothing wrong with trying to empathize with an animal, but we shouldn't forget that ultimately animals live *animal* lives.

Animal structures let us have it both ways—we can be struck with a strange wonder, and we can empathize right away, too. Seeing a vast spiderweb, taut and glistening between two bushes, it's easy to think, "I have no idea how that is done; the engineering is awesome." But it is just as easy to imagine climbing across the bright strands, springing from one to the next as if the web were a new Epcot attraction, the Invisible Flying Flexible Space Orb. That a clear artifact of an animal's wits and agility stands right there in front of us—that we can touch it, look at it from different angles, sometimes take it home—inspires our imagination as only a strange reality can. We needn't move into a molehill to experience a life of darkness and digging; our creative wonder takes us down there in a second, without even getting our hands dirty.

But what if we discover some of the mechanics of how the web is made? Once we see how the spider works (or the humming-bird, or the bee), is the engineering no longer awesome? This would be too bad: we don't want to lose our sense of wonder just because we gain understanding.

And we certainly do *not* lose it. In fact, seeing how an animal makes its nest or egg case or food storage vaults has the effect of increasing our amazement. The builder's energy, concentration, and athletic adroitness[12] are qualities we can readily admire and envy. Even more startling is the recognition that the animal is working from a precise design in its head, a design that is exactly replicated[13] time after time. This knowledge of architecture—knowing where to build, what materials to use, how to put them together—remains one of the most intriguing[14] mysteries of animal behavior. And the more *we* develop that same knowledge, the more we appreciate the instincts and intelligence of the animals.

---

12. **adroitness** (ə droit′nes), skillfulness in the use of the body.
13. **replicate** (rep′lə kāt), *v.* copy exactly or reproduce.
14. **intriguing** (in trē′ging), exciting the curiosity and interest.

The author compares a spider web to a new Epcot attraction. What else does this web remind you of? ➤

After Reading

Making Connections

1. What part of this essay is most interesting to you? Why?

2. Which description do you think was easiest to picture or understand?

3. How is this essay different from a chapter on wasps you might read in a science textbook?

4. What sentence best conveys the author's **main idea?**

5. This is nonfiction, but it has some elements of a short story or other work of fiction. Where in this essay does the author use **suspense,** as you might find in a mystery story?

6. Do you think humans can ever understand life from an animal's point of view? Why or why not?

7. Thousands of scientists across the world study animal behavior. Of what use to humans do you think such studies can be?

Literary Focus: Imagery

When we think of the word *image,* we might first think of pictures. A visual image is a picture, and it is created in writing by giving details that a reader can see: "a vast spiderweb, taut and glistening between two bushes. . . ." Sensory **images** in literature are words or phrases that appeal not only to sight, but also to sound, touch, smell, and taste. Often these senses are combined. "I stepped on the bottom rung of the ladder—slick with frost. . . ." You could see the frost, feel the slickness, and even feel the cold as you stepped on the ladder.

Review "Animal Craftsmen" and find at least three other examples of images. For each, tell what sense or senses are appealed to.

Vocabulary Study

intricately
uncanny
vigil
devise
aperture
homage
habitable
ingenious
empathy
replicate

Decide if the following pairs of words are synonyms or antonyms. On your paper write *S* for synonym or *A* for antonym.

1. intricately—simply
2. uncanny—weird
3. vigil—lookout
4. devise—design
5. aperture—closing

6. homage—disrespect
7. habitable—livable
8. ingenious—brilliant
9. empathy—detachment
10. replicate—duplicate

Expressing Your Ideas

Writing Choices

Such Beautiful Paper . . . Use the author's description of the wasp nest as a starting place and create a **poem** about the wasp nest. Begin by collecting five or six images of the nest from the essay. Organize these images so that the poem will "flow" from beginning to end.

Those Strange Humans! "Animal Craftsmen" looks from a human perspective at the "artifact of an animal's wits"—the wasp nest. Reverse the perspective and write a **description** of a human artifact—a structure or machine—from the perspective of an animal or insect. For example, how would a whale describe a submarine? Remember that the animal will not know the name of the artifact and will not fully understand it. Try to keep the sense of uncertainty and wonder the author had in "Animal Craftsmen."

The Main Thing Here . . . Create a **main idea** map for "Animal Craftsmen," using the structure of the map below. Review the essay to find the main idea. (Is the wasp nest the main idea or a supporting detail?) Write the main idea in the top box. In the next row, write details that support the main idea. In the bottom row, write more details and examples that extend the supporting details.

Other Options

Sketch the Natural World Find your own example of animal or insect craftsmanship and draw a **sketch** that shows what is amazing or remarkable about the structure. If you can't find a structure to sketch, find a photograph of such a structure and explain to the class how author Bruce Brooks might describe it.

Those Strange Humans, Part II With a partner, improvise a **dialogue** between two wasps or other animals who are discussing their human observers. What would they say about us? What do they find strange, fascinating, or terrifying?

How Do They Do That? Research an animal structure, such as a beaver dam, spider web, or bird's nest, and build **a model** of the structure. Use your model to explain to the class how and why the animal builds that structure.

Main Idea

Details   **Details**   **Details**

Before Reading

Keepsakes by Deloras Lane

Without Commercials by Alice Walker

Deloras Lane
born 1953

It's never too late—or too early—to become a poet. Deloras Lane, of Cherokee heritage, began composing poems almost as soon as she learned to write, before she was five years old.

Alice Walker
born 1944

Alice Walker, perhaps best known for her novel *The Color Purple,* has also written many books of poetry. She started to write poetry as a teenager, but writes now about different subjects: ". . . I think that my poems today are more about the world outside myself."

Building Background

Allusions to Eden An **allusion** is an indirect reference to something else, usually a person, place, or event in literature, myth, or religion. To call a job a "Herculean task," for example, is to allude to Hercules, the strongman in Greek mythology. This allusion is a shorthand way of saying the task is huge, if not impossible, and requires the strength of a superman like Hercules. In "Without Commercials," the references to Eden, Adam, and Eve are allusions to the Biblical story of creation. In the Bible, Adam and Eve are the first humans, created by God and placed in a beautiful garden called Eden.

Getting into the Poetry

Writer's Notebook When you get ready to go to school or go out in the evening, are there any steps you take to make yourself more attractive? What look are you after? Popular magazines for people of different ages feature advertisements and articles that have to do with changing your physical appearance. There seem to be conventional or "right" images for being attractive. In your notebook, write an answer to this question: What are the "rules" for how you are supposed to look?

Reading Tip

Reading Poetry One important difference between prose and poetry is that prose is organized in sentences and paragraphs, while poetry is organized in lines and stanzas, or line groups. Poets are careful about establishing **line breaks,** deciding how many words to put in each line. One of the poems to follow begins with these words: "Listen, stop tanning yourself and talking about fishbelly white." In the poem, however, these words make up five lines. As you read the poems, think about the effects of the line breaks. Because of the poets' choices, what words are emphasized? What features stand out?

Keepsakes

(Conversation with a twelve-year-old)

Deloras Lane

Why don't you dye your hair black
and cover the grey so
you don't look old,
my niece asked last week.
5 Oh no, I said,
those grey hairs are mistakes I made
and spun into lessons
of silver thread. Besides
I think they're rather attractive.

10 How about a little make-up
to hide those lines
around your eyes?
I like those lines, I
told her,
15 they are autographs
of smiles.

Let's go for a walk then,
she urged,
walking briskly
20 every day would help you lose
those extra pounds.
Ah those,
I answered,
are pizzas and banana-splits
25 shared with you—
and I savored[1] every one.

But let's take a walk anyway
and see if Mr. Bennett's
roses have
30 bloomed.

---

1. **savor** (sā′vər), *v.* enjoy or appreciate.

WITHOUT Commercials
Alice Walker

What's going on here? Can you think of a good title for this illustration by Lonni Sue Johnson?

Listen,
stop tanning yourself
and talking about
fishbelly
5 white.
The color white
is not bad at all.
There are white mornings
that bring us days.
10 Or, if you must,
tan only because
it makes you happy
to be brown,
to be able to see
15 for a summer
the whole world's
darker
face
reflected
20 in your own.

Stop unfolding
your eyes.
Your eyes are
beautiful.
25 Sometimes
seeing you in the street
the fold zany
and unexpected
I want to kiss
30 them
and usually
it is only
old
gorgeous
35 black people's eyes
I want
to kiss.

Stop trimming
your nose.
40 When you
diminish[1]
your nose

your songs
become little
45 tinny, muted
and snub.
Better you should
have a nose
impertinent
50 as a flower,
sensitive
as a root;
wise, elegant,[2]
serious and deep.
55 A nose that
sniffs
the essence[3]
of Earth. And knows
the message
60 of every
leaf.

Stop bleaching
your skin
and talking
65 about
so much black
is not beautiful
The color black
is not bad
70 at all.
There are black nights
that rock
us
in dreams.
75 Or, if you must,
bleach only
because it pleases you
to be brown,
to be able to see
80 for as long
as you can bear it
the whole world's
lighter face
reflected
85 in your own.

As for me,
I have learned
to worship
the sun
90 again.
To affirm[4]
the adventures
of hair.

For we are all
95 *splendid*
descendants
of Wilderness,
Eden:
needing only
100 to see
each other
without
commercials
to believe.

105 Copied skillfully
as Adam.

Original

as Eve.

---

1. diminish (də min′ish), v. make smaller.
2. elegant (el′ə gənt), *adj.* graceful, showing good taste.
3. essence (es′ns), *n.* that which makes a thing what it is; the necessary part.
4. affirm (ə fėrm′), v. declare to be true.

After Reading

Making Connections

1. Before you read the poem, what was your first reaction to the title, "Without Commercials"?

2. After reading the poem, how did your reaction change? What does the title mean to you now?

3. Why do you think Walker mentions Adam and Eve in her poem?

4. In "Keepsakes," what is an appropriate **tone** to use for reading the words of the niece? for the words of the aunt?

5. How would you describe the explanations the aunt gives for her grey hair, her wrinkles, and her extra pounds?

6. ☞ How is your **perspective** on beauty shaped by our culture? What role do you think commercials play in that cultural shaping?

Literary Focus: Similes and Metaphors

Do these words—". . . impertinent . . . sensitive . . . elegant . . . serious . . . deep"—describe your nose? Alice Walker uses some of these words in figures of speech to tell how a nose should be:

> ". . . impertinent
> as a flower,
> sensitive
> as a root. . . ."

These are examples of **simile,** a special kind of comparison that brings together two things not commonly thought of as similar. A simile uses *like* or *as* to establish the comparison between nose and flower or nose and root. In another figure of speech, a **metaphor,** the same kind of comparison is made, but without using *like* or *as.* "Keepsakes" uses this metaphor in the opening stanza:

> ". . . those grey hairs are mistakes I made
> and spun into lessons
> of silver thread. . . ."

List these and any other similes and metaphors you find in the two poems in your notebook, and graph the comparisons that are being made. One has been done for you below.

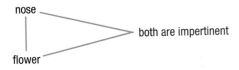

Vocabulary Study

savor
diminish
elegant
essence
affirm

Write the letter of the word that is not related in meaning to the other words in the set.

1. **a.** diminish **b.** increase **c.** reduce **d.** decrease

2. **a.** clumsy **b.** refined **c.** elegant **d.** tasteful

3. **a.** core **b.** essence **c.** center **d.** detail

4. **a.** deny **b.** proclaim **c.** insist **d.** affirm

5. **a.** savor **b.** relish **c.** ignore **d.** devour

Expressing Your Ideas

Writing Choices

Why Don't You . . .? "Keepsakes" is composed of three questions or suggestions from the niece, and three responses from the aunt. Think like a twelve-year-old and write one more **stanza** for the poem. The stanza should contain a question or suggestion for the aunt, and a response from the aunt.

Advice to Teenagers Bring together two of the speakers—the aunt from "Keepsakes" and the narrator from "Without Commercials"—and write the **dialogue** they might have on advice they would give to teenagers about how to respond to the physical appearance of the people they meet.

Counterpoint Suppose you are a plastic surgeon or own a cosmetic company. What would you say to these two poets? Write a **rebuttal,** or counter-argument, in which you defend the right of individuals to change how they look.

Other Options

Readers' Theater Work with a partner to do an **oral interpretation** of "Keepsakes" for your classmates. One of you take the part of the niece, the other take the part of the aunt. Read the poem carefully to decide on the feelings behind the words. Plan how to convey those feelings with your voice.

Debate! Stage a **debate** on whether people should spend large amounts of time and money on personal appearance. Divide into two teams, each of which will develop arguments to defend their side. Poll your classmates on their opinions and research the issue before holding your debate.

Need a Lift? Research one type of cosmetic surgery, and if possible interview a plastic surgeon to find out how the procedure is done. **Report** back to your classmates on the procedure, its cost, and possible dangers.

Before Reading

The Enchanted Raisin

by Jacqueline Balcells

Jacqueline Balcells
born 1950

If you were to have children someday, what kinds of stories would you tell them or read to them? If you wrote a story for them, what would it be like? "The Enchanted Raisin" was written by a mother for her own children. Jacqueline Balcells, a Chilean journalist, wrote this for her children while living in Paris. It was first written in French, then translated into Spanish, and then into English. In any language, the story makes some interesting points about human behavior, both of children and adults.

Building Background

Tales of the Fantastic Stories of enchantment and fantasy, from fairy tales such as "Hansel and Gretel" to modern novels like Madeleine L'Engle's *A Wrinkle in Time,* have some elements in common. First, of course, they contain magic or fantastic events that couldn't possibly happen in real life. Second, characters are usually not fully developed and realistic, but instead are broadly drawn figures who represent a type of personality—innocent, greedy, evil, foolish, or cruel, for example. In this fantasy, you'll encounter several types of characters: misbehaving children, a long-suffering mother, a father who is completely in the dark, and that much maligned **stock character** of fairy tales, the wicked stepmother.

Getting into the Story

Discussion Many stories have a character who is always getting into trouble—the bratty kid or misbehaving child who gets into all kinds of mischief. In a group, brainstorm characters you remember from cartoons, stories, TV shows, or movies who fit that description. For each character you recall, decide whether he or she "learned his lesson" or was unreformed in the end. Create a web like the one shown to record your ideas.

never learns

Dennis the Menace

Problem Child

Reading Tip

The Teaching in the Tale Some say that the purpose of literature is to entertain. Others believe literature should teach important lessons. One writer combined the teaching and entertaining aspects of literature into a metaphor: literature should be a sugar-coated pill. The pill is the medicine or lesson. The sugar coating is what allows us to swallow the pill by covering up the taste. In the story that follows, identify the parts you think make up the "pill." Also identify the parts that make up the sugar coating.

THE ENCHANTED RAISIN

ONCE UPON A TIME, THERE WAS A MOM WHO HAD THREE ABSOLUTELY UNBEARABLE CHILDREN. THEY DID EVERY BAD AND STUPID THING IMAGINABLE, AS WELL AS THE UNIMAGINABLE ONES. Several times they almost burned down the house, and they flooded it a hundred times. They broke the furniture, smashed the plates, fought and screamed like crazy people, spilled ink on the white sheets, and swung from the curtains as if they were monkeys in the jungle. And why bother saying what happened when they were sent outside: they spread panic throughout the neighborhood.

Their dad was almost never home, and their poor mother couldn't manage these three little devils. She was completely exhausted at the end of the day from chasing after them.

"My children," she said to them, "please stop your foolishness, if only this once. Look at me: each one of your pranks and screams is a wrinkle on my face. I am becoming an old lady."

And it was true. This woman, who had been tall and beautiful, was wrinkling and shrinking from one day to the next.

Her children didn't notice anything. But one day, when she went to meet them after school, their friends asked with astonishment, "Why does your grandmother come to get you now?"

The children felt bad for a moment; they were upset that their mother was mistaken for their grandmother. But they didn't think about it for long—they had so much to do!

The poor woman continued to wrinkle and shrink at an incredible rate. The moment arrived when she could no longer walk: her legs had become two little sticks that were so skinny they were like cherry stems, and her back was so curved she

JACQUELINE BALCELLS

could barely see in front of her. Nevertheless, her three children did not stop inventing more and more horrible pranks:

"Let's take the feathers out of the pillows!"

"Let's pull out the dog's fur!"

"Let's cut off the cat's ears!"

"Let's dig a hole in the field for the gardener to fall into!"

By now, their mother was so small that, standing, she did not reach her youngest child's knees. She sighed, "Children, enough! Look at my size, my wrinkles. If this continues, I will shrink so much that you won't even be able to see me." But she never thought this would happen.

One night after supper, she dragged herself to her room, exhausted. She put on her nightgown, which was now one hundred times too big. She climbed on her bed, rolled herself into a ball, and fell deeply asleep.

The next morning when they woke up, the children did what they always did. They jumped on their beds like devils and began to yell, "Moooooommm, bring us our breakfast!"

There was no response. They yelled louder, with no success. They began to howl, once, twice, ten times, thirty times. After the fifty-first shout, with their throats sore, they decided to go to their mother's room.

Her bed was unmade, but she was nowhere to be found. The children realized that something strange was happening. Suddenly, the youngest child bent over the pillow and screamed.

"What's the matter?" his brother asked.

"Look, look there!" he shouted.

Between the folds of their mother's nightgown was a small, dark ball. It was a raisin.

The children were frightened. They called louder and louder, "Mooooommy, Moooommy, . . . !"

Like the other times, there was no answer, but the oldest child realized that with each shout, the raisin on the pillow moved slightly. They were quiet and watched it: the raisin

didn't move. They shouted "Mom!" and the raisin shook a little.

Then they remembered their mother's words: "If this continues, I will shrink so much that you won't be able to see me." And horrified, they realized that this raisin that moved when they yelled "Mom" was all that remained of their mother, who in that way tried to make them recognize her. How they cried and wailed!

"Poor us! What are we going to do now that Mom is a raisin? What is Dad going to say when he gets home and sees her?"

Their father had been on a business trip for several weeks but was due to return home that very night. The children, frightened and not knowing what to do, waited for him in their room all day long. Once in a while, to reassure themselves, they approached the raisin and called "Mom!" The raisin invariably[1] moved.

That evening, their father arrived home. He opened the door, dropped his briefcase, took off his hat and coat, and called his wife from the hall: "Hello, are you there? Aren't you going to welcome me home? Aren't you going to give me a hug and bring me a glass of wine?"

Instead of his wife, his children appeared walking one behind the other with their heads bowed. The oldest held a matchbox in his hands.

"What's going on? Why aren't you in bed? And where's your mother?"

"She's in this box," the oldest answered in a mournful tone. "She turned into a raisin."

His father became angry. "You know that I hate jokes! Go to bed immediately!"

He searched the house for his wife. It was useless to tell him he would not find her. He then said, "She must have gone out for a

---

1. invariably (in ver′ē ə blē), *adv.* without changing; always in the same way.

▲ *Weeping Woman* was painted by Pablo Picasso in 1937. Picasso's style at the time was to show several views of a subject at once. How does he portray deep sorrow in this painting?

walk!" But an hour later, as she had not appeared, he began to worry.

He put on his hat and left. He walked around the neighborhood, went to the houses of his neighbors, relatives, and friends. He asked everyone, "Have you seen my wife?" Then he went to the police station. But they couldn't tell him anything either.

One night passed, a day and another night. And while the time passed and his wife continued to be missing, the father began to ask himself with great pain if his wife had died.

"She must have taken a walk by the lake and drowned! And the worst thing is, I will never know the truth!" he lamented[2] in anguish.

The months passed with no news. Feeling very lonely, the man finally decided to remarry.

"A new wife would help me take care of these wild animals. . . ."

So he chose a wife who was not as pretty as the first one—not to say frightful—but she seemed sweet and self-sacrificing. In reality, her face was as ugly as her heart was hard: she led him to believe that she adored the children, but the truth is that she detested[3] them.

The father didn't realize anything. But the three children immediately understood that their stepmother was evil, and they did not trust her. Also, they knew that their real mother was still alive in the matchbox that they guarded so carefully. They were certain she would stop being a raisin and return to her former self.

From time to time at night, the children circled the box, removed the cover, and called softly, "Mom, Mom."

And each time, the raisin responded by rocking gently.

OPEN IT UP, LITTLE MONSTERS!

One day when their father was in a good mood, they again asked him to go to their room to see what happened with the raisin. Perhaps he would understand! But their father didn't want to know anything; on the contrary, he became furious: "How long is this stupid joke going to continue? Little devils . . . if you keep up these stories, you are going to get it. I don't want to hear you mention that raisin again!"

Frightened, the children watched over the box.

But, horrors, the stepmother overheard the conversation from behind the door, and she believed them! For a while, she had had her suspicions about the matchbox that the children watched over with such anxiety.

At the beginning, she didn't say anything. But a few days later, one afternoon when the father wasn't home, she called the children and said to them: "Children, I am going to make a raisin cake, and I am short one raisin. I believe you have one. Go get it right now!" The stepmother had an evil expression on her face.

The children didn't dare protest.[4] They went to their room and asked each other, "What should we do? We can't give her our mother so she can throw her in the oven!" The oldest decided, "Let's go up to the attic. We will hide the box and tell our stepmother that we lost it."

Unfortunately, the evil woman had followed them and once again listened to their conversation from behind the door. She entered the room like a whirlwind and yelled, "Don't you dare trick me! Give me the raisin now; I already have the oven hot!"

The oldest child had just enough time to

---

2. lament (lə ment′), v. express grief.
3. detest (di test′), v. intensely dislike, hate.
4. protest (prə test′), v. object to.

grab the box. He yelled for his brothers to follow him, and ran upstairs as fast as he could. On his way out, he pushed the stepmother, who fell to the floor with a loud rattling of her bones because she was very thin.

The children ran up to the attic, closed the door, and blocked the entrance with a large bureau. Meanwhile, the stepmother got up painfully, brushed herself off, and quickly headed toward the attic. "Open the door, brats! Open it up, little monsters! You'll see what will happen when your father gets home!" But the children, mute with fear, didn't budge.

Then, a cold, wicked, and terrible fury invaded her.

"You don't want to open the door? Very well, you will stay locked there as long as it takes. And when you are dying from hunger . . . you will eat the raisin!" She took a key from her pocket and turned it in the lock. Then she laughed three times, "Ha, ha, ha," with a sharp and evil crackle that was unlike the musical laughs she let her husband hear.

At nightfall, her husband came home and asked, "Where are the children?"

She answered, feigning surprise, "Don't you remember? They left to visit their grandmother in the country for a few days." She lied so convincingly that he said, distracted, "That's true, I had forgotten."

Meanwhile, above in the attic, the three children celebrated the victory of having escaped from the cruel woman. But as the hours passed and they became tired of being prisoners, they began to think about how they would escape. The only opening besides the sealed door was a small skylight that was difficult to reach since it was high above the floor in the rafters. And it was at least ten meters above the ground, over the garden.

"We could never jump," they said. "We would need a parachute or a rope."

But in the attic, they couldn't find anything. Suddenly, in the middle of their reflections, the three children realized with surprise that they hadn't fought, whined, or played pranks for a long time. It was possible for them to behave! They were so happy with this discovery that they hugged each other and promised to continue their good behavior as long as they could.

But now it was vital[5] that they find a way to escape. Night was falling, and with it they felt the first signs of cold and hunger. The oldest sighed, "If only I had my bed and a good blanket." "And a large glass of warm milk," added the second. "And our beautiful mother," murmured the youngest. Not knowing what else to do, the children curled up on the floor in a corner, cuddling each other, with the matchbox in the middle. They stayed like that until they fell asleep.

In the morning, the growling of their stomachs woke them. They had never been so hungry before. "We must eat something!" they said. Then they looked at the matchbox. "Oh no," said the oldest, "We are not going to eat the raisin, never!" After thinking for a moment, he continued in a serious tone, "Brothers, remember the stories of lost explorers or shipwrecked people who are left without food? They end up eating anything or anyone. . . . This must not happen to us!"

The youngest then said, "Let's separate ourselves from our mother so we can be sure we will not eat her."

"Yes," said the middle child. "If we throw her from the skylight, she will land on the grass in the garden, and since it is soft, she won't get hurt."

The children looked at the small raisin for the last time. Their eyes filled with tears. It was hard for them to separate from their mother!

But how could they reach the skylight to throw her into the garden? They could drag over the bureau that was against the door and climb on top of it, but they ran the risk that

---

5. **vital,** necessary to life.

the evil stepmother would choose that moment to search for them. No! The best thing was to try to climb on top of each other to reach the skylight. The oldest would stand on a chair; the middle child would balance on the very top and open the skylight.

The More They Cried, The More The Raisin Grew.

And that is what they did. Or it is what they almost did, because the chair was broken, which did not help the operation.

"Can you reach it? Can you touch the skylight?" the older children asked the youngest, who was balancing on top of them.

"Yes . . . , I found it . . . pass me the box!"

"What? Don't you have it?"

"No! I left it on the floor . . ."

They had to start over!

There was a small argument: each accused the other of having forgotten the box. But they soon made up.

"We'll just begin again," said the oldest child.

And they climbed on top of each other again: the oldest on the chair, the middle child on top of the oldest, and the youngest on top of the middle child, like acrobats. The youngest child reached the window and was about to open it when suddenly, crack, the chair broke in two and the children fell to the floor with a great crash.

At that very moment their father was entering the house. He heard the noise and said to his wife, "Go see what is happening!"

She disappeared for a moment and returned saying, "It isn't anything, just some mice running through the attic."

Meanwhile, in the attic, the three children were crying. Large tears of pain ran down their cheeks: tears of pain, because they had hurt themselves in the fall, and of frustration, because how were they going to reach the skylight now that the chair was broken? To console themselves, they opened the matchbox and looked at the raisin. But just seeing the raisin made them even sadder, and they started to cry over it as hard as they could.

The children's tears fell in torrents[6] on the matchbox, so that it flooded, and the raisin was left floating in a small, warm puddle.

Suddenly, the oldest child shouted, "Look! It's growing!"

It was true. The raisin, swollen from the children's tears, had begun to grow. The more they cried, the more the raisin grew. And seeing it grow, the children cried more, but now from happiness.

The raisin continued inflating, stretching, enlarging, growing more and more. Until . . . before the children's disbelieving eyes, it changed form and . . .

"Mommmmmmm!" they yelled.

It was their mother, as tall and as beautiful as before she had shriveled up. The mother took her children in her arms and, laughing and crying, hugged them against her for a long time.

Meanwhile, on the first floor, the father was wondering about the strange noises that were coming from the attic. Finally, he could stand it no longer, and he said to his wife, "Those mice in the attic have a strange way of squeaking. It is as if they were crying. Give me the keys. . . . I am going to see what is happening."

His wife tried every way to stop him, but her efforts were in vain.[7] He went upstairs, tried to open the door with the key, and, when it wouldn't open, pushed it with all his might. Imagine his surprise to find his three children in the arms of his first, beautiful wife! The four, hugging tightly, looked at him without saying anything.

---

6. **torrent,** a rushing stream of water.
7. **in vain,** without success.

Then this man, who wasn't as bad as he seemed, felt as if he would die from remorse[8] and joy. He covered his children with kisses, and then, kneeling at his wife's feet, he begged forgiveness for having doubted her.

He was immediately forgiven, and father, mother, and children walked downstairs hand in hand to have dinner, with their hearts full of happiness.

The stepmother hadn't waited for them. Guessing what had happened, she had run off at full speed with her bags.

The raisin cake in the oven was completely burnt.

The mother threw it in the trash and quickly made another, delicious cake full of candied fruit.

The whole family happily and hungrily ate this new cake that didn't contain a single raisin.

---

8. remorse (ri môrs'), *n.* deep, painful regret for having done wrong.

▲ In *Soft-Boiled Eggs,* a 1946 painting by Will Barnet, a mother is surrounded by her children. Barnet felt it was unnecessary for a painter to create the illusion of space on a flat canvas. Do you think he was successful in expressing the personalities of these four individuals, despite the lack of realism in his style?

After Reading

Making Connections

1. What character in the story would you most want to talk with about this adventure? Why?

2. How is the mother **characterized?** Give some examples to support your opinion.

3. The **theme** for this unit is conflict. What do you think the central conflict is in this story?

4. Who is more affected by the children's misbehavior, their mother or their father? Support your answer with specific evidence or quotes from the story.

5. ☙ In this story, how do the children treat their mother at first? How does their **perspective** on their mother change during the story? In what ways do you think their treatment of their mother may be influenced by cultural beliefs?

6. Do you think this story is a good one to read or tell to young children? Give reasons for your answer.

Literary Focus: Stereotypes

Sometimes characters in stories are flat and one-dimensional. A flat character who represents a group of people rather than an individual is called a **stereotype.** These characters are not meant to be realistic. Realistic characters, like real people, are a mix of good and bad traits. Stereotyped characters are one-dimensional and tend to represent a single trait: evil, greed, stupidity, or goodness. A common stereotype is to equate goodness with beauty and youth and to equate evil with ugliness and old age.

In "The Enchanted Raisin," what stereotypes do you notice? With your classmates, discuss these questions:

- Why is it sometimes useful for an author to use stereotypes rather than realistic characters?

- Why do you think the author of *this* story used stereotyped characters?

- How can stereotypes be harmful?

Vocabulary Study

invariably
lament
protest
remorse
detest

Write an antonym from the listed words to complete each phrase.

1. not adore, but ____
2. not applaud, but ____
3. not celebrate, but ____
4. not occasionally, but ____
5. not pride, but ____

Expressing Your Ideas

Writing Choices

What, Three Parents? Make a **comparison chart** of the qualities of the mother, the father, and the stepmother in this story. Review the story to find direct descriptions, actions, thoughts and speeches, and comments made by other characters that reveal character traits. List your evidence in a separate column for each character. Finish with a brief comment about how these characters are portrayed.

Help! Help! (Wanted) "I am becoming an old lady," says the mother. Because she feels that she will soon not be able to take care of her children, she decides to hire a baby-sitter or nanny. Write the newspaper **classified advertisement** you think she would write to find a nanny for her children. Examine the classified ad section of a newspaper to see the style of employment ads.

No More Stereotypes! Pick a stock character in "The Enchanted Raisin," and write a **persuasive essay** arguing against the continued use of such characters in literature. For example, consider how a real stepmother might feel reading this story.

Other Options

Daddy, I Shrunk Our Mother! In a small group, plan a **sequel** to "The Enchanted Raisin" in which Mom gets shrunk again. Plot a few close calls for Mom, and figure out a happy ending. Prepare a plot outline, with sketches showing key scenes.

Wait Till I Tell You The stepmother in this story ran off at full speed with her bags. Imagine she ran into several of your classmates at a coffee shop. Work with one or two classmates to plan a **role play** for a meeting with this character. How would the stepmother explain what had happened?

Making a Story Map Make a **plot structure map** for "The Enchanted Raisin." Copy the map outline below. Then list the events that lead to the climax of the story, as well as the climax itself. Finally, include the events that lead to the resolution and the resolution itself.

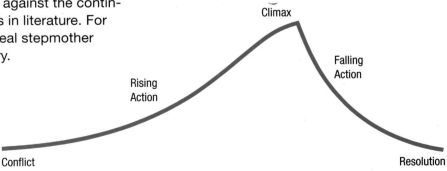

Climax

Rising
Action

Falling
Action

Conflict

Resolution

Things Are Not As They Seem

Deceiving to the Eye

Life Science Connection

Many plants and animals are not what they seem. Nature has provided them with the ability to camouflage themselves in order to survive. Look closely—nature's patterns are deceiving to the eye.

CAMOUFLAGE
THE BIG COVER-UP

Bengal tiger

Long-nosed hawkfish

Treehopper

Snowshoe hare

by Mary Batten

One of the best ways to hide is to look like part of the environment. This type of disguise is called *camouflage.*

For centuries, soldiers and hunters have used leaves, branches, reeds, vines, and other bits and pieces of the environment to cover themselves so they could hide from their enemies or their prey. Armies issue uniforms that mimic the colors and patterns of particular environments: green for tropical forests, white for snow country, beige for the desert. But people did not invent camouflage. It is another of nature's fantastic tricks.

There are two kinds of camouflage in nature: animals with built-in disguises and animals that use bits of the environment to camouflage themselves.

READY-MADE DISGUISES

Flatfishes such as flounder and sole are good examples of animals with built-in camouflage. These two groups of fishes can change color and pattern quickly to match the sandy ocean bottom where they live. Their skin contains several groups of pigment, or color, cells. Many colors and patterns can be produced by bringing these groups of pigments into action.

The pigment cells can work together or separately to spread color over a very large area or to reduce color to a tiny area of the fish's body. All of this happens in response to the particular environment in which the fish finds itself. The fish's eyes act as master switches in controlling the color changes. The fish sees the bottom, and this triggers the pigment cells to produce a particular color and pattern. The result is complete camouflage. The fish becomes invisible, seeming to disappear right before its predator's eyes.

Other fishes with built-in camouflage are the trumpet fish, whose body resembles the long, thick stalks of gorgonian corals among which it lives, and the spiny box fish, whose body looks like a chunk of rock.

Many land creatures also have built-in camouflage. The chameleon, which changes colors to match its background, is well known. Less well known are the tropical bark bugs that spend their lives exposed on tree trunks. When wet with rain, bark is darker than when it is dry. So the bark bugs must change color, too. On contact with raindrops or water streaming down the trunk, the bark bugs darken immediately. They return to a lighter color when they dry out.

Similarly, Arctic mammals such as the snowshoe hare and Arctic birds such as the ptarmigan change colors with the seasons: brown in summer and white in winter.

BEING YOUR OWN EXTERIOR DECORATOR

Spider crabs, also known as decorator crabs, rely on the second kind of camouflage—the kind an animal collects and attaches to itself. Decorator crabs camouflage themselves by hooking all kinds of things on their shells.

These crabs live on a soft bottom of mud or sand. Using their pair of front legs as little pincers, they gather a variety of decorating materials: algae, sponges, segments of simple water animals called *hydroids*, fragments of worm tubes, horny corals such as sea fans, wood chips, and even leaves of land plants that have fallen into the water.

With its pincers, the crab moves the material to its mouth and chews it until the edges are rough. Then it takes the roughened pieces of material and attaches them to tiny hook-shaped bristles found on various parts of its shell. When it has finished decorating its shell, it no longer looks like a crab. Decorator crabs use camouflage to protect themselves from predators such as European lobsters, sea otters, a wide variety of fishes, octopuses, starfishes, spiny lobsters, and other crabs.

Camouflage and mimicry are tricks that animals and plants have developed to survive. Those that use tricks reproduce more than those that don't. This means that the ability to deceive is passed on from generation to generation, producing more and better tricksters all the time. It also means that many things in nature are not what they seem. One must look closely and pay attention to every detail in order to catch a trickster in the act.

The giraffe's irregular pattern of light and dark allows it to blend with the dark-barked trees and filtered sunlight where it feeds.

PATTERNS

The small, regular pattern and variegated colors of the Pueblan kingsnake allow it to blend with its rocky Mexican habitat.

The regular, circular pattern of this sunflower seems to reflect the harmony found in nature.

IN NATURE

The green sea turtle of the Cayman Islands has a regular, geometric shape on its shell. Can you identify the shape?

Responding

1. Why do you think the ability to camouflage themselves is more important to some species than to others?

2. In a magazine, science text, or other book, look for more examples of patterns in nature. Bring your materials to class and share them with your classmates.

Mathematics Connection

Nature seems to be filled with conflict—struggle among the species for survival. Yet, at the heart of the natural world is order. Order and symmetry can be as simple as the bright circle of a harvest moon, or as complex as the tessellations of a honeybee hive.

What Is a Tessellation?

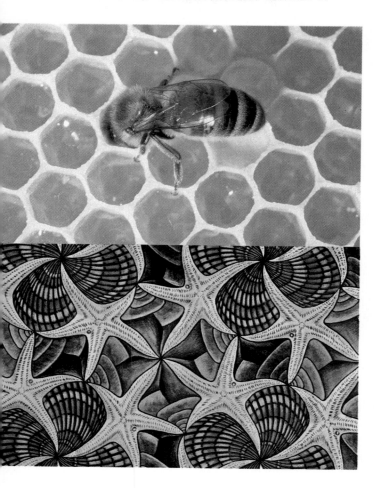

Pictured below is a honeybee in its beehive. Each hexagon behind the bee is a cell in which the bee stores honey. Bees are naturally talented at making such cells, so the pattern of hexagons is close to perfect. The pattern of hexagons is an example of a *tessellation*.

A **tessellation** is a filling up of a two-dimensional space by congruent copies of a figure that do not overlap. The figure that is copied is called the **fundamental region** or **fundamental shape** for the tessellation. Tessellations can be formed by combining translation, rotation, and reflection images of the fundamental region.

SHAPES THAT TESSELLATE

In the beehive the fundamental region is a **regular hexagon**. A **regular polygon** is a convex polygon whose sides all have the same length and angles all have the same measure. A regular polygon with six sides is a regular hexagon.

Only two other regular polygons tessellate. They are the square and the **equilateral triangle**. Pictured here are parts of tessellations using them. A fundamental region is shaded in each drawing.

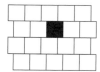

Variations of these regular polygons can also tessellate. There are many different ways to modify the sides of a regular fundamental region so that the resulting figure will tessellate.

Many other shapes can be fundamental regions for tessellations. The Dutch artist Maurits Escher became famous for the unusual shapes he used in tessellations. On the left is part of one of his drawings.

Some shapes do not tessellate. For instance, there can be no tessellation using only congruent regular *pentagons*. (You may want to try, but you will not succeed.)

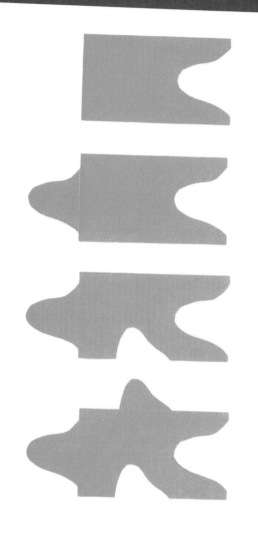

YOUR TURN

Modify a rectangle to create a new tessellation.

1. Draw and cut any shape out of any side of an index card.

2. Slide the cut-out piece *straight across* to the opposite side. Do not flip it over. Tape it to the opposite side.

3. Pick an uncut side of the rectangle. Draw and cut another shape out of this side, slide it straight across to the opposite side, and tape it to the opposite side.

4. On a large sheet of paper, trace around the figure you made.

5. Slide the figure until part of it fits (like a jigsaw puzzle) into part of the tracing you drew. Trace around the figure again.

6. Repeat Step 5 again and again until the page is filled.

Responding

1. Draw or take photographs of other natural or man-made tessellations. Display them in your classroom.

2. Try to make a tessellation using a geometric shape other than a hexagon or a rectangle. Discuss with the class which shapes work best and which are problematic.

Reading Mini-Lesson

Classifying Ideas

We classify objects so that we can store and locate them easily. If you go to a music store, you might find fifteen different classifications of recordings. Once you find the category you're looking for, you can look for the individual recording you want.

We classify ideas so that we can "store" and "locate" them also. In informational articles, ideas are "filed" for you in the writer's system of classification. Headings offer readers clues to the organization of ideas. In "Camouflage: The Big Cover-Up," there are two main headings: "Ready-Made Disguises" and "Being Your Own Exterior Decorator." These represent two main categories for the subject of the article, camouflage. The author also gives you a clue to the organization of the article in the last sentence on page 324, the one that starts, "There are two kinds of camouflage in nature. . . ."

When you take notes, you can show an article's classification system. On the left are two ways to take notes on "Ready-Made Disguises," using a traditional outline or a semantic map. Both are good ways to show classification.

Ready-Made Disguises

1. **Sea creatures**

   flounder and sole

   trumpet fish

   spiny box fish

2. **Land creatures**

   chameleon

   bark bugs

   Arctic mammals
   (snowshoe hare)

   Arctic birds (ptarmigan)

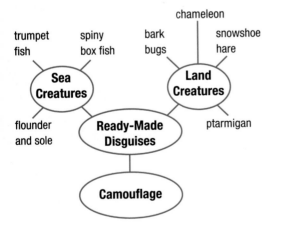

Activity Options

1. "Camouflage" has headings listed only for the middle of the article. Does that mean there is no way to classify the rest of the article? Of course not. Read through this article again and make up headings for the beginning and end of the article. Where would you place the last heading?

2. A semantic map highlights a concept important to a selection or topic. There may be more than one important idea on the map. Complete the semantic map that is shown by filling it in with information from the rest of the article.

3. Locate another informational article in a magazine or book and show the classification of ideas in two different ways. First, make an outline. Second, make a semantic map of the information. Which approach do you prefer? Why?

Writing Workshop

Examining Points of View

Assignment In the selections you read, things are not always as they first appeared. Now, assume the role of two different characters from a selection and recount the same event from two points of view. See the Writer's Blueprint for details.

WRITER'S BLUEPRINT

Product	Two interior monologues
Purpose	To recount the events of a story from two points of view
Audience	Your classmates, teacher, and family
Specs	As the writer of successful monologues, you should:

❑ Begin by assuming the role of a character from one of the selections.

❑ Go on to briefly summarize a key story scene from this character's point of view.

❑ Include observations, thoughts, feelings, and reactions that only you, as this character, would have.

❑ Next, assume the role of a different character from the same selection and summarize the same incident from this new point of view.

❑ Use transitional expressions to link paragraphs smoothly.

❑ Follow the rules for grammar, usage, spelling, and mechanics. Be careful not to confuse adjectives and adverbs.

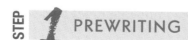

STEP **1** PREWRITING

Chart points of view from the literature. To help determine different points of view from the literature, choose three selections and chart the points of view of two characters. For example, you might consider the boy's encounter with the wasp nest in "Animal Craftsmen" from both the boy's and a wasp's point of view. Here is a chart for "The Enchanted Raisin."

Story: The Enchanted Raisin	
Character	Point of View
1. One of the children	Wants to protect the raisin because it is his/her mother.
2. Stepmother	Wants to get rid of the raisin so she can take over the household.

Review the characters' thoughts and feelings. Select two characters from the same selection and explore their points of view about the same scene or subject. Look for evidence of each character's feelings by reviewing the literature. Use the details you find to create a web for each character.

OR . . .
Instead of a quickwrite, write the scene in cartoon bubbles over each character's head. Then write what each would say about the scene.

Try a quickwrite. For a few minutes, assume that you are one of the characters that you selected. As that character jot down ideas about an important scene from the story. Include observations and feelings about the scene. Then assume the role of the other character that you chose and write about the same scene from the second character's point of view. Be sure to use first-person point of view as if you are the character. You should use the pronouns *I, me, we,* and *us.* Here is part of one student's quickwrite.

○

○   My brothers and I were so bad we probably helped turn my mother into an old woman. She tried to make us stop but we didn't. Even when she was gone, we didn't really understand what had happened. I especially remember when a friend noticed how wrinkled Mom was getting. We didn't

○   even know what was happening.

Ask yourself: *Am I really summarizing the scene from my characters' points of view?* Look at your quickwrite. If you feel that you are summarizing the scene from your point of view instead of the characters', try one of these.

- Review the literature to find more details about the characters' points of view.

- Be the characters as you write. What words would each one use?

Plan the monologues. Use your quickwrite to help you divide your ideas into two separate points of view. Create a chart similar to this one to determine what information to include at which point of your summary. Be sure to follow the points in the Writer's Blueprint and consider the character's thoughts and feelings.

Child	Stepmother
Upset about mother, wants to protect her, hopes she will turn back	Wants to get rid of the raisin Tries to come up with a scheme to get rid of the raisin

STEP 2 DRAFTING

Before you write, review your quickwrite, writing plan, and your other notes. Reread the Writer's Blueprint. Look ahead to the Revising Strategy on page 334 for help with using transitional devices to make smooth shifts between paragraphs. Here are some ideas for getting started.

- Have the first character explain what led up to the situation that you'll be describing.

- Begin by summarizing the first character's general feelings about this type of situation, and then introduce the specific situation as an example.

3 REVISING

Ask your partner for comments on your draft before you revise it.

✔ Have I followed the specs in the Writer's Blueprint?

✔ Do I show two different points of view? Is each character's clear?

✔ Have I used appropriate transitional devices?

Revising Strategy

Using Transitional Devices

Words, phrases, or sentences that smoothly connect one piece of writing to another are called **transitions.** They can smooth the connection between either paragraphs or ideas. See the Literary Source. Try using these transition words:

- To show addition—*and, furthermore, second, finally, again, also, in addition*

- To show contrast—*although, but, however, neither, or, still*

- To show time—*after a while, afterward, before, earlier, meanwhile, since, then, until*

- To show conclusion—*as a result, finally, in conclusion, therefore*

- To show as an example—*for example, for instance, that is*

Find the transitions in the student writing below.

By now mom couldn't even reach my knees, although I'm the youngest and shortest. That night mom tried to yell at us and tried to get us to stop our pranks. Still, we didn't stop.

STUDENT MODEL

4 EDITING

Ask a partner to review your revised draft before you edit. When you edit, watch for errors in grammar, usage, spelling, and mechanics. Pay special attention to not confusing adjectives with adverbs.

Editing Strategy

Confusing Adjectives with Adverbs

How do you know whether to use an adjective or an adverb after the verb in a sentence? It depends on what word is being modified. Use adjectives to modify nouns and pronouns (e.g., The **nest** was **perfect**). Use adverbs to modify action verbs (e.g., The nest was **designed perfectly**). To avoid confusion, make sure you know which word you are modifiying.

Notice which words are modified by these easily confused adjectives and adverbs.

> **FOR REFERENCE . . .**
> More rules for using adjectives and adverbs correctly are listed in the Language and Grammar Handbook.

Adjective	**Adverb**
Dad's **stories** are **good.**	Dad **tells** stories **well.**
Our **stepmother** was **bad.**	Our stepmother **behaved badly.**

How did the writer of the draft below pay attention to using adjectives and adverbs?

○   *well* Dad chose another wife. This lady was mean. She didn't cook or

clean good. We wanted our real mother back bad. Dad still thought it was

○   a joke about the raisin.    *badly*

STUDENT MODEL

5 PRESENTING

Here are two ideas for presenting your monologues.

- Turn your monologues into a two-act radio drama. Treat the program as a flashback in which two characters tell their sides of a story. Tape your program and present it to the class.

- Read your monologues aloud in small groups. After each person reads, discuss why each of the characters might have perceived the situation as they did.

6 LOOKING BACK

Self-evaluate. What grade would you give your paper? Look back at the Writer's Blueprint and evaluate yourself on each point, from 6 (superior) down to 1 (weak).

Reflect. Think about what you learned from writing your narratives as you write answers to these questions.

✔ Do you see each of your characters differently now that you have written the monologues? How has your view of each changed?

✔ Was it easier to write from one character's point of view than the other? If so, why?

For Your Working Portfolio: Add your monologues and your reflection responses to your working portfolio.

Beyond Print

Living with Commercials

At the end of Alice Walker's poem, "Without Commercials," she says we are all "*original* as Eve." Are you *original?* How are you original? Does the influence of commercials make you less original? Would you be different without commercials? What if there were no television, magazine, or radio commercials? Would your life be different? Would you look different?

Advertisers spend billions of dollars each year targeting teenagers. Most likely, much of what you wear and eat has been pitched to you on TV commercials. In many ways, you may benefit from commercials and the choices of products available. Commercials can inform you, persuade you, anger or delight you. Sometimes, however, if they are done well, ads can manipulate you. Your goal is to become aware of how commercials affect you. If you can figure out how commercials influence your life, you are less likely to be manipulated by them.

Advertising Scale

5—Most powerful: This commercial heavily influenced my decision to buy this product.

4—Powerful: This commercial influenced my decision to buy this product.

3—Somewhat powerful: This commercial may have played a role in influencing my decision to buy the product.

2—Not very powerful: I doubt if the commercial influenced my decision to buy this product.

1—No power: The commercial had nothing to do with my decision to buy the product.

Activity

Make a list of all the items you buy that are advertised. Next to each item write where you have seen or heard the ad and briefly describe it. Then rank the power of the ad based on the scale in the margin. After the ranking, briefly explain your reasoning. Finally, explain how the product impacts your life in a positive or negative way. For instance, does fast food have an impact on your health? Do the shoes you wear have an impact on your popularity?

Activity Extensions

1. Place your list of items on a posterboard. Share your list with the class. Discuss the influence of commercials on your life. Are there products you will not buy because of the commercials? Explain.

2. Discuss the differences among TV ads, radio ads, and magazine ads. Which medium is most effective? Why?

Projects for Collaborative Study

Theme Connection

Rules for Resolving Conflict Work with your classmates to develop a list of rules for clear communication during conflicts. Draw upon what you learned in this unit about looking at things from different perspectives.

■ In a group, brainstorm what you already know about communicating clearly during conflicts.

■ Invite a school counselor or health teacher to speak to your group about ways that communication can help resolve conflicts. Before the talk, work together on interview questions you will ask the speaker.

■ Explore library resources on conflict resolution and communication skills.

■ As a wrap-up, create a poster listing your rules and display it in your classroom or school.

Literature Connection

Moody Language Mood plays an important part in several of the selections in this unit. Working with a group, select two or three selections in the unit and discuss:

■ What **mood** was created by the author?

■ What **imagery** did the author use to create the mood?

With your classmates, prepare a chart for each story you chose, naming its mood and listing specific images from the selection that helped create that mood. You might want to include a **simile** or **metaphor** on your chart.

Life Skills Connection

My Pledge The Pledge of Allegiance to the U.S. flag expresses belief in unity, liberty, and justice for all, values important to many Americans. In this activity, you examine what you honor in your life.

In your notebook, respond to these questions:

• What values and beliefs are the most important for you?

• Where are you willing to take a stand in your life?

Then choose one of these options for expressing your beliefs:

• Develop your own Personal Pledge that expresses your truths or commitments.

• Create a poem, song, drawing, or other statement of your Personal Pledge.

As a class, share your pledges and discuss common themes.

Multicultural Connection

Cultural Conflicts With your classmates, examine local newspapers to find a situation in your own community in which people in two **groups** have a disagreement. What groups are involved? How do they see things differently? Assign some students to study one group's **perspective** while others study the other perspective. Then stage a debate in which students present the perspective of the group they studied. Afterwards, discuss what compromises are possible.

Read More About Conflict

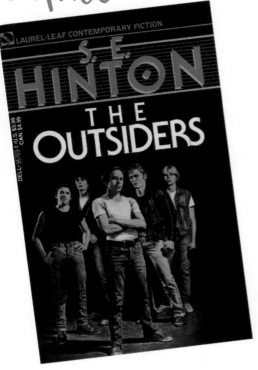

The Outsiders (1967) by S. E. Hinton. The author, who was seventeen when she wrote this novel, explores the confrontations between two rival groups of teenagers, one from the middle class and one from the lower class.

Cousins (1990) by Virginia Hamilton. The author of "He Lion, Bruh Bear, and Bruh Rabbit" weaves a tale of a young girl's struggle to deal with a family tragedy that brings her to the brink of despair.

More Good Books

A Day No Pigs Would Die (1973) by Robert Newton Peck. A maturing thirteen-year-old boy, growing up in rural Vermont in the 1930s, struggles with his father's decision to kill a pig he has raised as a pet.

Shane (1949) by Jack Schaefer. The conflict between cattle ranchers and homesteaders, and the trials and tribulations of an ex-gunfighter trying to escape his past, are the subjects of this novel set in 1889 Wyoming.

The Red Pony (1937) by John Steinbeck. This classic tale, in four vignettes, tells the story of a young boy growing up on a California farm.

Walking Stars: Stories of Magic and Power (1994) by Victor Villaseñor. This collection of stories features factual material about the author's Mexican family combined with elements from Native American folk tales and Mexican history.

Across Five Aprils (1964) by Irene Hunt. This novel chronicles the life of an Illinois family in which one son fights for the South and the others for the North during the Civil War (1861–1865).

The Sign of the Beaver (1983) by Elizabeth George Speare. A young boy, left alone to guard his family's wilderness home in eighteenth-century Maine, learns survival skills from the local Indians.

Relationships

Working Things Out
Part One, pages 344–401

Appreciating Each Other
Part Two, pages 402–471

Talking About
RELATIONSHIPS

Our lives are built around relationships—those with our family, our friends, and our classmates. Successful relationships require a lot of work, not to mention humor, patience, and understanding.

For the first time in my life, I saw love at work. Not movie love. . . . But love like something alive and tender, asking nothing in return.

from "The Moustache" by Robert Cormier, page 416

"Why aren't relationships like in the movies?"

Jason—Ontario, CA

"Relationships at our age should be about learning how to get along.

Martha—Boston, MA

Although neither later could remember what the quarrel was about, the pain grew stronger...

from "Strawberries" by Gayle Ross, page 390

She discovered that if she listened carefully, she could find something in common with almost everyone.

from "Beni Seballos" by Phillip Hoose, page 377

"I like this theme because people will learn to get along with different people."

Eric—Garland, TX

Part One

Working Things Out

Problems are part of life. Learning to resolve them often takes time and practice. By helping us to see things in a different light or from a different perspective, friends and family members can help us find solutions to seemingly unsolvable problems.

 Multicultural Connection **Communication** involves building cultural bridges. People who may have differences arising from age, gender, religion, language, ethnicity, or race can learn from each other through bridges of communication. What do the characters in these selections learn by communicating with each other?

Literature

Judie Angell	**Dear Marsha** ◆ short story	.346
Walter Dean Myers	**The Treasure of Lemon Brown** ◆ short story	.362
Phillip Hoose	**Beni Seballos** ◆ biography	.374
William Carlos Williams	**This Is Just to Say** ◆ poem	.382
Kenneth Koch	**Variations on a Theme by**	
	William Carlos Williams ◆ poem	.383
	Writing Mini-Lesson ◆ Maintaining Your Working Portfolio	.386
Zora Neale Hurston	**How the Snake Got Poison**	
	◆ African American folk tale	.388
Gayle Ross	**Strawberries** ◆ Cherokee legend	.390
Carl Sandburg	**Primer Lesson** ◆ poem	.392

Interdisciplinary Study In Harmony

In Balance with Nature by Vine Deloria, Jr. ◆ anthropology	.395
Native American Spirituality ◆ art	.398
Reading Mini-Lesson ◆ Generalizing	.401

Before Reading

Dear Marsha

by Judie Angell

Judie Angell
born 1937

The author says, "I think growing up heads the list of The Hardest Things to Do in Life. It's so hard, in fact, that some of us never get there. But even if the world changes as rapidly as it does, the feelings we have while coping with those changes don't." Angell has worked as an elementary teacher and a magazine editor, but currently devotes much of her time to writing stories for children and teenagers. She likes cats, singing, painting, and listening to music. Two other books she has written about growing up are *Don't Rent My Room* and *Leave the Cooking to Me*.

Building Background

Confiding in People Most health professionals believe that people who talk to others about their problems are generally healthier than people who keep it all inside. Talking with friends or family members helps people sort out their feelings and put things in a proper perspective.

Getting into the Story

Writer's Notebook Sharing your problems with someone can be very helpful. However, in some cases, such an outpouring of honesty can backfire. What problems might arise when you share a problem with someone? In your notebook, make a list, similar to the one below, of the advantages and disadvantages of sharing a problem with another person. Then, in a small group, discuss your lists.

Advantages	Disadvantages
You might gain a new perspective.	The person might tell someone else.

Reading Tip

Slang and Idioms In this selection the author uses informal language to convey a sense of closeness between the two main characters. Angell makes good use of two forms of informal language—slang and idioms. **Slang** refers to words or phrases that may be descriptive but are not generally used in formal English. For example, *tops, neat, cool, groovy, out of sight,* and *gnarly* are slang words that have been used by various generations as words of approval. Slang words are very short-lived. What was cool yesterday might be totally uncool tomorrow. **Idioms** are phrases or expressions whose meanings cannot be understood from the ordinary meanings of the words in them. For example, *hold one's tongue* (be quiet) can only be understood by someone familiar with the entire phrase.

I remember that assignment. Some of the kids really got into it when they got letters from your class and they're still writing back and forth. The friendships are terrific because everybody feels safe with them, you know? ...cause we're so far away no one k... And sinc... say... d... instead of them, ...as

Dear Marsha

Judie Angell

July 13

Dear Anne Marie,

I guess this letter is probably a big surprise to you . . . I mean, you probably looked at the return address and sign-off and all and saw that it's from nobody you ever heard of, right? Well, here's the reason I'm writing.

Maybe you remember this assignment that the kids in our English class got back in February. Our teacher (Ms. Bernardi, maybe that rings a bell) wrote to your English teacher and she asked him if he'd like to do this experiment: He would send a list of all the kids in your class with their names and addresses and we would pick those names out of a hat and write a letter to the name we picked. See, you all lived far away and the idea was to see if we could form a "relation-ship" (Ms. Bernardi grew up in the sixties) with a perfect stranger, using only pen and paper. (Or typewriter, I mean, YOU know.) Anyway, Ms. Bernardi said she wasn't going to grade the assignment, or even see it or anything because this assignment was personal, just for ourselves. You know, to "express ourselves" with a perfect stranger. Whatever. So naturally, if it didn't mean a grade or anything, I didn't do it.

But the thing is—I picked your name out of the hat and I just sort of kept it, you know, and now it's summer and hot and practically all of my friends are away, so . . . Here's a letter. You're a stranger even if you may not be perfect (or maybe you are perfect, I don't know), but here I am, trying to form this "relationship" using only two fingers on the type-writer (please excuse the mistakes, I'm taking Business Typing next semester) and you're the one I'm supposed to try it with.

Well, I'm not going to say anything more until I hear back from you—Hope you turn out to be cool.

Your new pen pal (maybe)

Marsha

July 18

Dear Marsha,

Your letter was great! It really picked up a slow summer for me.

I remember that assignment. Some of the kids really got into it when they got letters from your class and they're still writing back and forth. The friendships are terrific because everybody feels safe with them, you know? I mean, because we're so far away no one knows anyone the pen pal knows. And since you never have to meet, you feel freer to say whatever you want with no one coming down on you or whatever, you know.

So I'm glad you wrote and I'm also glad it's now instead of then, because back in Feb. I was really WIPED, I mean really. See, my dad died, it wasn't sudden or anything, he was sick a long time, but still it was very hard on everybody as you can probably figure out. So now it's just my mom and my sister and me and . . . we miss Dad, so sometimes we get on each other's nerves.

I guess if you wanted me to be the first one to give out personal stuff I guess there's that. Plus . . . let's see. . . . If you're thinking about "m-e-n," I don't go out a whole lot, but there's one guy I like at school. The thing is, he's YOUNGER than I am and I get embarrassed about that and since he doesn't even know I like him . . . I guess you can't count it as a "relationship." (That word bugs me too.)

I hope this is enough for you to think that maybe we could be friends, and I like the idea of a pen pal.

From
Anne Marie

July 21

Dear Anne Marie,

You are DEFINITELY the coolest person! I couldn't wait to hear back from you so I'm writing you the same day I got your letter.

I'm sorry about your dad. That must be tough to deal with. I mean, I have both of my parents and it never occurred to me that one of them could die. I know that sounds stupid, but I just never thought about it. They're okay most of the time, but really, I guess I just take them for granted, to be honest about it.

So now I'll tell you more about myself.

I'm a senior in high school, or at least I will be starting September. Which is okay, because the sooner I graduate the sooner I can start My Life. My dad says I could go to college if I want (HE'S the one who really wants me to go), but I'm not sure I could stand all that much school. I'm thinking about it more this summer, though, because I have this job at our local five-and-ten as a checkout girl and if anything is bor-ing, that is IT! Here's what you get: "Mar-sha, last week you had green grosgrain[1] in the sewing department and now it isn't there, why NOT?" And—"Mar-sha, you took ten minutes extra for lunch yesterday and it came off MY time, so you better come back ten minutes early today." That kind of stuff. Borrrr-ing.

Okay, well—I'm five feet five inches tall, which is about average, I guess, and I have black hair which in this weather I wear either in a chignon (sp.?) or in a ponytail. It's pretty long and straight and I guess it's my nicest feature. I'm a cheerleader and I think my hair looks good flopping up and down when I jump. (I'm not really as conceited[2] as that sounds!) Also I have brown eyes and no-more-BRACES. I'm pretty thin, which isn't too great when you wear a bathing suit. What do you look like? I picture Anne Marie as a blonde.

I don't have a boyfriend right now, although there's a very nice guy who works in the stockroom at the five-and-ten. Hmmm . . . maybe. . . .

Most of my friends got jobs at resorts and hotels in the mountains. I should have applied to one of them but as usual I was late and lazy, so here I am, bored at the five-and-ten. Write soon.

Your friend,

Marsha

---

1. **grosgrain,** a closely woven silk or rayon cloth with heavy cross threads and a dull finish, often used for ribbons.
2. conceited (kən sēt′əd), *adj.* having too high an opinion of oneself.

July 25

Dear Marsha,

   Boy, do I know what you mean about boredom! I'm working part time at my school—office stuff, and the rest of the time I'm at home because my mom and sister really need for us all to be together. Your town sounds like the same kind of hick burg mine is. You have one movie house and it's just got around to showing talkies, right? And: one Laundromat, a drugstore (NO BARE FEET, THIS MEANS YOU), a post office, and if you're real lucky, one of those no-alcohol bars for kids to hang out in on weekends.

   One nice thing here, though—there is a lake we can go to. In fact, our family has always had a cabin there. It's called Lake Michigan, which was someone's idea of a joke because it's more of a pond than a lake and it has a lot more brambly woods than pond. But this summer no one in my house seems to have the energy for going up there a lot.

   I'm a little shorter than you—five two exactly—and I do have blondish-brownish hair that's short and curly. I always wanted long black hair like yours. You sound really pretty and I bet that guy in the stockroom notices you pretty soon! I used to wear glasses but I got contacts finally and I think I look better now. Wish I had more to write but I don't, so let's hope things start to get more exciting for both of us!

                    Love,
                    Anne Marie

August 2

Dear Anne Marie,

It took me a while before I could write again. It's not that I didn't want to, but some stuff happened and I've been kind of scared and depressed ever since.

What happened was, this girl at work—she's the one I was kidding about in my last letter, the one who whines about my coming back late from lunch. Her name is Claudia and we alternate[3] shifts. Anyway, when I realized she was actually counting every one of my lunchtime minutes, I started coming back really on time, you know? Sometimes, even early. Well, last week when I relieved her, I counted up the receipts[4] and the money in the register and stuff and it seemed to me that I was coming up short. The receipts and the money didn't check out, you know? But I figured it was me, I must've done something wrong. I mean, my math is hardly the greatest. So I let it go and when Claudia came back at four o'clock, I told her to check it out. So she did and said I was wrong and dumb and everything was okay and blah, blah, blah. But the next thing I know, Mrs. Handy, the manager, started checking everything between shifts because she said we were losing some money.

Listen, I won't drag this on, but accusations[5] were thrown around and Claudia accused me of stealing. That was when I caught on that she was the one who was stealing and I knew that one time I got back too early for her to be able to hide it.

Well, of course she said I was the one and since it was her word against mine and she's a full-time worker and I'm only part time and no one noticed any shortage before I got there— naturally I got blamed. I wasn't arrested or anything because no one could prove I did it, but I did get fired. And as you put it so well, this IS a hick burg, and I stand about as much chance of getting another job as I have of spreading wings and flying away. Which I'd sure like to do. I really didn't steal, Anne Marie. I hope you believe me. The cute boy in the stock-room sure doesn't. You should have seen the look he gave me.

So . . . things got exciting for a while, anyway.

Love,
Marsha

---

3. **alternate** (ôl′tər nāt), *v.* take turns with.
4. **receipt** (ri sēt′), *n.* a written record of money that has been received.
5. **accusation** (ak′yə zā′shən), *n.* charge of wrongdoing.

August 5

Dear Marsha,

    I got your letter and broke into tears, I swear I did. Of course I believe you didn't steal anything. But they will find out eventually. Claudia won't stop stealing and I bet she does the same thing with the next person they hire and they will all catch on.

    I feel so bad for you, I don't know what to say. After I read your letter I told my mom and sister that I just had to get away for a while, so I took the bus up to our cabin and that's where I am now. I'm sitting on the porch and looking out at (ha-ha) Lake Michigan and thinking about you. People can be so mean. But I bet there are lots of people in the town who know you well enough to know it was all a lie and will be glad to hire you.

    It's so peaceful up here, really. Just about an hour and fifteen minutes north of my house, but it feels like another world. Wait a minute, Marsha. . . .

    You won't believe it! I'm back now, but I had to go inside and close the windows and doors and spray everything with Lysol! While I was sitting there describing all the peace and quiet, this SKUNK marches right up on the porch and lets me have some of what skunks do best! YUUUUCH! This is just AWFUL, did you ever get a whiff of skunk? They say tomato juice takes the smell away, but I don't have any and what are you supposed to do, bathe in it or what? PEEEEW!

    So I'm sitting here in this locked cabin wondering which smells worse, the Lysol or the skunk or the mixture of both, and thinking of you.

        Love,
        Anne Marie

August 10

Dear Anne Marie,

Your letter gave me the first good laugh I've had in a while! I'm still laughing because I think I can smell that combination of stuff you mentioned on the pages of the letter! You can't even imagine how much I wish I had a place to go like Lake Michigan (without the skunk!) but we're pretty far from any quiet place with water and woods. I mean, there's a pool at the town recreation center, but that's not exactly what I had in mind. The closest I can get to coolness and peace and quiet is my basement, but THAT smells of cat litter and Clorox, ALMOST as bad as your place!

Well, my mom and dad believe I didn't take any money or anything else, but it's hard for them because everyone they know heard about what happened. And so when people say, "Oh, Marsha, wasn't that awful, we just KNOW you'd never" and all that, I somehow get the feeling they're really thinking Maybe she did, you know these kids today. . . .

Anyway, tell me something good to cheer me up. Your letters are the only nice thing to happen this whole stinking summer—NO PUN INTENDED!

Love,

Marsha

August 16

Dear Marsha,

I hope by the time this gets to you that you're feeling better. I want you to know I really do think about you all the time.

Maybe this will cheer you up a little. . . . Did you ever have a carnival come to your town? Our firehouse sits on a tract of land of about twelve acres and every year they put on a really terrific carnival. Picture this: There's a high booth on wheels with a glass window where you can watch a boy spin pink cotton candy around and around. Close your eyes now, and you can smell it, all sickly sweet and gorgeous, and you can make mustaches and beards and eyebrows and earrings all over your face with it, you know? And they also have this huge plastic bubble, all different colors, with a foam bottom and you can go in there and jump your heart out. You fall over a lot, of course, but you don't get hurt even if you fall on your face because it's so soft. And there are these booths where you can throw baseballs at little Indian teepees and win neat stuff like plush polar bear dolls and clock radios and blow-dryers with three speeds and makeup mirrors and everything. And best of all is the Ferris wheel, because they stop it for a few minutes when you get to the top, and it's like you really are on top of the world. So picture yourself on top of the world and that's where you'll be.

That's where I was last night. And when I got to the top I thought about you and made a wish, so I know things will get better soon for you.

And also, guess what? At the shooting gallery, guess who I met? That younger guy I told you about. And we went on the Whip together. And I'm going back tonight, so . . . who knows?

Love,
Anne Marie

August 20

Dear Anne Marie,

I have read your letter about eight hundred times. Where you live sounds so great. I pictured the carnival. I really tasted the cotton candy. I won a stuffed bear. I rode on the Ferris wheel with you and I think the "younger man" is cute. I liked being on top of the world, even if it was only for a few minutes.

Things here only seem to be getting worse. One of my girlfriends is back from her hotel job and you wouldn't believe how she sounded on the phone when I called her up. I feel like everyone's looking at me whenever I walk down the street.

Now I'm seriously starting to think about college, if only to get away from here. My dad says he's sorry it took something like this to get me thinking about it, but he's glad I am, he says. A blessing in disguise, he says. Ha, some blessing! But even if I do go to college, I still have a year of high school left and I honestly don't know how I'm going to stand it.

Tell me something else to smell and taste and ride on.

Love,

Marsha

August 25

Dear Marsha,

    I think it's neat you're thinking about college. If you're lucky enough to be able to go, I really think that's what you should do. It's just my opinion, but that's what I think.

    Marsha, did you ever see kittens being born? You have NEVER seen anything so incredible in your whole life! My Y-M (younger man) works at his dad's carpentry shop in the summer and they have this mamma cat who was about to give birth and he asked me if I'd like to watch. Well, it took from six o'clock to around ten. The mama had a litter of seven kittens, and they came out two, two, one and two, over all those four hours. They each came out wrapped in a shiny silver cover, which the mama licked up and ate. I know it sounds really gross, but it was honestly beautiful. Their teeny eyes were shut tight and they made these little squeaky noises and they looked at first as if they had no fur, but they do. Y-M says I can have one.

    Keep thinking about college and you'll see how quickly the year will go.

                Love,
                Anne Marie

September 1

Dear Anne Marie,

It's Labor Day weekend and I'm spending it crying. The cheerleading squad is meeting Tuesday, the day before school starts, and I'm "not welcome" on it anymore. I got the word straight from the captain herself. "Oh, I don't believe any of it, Marsha," she says, "but you know how people think of cheerleaders, they're supposed to represent the school's highest standards" and blah, blah, blah! "I know you'll sacrifice," she says, "for the good of the school." Right. Can you BELIEVE it? Anne Marie, it's SO not fair!

Well, I can't handle it, Anne Marie, I really can't. I just can't spend an entire year at school like this. So I've made this decision, and I just know being the kind of person you are and with the kind of family you say you have, that you might be happy about it. This decision, I mean.

I know my mom and dad are on my side, but they're not, you know, the same as a FRIEND or anything. And this summer, I guess you know that you became my very best friend.

I want to be where I can sit on top of the world on a Ferris wheel and watch little kittens being born and chase skunks away from a cabin porch. And spend all my time with a true friend, who's sensitive and caring and growing up with the same kinds of feelings I have. That stupid school assignment was the best thing that every happened to me, Anne Marie, and I know I'm dragging this out, but here's my idea:

Could I spend the year with you? I swear on my own life I won't be any trouble, in fact, I'll be a help. With your dad gone, I can help make up for the work he did around the house. I'm very handy, I really am, I can do all kinds of things.

And best of all, we could go to school together, and do our homework together, and sit up nights and talk, and bake stuff and double date and go to the prom and make Senior Year everything it's supposed to be! And I'll bring my tapes—I bet I have the best rock and roll tape collection you ever heard!

Don't you think it would be great? Don't you? School's starting next week, Anne Marie. . . . Please let me know. . . .

Love,

Marsha

1201-S

WESTERN UNION

SIGNS

DL	= Day Letter
NM	= Night Message
NL	= Night Letter
LCO	= Deferred Cable
NLT	= Cable Night Letter
WLT	= Week-End Letter

Received at

NIGHT LETTER TUES SEPT 5

DEAR MARSHA—YOU MUST STAY IN SCHOOL, RIGHT THERE IN YOUR OWN TOWN—IT WILL BE HARD, VERY HARD, BUT YOU MUST DO IT—REMEMBER, YOU DIDN'T DO ANYTHING WRONG AND THEREFORE YOU MUST NOT RUN AWAY—YOU MUST NEVER LET STUPID AND CRUEL PEOPLE GET THE BEST OF YOU—I AM SURE YOUR MOM AND DAD HAVE TOLD YOU THE SAME—HOLD YOUR HEAD UP AS HIGH AS YOU CAN AND GIVE THAT CHEERLEADING SQUAD A GOOD RASPBERRY—

MARSHA, I CANNOT TELL YOU HOW SORRY I AM FOR THIS—MY NAME WAS NOT SUPPOSED TO BE INCLUDED IN THAT LIST YOUR TEACHER RECEIVED FROM OUR TEACHER—SOMEONE MUST HAVE PUT IT IN AS A JOKE—BUT I DIDN'T MIND BECAUSE YOUR FIRST LETTERS WERE SUCH A JOY THAT I SIMPLY HAD TO ANSWER THEM IN KIND—THEN WHEN YOUR TROUBLE BEGAN, ALL I WANTED WAS TO MAKE YOU FEEL BETTER—MARSHA, I HOPE YOU WON'T MIND THIS—I HOPE IT DOESN'T MAKE ANY DIFFERENCE TO YOU—I HOPE WE CAN CONTINUE TO WRITE AND BE FRIENDS—

DEAR MARSHA, MY DAD DID DIE LAST WINTER AND I DO LIVE WITH MY MOTHER AND SISTER—THEY ARE EIGHTY-THREE AND SIXTY-THREE, RESPECTIVELY[6]—I'M THE PRINCIPAL OF OUR SCHOOL AND I'M SIXTY-ONE YEARS OLD—

ALL MY BEST LOVE, ANNE MARIE

---

6. **respectively** (ri spek′tiv lē), *adv.* as regards each of several persons or things in turn or in the order mentioned.

After Reading

Making Connections

1. Was Anne Marie right or wrong to pretend that she was a teenager? Draw a line like the one below, circling the appropriate number. Explain your choice.

   very wrong _____ very right

        1   2   3   4   5

2. Below is a Venn diagram. One circle represents Marsha, and the other represents Anne Marie. In Marsha's circle, list some of her **characteristics.** Do the same for Anne Marie. Where the circles overlap, list the traits that they both share—the traits that make it possible for them to be friends.

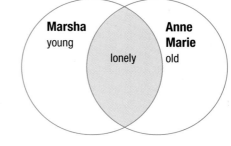

3. Look back at your list of advantages and disadvantages of sharing a problem with someone. Use it to explain how Marsha and Anne Marie managed to become friends through their letters.

4. If this story were written today, what new **slang words** or **idioms** might the author have used?

5. Not all letters are personal or between friends. In what other ways are letters used to state opinions and solve problems?

6. 👣 What cultural differences might make it difficult for a young person and an older person to **communicate?** How could they bridge those differences?

Literary Focus: Language Choice

Look through the story and find examples of **slang words** and **idioms.** Make a list such as the one below of the words or expressions you find. Then write a formal substitute for the slang word or idiom.

Expression	Slang or Idiom	Formal Expression
rings a bell	idiom	helps you remember
cool	slang	

Vocabulary Study

On a separate piece of paper, write the word from the list that best completes each sentence in the letter.

conceited
alternate
receipt
accusation
respectively

Dear Marsha,

Good news! Jill and I have been voted in as president and vice president of the student council, ___(1)___ . I hope you don't think I'm being ___(2)___ , but I feel very proud and want to boast a bit. Jill's victory was rather a surprise, considering the ___(3)___ made by Tom that she had some unreported campaign contributions. Thank goodness she found the missing ___(4)___! Oh, and by the way, Sam and Manuel will ___(5)___ as treasurer every other month because of a tie. I hope they both do well. Need to run now . . .

Tina

Expressing Your Ideas ——————

Writing Choices

To Whom It May Concern Write a **letter** to the captain of the cheerleading squad, trying to convince her that Marsha should be allowed on the team. You could use a diplomatic approach, simply citing all of Marsha's good qualities, or you could play "hardball" by hinting at the possibility of a lawsuit.

Dear Anne Marie Imagine what Marsha felt when she discovered that her pen pal was a high-school principal! Write Marsha's next **letter** to Anne Marie.

Listen Very Carefully Review Anne Marie's description of the carnival and the birth of the kittens. Choose an incident or event you've experienced and write a **paragraph** that describes it. Try to include the sense of smell as well as sight. Read the paragraph aloud to someone to see if the description sounds realistic.

Other Options

Words from the Heart Using library resources, find a poem that Anne Marie could send to Marsha to help cheer her up. Then read it to the class. Perhaps you and another student might like to jointly **illustrate** the poem.

Back to the Drawing Board Using Anne Marie's descriptions, **draw** the cottage on the lake or the carnival. As a class, display and discuss the drawings. What similarities do the drawings have? How are they different?

Marsha and Anne Marie Meet With a partner, **act out** the first face-to-face meeting between Marsha and Anne Marie. What would they say to each other? Do you think Marsha will be angry at Anne Marie for deceiving her? How will Anne Marie explain why she pretended to be a teenager?

Before Reading

The Treasure of Lemon Brown

by Walter Dean Myers

Walter Dean Myers
born 1937

"I'd hate to see what kind of biography my cat, Tarik, would write about me. Probably something like, 'Walter Dean Myers had enormous feet, didn't feed me on time, and often sat in my favorite chair,'" says the author. He adds, "Writing for me has been many things. It was a way to overcome the hindrance of speech problems as I tried to reach out to the world. It was a way of establishing my humanity in a world that often ignores the humanity of those in less favored positions." Myers has written a variety of fiction and nonfiction books for children as well as adults. Among other motivations for writing, Myers wants to "tell Black children about their humanity and about their history."

Building Background

The Author and His Story To make their stories more believable and realistic, writers are often encouraged to set their fictional stories in places with which they are familiar. In "The Treasure of Lemon Brown," Walter Dean Myers takes this advice by setting the story in Harlem, the New York City community where he grew up in the 1940s and early 1950s with his adoptive parents, the Deans. Like Greg, the main character of the story, the author found Harlem to be a place where African American kids grew up early, toughened by harsh economic realities and racial injustice. Despite these realities, however, the author has some warm memories of Harlem. He remembers it "as a great place. Full of lively, warm people, most of whom meant you nothing but good."

Getting into the Story

Writer's Notebook "The Treasure of Lemon Brown" is about a man's treasure, something that he cherishes and values very much. What are some of the things that *you* treasure? In your notebook, make a list of these items. They do not necessarily have to be of monetary value. Then choose the object you value the most from the list and write a paragraph about why it is important to you.

Reading Tip

Setting "The dark sky, filled with angry, swirling clouds, reflected Greg Ridley's mood as he sat on the stoop of his building." **Setting,** the time and place in which the events of a narrative occur, often is used by the author to establish a **mood** or to show a shift in mood. A thunderstorm begins just as the main character encounters his worst problems; the clouds part and the sun comes out at the point in the story when problems are resolved. As you read this story, note what kind of mood is created by the setting. Does the setting change at certain points? Does the mood change too?

The Treasure of Lemon Brown

Walter Dean Myers

The dark sky, filled with angry, swirling clouds, reflected Greg Ridley's mood as he sat on the stoop of his building. His father's voice came to him again, first reading the letter the principal had sent to the house, then lecturing endlessly about his poor efforts in math.

"I had to leave school when I was thirteen," his father had said, "that's a year younger than you are now. If I'd had half the chances that you have, I'd . . ."

Greg had sat in the small, pale green kitchen listening, knowing the lecture would end with his father saying he couldn't play ball with the Scorpions. He had asked his father the week before, and his father had said it depended on his next report card. It wasn't often the Scorpions took on new players, especially fourteen-year-olds, and this was a chance of a lifetime for Greg. He hadn't been allowed to play high school ball, which he had really wanted to do, but playing for the Community Center team was the next best thing. Report cards were due in a week, and Greg had been hoping for the best. But the principal had ended the suspense early when she sent that letter saying Greg would probably fail math if he didn't spend more time studying.

▲ *Shivered Glass* was painted by Clarence Holbrook Carter in 1932. What mood is created by the image?

"And you wanted to play *basketball?*" His father's brows knitted over deep brown eyes. "That must be some kind of a joke. Now you just get into your room and hit those books."

That had been two nights before. His father's words, like the distant thunder that now echoed through the streets of Harlem, still rumbled softly in his ears.

It was beginning to cool. Gusts of wind made bits of paper dance between the parked cars. There was a flash of nearby lightning, and soon large drops of rain splashed onto his jeans. He stood to go upstairs, thought of the lecture that probably awaited him if he did anything except shut himself in his room with his math book, and started walking down the street instead. Down the block there was an old tenement[1] that had been abandoned for some months. Some of the guys had held an impromptu checker tournament there the week before, and Greg had noticed that the door, once boarded over, had been slightly ajar.[2]

Pulling his collar up as high as he could, he checked for traffic and made a dash across the street. He reached the house just as another flash of lightning changed the night to day for an instant, then returned the graffiti-scarred building to the grim shadows. He vaulted over the outer stairs and pushed tentatively[3] on the door. It was open, and he let himself in.

The inside of the building was dark except for the dim light that filtered through the dirty windows from the streetlamps. There was a room a few feet from the door, and from where he stood at the entrance, Greg could see a squarish patch of light on the floor. He entered the room, frowning at the musty smell. It was a large room that might have been someone's parlor at one time. Squinting, Greg could see an old table on its side against one wall, what looked like a pile of rags or a torn mattress in the corner, and a couch, with one side broken, in front of the window.

He went to the couch. The side that wasn't broken was comfortable enough, though a little creaky. From this spot he could see the blinking neon sign over the bodega[4] on the corner. He sat awhile, watching the sign blink first green then red, allowing his mind to drift to the Scorpions, then to his father. His father had been a postal worker for all Greg's life, and was proud of it, often telling Greg how hard he had worked to pass the test. Greg had heard the story too many times to be interested now.

PREDICT: Given the setting—alone in a dark room with a storm outside—what is going to happen next?

For a moment Greg thought he heard something that sounded like a scraping against the wall. He listened carefully, but it was gone.

Outside the wind had picked up, sending the rain against the window with a force that shook the glass in its frame. A car passed, its tires hissing over the wet street and its red taillights glowing in the darkness.

Greg thought he heard the noise again. His stomach tightened as he held himself still and listened intently. There weren't any more scraping noises, but he was sure he had heard something in the darkness—something breathing!

---

1. tenement (ten′ə mənt), *n.* apartment building, especially in a poor section of town.
2. ajar (ə jär′), *adj.* slightly open.
3. tentatively (ten′tə tiv lē), *adv.* hesitatingly, with caution.
4. bodega (bō dä′gə), *n.* a grocery store in a Spanish-speaking neighborhood.

He tried to figure out just where the breathing was coming from; he knew it was in the room with him. Slowly he stood, tensing. As he turned, a flash of lightning lit up the room, frightening him with its sudden brilliance. He saw nothing, just the overturned table, the pile of rags and an old newspaper on the floor. Could he have been imagining the sounds? He continued listening, but heard nothing and thought that it might have just been rats. Still, he thought, as soon as the rain let up he would leave. He went to the window and was about to look out when he heard a voice behind him.

"Don't try nothin' 'cause I got a razor here sharp enough to cut a week into nine days!"

Greg, except for an involuntary[5] tremor in his knees, stood stock still. The voice was high and brittle, like dry twigs being broken, surely not one he had ever heard before. There was a shuffling sound as the person who had been speaking moved a step closer. Greg turned, holding his breath, his eyes straining to see in the dark room.

The upper part of the figure before him was still in darkness. The lower half was in the dim rectangle of light that fell unevenly from the window. There were two feet, in cracked, dirty shoes from which rose legs that were wrapped in rags.

"Who are you?" Greg hardly recognized his own voice.

"I'm Lemon Brown," came the answer. "Who're you?"

"Greg Ridley."

"What you doing here?" The figure shuffled forward again, and Greg took a small step backward.

"It's raining," Greg said.

"I can see that," the figure said.

The person who called himself Lemon Brown peered forward, and Greg could see him clearly. He was an old man. His black, heavily wrinkled face was surrounded by a halo of crinkly white hair and whiskers that seemed to separate his head from the layers

> ... he was sure he had heard something in the darkness— something breathing!

of dirty coats piled on his smallish frame. His pants were bagged to the knee, where they were met with rags that went down to the old shoes. The rags were held on with strings, and there was a rope around his middle. Greg relaxed. He had seen the man before, picking through the trash on the corner and pulling clothes out of a Salvation Army box. There was no sign of the razor that could "cut a week into nine days."

"What are you doing here?" Greg asked.

"This is where I'm staying," Lemon Brown said. "What you here for?"

"Told you it was raining out," Greg said, leaning against the back of the couch until he felt it give slightly.

"Ain't you got no home?"

"I got a home," Greg answered.

"You ain't one of them bad boys looking for my treasure, is you?" Lemon Brown cocked his head to one side and squinted one eye. "Because I told you I got me a razor."

"I'm not looking for your treasure," Greg answered, smiling. "*If* you have one."

"What you mean, *if* I have one," Lemon Brown said. "Every man got a treasure. You don't know that, you must be a fool!"

"Sure," Greg said as he sat on the sofa and put one leg over the back. "What do you have, gold coins?"

---

5. involuntary (in vol′ən ter′ē), *adj.* not controlled by one's will.

"Don't worry none about what I got," Lemon Brown said. "You know who I am?"

"You told me your name was orange or lemon or something like that."

"Lemon Brown," the old man said, pulling back his shoulders as he did so, "they used to call me Sweet Lemon Brown."

"Sweet Lemon?" Greg asked.

"Yessir. Sweet Lemon Brown. They used to say I sung the blues so sweet that if I sang at a funeral, the dead would commence[6] to rocking with the beat. Used to travel all over Mississippi and as far as Monroe, Louisiana, and east on over to Macon, Georgia. You mean you ain't never heard of Sweet Lemon Brown?"

"Afraid not," Greg said. "What . . . what happened to you?"

"Hard times, boy. Hard times always after a poor man. One day I got tired, sat down to rest a spell and felt a tap on my shoulder. Hard times caught up with me."

"Sorry about that."

"What you doing here? How come you didn't go on home when the rain come? Rain don't bother you young folks none."

"Just didn't." Greg looked away.

"I used to have a knotty-headed boy just like you." Lemon Brown had half walked, half shuffled back to the corner and sat down against the wall. "Had them big eyes like you got. I used to call them moon eyes. Look into them moon eyes and see anything you want."

"How come you gave up singing the blues?" Greg asked.

"Didn't give it up," Lemon Brown said. "You don't give up the blues; they give you up. After a while you do good for yourself, and it ain't nothing but foolishness singing about how hard you got it. Ain't that right?"

"I guess so."

"What's that noise?" Lemon Brown asked, suddenly sitting upright.

Greg listened, and he heard a noise out-side. He looked at Lemon Brown and saw the old man was pointing toward the window.

Greg went to the window and saw three men, neighborhood thugs, on the stoop. One was carrying a length of pipe. Greg looked back toward Lemon Brown, who moved quietly across the room to the window. The old man looked out, then beckoned frantically for Greg to follow him. For a moment Greg couldn't move. Then he found himself following Lemon Brown into the hallway and up darkened stairs. Greg followed as closely as he could. They reached the top of the stairs, and Greg felt Lemon Brown's hand first lying on his shoulder, then probing[7] down his arm until he finally took Greg's hand into his own as they crouched in the darkness.

"They's bad men," Lemon Brown whispered. His breath was warm against Greg's skin.

"Hey! Rag man!" A voice called. "We know you in here. What you got up under them rags? You got any money?"

Silence.

"We don't want to have to come in and hurt you, old man, but we don't mind if we have to."

Lemon Brown squeezed Greg's hand in his own hard, gnarled fist.

There was a banging downstairs and a light as the men entered. They banged around noisily, calling for the rag man.

"We heard you talking about your treasure." The voice was slurred.[8] "We just want to see it, that's all."

"You sure he's here?" One voice seemed to come from the room with the sofa.

---

6. **commence** (kə mens′), v. begin.
7. **probe** (prōb), v. search.
8. **slurred** (slėrd), adj. pronounced unclearly, indistinctly.

▲ *Ben* was painted by Hubert Shuptrine in 1976. What type of "story" is revealed by the man's face and expression? Do you think this story is similar to Lemon Brown's?

"Yeah, he stays here every night."

"There's another room over there; I'm going to take a look. You got that flashlight?"

"Yeah, here, take the pipe too."

Greg opened his mouth to quiet the sound of his breath as he sucked it in uneasily. A beam of light hit the wall a few feet opposite him, then went out.

"Ain't nobody in that room," a voice said. "You think he gone or something?"

"I don't know," came the answer. "All I know is that I heard him talking about some kind of treasure. You know they found that shopping bag lady with that money in her bags."

"Yeah. You think he's upstairs?"

"HEY, OLD MAN, ARE YOU UP THERE?" Silence.

"Watch my back, I'm going up."

There was a footstep on the stairs, and the beam from the flashlight danced crazily along the peeling wallpaper. Greg held his breath. There was another step and a loud crashing noise as the man banged the pipe against the wooden banister. Greg could feel his temples throb as the man slowly neared them. Greg thought about the pipe, wondering what he would do when the man reached them—what he *could* do.

Then Lemon Brown released his hand and moved toward the top of the stairs. Greg looked around and saw stairs going to the next floor. He tried waving to Lemon Brown, hoping the old man would see him in the dim light and follow him to the next floor. Maybe, Greg thought, the man wouldn't follow them up there. Suddenly, though, Lemon Brown stood at the top of the stairs, both arms raised high above his head.

"There he is!" A voice cried from below.

"Throw down your money, old man, so I won't have to bash your head in!"

Lemon Brown didn't move. Greg felt himself near panic. The steps came closer, and still Lemon Brown didn't move. He was an eerie[9] sight, a bundle of rags standing at the top of the stairs, his shadow on the wall looming over him. Maybe, the thought came to Greg, the scene could be even eerier.

Greg wet his lips, put his hands to his mouth and tried to make a sound. Nothing came out. He swallowed hard, wet his lips once more and howled as evenly as he could.

"What's that?"

As Greg howled, the light moved away from Lemon Brown, but not before Greg saw him hurl his body down the stairs at the men who had come to take his treasure. There was a crashing noise, and then footsteps. A rush of warm air came in as the downstairs door opened, then there was only an ominous[10] silence.

> Suddenly, . . . Lemon Brown stood at the top of the stairs, both arms raised high above his head.

Greg stood on the landing. He listened, and after a while there was another sound on the staircase.

"Mr. Brown?" he called.

"Yeah, it's me," came the answer. "I got their flashlight."

Greg exhaled in relief as Lemon Brown made his way slowly back up the stairs.

"You OK?"

"Few bumps and bruises," Lemon Brown said.

"I think I'd better be going," Greg said, his

9. **eerie** (ir′ē), *adj.* something that is weird or strange and causes fear.
10. **ominous** (om′ə nəs), *adj.* threatening.

breath returning to normal. "You'd better leave, too, before they come back."

"They may hang around outside for a while," Lemon Brown said, "but they ain't getting their nerve up to come in here again. Not with crazy old rag men and howling spooks. Best you stay a while till the coast is clear. I'm heading out west tomorrow, out to east St. Louis.

"They were talking about treasures," Greg said. "You *really* have a treasure?"

"What I tell you? Didn't I tell you every man got a treasure?" Lemon Brown said. "You want to see mine?"

"If you want to show it to me," Greg shrugged.

"Let's look out the window first, see what them scoundrels[11] be doing," Lemon Brown said.

They followed the oval beam of the flashlight into one of the rooms and looked out the window. They saw the men who had tried to take the treasure sitting on the curb near the corner. One of them had his pants leg up, looking at his knee.

"You sure you're not hurt?" Greg asked Lemon Brown.

"Nothing that ain't been hurt before," Lemon Brown said. "When you get as old as me all you say when something hurts is, 'Howdy, Mr. Pain, sees you back again.' Then when Mr. Pain see he can't worry you none, he go on mess with somebody else."

Greg smiled.

"Here, you hold this." Lemon Brown gave Greg the flashlight.

He sat on the floor near Greg and carefully untied the strings that held the rags on his right leg. When he took the rags away, Greg saw a piece of plastic. The old man carefully took off the plastic and unfolded it. He revealed some yellowed newspaper clippings and a battered harmonica.

"There it be," he said, nodding his head. "There it be."

Greg looked at the old man, saw the distant look in his eye, then turned to the clippings. They told of Sweet Lemon Brown, a blues singer and harmonica player who was appearing at different theaters in the South. One of the clippings said he had been the hit of the show, although not the headliner. All of the clippings were reviews of shows Lemon Brown had been in more than fifty years ago. Greg looked at the harmonica. It was dented badly on one side, with the reed holes on one end nearly closed.

"I used to travel around and make money for to feed my wife and Jesse—that's my boy's name. Used to feed them good, too. Then his mama died, and he stayed with his mama's sister. He growed up to be a man, and when the war come he saw fit to go off and fight in it. I didn't have nothing to give him except these things that told him who I was, and what he come from. If you know your pappy did something, you know you can do something too.

"Anyway, he went off to war, and I went off still playing and singing. 'Course by then I wasn't as much as I used to be, not without somebody to make it worth the while. You know what I mean?"

"Yeah," Greg nodded, not quite really knowing.

"I traveled around, and one time I come home, and there was this letter saying Jesse got killed in the war. Broke my heart, it truly did.

"They sent back what he had with him over there, and what it was is this old mouth fiddle and these clippings. Him carrying it around with him like that told me it meant something to him. That was my treasure, and when I give it to him he treated it just like that, a treasure. Ain't that something?"

---

11. **scoundrel** (skoun′drəl), *n.* wicked person; someone without honor or principles.

"Yeah, I guess so," Greg said.

CLARIFY: What was Lemon Brown's treasure, and why was it important?

"You *guess* so?" Lemon Brown's voice rose an octave as he started to put his treasure back into the plastic. "Well, you got to guess 'cause you sure don't know nothing. Don't know enough to get home when it's raining."

"I guess . . . I mean, you're right."

"You OK for a youngster," the old man said as he tied the strings around his leg, "better than those scalawags what come here looking for my treasure. That's for sure."

"You really think that treasure of yours was worth fighting for?" Greg asked. "Against a pipe?"

"What else a man got 'cepting what he can pass on to his son, or his daughter, if she be his oldest?" Lemon Brown said. "For a bigheaded boy you sure do ask the foolishest questions."

Lemon Brown got up after patting his rags in place and looked out the window again.

"Looks like they're gone. You get on out of here and get yourself home. I'll be watching from the window so you'll be all right."

Lemon Brown went down the stairs behind Greg. When they reached the front door the old man looked out first, saw the street was clear and told Greg to scoot on home.

"You sure you'll be OK?" Greg asked.

"Now didn't I tell you I was going to east St. Louis in the morning?" Lemon Brown asked. "Don't that sound OK to you?"

"Sure it does," Greg said. "Sure it does. And you take care of that treasure of yours."

"That I'll do," Lemon said, the wrinkles about his eyes suggesting a smile. "That I'll do."

The night had warmed and the rain had stopped, leaving puddles at the curbs. Greg didn't even want to think how late it was. He thought ahead of what his father would say and wondered if he should tell him about Lemon Brown. He thought about it until he reached his stoop, and decided against it. Lemon Brown would be OK, Greg thought, with his memories and his treasure.

Greg pushed the button over the bell marked Ridley, thought of the lecture he knew his father would give him, and smiled.

After Reading

Making Connections

1. What was a particularly memorable **image** from the story? What made it so?

2. Why do you think Greg smiles at the end of the story?

3. Do you think Greg will change because of his encounter with Lemon Brown? Why or why not?

4. What do you think the author was really saying about treasures?

5. Would *you* fight someone with a pipe or other dangerous weapon for your treasure? Explain.

6. What type of **mood** is created by the story's **setting?**

7. 👣 What do Greg and Lemon Brown learn by **communicating** with each other?

Literary Focus: Plot

The **plot** of a story is a series of related events selected by the author to present and bring about the resolution of some conflict. There are many conflicts in this story. Some are external, such as the conflict between Greg and his father. Some are internal, such as Greg's inner conflict between what he loves to do and what he knows he should do. To help you better understand the conflicts in this story and their relationship to the plot, make a chart like the one below.

Conflict Between . . .	Brief Description	Impact on the Story
Greg and his father	Greg wants to play basketball, but his father won't let him.	Greg goes into the tenement instead of going home to avoid a fight with his father.

Vocabulary Study

tenement
ajar
tentatively
involuntary
commence
probe
slurred
eerie
ominous
scoundrel

A. Decide if the following pairs of words are synonyms or antonyms. Record your answers on a separate sheet of paper.

1. ajar–open
2. tentatively–assuredly
3. commence–end
4. eerie–weird

B. On a separate sheet of paper, write the vocabulary word that matches each clue.

5. This is a good name for someone who cheats or lies.
6. Your dentist will do this with an instrument.
7. Your speech might sound this way with a mouth full of marbles.
8. This word could be used to describe a back spasm or blinking.
9. This word would be useful in describing threatening clouds.
10. This building houses many different families.

Expressing Your Ideas

Writing Choices

To the Boy with the Moon Eyes Imagine that you are Lemon Brown and that a year has passed since you met Greg at the tenement. Write a **letter** to Greg explaining what you have been doing. Include several questions that Lemon Brown would have for his young friend.

What About You? Have you ever met someone whose words or actions helped you to see things in a new light? Who was this person, and how did he or she affect you? Put down your thoughts about this person in a **poem**.

Uh, Oh, They're Not Leaving What would have happened if the thugs had not been scared off? Write another **story ending** for "The Treasure of Lemon Brown." If you think it is appropriate, create a new title.

Other Options

Say It Aloud Review the author's description of Lemon Brown's voice and his way of speaking. Practice a few of his lines to see if you can sound like him. Work with a partner who can create a voice for Greg. After you've both practiced, select some **dialogue** from the story to read to the class.

Hi, Dad With a partner, act out for the class the **conversation** Greg probably had with his father after returning home from his visit with Lemon Brown. You can either prepare some dialogue in advance or improvise.

Singing the Blues In small groups, use library resources to research and create a **bulletin board display** of the history of the blues. One person might like to do a time line; one person could find pictures and illustrations; another could create a collage, and so on.

Before Reading

Beni Seballos

by Phillip Hoose

Phillip Hoose
born 1947

Phillip Hoose is the author of the book *It's Our World, Too! Stories of Young People Who Are Making a Difference.* His book contains fourteen stories of children and adolescents who are working, or who worked, to change the world. There are stories of people who stood up to gangs, who fought against big companies, and who organized to protect the environment. The book also has a lot of information about how to get organized and raise money for an issue that may concern you.

Building Background

Extended Families The main character of this selection, Beni Seballos, immigrated from the Philippines to the United States. The Philippines is a nation of more than 7,000 islands in the southwest Pacific. There, most people belong to large extended families that live and often work together. An extended family includes not only parents and their children but also grand-parents, aunts, uncles, cousins, and in-laws. As you will read, Beni's family is no exception. Are large extended families a rule or an exception in the U.S.?

Getting into the Story

Writer's Notebook Volunteers such as Beni Seballos play an important role in our society. In your notebook, make a list similar to the one below of jobs that people volunteer to do. Then make a list of possible motivations they might have for volunteering.

Types of Jobs Volunteers Do	Motivations for Volunteering
bringing hot meals to the elderly	to feel needed

Reading Tip

Problem Solving There's almost always a solution to any given problem. Finding that solution can be made easier if a person follows an organized plan. The first step is to identify the problem, which means actually naming it. Then it's time to collect information about the problem and identify possible causes. Only after figuring out what is causing the problem will you be able to figure out some possible solutions. Then you can select one of these solutions, try it, and if it doesn't work, try another. As you read, think about the problem-solving process that Beni Seballos goes through as she tries to change her relationship with her grandmother.

Beni Seballos

Phillip Hoose

Volunteering to take care of others can be just as important to a community as standing up to an injustice. It can be just as challenging, too. Beni Seballos of Racida, California, overcame her self-doubt and volunteered to take care of older people with diseases that affect their ability to think, remember, and move. The things she learned gave her confidence and helped her solve one of the biggest problems in her own life.

One day when she was fifteen, Beni Seballos stepped onto a plane with ten of her aunts, uncles, cousins, nieces, and nephews and said good-bye to everything she loved. Soon her home, her friends, and her school in the Philippines were far behind her.

When they arrived in Los Angeles, they drove to a small house. There they would stay with her aunt and grandparents until they could find enough money to buy a home of their own.

The fourteen of them tried their best to be cheerful. For Beni, the hardest part was trying to get along with her grandmother. She was a stern,[1] quiet woman, used to the respect that elders commanded in the Philippines. Beni was noisy and opinionated.[2] Her grandmother always seemed to disapprove of her. Each day Beni would ask her grandmother if she could help with dinner, and the answer was always no. That "no" filled the kitchen, leaving no space for Beni. She always left the room in anger, wondering how long she could take living there.

---

1. **stern** (stėrn), *adj.* harshly firm; strict.
2. **opinionated** (ə pin′yə nā′tid), *adj.* firm, even stubborn, with regard to one's opinion.

Racida High School was no better. She didn't know anybody at first. She made the basketball team but rarely got in the games. "Academic Decathlon[3] was even worse," Beni recalls. "A team of kids from Racida High tried to answer questions faster than a team from another school. It wasn't about learning. I hated it."

The one thing she really liked was a volunteer organization called Youth Community Services, or YCS. After hearing about it at school, Beni went on a weekend field trip to plant trees in a farm area. There was no feeling of competition here. Everyone was working together. She volunteered for YCS at a blood bank, at a recycling center, and with a program that helped keep young kids off drugs. At last, she was having fun in the United States.

Her parents didn't understand. To them, volunteering just kept her away from home. She wasn't even getting school credit for it. When Beni put on her jacket to go to a YCS event, her grandmother would glare, and her mother would say, softly but pointedly, "Oh, you're going off again, aren't you, Beni?"

During the summer break, a YCS counselor urged Beni to volunteer at a senior citizens center. The staff needed volunteers to help take care of old people who had Alzheimer's and Parkinson's diseases. Think of all you could learn, the counselor kept saying.

Beni wasn't so sure. She found herself wondering what a sixteen-year-old could really have in common with someone who was seventy-five or eighty. She hated to admit it to herself, but old people sounded boring. Even worse, what if they all treated her the way her grandmother did?

But maybe the counselor was right. After all, she thought, you learn most by doing what you understand least. Beni signed up for four days a week, five hours a day, and then walked to the library to find out about Alzheimer's and Parkinson's diseases.

A medical encyclopedia said that both diseases affect the brain's ability to function. Alzheimer's patients gradually lose their memories, and Parkinson's patients gradually lose control of their muscles. After reading less than a page, Beni closed the book, unable to go on. "I was terrified," she remembers. "I could see myself having to force-feed these drooling people. I'd have to pick them up off the ground all the time. I thought they'd be vegetables.

"I practically ran out of the library. I was ready to quit before I had ever met a single patient. By the time I got home, I was wondering, 'What did I get myself into?'"

"What Do You Think About This?"

The first day, Beni introduced herself to the center's supervisor, Kathleen, and the six other volunteers, all in their forties and fifties. They were friendly, but she wondered if they really believed a teenager could handle the work.

Kathleen explained that the volunteers were supposed to feed the patients, take them for walks, and help give them their medicine. She went over each patient's medicine and diet. She kept looking at Beni and saying, "Don't worry, you'll do fine."

Then Kathleen opened the door, and they all walked out into the hallway, where about fifteen patients and their relatives were waiting. Some patients were in wheelchairs. Others were in walkers. A few leaned on canes.

Beni hung back and watched as the other

---

3. **decathlon** (di kath′lon), *n.* originally a ten-part track-and-field contest. An Academic Decathlon is a competition with questions about subjects like history and science.

volunteers rushed forward to greet the patients. Was she supposed to help them into their wheelchairs? How did you do it, anyway? What if she dropped someone? "I could see some of the patients' relatives looking at me. I felt them thinking, She's just a kid. She doesn't look like she knows what she's doing."

She followed the crowd into a big room, where the volunteers were supposed to serve the patients coffee and doughnuts. Beni's mind went blank. She couldn't remember who was supposed to have only half a doughnut and who wasn't supposed to get a doughnut at all. Kathleen was nowhere in sight. Beni fought back tears. This was terrible. It was the Alzheimer's patients who were supposed to have memory problems, not her.

After coffee, Kathleen was reading a newspaper article to a group of patients when one of them interrupted. He pointed to Beni. "You're a young person," he said. "What do you think about this?" Beni was startled. An older person actually wanted her opinion? This was certainly different from home. Well, actually she *did* have an opinion on the topic of the article, and so she gave it. They listened carefully and discussed it. This part isn't so bad, Beni thought.

"You're a young person," he said. "What do you think about this?"

She went home that night exhausted and determined to do better tomorrow. As always, her grandmother was in the kitchen. They went through the usual routine again, with Beni offering to help and her grandmother refusing her. Beni walked out fuming. She had to get out of there.

The next morning, Beni went to the center early and memorized the patients' names. When the patients arrived, she sat down beside a frail woman named Lil with a sparse[4] crown of thin white hair. Beni peeled an orange for her and filled up her cup of coffee halfway with a single lump of sugar, just as Lil's chart said. As she was working, Beni told Lil about what it had been like to move from the Philippines.

Lil began to talk, too. She said she had spent much of her life raising five wonderful children.

"Where are they now?" Beni asked.

"Who?"

"Your children."

"What?"

"Your children. You were saying you have five children."

Lil rung the hem of her dress in her hands, looking frantically around the room. "What do you mean? I-I-I can't remember." She seemed to be growing more desperate by the second. Beni quickly changed the subject to her own college plans, and gradually Lil relaxed. It was Beni's first real contact with Alzheimer's disease. It taught her that she had to listen and be flexible,[5] alert to each patient's needs. Patients wouldn't always be able to stick to the same subject for very long.

Later that week, Beni was leading a patient named Oscar outside for a game of shuffleboard when she heard the sharp scrape of metal behind her. His walker had become caught between two chairs. Trembling, he tried to shake loose. Beni knelt to pry the walker free, but it was no use. Oscar was growing enraged and started to shout. His face was turning red. Here it is, Beni thought, the emergency I can't handle. She sprinted into the kitchen to get help. Three volunteers and Kathy rushed out, and in a moment, they had

---

4. **sparse** (spärs), *adj.* thinly scattered.
5. **flexible** (flek′sə bəl), *adj.* mentally able to adapt to changing circumstances.

Beni Seballos helps one of the patients play shuffleboard, a popular game at the senior citizens center. How do you think playing a game together could help younger and older people learn to **communicate** better?

him free. "You handled it well," Kathy said to Beni later. "Just get help."

As the summer went by, Beni faced many different kinds of challenges. A few patients tried to wander off. Some became angry because they couldn't remember when to take their medicine. One refused to go back inside after a walk.

After a few weeks at the center, Beni found herself thinking differently about the patients. She could no longer think of them as "old people" or "senior citizens," or "Alzheimer's patients" or even "patients." They had become individuals, like her, who just happened to be at a different stage of their lives. Like her, they all had their own interests and families, hopes and fears, opinions and problems.

She discovered that if she listened carefully, she could find something in common with almost everyone. Alex wrote poetry, just like Beni. Sometimes at the shuffleboard court, they recited their poems to each other. Beni and Oscar spoke Spanish together. Blackie told her World War II stories. Mary taught her a few words of Czech. Lil loved to talk about children.

By the end of the summer, it seemed to Beni that being young had been an advantage, not a handicap, at the center. "I was special to some of the Alzheimer's patients," she says. "I think maybe having me around helped them remember how they were when they were young themselves."

Beans and Friendship

In September, Beni said a tearful good-bye to the patients and staff and took a week off before school started. She had some unfinished business.

All summer long, things had gotten worse and worse with her grandmother until finally she had moved out of her aunt's house in order to find some peace in her life. But she didn't feel at peace. She loved her grandmother, and she wanted to put things right between them.

For a while it had seemed strange that she could have fun with Lil or Oscar or Alex but not her own grandmother. Then it came to her: When things got tough with a patient at the center, she kept trying patiently until she found a way to get through. But when things got tough with her grandmother, she gave up.

So one afternoon, she walked over to her aunt's house, determined to treat her grandmother as she had learned to treat the people at the center.

As usual, Beni's grandmother was in the kitchen. "Hi," Beni said. "Is there anything I can do?" "No," said her grandmother. This time Beni didn't leave. She noticed a bowl of string beans on the counter and carried them to the kitchen table. She sat down, picked up a bean, and snapped off the end.

She began to tell her grandmother about her summer. Though her grandmother didn't say anything, Beni could sense that she was listening. After a while, her grandmother wiped her hands on a towel, pulled up a chair, and sat down at the other end of the table. She picked up a bean and snapped the top off. A half hour later, there was a big pile of beans between them—and the beginning of a friendship.

Beni says that friendship was maybe the greatest gift of the summer. It couldn't have happened until she herself changed, and volunteering at the center was the key that opened doors within her. "The summer started working for me when I began to share myself with the patients, not just log time," she says. "Then it was fun. I know I did a good job at the center, but I probably got more out of it than the patients. I learned that caring is like a muscle. The more you exercise it, the more you *can* share."

I feel myself
   grow old
My eyes go blind
   My hands shake
Please, Lord, let
   someone also
   help me out
When tomorrow's dawns
   grow dark on
   me.
—Beni Seballos

After Reading

Making Connections

1. Does Beni remind you of someone? What characteristics does this person share with Beni?

2. What does Beni's poem at the end of the selection tell you about what she learned?

3. Did Beni use the problem-solving steps outlined in the Reading Tip on page 373 to repair her relationship with her grandmother? Explain.

4. Why do you think the author chose to write about someone like Beni?

5. ⚬ In what ways did Beni learn to overcome her differences with the various people at the center and effectively **communicate** with them?

6. Look at the list of volunteer work you made before reading the story. What kind of volunteer activity would you choose for yourself? Why?

Literary Focus: Characterization

Characterization is the way an author describes a character. The author may give physical or personality traits, have the character speak so that the reader can "hear" him or her, or have another person describe the character. The author may also describe the person's feelings and opinions so that the reader knows how the character thinks. What methods does the author use to describe Beni? Read through the story for clues in order to fill out a chart like the one below.

Information from the Text	What It Tells the Reader
Beni moves to the United States.	She may be lonely or confused.
"It wasn't about learning."	She doesn't like competition.

Vocabulary Study

stern
opinionated
decathlon
sparse
flexible

On a separate piece of paper, fill in each blank with one of the words from the list.

The volunteers busily decorated the rather __(1)__ walls of the cafeteria with colorful posters, balloons, and streamers. Cynthia, a rather __(2)__ person, told some of the volunteers they were doing everything wrong. Manuel, level-headed as always, took Cynthia aside. "Don't be so __(3)__ with them," he pleaded. "We're all just trying to help out. Be a little more __(4)__. There's more than one right way to do things." After their talk everything went more smoothly. By the time the volunteers had finished decorating, however, they all felt as if they had just competed in a tough __(5)__.

Expressing Your Ideas

Writing Choices

A Recipe for Success In the form of a **recipe,** write Beni's ingredients for improving a relationship between a young person and his or her grandparents. Write your recipe on a notecard. Perhaps you and your classmates could collect the recipes and put them together in a "cookbook."

Another Act of Kindness Write a brief **biographical sketch** about someone who is very caring toward others. You could write about a friend of yours or someone who is famous for his or her work with others.

Problem Solving Read several letters from one or more of the advice columns that appear in most newspapers. Choose a letter from someone who has a problem and who has requested help in finding a solution. Using the problem-solving steps described on page 373, write a **response** to the letter writer.

Other Options

What's It Really Like? With a partner, arrange to visit a local nursing home. **Interview** someone who lives or works there. Before your visit, brainstorm questions that you'd like to ask. Prepare an oral report for the class describing your visit and interview.

Investigate Use the *Readers' Guide to Periodical Literature* in your community or school library to locate articles dealing with Alzheimer's or Parkinson's disease, two diseases that affect many elderly people. In an **oral report,** share this information with the class.

Volunteers? Take a **survey** of people in your class and find out what kind of activities they volunteer for—or would volunteer for, if they could. To encourage honest responses, assure your classmates that their responses will be anonymous. Tally the results and record the responses on the board.

Before Reading

This Is Just to Say by William Carlos Williams

Variations on a Theme by William Carlos Williams by Kenneth Koch

William Carlos Williams
1883–1963

Williams was born in New Jersey. His father was English, and his mother was Puerto Rican. He was a pediatrician, as well as a poet, playwright, and novelist. He used the lives of people he knew, his patients, and his own imagination to create distinctly American verse.

Kenneth Koch
born 1925

Kenneth Koch is a poet living in New York. In addition to poetry, he has written stories, plays, and nonfiction. He says, "I think some of my work is funny, but if it's not also serious, then I'm wasting my time."

Building Background

The Poet's Work William Carlos Williams's poems are based on everyday occurrences. He thought that a poet should create concrete images for the reader, images that left no guesswork, so that the poem would evoke emotions and thoughts in the reader. Unlike many of his contemporaries, who wrote hard-to-understand poems full of references to ancient literature and history, Williams wrote poetry about things that were typical in American life. He wanted to celebrate everyday life, and he wanted the people who read his poetry to be able to celebrate too.

Getting into the Poetry

Writer's Notebook Oh, dear, you just ate something that was in the refrigerator, and you suddenly realize that someone was probably saving it. In your notebook, write a short apology to that person. The note should be sincere yet contain some humor about the incident. It should be the type of note you'd affix to the refrigerator with a magnet.

Dear _____,
I'm sorry, but I just ate _____
_____
_____

Reading Tip

Parody A humorous imitation of another piece of writing is called a **parody.** A parody follows the form of the original but changes sense to nonsense in order to make fun of the original piece or writer. "Variations on a Theme by William Carlos Williams" is a parody of Williams's poem, "This Is Just to Say." As you read, think about some of the reasons why Kenneth Koch might have wanted to parody Williams's poem.

This Is Just to Say

William Carlos Williams

I have eaten
the plums
that were in
the icebox

5 and which
you were probably
saving
for breakfast

Forgive me
10 they were delicious
so sweet
and so cold

▲ The still life *Plums, Apricots, in a Bowl* was painted by Jacob Van Hulsdonck. Why do you think the artist chose to combine purple plums and yellow apricots in this painting?

Variations on a Theme by William Carlos Williams

Kenneth Koch

1

I chopped down the house that you have been saving to live in next summer.
I am sorry, but it was morning, and I had nothing to do
and its wooden beams were so inviting.

2

We laughed at the hollyhocks together
5   and then I sprayed them with lye.
Forgive me. I simply do not know what I am doing.

3

I gave away the money that you have been saving to live on for the next
    ten years.
The man who asked for it was shabby
and the firm March wind on the porch was so juicy and cold.

4

10 Last evening we went dancing and I broke your leg.
Forgive me. I was clumsy, and
I wanted you here in the wards, where I am the doctor!

After Reading

Making Connections

1. If someone had left William Carlos Williams's poem on your refrigerator, what would your reaction have been? Why?

2. Williams wanted his poems to celebrate everyday life. Has he succeeded with "This Is Just to Say"? Why or why not?

3. **Tone** is the author's attitude, stated or implied, toward the subject and toward the audience. Some possible attitudes are joy, seriousness, and bitterness. What would you say is the tone of "This Is Just to Say"?

4. Which words tell what the plums were like? To what **senses** do the words appeal?

5. What would you say is the relationship of the **narrator** to the person for whom the poem is intended?

6. What was your first reaction to Kenneth Koch's "Variations"?

7. Why do you think Koch chose to **parody** the poem, "This Is Just to Say"?

8. How would you have reacted to Koch's poem had you not known it was a parody?

Literary Focus: Rhythm

Rhythm is everywhere, in the way we walk and talk, in music, in traffic—everywhere. Most of the poetry we know has a regular rhythm, such as in "TWINkle TWINkle LITTle STAR." Some poets, however, make use of more irregular rhythms. One way that poets do this is to have one line overflow into the next. This technique, which is used by William Carlos Williams in "This Is Just to Say," breaks up the rhythm and makes the reader focus more on the poem's meaning rather than the rhythm. Read the poem again, this time concentrating on the poet's sense of rhythm. How would you describe it? Then read the poem aloud, tapping out the rhythm.

Expressing Your Ideas

Writing Choices

Be a Humorist With the help of a witty, sarcastic partner, write a **parody** of one of the other selections you have read in this book. If the selection you choose is rather lengthy, you may parody an appropriate section of the piece. Present the parody to the class.

Tell It Like It Is Read some more of Williams's poetry. Then write a **critique** of the poet's works. Comment on such areas as rhythm, mood, tone, applicability to real life, and so on. Read your critique to the class, ending it, like many movie critics do, with a ranking based on four stars:

- Four stars will stand for EXCELLENT,
- Three for VERY GOOD,
- Two for OK,
- And one for NOT RECOMMENDED.

If you'd like, invent your own rating system.

Roses Are Red . . . William Carlos Williams believed in writing about the common events and subjects of his day. Pretend that you are a modern-day William Carlos Williams. Write a **poem** that he might have written if he were alive today.

Other Options

Be a Political Cartoonist Create a **political cartoon** that parodies someone or something in the news. Before you begin, read political cartoons in newspapers and magazines to get an idea of how to proceed. To be effective, you'll need to tackle a subject with which most people are familiar. With your classmates, create a bulletin board display of the cartoons.

Find Other Examples Parody exists in art, music, and other areas, as well as in literature. Using library resources, find some examples of parody in other areas. Prepare a **bibliography** of parody writing that interested readers can use.

Sing About It Have you heard any of Weird Al Yankovich's parodies of well-known rock songs? Bring in an example of a **song** that parodies another song to play for your classmates. Then try your hand at writing a musical parody of a well-known song. Perform it for the class.

Writing Mini-Lesson

Maintaining Your Working Portfolio

Whether you have been keeping your working portfolio or your teacher has been keeping it, now is the time to review it.

- First, review your statement of your goals. Do you have pieces in your portfolio that show that you are working on or have met each goal? If not, what kinds of writing do you need?

- Next, look at your writing samples. Do you have planning pieces, first drafts, revised and edited drafts, and the final copies for all your samples? Do you have some different kinds of writing—critical writing, reports, narratives, poems?

- Finally, is there anything in your portfolio that you don't think should be there? What pieces do you really like? What pieces are not examples of your best work? Make a list of items that you need to add or remove before you prepare your presentation portfolio at the end of the year.

Making a Mid-Course Correction

What about the goals themselves? Review your goals. Are they still the ones that you want to reach? Also, think about your progress in reaching the goals. Did you take on more than you can accomplish, or did you underestimate yourself? You might ask a partner for a second opinion on your goals and the written pieces you have produced.

Take some time to rewrite your goals. If you have already met your goals, then set some new ones. Be sure to include the changes you want to make in your portfolio and what you plan to accomplish for the next grading period.

Before Reading

How the Snake Got Poison by Zora Neale Hurston

Strawberries by Gayle Ross

Zora Neale Hurston
1891–1960

In addition to retelling African American folk tales, Hurston wrote articles, short stories, novels, and movie scripts. She also taught drama at an African American college in North Carolina and worked as an anthropologist.

Gayle Ross
born 1951

Gayle Ross is a descendant of a Cherokee Indian chief, John Ross. She enjoys telling Cherokee animal stories to children and researching the sacred myths and creation stories of her ancestors.

Building Background

Words and the Oral Tradition Long before the advent of writing, people orally passed on stories from generation to generation. Thankfully, many of these stories now exist in written form, because of the efforts of people such as Zora Neale Hurston, who collected and interpreted the African American folklore she grew up with in Eatonville, Florida. "How the Snake Got Poison" is one of these tales. Another collector of tales was James Mooney, an expert on Cherokee customs and myths. In 1900 he published a treasure-trove of Cherokee stories. Gayle Ross, a professional storyteller, discovered "Strawberries" while studying Mooney's collections.

Getting into the Stories

Discussion You have come across many types of **dialect** in your reading, especially if you read "He Lion, Bruh Bear, and Bruh Rabbit." What exactly *is* dialect? Why do writers use it? What purpose does it serve? In small groups, explore these questions.

Reading Tip

Cause and Effect Cause-and-effect relationships are important elements in most stories. In order to identify the **effects** in a piece of writing you need to ask "What happened?" To identify the **causes,** ask "Why?" In some cases, causes and effects are not always stated directly. As you read, record some of the causes and effects that you identify in a chart like the one below.

How the Snake Got Poison	
Causes	**Effects**
God wanted to decorate the ground. ➤	God created the snake

How the Snake Got Poison

Zora Neale Hurston

Well, when God made de snake he put him in de bushes to ornament[1] de ground. But things didn't suit de snake so one day he got on de ladder and went up to see God.

"Good mawnin', God."

"How do you do, Snake?"

"Ah ain't so many, God, you put me down there on my belly in de dust and everything trods[2] upon me and kills off my generations.[3] Ah ain't got no kind of protection at all."

God looked off towards immensity and thought about de subject for awhile, then he said, "Ah didn't mean for nothin' to be stompin' you snakes lak dat. You got to have some kind of a protection. Here, take dis poison and put it in yo' mouf and when they tromps on you, protect yo' self."

So de snake took de poison in his mouf and went on back.

So after awhile all de other varmints went up to God.

"Good evenin', God."

"How you makin' it, varmints?"

"God, please do somethin' 'bout dat snake. He' layin' in de bushes there wid poison in his mouf and he's strikin' everything dat shakes de bush. He's killin' up our generations. Wese skeered to walk de earth."

So God sent for de snake and tole him:

"Snake, when Ah give you dat poison, Ah didn't mean for you to be hittin' and killin' everything dat shake de bush. I give you dat poison and tole you to protect yo'self when they tromples on you. But you killin' everything dat moves. Ah didn't mean for you to do dat."

De snake say, "Lawd, you know Ah'm down here in de dust. Ah ain't got no claws to fight wid, and Ah ain't got no feets to git me out de way. All Ah kin see is feets comin' to tromple me. Ah can't tell who my enemy is and who is my friend. You gimme dis protection in my mouf and Ah uses it."

---

1. ornament (ôr′nə mənt), *v.* decorate or add beauty to.
2. trod (trod), *v.* walk on or trample.
3. generation (jen′ə rā′shən), *n.* all of the people born about the same period. Parents belong to one generation and their children to the next.

God thought it over for a while then he says:

"Well, snake, I don't want yo' generations all stomped out and I don't want you killin' everything else dat moves. Here take dis bell and tie it to yo' tail. When you hear feets comin' you ring yo' bell and if it's yo' friend, he'll be keerful. If it's yo' enemy, it's you and him."

So dat's how de snake got his poison and dat's how come he got rattles.

Biddy, biddy, bend my story is end.

Turn loose de rooster and hold de hen.

STRAWBERRIES

Gayle Ross

Long ago, in the very first days of the world, there lived the first man and the first woman. They lived together as husband and wife, and they loved one another dearly.

But one day, they quarreled.[1] Although neither later could remember what the quarrel was about, the pain grew stronger with every word that was spoken, until finally, in anger and in grief, the woman left their home and began walking away—to the east, toward the rising sun.

The man sat alone in his house. But as time went by, he grew lonelier and lonelier. The anger left him and all that remained was a terrible grief and despair, and he began to cry.

A spirit heard the man crying and took pity on him. The spirit said, "Man, why do you cry?"

The man said, "My wife has left me."

The spirit said, "Why did your woman leave?"

The man just hung his head and said nothing.

The spirit asked, "You quarreled with her?" And the man nodded.

"Would you quarrel with her again?" asked the spirit.

The man said, "No." He wanted only to live with his wife as they had lived before—in peace, in happiness, and in love.

"I have seen your woman," the spirit said. "She is walking to the east toward the rising sun."

The man followed his wife, but he could not overtake her. Everyone knows an angry woman walks fast.

Finally, the spirit said, "I'll go ahead and see if I can make her slow her steps." So the spirit found the woman walking, her footsteps fast and angry and her gaze fixed straight ahead. There was pain in her heart.

The spirit saw some huckleberry bushes growing along the trail, so with a wave of his hand, he made the bushes burst into bloom and ripen into fruit. But the woman's gaze remained fixed. She looked neither to the right nor the left, and she didn't see the berries. Her footsteps didn't slow.

---

1. **quarrel** (kwôr′əl), *v.* disagree angrily.

▲ *Woman of Taos* was painted by the California impressionist Selden Gile in 1931. How would you describe the woman's expression? If she were the woman in the tale, would she be at the beginning or end of her journey? Why?

Again, the spirit waved his hand, and one by one, *all* of the berries growing along the trail burst into bloom and ripened into fruit. But still the woman's gaze remained fixed. She saw nothing but her anger and pain, and her footsteps didn't slow.

And again, the spirit waved his hand, and, one by one, the trees of the forest—the peach, the pear, the apple, the wild cherry—burst into bloom and ripened into fruit. But still, the woman's eyes remained fixed, and even still, she saw nothing but her anger and pain. And her footsteps didn't slow.

Then finally, the spirit thought, "I will create an entirely new fruit—one that grows very, very close to the ground so the woman must forget her anger and bend her head for a moment." So the spirit waved his hand, and a thick green carpet began to grow along the trail. Then the carpet became starred with tiny white flowers, and each flower gradually ripened into a berry that was the color and shape of the human heart.

As the woman walked, she crushed the tiny berries, and the delicious aroma[2] came up through her nose. She stopped and looked down, and she saw the berries. She picked one and ate it, and she discovered its taste was as sweet as love itself. So she began walking slowly, picking berries as she went, and as she leaned down to pick a berry, she saw her husband coming behind her.

The anger had gone from her heart, and all that remained was the love she had always known. So she stopped for him, and together, they picked and ate the berries. Finally, they returned to their home where they lived out their days in peace, happiness, and love.

And that's how the world's very first strawberries brought peace between men and women in the world, and why to this day they are called the berries of love.

---

2. aroma (ə rō′mə), *n.* distinctive fragrance.

Another Voice

Primer Lesson
Carl Sandburg

Look out how you use proud words.
When you let proud words go, it is
    not easy to call them back.
They wear long boots, hard boots; they
5   walk off proud; they can't hear
        you calling—
Look out how you use proud words.

After Reading

Making Connections

1. Which story do you like better? Why?

2. What do the two stories have in common? How are they different?

3. According to "How the Snake Got Poison," what was the **cause** of the snake's poison?

4. What broader message do you think "How the Snake Got Poison" might be making?

5. According to "Strawberries," what are some of the **causes** that brought about the creation of strawberries?

6. How do "proud words" play a part in "Strawberries"?

7. Do you agree that there is now peace between men and women in the world?

8. Why do you think people find it so difficult to overcome anger after a serious quarrel?

9. Based on these readings, what advice do you have for how to become friends with someone again after a quarrel?

Literary Focus: Dialect

Think about your responses to the questions about dialect on page 387. Now answer the same questions, but this time in reference to "How the Snake Got Poison." Why would Hurston use this dialect? What purpose does it serve in this story? What are some particular examples that you either liked or found confusing?

Vocabulary Study

ornament
trod
generation
quarrel
aroma

Decide if the underlined words are used correctly in the sentences below. Write *Correct* or *Incorrect* on your paper and if a sentence is incorrect, explain why.

1. The Cherokee boy and his grandfather are from the same generation.

2. The aroma from the strawberry pie smelled heavenly.

3. She gingerly trod through the strawberry patch, being careful not to step on the strawberries.

4. The crimson-red strawberries will nicely ornament the barren ground.

5. The man and woman would never quarrel over something so trivial.

Expressing Your Ideas

Writing Choices

Well, Dis Is How It Goez Practice writing a **story** in a particular dialect. Try a favorite fairy tale.

Emotional Words Choose words of emotion from the stories, such as *quarrel, pain, anger, grief*, and *love*. Use these words to write a **poem.**

A Personal Mythology Create your own **legend** based on the painting below, *Chouette au Coucher de Soleil* by Maria Christen. Before you begin, decide what effect you want to explain in your legend— for example, "how the owl got its big eyes." Then create a cause that explains that effect.

Other Options

Another da Vinci? **Draw** a favorite scene from one of the selections. Write a descriptive caption beneath the drawing.

Convincing Words Plan and write a radio, magazine, or newspaper **advertisement** or **TV commercial** sponsored by the Strawberry Council that will encourage people to buy and eat strawberries.

Squirmin' Along Find another tale about snakes to **read aloud** to your class or a class of younger students. Use your library's card catalog or an on-line database to locate titles.

Rattler Diagram Research rattlesnakes to find out more about their poison and rattles. Draw a **diagram** of a rattlesnake that shows where the rattles are and how the snake delivers poison to its victims.

Working Things Out

In Harmony

Anthropology Connection

In many areas, human beings have made remarkable advancements in the past few centuries—in science, technology, and education, to name a few. In other areas we have fallen sadly behind. Just a short time ago, Native Americans lived in harmony with the earth and its wildlife. Somewhere along the way we have forgotten to respect the land and what it gives us. As a result, we are just now working things out, trying to strike a balance in the relationship between the technology we have created and the land that supports us.

In BALANCE with NATURE

by Vine Deloria, Jr.

O ur knowledge of birds, animals, and the natural world is derived primarily from television, textbooks, and unfortunately, from cartoons that feature cuddly and all-too-human bears, energetic roadrunners, and inept coyotes. Few of our children ever see animals, and they never see them in their natural habitats.

Native North Americans saw themselves as participants in a great natural order of life, related in some fundamental manner to every other living species. It was said that each species had a particular knowledge of the universe and specific skills for living in it. Human beings had a little bit of knowledge and some basic skills, but we could not compare with any other animals as far as speed, strength, cunning, and intelligence. Therefore it was incumbent on us to respect every other form of life. Man was the youngest member of the web of life and, therefore, had to have some humility in the face of the talents and experience of other species.

Native North Americans made a point of observing the other creatures and modeling their own behavior after them. Many of the social systems of the tribes were patterned after their observations of the birds and animals, and in those tribes that organized themselves in clans, every effort was made to follow the behavior of the clan totem animal or bird. Teaching stories for children emphasized the virtue of the animals, and children were admonished to be wise, gentle, brave, or cheerful in the same manner as certain birds and animals.

The technical skills of birds, animals, and reptiles were such that Native North Americans could take cues from them for their own welfare. If birds consistently built nests out of certain materials, it meant that they recognized and adjusted to the fact of harsh or mild weather in

Much of the religious ceremony and ritual of the tribes was derived from information provided to them by birds, animals, and reptiles.

a certain location. The building of beaver dams in certain parts of rivers gave information on the depth of water, its purity, the kinds of fish and other water creatures in the locale, and the kinds of roots, berries, and medicine roots that would be available at that place. Animal trails were carefully observed by the people because inevitably the game animals would take the shortest and easiest path through mountains, prairies, and desert and would not be far from water and edible plants.

Much of the religious ceremony and ritual of the tribes was derived from information provided to them by birds, animals, and reptiles. The famous Hopi "Snake Dance" enabled the people to live in an arid high plateau desert because the snakes could bring water to assist the Hopi in growing corn.

The relationship was so close between humans and other forms of life that it was believed humans could take the shape of the birds and animals for some time after their deaths. Thus it was not uncommon, following the death of an old person, to see a hawk or woodpecker circling the camp or village. Owls sometimes gathered in large numbers on the approaching death of a medicine man.

Interestingly, many tribes had classifications among the birds and animals that enabled them to explain complicated relationships. Thus the Plains Indians saw a grand distinction between two-legged and four-legged creatures. Among the two-leggeds were humans, birds, and bears. Bears were included because when feeding, they often stand on two legs. Since the two-leggeds are responsible for helping to put the natural world back into balance when it becomes disordered, birds, bears, and humans share a responsibility to participate in healing ceremonies.

We must carefully accord these other creatures the respect that they deserve and the right to live without unnecessary harm.

(above) *Journey to the Butterfly World* was sculpted by Navajo artist Alvin Marshall. As the people at the bottom perform a ceremony, the smoke from their fire travels up to the Butterfly Lady, signifying harmony with nature.

(opposite page) Hopi butterfly dancers appear over the edge of Second Mesa, Arizona.

Responding

Use a chart or diagram to illustrate how the Native Americans viewed their relationship to the earth and its creatures. Make a second diagram that shows how modern Americans relate to their environment. Write a short paragraph that explains the differences.

397

Art Connection

Each Native American tribe had its own distinct beliefs, customs, and ceremonies. Yet, there was a common thread that bound them all together. They had a great respect for nature. They worked to maintain a balance in the natural order of the universe. Native Americans strove to live in harmony with all creatures. That common philosophy is woven into the tapestry of Native American art from across the continent.

Decorated with a frog design made of seashells, this dance shirt was likely owned by a wealthy man. Shells were collected and traded for European goods such as wool, metal items, and weapons. The shells sewn on this shirt were probably more valuable than the shirt alone.

Tribal healers of some Northeast tribes carved masks from a living tree. This Mohawk mask is an example. A mask begun in the morning was painted red. Black was the color of a mask made in the afternoon. Wearing the mask, a healer would go to the longhouse of a sick person and perform healing ceremonies.

This Cherokee mask was made of woodchuck hide with pieces of deer tail for ears. Worn for hunting rituals, the mask represents the power of the wildcat.

NATIVE AMERICAN *Spirituality*

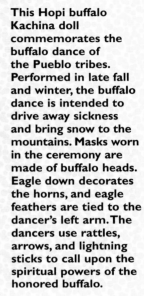

This Hopi buffalo Kachina doll commemorates the buffalo dance of the Pueblo tribes. Performed in late fall and winter, the buffalo dance is intended to drive away sickness and bring snow to the mountains. Masks worn in the ceremony are made of buffalo heads. Eagle down decorates the horns, and eagle feathers are tied to the dancer's left arm. The dancers use rattles, arrows, and lightning sticks to call upon the spiritual powers of the honored buffalo.

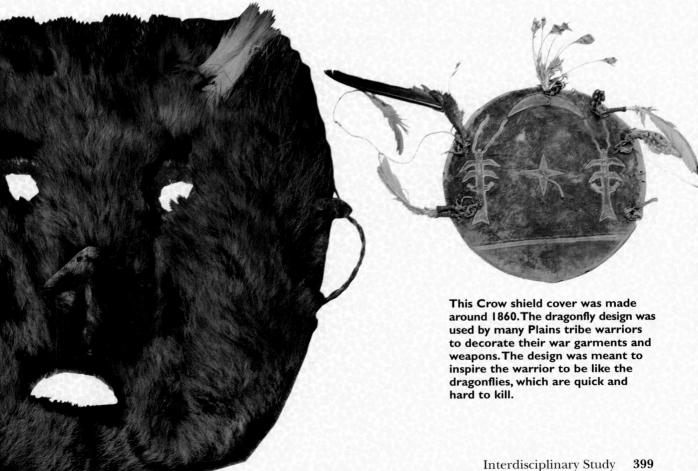

This Crow shield cover was made around 1860. The dragonfly design was used by many Plains tribe warriors to decorate their war garments and weapons. The design was meant to inspire the warrior to be like the dragonflies, which are quick and hard to kill.

Tribes of the Northwest coast used drums in both social and religious ceremonies. A symbol of unity, this drum is decorated with intricate paintings of a killer whale and a bear.

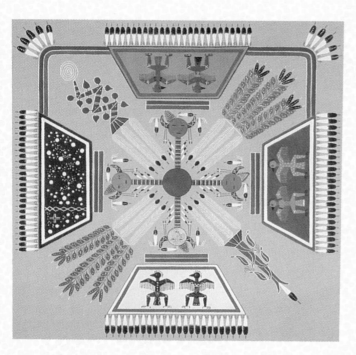

The Skies, a Navaho sandpainting by Herbert Ben, Sr., depicts the Sky world. White is the dawn, blue the day, yellow the sunset, and black the night sky. The corn, beans, and squash represent the earth. The birds are messengers connecting the sky to the earth. The rainbow connects the skies. All elements of the painting are in perfect balance, expressing the view that nature is a complex whole made up of parts that balance each other.

Responding

1. Native American art often depicts harmony in nature. How do the examples of Native American art on these pages show this harmony?

2. Create your own design that represents balance in nature. Write a short explanation of your work.

Reading Mini-Lesson

Generalizing

Making a generalization involves drawing conclusions from a series of observations. For example, suppose you experiment with containers of water to see what happens when you lower the temperature. Each time, you observe that the water freezes when the temperature reaches 32°F. After seeing this happen many times, you generalize that "water always freezes at 32°F."

Now suppose your science teacher gives a quiz every Thursday for the first three weeks of class. You might generalize that "Science quizzes always come on Thursday." Then the next quiz comes on Wednesday. That would show that you made a faulty generalization. Perhaps the correct generalization is that "Science quizzes *usually* come on Thursday." You would have to wait a few more weeks to see if that was true.

"In Balance with Nature" begins with a generalization about our knowledge of birds, animals, and the natural world. Although we don't see the evidence for this generalization, we can imagine that it comes from the writer's observations. A good thing to do with generalizations is to ask what observations led to each one. The following activities help you connect generalizations with evidence.

Activity Options

1. The author says on page 395: "The technical skills of birds, animals, and reptiles were such that Native North Americans could take cues from them for their own welfare." What evidence does he give for this generalization?

2. What generalization in the article is based on this evidence?

   A. Children were taught to behave in the same ways as birds or animals.

   B. Each clan tried to follow the behavior of the clan animal or bird.

3. Based on your reading of the entire article, what generalization can you make about Native North Americans and their knowledge of the natural world? Write your generalization and the evidence (at least two observations) on which it was based.

Part Two

Appreciating Each Other

Seen from a distance, unfamiliar people, experiences, and objects may make us uncomfortable, embarrassed, or even angry. The individuals in these selections discover that the first step toward appreciating others is increased understanding, and that increased understanding leads to stronger relationships.

Multicultural Connection **Interactions** across cultures occur when people of different backgrounds come into close contact. Sometimes an individual whose family background includes more than one cultural tradition must balance conflicting pressures and expectations. How do the people in these selections seek ways to balance the pressures of two cultures?

Literature

Merrill Markoe	**Greeting Disorder** ♦ play	.404
Rosalie Moore	**Catalogue** ♦ poem	.406
Robert Cormier	**The Moustache** ♦ short story	.410
	Language Mini-Lesson ♦ Punctuating for Clarity	.420
Carol Saline	**Coretta and Edythe: The Scott Sisters** ♦ letters	.422
Robert Frost	**A Time to Talk** ♦ poem	.429
Teresa Palomo Acosta	**My Mother Pieced Quilts** ♦ poem	.430
Virginia Driving Hawk Sneve	**The Medicine Bag** ♦ short story	.435
Gerald Haslam	**The Horned Toad** ♦ short story	.446

Interdisciplinary Study **Generations Together**

They Won't Let Me Grow Up by Lauren Tarshis ♦ psychology 456
Search for Your "Roots" by A. Elwood and C. Orsag ♦ history 460
            Reading Mini-Lesson ♦ Recalling Details 462

Writing Workshop **Expository Writing**

Letter of Thanks 463

Beyond Print **Effective Listening**

Feel Like You're Talking to a Wall? 469

Before Reading

Greeting Disorder

by Merrill Markoe

Merrill Markoe
born 1949

If you watch late-night television, chances are that you've seen Merrill Markoe's work, even if you haven't heard her name. For many years, she was the head writer for the *Late Night with David Letterman* show, a program famous for its "stupid pet tricks." Markoe won three Emmy Awards for her work on the show. This selection is from her book *How to Be Hap-Hap-Happy Like Me.* She writes regularly for several national magazines and lives in Malibu, California, with quite a few dogs.

Building Background

Pet Appreciation Pets today are popular and pampered. For dogs and cats, you can buy clothes, toys, vitamins, and many other items. Not only can you visit the vet, but you can also see the pet therapist if your schnauzer is having psychological problems! We benefit from this popularity too. Researchers have found there are health benefits to caring for an animal. In fact, your blood pressure actually goes down when you pet your dog or cat!

Getting into the Play

Discussion Experimenters have shown that we have invisible boundary lines around us and that we respond when a line is crossed and our space has been invaded. Try this boundary experiment with a partner: *Stand and face each other, starting about ten feet apart. Each take one step closer. Then each take another step. Then another. Then another. Continue until your toes are almost touching your friend's toes.* As you do this experiment, keep mental notes of when you start to feel uncomfortable and how you want to react. When you are done, discuss the results of your experiment. Do different people in your class have different needs for their own space?

Reading Tip

Making Inferences Have you ever wondered what a dog or cat was thinking? They may not have human faces, but animals certainly have different expressions, and these expressions make us think of human moods, feelings, and thoughts. We may be wrong, but we often **infer** or conclude from their behavior that our pets have thoughts or feelings similar to our own.

In this selection, you have the opposite problem. The writer tells you what the dogs say, and you have to infer what the dogs actually do. As you read "Greeting Disorder," notice how the dogs' behavior is suggested through the **dialogue**—what they say to their owner and each other. Try to picture in your mind how the dogs are acting as they speak.

GREETING DISORDER

MERRILL MARKOE

One afternoon, having arrived home in a bad mood after a long series of thankless chores, it occurred to me that it was time to confront[1] my dogs about an issue between us that was building to insurmountable[2] proportions. I called for the two largest ones, Lewis and Tex, to join me in my office. Since they never come when I call, the two others arrived. I locked them in there and cornered Lewis and Tex in the front room, where we finally thrashed the whole thing out.[3]

ME. Okay, you two, LISTEN CAREFULLY. In the future it is neither necessary nor desirable for you to greet me every single time I walk in the door. Unless a minimum of two hours has passed, the previous greeting is still in effect. In other words, if I come IN the door, and you greet me, and then several minutes later I go OUT the door, only to return in a matter of seconds, you do NOT have to greet me again.

LEWIS. Ha-ha. Good one.

ME. I am serious. Maybe it would be best at this point to discuss the PURPOSE of a greeting.

TEX. What is she talking about?

LEWIS. Play along. We don't eat for about an hour.

ME. A GREETING is what you give someone you have not seen IN A WHILE. A WHILE is a period of time of more than two hours. Try another example. I come in the door after a day of work . . .

TEX. I would be so glad to see you that I would rush up and hurl myself

---

1. **confront** (kən frunt′), *v.* face boldly.
2. **insurmountable** (in′sər moun′tə bəl), *adj.* that cannot be overcome.
3. **thrash out** *v.* settle by thorough discussion.

at you. Then I would get up on my back legs, knocking you over, causing you to drop whatever you were carrying . . .

LEWIS. Listen to what you're saying, bro. You know we're not supposed to get UP on her.

ME. Very good, Lewis. Thank you.

LEWIS. Which is why the approach *I* take is to circle closely, using body blocks. Throwing my whole weight against her legs so that she falls over and drops everything. Same exact result. I never have to get UP on her at all.

ME. You're missing the point. All that is required from a greeting is a simple show of enthusiasm. Eyes filled with a certain amount of joy, a bit of tail-wagging. THAT'S IT.

TEX. What did she say?

LEWIS. Just go with it. She likes to hear herself talk.

ME. Now that we've defined a greeting . . .

LEWIS. And by the way, I like to make mine last until she's down on her knees, if not flat on her back . . .

TEX. I've seen your work, buddy. You're an artist.

ME. . . . Let's try one more exercise to see if you are getting the point. Okay. Imagine this. I decide to take out the garbage. I walk to the door . . .

LEWIS. I'm right there with you.

TEX. I beat you there.

LEWIS. The hell you do.

ME. I exit. About eight seconds later I come back *in* the door. What would be your response?

TEX. I'd be so thrilled to see you that I'd run up to you,

hurl myself at you, then I'd get up on my back legs and . . .

LEWIS. Dolt.[4] You don't listen. We just went through this a second ago. It's circle and hurl, circle and lean . . . and hurl. Circle and hurl.

ME. STOP! Listen to me! The point was that you do not have to greet me again. You just greeted me seconds before. I'm sorry if this seems confusing, but I'd like you just to blindly accept this rule and obey it. DO NOT GREET ME EVERY TIME I COME IN THE DOOR.

LEWIS. So you're asking us to be rude.

TEX. No, no, I hear you. Tell me if I've got it straight. You go OUT the door, and then you come RIGHT BACK IN. We do NOT get up on you. No. We circle and hurl, circle and lean and hurl . . .

LEWIS. There you go. Step on her feet and trip her. Tangle her up, and lean on her and at the same time circle . . .

TEX. I can definitely do that.

LEWIS. Where is she going?

TEX. Looks like the bedroom. Whoa. She closed the door. How long is she going to be gone?

LEWIS. I don't know. All I know is suddenly we're very alone.

TEX. How long has it been since we saw her?

LEWIS. I don't know. A month? A year?

TEX. Wait! The door is opening. . . . She's back!

LEWIS. . . . She's back! Welcome back!

TEX. Come let me get up on you and give you a nice big kiss.

---

4. **dolt** (dōlt), *n.* a dull, stupid person.

Greeting Disorder **405**

Catalogue

Rosalie Moore

Suggest one more line for the poem "Catalogue" based on this illustration by Mary Lempa.

Cats sleep fat and walk thin.
Cats, when they sleep, slump;
When they wake, stretch and begin
Over, pulling their ribs in.
5 Cats walk thin.

Cats wait in a lump,
Jump in a streak.
Cats, when they jump, are sleek
As a grape slipping its skin—
10 They have technique.
Oh, cats don't creak.
They sneak.

Cats sleep fat.
They spread out comfort underneath them
15 Like a good mat,
As if they picked the place
And then sat;
You walk around one
As if he were the City Hall
20 After that.

If male,
A cat is apt to sing on a major scale;
This concert is for everybody, this
Is wholesale.
25 For a baton, he wields a tail.

(He is also found,
When happy, to resound
With an enclosed and private sound.)

A cat condenses.[1]
30 He pulls in his tail to go under bridges,
And himself to go under fences.
Cats fit
In any size box or kit,
And if a large pumpkin grew under one,
35 He could arch over it.

When everyone else is just ready to go out,
The cat is just ready to come in.
He's not where he's been.
Cats sleep fat and walk thin.

---

1. **condense** (kən dens′), *v.* make more compact.

After Reading

Making Connections

1. Do you find this play believable? If dogs could talk, do you think they would sound like this?

2. Give two examples of **humor** from the play. What makes them funny?

3. Cite a passage that gave you a clear picture of the dogs' behavior. Describe how you pictured the dogs as you read that passage.

4. How do you think the author of "Greeting Disorder" wanted you to feel about the dogs?

5. There are no stage directions or descriptions in the play. How can you tell what action is taking place during the conversation?

6. How does the author of "Catalogue" seem to feel about cats? What lines especially suggest these feelings?

7. Even though they seem to speak the same language, the human is having trouble communicating with the dogs in "Greeting Disorder." What advice can you give for how to communicate clearly with friends and family?

Literary Focus: Personification

It's easy to see how Tex and Lewis are like dogs, but it might be more fun to see how they are like people—two different people. The author **personifies** each dog by giving it a distinct personality. Review the story for details about each dog. Since you will have to draw conclusions about their personalities, be sure to examine what each dog says. Use concept webs like the ones below to organize your ideas. Note four or five personality characteristics for each dog. Use your web to compose a short "personality sketch" of each dog. Include examples from the play to support your ideas.

 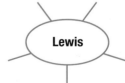

Vocabulary Study

confront
insurmountable
thrash out
dolt
condense

Answer the following questions.

1. Which of these things would be the easiest to <u>condense</u>?

   a. rock   **b.** a sponge   **c.** glass   **d.** cement

2. Which of these might be considered <u>insurmountable</u>?

   a. a mountain   **b.** a bump   **c.** a sidewalk crack   **d.** an ant hill

3. Which of these is another meaning for <u>dolt</u>?

   a. genius   **b.** fireman   **c.** blockhead   **d.** skydiver

4. Which of these acts might your parents <u>confront</u> you about?

   a. picking on your younger sister   **b.** washing the car

   c. cleaning your room   **d.** watching a baseball game

5. When would people NOT have to <u>thrash</u> something <u>out</u>?

   a. deciding who gets to eat the last piece of cake

   b. assigning chores

   c. figuring out how much allowance you deserve

   d. switching on the light

Expressing Your Ideas

Writing Choices

I Draw the Line Here! For the others in your family, write **guidelines** for respecting your personal space and privacy within your home. Explain when they have a right to invade your privacy and when they do not.

We Need to Talk Your pet isn't perfect. You'd like a few things changed about the animal's behavior. Write a **dialogue** between you and your real or imaginary pet in which you discuss the changes you'd like to see. Be sure that your pet's words match its "personality."

Well, Tex, What Do You Think? Continue the play by writing a new **scene** in which Lewis and Tex talk about what to do when the human returns.

Other Options

Welcome Home! What will be the result of "thrashing it all out"? Make a **drawing** of the scene that you think will take place the next time the person comes home.

Dog Song What kind of song would Tex and Lewis sing about themselves? Using words and phrases from either "Greeting Disorder" or "Catalogue," write a dog or cat **song** and put it to music.

Circle and Hurl, Circle and Lean . . . Working with two classmates, take the roles of the human and the two dogs and **act out** the scene. Review the dialogue carefully to be sure when each character needs to move.

Before Reading

The Moustache

by Robert Cormier

Robert Cormier
born 1925

Robert Cormier (côr mē ā´) wanted to become a fiction writer from the time he was in the eighth grade. Yet he was almost fifty years old before his stories won national recognition. Early in his career he worked as a reporter for New England newspapers, winning numerous awards for journalism. It was Cormier's novels for adolescents, however, that gained him popularity, critical recognition, and controversy.

Cormier's stories do not have pat endings but portray life realistically—often harshly. *The Chocolate War* (1974), *I Am the Cheese* (1977), and *After the First Death* (1979) each won the *New York Times* Outstanding Book of the Year Award.

Building Background

No Sugar Coating "That story was kid stuff." Not many readers have that reaction to stories by Robert Cormier. The mark of a Cormier story is that realistic things happen to realistic characters. Perhaps another reason for the great popularity of Cormier's stories is that they stem from real-life experiences with strong emotion. He says, "I *want* the reader to feel the emotion of the characters. And I would use any word, any unpretty image, to communicate that emotion."

Getting into the Story

Discussion Make a list of the older people in your family: parents, aunts and uncles, grandparents. Suppose you had to write about the life of one of these people. Could you write very much? Would it be easier to write about one of your friends? Sometimes it seems that we know our friends better than we know our own family members. In a group, discuss why you think it may be hard to get to know the older people in your family.

Reading Tip

Discovering Themes in Literature Different readers will have different ideas of what a story is about. Why? All readers see the same words. If asked to summarize the plot, most would include the same events. What differs is readers' responses to the words and events. A **theme** results when you consider the main events of the plot and ask, "What does it all mean?" For example, remember the popular story *Charlotte's Web?* You could summarize the **plot** of that story by saying that it is about how a spider saves a pig's life by weaving messages about the pig into her webs. How would you state the theme? Well, it certainly is about friendship. Perhaps you would say, "Friendship is an important part of life," or "Friends can be found in unexpected places," or "Friendship involves sacrifice."

As you read "The Moustache," copy words or sentences that you think suggest a theme. When you finish reading, be prepared to discuss themes you've found in the story.

The Moustache

Robert Cormier

Why do you think the artist, Maryann Thomas, chose such an unusual perspective for this painting?

At the last minute Annie couldn't go. She was invaded by one of those twenty-four-hour flu bugs that sent her to bed with a fever, moaning about the fact that she'd also have to break her date with Handsome Harry Arnold that night. We call him Handsome Harry because he's actually handsome, but he's also a nice guy, cool, and he doesn't treat me like Annie's kid brother, which I am, but like a regular person. Anyway, I had to go to Lawnrest alone that afternoon. But first of all I had to stand inspection. My mother lined me up against the wall. She stood there like a one-man firing squad, which is kind of funny because she's not like a man at all, she's very feminine, and we have this great relationship—I mean, I feel as if she really likes me. I realize that sounds strange, but I know guys whose mothers love them and cook special stuff for them and worry about them and all but there's something missing in their relationship.

Anyway. She frowned and started the routine.

"That hair," she said. Then admitted: "Well, at least you combed it."

I sighed. I have discovered that it's better to sigh than argue.

"And that moustache." She shook her head. "I still say a seventeen-year-old has no business wearing a moustache."

"It's an experiment," I said. "I just wanted to see if I could grow one." To tell the truth, I had proved my point about being able to grow a decent moustache, but I also had learned to like it.

"It's costing you money, Mike," she said.

"I know, I know."

The money was a reference to the movies. The Downtown Cinema has a special Friday night offer—half-price admission for high school couples, seventeen or younger. But the woman in the box office took one look at my moustache and charged me full price. Even when I showed her my driver's license. She charged full admission for Cindy's ticket, too, which left me practically broke and unable to take Cindy out for a hamburger with the crowd afterward. That didn't help matters, because Cindy has been getting impatient recently about things like the fact that I don't own my own car and have to concentrate on my studies if I want to win that college scholarship, for instance. Cindy wasn't exactly crazy about the moustache, either.

Now it was my mother's turn to sigh.

"Look," I said, to cheer her up. "I'm thinking about shaving it off." Even though I wasn't. Another discovery: You can build a way of life on postponement.[1]

CLARIFY: What does it mean to "build a way of life on postponement"?

"Your grandmother probably won't even recognize you," she said. And I saw the shadow fall across her face.

Let me tell you what the visit to Lawnrest was all about. My grandmother is seventy-three years old. She is a resident—which is supposed to be a better word than *patient*—at the Lawnrest Nursing Home. She used to make the greatest turkey dressing in the world and was a nut about baseball and could even quote batting averages, for crying out loud. She always rooted for the losers. She was in love with the Mets until they started to win. Now she has arteriosclerosis,[2] which the dictionary says is "a chronic disease characterized by abnormal thickening and hardening of the

---

1. postponement (pōst pōn′mənt), *n.* delay.
2. **arteriosclerosis** (är tir′ē ō sklə rō′sis).

arterial walls." Which really means that she can't live at home anymore or even with us, and her memory has betrayed[3] her as well as her body. She used to wander off and sometimes didn't recognize people. My mother visits her all the time, driving the thirty miles to Lawnrest almost every day. Because Annie was home for a semester break from college, we had decided to make a special Saturday visit. Now Annie was in bed, groaning theatrically—she's a drama major—but I told my mother I'd go anyway. I hadn't seen my grandmother since she'd been admitted to Lawnrest. Besides, the place is located on the Southwest Turnpike, which meant I could barrel along in my father's new LeMans.[4] My ambition was to see the speedometer hit seventy-five. Ordinarily, I used the old station wagon, which can barely stagger up to fifty.

> "Mike, Mike, I didn't think you'd come. . . ."

Frankly, I wasn't too crazy about visiting a nursing home. They reminded me of hospitals and hospitals turn me off. I mean, the smell of ether makes me nauseous, and I feel faint at the sight of blood. And as I approached Lawnrest—which is a terrible cemetery kind of name, to begin with—I was sorry I hadn't avoided the trip. Then I felt guilty about it. I'm loaded with guilt complexes. Like driving like a madman after promising my father to be careful. Like sitting in the parking lot, looking at the nursing home with dread and thinking how I'd rather be with Cindy. Then I thought of all the Christmas and birthday gifts my grandmother had given me and I got out of the car, guilty as usual.

PREDICT: What do you think guilt might have to do with this story?

Inside, I was surprised by the lack of hospital smell, although there was another odor or maybe the absence of an odor. The air was antiseptic,[5] sterile. As if there was no atmosphere at all or I'd caught a cold suddenly and couldn't taste or smell.

A nurse at the reception desk gave me directions—my grandmother was in East Three. I made my way down the tiled corridor and was glad to see that the walls were painted with cheerful colors like yellow and pink. A wheelchair suddenly shot around a corner, self-propelled by an old man, white-haired and toothless, who cackled merrily as he barely missed me. I jumped aside—here I was, almost getting wiped out by a two-mile-an-hour wheelchair after doing seventy-five on the pike. As I walked through the corridor seeking East Three, I couldn't help glancing into the rooms, and it was like some kind of wax museum—all these figures in various stances and attitudes, sitting in beds or chairs, standing at windows, as if they were frozen forever in these postures. To tell the truth, I began to hurry because I was getting depressed. Finally, I saw a beautiful girl approaching, dressed in white, a nurse or an attendant, and I was so happy to see someone young, someone walking and acting normally, that I gave her a wide smile and a big hello and I must have looked like a kind of nut. Anyway, she looked right through me as if I were a window, which is about par for the course whenever I meet beautiful girls.

I finally found the room and saw my grandmother in bed. My grandmother looks like Ethel Barrymore. I never knew who Ethel Barrymore was until I saw a terrific movie, *None But the Lonely Heart*, on TV, starring Ethel Barrymore and Cary Grant. Both my grand-

---

3. betray (bi trā′), v. be disloyal to.
4. **LeMans** (lə mänz′).
5. antiseptic (an′tə sep′tik), adj. having a sterilized or sterile quality; cold, barren, lifeless, etc.

mother and Ethel Barrymore have these great craggy[6] faces like the side of a mountain and wonderful voices like syrup being poured. Slowly. She was propped up in bed, pillows puffed behind her. Her hair had been combed out and fell upon her shoulders. For some reason, this flowing hair gave her an almost girlish appearance, despite its whiteness.

She saw me and smiled. Her eyes lit up and her eyebrows arched and she reached out her hands to me in greeting. "Mike, Mike," she said. And I breathed a sigh of relief. This was one of her good days. My mother had warned me that she might not know who I was at first.

I took her hands in mine. They were fragile.[7] I could actually feel her bones, and it seemed as if they would break if I pressed too hard. Her skin was smooth, almost slippery, as if the years had worn away all the roughness the way the wind wears away the surfaces of stones.

"Mike, Mike, I didn't think you'd come," she said, so happy, and she was still Ethel Barrymore, that voice like a caress. "I've been waiting all this time." Before I could reply, she looked away, out the window. "See the birds? I've been watching them at the feeder. I love to see them come. Even the blue jays. The blue jays are like hawks—they take the food that the small birds should have. But the small birds, the chickadees, watch the blue jays and at least learn where the feeder is."

She lapsed into silence, and I looked out the window. There was no feeder. No birds. There was only the parking lot and the sun glinting on car windshields.

She turned to me again, eyes bright. Radiant, really. Or was it a medicine brightness? "Ah, Mike. You look so grand, so grand. Is that a new coat?"

"Not really," I said. I'd been wearing my Uncle Jerry's old army-fatigue jacket[8] for months, practically living in it, my mother said. But she insisted that I wear my raincoat for the visit. It was about a year old but looked new because I didn't wear it much. Nobody was wearing raincoats lately.

"You always loved clothes, didn't you Mike?" she said.

I was beginning to feel uneasy because she regarded me with such intensity. Those bright eyes. I wondered—are old people in places like this so lonesome, so abandoned that they go wild when someone visits? Or was she so happy because she was suddenly lucid[9] and everything was sharp and clear? My mother had described those moments when my grandmother suddenly emerged from the fog that so often obscured[10] her mind. I didn't know the answers, but it felt kind of spooky, getting such an emotional welcome from her.

"I remember the time you bought the new coat—the Chesterfield," she said, looking away again, as if watching the birds that weren't there. "That lovely coat with the velvet collar. Black, it was. Stylish. Remember that, Mike? It was hard times, but you could never resist the glitter."

I was about to protest—I had never heard of a Chesterfield, for crying out loud. But I stopped. Be patient with her, my mother had said. Humor her. Be gentle.

We were interrupted by an attendant who pushed a wheeled cart into the room. "Time for juices, dear," the woman said. She was the standard forty- or fifty-year-old woman: glasses, nothing hair, plump cheeks. Her manner was cheerful but a businesslike kind of cheerfulness. I'd hate to be called "dear" by someone getting paid to do

---

6. craggy (krag′ē), *adj.* rough; uneven.
7. fragile (fraj′əl), *adj.* delicate; frail.
8. **army-fatigue jacket,** military work clothing worn in the field or whenever dress uniform is not required.
9. lucid (lü′sid), *adj.* clear, sane.
10. obscure (əb skyür′), *v.* cloud, darken.

it. "Orange or grape or cranberry, dear? Cranberry is good for the bones, you know."

My grandmother ignored the interruption. She didn't even bother to answer, having turned away at the woman's arrival, as if angry about her appearance.

The woman looked at me and winked. A conspiratorial[11] kind of wink. It was kind of horrible. I didn't think people winked like that anymore. In fact, I hadn't seen a wink in years.

"She doesn't care much for juices," the woman said, talking to me as if my grandmother weren't even there. "But she loves her coffee. With lots of cream and two lumps of sugar. But this is juice time, not coffee time." Addressing my grandmother again, she said, "Orange or grape or cranberry, dear?"

"Tell her I want no juices, Mike," my grandmother commanded regally,[12] her eyes still watching invisible birds.

The woman smiled, patience like a label on her face. "That's all right dear. I'll just leave some cranberry for you. Drink it at your leisure. It's good for the bones."

She wheeled herself out of the room. My grandmother was still absorbed in the view. Somewhere a toilet flushed. A wheelchair passed the doorway—probably that same old driver fleeing a hit-run accident. A television set exploded with sound somewhere, soap-opera voices filling the air. You can always tell soap-opera voices.

I turned back to find my grandmother staring at me. Her hands cupped her face, her index fingers curled around her cheeks like parenthesis marks.

"But you know, Mike, looking back, I think you were right," she said, continuing our conversation as if there had been no interruption. "You always said, 'It's the things of the spirit that count, Meg.' The spirit! And so you bought the baby-grand piano—a baby grand in the middle of the Depression.[13] A knock came on the door and it was the deliveryman. It took five of them to get it into the house." She leaned back, closing her eyes. "How I loved that piano, Mike. I was never that fine a player, but you loved to sit there in the parlor, on Sunday evenings, Ellie on your lap, listening to me play and sing." She hummed a bit, a fragment of melody I didn't recognize. Then she drifted into silence. Maybe she'd fallen asleep. My mother's name is Ellen, but everyone always calls her Ellie. "Take my hand, Mike," my grandmother said suddenly. Then I remembered—my grandfather's name was Michael. I had been named for him.

"Ah, Mike," she said, pressing my hands with all her feeble strength. "I thought I'd lost you forever. And here you are, back with me again. . . ."

QUESTION: What questions do you have at this point?

Her expression scared me. I don't mean scared as if I were in danger but scared because of what could happen to her when she realized the mistake she had made. My mother always said I favored her side of the family. Thinking back to the pictures in the old family albums, I recalled my grandfather as tall and thin. Like me. But the resemblance[14] ended there. He was thirty-five when he died, almost forty years old. And he wore a moustache. I brought my hand to my face. I also wore a moustache now, of course.

---

11. **conspiratorial** (kən spir′ə tôr′ē əl), *adj.* having to do with secret plans with others to do something wrong; plotting or scheming.
12. **regally** (rē′gəl lē), *adv.* royally; like a king or queen.
13. **the Depression,** a period during the 1930s when the stock market crashed, banks failed, and many people lost their jobs.
14. **resemblance** (ri zem′bləns), *n.* similar appearance; likeness.

"I sit here these days, Mike," she said, her voice a lullaby, her hand still holding mine, "and I drift and dream. The days are fuzzy sometimes, merging together. Sometimes it's like I'm not here at all but somewhere else altogether. And I always think of you. Those years we had. Not enough years, Mike, not enough. . . ."

Her voice was so sad, so mournful that I made sounds of sympathy, not words exactly but the kind of soothings that mothers mur- mur to their children when they awaken from bad dreams.

"And I think of that terrible night, Mike, that terrible night. Have you ever really for- given me for that night?"

"Listen . . .," I began. I wanted to say: "Nana, this is Mike your grandson, not Mike your husband."

"Sh . . . sh . . .," she whispered, placing a finger as long and cold as a candle against my lips. "Don't say anything. I've waited so

Still Life #3 was painted by G.G. Kopilak in 1942. In what ways does this painting reflect the situation of Mike's grandmother?

long for this moment. To be here. With you. I wondered what I would say if suddenly you walked in that door like other people have done. I've thought and thought about it. And I finally made up my mind—I'd ask you to forgive me. I was too proud to ask before." Her fingers tried to mask her face. "But I'm not proud anymore, Mike." That great voice quivered and then grew strong again. "I hate you to see me this way—you always said I was beautiful. I didn't believe it. The Charity Ball when we led the grand march and you said I was the most beautiful girl there . . ."

"Nana," I said. I couldn't keep up the pretense any longer, adding one more burden to my load of guilt, leading her on this way, playing a pathetic game of make-believe with an old woman clinging to memories. She didn't seem to hear me.

"But that other night, Mike. The terrible one. The terrible accusations I made. Even Ellie woke up and began to cry. I went to her and rocked her in my arms and you came into the room and said I was wrong. You were whispering, an awful whisper, not wanting to upset little Ellie but wanting to make me see the truth. And I didn't answer you, Mike. I was too proud. I've even forgotten the name of the girl. I sit here, wondering now—was it Laura or Evelyn? I can't remember. Later, I learned that you were telling the truth all the time, Mike. That I'd been wrong . . ." Her eyes were brighter than ever as she looked at me now, but tear-bright, the tears gathering. "It was never the same after that night, was it, Mike? The glitter was gone. From you. From us. And then the accident . . . and I never had the chance to ask you to forgive me . . ."

My grandmother. My poor, poor grandmother. Old people aren't supposed to have those kinds of memories. You see their pictures in the family albums and that's what they are: pictures. They're not supposed to come to life. You drive out in your father's LeMans doing seventy-five on the pike and all you're doing is visiting an old lady in a nursing home.

A duty call. And then you find out that she's a person. She's *somebody*. She's my grandmother, all right, but she's also herself. Like my own mother and father. They exist outside of their relationship to me. I was scared again. I wanted to get out of there.

> . . . I learned that you were telling the truth all the time, Mike. That I'd been wrong. . . .

"Mike, Mike," my grandmother said. "Say it, Mike."

I felt as if my cheeks would crack if I uttered a word.

"Say you forgive me, Mike. I've waited all these years . . ."

I was surprised at how strong her fingers were.

"Say, '*I forgive you, Meg.*'"

I said it. My voice sounded funny, as if I were talking in a huge tunnel. "I forgive you, Meg."

Her eyes studied me. Her hands pressed mine. For the first time in my life, I saw love at work. Not movie love. Not Cindy's sparkling eyes when I tell her that we're going to the beach on a Sunday afternoon. But love like something alive and tender, asking nothing in return. She raised her face, and I knew what she wanted me to do. I bent and brushed my lips against her cheek. Her flesh was like a leaf in autumn, crisp and dry.

She closed her eyes and I stood up. The sun wasn't glinting on the cars any longer. Somebody had turned on another television set, and the voices were the show-off voices of the panel shows. At the same time you could still hear the soap-opera dialogue on the other television set.

I waited awhile. She seemed to be sleeping, her breathing serene and regular. I buttoned my raincoat. Suddenly she opened her eyes again and looked at me. Her eyes were still bright, but they merely stared at me. Without recognition or curiosity. Empty eyes. I smiled at her, but she didn't smile back. She made a kind of moaning sound and turned away on the bed, pulling the blankets around her.

I counted to twenty-five and then to fifty and did it all over again. I cleared my throat and coughed tentatively. She didn't move; she didn't respond. I wanted to say, "Nana, it's me." But I didn't. I thought of saying, "Meg, it's me." But I couldn't.

Finally I left. Just like that. I didn't say goodbye or anything. I stalked through the corridors, looking neither to the right nor the left, not caring whether that wild old man with the wheelchair ran me down or not.

On the Southwest Turnpike I did seventy-five—no, eighty—most of the way. I turned the radio up as loud as it could go. Rock music—anything to fill the air. When I got home, my mother was vacuuming the living-room rug. She shut off the cleaner, and the silence was deafening. "Well, how was your grandmother?" she asked.

I told her she was fine. I told her a lot of things. How great Nana looked and how she seemed happy and had called me Mike. I wanted to ask her—hey, Mom, you and Dad really love each other, don't you? I mean—there's nothing to forgive between you, is there? But I didn't.

Instead I went upstairs and took out the electric razor Annie had given me for Christmas and shaved off my moustache.

After Reading

Making Connections

1. Mike compares his grandmother to an actress, Ethel Barrymore. What actor would you choose to play the role of Mike? Why?

2. How does this story make you feel about Mike? About his grandmother?

3. Do you think Mike was right to pretend to be his grandfather? Give reasons for your answer.

4. Choose a significant passage or phrase that you noted as you were reading, and explain how it expresses a **theme** of the story.

5. What do you think the **title** of this story means?

6. Why do you think the story ends with Mike shaving off his moustache?

7. During his **interactions** with his grandmother, Mike thinks, "Old people aren't supposed to have those kinds of memories." What might be some reasons teenagers have trouble seeing older people as human beings with feelings?

Literary Focus: Characterization

There are two Mikes in this story, the grandson and the grandfather. Use a Venn diagram like the one below to show which **character traits** are shared by the two Mikes and which are unique to one or the other. Include both physical characteristics and personality traits. When you have completed the Venn diagram, tell why you think the similarities and the differences between characters are important to understanding this story.

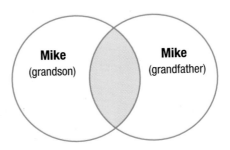

Mike
(grandson)

Mike
(grandfather)

Vocabulary Study

postponement
betray
antiseptic
craggy
fragile
lucid
obscure
conspiratorial
regally
resemblance

Draw the crossword puzzle on your paper and complete it with the words in the list at the left.

Across

2. something procrastinators enjoy

6. glass is, plastic isn't

7. how Queen Elizabeth speaks

10. jagged

Down

1. conceal by darkening

3. people plotting in secret act this way

4. similarity

5. what a hospital should be

8. making sense; sane

9. give away a secret

Expressing Your Ideas

Writing Choices

I'd Like You to Meet. . . List key phrases that describe Mike's grandmother, Meg. Then write the **script** you would use to introduce Mike's grandmother to a person interviewing her for an article on the Depression.

Similes, Similes Robert Cormier's style is marked by vivid description and use of figurative language. One of his favorite figures of speech is the simile. While inspecting him, Mike's mother "stood there like a one-man firing squad." Find four other **similes** the author uses to develop characters or show the emotions of a situation. Then write your own **character description** of a real or fictional person, using at least one simile.

Other Options

Title, Please? Working in a group, brainstorm five other **titles** that could be used with this story. For each title, be ready to explain how the change in title would affect a reader's first impression of the story.

So, How Was Nana? Mike doesn't tell his mother about being mistaken for his grandfather. Work with a partner to create a continuation of the story, just one more **scene.** After Mike shaves off the moustache, he finds his mother and starts the scene by saying, "Mom, there's more." You and your partner act out the final scene for the class.

Language Mini-Lesson

Punctuating for Clarity

Commas and Semicolons Using commas and semicolons to punctuate items in a series can help clarify information for readers. Notice how the correct punctuation makes it easier to read these sentences.

WITHOUT COMMAS	Maria's favorite sports include basketball swimming archery and tennis.
WITH COMMAS	Maria's favorite sports include basketball, swimming, archery, and tennis.
WITHOUT SEMICOLONS	Keith's family visited San Diego, California, Albuquerque, New Mexico, and Phoenix, Arizona, on their vacation.
WITH SEMICOLONS	Keith's family visited San Diego, California; Albuquerque, New Mexico; and Phoenix, Arizona, on their vacation.

Writing Strategy Use commas to separate items in a series that are not already punctuated with a comma. When the items are already punctuated with commas, as with dates and some place names, separate the items with semicolons.

Activity Options

1. On separate slips of paper, write ten sentences with series that need commas or semicolons to make them clear. Punctuate half of them. Combine your slips of paper with other students and then take turns drawing out sentences and trying to read them aloud.

2. Write a paragraph with at least three series in it. Then read it aloud while class members try to signal when punctuation is needed. For example, they might snap for commas and clap for semicolons. It's a good idea to read your paragraph aloud once with no response and then have everyone signal on the second time .

3. Look through the literature to find examples of punctuating for series clarity with commas and semicolons. Share your favorites with the class.

Before Reading

Coretta and Edythe: The Scott Sisters

by Carol Saline

Carol Saline
born 1939

The following selection comes from a book called *Sisters,* a book dedicated to the sisters of the writer, Carol Saline, and the photographer, Sharon Wohlmuth. The idea to work together on the book came out of a discussion they had one day about the power of the relationship between sisters. Once they had decided to do the book, they interviewed and photographed sisters to discover the many features of the sisterly relationship. Carol Saline is a senior editor at *Philadelphia Magazine.*

Building Background

Coretta Scott King Coretta Scott King is a civil rights activist and the widow of Dr. Martin Luther King, Jr., the famous civil rights leader who wrote, spoke, and acted on his belief that nonviolence is the solution to the world's human problems. Coretta supported her husband's work during his lifetime by giving speeches and concert recitals. She continued these activities after Dr. King's assassination in 1968.

Getting into the Selection

Writer's Notebook In the introduction to the book *Sisters,* from which this selection is taken, author Carol Saline says:

"Sisters are girlfriends, rivals, listening posts, shopping buddies, confidantes, and so much more."

Write your reactions to this statement. In what ways do you think it is true? In what ways do you think it is not so true? What experiences have formed your views? If you do not have a sister, base your reflections on what you've seen of sisters in other families or on what you imagine it would be like to have a sister.

Reading Tip

Cause-and-Effect Relationships In this selection you will see that each sister has influenced the other in the past, and that the act of one sister writing has also caused a response from the other. Sometimes we might think of **cause** and **effect** as working in a straight line: one cause produces one effect. Life is rarely that simple, however. To trace cause and effect in real-life situations, we'd need a more complicated map. As you read this selection, keep track of how each sister influences the other.

Edythe's Effects on Coretta	Coretta's Effects on Edythe

Coretta and Edythe

The Scott Sisters

Carol Saline

My dear sister Coretta,

I am sitting here tonight thinking about us. How close we were as children, sharing everything, doing everything together, always the leaders, always picked for the plays and the concerts because we were talented and attractive. The kind of kids teachers just knew would cooperate. When I went to Antioch before you, I learned about sibling[1] rivalry in one of my courses, and I didn't believe there could be such a thing. We certainly never competed or were jealous—even if you did have more boyfriends. And you've forgiven me for telling you there was no Santa Claus.

> . . . we've pulled each other up, supported each other, and taken care of each other.

Do you remember when you were five, already so physically strong, and you helped me pull the first bucket of water from the well outside of our house? That became a metaphor for our lives. All these years we've pulled each other up, supported each other, and taken care of each other. Even Martin[2] saw that. He called us the twins. He'd be giving a speech in some big auditorium and he'd say, "My wife isn't here tonight. But her sister is in the audience—so if I want to see Coretta, I just look down there at Edythe."

---

1. **sibling** (sib′ling), *n.* a brother or sister.
2. **Martin,** Dr. Martin Luther King, Jr., Coretta's husband.

Preparing to fly to Oslo for Dr. King's acceptance of the Nobel Peace Prize on December 5, 1964, are Dr. King's parents, the Reverend and Mrs. Martin Luther King, Sr.; his wife, Mrs. Coretta King; and his sister, Mrs. Christine Farris. ➤

I've never told you this, but Martin comes back to me in my dreams. It's always when we're up against the wall and you don't know what to do. He comes to me smiling and joking and says it's going to be all right. That's when I call you and get very positive and tell you we'll find a way. Sometimes I think we would have been even closer if Martin hadn't died. You were my best friend for so long, but now there are always so many others around you, wanting a piece of you, there isn't always as much room for the two of us.

When we were growing up you always told people you thought I was the smarter one, that I knew everything. But I have learned from you. You've taught me to live each day as fully as I can, because no one knows what tomorrow will bring. You taught me to rely on the spiritual force in the universe, how not to worry or to be afraid. And I hope I've made you laugh and brought some joy into your very serious life.

I was trying to explain to someone what keeps our relationship working, and I used that phrase from *The Prophet* by Kahlil Gibran.[3] I said, "We have spaces in our togetherness." Doesn't that describe us well? We've never been the kind to say things; we just do for each other. So, for once, I wanted to tell you how blessed I feel to have a sister that I'm comfortable with and that I like as well as love.

Edythe

Dear Edythe,

Your beautiful letter carried me back to those days when it was more common for us to pick up a pen than a telephone. I particularly remembered a letter you'd written to me when I was in Boston studying music at the New England Conservatory. I hadn't told you that Martin had proposed to me on our first date, several months earlier. Because this was the most important decision I could make in terms of my future, I wanted to make it myself, without your influence. I prayed and struggled and then I had a revelation in a dream. I saw Daddy King, Martin's father, smiling at me approvingly. The next morning I woke up with a sense of inner peace that I interpreted to mean the relationship would work out. Right after that, your letter came, as if you'd read my mind. "Don't be silly, girl," you wrote. "You know how difficult it is to find intelligent, stable, well-adjusted men"—a whole string of adjectives. And then you wrote, "You won't have your career as you dreamed it, but you will have your career."

That summer you came to live with me in Boston and we used to play games with Martin on the phone because he couldn't tell us apart. And remember how he wanted to test me on my cooking? You and I prepared this fine dinner for him. We really were old-fashioned girls who knew how to cook. Afterwards he'd tell people, "I asked Coretta to cook a meal for me and she dispatched[4] Edythe. The two of them teamed up on me!"

You've always known instinctively[5] just how to make me comfortable and support me. I

---

3. **Kahlil Gibran** (kä lel′ jŭ brän′), 1883–1931, Syrian poet and painter.
4. dispatch (dis pach′), *v.* send off to some place or for some purpose.
5. instinctively (in stingk′tiv lē), *adv.* of or having to do with instinct, intuition, or unlearned behavior.

will never forget the day after Martin's funeral, when you packed up your son and came to stay with me. The fact that I never had to ask meant so much to me. You just knew ahead of time how deeply I was going to need you and you were there. I will always be grateful for your foresight[6] and your presence. Having

. . . I can be myself and know you'll love and understand me no matter what.

you, my sister, in the house for two years with me and as a surrogate[7] mother to my children, especially when I had to be away so often, was a comfort no one else could have provided. And when there were little frictions among my staff, you were always careful to keep negative things away from me so that I wouldn't worry.

I'm so glad you've been with me whenever anything important has happened, although I still regret that you were ill and couldn't come to Oslo for the Nobel Peace Prize.[8] But I have wonderful memories of all the times you traveled with me on special occasions, giving advice and helping me write letters and speeches. Writing was never my forte, but you had that talent back in high school when you were editor of the paper. I always admired that you had such a good mind and a grasp of things. You did so much reading and thinking. I was more an activist kind of child. It seemed to me you always had so much information—you had that way of eavesdropping on the adults—and I loved when you'd tell me things and share the secrets you'd found out.

If you hadn't gone to Antioch College first and made a place for me and pulled me in, I'd have missed having the experience that prepared me for my role today. The emphasis on multiculturalism and the democratic community there were the perfect training for my life's work.

I wish that your teaching commitments at Cheyney State and my busy schedule would allow us to visit more often. When you're around I laugh more, and I need that because I tend to be so serious-minded. You have a way of finding humor in anything. You can pull the theater out of life. Being with you, I can be completely myself. You appreciate the stresses I have being a public figure, meeting people's expectations, fulfilling a role. When it's just us, I can be myself and know you'll love and understand me no matter what. You don't want anything from me except my happiness.

I'm very lucky. I don't have a husband, but I do have a sister. A sister I can talk to about personal things I wouldn't tell anyone else. A sister who does things for me, consoles me, comforts me. A sister with whom I can share my burdens and my joys. It's very hard in this world to find someone who can walk in your shoes, but you come closer to that than anybody. A lot of sisters are not friends. You, Edythe, like Maya Angelou has said, are my sister-friend.

Coretta

---

6. **foresight** (fōr′sīt′), *n.* power to see or know beforehand what is likely to happen.
7. **surrogate** (sėr′ə gāt, sėr′ə git), *adj.* substitute.
8. **Nobel Peace Prize:** Dr. Martin Luther King, Jr., Coretta's husband, won the Nobel Peace Prize in 1964 for his nonviolent civil rights protests. This annual prize for outstanding efforts toward world peace is presented at a ceremony in Oslo, Norway.

After Reading

Making Connections

1. Edythe was a "reader and a thinker," while Coretta was "an activist child." Which of them would you prefer as a friend? Why?

2. Do you think the Scott sisters are typical sisters? Why or why not?

3. What might have caused Edythe to write the letter to Coretta?

4. What do the letters reveal about the family life of the sisters?

5. Coretta's husband Martin is mentioned in both letters. What do you learn about him?

6. What is the effect of the writers' use of specific examples in the two letters?

7. If you have a brother or a sister, do you think that relationship will change as you grow older? In what ways?

Literary Focus: Tone

Tone in a literary work is much like tone in speaking to another person: it shows an attitude toward the subject and/or the audience. In speaking you convey a tone through facial expression, body language, and how you say the words. In writing, tone must be conveyed through word choice and style. Take this passage from a previous selection in this unit, "Greeting Disorder":

LEWIS. Dolt. You don't listen. We just went through this a second ago. It's circle and hurl, circle and lean . . . and hurl.

Sentence structure, word connotations, figurative language, and the sounds of words all tell you whether the author's tone is respectful or disrespectful, serious or mocking, positive, negative, or neutral. In the passage above, you know the tone is humorous and sarcastic by the use of short sentences and words like *dolt*.

Review the letters from Coretta and Edythe and find words or phrases you think best show the tone of their letters. Copy this chart into your notebook and use it to take notes.

Tone:	
Word Choice	
Sentence Structure	
Figurative Language	

Vocabulary Study

instinctively
surrogate
sibling
foresight
dispatch

On your paper, write the word from the list at the left that best completes each sentence.

1. Coretta was Edythe's ____, or sister.

2. When Coretta couldn't go somewhere, she would ____ Edythe.

3. Edythe always seemed to know ahead of time what Coretta needed; Coretta was amazed at her sister's ____.

4. Edythe acted as a ____ mother to Coretta's children when Coretta was away.

5. Sometimes one sister would ____ know what the other sister was thinking.

Expressing Your Ideas

Writing Choices

I Was Thinking About Us. . . . Write a **letter** to your sister, brother, or another person telling what you appreciate about him or her. Use specific examples to show what experiences you have shared that have had an impact on your life.

Edythe and Coretta Review the letters and make a **list** of the qualities that each sister admired in the other. Give an example of each quality you listed.

The Larger Story You have seen a small part of the life of Coretta Scott King. Now discover more of her story. Research and write a **biographical sketch** of Coretta that includes important events from her childhood and her adult life. You may wish to include pictures by scanning them into a Hypercard report. Don't forget electronic sources, such as online databases, as you do your research.

Other Options

Dear Edythe. . . . Read aloud Coretta's letter to Edythe. As you rehearse, think about the **tone** you will use. What should it show about Coretta's feelings for her sister? What words and phrases will you emphasize?

Along Parallel Lines? Make a **chart** that traces how near or far apart Edythe and Coretta were at various points in their lives. Use a straight horizontal line to show Coretta's life. Above that line start a parallel line to show Edythe's life. (Should this line start near or far away?) When she is close to Coretta, Edythe's line should drop to meet Coretta's. When they are apart, Edythe's line should rise to move away. Label events that bring them together.

Edythe: – – – –
Coretta: ——————————
　　　　 childhood

Before Reading

A Time to Talk by Robert Frost
My Mother Pieced Quilts by Teresa Palomo Acosta

Robert Frost
1874–1963

Robert Frost may be America's most famous poet. He is certainly one of our most honored writers, winning the Pulitzer Prize four times. Although some reviewers criticized his work as being too folksy and informal, the natural speech of New England is the mark of this writer's style.

Teresa Palomo Acosta
born 1949

Teresa Palomo Acosta grew up in Texas, where she listened to her grandfather's stories about his childhood in Mexico. She first wrote "My Mother Pieced Quilts" as a college writing assignment.

Building Background

Those Crazy Quilts! Quilts are made by stitching together two layers of fabric, usually with another soft, thick layer between them. The outside layer of the quilt is usually fastened by stitching fabric pieces together as patchwork. The patchwork follows a design laid out on a large frame. Often the entire quilt tells a series of stories through pictures.

Getting into the Poetry

Discussion Suppose you were busy and a friend or family member wanted you to stop and talk. How would you react? In a group, discuss these questions:

- What do you do if someone wants to talk to you at a time when it would be inconvenient to stop what you are doing?

- How do you resolve the conflicts between the time you need to spend at work and the time you want to spend talking to friends and family members?

Reading Tip

Reading Poetry "A Time to Talk" and "My Mother Pieced Quilts" are both poems, but their differences are as important as their similarities. The Frost poem has ten lines with rhyme, capitalization, and end punctuation. It is easy to read, either silently or aloud.

The Acosta poem has many lines in stanzas of varying length, no regular rhyme, little punctuation, and not a single capital letter. When you read this work, you have to make your own decisions on beginnings and endings of lines, words to emphasize, and the flow and movement of the poem. As you read, start by considering each stanza as a unit of thought.

Robert Frost

A Time to TALK

When a friend calls to me from the road
And slows his horse to a meaning walk,
I don't stand still and look around
On all the hills I haven't hoed,
5 And shout from where I am, "What is it?"
No, not as there is a time to talk.
I thrust my hoe in the mellow ground,
Blade-end up and five feet tall,
And plod: I go up to the stone wall
10 For a friendly visit.

An idealized image of American farmland, *Spring Plowing* was painted by Grant Wood in 1932. Why do you think the painter set the farmer and his horses so far off in the distance and barely visible in the painting? ▼

My Mother Pieced

Teresa Palomo Acosta

they were just meant as covers
in winters
as weapons
against pounding january winds

5 but it was just that every morning I
       awoke to these
october ripened canvases[1]
passed my hand across their cloth faces
and began to wonder how you pieced
all these together
10 these strips of gentle communion cotton
       and flannel nightgowns
wedding organdies[2]
dime store velvets

how you shaped patterns square and
       oblong and round
positioned
15 balanced
then cemented them
with your thread
a steel needle
a thimble

20 how the thread darted in and out
galloping along the frayed edges,
       tucking them in
as you did us at night
oh how you stretched and turned and
       rearranged
your michigan spring faded curtain
       pieces

25 my father's santa fe work shirt
the summer denims, the tweeds of fall

in the evening you sat at your canvas
—our cracked linoleum floor the
       drawing board
me lounging on your arm
30 and you staking out the plan:
whether to put the lilac purple of easter
       against the red plaid of
       winter-going-
into-spring

whether to mix a yellow with blue and
       white and paint the
corpus christi[3] noon when my father
       held your hand
35 whether to shape a five-point star from the
somber black silk you wore to
       grandmother's funeral

you were the river current
carrying the roaring notes . . .
forming them into pictures of a little boy
       reclining
40 a swallow flying
you were the caravan[4] master at the reins
driving your threaded needle artillery[5]
       across the mosaic[6] cloth bridges
delivering yourself in separate
       testimonies

Quilts

oh mother you plunged me sobbing and
    laughing
45 into our past
into the river crossing at five
into the spinach fields
into the plainview[7] cotton rows
into tuberculosis wards
50 into braids and muslin dresses
sewn hard and taut[8] to withstand the
    thrashings of twenty-five years

stretched out they lay
armed/ready/shouting/celebrating

knotted with love
55 the quilts sing on

---

1. **canvas** (kan′vəs), *n.* a piece of strong cloth to be painted on.
2. **organdy,** fine muslin cloth used for curtains, dresses.
3. **corpus christi:** Corpus Christi is a Texas city named for a Catholic holiday.
4. **caravan** (kar′ə van), *n.* group traveling together for safety.
5. **artillery** (är til′ər ē), *n.* weapons, usually large.
6. **mosaic** (mō zā′ik), *adj.* resembling a decoration made of small pieces of glass, wood, etc., to form a picture or design.
7. **plainview:** Plainview is a city in Texas.
8. **taut** (tôt), *adj.* tightly drawn.

Improvisational Blocks, a quilt made by Monin Brown and/or her sister Hattie Mitchell in 1932, shows the creativity that can come of **interactions** between cultures. The sisters made most of their quilts for the white Johnston family they worked for in Macon, Georgia. They used traditional European designs in new ways, improvising to create a unique African American style. ➤

After Reading

Making Connections

1. Which poem do you like better? Why?

2. Choose a key word from each poem and explain how that word expresses what the poem is about.

3. In "A Time to Talk," why do you think the speaker stops work to talk to the friend?

4. What is meant by the "meaning walk" in line 2?

5. Do you think it is important to stop work or another activity when a friend or family member wants to talk? Explain your answer.

6. How does the **mood** of "My Mother Pieced Quilts" change from beginning to end?

7. What is the most striking **image** in "My Mother Pieced Quilts"?

8. What do you think Acosta is saying in her poem about the role of her mother in her family?

Literary Focus: Metaphors

On the literal level, "My Mother Pieced Quilts" explains how a quilt maker selected fabrics and stitched them together into a patchwork quilt. Yet the author's use of metaphors suggests other meanings as well. **Metaphors** are implied comparisons between one thing and another. Look at these lines from the poem:

> how the thread darted in and out
> galloping along the frayed edges, . . .

In the metaphor, the "galloping" thread is compared to a horse, suggesting power and speed. Review the poem and find at least one more metaphor and explain what is suggested by the comparison.

Vocabulary Study

canvas
caravan
artillery
mosaic
taut

On your own paper, write the word from the list that best completes each sentence.

1. The artist brushed the first dab of paint on her ____.
2. The cloth on which she painted was stapled to a wooden frame to keep it ____.
3. He admired the colorful ____ pattern in the picture.
4. The design showed a large ____ traveling across the desert.
5. The people in the picture were carrying ____ to defend themselves.

Expressing Your Ideas

Writing Choices

It's Not *Always* Time to Talk In response to the Frost poem, write a **poem** that disagrees with the poet's main idea. Create a circumstance that shows that it's not always necessary or desirable to stop what you're doing just because someone wants to talk. Make your poem about the same length as "A Time to Talk," and try to use Frost's conversational style.

Q Is for Quilting Bee Research quilts in your library and prepare a brief **report** on one of these topics:

- how quilts are made
- fabrics used in quilts
- quilting bees
- famous quilts in American history

I Remember the Time When . . . Select three images from "My Mother Pieced Quilts" and make up the **stories** that could be behind the images. Start by identifying the three images you want to work with. Then use your imagination to write an event based on clues from the poem.

Other Options

A Stitch in Time Interview the older people in your family to find some interesting bits of family history. Then make a **sketch** of quilt sections or pieces you might make from these family "pictures."

More Than a Comforter If you have a quilt in the family, bring it to class and **explain** its history. Tell who made or bought it, how it was made, who has owned it, and anything else that might be of historical interest.

Class History Working in a group, plan a **quilt** for your class that includes squares for a dozen important features or events of the year. Start by listing the events and features you want to quilt into history. Then divide a piece of 18" x 24" paper or posterboard into twelve 6-inch squares (you may decide to use varying shapes). Decide how you will arrange your twelve "pieces," and draw or paint the pieces into your design.

Before Reading

The Medicine Bag

by Virginia Driving Hawk Sneve

Virginia Driving Hawk Sneve
born 1933

The author, who grew up on the Rosebud Sioux reservation in South Dakota, is the child of James H. Sneve, an Episcopal priest, and Rose Driving Hawk, a Sioux Indian. This heritage has led her to live and work in both worlds. She has taught in public schools and Indian schools. She has compiled history for the South Dakota Episcopal Church and served on the board of directors for the United Sioux Tribes Cultural Arts. She explains her work this way: "I try to present an accurate portrayal of American Indian life as I have known it. I also attempt to interpret history from the viewpoint of the American Indian; in so doing, I hope to correct the many misconceptions and untruths which have been too long perpetrated by non-Indian authors."

Building Background

The History of a Name Would you like it if someone changed your family name—without asking you what you wanted to be called? That is what happened to an entire nation of Native Americans, the nation that came to be known as the Sioux. Early French settlers gave them that name, but in a roundabout way. The Chippewa Indians, enemies of the Sioux, called them *Nadowessi,* which means "enemy" or "poisonous snake." The French changed the spelling to *Nadowessiousj* and eventually shortened the name to *Sioux.* Today many members of this Indian nation prefer to be called Lakota, Dakota, or Nakota, depending on the division to which they belong.

Getting into the Story

Writer's Notebook In traditional Sioux culture, a boy became a man by going on a **vision quest.** First, the boy purified himself by bathing in the steam of a sweat lodge (a sort of sauna). Then he went off alone to a hilltop, where he was expected to stay until he received a vision. This vision provided the boy with a purpose for his life and ushered him into adulthood. He returned from his quest a man.

How do you think you will know when *you* are an adult? In your notebook, write about an event coming up in your life that will mean you are an adult. Will there be a public event—a bar mitzvah, graduation ceremony, or wedding—that will mean you are grown up? Or do you imagine a more private experience of becoming an adult?

Reading Tip

Unfamiliar Terms It is confusing to read a story filled with references that are unfamiliar to you. Do you know what a medicine bag is? Sacred sage? A vision quest? These are all important features of this story. When you come across an unfamiliar word or reference in your reading of this story, stop and make sure you figure out what the object, event, or idea really is.

THE MEDICINE BAG

Virginia Driving Hawk Sneve

My kid sister Cheryl and I always bragged about our Sioux grandpa, Joe Iron Shell. Our friends, who had always lived in the city and only knew about Indians from movies and TV, were impressed by our stories. Maybe we exaggerated and made Grandpa and the reservation[1] sound glamorous, but when we'd return home to Iowa after our yearly summer visit to Grandpa we always had some exciting tale to tell.

We always had some authentic[2] Sioux article to show our listeners. One year Cheryl had new moccasins that Grandpa had made. On another visit he gave me a small, round, flat, rawhide drum which was decorated with a painting of a warrior riding a horse. He taught me a real Sioux chant to sing while I beat the drum with a leather-covered stick that had a feather on the end. Man, that really made an impression.

---

1. **reservation** (rez′ər vā′shən), *n.* land set aside by the government for a special purpose.
2. **authentic** (ô then′tik), *adj.* real, not copied.

We never showed our friends Grandpa's picture. Not that we were ashamed of him, but because we knew that the glamorous tales we told didn't go with the real thing. Our friends would have laughed at the picture, because Grandpa wasn't tall and stately like TV Indians. His hair wasn't in braids, but hung in stringy, gray strands on his neck, and he was old. He was our great-grandfather, and he didn't live in a tipi, but all by himself in a part log, part tar-paper shack on the Rosebud Reservation in South Dakota. So when Grandpa came to visit us, I was so ashamed and embarrassed I could've died.

There are a lot of yippy poodles and other fancy little dogs in our neighborhood, but they usually barked singly at the mailman from the safety of their own yards. Now it sounded as if a whole pack of mutts were barking together in one place.

I got up and walked to the curb to see what the commotion was. About a block away I saw a crowd of little kids yelling, with the dogs yipping and growling around someone who was walking down the middle of the street.

I watched the group as it slowly came closer and saw that in the center of the strange procession was a man wearing a tall black hat. He'd pause now and then to peer at something in his hand and then at the houses on either side of the street. I felt cold and hot at the same time as I recognized the man. "Oh, no!" I whispered. "It's Grandpa!"

I stood on the curb, unable to move even though I wanted to run and hide. Then I got mad when I saw how the yippy dogs were growling and nipping at the old man's baggy pant legs and how wearily he poked them

I WAS SO ASHAMED AND EMBARRASSED I COULD'VE DIED.

away with his cane. "Stupid mutts," I said as I ran to rescue Grandpa.

When I kicked and hollered at the dogs to get away, they put their tails between their legs and scattered. The kids ran to the curb where they watched me and the old man.

"Grandpa," I said and felt pretty dumb when my voice cracked. I reached for his beat-up old tin suitcase, which was tied shut with a rope. But he set it down right in the street and shook my hand.

"*Hau, Takoza*, Grandchild," he greeted me formally in Sioux.

All I could do was stand there with the whole neighborhood watching and shake the hand of the leather-brown old man. I saw how his gray hair straggled from under his big black hat, which had a drooping feather in its crown. His rumpled black suit hung like a sack over his stooped frame. As he shook my hand, his coat fell open to expose a bright-red, satin shirt with a beaded bolo tie under the collar. His getup wasn't out of place on the reservation, but it sure was here, and I wanted to sink right through the pavement.

"Hi," I muttered with my head down. I tried to pull my hand away when I felt his bony hand trembling, and looked up to see fatigue[3] in his face. I felt like crying. I couldn't think of anything to say so I picked up Grandpa's suitcase, took his arm, and guided him up the driveway to our house.

Mom was standing on the steps. I don't know how long she'd been watching, but her hand was over her mouth and she looked as if she couldn't believe what she saw. Then she ran to us.

---

3. fatigue (fə tēg'), *n.* weariness caused by hard work or effort.

"Grandpa," she gasped. "How in the world did you get here?"

She checked her move to embrace Grandpa, and I remembered that such a display of affection is unseemly[4] to the Sioux and would embarrass him.

"*Hau*, Marie," he said as he shook Mom's hand. She smiled and took his other arm.

As we supported him up the steps the door banged open and Cheryl came busting out of the house. She was all smiles and was so obviously glad to see Grandpa that I was ashamed of how I felt.

"Grandpa!" she yelled happily. "You came to see us!"

Grandpa smiled, and Mom and I let go of him as he stretched out his arms to my ten-year-old-sister, who was still young enough to be hugged.

"*Wicincala*, little girl," he greeted her and then collapsed.

He had fainted. Mom and I carried him into her sewing room, where we had a spare bed.

After we had Grandpa on the bed Mom stood there helplessly patting his shoulder.

"Shouldn't we call the doctor, Mom?" I suggested, since she didn't seem to know what to do.

"Yes," she agreed with a sigh. "You make Grandpa comfortable, Martin."

I reluctantly moved to the bed. I knew Grandpa wouldn't want to have Mom undress him, but I didn't want to, either. He was so skinny and frail that his coat slipped off easily. When I loosened his tie and opened his shirt collar, I felt a small leather pouch[5] that hung from a thong around his neck. I left it alone and moved to remove his boots. The scuffed old cowboy boots were tight and he moaned as I put pressure on his legs to jerk them off.

I put the boots on the floor and saw why they fit so tight. Each one was stuffed with money. I looked at the bills that lined the boots and started to ask about them, but Grandpa's eyes were closed again.

Mom came back with a basin of water. "The doctor thinks Grandpa is suffering from heat exhaustion," she explained as she bathed Grandpa's face. Mom gave a big sigh, "*Oh hinh*, Martin. How do you suppose he got here?"

We found out after the doctor's visit. Grandpa was angrily sitting up in bed while Mom tried to feed him some soup.

"Tonight you let Marie feed you, Grandpa," spoke my dad, who had gotten home from work just as the doctor was leaving. "You're not really sick," he said as he gently pushed Grandpa back against the pillows. "The doctor said you just got too tired and hot after your long trip."

Grandpa relaxed, and between sips of soup he told us of his journey. Soon after our visit to him Grandpa decided that he would like to see where his only living descendants lived and what our home was like. Besides, he admitted sheepishly, he was lonesome after we left.

I knew everybody felt as guilty as I did—especially Mom. Mom was all Grandpa had left. So even after she married my dad, who's a white man and teaches in the college in our city, and after Cheryl and I were born, Mom made sure that every summer we spent a week with Grandpa.

I never thought that Grandpa would be lonely after our visits, and none of us noticed how old and weak he had become. But Grandpa knew and so he came to us. He had ridden on buses for two and a half days. When he arrived in the city, tired and stiff from sitting for so long, he set out, walking, to find us.

---

4. unseemly (un sēm′lē), *adj.* not suitable; improper.
5. pouch (pouch), *n.* small bag or sack.

He had stopped to rest on the steps of some building downtown, and a policeman found him. The cop, according to Grandpa, was a good man who took him to the bus stop and waited until the bus came and told the driver to let Grandpa out at Bell View Drive. After Grandpa got off the bus, he started walking again. But he couldn't see the house numbers on the other side when he walked on the sidewalk so he walked in the middle of the street. That's when all the little kids and dogs followed him.

I knew everybody felt as bad as I did. Yet I was proud of this eighty-six-year-old man, who had never been away from the reservation, having the courage to travel so far alone.

"You found the money in my boots?" he asked Mom.

"Martin did," she answered, and roused herself to scold. "Grandpa, you shouldn't have carried so much money. What if someone had stolen it from you?"

Grandpa laughed. "I would've known if anyone tried to take the boots off my feet. The money is what I've saved for a long time—a hundred dollars—for my funeral. But you take it now to buy groceries so that I won't be a burden to you while I am here."

"That won't be necessary, Grandpa," Dad said. "We are honored to have you with us and you will never be a burden. I am only sorry that we never thought to bring you home with us this summer and spare you the discomfort of a long trip."

Grandpa was pleased. "Thank you," he answered. "But do not feel bad that you didn't bring me with you, for I would not have come then. It was not time." He said this in such a way that no one could argue with him. To Grandpa and the Sioux, he once told me, a thing would be done when it was the right time to do it, and that's the way it was.

"Also," Grandpa went on, looking at me, "I have come because it is soon time for Martin to have the medicine bag."

We all knew what that meant. Grandpa thought he was going to die, and he had to follow the tradition of his family to pass the medicine bag, along with its history, to the oldest male child.

"Even though the boy," he said still looking at me, "bears a white man's name, the medicine bag will be his."

I didn't know what to say. I had the same hot and cold feeling that I had when I first saw Grandpa in the street. The medicine bag was the dirty leather pouch I had found around his neck. "I could never wear such a thing," I almost said aloud. I thought of having my friends see it in gym class, at the swimming pool, and could imagine the smart things they would say. But I just swallowed hard and took a step toward the bed. I knew I would have to take it.

But Grandpa was tired. "Not now, Martin," he said, waving his hand in dismissal, "it is not time. Now I will sleep."

So that's how Grandpa came to be with us for two months. My friends kept asking to come see the old man, but I put them off. I told myself that I didn't want them laughing at Grandpa. But even as I made excuses I knew it wasn't Grandpa that I was afraid they'd laugh at.

Nothing bothered Cheryl about bringing her friends to see Grandpa. Every day after school started there'd be a crew of giggling little girls or round-eyed little boys crowded around the old man on the patio, where he'd gotten in the habit of sitting every afternoon.

Grandpa would smile in his gentle way and patiently answer their questions, or he'd tell them stories of brave warriors, ghosts, animals, and the kids listened in awed silence. Those little guys thought Grandpa was great.

Finally, one day after school, my friends came home with me because nothing I said stopped them. "We're going to see the great

▲ *The Tribesman* is a portrait of James "Going Back" Chiltoskey, a Cherokee Indian whose wood sculptures have been exhibited at the Smithsonian Institution. What qualities of the man do you think the artist, Hubert Shuptrine, conveys through the painting?

Indian of Bell View Drive," said Hank, who was supposed to be my best friend. "My brother has seen him three times, so he oughta be well enough to see us."

When we got to my house Grandpa was sitting on the patio. He had on his red shirt, but today he also wore a fringed leather vest that was decorated with beads. Instead of his usual cowboy boots he had solidly beaded moccasins on his feet that stuck out of his black trousers. Of course, he had his old black hat on—he was seldom without it. But it had been brushed and the feather in the beaded headband was proudly erect, its tip a brighter white. His hair lay in silver strands over the red shirt collar.

I stared just as my friends did, and I heard one of them murmur, "Wow!"

Grandpa looked up and when his eyes met mine they twinkled as if he were laughing inside. He nodded to me and my face got all hot. I could tell that he had known all along I was afraid he'd embarrass me in front of my friends.

"*Hau, hoksilas,* boys," he greeted and held out his hand.

My buddies passed in a single file and shook his hand as I introduced them. They were so polite I almost laughed. "How, there, Grandpa," and even a "How-do-you-do, sir."

"You look fine, Grandpa," I said as the guys sat on the lawn chairs or on the patio floor.

"*Hanh,* yes," he agreed. "When I woke up this morning it seemed the right time to dress in the good clothes. I knew that my grandson would be bringing his friends."

"You guys want some lemonade or something?" I offered. No one answered. They were listening to Grandpa as he started telling how he'd killed the deer from which his vest was made.

WHEN YOU COME HOME IT WILL BE TIME TO GIVE YOU THE MEDICINE BAG.

Grandpa did most of the talking while my friends were there. I was so proud of him and amazed at how respectfully quiet my buddies were. Mom had to chase them home at supper time. As they left they shook Grandpa's hand again and said to me:

"Martin, he's really great!"

"Yeah, man! Don't blame you for keeping him to yourself."

"Can we come back?"

But after they left, Mom said, "No more visitors for a while, Martin. Grandpa won't admit it, but his strength hasn't returned. He likes having company, but it tires him."

That evening Grandpa called me to his room before he went to sleep. "Tomorrow," he said, "when you come home, it will be time to give you the medicine bag."

I felt a hard squeeze from where my heart is supposed to be and was scared, but I answered, "OK, Grandpa."

All night I had weird dreams about thunder and lightning on a high hill. From a distance I heard the slow beat of a drum. When I woke up in the morning I felt as if I hadn't slept at all. At school it seemed as if the day would never end and, when it finally did, I ran home.

Grandpa was in his room, sitting on the bed. The shades were down and the place was dim and cool. I sat on the floor in front of Grandpa, but he didn't even look at me. After what seemed a long time he spoke.

"I sent your mother and sister away. What you will hear today is only for a man's ears. What you will receive is only for a man's hands." He fell silent and I felt shivers down my back.

"My father in his early manhood," Grandpa began, "made a vision quest[6] to find a spirit guide for his life. You cannot understand how it was in that time, when the great Teton Sioux were first made to stay on the reservation. There was a strong need for guidance from *Wakantanka,* the Great Spirit. But too many of the young men were filled with despair and hatred. They thought it was hopeless to search for a vision when the glorious life was gone and only the hated confines of a reservation lay ahead. But my father held to the old ways.

"He carefully prepared for his quest with a purifying[7] sweat bath, and then he went alone to a high butte[8] top to fast[9] and pray. After

---

6. **quest** (kwest), *n.* search or hunt.
7. **purifying** (pyür′ə fī ing), *adj.* making pure, clean, or free from evil.
8. **butte** (byüt), *n.* a steep, flat-topped hill standing alone.
9. **fast** (fast), *v.* go without food; eat little or nothing.

three days he received his sacred dream—in which he found, after long searching, the white man's iron. He did not understand his vision of finding something belonging to the white people, for in that time they were the enemy. When he came down from the butte to cleanse himself at the stream below, he found the remains of a campfire and the broken shell of an iron kettle. This was a sign which reinforced his dream. He took a piece of the iron for his medicine bag, which he had made of elk skin years before, to prepare for his quest.

"He returned to his village, where he told his dream to the wise old men of the tribe. They gave him the name *Iron Shell*, but neither did they understand the meaning of the dream. This first Iron Shell kept the piece of iron with him at all times and believed it gave him protection from the evils of those unhappy days.

"Then a terrible thing happened to Iron Shell. He and several other young men were taken from their homes by the soldiers and sent far away to a white man's boarding school. He was angry and lonesome for his parents and the young girl he had wed before he was taken away. At first Iron Shell resisted the teachers' attempts to change him and he did not try to learn. One day it was his turn to work in the school's blacksmith shop. As he walked into the place he knew that his medicine had brought him there to learn and work with the white man's iron.

"Iron Shell became a blacksmith and worked at the trade when he returned to the reservation. All of his life he treasured the medicine bag. When he was old, and I was a man, he gave it to me, for no one made the vision quest any more."

Grandpa quit talking, and I stared in disbelief as he covered his face with his hands. His shoulders were shaking with quiet sobs, and I looked away until he began to speak again.

Kam Mak has combined modern and traditional elements in this painting. What details give the painting an ancient, timeless feeling? What details make it seem modern?

The Medicine Bag   **441**

"I kept the bag until my son, your mother's father, was a man and had to leave us to fight in the war across the ocean. I gave him the bag, for I believed it would protect him in battle, but he did not take it with him. He was afraid that he would lose it. He died in a faraway place."

Again Grandpa was still and I felt his grief around me.

"My son," he went on after clearing his throat, "had only a daughter, and it is not proper for her to know of these things."

He unbuttoned his shirt, pulled out the leather pouch, and lifted it over his head. He held it in his hand, turning it over and over as if memorizing how it looked.

"In the bag," he said as he opened it and removed two objects, "is the broken shell of the iron kettle, a pebble from the butte, and a piece of the sacred sage."[10] He held the pouch upside down and dust drifted down.

"After the bag is yours you must put a piece of prairie sage within and never open it again until you pass it on to your son." He replaced the pebble and the piece of iron, and tied the bag.

I stood up, somehow knowing I should. Grandpa slowly rose from the bed and stood upright in front of me holding the bag before my face. I closed my eyes and waited for him to slip it over my head. But he spoke.

"No, you need not wear it." He placed the soft leather bag in my right hand and closed my other hand over it. "It would not be right to wear it in this time and place where no one will understand. Put it safely away until you are again on the reservation. Wear it then, when you replace the sacred sage."

Grandpa turned and sat again on the bed. Wearily he leaned his head against the pillow. "Go," he said, "I will sleep now."

"Thank you, Grandpa," I said softly and left with the bag in my hands.

That night Mom and Dad took Grandpa to the hospital. Two weeks later I stood alone on the lonely prairie of the reservation and put the sacred sage in my medicine bag.

---

10. sage (sāj), *n.* a small shrub whose leaves are used for seasoning and medicines.

After Reading

Making Connections

1. For you, what is the most memorable moment or scene in the story? What words or phrases make this scene stand out?

2. Would you wear something (like a medicine bag) that sets you apart from your peers but identifies you with your culture? Why or why not?

3. Is this a good story to include in a group of selections with the **theme** of "Appreciating Each Other"? Explain.

4. Why do you think Cheryl isn't embarrassed by Grandpa the way Martin is?

5. 👋 What conflict does Martin feel between his Native American and white identity? How do his **interactions** with his grandfather help him resolve this conflict?

6. Why do you think the author chose to tell the story from Martin's **point of view?**

7. From Grandpa's explanation of the history of his family, what general conclusions can you draw about the history of the Sioux or of Native Americans?

Literary Focus: Symbolism

"The *pen* is mightier than the *sword.*" This statement, of course, does not make literal sense. It only makes sense when interpreted **symbolically.** You must recognize the pen as a symbol for writing and persuasion, and the sword as a symbol for weapons and brute force. In literature you will find objects that have a literal meaning but also suggest symbolic meanings. Consider the medicine bag as a symbol. Review the story and jot down each mention of the bag. Then write a summary statement of its symbolic value: besides a container of objects, what other meanings does the bag suggest to you? Use a diagram like the one below to organize your thoughts.

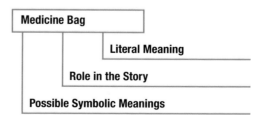

Vocabulary Study

authentic
butte
reservation
sage
fast
unseemly
quest
purifying
pouch
fatigue

Write the word from the list that best completes each sentence.

This medicine bag is not fake: it is a(n) (1) bag worn by a Sioux Indian. A medicine bag is a small (2) used to carry special items. Perhaps a piece of (3) , or another medicinal plant, will be carried in the bag. A sacred item may be added to the medicine bag after a Sioux boy has gone on his (4) , seeking a vision to guide his life.

Before seeking a vision, a boy must take a sweat bath that is meant to be (5) , cleansing his spirit. He will travel to a high spot, such as a mountain or (6) . He is expected to (7) , or go without food, while he prays. Alone, without food or rest, the boy may experience (8) , but he must continue his efforts until he receives a sacred vision. A man would never discuss such private things with a woman, because that would be considered (9) . Even now that they live on a government (10) , many Sioux continue to practice these ancient traditions.

Expressing Your Ideas

Writing Choices

Your Turn, Grandpa In the story we see Grandpa through Martin's eyes. Now, change points of view. Review the story to find important details, and write a **description** of Martin from Grandpa's point of view.

The Vision Quest Find out more about the Sioux tradition of the vision quest and write a **report** to your class about the tradition. As an alternative, prepare a report on the history of the Sioux or on how they are preserving their traditional way of life today. Don't ignore online services you or your library may have to aid in your research.

Not Like in the Movies Compare and contrast Martin's grandfather with Indians as they are portrayed in movies and on television. Review the story for details, and write a **comparison/contrast essay.**

Other Options

Your Own Bag Make a **"medicine bag"** to pass on to someone you care about. What container would you choose? What special objects would you put inside? Which object would the new owner have to replace?

Mike, Meet Martin Choose a character from another story in this part of the unit. Imagine that this character and Martin, years later, both attend a **panel discussion** on the topic "Appreciating Older Generations." You and a partner act out the discussion they might have when they share the understandings they gained through the events of the stories.

Mapping Grandpa's Quest Make a **map** to show how Grandpa traveled from the Rosebud Reservation to Martin's house.

The Horned Toad

by Gerald Haslam

Gerald Haslam
born 1937

In the 1850s, some of Gerald Haslam's ancestors began to move north from Mexico to the United States. Several generations of life in the U.S. have resulted in the Anglo-Hispanic family of which he writes in this selection.

Proud of both his Anglo and his Hispanic heritage, he writes here of the tensions between languages and cultures. For this writer, family is the "melting pot" in which all cultural elements come together. Haslam says, "I was raised in a richly varied area—California's San Joaquin Valley—where oral tale-telling was a fine art. . . . It is a continuing source of both wonder and satisfaction to me that I have evolved into a storyteller."

Building Background

Questions and Answers *Does a horned toad have horns?* Not exactly, but it has sharp spikes that stick out from the head, and smaller ones that cover the rest of the body. These protective features help to discourage attackers.

Is a horned toad a toad? Not exactly, but it is a lizard with a squat shape that makes it look like a toad.

Can a horned toad shoot poison from its eyes? Not exactly, but it can shoot small spurts of a bloodlike fluid from its eyes when it is attacked or otherwise disturbed.

Getting into the Story

Writer's Notebook Did you ask to be in the family you belong to? Probably not, but you're in it just the same. Just as is true with any other group, with membership comes responsibility. Make a chart of the responsibilities *you* have to the rest of your family. Set up your chart like the sample that follows.

Family Member	My Responsibilities
Mom	Tell her when I'm going to be late coming home.
Dad	

Reading Tip

Dealing with a Foreign Language This story, because it is about people who speak two languages, is written in two languages. In "The Horned Toad" you will find more than a dozen Spanish words and expressions. You will understand most of them if you pay attention to clues. Often the clue comes after the Spanish words. The story begins like this: *"Expectoran su sangre!"* At the end of the first paragraph, the sentence is translated for you by a character. In other cases, there are clues from the narration and from what the characters say. It is important to understand the meanings of these expressions, but it is also important to catch their *flavor.* Use the pronunciation notes to sound out the Spanish words.

The HORNED TOAD

Gerald Haslam

"*¡Expectoran su sangre!*"[1] exclaimed Great-Grandma when I showed her the small horned toad I had removed from my breast pocket. I turned toward my mother, who translated: "They spit blood."

"*De los ojos,*"[2] Grandma added. "From their eyes," Mother explained, herself uncomfortable in the presence of the small beast.

I grinned, "Awwwwww."

But my great-grandmother did not smile. "*Son muy tóxicos,*"[3] she nodded with finality. Mother moved back an involuntary step, her hands suddenly busy at her breast. "Put that thing down," she ordered.

"His name's John," I said.

"Put John down and not in your pocket, either," my mother nearly shouted. "Those things are very poisonous. Didn't you understand what Grandma said?"

I shook my head.

"Well . . ." Mother looked from one of us to the other—spanning four generations of California, standing three feet apart—and said, "Of course you didn't. Please take him back where you got him, and be careful. We'll all feel better when you do." The tone of her voice told me that the discussion had ended, so I released the little reptile where I'd captured him.

During those years in Oildale, the mid-1940s, I needed only to walk across the street to find a patch of virgin desert. Neighborhood kids called it simply "the vacant lot," less than an acre without houses or sidewalks. Not that we were desperate for desert then, since we could walk into its scorched skin a mere half-mile west, north, and east. To the south, incongruously, flowed the icy Kern River, fresh from the Sierras and surrounded by riparian[4] forest.

---

1. *Expectoran su sangre* (eks pek to′ran sü san′gre)
2. *De los ojos* (de los o′hos).
3. *Son muy tóxicos* (son mwē tok′sē kos), They are very poisonous.
4. **riparian** (rə per′ē ən), of or on a bank of a river.

▲ In *A Medio Dia/Pedacito de mi Corazón (At High Noon/A Little Piece of My Heart)*, Carmen Lomas Garza adds to her desert scene touches of juicy red sweetness in the little pieces of fruit being eaten by horned toads. Why do you think the artist used the title she did?

Ours was rich soil formed by that same Kern River as it ground Sierra granite and turned it into coarse sand, then carried it down into the valley and deposited it over millennia along its many changes of channels. The ants that built miniature volcanoes on the vacant lot left piles of tiny stones with telltale markings of black on white. Deeper than ants could dig were pools of petroleum that led to many fortunes and lured men like my father from Texas. The dry hills to the east and north sprouted forests of wooden derricks.

. . . she barked orders in Spanish from the moment she emerged from Manuel and Toni's car.

Despite the abundance of open land, plus the constant lure of the river where desolation[5] and verdancy[6] met, most kids relied on the vacant lot as their primary playground. Even with its bullheads and stinging insects, we played everything from football to kick-the-can on it. The lot actually resembled my father's head, bare in the middle but full of growth around the edges: weeds, stickers, cactuses, and a few bushes. We played our games on its sandy center, and conducted such sports as ant fights and lizard hunts on its brushy periphery.[7]

That spring, when I discovered the lone horned toad near the back of the lot, had been rough on my family. Earlier, there had been quiet, unpleasant tension between Mom and Daddy. He was a silent man, little given to emotional displays. It was difficult for him to show affection, and I guess the openness of Mom's family made him uneasy. Daddy had

no kin in California and rarely mentioned any in Texas. He couldn't seem to understand my mother's large, intimate family, their constant noisy concern for one another, and I think he was a little jealous of the time she gave everyone, maybe even me.

I heard her talking on the phone to my various aunts and uncles, usually in Spanish. Even though I couldn't understand—Daddy had warned her not to teach me that foreign tongue because it would hurt me in school, and she'd complied[8]—I could sense the stress. I had been afraid they were going to divorce, since she only used Spanish to hide things from me. I'd confronted her with my suspicion, but she comforted me, saying, no, that was not the problem. They were merely deciding when it would be our turn to care for Grandma. I didn't really understand, although I was relieved.

I later learned that my great-grandmother—whom we simply called "Grandma"—had been moving from house to house within the family, trying to find a place she'd accept. She hated the city, and most of the aunts and uncles lived in Los Angeles. Our house in Oildale was much closer to the open country where she'd dwelled all her life. She had wanted to come to our place right away because she had raised my mother from a baby when my own grandmother died. But the old lady seemed unimpressed with Daddy, whom she called *"ese gringo."*[9]

In truth, we had more room, and my dad made more money in the oil patch than almost anyone else in the family. Since my mother was the closest to Grandma, our place

---

5. **desolation** (des′ə lā′ shən), *n.* barren or deserted condition.
6. **verdancy** (vėrd′n sē), greenness.
7. periphery (pə rif′ər ē), *n.* an outside boundary.
8. comply (kəm plī), *v.* act in agreement with a request or command.
9. *ese gringo* (e′se grēn′go), that American.

was the logical one for her, but Ese Gringo didn't see it that way, I guess, at least not at first. Finally, after much debate, he relented.[10]

In any case, one windy afternoon, my Uncle Manuel[11] and Aunt Toni drove up and deposited four-and-a-half feet of bewigged, bejeweled Spanish spitfire: a square, pale face topped by a tightly-curled black wig that hid a bald head—her hair having been lost to typhoid nearly sixty years before—her small white hands veined with rivers of blue. She walked with a prancing bounce that made her appear half her age, and she barked orders in Spanish from the moment she emerged from Manuel and Toni's car. Later, just before they left, I heard Uncle Manuel tell my dad, "Good luck, Charlie. That old lady's dynamite." Daddy only grunted.

She had been with us only two days when I tried to impress her with my horned toad. In fact, nothing I did seemed to impress her, and she referred to me as *el malcriado*,[12] causing my mother to shake her head. Mom explained to me that Grandma was just old and lonely for Grandpa and uncomfortable in town. Mom told me that Grandma had lived over half a century in the country, away from the noise, away from clutter, away from people. She refused to accompany my mother on shopping trips, or anywhere else. She even refused to climb into a car, and I wondered how Uncle Manuel had managed to load her up in order to bring her to us.

She disliked sidewalks and roads, dancing across them when she had to, then appearing to wipe her feet on earth or grass. Things too civilized simply did not please her. A brother of hers had been killed in the great San Francisco earthquake and that had been the end of her tolerance of cities. Until my great-grandfather died, they lived on a small rancho near Arroyo Cantua, north of Coalinga.[13] Grandpa, who had come north from Sonora as a youth to work as a *vaquero*,[14] had bred horses and cattle, and cowboyed for other ranchers, scraping together enough of a living to raise eleven children.

He had been, until the time of his death, a lean, dark-skinned man with wide shoulders, a large nose, and a sweeping handlebar moustache that was white when I knew him. His Indian blood darkened all his progeny[15] so that not even I was as fair-skinned as my great-grandmother, Ese Gringo for a father or not.

As it turned out, I didn't really understand very much about Grandma at all. She was old, of course, yet in many ways my parents treated her as though she were younger than me, walking her to the bathroom at night and bringing her presents from the store. In other ways—drinking wine at dinner, for example—she was granted adult privileges. Even Daddy didn't drink wine except on special occasions. After Grandma moved in, though, he began to occasionally join her for a glass, sometimes even sitting with her on the porch for a pre-meal sip.

PREDICT: What do you think will happen between Grandma and the boy's father?

She held court on our front porch, often gazing toward the desert hills east of us or across the street at kids playing on the lot.

---

10. **relent** (ri lent′), *v.* become less harsh or cruel; be more tender and merciful.
11. **Manuel** (man wel′).
12. *el malcriado* (el mal krē a′do), the spoiled boy.
13. **Arroyo Cantua** (a rro′yo kan′tŭa), **Coalinga** (ko a lēn′ga).
14. *vaquero* (ba ke′ro), cowboy.
15. **progeny** (proj′ə nē), *n.* children; offspring.

Occasionally, she would rise, cross the yard and sidewalk and street, skip over them, sometimes stumbling on the curb, and wipe her feet on the lot's sandy soil, then she would slowly circle the boundary between the open middle and the brushy sides, searching for something, it appeared. I never figured out what.

One afternoon I returned from school and saw Grandma perched on the porch as usual, so I started to walk around the house to avoid her sharp, mostly incomprehensible,[16] tongue. She had already spotted me. *"¡Venga aquí!"*[17] she ordered, and I understood.

I approached the porch and noticed that Grandma was vigorously chewing something. She held a small white bag in one hand. Saying *"¿Qué deseas tomar?"*[18] she withdrew a large orange gumdrop from the bag and began slowly chewing it in her toothless mouth, smacking loudly as she did so. I stood below her for a moment trying to remember the word for candy. Then it came to me: *"Dulce,"*[19] I said.

Still chewing, Grandma replied, *"¿Mande?"*[20]

Knowing she wanted a complete sentence, I again struggled, then came up with *"Deseo dulce."*[21]

She measured me for a moment, before answering in nearly perfect English, "Oh, so you wan' some candy. Go to the store an' buy some."

I don't know if it was the shock of hearing her speak English for the first time, or the way she had denied me a piece of candy, but I suddenly felt tears warm my cheeks and I sprinted into the house and found Mom, who stood at the kitchen sink. "Grandma just talked English," I burst between light sobs.

"What's wrong?" she asked as she reached out to stroke my head.

"Grandma can talk English," I repeated.

"Of course she can," Mom answered. "What's wrong?"

I wasn't sure what was wrong, but after considering, I told Mom that Grandma had teased me. No sooner had I said that than the old woman appeared at the door and hiked her skirt. Attached to one of her petticoats by safety pins were several small tobacco sacks, the white cloth kind that closed with yellow drawstrings. She carefully unhooked one and opened it, withdrawing a dollar, then handed the money to me. *"Para su dulce,"*[22] she said. Then, to my mother, she asked, "Why does he bawl like a motherless calf?"

"It's nothing," Mother replied.

"Do not weep, little one," the old lady comforted me, "Jesus and the Virgin love you." She smiled and patted my head. To my mother she said as though just realizing it, "Your baby?"

Somehow that day changed everything. I wasn't afraid of my great-grandmother any longer and, once I began spending time with her on the porch, I realized that my father had also begun directing increased attention to the old woman. Almost every evening Ese Gringo was sharing wine with Grandma. They talked out there, but I never did hear a real two-way conversation between them. Usually Grandma rattled on and Daddy nodded. She'd chuckle and pat his hand and he might grin, even grunt a word or two, before she'd begin talking again. Once I saw my mother standing by the front window watching them together, a smile playing across her face.

---

16. **incomprehensible** (in′kom pri hen′sə bəl), *adj.* impossible to understand.
17. *¡Venga aquí!* (ben′ga a kē′), Come here!
18. *¿Qué deseas tomar?* (ke de se′as to mar′), What would you like to eat?
19. *dulce* (dül′se), candy.
20. *¿Mande?* (man′de), What?
21. *Deseo dulce* (de se′o dül′se), I would like candy.
22. *Para su dulce* (pa′ra sü dül′se), For your candy.

No more did I sneak around the house to avoid Grandma after school. Instead, she waited for me and discussed my efforts in class gravely, telling Mother that I was a bright boy, *"muy inteligente,"*[23] and that I should be sent to the nuns who would train me. I would make a fine priest. When Ese Gringo heard that, he smiled and said, "He'd make a fair-to-middlin' Holy Roller preacher, too." Even Mom had to chuckle, and my great-grandmother shook her finger at Ese Gringo. "Oh you debil, Sharlie!" she cackled.

Frequently, I would accompany Grandma to the lot where she would explain that no fodder[24] could grow there. Poor pasture or not, the lot was at least unpaved, and Grandma greeted even the tiniest new cactus or flowering weed with joy. "Look how beautiful," she would croon. "In all this ugliness, it lives." Oildale was my home and it didn't look especially ugly to me, so I could only grin and wonder.

Because she liked the lot and things that grew there, I showed her the horned toad when I captured it a second time. I was determined to keep it, although I did not discuss my plans with anyone. I also wanted to hear more about the bloody eyes, so I thrust the small animal nearly into her face one afternoon. She did not flinch. *"Hola señor sangre de ojos,"*[25] she said with a mischievous grin. *"¿Qué tal?"*[26] It took me a moment to catch on.

"You were kidding before," I accused.

"Of course," she acknowledged, still grinning.

"But why?"

"Because the little beast belongs with his own kind in his own place, not in your pocket. Give him his freedom, my son."

I had other plans for the horned toad, but I was clever enough not to cross Grandma. "Yes, Ma'am," I replied. That night I placed the reptile in a flower bed cornered by a

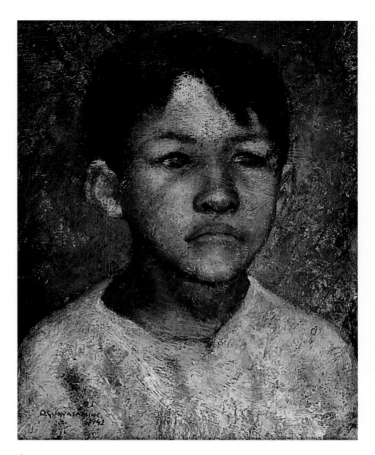

My Brother was painted in 1942 by Oswaldo Guayasamín Calero, one of the best-known artists in Latin America. How does the style of this artist differ from that of Carmen Lomas Garza on page 447?

brick wall Ese Gringo had build the previous summer. It was a spot rich with insects for the toad to eat, and the little wall, only a foot high, must have seemed massive to so squat an animal.

Nonetheless, the next morning, when I searched for the horned toad it was gone. I had no time to explore the yard for it, so I

---

23. *muy inteligente* (mwē ēn tel ē hen′te), very intelligent.
24. fodder (fod′ər), *n.* coarse food, such as hay and cornstalks, for a horse, cattle, etc.
25. *Hola señor sangre de ojos* (o′la sen yor′ san′gre de o′hos), Hello mister blood-from-the-eyes.
26. *¿Qué tal?* (ke tal), How are you?

trudged off to school, my belly troubled. How could it have escaped? Classes meant little to me that day. I thought only of my lost pet—I had changed his name to Juan,[27] the same as my great-grandfather—and where I might find him.

PREDICT: What do you think might have happened to the toad?

I shortened my conversation with Grandma that afternoon so I could search for Juan. "What do you seek?" the old woman asked me as I poked through flower beds beneath the porch. "Praying mantises," I improvised,[28] and she merely nodded, surveying me. But I had eyes only for my lost pet, and I continued pushing through branches and brushing aside leaves. No luck.

Finally, I gave in and turned toward the lot. I found my horned toad nearly across the street, crushed. It had been heading for the miniature desert and had almost made it when an automobile's tire had run over it. One notion immediately swept me: if I had left it on its lot, it would still be alive. I stood rooted there in the street, tears slicking my cheeks, and a car honked its horn as it passed, the driver shouting at me.

Grandma joined me, and stroked my back. "The poor little beast," was all she said, then she bent slowly and scooped up what remained of the horned toad and led me out of the street. "We must return him to his own place," she explained, and we trooped, my eyes still clouded, toward the back of the vacant lot. Carefully, I dug a hole with a piece of wood. Grandma placed Juan in it and covered him. We said an Our Father and a Hail Mary, then Grandma walked me back to the house.

"Your little Juan is safe with God, my son," she comforted. We kept the horned toad's death a secret, and we visited his small grave frequently.

Grandma fell just before school ended and summer vacation began. As was her habit, she had walked alone to the vacant lot but this time, on her way back, she tripped over the curb and broke her hip. That following week, when Daddy brought her home from the hospital, she seemed to have shrunken. She sat hunched in a wheelchair on the porch, gazing with faded eyes toward the hills or at the lot, speaking rarely. She still sipped wine every evening with Daddy and even I could tell how concerned he was about her. It got to where he'd look in on her before leaving for work every morning and again at night before turning in. And if Daddy was home, Grandma always wanted him to push her chair when she needed moving, calling, "Sharlie!" until he arrived.

I was tugged from sleep on the night she died by voices drumming through the walls into darkness. I couldn't understand them, but was immediately frightened by the uncommon sounds of words in the night. I struggled from bed and walked into the living room just as Daddy closed the front door and a car pulled away.

Mom was sobbing softly on the couch, and Daddy walked to her, stroked her head, then noticed me. "Come here, son," he gently ordered.

I walked to him and, uncharacteristically, he put an arm around me. "What's wrong?" I asked, near tears myself. Mom looked up, but before she could speak, Daddy said, "Grandma died." Then he sighed heavily and stood there with his arms around his weeping wife and son.

---

27. **Juan** (hwän)
28. improvise (im′prə vīz), v. make up on the spur of the moment.

The next day my Uncle Manuel and Uncle Arnulfo, plus Aunt Chintia,[29] arrived and over food they discussed with my mother where Grandma should be interred.[30] They argued that it would be too expensive to transport her body home and, besides, they could more easily visit her grave if she was buried in Bakersfield. "They have such a nice, manicured grounds at Greenlawn," Aunt Chintia pointed out. Just when it seemed they had agreed, I could remain silent no longer. "But Grandma has to go home," I burst. "She has to! It's the only thing she really wanted. We can't leave her in the city."

Uncle Arnulfo, who was on the edge, snapped to Mother that I belonged with the other children, not interrupting adult conversation. Mom quietly agreed, but I refused. My father walked into the room then. "What's wrong?" he asked.

"They're going to bury Grandma in Bakersfield, Daddy. Don't let 'em, please."

"Well, son . . ."

"When my horny toad got killed and she helped me to bury it, she said we had to return him to his place."

"Your horny toad?" Mother asked.

"He got squished and me and Grandma buried him in the lot. She said we had to take him back to his place. Honest she did."

No one spoke for a moment, then my father, Ese Gringo, who stood against the sink, responded: "That's right . . ." He paused, then added, "We'll bury her." I saw a weary smile cross my mother's face. "If she wanted to go back to the ranch then that's where we have to take her," Daddy said.

I hugged him and he, right in front of everyone, hugged back.

No one argued. It seemed, suddenly, as though they had all wanted to do exactly what I had begged for. Grown-ups baffled[31] me. Late that week the entire family, hundreds it seemed, gathered at the little Catholic church in Coalinga for mass, then drove out to Arroyo Cantua and buried Grandma next to Grandpa. She rests there today.

"If she wanted to go back to the ranch then that's where we have to take her. . . ."

My mother, father, and I drove back to Oildale that afternoon across the scorching westside desert, through sand and tumbleweeds and heat shivers. Quiet and sad, we knew we had done our best. Mom, who usually sat next to the door in the front seat, snuggled close to Daddy, and I heard her whisper to him, "Thank you, Charlie," as she kissed his cheek.

Daddy squeezed her, hesitated as if to clear his throat, then answered, "When you're family, you take care of your own."

29. **Arnulfo** (ar nül′fo), **Chintia** (chēn′tē a)
30. inter (in tèr′), v. put (a dead body) into a grave or tomb; bury.
31. baffle (baf′əl), v. bewilder.

After Reading

Making Connections

1. What are the first words that come to mind when you think about Grandma?

2. Would you like to have someone like Grandma in your family? Why or why not?

3. 🐾 How did the boy's **interactions** with Grandma change his appreciation of the Mexican side of his family background?

4. What is the significance of the boy learning to speak Spanish to Grandma?

5. Is "The Horned Toad" a good **title** for this story? Explain your reasoning.

6. In what way does Grandma's relationship with the father change during the story? Tell the reasons for this change.

7. Why does Grandma insist that the toad be buried in the vacant lot?

8. Father warned that teaching the boy Spanish would hurt him in school. Do you think learning a second language at home would be harmful or helpful to success at school? Give reasons for your answer.

Literary Focus: Setting

Every story has to take place somewhere, and that somewhere is called the **setting.** We usually say that the setting is the time and place of the work, but there can be several levels of time and place in a story. Places can include countries, states, cities, and specific locations, such as a vacant lot, a house, or a front porch. Times can include centuries, decades, years, times of year, days of the week, and hours and minutes of the day. For this story, make a list of all the kinds of places and times mentioned above and tell if each is important to the story.

The Horned Toad	
Times	**Places**

Vocabulary Study

Write the letter of the word that is not related in meaning to the other words in that set.

desolation
periphery
comply
relent
progeny
incomprehensible
fodder
improvise
inter
baffle

1. **a.** emptiness **b.** loneliness **c.** fullness **d.** desolation
2. **a.** periphery **b.** area **c.** perimeter **d.** edge
3. **a.** agree **b.** comply **c.** disagree **d.** accept
4. **a.** relent **b.** harshen **c.** soften **d.** give in
5. **a.** progeny **b.** children **c.** offspring **d.** ancestors
6. **a.** understandable **b.** puzzling **c.** mysterious **d.** incomprehensible
7. **a.** oats **b.** water **c.** fodder **d.** barley
8. **a.** schedule **b.** make up **c.** improvise **d.** invent
9. **a.** bury **b.** cremate **c.** inter **d.** entomb
10. **a.** baffle **b.** bewilder **c.** astonish **d.** instruct

Expressing Your Ideas

Writing Choices

I Remember Grandma One responsibility family members sometimes have is to speak at the funeral of a relative. Such a speech is called a **eulogy.** Write a eulogy that the boy might read at Grandma's funeral. Think about the boy's relationship with her as you plan what he might want to remember about her.

Tell It Your Way The mother and father in this story are important characters, but Grandma and the boy are the stars. Most of the action centers on Grandma, and the boy tells the story. Give somebody else a chance. **Retell** this story from the point of view of either the mother or the father. Before you start, review the story to see what events the new narrator would know about.

Other Options

An Anglo-Hispanic Tree Draw a **family tree** of the boy's family, including key information about each family member. Review the story to trace the boy's heritage.

Guide to Lot Fauna The word *fauna* refers to animals that live in a certain location. Make a **guide** to fauna living in or near the vacant lot: ants, horned toads, lizards, and praying mantises. Use the list below as a checklist to help you gather information.

- Life Span
- Food
- Appearance
- Social Organization

It Happened Right Here Do a **drawing** of the main setting of the story, including the vacant lot, the street, and the house where the family lives. Mark important events that took place at each point of the setting.

Appreciating Each Other

Generations Together

Psychology Connection
Family relationships don't always run smoothly. Even though there are rough spots, it is important to take time to appreciate each other.

They Won't Let Me Grow Up
by Lauren Tarshis

Last October, for Philip's fourteenth birthday, he and his family went into New York City for a full day of sightseeing, splurging, and celebrating. The pictures from that day show Philip, dressed in the green cotton sweater his mother had chosen for him as a gift, smiling with his family in various Manhattan settings. A year later, as Philip looks through those pictures, he winces as he sees himself fraternizing with people—his parents and two younger sisters—he now considers unfit for his company. "I only spend time with them when I can't get out of it," he says.

What have Philip's parents done to earn Philip's contempt? "They don't understand me," says Philip. "They want me to be a certain way—like they were when they were young. And I refuse. That's not who I am."

Who Philip *is* is a tenth-grader with family problems typical of teenagers around the country and probably the world. Philip's relationship with his parents has changed radically as he's entered his teens. Philip says he's spent many twilight hours wondering what went wrong. His analysis: His parents aren't adjusting fast enough to the fact that Philip is no longer a child. He says that he's changed dramatically in the past year. He gave up his place on his school's basketball team so he could devote more time to the guitar. He enjoys sleeping late on weekends and doesn't feel like accompanying his family to the mall or the beach.

Most important, he now resists the ground rules his parents set up for him and that he used to follow as unquestioningly as a Marine recruit in boot camp—his 11:30 curfew, homework before television, only one hour of MTV a day, to name a few.

Curfews, Chores, and Money

Adolescence deserves its reputation as one of life's more difficult phases. It's a time of changes—physical, emotional, intellectual—that can happen quickly. Certainly, family problems are a fact of life that many of us deal with from the day we are born until after we have kids of our own. But experts agree that adolescence is often the most explosive time between parents and children. Why is it so tough? Why do some of the closest family bonds seem to rupture as children hit their teens? And what can you do to make things better with your family?

First, you should step back and understand that clashing with your parents is a normal and necessary part of your development—and your parents' too.

They want me to be a certain way—like they were when they were young.

New Identities

That's because you and your parents are often working at cross purposes.

Your job during your teens is to stake out a place in the world apart from your family and to develop the independence that will make you a successful adult. "Some rebellion is completely normal during adolescence as kids establish their own identity, apart from their family," says Karen Zager, a New York City psychologist who works with teens and their families. "And during this rebellion, there are going to be arguments."

Your parents' job during this time is tricky. They need to keep you safe and secure. They need to provide you with clear guidelines to help you navigate through the labyrinth that will lead you to adulthood. In short, they need to make sure you don't do something dumb that will mess up your life.

Other Perspectives

Most of you admit that you often understand your parents' perspective on the issues you fight about. "I resent my mother prying into my life and not letting me do things," says seventeen-year-old Andrea. "But I know that she does it because I'm her child. I'm sure I'm going to be the same way with my child."

But this understanding doesn't stop many of you from heaping much of the blame for the tensions at home on your parents. "My parents are dictators," says Sean. "My parents are afraid to let me grow up," says Misty. The biggest problem with blaming your parents for every conflict is that you deprive yourself of any power to improve the relationship; you turn yourself into a victim. "If you're willing to admit that it's a two-way street, then you suddenly realize that you do have some control over the quality of your relationship," says Shari Shapiro, executive director of The Youth Shelter/Kids in Crisis, two shelters in Greenwich, Connecticut. "Once that happens, things can start to get better."

Communicate

Make an effort to talk to your parents and to clue them in to what's going on in your life.

Put in Some Face Time

Try to put aside at least some time every week to spend with your parents doing something you all enjoy.

Be Willing to Prove Yourself

If you're itching for a later curfew or more freedom and privileges, discuss it with your parents and find out what they expect in return. If it's a later curfew you want, show them that you respect your existing curfew first.

Be a Student of Your Parents' Lives

While you're struggling through the changes that come during the teen years, your parents are probably grappling with transitions of their own. Pay attention to what your parents are going through—job changes, sick relatives, money strains, marital conflicts. These issues are likely to affect the way your parents deal with you. And they might require that you devote more of yourself to your family.

Pick Your Battles

Save your energy and spirit for issues that really matter to you. Don't get sucked into conflicts over petty issues. By heading off battles over small issues, you put yourself into a better position when you're negotiating for something you really care about.

Be Patient

Few families are spared from the clashes that hit during a child's adolescence. And while life at home might feel unbearable when you're in the midst of a storm, things almost always get better with time.

Get Help

If you feel that you and your parents can't work out your problems on your own, or if your family situation becomes abusive or violent, seek outside help. Talk to your high school counselor, a friend's parent, or a trusted adult.

Responding

1. What kinds of problems do you think the generation before yours had in dealing with their parents? Do you think it was easier to grow up then?

2. What is one way your family deals with conflict?

History Connection

Not long ago, it was common for children, their parents, and grandparents all to live in the same house. There was so much to be gained when several generations lived and worked together. Although times have changed, you can still tap the wonderful source of information that is your grandparents.

What were your grandparents like as children and teenagers? What did they daydream about? What did they look like? What problems did they have? What were their lives like when they grew up?

Most young people know very little about the history of their families. There are many unanswered questions about the past. A science called genealogy can help you to discover your "roots." There is an easy way to get many of the interesting facts—through a branch of genealogy called oral history. That means interviewing older members of your family.

The best people to interview are your grandparents, and the easiest way to do an interview is with a tape recorder. If you can't get a tape recorder, you will have to take good notes throughout the interview.

Pick one grandparent to begin with, for interviews should always be done one at a time. But what if all of your grandparents live too far away? In that case, you will have to pick another relative. Choose one of the family's best storytellers, but—and this is important—be sure to pick someone who is old enough to have had a different lifestyle than your own. Here are suggestions to help you get ready for the big interview.

Getting Ready for the Interview

Like any good reporter, you should do a little advance work. Get some facts about your grandparent before the interview. Talk to your parents, and ask them what they know. These leads will help you to make up a list of good questions.

Tips on Being a Good Reporter

1. Try to limit the interview to one hour. This means you can't ask too many questions, so choose your questions carefully.
2. Ask short questions.
3. Be a good listener.
4. Check the tape recorder.
5. Take a few notes during the interview, especially about the spellings of places and people.
6. Your grandparent may not want to answer some of your questions. Move on to other ones.

Search for Your "Roots":

Interviewing Your

by Ann Elwood and Carol Orsag

Questions

IMPORTANT: Prepare your list of questions in advance. Have them in front of you at the interview.

Be sure to ask interesting questions. You don't want your grandparent to answer only yes or no. For instance, you may ask, "Were you a soldier in World War II?" But follow it up with, "What are the three things you remember most about the war?"

Here is a list of sample questions to give you a head start.

Childhood

1. When and where were you born?
2. What did your parents (my great-grandparents) look like? Where were they born? What did they do for a living?
3. Who was the most unusual relative you can remember? Why?
4. How many brothers and sisters did you have? Were you a close family?

Grandparents

5. At what age did your family consider a person grown up?
6. What kind of chores did you have to do as a child?
7. What can you remember about school?
8. What was the biggest holiday that your family celebrated? How did you celebrate?
9. How did your family survive the Great Depression?

Marriage and Family

1. Where and how did you and Grandmother (Grandfather) meet?
2. What was the first thing you noticed about her (him)?
3. How long did you know her (him) before you got married? What did your parents think about the marriage?
4. What was your wedding like?
5. What did your house or apartment look like?

Work and Money

1. How many different jobs have you had? Which one did you like the most?
2. If you could have picked a "dream job," what would you have picked?

Writing the Article from the Tape

1. Play back the tape. Take notes on what you think are the most interesting parts of the interview.
2. Organize your notes and write the article.
3. Make sure you have the right spellings for names and places.

Responding

Interview one of your grandparents. Use the steps listed in this article to prepare for and to conduct the interview. When finished, use the interview to write a one-page article about your grandparent. Read your article to the class.

Reading Mini-Lesson

Recalling Details

How do you study when you need to remember details? Although not all people remember things in the same ways, studies have shown that certain rules seem to hold true for most people:

1. Information you understand is easier to remember than information you don't understand.

2. A framework or organizing pattern helps you remember details.

3. The more ways you use the information, the more likely you are to remember it.

Let's look at Rule 1. One way to better understand new information is to link it to what you already know. Using a **K-W-L Chart** will help you do that. Try this out with the preceding article, "Search for Your 'Roots.'" First scan the article to get clues about the topic: interviewing grandparents. Then draw a K-W-L Chart like the one to the left and fill in the K column with what you already know about interviewing techniques. Add any questions you have to the W column. As you read, you will notice details that answer your questions and you will connect new information to what you already know about interviewing. Jot down what you learn in the L column of the chart.

What about Rule 2? Discovering the organizing pattern of an article will often help you recall details. Making an **outline** or a **semantic web** of the article is a tool for organizing details. Review the Reading Mini-Lesson on page 330 for more information.

What We K now

Think of questions ahead of time.

Take good notes.

Use a tape recorder.

What We W ant to Know

What kinds of questions should I ask?

What We L earned

Activity Options

1. Use the headings as a starting place and make an outline of "They Won't Let Me Grow Up" (page 456).

2. Organize the information in "They Won't Let Me Grow Up" in a semantic web. Write the main topic in a center circle and note the important details at the end of spokes around the circle.

3. Practice using a K-W-L Chart on another informational article in a book or magazine. Fill out the K and W columns before reading, and complete the L column after reading.

Writing Workshop

Letters of Thanks

Assignment Many characters you read about receive gifts from someone close to them. Write a letter in which you thank someone for a special gift. See the Writer's Blueprint for details.

WRITER'S BLUEPRINT

Product A personal letter and speech

Purpose To thank someone for a special gift and to explain its importance to you

Audience The giver of the gift

Specs As the writer of a successful letter, you should:

❑ Think of a few items that could represent aspects of your relationship. For example, a fishing pole, an empty coffee can, and a wild-looking lure could represent time you and a relative have spent fishing together.

❑ Imagine that you received all of these items in a gift bag from your special person. Begin your letter by explaining that you are writing to thank him or her for the gifts.

❑ Go on to name each gift and explain its importance to you.

❑ Close your letter by telling the person what he or she means to you.

❑ Make your letter more interesting by using a variety of sentence patterns.

❑ Follow the rules of grammar, usage, spelling, and mechanics. Use the correct form for a friendly letter.

The following instructions will help you write a successful letter.

Chart characters from the literature. Review three of the stories from this part. Use a chart like the one below to indicate gifts, givers, and how the gifts are received.

Who gives the gift?	What is the gift?	How is the gift received?
Lewis and Tom	A joyous greeting	She wishes they would stop doing it.

Brainstorm important people in your life. Make a list of important people in your life. Choose people who have influenced you.

Draw items that stand for a special gift. In "The Medicine Bag," Grandpa gives his great-grandson some items in a small pouch. Each item has a special meaning. Together they represent the gift of grand-father's Sioux tradition. Think about your special person. What items stand for the gift that person has given you? On a separate sheet of paper, draw an outline sketch of a medicine bag. Inside the bag, draw pictures of the items that represent the gift. Choose items that stand for ideas. For example, a recipe, a lace handkerchief, and a clothes-pin might stand for values learned from an older relative. A book, a pencil, and a gold star might stand for a teacher who helped you gain confidence in yourself.

Try a quickwrite. Beneath your medicine bag, briefly write down information about each item. Explain what each item stands for and why it is important to you.

Provide details. Think about each of the items you drew in your medicine bag. How would you describe each one? What does it rep-resent about your relationship? Why is each one meaningful? Record your details in a chart like the one below.

OR . . . You may already have selected the person you want to write to. In that case, jump ahead to the "Draw items that stand for a special gift" step.

OR . . . Instead of doing a quick-write, you might want to describe each item to a partner. Can you explain what the items stand for?

Gift	Details	What it represents	Why it's important
Fishing pole	Long, plastic and wood, flexible, old-fashioned reel	Times we've spent together fishing	You love to fish and you've passed that hobby on to me.
Hourglass	Curved glass body with ornately carved wooden base	Your patience with me as I've learned and grown	You've taught me to believe in myself. You never gave up on me even when it took a long time.

Plan your letter. Imagine that the special person has given you a medicine bag filled with items from your charts and drawings. Now, plan out how you will thank this person.

  DRAFTING

Before you write, review the Writer's Blueprint. Look over your chart, drawing, and quickwrite.

As you draft, vary your sentence structure. Look ahead to the Revising Strategy for ideas on how to do this. Don't worry about mistakes with spelling and punctuation. Concentrate on getting the events and details down on paper. Here are some ideas for getting started.

- Begin by describing how the person looks doing something you vividly remember. Include one of the items he or she gave to you if appropriate.

- Begin by telling how this person has affected your life.

- Begin by describing a trait of this person's character you think is important.

> **OR...**
> You might begin by recalling an incident you remember with the person. Then you can go on to tell why the person's gift is important to you.

  REVISING

Ask your partner for comments on your draft before you revise it.

✔ Have I followed the Specs in the Writer's Blueprint?

✔ Have I communicated how important the giver is to me and how meaningful the gift is?

✔ Have I included a variety of sentence structures?

Revising Strategy

Sentence Variety

Writers vary the structure of their sentences to make their writing more interesting. A string of declarative sentences can make for dull reading. Look at the three sentences in the Literary Source. How has the author created variety in these sentences?

It takes practice, but with time you'll find that sentence variety comes naturally as you put your ideas on paper. Here are some suggestions that will help you achieve sentence variety.

- Vary sentence length, using short, declarative sentences and longer compound or complex sentences.

- Vary sentence beginnings by using adjective or adverb phrases and clauses.

- Combine short sentences with similar ideas into longer sentences.

- Vary the types of sentences you use. Sometimes a declarative sentence is more effective if it is phrased as a question.

Notice how the writer of the passage below revised to create varied sentence structure.

> *As*
> I took the train set out of the box, I was reminded of how
> *While*
> you helped me set it up every Christmas. Mom would be in the
> *and*
> kitchen fixing Christmas dinner. The relatives would be in the
> dining room talking and laughing. We would be happily playing with
> the train under the tree.

STUDENT MODEL

4 EDITING

Ask a partner to review your revised draft before you edit. When you edit, watch for errors in grammar, usage, spelling, and mechanics. Make sure you've used the correct form for a friendly letter.

Editing Strategy

Form for a Friendly Letter

The format you use in a letter changes depending on the type of letter you're writing. The example below shows the format for a friendly letter.

673 Grandview Circle
Tacoma, WA 73642
August 12, 1999

Dear Aunt Eve,

I just wanted to let you know that my travel plans are all set. Mom and Dad are taking me to the airport on Saturday morning. I'll be arriving in Orlando at 11:00 AM. My return flight is on Friday. I'll see you soon!

Love,

Emily

Notice how the writer of this draft corrected errors in letter format.

3608 N. Wilton Ave.
Chicago, IL 60613
April 20, 1999

Dear Dad,

Thanks for sending all my childhood toys back to me. When I moved out at twenty-one, I never imagined that twenty years later, I'd have kids of my own who'd want to play with my old toys. Those toys set off a whole string of memories for me, and they reminded me how important you've always been to me.

Love,
Greg

STUDENT MODEL

STEP 5 PRESENTING

Turn your letter into a testimonial which you deliver at a ceremony honoring the person you wrote to.

Make note cards for your speech. Review your letter and list the main ideas and details. Then use these note cards to deliver your speech, instead of simply reading your essay.

Here are some tips for delivering your speech.

- **Rehearse.** Practice out loud, by yourself, in front of others, and as often as you need to. Try out different gestures and different kinds of vocal emphasis.

- **Get organized.** Have everything ready before you get up in front of your audience.

- **Maintain eye contact.** Look at your audience and talk to them. Pick out different people and direct a sentence or two at each one.

- **Speak loudly and clearly,** but don't shout. Your speech is worthless if your audience can't hear you.

STEP 6 LOOKING BACK

Self-evaluate. What grade would you give your paper? Look back at the Writer's Blueprint and evaluate yourself on each point, from 6 (superior) down to 1 (weak).

Reflect. Think about what you learned from writing your letter as you write answers to these questions.

✔ How has your gift changed you? How has knowing the giver changed you? How has reflecting upon the gift changed you?

✔ If you could rewrite your letter, is there anything you would change? Are there things you'd like to put in or take out?

For Your Working Portfolio: Add your letter, speech, and reflection responses to your working portfolio.

Beyond Print

Feel Like You're Talking to a Wall?

Are there times when you need someone to listen? Of course there are. When you have something to say, are you always happy with the way your friends or family listen to you? Have you ever been interrupted in the middle of a thought? Did you ever begin telling a friend about a problem and before you were half done explaining it, he or she was offering a solution? Do you remember times when all you wanted to do was get something off your chest, but all your friendly listener could do was offer all kinds of unsolicited advice? All of us have firsthand experience with these types of situations. They are all examples of a widespread problem called "poor listening."

Listening Tips

Think Look in the speaker's eyes and relate what the speaker is saying to your personal experience.

Feedback Tell the speaker what you heard until you get it right.

Don't Interrupt Give the speaker plenty of time to finish his or her statement. Allow for pauses so the speaker has time to think. Do not be afraid of silence. Make sure the speaker is finished before you speak.

Take Notes You may want to jot down what you hear. You will not have time to write down what the speaker is saying word for word.

Make a Mental Picture For example, if the speaker describes a sport, picture the sport in your mind.

Activity

How does one become a better listener? The Listening Tips in the margin will be helpful. Study them before doing the following activity.

1. In pairs, create a list of about five general questions you will ask each other. Examples: What are your favorite hobbies? Who are your heroes? What traits do you look for in a friend?

2. One person is the interviewer/listener. This person selects the five questions and asks her/his partner to respond.

3. It is the job of the interviewer/listener to listen as well as possible to the answers.

4. The interviewer/listener reports to the class on the interview, summarizing what she/he heard as accurately as possible.

5. Do the activity again, but switch roles.

Activity Extensions

1. Have the person you listened to critique your class summary. If you missed more than a couple items by either omitting them or getting them wrong, do the activity again.

2. Practice some of the tips you learned here when you listen to your friends. Maybe you will become a better listener and friend.

Projects for Collaborative Study

Theme Connection

Relationship Mixer In "Beni Seballos," Beni learned that "if she listened carefully, she could find something in common with almost everyone." Here's a game that helps people find things they have in common. First, write the answers to these questions:

1. If I could be any animal I would be a ____.

2. My personality is the color of a ____.

3. No one knows that I secretly listen to ____.

4. The sport I find most interesting is ____.

5. An adjective that describes me is ____.

■ Next, compare your list to that of others in your class. Find the person or people who have the most answers like yours.

■ Finally, work together to chart your new group by name, number, and answers.

Literature Connection

What a Character! In this unit, authors develop characters in various ways. In "Dear Marsha," for example, we only find out what the main characters tell about themselves in their letters. In "The Horned Toad," however, we learn a lot about Grandma. We find out how she looks, what she says, how she acts, and what several members of her family think of her. Choose two or three selections in the unit, and in a small group, discuss how each character was developed.

■ Work in a small group to extend one of the selections in the unit using the method of characterization you like best. Together, write your story, dramatize it, or tell it aloud.

Life Skills Connection

First Impressions When people meet for the first time, they usually form an opinion of each other quickly. After people spend time together, their initial impressions may get stronger, or they may change their opinions.

■ In your notebook, list some people you have met for the first time in the past year. What was your initial impression of each?

■ As you got to know these people better, were your initial opinions (negative or positive) reinforced or did they change? Why? What happened?

As a class, discuss what it would take to keep an open mind toward others.

Multicultural Connection

Let's Talk In "The Horned Toad," the boy is not allowed to learn Spanish, because his father thinks it will hurt him in school. However, **communication** in more than one language can open up rich possibilities for **interactions** among people. In a small group, work on one of these projects:

■ Find out how many people in the United States speak more than one language. What languages do they speak? Create charts and graphs that show these findings.

■ Prepare a report on the Canadian system of two official languages. What laws support a bilingual society in Canada?

■ Organize a panel discussion with people who speak two languages. Do they speak English in some situations and another language in others? What problems and rewards are there in speaking two languages?

Read More About Relationships

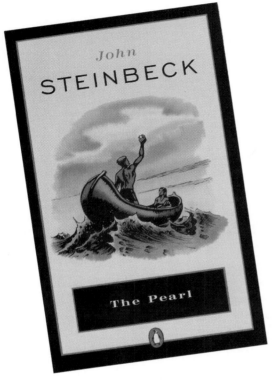

The Pearl (1947) by John Steinbeck. A poor fisherman finds a valuable pearl that brings on a series of mishaps and disasters that threaten his family.

Join In: Multiethnic Short Stories by Outstanding Writers for Young Adults (1993) edited by Donald R. Gallo. Contemporary authors write about the problems and concerns experienced by American teenagers.

More Good Books

An Island Like You: Stories of the Barrio (1995) by Judith Ortiz Cofer. Drawing upon her childhood experiences, the author presents twelve short stories that explore the lives of Puerto Rican teenagers growing up in a New Jersey barrio.

A Solitary Blue (1983) by Cynthia Voight. Feeling abandoned and neglected by his parents, a young boy struggles to make sense of his life. A summer spent with his mother, who left him and his father several years earlier, changes his life forever.

The Pigman (1968) by Paul Zindel. Two alienated teenagers befriend a lonely, good-hearted widower who later regrets entrusting them with his treasured ceramic pig collection.

The Golden Pasture (1986) by Joyce Carol Thomas. A magnificent horse helps bring together a boy, his father, and his grandfather who had been divided by anger for many years.

The Year Without Michael (1987) by Susan Beth Pfeffer. This suspenseful novel is centered around the disappearance of thirteen-year-old Michael and the impact this traumatic event has on his family.

Justice

Life's Not Always Fair
Part One, pages 476–534

The Triumph of the Spirit
Part Two, pages 535–627

Talking About
JUSTICE

When you hear the word *justice,* you may think of peace or freedom or liberty. For many people, *justice* calls up images of police, judges, and lawyers. For nearly everyone, justice means being treated fairly. Americans value justice. Yet there are probably times when you wonder, "Is there any justice in the world?"

> My parents let Miguel do almost whatever he wants. They tell me, "later when you're older."
>
> *from* "Inequalities" by Nereida Román, page 480

> Because the old man was out of sight, he was often neglected. Sometimes he even went hungry.
>
> *from* "The Boy and His Grandfather" by Rudolfo A. Anaya, page 518

> In September we were told that we were to be shipped to Poland. . . The men to one camp. The women to another.
>
> *from The Diary of Anne Frank* by Frances Goodrich and Albert Hackett, page 606

"Justice is being treated fairly by teachers and parents."

Lindsay—Baltimore, MD

"All people should be treated with respect."

Dantrell—Los Angeles, CA

"Everyone needs to be treated equally and fairly—all races and religions."

Lisa—Portland, WA

Part One

Life's Not Always Fair

Have you ever been treated unfairly because of your race, your religion, the way you look, or just because you are "different"? Unfortunately, many of us have. Although the world will never be perfect, we can all help erase some of its unfairness. A little knowledge, patience, and understanding will go a long way toward achieving that goal.

🐾 Multicultural Connection The unique ways in which a person speaks, acts, and views the world make up his or her **individuality.** Although individuality is important, people also need to belong to groups and want to be treated fairly by others. As you read these selections, look for ways in which the characters struggle to be themselves while also being accepted by others.

Literature

Ophelia Rivas	**Indians** ◆ poem	.479
Nereida Román	**Inequalities** ◆ essay	.480
Judith Ortiz Cofer	**The Changeling/Transformación** ◆ poems	.481
Daniel Keyes	**Flowers for Algernon** ◆ short story	.485
	Language Mini-Lesson ◆ Sentence Conciseness	.516
Rudolfo A. Anaya	**The Boy and His Grandfather**	
	◆ American folk tale	.518
Dell J. McCormick	**Paul Bunyan Digs the St. Lawrence River**	
	◆ American folk tale	.522
Traditional	**John Henry** ◆ American folk ballad	.524

Interdisciplinary Study **All Work, No Play**

Mother Jones Seeks Justice for the Mill Children
by Penny Colman ◆ U.S. history 528

Too Much Work = Poor Grades by Rahul Jacob ◆ sociology 532

Child Labor and Rules of Reason ◆ sociology 533

Reading Mini-Lesson ◆ Distinguishing Between Fact
and Opinion 534

Before Reading

Indians by Ophelia Rivas

Inequalities by Nereida Román

The Changeling/Transformación by Judith Ortiz Cofer

Building Background

Waking Up to Reality Discovering that inequalities are a fact of life does not necessarily make them easier to deal with. What do people do when they are treated unfairly? Trying to understand why a particular inequality exists is a good first step. Knowledge can help us discover what actions to take. It can also help us determine when the best thing to do is nothing at all. As with other problems in life, it sometimes helps to write down our thoughts when we feel we are being treated unfairly. Two of the following selections are by young authors who did just that.

Getting into the Selections

Discussion Two of the pieces you will read are about girls who feel their parents treated them differently than their brothers. Of course, *differently* can be either positive or negative. In your experience, do parents treat girls differently than they treat boys? Are girls treated better or worse than boys? In other words, is there a double standard in place? Discuss these questions within a small group.

Reading Tip

Main Idea and Supporting Details An **essay,** which is a brief composition in prose that presents a point of view, always has a **main idea.** The author's viewpoint is elaborated by **supporting details,** which provide evidence to support, or back up, the writer's opinion. In Nereida Román's essay, find the main idea. Then locate the supporting details. Put your information in a chart like the one below.

Main Idea: _____

_____

Supporting detail 1: _____

Supporting detail 2: _____

Supporting detail 3: _____

Ophelia Rivas
born 1956

Ophelia Rivas, of Tohono O'odham heritage, was an eighth-grade student at Santa Rosa school in Arizona when her poem "Indians" won a creative writing contest sponsored by the Bureau of Indian Affairs. As part of her award, Rivas's poem was published in 1971. In addition, her poem was chosen to appear in *Rising Voices: Writings of Young Native Americans,* which was published in 1992.

Nereida Román
born 1976

When she wrote "Inequalities," Nereida Román was a member of Las Mujeres Hispañas, a group of Hispanic American teenage women at Manhattan East, an alternative high school in New York City. During the course of a year, this group explored many of the issues affecting Hispanic American women today. They read and discussed the works of prominent female Hispanic authors, such as Judith Ortiz Cofer. Thus inspired, they wrote poetry, essays, and stories about some of the issues that affect their lives. Their pieces were then combined with those of some famous female Hispanic authors, Judith Ortiz Cofer included, and published in a book titled *Hispanic, Female and Young: An Anthology.* The work was published in 1994.

Judith Ortiz Cofer
born 1952

Judith Ortiz Cofer is an accomplished poet who has also written plays, essays, and a novel. Much of her writing deals with her extended family, part of which is in her native Puerto Rico, and part of which is in the United States. She says that "the infinite variety and power of language interest me. I never cease to experiment with it. As a native Puerto Rican, my first language was Spanish. It was a challenge, not only to learn English, but to master it enough to teach it and—the ultimate goal—to write poetry in it." Cofer's first novel, *The Line of the Sun,* was published in 1989. Not surprisingly, the work has been praised for its poetic quality.

Indians

Ophelia Rivas

Indians are native people
    here before the Pilgrims came
    here before Columbus came
    here before the Vikings came
5 Yet, we are treated
As though we don't belong here
Indians are native people
    here before the Pilgrims came
    here before Columbus came
10   here before the Vikings came
Yet, we are treated
As though we just got here.

These baskets were crafted by Tohono O'odham
weavers, using traditional designs. How do you think
each weaver expressed his or her **individuality** in
designing a basket?

INEQUALITIES

Nereida Román

Not only in the Hispanic culture but in every culture males and females are treated differently. My family isn't an exception.[1] I have an older brother named Miguel. He is a year and nine months older than me, but my parents treat me as if I were much younger. My parents let Miguel do almost whatever he wants. They tell me, "later when you're older." They have been giving me that same line for over a year. I'm sick of hearing that same line.

I remember once last summer I was going to the store, and my mother wouldn't let me go to the store by myself. She said, "You can't go alone, take Carlos with you." Carlos is my younger brother—at the time he was only eight years old.

A few days later Carlos, my father, and I went to a park. Carlos asked my father if he could go to the store. My father said, "Okay son, need some money?" Later on that same day I asked my father if I could go to the store. He made me take my brother.

I'm sure that I'm not alone. I know a lot of people with the same problem. I seem to be the first to speak out about it. I hope that this story will encourage more girls with the same problem as I have to speak out.

---

1. **exception** (ek sep′shən), *n.* a case that does not follow the rule.

These clay puppets were fashioned in Mexico City by Manuel Ibarra Ramírez. Why do you think children around the world play with puppets and dolls? ➤

THE CHANGELING

Judith Ortiz Cofer

As a young girl
vying[1] for my father's attention,
I invented a game that made him look up
from his reading and shake his head
5 as if both baffled and amused.

In my brother's closet, I'd change
into his dungarees—the rough material
molding me into boy-shape; hide
my long hair under an army helmet
10 he'd been given by Father, and emerge
transformed[2] into the legendary Ché
of grown-up talk.

Strutting[3] around the room,
I'd tell of life in the mountains,
15 of carnage and rivers of blood,
and of manly feasts with rum and music
to celebrate victories *para la libertad.*
He would listen with a smile
to my tales of battles and brotherhood
20 until Mother called us to dinner.

She was not amused
by my transformations,[4] sternly
forbidding me
from sitting down with them as a man.
She'd order me back to the dark cubicle
25 That smelled of adventure, to shed
my costume, to braid my hair furiously
with blind hands, and to return invisible,
as myself,
to the real world of her kitchen.

---

1. vie (vī), *v.*; compete; strive for superiority.
2. transformed (tran sfôrmd), *adj.* changed.
3. strut (strut), *v.* walk in a self-important manner.
4. transformation (tran′sfər mā′shən), *n.* a change in
   form or appearance.

TRANSFORMACION

Translated from the English by
Johanna Vega

Cuando era pequeña,
compitiendo por la atención de mi padre,
inventé un juego que lo hacía levantar
la vista
de lo que leía y mover la cabeza
5 Como si estuviera a la vez sorprendido y
divertido.

En el armario de mi hermano, me ponía
sus pantalones—el áspero material hacía
que mi cuerpo pareciera el de un chico;
escondía
mi pelo largo en el casco
10 que le había regalado papá y salía
transformada en el legendario Ché
de las conversaciones adultas.

Pavoneándome en el cuarto,
hablaba de la vida en las montañas,
15 de las matanzas y los ríos de sangre,
y de los banquetes masculinos con ron y
música
para celebrar los triunfos para la libertad.
Con una sonrisa él escuchaba
mis cuentos de batallas y fraternidad
20 hasta que mamá nos llamaba a cenar.

A ella no le divertían
mis transformaciones, prohibiéndome
severamente
que me sentara con ellos como hombre.
Me ordenaba que volviera al cubículo
25 que olía a aventuras para quitarme
el disfraz, para trenzarme el pelo
furiosamente
con manos ciegas y que regresara
invisible,
como yo misma,
al mundo real de su cocina.

After Reading

Making Connections

1. To which selection did you most relate? Why?

2. Look at the first statement in "Inequalities." Is it a **fact** (an indisputable truth) or an **opinion** (a belief)? How could you prove or disprove this?

3. What are some of the **supporting details** from "Inequalities"?

4. In "Indians," the writer repeats the phrase "here before" six times. How does the use of **repetition** affect the poem?

5. Describe the life of the narrator of "The Changeling."

6. What defense do you think the parents of "The Changeling" and "Inequalities" could put up to explain and justify their behavior?

7. 👁 How does the author of "Inequalities" express her special qualities, her **individuality?**

8. Do you believe that life isn't always fair? Explain.

Literary Focus: Point of View

All stories are told from a particular **point of view.** In a first-person narrative, a story is told from one person's point of view. The person may be speaking for himself or herself or for a group. The use of the pronouns *I* and *we* are clear indicators that the story is in the first person. For example, "*I* went to the store," or "*We* discovered the treasure." A story in the third person is told by a person who is outside of the action. Third-person writing can be recognized by the pronouns *he, she,* and *they.* Look through some of the stories you have read and decide whether they are first- or third-person narratives. Record your findings in a chart like the one below.

Selection	First Person	Third Person
"The Treasure of Lemon Brown"		✔

Vocabulary Study

On a sheet of paper, write the vocabulary word that completes each sentence.

Most brothers are slobs, and my brother is no __(1)__. Despite his grungy appearance, however, he's rather self-assured. You'd know what I mean if you saw him __(2)__ down the street. He's competitive. Whenever we __(3)__ for anything, he invariably wins.

The other day I read a story to my little sister about a frog who was __(4)__ into a prince. It made me wonder whether my brother will ever undergo a __(5)__ of his own—one that turns him into a human being. Oh, well, despite his faults, he's really not all that bad—for a brother, that is.

Expressing Your Ideas

Writing Choices

Details, Details Write an **essay** on whether or not girls are treated differently than boys. Start with a main idea and then add supporting details from *your* experience.

What's Going On? Write a two- or three-sentence **caption** for this "storyteller" sculpture by Helen Cordero of Cochito Pueblo, New Mexico. Try to work the words *communication* and *culture* into the caption.

Other Options

That's Debatable Organize a **debate** about gender equality. The question to be debated is: Are men and women equal? Try to make the teams as equal as possible in terms of gender.

A Sure Oscar With a partner, **role-play** a discussion between a girl and her mother. Choose either the mother in "Inequalities" or the mother in "The Changeling." What would the mother say to defend her point of view?

Pictures Don't Lie Look through magazines to find examples of how expectations for men and women are expressed through advertisements. If possible, locate magazines from different countries or cultures to see if expectations differ. Make a **collage** that shows the ways in which men and women are portrayed in advertisements.

Before Reading

Flowers for Algernon

by Daniel Keyes

Daniel Keyes
born 1927

Of "Flowers for Algernon" Daniel Keyes writes, "I recall clearly the brief note in my 'idea folder,' something like: 'What would happen if a person's intelligence could be increased by surgery or something like that?' But that's all it was—an idea—until more than five years later a retarded boy said to me: 'Mr. Keyes, if I try hard and become smart will they put me into a regular class and let me be like everyone else?' The impact of those words stayed with me for a long time afterwards, until one day idea fused with character and I began to write 'Flowers for Algernon.' "

Building Background

The Story "Flowers for Algernon" was first published in *The Magazine of Fantasy and Science Fiction* in 1959. The story was expanded into a full-length novel, and then made into a movie called *Charly,* a musical play, and a TV production. For many people, it is a perfect example of good science fiction, because the hero is an ordinary man, and what happens to him seems to be something that might be possible a few years from now.

Getting into the Story

Writer's Notebook Make a list of the ways in which you have changed since you were in second grade. You may want to structure your list in this way:

When I was in second grade I:	Now I:
• wrote in pencil	• write in ink
• played with dolls	• play video games

Reading Tip

Keeping a Reading Log To help you keep track of the events and the characters in "Flowers for Algernon," set up a **double-entry log** in a format similar to the one below. First, draw a line down the middle of a page in your notebook. As you read, stop periodically and copy a **phrase** or a few words from the story. These entries will go on the left side of the page. On the other side, you will respond to what you have read by **questioning, clarifying, predicting, summarizing,** or **evaluating.**

Left Side of Page	Right Side of Page
Page **486** **Phrase:** "I had my rabits foot"	**Clarify:** He's superstitious. **Evaluate:** He's a bad speller. **Question:** Is he uneducated?

Flowers for Algernon

Daniel Keyes

Flowers is by Pablo Picasso. How does this image complement the Charlie Gordon that we meet at the beginning of this story?

progris riport 1—martch 5 1965

Dr. Strauss says I shud rite down what I think and evrey thing that happins to me from now on. I dont know why but he says its importint so they will see if they will use me. I hope they use me. Miss Kinnian says maybe they can make me smart. I want to be smart. My name is Charlie Gordon. I am 37 years old and 2 weeks ago was my brithday. I have nuthing more to rite now so I will close for today.

progris riport 2—march 6

I had a test today. I think I faled it. and I think that maybe now they wont use me. What happind is a nice young man was in the room and he had some white cards with ink spillled all over them. He sed Charlie what do you see on this card. I was very skared even tho I had my rabits foot in my pockit because when I was a kid I always faled tests in school and I spillled ink to.

I told him I saw a inkblot. He said yes and it made me feel good. I thot that was all but when I got up to go he stopped me. He said now sit down Charlie we are not thru yet. Then I don't remember so good but he wantid me to say what was in the ink. I dint see nuthing in the ink but he said there was picturs there other pepul saw some picturs. I couldnt see any picturs. I reely tryed to see. I held the card close up and then far away. Then I said if I had my glases I could see better I usally only ware my glases in the movies or TV but I said they are in the closit in the hall. I got them. Then I said let me see that card agen I bet Ill find it now.

I tryed hard but I still coudnt find the picturs I only saw the ink. I told him maybe I need new glases. He rote somthing down on a paper and I got skared of faling the test. I told him it was a very nice inkblot with littel points all around the eges. He looked very sad so that wasnt it. I said please let me try agen. Ill get it in a few minits becaus Im not so fast somtimes. Im a slow reeder too in Miss Kinnians class for slow adults but Im trying very hard.

He gave me a chance with another card that had 2 kinds of ink spillled on it red and blue.

He was very nice and talked slow like Miss Kinnian does and he explaned it to me that it was a *raw shok*.[1] He said pepul see things in the ink. I said show me where. He said think. I told him I think a inkblot but that wasnt rite eather. He said what does it remind you—pretend something. I closd my eyes for a long time to pretend. I told him I pretned a fowntan pen with ink leeking all over a table cloth. Then he got up and went out.

I dont think I passd the *raw shok* test.

SUMMARIZE: What do you know about Charlie so far?

progris report 3—martch 7

Dr Strauss and Dr Nemur say it dont matter about the inkblots. I told them I dint spill the ink on the cards and I coudnt see anything in the ink. They said that maybe they will still use me. I said Miss Kinnian never gave me tests like that one only spelling and reading. They said Miss Kinnian told that I was her bestist pupil in the adult nite scool becaus I tryed the hardist and I reely wantid to lern. They said how come you went to the adult nite scool all by yourself Charlie. How did you find it. I said I askd pepul and sumbody told me where I shud go to lern to read and spell good. They said why did you want to. I told them becaus all my life I wantid to be smart and not dumb. But its very hard to be smart. They said you know it will probly be tempirery. I said yes. Miss Kinnian told me. I dont care if it herts.

Later I had more crazy tests today. The nice lady who gave it me told me the name and I asked her how do you spellit so I can rite it in my progris riport. THEMATIC APPERCEPTION TEST.[2] I dont know the frist 2 words but I know what *test* means. You got to pass it or you get bad marks. This test lookd easy becaus I could see the picturs. Only this time she dint want me to tell her the picturs.

---

1. **raw shok:** Charlie means the Rorschach (rô′shōk) test, a psychological test used to gain information about personality traits and intellect.
2. **Thematic Apperception Test,** another psychological test.

That mixd me up. I said the man yesterday said I should tell him what I saw in the ink she said that dont make no difrence. She said make up storys about the pepul in the picturs.

I told her how can you tell storys about pepul you never met. I said why shud I make up lies. I never tell lies any more becaus I always get caut.

She told me this test and the other one the raw-shok was for getting personalty. I laffed so hard. I said how can you get that thing from inkblots and fotos. She got sore and put her picturs away. I dont care. It was sily. I gess I faled that test too.

Later some men in white coats took me to a difernt part of the hospitil and gave me a game to play. It was like a race with a white mouse. They called the mouse Algernon. Algernon was in a box with a lot of twists and turns like all kinds of walls and they gave me a pencil and a paper with lines and lots of boxes. On one side it said START and on the other end it said FINISH. They said it was *amazed* [3] and that Algernon and me had the same *amazed* to do. I

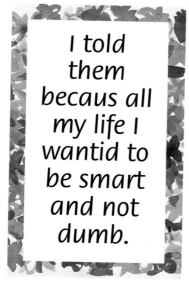

I told them becaus all my life I wantid to be smart and not dumb.

dint see how we could have the same *amazed* if Algernon had a box and I had a paper but I dint say nothing. Anyway there wasnt time because the race started.

One of the men had a watch he was trying to hide so I woudnt see it so I tryed not to look and that made me nervus.

Anyway that test made me feel worser than all the others because they did it over 10 times with difernt *amazeds* and Algernon won every

time. I dint know that mice were so smart. Maybe thats because Algernon is a white mouse. Maybe white mice are smarter than other mice.

progris riport 4—Mar 8

Their going to use me! Im so exited I can hardly write. Dr Nemur and Dr Strauss had a argament about it first. Dr Nemur was in the office when Dr Strauss brot me in. Dr Nemur was worryed about using me but Dr Strauss told him Miss Kinnian rekemmended me the best from all the people who she was teaching. I like Miss Kinnian becaus shes a very smart teacher. And she said Charlie your going to have a second chance. If you volenteer for this experament you mite get smart. They dont know if it will be perminint but theirs a chance. Thats why I said ok even when I was scared because she said it was an operashun. She said dont be scared Charlie you done so much with so little I think you deserv it most of all.

So I got scaird when Dr Nemur and Dr Strauss argud about it. Dr Strauss said I had something that was very good. He said I had a good *motor-vation*. I never even knew I had that. I felt proud when he said that not every body with an eye-q of 68 [4] had that thing. I dont know what it is or where I got it but he said Algernon had it too. Algernons *motor-vation* is the cheese they put in his box. But it cant be that because I didnt eat any cheese this week.

Then he told Dr Nemur something I dint understand so while they were talking I wrote down some of the words.

He said Dr Nemur I know Charlie is not what you had in mind as the first of your new brede of intelek** (coudnt get the word)

---

3. **amazed,** Charlie means a maze, a confusing network of paths through which one must find one's way.
4. **eye-q of 68.** An average I.Q. is 100.

superman. But most people of his low ment** are host** and uncoop** they are usualy dull apath** and hard to reach. He has a good natcher hes intristed and eager to please.

Dr Nemur said remember he will be the first human beeng ever to have his intelijence trippled by surgicle meens.

Dr Strauss said exakly. Look at how well hes lerned to read and write for his low mentel age its as grate an acheve** as you and I lerning einstines therey of **vity without help. That shows the intenss motorvation. Its comparat** a tremen** achev** I say we use Charlie.

I dint get all the words and they were talking to fast but it sounded like Dr Strauss was on my side and like the other one wasnt.

Then Dr Nemur nodded he said all right maybe your right. We will use Charlie. When he said that I got so exited I jumped up and shook his hand for being so good to me. I told him thank you doc you wont be sorry for giving me a second chance. And I mean it like I told him. After the operashun Im gonna try to be smart. Im gonna try awful hard.

PREDICT: What do you think will happen to Charlie?

progris ript 5—Mar 10

Im skared. Lots of people who work here and the nurses and the people who gave me the tests came to bring me candy and wish me luck. I hope I have luck. I got my rabits foot and my lucky penny and my horse shoe. Only a black cat crossed me when I was comming to the hospitil. Dr Strauss says dont be supersitis Charlie this is sience. Anyway Im keeping my rabits foot with me.

I asked Dr Strauss if Ill beat Algernon in the race after the operashun and he said maybe. If the operashun works Ill show that mouse I can be as smart as he is. Maybe

smarter. Then Ill be abel to read better and spell the words good and know lots of things and be like other people. I want to be smart like other people. If it works perminint they will make everybody smart all over the wurld.

They dint give me anything to eat this morning. I dont know what that eating has to do with getting smart. Im very hungry and Dr Nemur took away my box of candy. That Dr Nemur is a grouch. Dr Strauss says I can have it back after the operashun. You cant eat befor a operashun . . .

Progress Report 6—Mar 15

The operashun dint hurt. He did it while I was sleeping. They took off the bandijis from my eyes and my head today so I can make a **PROGRESS REPORT**. Dr Nemur who looked at some of my other ones says I spell **PROGRESS** wrong and he told me how to spell it and **REPORT** too. I got to try and remember that.

I have a very bad memary for spelling. Dr Strauss says its ok to tell about all the things that happin to me but he says I shoud tell more about what I feel and what I think. When I told him I dont know how to think he said try. All the time when the bandijis were on my eyes I tryed to think. Nothing happened. I dont know what to think about. Maybe if I ask him he will tell me how I can think now that Im suppose to get smart. What do smart people think about. Fancy things I suppose. I wish I knew some fancy things alredy.

Progress Report 7—mar 19

Nothing is happining. I had lots of tests and different kinds of races with Algernon. I hate that mouse. He always beats me. Dr Strauss said I got to play those games. And he said some time I got to take those tests over again. Thse inkblots are stupid. And those pictures are stupid too. I like to draw a picture of a man and a woman but I wont make up lies about people.

I got a headache from trying to think so much. I thot Dr Strauss was my frend but he dont help me. He dont tell me what to think or when Ill get smart. Miss Kinnian dint come to see me. I think writing these progress reports are stupid too.

Progress Report 8—Mar 23

Im going back to work at the factery. They said it was better I shud go back to work but I cant tell any- one what the operashun was for and I have to come to the hospitil for an hour evry night after work. They are gonna pay me mony every month for lern- ing to be smart.

Im glad Im going back to work because I miss my job and all my frends and all the fun we have there.

Dr Strauss says I shud keep writing things down but I dont have to do it every day just when I think of something or something speshul happins. He says dont get discoridged because it takes time and it happins slow. He says it took a long time with Algernon before he got 3 times smarter then he was before. Thats why Algernon beats me all the time because he had that operashun too. That makes me feel better. I coud probly do that *amazed* faster than a reglar mouse. Maybe some day Ill beat Algernon. Boy that would be some- thing. So far Algernon looks like he mite be smart perminent.

Mar 25 (I dont have to write PROGRESS REPORT on top any more just when I hand it

in once a week for Dr Nemur to read. I just have to put the date on. That saves time)

We had a lot of fun at the factery today. Joe Carp said hey look where Charlie had his operashun what did they do Charlie put some brains in. I was going to tell him but I remembered Dr Strauss said no. Then Frank Reilly said what did you do Charlie forget your key and open your door the hard way. That made me laff. Their really my friends and they like me.

Sometimes somebody will say hey look at Joe or Frank or George he really pulled a Charlie Gordon. I dont know why they say that but they always laff. This morning Amos Borg who is the 4 man at Donnegans used my name when he shouted at Ernie the office boy. Ernie lost a packige. He said Ernie what are you trying to be a Charlie Gordon. I dont understand why he said that. I never lost any packiges.

Mar 28 Dr Strauss came to my room tonight to see why I dint come in like I was suppose to. I told him I dont like to race with Algernon any more. He said I dont have to for a while but I shud come in. He had a present for me only it wasnt a present but just for lend. I thot it was a little televi- sion but it wasnt. He said I got to turn it on when I go to sleep. I said your kidding why shud I turn it on when Im going to sleep. Who ever herd of a thing like that. But he said if I want to get smart I got to do what he says. I told him I dint think I was going to get smart and he put his hand on my sholder and said Charlie you dont know it yet but your getting smarter all the time. You wont notice for a while. I think he was just being nice to make me feel good because I dont look any smarter.

Oh yes I almost forgot. I asked him when I can go back to the class at Miss Kinnians school. He said I wont go their. He said that soon Miss Kinnian will come to the hospitil to

> If the operashun works Ill show that mouse I can be as smart as he is.

start and teach me speshul. I was mad at her for not comming to see me when I got the operashun but I like her so maybe we will be frends again.

Mar 29 That crazy TV kept me up all night. How can I sleep with something yelling crazy things all night in my ears. And the nutty pictures. Wow. I dont know what it says when Im up so how am I going to know when Im sleeping.

Dr Strauss says its ok. He says my brains are lerning when I sleep and that will help me when Miss Kinnian starts my lessons in the hospitl (only I found out it isnt a hospitil its a labatory). I think its all crazy. If you can get smart when your sleeping why do people go to school. That thing I dont think will work. I use to watch the late show and the late late show on TV all the time and it never made me smart. Maybe you have to sleep while you watch it.

PROGRESS REPORT 9—April 3

Dr Strauss showed me how to keep the TV turned low so now I can sleep. I dont hear a thing. And I still dont understand what it says. A few times I play it over in the morning to find out what I lerned when I was sleeping and I dont think so. Miss Kinnian says Maybe its another langwidge or something. But most times it sounds american. It talks so fast faster then even Miss Gold who was my teacher in 6 grade and I remember she talked so fast I coudnt understand her.

I told Dr Strauss what good is it to get smart in my sleep. I want to be smart when Im awake. He says its the same thing and I have two minds. Theres the *subconscious* and the *conscious* (that's how you spell it). And one dont tell the other one what its doing. They dont even talk to each other. Thats why I dream. And boy have I been having crazy dreams. Wow. Ever since that night TV. The late late late late late show.

I forgot to ask him if it was only me or if everybody had those two minds.

(I just looked up the word in the dictionary Dr Strauss gave me. The word is *subconscious. adj. Of the nature of mental operations yet not present in consciousness; as, subconscious conflict of desires.*) Theres more but I still don't know what it means. This isnt a very good dictionary for dumb people like me.

Anyway the headache is from the party. My frends from the factery Joe Carp and Frank Reilly invited me to go with them to Muggsys Saloon for some drinks. I dont like to drink but they said we will have lots of fun. I had a good time.

Joe Carp said I shoud show the girls how I mop out the toilet in the factory and he got me a mop. I showed them and everyone laffed when I told that Mr Donnegan said I was the best janiter he ever had because I like my job and do it good and never come late or miss a day except for my operashun.

I said Miss Kinnian always said Charlie be proud of your job because you do it good.

Everybody laffed and we had a good time and they gave me lots of drinks and Joe said Charlie is a card when hes potted. I dont know what that means but everybody likes me and we have fun. I cant wait to be smart like my best frends Joe Carp and Frank Reilly.

I dont remember how the party was over but I think I went out to buy a newspaper and coffe for Joe and Frank and when I came back there was no one their. I looked for them all over till late. Then I dont remember so good but I think I got sleepy or sick. A nice cop brot me back home. Thats what my landlady Mrs Flynn says.

But I got a headache and a big lump on my head and black and blue all over. I think maybe I fell but Joe Carp says it was the cop they beat up drunks some times. I don't think

This painting by Etienne Delessert was done to illustrate "Flowers for Algernon." Why do you think it shows the mouse and the maze inside the man's head? ➤

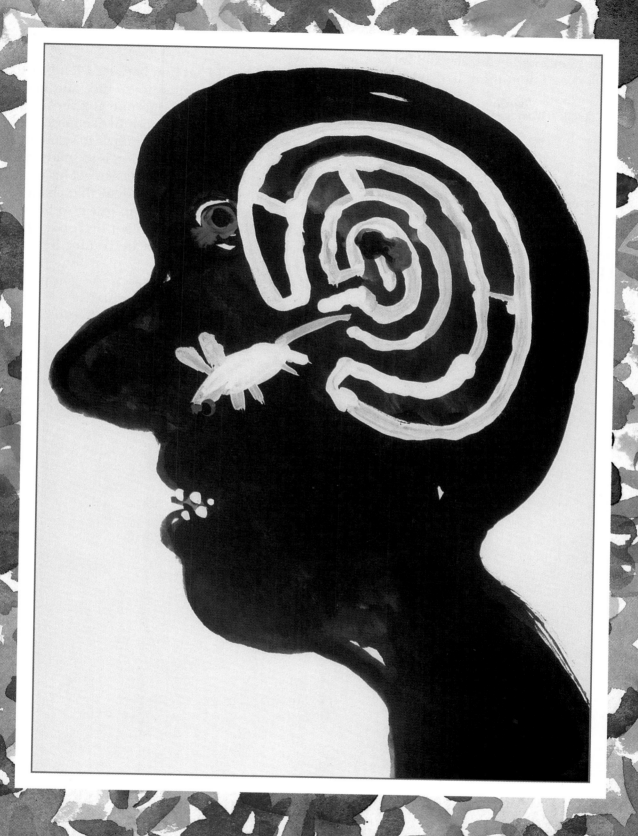

so. Miss Kinnian says cops are to help people. Anyway I got a bad headache and Im sick and hurt all over. I dont think Ill drink anymore.

CLARIFY: What are Charlie's friends like?

April 6 I beat Algernon! I dint even know I beat him until Burt the tester told me. Then the second time I lost because I got so exited I fell off the chair before I finished. But after that I beat him 8 more times. I must be getting smart to beat a smart mouse like Algernon. But I dont *feel* smarter.

I wanted to race Algernon some more but Burt said thats enough for one day. They let me hold him for a minit. Hes not so bad. Hes soft like a ball of cotton. He blinks and when he opens his eyes their black and pink on the edges.

I said can I feed him because I felt bad to beat him and I wanted to be nice and make frends. Burt said no Algernon is a very specshul mouse with an operashun like mine, and he was the first of all the animals to stay smart so long. He told me Algernon is so smart that every day he has to solve a test to get his food. Its a thing like a lock on a door that changes every time Algernon goes in to eat so he has to lern something new to get his food. That made me sad because if he coudnt lern he would be hungry.

I dont think its right to make you pass a test to eat. How woud Dr Nemur like it to have to pass a test every time he wants to eat. I think Ill be frends with Algernon.

After Reading

Making Connections (pages 485–492)

1. Describe your first impression of Charlie.

2. What are some of the ways in which the author indicates through Charlie's writing that Charlie's intelligence is below average?

3. How do you think this story relates to the **theme** "Life's Not Always Fair"?

4. What do you think is Charlie's most important **character trait?** Is it his kindness? His drive and determination? Something else? Explain.

5. The author utilizes **dramatic irony** when he lets the reader know that Charlie's friends are laughing at him instead of with him. What effect does this use of irony have on the reader?

6. What might be some of the things that are right about conducting experiments involving the human mind? What might be some things that are wrong about such experiments?

Expressing Your Ideas

Measure Your Smarts Working with several other students, use library resources to find out more about IQ. What *is* an IQ? How is it measured? What is an average IQ? Why is it considered something worth measuring? Why do some experts believe that IQs are not a reliable measure of intelligence? Prepare an **oral report** based on your findings.

I See a . . . Make your own inkblots for a Rorschach test. Dab one or two colors of paint on a card, then fold the card in half to spread the paint. Open the card again to let the paint dry. Then **interview** each of your classmates to find out what "pictures" they see. Record the anonymous responses on the board and discuss them with your classmates. Are there any patterns?

Fill in the Blank Go back and **complete** the asterisked (*) unfinished words from Charlie's March 8 report. Compare your answers with a classmate's. Do your answers match?

PROGRESS REPORT 10

April 9 Tonight after work Miss Kinnian was at the laboratory. She looked like she was glad to see me but scared. I told her dont worry Miss Kinnian Im not smart yet and she laffed. She said I have confidence in you Charlie the way you struggled so hard to read and right better than all the others. At werst you will have it for a littel wile and your doing somthing for sience.

We are reading a very hard book. I never read such a hard book before. Its called *Robinson Crusoe* about a man who gets merooned on a dessert Iland. Hes smart and figers out all kinds of things so he can have a house and food and hes a good swimmer. Only I feel sorry because hes all alone and has no frends. But I think their must be somebody else on the iland because theres a picture with his funny umbrella looking at footprints. I hope he gets a frend and not be lonly.

April 10 Miss Kinnian teaches me to spell better. She says look at a word and close your eyes and say it over and over until you remember. I have lots of truble with *through* that you say *threw* and *enough* and *tough* that you don't say *enew* and *tew*. You got to say *enuff* and *tuff*. Thats how I use to write it before I started to get smart. Im confused but Miss Kinnian says theres no reason in spelling.

Apr 14 Finished *Robinson Crusoe*. I want to find out more about what happens to him but Miss Kinnian says thats all there is. *Why*

QUESTION: What is happening to Charlie?

April 15 Miss Kinnian says Im lerning fast. She read some of the Progress Reports and she looked at me kind of funny. She says Im a fine person and Ill show them all. I asked her why. She said never mind but I shoudnt feel bad if I find out that everybody isnt nice like I think. She said for a person who god gave so little to you done more then a lot of people with brains they never even used. I said all my frends are smart people but there good. They like me and they never did anything that wasnt nice. Then she got something in her eye and she had to run out to the ladys room.

Apr 16 Today, I lerned, the *comma*, this is a comma (,) a period, with a tail, Miss Kinnian, says its importent, because, it makes writing, better, she said, sombeody, coud lose, a lot of money, if a comma, isnt, in the, right place, I dont have, any money, and I dont see, how a comma, keeps you, from losing it,

But she says, everybody, uses commas, so Ill use, them too,

Apr 17 I used the comma wrong. Its punctuation. Miss Kinnian told me to look up long words in the dictionary to lern to spell them. I said whats the difference if you can read it anyway. She said its part of your education so now on Ill look up all the words Im not sure how to spell. It takes a long time to write that way but I think Im remembering. I only have to look up once and after that I get it right. Anyway thats how come I got the word *punctuation* right. (Its that way in the dictionary). Miss Kinnian says a period is punctuation too, and there are lots of other marks to lern. I told her I thot all the periods had to have tails but she said no.

You got to mix them up, she showed? me" how. to mix! them (up,. and now; I can! mix up all kinds" of punctuation, in! my writing? There, are lots! of rules? to lern; but Im gettin'g them in my head.

One thing I? like about, Dear Miss Kinnian: (thats the way it goes in a business letter if I ever go into business) is she, always gives me' a reason" when—I ask. She's a gen'ius! I wish! I cou'd be smart" like, her;

(Punctuation, is; fun!)

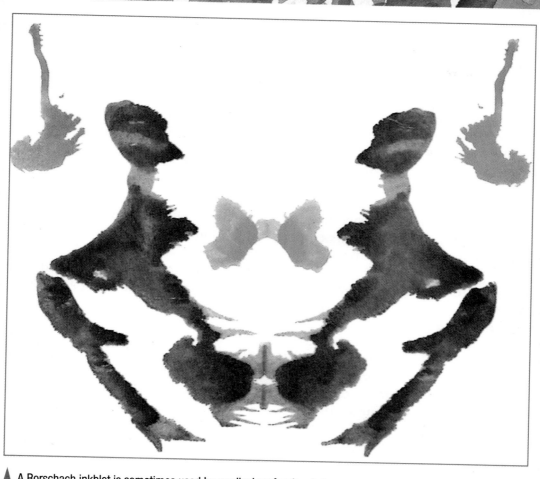

▲ A Rorschach inkblot is sometimes used by medical professionals to measure personality traits and general intelligence. It is made by dropping ink on a page and folding it in half. Why do you think this kind of image might reveal personality traits?

April 18 What a dope I am! I didn't even understand what she was talking about. I read the grammar book last night and it explanes the whole thing. Then I saw it was the same way as Miss Kinnian was trying to tell me, but I didn't get it. I got up in the middle of the night, and the whole thing straightened out in my mind.

Miss Kinnian said that the TV working in my sleep helped out. She said I reached a plateau.[1] Thats like the flat top of a hill.

After I figgered out how punctuation worked, I read over all my old Progress

---

1. **plateau** (pla tō′), *n.* period or state of stability or little or no growth.

Reports from the beginning. Boy, did I have crazy spelling and punctuation! I told Miss Kinnian I ought to go over the pages and fix all the mistakes but she said, "No, Charlie, Dr. Nemur wants them just as they are. That's why he let you keep them after they were photostated, to see your own progress. You're coming along fast, Charlie."

That made me feel good. After the lesson I went down and played with Algernon. We don't race anymore.

April 20 I feel sick inside. Not sick like for a doctor, but inside my chest it feels empty like getting punched and a heartburn at the same time.

I wasn't going to write about it, but I guess I got to, because it's important. Today was the first time I ever stayed home from work.

Last night Joe Carp and Frank Reilly invited me to a party. There were lots of girls and some men from the factory. I remembered how sick I got last time I drank too much, so I told Joe I didn't want anything to drink. He gave me a plain Coke instead. It tasted funny, but I thought it was just a bad taste in my mouth.

We had a lot of fun for a while. Joe said I should dance with Ellen and she would teach me the steps. I fell a few times and I couldn't understand why because no one else was dancing besides Ellen and me. And all the time I was tripping because somebody's foot was always sticking out.

Then when I got up I saw the look on Joe's face and it gave me a funny feeling in my stomach. "He's a scream," one of the girls said. Everybody was laughing.

Frank said, "I ain't laughed so much since we sent him off for the newspaper that night at Muggsy's and ditched him."

"Look at him. His face is red."

"He's blushing. Charlie is blushing."

"Hey, Ellen, what'd you do to Charlie? I never saw him act like that before."

I didn't know what to do or where to turn. Everyone was looking at me and laughing and I felt naked. I wanted to hide myself. I ran out into the street and I threw up. Then I walked home. It's a funny thing I never knew that Joe and Frank and the others liked to have me around all the time to make fun of me.

Now I know what it means when they say "to pull a Charlie Gordon."

I'm ashamed.

PROGRESS REPORT 11

April 21 Still didn't go into the factory. I told Mrs. Flynn my landlady to call and tell Mr. Donnegan I was sick. Mrs. Flynn looks at me very funny lately like she's scared of me.

I think it's a good thing about finding out how everybody laughs at me. I thought about it a lot. It's because I'm so dumb and I don't even know when I'm doing something dumb. People think it's funny when a dumb person can't do things the same way they can.

Anyway, now I know I'm getting smarter every day. I know punctuation and I can spell good. I like to look up all the hard words in the dictionary and I remember them. I'm reading a lot now, and Miss Kinnian says I read very fast. Sometimes I even understand what I'm reading about, and it stays in my mind. There are times when I can close my eyes and think of a page and it all comes back like a picture.

Besides history, geography, and arithmetic, Miss Kinnian said I should start to learn a few foreign languages. Dr. Strauss gave me some more tapes to play while I sleep. I still don't understand how that conscious and unconscious mind works, but Dr. Strauss says not to worry yet. He asked me to promise that when I start learning college subjects next week I wouldn't read any books on psychology—that is, until he gives me permission.

I feel a lot better today, but I guess I'm still a little angry that all the time people were laughing and making fun of me because I wasn't so smart. When I become intelligent like Dr. Strauss says, with three times my I.Q. of 68, then maybe I'll be like everyone else and people will like me and be friendly.

I'm not sure what an I.Q. is. Dr. Nemur said it was something that measured how intelligent you were—like a scale in the drugstore weighs pounds. But Dr. Strauss had a big argument with him and said an I.Q. didn't weigh intelligence at all. He said an I.Q. showed how much intelligence you could get, like the numbers on the outside of a measuring cup. You still had to fill the cup up with stuff.

Then when I asked Burt, who gives me my intelligence tests and works with Algernon, he said that both of them were wrong (only I had to promise not to tell them he said so). Burt says that the I.Q. measures a lot of different things including some of the things you learned already, and it really isn't any good at all.

So I still don't know what I.Q. is except that mine is going to be over 200 soon. I didn't want to say anything, but I don't see how if they don't know *what* it is, or *where* it is—I don't see how they know *how much* of it you've got.

Dr. Nemur says I have to take a *Rorshach Test* tomorrow. I wonder what *that* is.

PREDICT: When Charlie's I.Q. triples, do you think people will like him?

April 22 I found out what a *Rorschach* is. It's the test I took before the operation—the one with the inkblots on the pieces of cardboard. The man who gave me the test was the same one.

I was scared to death of those inkblots. I knew he was going to ask me to find the pictures and I knew I wouldn't be able to. I was thinking to myself, if only there was some way of knowing what kind of pictures were hidden there. Maybe there weren't any pictures at all. Maybe it was just a trick to see if I was dumb enough to look for something that wasn't there. Just thinking about that made me sore at him.

"All right, Charlie," he said, "you've seen these cards before, remember?"

"Of course I remember."

The way I said it, he knew I was angry, and he looked surprised. "Yes, of course. Now I want you to look at this one. What might this be? What do you see on this card? People see all sorts of things in these inkblots. Tell me what it might be for you—what it makes you think of."

I was shocked. That wasn't what I had expected him to say at all. "You mean there are no pictures hidden in those inkblots?"

He frowned and took off his glasses. "What?"

"Pictures. Hidden in the inkblots. Last time you told me that everyone could see them and you wanted me to find them too."

He explained to me that the last time he had used almost the exact same words he was using now. I didn't believe it, and I still have the suspicion that he misled me at the time just for the fun of it. Unless—I don't know any more—could I have been *that* feeble-minded?

We went through the cards slowly. One of them looked like a pair of bats tugging at something. Another one looked like two men fencing with swords. I imagined all sorts of things. I guess I got carried away. But I didn't trust him any more, and I kept turning them around and even looking on the back to

> After the lesson I went down and played with Algernon. We don't race anymore.

see if there was anything there I was supposed to catch. While he was making his notes, I peeked out of the corner of my eye to read it. But it was all in code that looked like this:

WF + A DdF-Ad orig. WF-A SF + obj

The test still doesn't make sense to me. It seems to me that anyone could make up lies about things that they didn't really see. How could he know I wasn't making a fool of him by mentioning things that I didn't really imagine? Maybe I'll understand it when Dr. Strauss lets me read up on psychology.

April 25 I figured out a new way to line up the machines in the factory, and Mr. Donnegan says it will save him ten thousand dollars a year in labor and increased production. He gave me a twenty-five-dollar bonus.

I wanted to take Joe Carp and Frank Reilly out to lunch to celebrate, but Joe said he had to buy some things for his wife, and Frank said he was meeting his cousin for lunch. I guess it'll take a little time for them to get used to the changes in me. Everybody seems to be frightened of me. When I went over to Amos Borg and tapped him on the shoulder, he jumped up in the air.

People don't talk to me much any more or kid around the way they used to. It makes the job kind of lonely.

April 27 I got up the nerve today to ask Miss Kinnian to have dinner with me tomorrow night to celebrate my bonus.

At first she wasn't sure it was right, but I asked Dr. Strauss and he said it was okay. Dr. Strauss and Dr. Nemur don't seem to be getting along so well. They're arguing all the time. This evening when I came in to ask Dr. Strauss about having dinner with Miss Kinnian, I heard him shouting. Dr. Nemur was saying that it was *his* experiment and *his* research, and Dr. Strauss was shouting back that he contributed just as much, because he

found me through Miss Kinnian and he performed the operation. Dr. Strauss said that someday thousands of neurosurgeons might be using his technique all over the world.

Dr. Nemur wanted to publish the results of the experiment at the end of this month. Dr. Strauss wanted to wait a while longer to be sure. Dr. Strauss said that Dr. Nemur was more interested in the Chair of Psychology at Princeton[2] than he was in the experiment. Dr. Nemur said that Dr. Strauss was nothing but an opportunist[3] who was trying to ride to glory on *his* coattails.

It worked, didn't it? Even Algernon is still smart.

When I left afterwards, I found myself trembling. I don't know why for sure, but it was as if I'd seen both men clearly for the first time. I remember hearing Burt say that Dr. Nemur had a shrew of a wife who was pushing him all the time to get things published so that he could become famous. Burt said that the dream of her life was to have a big-shot husband.

Was Dr. Strauss really trying to ride on his coattails?

April 28 I don't understand why I never noticed how beautiful Miss Kinnian really is. She has brown eyes and feathery brown hair that comes to the top of her neck. She's only thirty-four! I think from the beginning I had

---

2. **Chair of Psychology at Princeton,** a high-ranking professor of psychology at Princeton University.
3. **opportunist** (op/ər tü/nist), *n.* a person who uses every opportunity to gain some advantage, regardless of right or wrong.

the feeling that she was an unreachable genius—and very, very old. Now, every time I see her she grows younger and more lovely.

We had dinner and a long talk. When she said that I was coming along so fast that soon I'd be leaving her behind, I laughed.

"It's true, Charlie. You're already a better reader than I am. You can read a whole page at a glance while I can take in only a few lines at a time. And you remember every single thing you read. I'm lucky if I can recall the main thoughts and the general meaning."

"I don't feel intelligent. There are so many things I don't understand."

She took out a cigarette and I lit it for her. "You've got to be a *little* patient. You're accomplishing in days and weeks what it takes normal people to do in half a lifetime. That's what makes it so amazing. You're like a giant sponge now, soaking things in. Facts, figures, general knowledge. And soon you'll begin to connect them, too. You'll see how the different branches of learning are related. There are many levels, Charlie, like steps on a giant ladder that take you up higher and higher to see more and more of the world around you.

"I can see only a little bit of that, Charlie, and I won't go much higher than I am now, but you'll keep climbing up and up, and see more and more, and each step will open new worlds that you never even knew existed." She frowned. "I hope . . . I just hope—"

"What?"

"Never mind, Charles. I just hope I wasn't wrong to advise you to go into this in the first place."

I laughed. "How could that be? It worked, didn't it? Even Algernon is still smart."

We sat there silently for a while and I knew what she was thinking about as she watched me toying with the chain of my rabbit's foot and my keys. I didn't want to think of that possibility any more than elderly people want to think of death. I *knew* that this was only the beginning. I knew what she meant about levels

because I'd seen some of them already. The thought of leaving her behind made me sad.

I'm in love with Miss Kinnian.

SUMMARIZE: How is Charlie's relationship with Miss Kinnian changing?

PROGRESS REPORT 12

April 30 I've quit my job with Donnegan's Plastic Box Company. Mr. Donnegan insisted that it would be better for all concerned if I left. What did I do to make them hate me so?

The first I knew of it was when Mr. Donnegan showed me the petition.[4] Eight hundred and forty names, everyone connected with the factory, except Fanny Girden. Scanning the list quickly, I saw at once that hers was the only missing name. All the rest demanded that I be fired.

Joe Carp and Frank Reilly wouldn't talk to me about it. No one else would either, except Fanny. She was one of the few people I'd known who set her mind to something and believed it no matter what the rest of the world proved, said, or did—and Fanny did not believe that I should have been fired. She had been against the petition on principle and despite the pressure and threats she'd held out.

"Which don't mean to say," she remarked, "that I don't think there's something mighty strange about you, Charlie. Them changes. I don't know. You used to be a good, dependable, ordinary man—not too bright maybe, but honest. Who knows what you done to yourself to get so smart all of a sudden. Like everybody around here's been saying, Charlie, it's not right."

"But how can you say that, Fanny? What's wrong with a man becoming intelligent and

---

4. **petition** (pə tish′ən), *n.* a formal request to an authority to have something done.

wanting to acquire knowledge and understanding of the world around him?"

She stared down at her work and I turned to leave. Without looking at me, she said: "It was evil when Eve listened to the snake and ate from the tree of knowledge. It was evil when she saw that she was naked. If not for that none of us would ever have to grow old and sick, and die."[5]

Once again now I have the feeling of shame burning inside me. This intelligence has driven a wedge between me and all the people I once knew and loved. Before, they laughed at me and despised me for my ignorance and dullness; now, they hate me for my knowledge and understanding. What do they want of me?

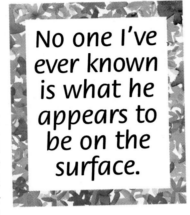

No one I've ever known is what he appears to be on the surface.

They've driven me out of the factory. Now I'm more alone than ever before . . .

May 15 Dr. Strauss is very angry at me for not having written any progress reports in two weeks. He's justified because the lab is now paying me a regular salary. I told him I was too busy thinking and reading. When I pointed out that writing was such a slow process that it made me impatient with my poor handwriting, he suggested that I learn to type. It's much easier to write now because I can type nearly seventy-five words a minute. Dr. Strauss continually reminds me of the need to speak and write simply so that people will be able to understand me.

I'll try to review all the things that happened to me during the last two weeks. Algernon and I were presented to the American Psychological Association sitting in convention with the World Psychological Association last Tuesday.

We created quite a sensation. Dr. Nemur and Dr. Strauss were proud of us.

I suspect that Dr. Nemur, who is sixty—ten years older than Dr. Strauss—finds it necessary to see tangible[6] results of his work. Undoubtedly the result of pressure by Mrs. Nemur.

Contrary to my earlier impressions of him, I realize that Dr. Nemur is not at all a genius. He has a very good mind, but it struggles under the spectre of self-doubt. He wants people to take him for a genius. Therefore, it is important for him to feel that his work is accepted by the world. I believe that Dr. Nemur was afraid of further delay because he worried that someone else might make a discovery along these lines and take the credit from him.

Dr. Strauss on the other hand might be called a genius, although I feel that his areas of knowledge are too limited. He was educated in the tradition of narrow specialization; the broader aspects of background were neglected far more than necessary—even for a neurosurgeon.

I was shocked to learn that the only ancient languages he could read were Latin, Greek, and Hebrew, and that he knows almost nothing of mathematics beyond the elementary levels of the calculus of variations. When he admitted this to me, I found myself almost annoyed. It was as if he'd hidden this part of himself in order to deceive me, pretending— as do many people I've discovered—to be what he is not. No one I've ever known is what he appears to be on the surface.

Dr. Nemur appears to be uncomfortable around me. Sometimes when I try to talk to him, he just looks at me strangely and turns away. I was angry at first when Dr. Strauss told

---

5. **"It was evil . . . die."** Fanny is referring to the biblical story of the fall of Adam and Eve and their expulsion by God from the Garden of Eden. [Genesis 3]

6. tangible (tan′jə bəl), *adj.* something that is real, actual, and definite.

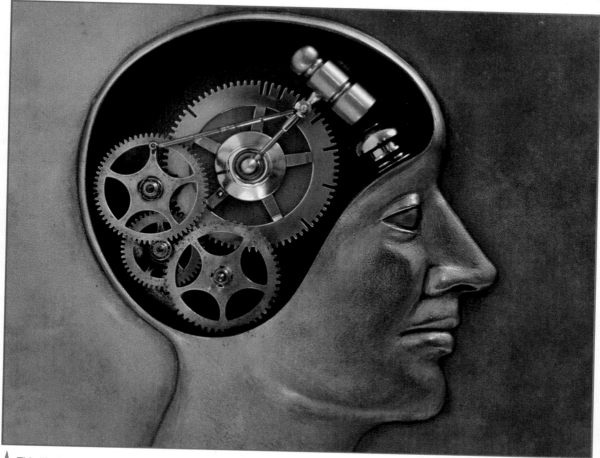

This illustration is by Mary Bono. What do the gears and the bell represent? Why is this image appropriate at this point in the story?

me I was giving Dr. Nemur an inferiority complex. I thought he was mocking me and I'm oversensitive at being made fun of.

How was I to know that a highly respected psychoexperimentalist like Nemur was unacquainted with Hindustani and Chinese? It's absurd when you consider the work that is being done in India and China today in the very field of his study.

I asked Dr. Strauss how Nemur could refute Rahajamati's attack on his method and results if Nemur couldn't even read them in the first place. That strange look on Dr. Strauss' face can mean only one of two things. Either he doesn't want to tell Nemur what they're saying in India, or else—and this worries me—Dr. Strauss doesn't know either. I must be careful to speak and write clearly and simply so that people won't laugh.

May 18 I am very disturbed. I saw Miss Kinnian last night for the first time in over a week. I tried to avoid all discussions of intellectual concepts and to keep the conversation on a simple, everyday level, but she just stared at me blankly and asked me what I meant about the mathematical variance equivalent in Dorbermann's *Fifth Concerto.*

When I tried to explain she stopped me and laughed. I guess I got angry, but I suspect I'm approaching her on the wrong level. No matter what I try to discuss with her, I am unable to communicate. I must review Vrostadt's equations on *Levels of Semantic Progression.* I find that I don't communicate with people much any more. Thank God for books and music and things I can think about. I am alone in my apartment at Mrs. Flynn's boardinghouse most of the time and seldom speak to anyone.

EVALUATE: Why do you think Charlie is still lonely?

May 20 I would not have noticed the new dishwasher, a boy of about sixteen, at the corner diner where I take my evening meals if not for the incident of the broken dishes.

They crashed to the floor, shattering and sending bits of white china under the tables. The boy stood there, dazed and frightened, holding the empty tray in his hand. The whistles and catcalls from the customers (the cries of "hey, there go the profits!" . . . *"Mazel tov!"*[7] . . . and "well, *he* didn't work here very long . . . " which invariably seem to follow the breaking of glass or dishware in a public restaurant) all seemed to confuse him.

When the owner came to see what the excitement was about, the boy cowered as if he expected to be struck and threw up his arms as if to ward off the blow.

"All right! All right, you dope," shouted the owner, "don't just stand there! Get the broom and sweep that mess up. A broom . . . a broom, you idiot! It's in the kitchen. Sweep up all the pieces."

The boy saw that he was not going to be punished. His frightened expression disappeared and he smiled and hummed as he came back with the broom to sweep the floor. A few

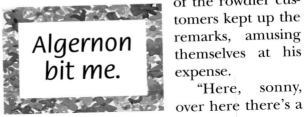

Algernon bit me.

of the rowdier customers kept up the remarks, amusing themselves at his expense.

"Here, sonny, over here there's a nice piece behind you . . . "

"C'mon, do it again . . . "

"He's not so dumb. It's easier to break 'em than to wash 'em . . . "

As his vacant eyes moved across the crowd of amused onlookers, he slowly mirrored their smiles and finally broke into an uncertain grin at the joke which he obviously did not understand.

I felt sick inside as I looked at his dull, vacuous[8] smile, the wide, bright eyes of a child, uncertain but eager to please. They were laughing at him because he was mentally retarded.

And I had been laughing at him too.

Suddenly, I was furious at myself and all those who were smirking at him. I jumped up and shouted, "Shut up! Leave him alone! It's not his fault he can't understand! He can't help what he is! But he's still a human being!"

The room grew silent. I cursed myself for losing control and creating a scene. I tried not to look at the boy as I paid my check and walked out without touching my food. I felt ashamed for both of us.

How strange it is that people of honest feelings and sensibility, who would not take

---

7. **Mazel tov!,** a Yiddish expression meaning "Congratulations!" or "Good luck!"

8. **vacuous** (vak′yü əs), *adj.* showing no thought or intelligence; stupid.

advantage of a man born without arms or legs or eyes—how such people think nothing of abusing a man born with low intelligence. It infuriated me to think that not too long ago I, like this boy, had foolishly played the clown.

And I had almost forgotten.

I'd hidden the picture of the old Charlie Gordon from myself because now that I was intelligent it was something that had to be pushed out of my mind. But today in looking at that boy, for the first time I saw what I had been. *I was just like him!*

Only a short time ago, I learned that people laughed at me. Now I can see that unknowingly I joined with them in laughing at myself. That hurts most of all.

I have often reread my progress reports and seen the illiteracy, the childish naïveté, the mind of low intelligence peering from a dark room, through the keyhole, at the dazzling light outside. I see that even in my dullness I knew that I was inferior, and that other people had something I lacked—something denied me. In my mental blindness, I thought that it was somehow connected with the ability to read and write, and I was sure that if I could get those skills I would automatically have intelligence too.

Even a feeble-minded man wants to be like other men.

A child may not know how to feed itself, or what to eat, yet it knows of hunger.

This then is what I was like, I never knew. Even with my gift of intellectual awareness, I never really knew.

This day was good for me. Seeing the past more clearly, I have decided to use my knowledge and skills to work in the field of increasing human intelligence levels. Who is better equipped for this work? Who else has lived in both worlds? These are my people. Let me use my gift to do something for them.

Tomorrow, I will discuss with Dr. Strauss the manner in which I can work in this area. I may be able to help him work out the prob-

lems of widespread use of the technique which was used on me. I have several good ideas of my own.

There is so much that might be done with this technique. If I could be made into a genius, what about thousands of others like myself? What fantastic levels might be achieved by using the technique on normal people? On *geniuses*?

There are so many doors to open. I am impatient to begin.

PROGRESS REPORT 13

May 23 It happened today. Algernon bit me. I visited the lab to see him as I do occasionally, and when I took him out of his cage, he snapped at my hand. I put him back and watched him for a while. He was unusually disturbed and vicious.

May 24 Burt, who is in charge of the experimental animals, tells me that Algernon is changing. He is less co-operative; he refuses to run the maze any more; general motivation[9] has decreased. And he hasn't been eating. Everyone is upset about what this may mean.

May 25 They've been feeding Algernon, who now refuses to work the shifting-lock problem. Everyone identifies me with Algernon. In a way we're both the first of our kind. They're all pretending that Algernon's behavior is not necessarily significant for me. But it's hard to hide the fact that some of the other animals who were used in this experiment are showing strange behavior.

Dr. Strauss and Dr. Nemur have asked me not to come to the lab any more. I know what they're thinking but I can't accept it. I am going ahead with my plans to carry their research forward. With all due respect to both

---

9. **motivation** (mō′tə vā′shən), *n.* the reason or force that makes people act.

of these fine scientists, I am well aware of their limitations. If there is an answer, I'll have to find it out for myself. Suddenly, time has become very important to me.

May 29 I have been given a lab of my own and permission to go ahead with the research. I'm on to something. Working day and night. I've had a cot moved into the lab. Most of my writing time is spent on the notes which I keep in a separate folder, but from time to time I feel it necessary to put down my moods and my thoughts out of sheer habit.

I find the *calculus of intelligence* to be a fascinating study. Here is the place for the application of all the knowledge I have acquired. In a sense it's the problem I've been concerned with all my life.

May 31 Dr. Strauss thinks I'm working too hard. Dr. Nemur says I'm trying to cram a lifetime of research and thought into a few weeks. I know I should rest, but I'm driven on by something inside that won't let me stop. I've got to find the reason for the sharp regression[10] in Algernon. I've got to know *if* and *when* it will happen to me.

---

10. regression (ri gresh′ən), *n.* a return to an earlier way of thinking or acting.

Ladders of Light #7: Yellow Hands was painted by Sherri Silverman. What do you think the painting symbolizes? What do the hands, the ladder, and the moon represent? ➤

After Reading

Vocabulary Study (pages 494–505)

A. Decide if the following pairs of words are synonyms or antonyms. On a separate piece of paper, write *S* for Synonym or *A* for Antonym.

plateau
opportunist
petition
tangible
vacuous
motivation
regression

1. tangible—unreal
2. vacuous—unintelligent
3. regression—progression
4. petition—request
5. motivation—incentive

B. On a sheet of paper, write the vocabulary word that completes each sentence.

Even if he has to lie and cheat, my neighbor tries to get ahead. He is a true __(1)__ . He always finds a way to gain an advantage and to produce __(2)__ results. What is his __(3)__ ? Perhaps it is his desire to prove a point to people who believe he's a __(4)__ simpleton. Or perhaps it is his need to attain constancy in his life—to reach a comfortable __(5)__ .

Expressing Your Ideas

Just for Fun Write a **paragraph** using lots of punctuation, the way Charlie did in his April 17 entry. Then switch paragraphs with another person so that you can correct the misplaced and misused marks.

Move Over, Oprah! Organize a **talk show** with the theme, "Why did you sign the petition?" Have people playing the parts of Mr. Donnegan, Joe Carp, Frank Reilly, and a few other people from Charlie's workplace sit at the front of the room. The talk show host will call on people from the audience to ask questions. If time permits, have Dr. Strauss and Dr. Nemur join the discussion a little while later.

June 4

LETTER TO DR. STRAUSS (copy)

Dear Dr. Strauss:

Under separate cover I am sending you a copy of my report entitled, "The Algernon-Gordon Effect: A Study of Structure and Function of Increased Intelligence," which I would like to have you read and have published.

As you see, my experiments are completed. I have included in my report all of my formulae, as well as mathematical analysis in the appendix. Of course, these should be verified.

Because of its importance to both you and Dr. Nemur (and need I say to myself, too?) I have checked and rechecked my results a dozen times in the hope of finding an error. I am sorry to say the results must stand. Yet for the sake of science, I am grateful for the little bit that I here add to the knowledge of the function of the human mind and of the laws governing the artificial increase of human intelligence.

I recall your once saying to me that an experimental *failure* or the *disproving* of a theory was as important to the advancement of learning as a success would be. I know now that this is true. I am sorry, however, that my own contribution to the field must rest upon the ashes of the work of two men I regard so highly.

Yours truly,
Charles Gordon

encl.: rept.

CLARIFY: What is Charlie really saying in the letter?

June 5   I must not become emotional. The facts and the results of my experiments are clear, and the more sensational aspects of my own rapid climb cannot obscure the fact that the tripling of intelligence by the surgical technique developed by Drs. Strauss and Nemur must be viewed as having little or no practical applicability (at the present time) to the increase of human intelligence.

As I review the records and data on Algernon, I see that although he is still in his physical infancy, he has regressed mentally. Motor activity is impaired;[1] there is a general reduction of glandular activity; there is an accelerated loss of co-ordination.

There are also strong indications of progressive amnesia.[2]

As will be seen by my report, these and other physical and mental deterioration[3] syndromes can be predicted with statistically significant results by the application of my formula.

The surgical stimulus to which we were both subjected has resulted in an intensification and acceleration of all mental processes. The unforeseen development, which I have taken the liberty of calling the *Algernon-Gordon Effect*, is the logical extension of the entire intelligence speed-up. The hypothesis here proven may be described simply in the following terms: Artificially increased intelligence deteriorates at a rate of time directly proportional to the quantity of the increase.

I feel that this, in itself, is an important discovery.

As long as I am able to write, I will continue to record my thoughts in these progress reports. It is one of my few pleasures. However, by all indications, my own mental deterioration will be very rapid.

I have already begun to notice signs of

1. **impaired** (im perd′), *adj.* damaged; weakened.
2. **amnesia** (am nē′zhə), *n.* partial or total loss of memory caused by injury to the brain, or by disease, shock, etc.
3. **deterioration** (di tir′ē ə rā′shən), *n.* when something wears down and becomes lower in quality.

emotional instability[4] and forgetfulness, the first symptoms of the burnout.

June 10 Deterioration progressing. I have become absentminded. Algernon died two days ago. Dissection[5] shows my predictions were right. His brain had decreased in weight and there was a general smoothing out of cerebral[6] convolutions as well as a deepening and broadening of brain fissures.[7]

I guess the same thing is or will soon be happening to me. Now that it's definite, I don't want it to happen.

I put Algernon's body in a cheese box and buried him in the back yard. I cried.

PREDICT: What is going to happen to Charlie?

June 15 Dr. Strauss came to see me again. I wouldn't open the door and I told him to go away. I want to be left to myself. I have become touchy and irritable. I feel the darkness closing in. It's hard to throw off thoughts of suicide. I keep telling myself how important this introspective[8] journal will be.

It's a strange sensation to pick up a book that you've read and enjoyed just a few months ago and discover that you don't remember it. I remembered how great I thought John Milton was, but when I picked up *Paradise Lost* I couldn't understand it at all. I got so angry I threw the book across the room.

I've got to try to hold on to some of it. Some of the things I've learned. Oh, God, please don't take it all away.

June 19 Sometimes, at night, I go out for a walk. Last night I couldn't remember where I lived. A policeman took me home. I have the strange feeling that this has all happened to me before—a long time ago. I keep telling myself I'm the only person in the world who can describe what's happening to me.

June 21 Why can't I remember? I've got to fight. I lie in bed for days and I don't know who or where I am. Then it all comes back to me in a flash. Fugues of amnesia. Symptoms of senility[9]—second childhood. I can watch them coming on. It's so cruelly logical. I learned so much and so fast. Now my mind is deteriorating rapidly. I won't let it happen. I'll fight it. I can't help thinking of the boy in the restaurant, the blank expression, the silly smile, the people laughing at him. No—please—not that again . . .

June 22 I'm forgetting things that I learned recently. It seems to be following the classic pattern—the last things learned are the first things forgotten. Or is that the pattern? I'd better look it up again. . . .

I reread my paper on the *Algernon-Gordon Effect* and I get the strange feeling that it was written by someone else. There are parts I don't even understand.

Motor activity impaired. I keep tripping

---

4. **instability** (in′stə bil′ə tē), *n.* being unstable; being unpredictable.
5. **dissection** (di sek′shən), *n.* the act of cutting apart an animal in order to study its structure.
6. **cerebral** (sə rē′brəl), *adj.* of the brain.
7. **"His brain . . . fissures."** There seems to be a relationship between intelligence and brain weight, and between intelligence and the number of cerebral convolutions (folds or ridges on the surface of the brain).
8. **introspective** (in′trə spek′tiv), *adj.* having to do with looking inward to examine one's own thoughts and feelings.
9. **senility** (sə nil′ə tē), *n.* the mental and physical deterioration often characteristic of old age.

Studio Arch was painted by Fran Beallor. How does this painting represent Charlie's situation at this point in the story? ➤

over things, and it becomes increasingly difficult to type.

June 23   I've given up using the typewriter completely. My co-ordination is bad. I feel that I'm moving slower and slower. Had a terrible shock today. I picked up a copy of an article I used in my research, Krueger's *Uber psychische Ganzheit*, to see if it would help me understand what I had done. First I thought there was something wrong with my eyes. Then I realized I could no longer read German. I tested myself in other languages. All gone.

June 30   A week since I dared to write again. It's slipping away like sand through my fingers. Most of the books I have are too hard for me now. I get angry with them because I know that I read and understood them just a few weeks ago.

I keep telling myself I must keep writing these reports so that somebody will know what is happening to me. But it gets harder to form the words and remember spellings. I have to look up even simple words in the dictionary now and it makes me impatient with myself.

Dr. Strauss comes around almost every day, but I told him I wouldn't see or speak to anybody. He feels guilty. They all do. But I don't blame anyone. I knew what might happen. But how it hurts.

SUMMARIZE: What are some of the changes you see in Charlie?

July 7   I don't know where the week went. Todays Sunday I know becuase I can see through my window people going to church. I think I stayed in bed all week but I remember Mrs. Flynn bringing food to me a few times. I keep saying over and over Ive got to do something but then I forget or maybe its just easier not to do what I say Im going to do.

I think of my mother and father a lot these days. I found a picture of them with me taken at a beach. My father has a big ball under his arm and my mother is holding me by the hand. I dont remember them the way they are in the picture. All I remember is my father drunk most of the time and arguing with mom about money.

He never shaved much and he used to scratch my face when he hugged me. My mother said he died but Cousin Miltie said he heard his mom and dad say that my father ran away with another woman. When I asked my mother she slapped my face and said my father was dead. I don't think I ever found out which was true but I don't care much. (He said he was going to take me to see cows on a farm once but he never did. He never kept his promises . . .)

July 10   My landlady Mrs Flynn is very worried about me. She says the way I lay around all day and dont do anything I remind her of her son before she threw him out of the house. She said she doesnt like loafers. If Im sick its one thing, but if Im a loafer thats another thing and she wont have it. I told her I think Im sick.

I try to read a little bit every day, mostly stories, but sometimes I have to read the same thing over and over again because I dont know what it means. And its hard to write. I know I should look up all the words in the dictionary but its so hard and Im so tired all the time.

Then I got the idea that I would only use the easy words instead of the long hard ones. That saves time. I put flowers on Algernons grave about once a week. Mrs. Flynn thinks Im crazy to put flowers on a mouses grave but I told her that Algernon was special.

July 14   Its sunday again. I dont have anything to do to keep me busy now because my television set is broke and I dont have any money to get it fixed. (I think I lost this months check from the lab. I dont remember)

I get awful headaches and asperin doesnt help me much. Mrs Flynn knows Im really sick and she feels very sorry for me. Shes a wonderful woman whenever someone is sick.

July 22 Mrs Flynn called a strange doctor to see me. She was afraid I was going to die. I told the doctor I wasnt too sick and that I only forget sometimes. He asked me did I have any friends or relatives and I said no I dont have any. I told him I had a friend called Algernon once but he was a mouse and we used to run races together. He looked at me kind of funny like he thought I was crazy.

He smiled when I told him I used to be a genius. He talked to me like I was a baby and he winked at Mrs Flynn. I got mad and chased him out because he was making fun of me the way they all used to.

July 24 I have no more money and Mrs. Flynn says I got to go to work somewhere and pay the rent because I havent paid for over two months. I dont know any work but the job I used to have at Donnegans Plastic Box Company. I dont want to go back there because they all knew me when I was smart and maybe theyll laugh at me. But I dont know what else to do to get money.

July 25 I was looking at some of my old progress reports and its very funny but I cant read what I wrote. I can make out some of the words but they dont make sense.

Miss Kinnian came to the door but I said go away I dont want to see you. She cried and I cried too but I wouldnt let her in because I didnt want her to laugh at me. I told her I didnt like her any more. I told her I didn't want to be smart any more. Thats not true. I still love her and I still want to be smart but I had to say that so shed go away. She gave Mrs Flynn money to pay the rent. I dont want that. I got to get a job.

Please . . . please let me not forget how to read and write . . .

July 27 Mr Donnegan was very nice when I came back and asked him for my old job of janitor. First he was very suspicious but I told him what happened to me then he looked very sad and put his hand on my shoulder and said Charlie Gordon you got guts.

Everybody looked at me when I came downstairs and started working in the toilet sweeping it out like I used to. I told myself Charlie if they make fun of you dont get sore because you remember their not so smart as you once thot they were. And besides they were once your friends and if they laughed at you that doesnt mean anything because they liked you too.

Please . . . please let me not forget how to read and write . . .

One of the new men who came to work there after I went away made a nasty crack he said hey Charlie I hear your a very smart fella a real quiz kid. Say something intelligent. I felt bad but Joe Carp came over and grabbed him by the shirt and said leave him alone you lousy cracker or Ill break your neck. I didnt expect Joe to take my part so I guess hes really my friend.

Later Frank Reilly came over and said Charlie if anybody bothers you or trys to take advantage you call me or Joe and we will set em straight. I said thanks Frank and I got choked up so I had to turn around and go into the supply room so he wouldnt see me cry. Its good to have friends.

July 28 I did a dumb thing today I forgot I wasnt in Miss Kinnians class at the adult center any more like I use to be. I went in and sat down in my old seat in the back of the room and she looked at me funny and she said Charles. I dint remember she ever called me that before only Charlie so I said hello Miss Kinnian Im redy for my lesin today only I lost my reader that we was using. She startid to cry and run out of the room and everybody looked at me and I saw they wasnt the same pepul who used to be in my class.

Then all of a suddin I rememberd some things about the operashun and me getting smart and I said holy smoke I reely pulled a Charlie Gordon that time. I went away before she come back to the room.

Thats why Im going away from New York for good. I dont want to do nothing like that agen. I dont want Miss Kinnian to feel sorry for me. Evry body feels sorry at the factery and I dont want that eather so Im going someplace where nobody knows that Charlie Gordon was once a genus and now he cant even reed a book or rite good.

Im taking a cuple of books along and even if I cant reed them Ill practise hard and maybe I wont forget every thing I lerned. If I try reel hard maybe Ill be a littel bit smarter then I was before the operashun. I got my rabits foot and my luky penny and maybe they will help me.

If you ever reed this Miss Kinnian dont be sorry for me Im glad I got a second chanse to be smart becaus I lerned a lot of things that I never even new were in this world and Im grateful that I saw it all for a littel bit. I dont know why Im dumb agen or what I did wrong maybe its becaus I dint try hard enuff. But if I try and practis very hard maybe Ill get a littl smarter and know what all the words are. I remember a littel bit how nice I had a feeling with the blue book that has the torn cover when I red it. Thats why Im gonna keep trying to get smart so I can have that feeling agen. Its a good feeling to know things and be smart. I wish I had it rite now if I did I would sit down and reed all the time. Anyway I bet Im the first dumb person in the world who ever found out somthing important for sience. I remember I did somthing but I dont remember what. So I gess its like I did it for all the dumb pepul like me.

Good-by Miss Kinnian and Dr Strauss and evreybody. And P.S. please tell Dr Nemur not to be such a grouch when pepul laff at him and he woud have more frends. Its easy to make frends if you let pepul laff at you. Im going to have lots of frends where I go.

P.P.S. Please if you get a chanse put some flowrs on Algernons grave in the bak yard . . .

Flowers, by Pablo Picasso, was also shown at the beginning of the story. Why do you think this image was chosen for this story? ➤

After Reading

Making Connections

1. Was this an easy story to read? Explain.

2. Do you think Charlie is better off at the end of the story than at the beginning? Why or why not?

3. Why do you suppose Charlie put flowers on Algernon's grave?

4. Were any of the **predictions** you made in your reading log correct? Which ones?

5. Choose one of the people in the story that Charlie was involved with and chart the changes in Charlie's awareness of and interactions with that person.

6. How would the story be different if it had been told from Dr. Strauss's **point of view?**

7. Were Joe Carp and Frank Reilly really Charlie's friends? Explain.

8. 🐾 Charlie wanted to develop as an **individual,** but he also wanted to "fit in" with the people around him. Was he ever accepted for who he was? Explain your answer.

9. How far do you believe science should go to change the basic qualities a person is born with? Consider both mental and physical characteristics.

Literary Focus: Foreshadowing

Foreshadowing is used by an author to give you clues about what might happen later on in the story. How are the events of Charlie's life foreshadowed in this story? Make a list of things that he writes in his reports that are clues to what will happen to him later on. Here's an example:

Quote	Foreshadows
Algernon bit me.	

Vocabulary Study

impaired
amnesia
deterioration
instability
dissection
cerebral
introspective
senility

On a sheet of paper, write the vocabulary word that best matches each clue. Some of the words are used more than once.

1. You might have this if you forget your name after bumping your head.

2. This word is related to *brain.*

3. You may have completed this procedure on a frog.

4. A word you might think of when looking at a smoking volcano.

5. You might describe someone's poor vision with this word.

6. A state that your sandwich would assume if you forget it in your locker over summer vacation.

7. A word you might think of when trying to describe a person who is capable of outbursts and tantrums.

8. A shy, quiet person might be described this way.

9. If you reach this state, you probably are at an advanced age.

10. You might use this word to describe the state of an abandoned building.

Expressing Your Ideas _____

Writing Choices

What if . . . ? What would happen if everyone became super-intelligent? Write a **short story** about such a society.

From One Respected Colleague to Another In the May 15 report Charlie mentions that researchers in India are criticizing Dr. Nemur's work. Imagining that you are one of these scientists, write a **letter** to Dr. Nemur, explaining your objections.

One More Time Write another **journal entry** for Charlie. Date the entry several months after Charlie left New York.

Other Options

Lights, Camera . . . Create a **poster** that could be used to advertise a new movie version of "Flowers for Algernon." Which Hollywood actor would you have play Charlie? Who would play the other characters? Include these names on your poster.

Voice Your Opinion After using library resources to locate information about IQs, conduct a **debate** about IQ measurements. Choose from among the three different positions on IQs that are expressed in the story.

Rock or Bach? Find **music** that captures the mood of the story. Bring the music to class and play it while you and several classmates **dramatize** parts of the story that contain dialogue.

Language Mini-Lesson

Sentence Conciseness: Avoiding Wordiness

Recognize wordy sentences. Have you heard the saying "Too many cooks spoil the broth"? In writing, too many words can spoil a sentence. Writing is more effective if it is concise and doesn't contain unnecessary words.

Writing concise sentences doesn't mean that we eliminate necessary details just to make things shorter. It means that we eliminate anything that doesn't add to the meaning or the freshness of the writing. Look at the following sentences. Notice how words were eliminated without changing the meaning of the sentence.

WORDY
The huge, towering, dark, black cloud rolled across the sky and pelted and hammered us with icy, frozen rain.

CONCISE
The towering, black cloud rolled across the sky and pelted us with freezing rain.

Writing Strategy Sentences can be made concise in several ways. Here are two to concentrate on in your writing.

- Avoid unnecessary repetition.

- Reduce parts of sentences—clauses can be reduced to phrases, and phrases can be reduced to single words.

Activity Options

1. Make the following paragraph more concise.

   When Kerry walked to the starting block of the race on the track, he knew that he would attempt to try and break the school record. As the gun sounded with a bang, Kerry shot off the starting line and ran the fifty yards to win the fifty-yard dash in record time.

2. Review your writing portfolio and find instances of wordiness. Try different ways of revising to make each piece less wordy.

3. Newspaper stories are frequently concisely written. Test your local newspaper. Work with a partner and read several stories in the newspaper for concise writing. Make notes of any examples of wordiness you find and share these with the class.

Before Reading

The Boy and His Grandfather

by Rudolfo A. Anaya

Rudolfo A. Anaya
born 1937

In addition to retelling *cuentos,* Anaya has written poetry, short stories, plays, screenplays, and novels. His novels, including *Bless Me, Ultima,* for which he is best known, tell about the lives and experiences of Hispanic Americans in the Southwest. Many of his works have been strongly influenced by American folk tales. He says, "In a real sense, the mythologies of the Americas are the only mythologies of all of us, whether we are newly arrived or whether we have been here for centuries. The land and the people force this mythology on us."

Building Background

Cuentos *Cuento* is the Spanish word for *story.* In the United States, the word refers to the legends, stories, and myths of the Hispanic culture of New Mexico and southern Colorado. *Cuentos* were first brought to the Southwest by the Spanish and Mexican settlers. The stories became mixed with Native American culture and were also influenced by the shape and forces of the land itself. "The Boy and His Grandfather" is one of these *cuentos.*

Getting into the Story

Discussion In small groups, brainstorm some of the advantages and disadvantages of living in an extended family. An extended family includes the nuclear family (parents and children) as well as other family members, such as grandparents, cousins, aunts, and uncles. Try to think of the perspectives of various family members as you brainstorm. Put your ideas on a chart like the one below. After your group has completed the chart, choose someone to copy it on the blackboard. Discuss the list as a class.

Living in an Extended Family	
Advantages	**Disadvantages**
• more people to do chores	• too crowded
• additional companions	•
•	•

Reading Tip

Characteristics of Folk Tales Folk tales are short tales handed down by word of mouth, expressing legends, beliefs, and customs of people. They are the stories of common, everyday people. Their purpose, according to Anaya, often is to "delight and instruct." As you read, think about other characteristics of folk tales.

THE BOY AND HIS GRANDFATHER

Rudolfo A. Anaya

In the old days it was not unusual to find several generations living together in one home. Usually, everyone lived in peace and harmony, but this situation caused problems for one man whose household included, besides his wife and small son, his elderly father.

It so happened that the daughter-in-law took a dislike to the old man. He was always in the way, she said, and she insisted he be removed to a small room apart from the house.

Because the old man was out of sight, he was often neglected. Sometimes he even went hungry. They took poor care of him, and in winter the old man often suffered from the cold. One day the little grandson visited his grandfather.

"My little one," the grandfather said, "go and find a blanket and cover me. It is cold and I am freezing."

The small boy ran to the barn to look for a blanket, and there he found a rug.

"Father, please cut this rug in half," he asked his father.

"Why? What are you going to do with it?"

"I'm going to take it to my grandfather because he is cold."

"Well, take the entire rug," replied his father.

"No," his son answered, "I cannot take it all. I want you to cut it in half so I can save the other half for you when you are as old as my grandfather. Then I will have it for you so you will not be cold."

His son's response was enough to make the man realize how poorly he had treated his own father. The man then brought his father back into his home and ordered that a warm room be prepared. From that time on he took care of his father's needs and visited him frequently every day.

▲ *Old Peasant* was painted by Vincent Van Gogh, one of the most famous and popular painters of modern art. How has Van Gogh expressed the energy and vitality of the man in his painting?

After Reading

Making Connections

1. Write three words that come to mind when you think about the story.
2. What are some of the cultural values shown by this story?
3. 👣 How did the young boy express his **individuality?** How did this action affect his relationship with his family?
4. What do you think is the lesson, or **moral,** of this story?
5. People over the age of fifty-five often get discounts for things such as movie tickets and hotel rooms. What do you think of these policies? Why do they exist?

Expressing Your Ideas

Writing Choices

What if? Change the setting, or the structure of the family, or even what the little boy does and **retell** this story from your own cultural perspective.

Two Sides of the Coin Using the list created before reading the story (see page 517), write an **essay** about the advantages and disadvantages of living in an extended family. Don't feel that you have to choose one side as "better"; your job is simply to explain both perspectives.

This Is How I Really Feel Write a **message** to the grandfather from the boy, telling him how he feels about him.

Other Options

Artistic License In a small group, prepare **illustrations** that would complement this tale. Write the text of the story under your pictures to make a picture book.

The Lives of Our Elders Using library resources, find out more about the treatment of older people in the United States, or look into an issue that concerns them, such as housing or Social Security. Present your findings to the class in an **oral report.**

The Golden Rule The Golden Rule is a rule of conduct stating that you should treat others as you would have them treat you. Using library resources, find another *cuento* that conveys the Golden Rule and **read** it to the class.

Before Reading

Paul Bunyan Digs the St. Lawrence River by Dell J. McCormick
John Henry Traditional Ballad

Dell McCormick
1892–1949

Dell McCormick was a collector of American tall tales. Quite a few of them, particularly those about Paul Bunyan, he first heard while working in a sawmill in northern Idaho during the early 1900s. Many of the versions of the Paul Bunyan stories we read now are due to McCormick's work and his book *Paul Bunyan Swings His Ax*. In addition to "Paul Bunyan Digs the St. Lawrence River," the book contains the tales "Johnnie Inkslinger and His Magic Pen," "The Popcorn Blizzard," and "The Red River Camp." A number of other tall tales told by McCormick appear in *Tall Timber Tales: More Paul Bunyan Stories*.

Building Background

Paul Bunyan and John Henry American tall tales are notorious for their use of **exaggeration.** People are taller than trees, stronger than oxen, and move faster than greased lightning. Paul Bunyan was a hero of the lumber industry, and stories about him have been told since the late 1800s. The story of John Henry is based on a real event and a real man named John Henry, an African American laborer who helped dig railroad tunnels in the 1870s. The ballad you are about to read, which is a classic confrontation between a person and a machine, developed from the stories that were told and passed on through the years. As you will discover, both of these men are "larger than life."

Getting into the Story

Writer's Notebook There are people even now who seem "larger than life." These people are very beautiful or very strong or very powerful. Newspapers and television news programs love to write about them. Try to think of at least three people who get a lot of attention from the press. Write down their names, the reasons why you think they are so popular, and some of the ways that news writers like to describe them. Share your lists and discuss them.

Reading Tip

Visualize In the beginning of the story about Paul Bunyan, you will learn about Billy Pilgrim's project—digging the St. Lawrence River! This is a project of major proportions, considering that the river starts at Lake Ontario (on the border of New York) and runs east for 744 miles to the Atlantic Ocean. The part that Billy Pilgrim is digging, which is the part that runs between northern New York and Montreal, Canada, is about 250 miles long. That's a lot of digging. So you'll have to s-t-r-e-t-c-h your imagination to picture these legendary heroes as they dig away!

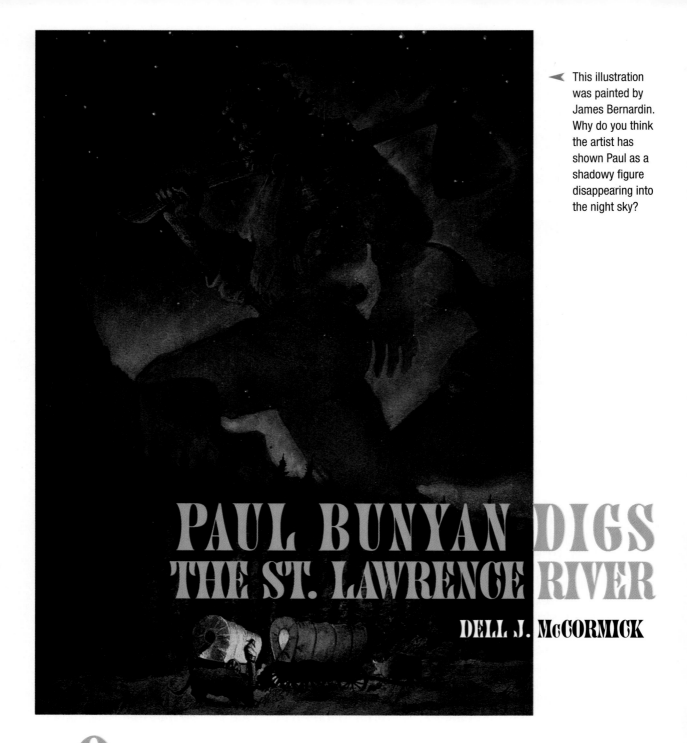

This illustration was painted by James Bernardin. Why do you think the artist has shown Paul as a shadowy figure disappearing into the night sky?

PAUL BUNYAN DIGS THE ST. LAWRENCE RIVER

DELL J. McCORMICK

One summer Paul decided to leave the North Woods and go back to Maine to visit his father and mother. When he arrived, they talked about old times, and Paul asked about Billy Pilgrim, the biggest man in that part of the country.

"What is this Billy Pilgrim doing?" asked Paul.

"He is digging the St. Lawrence River between the United States and Canada," said Paul's father. "There was nothing to separate the two countries. People never knew when they were in the United States and when they were in Canada."

Paul Bunyan went to see Billy. He found that Billy Pilgrim and his men had been digging for three years and had dug only a very small ditch. Paul laughed when he saw it.

"My men could dig the St. Lawrence River in three weeks," said Paul.

This made Billy angry for he thought no one could dig a large river in three weeks.

"I will give you a million dollars if you can dig the St. Lawrence River in three weeks!" said Billy Pilgrim.

So Paul sent for Babe the Blue Ox, Ole the Big Swede, Brimstone Bill, and all his woodsmen.

Paul told Ole to make a huge scoop shovel as large as a house. They fastened it to Babe with a long buckskin rope. He hauled many tons of dirt every day and emptied the scoop shovel in Vermont. You can see the large piles of dirt there to this day. They are called the Green Mountains.

Every night Johnnie Inkslinger, who did the arithmetic, would take his large pencil and mark one day off the calendar on the wall.

Billy Pilgrim was afraid they would finish digging the river on time. He did not want to pay Paul Bunyan the million dollars, for at heart he was a miser. So he thought of a plan to prevent Paul from finishing the work.

One night Billy called his men together and said, "When everybody has gone to bed we will go out and pour water on the buckskin rope so it will stretch, and Babe the Blue Ox will not be able to pull a single shovelful of dirt!"

The next day, Babe started toward Vermont with the first load of dirt. When he arrived there, he looked around and the huge scoop shovel was nowhere to be seen. For miles and

miles the buckskin rope had stretched through the forests and over the hills.

Babe didn't know what to do. He sat down and tried to think, but everyone knows an ox isn't very bright; so he just sat there. After a while the sun came out and dried the buckskin and it started to shrink to normal size.

Babe planted his large hoofs between two mountains and waited. The buckskin rope kept shrinking and shrinking. Soon the scoop shovel came into view over the hills. Then Babe emptied it and started back after another load.

In exactly three weeks the St. Lawrence River was all finished, but still Billy Pilgrim did not want to pay Paul the money.

"Very well," said Paul, "I will remove the water!" So he led Babe the Blue Ox down to the river, and Babe drank the St. Lawrence River dry.

Billy Pilgrim only chuckled to himself for he knew that the first rain would fill it again. Soon it began to rain, and the river became as large as ever.

So Paul picked up a large shovel.

"If you do not pay the money you owe me I will fill the river up again," said Paul.

He threw in a shovelful of dirt. He threw in another and another, but still Billy Pilgrim would not pay him the money.

"I will pay you half your money," said Billy.

Paul again picked up his shovel and tossed more dirt into the river.

"I will pay you two thirds of your money," said Billy.

Paul kept throwing more dirt into the river until he had thrown a thousand shovelfuls.

"Stop! I will pay you all your money!" cried Billy.

So Paul Bunyan was finally paid in full for digging the St. Lawrence River. The thousand shovelfuls of dirt are still there.

They are called the Thousand Islands.

John Henry

Traditional Song

▲ This illustration of John Henry was painted by Jerry Pinkney. What words and phrases from the song could you use to describe this picture?

John Henry was a lil baby,
Sittin' on his mama's knee,
Said: 'The Big Bend Tunnel on the C. & O. road
Gonna cause the death of me
5 Lawd, Lawd, gonna cause the death of me.'

Cap'n says to John Henry,
'Gonna bring me a steam drill 'round,
Gonna take that steam drill out on the job,
Gonna whop that steel on down,
10 Lawd, Lawd, gonna whop that steel on down.'

John Henry tol' his cap'n,
Lightnin' was in his eye:
'Cap'n, bet yo' las' red cent on me,
Fo' I'll beat it to the bottom or I'll die,
15 Lawd, Lawd, I'll beat it to the bottom or I'll die.'

Sun shine hot an' burnin',
Wer'n't no breeze a-tall,
Sweat ran down like water down a hill,
That day John Henry let his hammer fall,
20 Lawd, Lawd, that day John Henry let his hammer fall.

John Henry went to the tunnel,
An' they put him in the lead to drive,[1]
The rock so tall an' John Henry so small,
That he lied down his hammer an' he cried,
25 Lawd, Lawd, that he lied down his hammer an' he cried.

John Henry started on the right hand,
The steam drill started on the lef'—
'Before I'd let this steam drill beat me down,
I'd hammer my fool self to death,
30 Lawd, Lawd, I'd hammer my fool self to death.'

John Henry had a lil woman,
Her name were Polly Ann,
John Henry took sick an' had to go to bed,
Polly Ann drove steel like a man,
35 Lawd, Lawd, Polly Ann drove steel like a man.

John Henry said to his shaker,[2]
'Shaker, why don' you sing?
I'm throwin' twelve poun's from my hips on down,
Jes' listen to the col' steel ring,
40 Lawd, Lawd, jes' listen to the col' steel ring.'

---

1. John Henry's job is to tunnel out rocks for the railroad. He swings a hammer while someone else holds a steel bit against the rock for him.
2. **shaker** (shā′kər), the person who holds the steel bit.

Oh, the captain said to John Henry,
'I b'lieve this mountain's sinkin' in.'
John Henry said to his captain, oh my!
'Ain' nothin' but my hammer suckin' win',
45 Lawd, Lawd, ain' nothin' but my hammer suckin' win'.'

John Henry tol' his shaker,
'Shaker, you better pray,
For, if I miss this six-foot steel,
Tomorrow'll be yo' buryin' day,
50 Lawd, Lawd, tomorrow'll be yo' buryin' day.'

John Henry tol' his captain,
'Look yonder what I see—
Yo' drill's done broke an' yo' hole's done choke,
An' you cain' drive steel like me,
55 Lawd, Lawd, an' you cain' drive steel like me.'

The man that invented the steam drill,
Thought he was mighty fine.
John Henry drove his fifteen feet,
An' the steam drill only made nine,
60 Lawd, Lawd, an' the steam drill only made nine.

The hammer that John Henry swung,
It weighed over nine pound;
He broke a rib in his lef'-han' side,
An' his intrels fell on the groun',
65 Lawd, Lawd, an' his intrels fell on the groun'.

All the womens in the Wes',
When they heard of John Henry's death,
Stood in the rain, flagged the eas'-boun' train,
Goin' where John Henry fell dead,
70 Lawd, Lawd, goin' where John Henry fell dead.

John Henry's lil mother,
She was all dressed in red,
She jumped in bed, covered up her head,
Said she didn' know her son was dead,
75 Lawd, Lawd, didn' know her son was dead.

Dey took John Henry to the graveyard,
An' they buried him in the san',
An' every locomotive come roarin' by,
Says, 'There lays a steel-drivin' man,
80 Lawd, Lawd, there lays a steel-drivin' man.'

After Reading

Making Connections

1. Take a moment to describe how you pictured Paul Bunyan.

2. How did you picture John Henry? Describe the image of him that comes to mind.

3. Why do you think Paul refused to remove the thousand shovelfuls of dirt after he was paid?

4. What writer's techniques does the author use to convey Paul's and Babe's physical strength?

5. In your opinion, what is the **theme** of "John Henry"?

6. Compare the struggle between people and machines in the 1870s to the one that exists between people and computers today. What are the similarities? the differences?

7. Why do you think people continue to tell stories about folk characters such as Paul Bunyan and John Henry?

Literary Focus: Hyperbole

Hyperbole (hī pėr′ bə lē) is an exaggerated statement that is used to heighten effect. Let's say that your cousin is very tall. Instead of just stating that he's tall, you stretch things a bit by saying, "My cousin is as tall as a house." Tall tales use a great deal of hyperbole. Read through the two selections to find examples and record them in your notebook.

Expressing Your Ideas

Tell It Tall! Write your own **tall tale** about one of the people you listed as being "larger than life" before you read these tales. It may help to imagine that you are writing your tale a hundred years from now, when the person's reputation has had time to "grow."

How's That Again? Retell "John Henry" as a **short story.** If you wish to concentrate on one particular aspect, such as his strength or the idea of "man against machine," then do so. Don't feel that you need to keep every single detail from the ballad.

Other Heroes, Other Stories Find stories about other people of American folklore and legend, such as Johnny Appleseed, Sacagawea, and Davy Crockett. Costume yourself as one of these folk heroes and tell the class a **tale** about yourself.

Life's Not Always Fair

All Work, No Play

U.S. History Connection

"All work and no play make Jack a dull boy." For many nineteenth-century children, those words rang too true. Long workdays in factories were punctuated by exhaustion and danger. They were interrupted only by short nights and a few moments with family or friends. Life's not always fair, but Mary Harris Jones fought to make life better for working children.

MOTHER JONES Seeks Justice for the Mill Children

by Penny Colman

As if in uniform, Mother Jones usually wore a long, full black skirt and a black blouse with lace tucked around the neckline. She was about 5 feet (150 centimeters) tall and had a solid, trim body. Her eyes were deep-set, small, and sparkling blue. Her full lips, which she pressed tightly together, were red against her white skin. Her hair was even whiter than her skin. People who heard her speak remembered her voice— intense, powerful, and rhythmic. According to one listener, when Jones spoke, "suddenly everyone sat up alert and listened."

About 1894, Mother Jones got a job in a cotton mill in Cottondale, Alabama. "I wanted to see for myself if the grewsome [gruesome] stories of little children working in the mills were true," she wrote in her autobiography. The manager of the mill refused to hire her unless she "had a family that would work also." Jones lied and said that she had six children who would be coming to join her soon. The manager eagerly hired her and showed her a house for rent.

"The house he brought me to was a sort of two-story plank shanty. The windows were broken and the door sagged open. Its latch was broken. It had one room downstairs and an unfinished loft upstairs. Through the

1869
Knights of Labor was formed. (It was opened to all workers in 1879.)

1882
John D. Rockefeller formed Standard Oil Trust.

cracks in the roof the rain had come in and rotted the flooring. Downstairs there was a big old open fireplace in front of which were holes big enough to drop a brick through," she wrote.

According to Jones, the manager was "delighted with the house." When she pointed out that the wind and the cold would come through the holes, the manager laughed and said, "Oh, it will be summer soon and you will need all the air you can get."

Jones rented the house and reported to work in the cotton mill. She saw for herself that the stories were true:

Little girls and boys, barefooted, walked up and down between the endless rows of spindles, reaching thin little hands into the machinery to repair snapped threads. They crawled under machinery to oil it. They replaced spindles all day long [and all] night through. Tiny babies of six years old with faces of sixty did an eight-hour shift for ten cents a day. If they fell asleep, cold water was dashed in their faces, and the voice of the manager yelled above the ceaseless racket and whir of the machines. Toddling chaps of four years old were brought to the mills to "help" the older sister or brother of ten years but their labor was not paid. . . .

Child labor in America was nothing new. Children had always worked. During colonial times, children worked alongside their parents, on farms and in home industries such as weaving and candlemaking. As machines were invented and factories and mills were built, children worked there, too. . . .

By 1900 an estimated 2,250,000 children under the age of sixteen worked in various industries. The textile industry, the mills and factories that spun cotton and wove wool into such goods as sweaters, rugs, knit hats, and horse blankets, employed the greatest number of children. Some states had child labor laws, which set a minimum age at which a child could be hired and the maximum number of hours the child could work per day. Generally, the minimum age was twelve and the maximum hours were ten a day. But these laws were rarely enforced. Because workers' families desperately needed their wages, many children lied about their age. So did their parents, who would buy fake certificates to "prove" that their child

1886
At Haymarket Square in Chicago, workers rioted for an eight-hour workday.

1886
Samuel Gompers founded the American Federation of Labor.

1892
Andrew Carnegie formed the Carnegie Steel Company.

1893
The Illinois Factory Act was passed prohibiting child labor in factories.

Children usually were the workers who changed the spindles in the textile mills. They were small enough to climb on the machinery and reach the spindles.

was old enough to work. In addition to needing their children's wages, parents knew that they would probably lose their jobs or be evicted from their company-owned houses if their children didn't work.

Mother Jones once bought $500 worth of shoes for striking miners and their families.

Mother Jones was determined to do something about child labor, or "child slavery," as she called it. In 1903, at the age of seventy-three, Jones went to Philadelphia, Pennsylvania, where 100,000 textile workers including 16,000 children were on strike. The strike had been called by the Central Textile Workers' Union after mill owners refused to shorten the workweek from sixty hours to fifty-five.

The union leaders were particularly concerned about the effects of the long hours on children workers. "Long and incessant toil ruins their health. . . . The textile industry of Philadelphia rests on the bowed backs of young and helpless children," they said. The union was so concerned that all the workers were willing to take a cut in pay to get a fifty-five-hour workweek. (Today a workweek is forty hours.) But the owners refused. They said they couldn't afford it. So, workers at six hundred textile mills went on strike. . . .

1894
Pullman strike of the American Railway Union occurred.

1896
The League for Protection of the Family was formed to take children out of factories and enroll them in schools.

1896
Mothers Congress was formed. (It later became the National Congress of Parents and Teachers, the forerunner of today's PTA.)

On June 17, 1903, Mother Jones started getting publicity with a large demonstration at City Hall. "I put the little boys with their fingers off and hands crushed and maimed on a platform. I held up their mutilated hands and showed them to the crowd and made the statement that Philadelphia's mansions were built on the broken bones, the quivering hearts and drooping heads of these little children." She held up the children so city officials standing in their open office windows could see them and "pointed to their puny arms and legs and hollow chests." Jones talked about children being "sacrificed on the altar of profit" and about "millionaire manufacturers" who commit "moral murders."

Because of the size of the demonstration and Jones's dramatic speech, the newspapers published a report of the event. "That was what I wanted. Public attention on the subject of child labor," Jones wrote.

These boys, some as young as six, are sorting coal in a coal mine.

Mother Jones hoped to convince Congress to pass federal legislation preventing factories from hiring children. Such a law was passed in 1916, but it was declared unconstitutional by the U.S. Supreme Court. A similar law passed in 1918 was also struck down. Finally, in 1938, child labor was made illegal when the Supreme Court ruled in favor of the Fair Labor Standards Act.

The day-shift workers at a mill in Whitnel, North Carolina.

Responding

1. Mother Jones was so committed to her cause that she was willing to endure harassment, imprisonment, and even death threats. Make a list of five rights or causes that you think are important enough to fight for.

2. Mother Jones's opponents argued that she incited violence and was the cause rather than the cure for some of the workers' plights. Do you think that violence is ever justified? When? Give reasons for your responses.

1900
The ILGWU (International Ladies Garment Workers Union) was formed.

1904
The National Child Labor Committee was organized to eliminate child labor outside of factories

TOO MUCH WORK

= Poor Grades

by Rahul Jacob

Working after school is one of the verities of American life, right up there with baseball and apple pie. But while there's nothing wrong with teaching Junior the value of a buck or Janie self-reliance, too much work can be, well, too much.

Many studies show that, in general, the more kids work, the less time they have for homework, and the worse they perform in school. Says Laurence Steinberg, a psychology professor at Temple University: "We've reached a stage where for many youngsters their main concern is not school but work." Steinberg, who conducted a two-year survey of 10th- and 11th-grade students from nine schools in Wisconsin and California, found that teenagers who toiled more than twenty hours a week cut class more often and were less involved in their studies than those who worked moderate hours. Those who didn't work at all did best.

Some critics object not just to how much kids work but to *where* they work—overwhelmingly in fast-food restaurants. Says Joseph Kinney, executive director of the National Safe Workplace Institute: "Fast food is the wrong kind of work. It's repetitious and mindless." Sheer elitism, counters Mark Gorman, senior director for government affairs at the National Restaurant Association: "The argument is, 'If kids are not working, they'll be home studying. They'll go to Harvard and become computer engineers.'"

Still, it's hard to argue against reasonable restrictions on hours worked. In 1991, New York and Maine enacted laws that allow children under sixteen, for example, to work no more than eighteen hours a week when school is in session. In July [1993], Washington State will impose similar limits. Says Rich Berkowitz, a policy analyst with Washington State's House of Representatives: "What are kids going to learn in forty hours of work a week that they can't learn in twenty?"

Some state industry groups are also joining the charge to convince parents and kids that extra hours on homework offer a better long-term payoff than more time behind the cash register. Since September, Texas Restaurant Association President Bill Daniels has logged 30,000 miles visiting members in his state. The message: "Business must put education first."

Child Labor and RULES OF REASON

Chicago Tribune editorial,
August 5, 1995

There are sweatshops in New York, migrant labor camps in Florida, and assorted workers being paid less than the minimum wage by unscrupulous business-people from coast to coast.

But the U.S. Department of Labor has managed to find the time to investigate violations of child-labor laws by several suburban park districts in the Chicago area. Among the transgressions: letting underage Americans slave away at such grueling jobs as refereeing kids' soccer games and checking swimming pool passes.

This is not a joke. The Mt. Prospect Park District underwent a federal audit and paid nearly $16,000 in fines for a variety of

> The danger is not that kids work too much but that kids have nothing constructive to do.

offenses, such as letting a fifteen-year-old boy serve as scorekeeper for a basketball game that didn't end until the shocking hour of 7:35 P.M.—on a school night, no less.

In recent years, the feds have levied fines against five other suburban park districts for the crime of letting local teenagers do something useful, for pay, for too many hours or at the wrong hours.

The great nineteenth-century social reformer Jacob Riis would probably have trouble getting worked up over such incidents. In many suburbs, the danger is not that kids work too much but that kids have nothing constructive to do. A job teaching tennis or selling hot dogs gives them a valuable acquaintance with the world of work and lets them develop some rudimentary skills in a way that benefits their community. Considering the prevalence of drugs, alcohol, premarital sex, and gang involvement among modern teenagers, the danger posed by such modestly demanding employment seems minor indeed.

But the Labor Department says rules are rules, and the rules say children under sixteen may not work after 7 P.M. during the school year or 9 P.M. during the summer, and may not work more than forty hours in any week. These teenagers, a Labor Department official told *The Tribune,* "have yet to reach maturity physiologically, and they have a different labor tolerance. . . . They need special protection."

Not necessarily. The government has its regulations, but they ought to be leavened with common sense. A child picking lettuce in a sun-baked California field needs protection, but a middle-class fifteen-year-old swimming pool attendant may not. Some real harm or at least danger ought to be demonstrated before the department intervenes in cases like these.

Reasonableness, not literal application of rules, ought to prevail.

Responding

1. What do you think are reasonable age and time limits for working teens? Support your answer.

2. To what extent do you think the government should control working conditions for children?

533

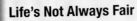

Reading Mini-Lesson

Distinguishing Between Fact and Opinion

Ask ten people this question: "What is the best new movie?" Each answer will be a personal opinion. Who starred in a movie will be a fact. Who directed it and how much money it made will be facts. How many Academy Awards it won will be a fact. But which movie is the best will still be an opinion, a personal view that may be based on facts.

What is a fact? How does it differ from an opinion? A **fact** can be proved to be true or false. Some facts can be demonstrated. In science class, you can demonstrate that the mineral feldspar is harder than the mineral talc. Many facts can be observed, and different observers would agree on the observations. Some facts are widespread agreements that continue over time. In the metric system, 1,000 millimeters equal one meter, a hundred years ago and today.

Opinions do not have to be demonstrated, they are not observable, and they certainly don't have to be agreed upon. Opinions are judgments, often involving words such as *good* or *bad, should* or *shouldn't.* Opinions are often based on facts, but are not themselves facts.

You saw in the article "Mother Jones Seeks Justice for the Mill Children" that Mother Jones acted on her opinions, and that her opinions were based on observations. She took the job in the cotton mill to observe for herself just what conditions were like.

Activity Options

1. Make a fact list for the first paragraph of "Mother Jones Seeks Justice for the Mill Children" (page 528). List every detail about Mother Jones that could have been demonstrated or observed.

2. Mother Jones believed that child labor laws were needed to stop the abuses in mills and factories, particularly in the textile industry. Can you find in the article seven facts that support this opinion? Look for facts about working conditions, housing, and injuries.

3. The two editorials on pages 532–533 express opposite opinions on current child labor laws. Summarize the main opinion of each editorial. Then list two or three facts that are given in each editorial in support of its opinion. Which do you find more persuasive? Why?

Part Two

The Triumph of the Spirit

It is a common theme in literature that the worst of times bring out not only the worst but also the best in people. Individuals faced with overwhelming odds, unbearable pressures, and monstrous evil are capable of extraordinary acts of courage and kindness. The dramatization of Anne Frank's diary has for millions of people shown that heroism is as much an attitude as an action. In this play, heroism is the keeping of faith, hope, and the human spirit while threatened by an inhuman evil.

Multicultural Connection **Interactions** between people of different cultural backgrounds can happen on a large scale or a small scale. In *The Diary of Anne Frank,* the large scale involves countries at war and the attempt by the Nazi government to systematically annihilate the Jews. As you read the play, notice how key characters—especially Anne and Peter—react on a small scale to this reality of the world they live in.

Literature

Frances Goodrich
and Albert Hackett   **The Diary of Anne Frank** ◆ play 538

      Writing Mini-Lesson ◆ Summarizing Information 611

Interdisciplinary Study Unshackled

A Spirit Unshackled by Frederick Douglass ◆ U.S. history 612

Music, Art, Crafts ◆ fine arts 615

Kin by James S. Kunen ◆ sociology 616

      Reading Mini-Lesson ◆ Using Cause-and-Effect Relationships 618

Writing Workshop Narrative Writing

Research Report 619

Beyond Print Media Literacy

Designing a Scale Model of a Set 625

Before Reading

The Diary of Anne Frank

by Frances Goodrich and Albert Hackett

Frances Goodrich (1890–1984) and **Albert Hackett** (1900–1995)

Frances Goodrich and Albert Hackett began writing scripts for plays and movies together in 1927. This husband-and-wife team is best known for their adaptation of Anne Frank's diary into a play and, later, a movie. To prepare for this project, they traveled to Amsterdam to interview Mr. Frank and see the attic where the Frank family had lived in hiding. They worked on the play from 1953 to 1955, writing eight drafts before they were satisfied. The play won a Pulitzer Prize and a Tony Award. Goodrich and Hackett wrote many other movies, including the perennial Christmas favorite, *It's a Wonderful Life.* However, they always felt that *The Diary of Anne Frank* was the high point of their writing career.

Building Background

Anne Frank: The Diary and the Play Anne Frank wrote the diary on which this play is based during World War II. The diary was returned to her father in 1945 and was published in England and the U.S. under the title *The Diary of a Young Girl*. The extraordinary power of the story is shown in a number of ways. Anne's diary was published in fifty-five languages. The play has been performed in more than twenty countries. Audiences have responded with awe to this real-life story of hope and heroism in the face of evil. The effect of the play when performed in Germany in the late 1950s was especially powerful: Audiences left the halls silently, without even applauding, so deeply were they moved.

Nazi Germany During World War II, much of Europe was occupied by Nazi Germany. In every country that the Nazis occupied, Jews, Gypsies, and other minorities were taken from their homes and sent to concentration camps, some to be used for forced labor and others to be killed. After 1940, Hitler ordered most of the prisoners killed. Belsen, the camp to which Anne was sent, was in Germany. On April 15, 1945, the camp at Belsen was liberated by the British army. The bodies of more than 10,000 people were found within the camp.

Getting into the Play

Writer's Notebook Think about a time when you were crowded or confined or limited physically in some way. Try to remember: Where were you? How old were you? How were you confined or limited? How long did it last? Who were you with? How did you feel? What did you do to cope with the stress of the confinement or overcrowding? In your notebook, answer this question: What did you find out about yourself and other people through this experience?

Reading Tip

Keeping a Reading Log Here's how to set up a **Double-Entry Reading Log.** First, draw a line down the middle of a page in your notebook. As you read, stop occasionally (at least two or three

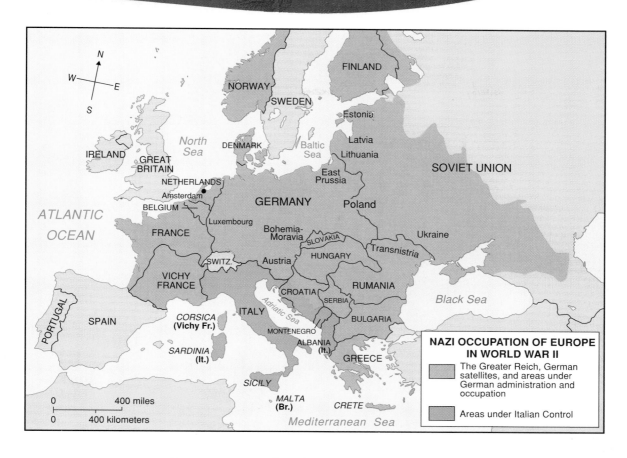

NAZI OCCUPATION OF EUROPE
IN WORLD WAR II

The Greater Reich, German
satellites, and areas under
German administration and
occupation

Areas under Italian Control

times per scene) and copy quotations from the play, both dialogue and stage directions, that you find especially memorable. Write them on the left side of your page, noting what page each quote is from. On the right side, respond to what you have read. Here are brief explanations for each type of response you might make.

Question express the questions you have at that moment

Predict make a reasoned guess about what might happen next

Clarify clear up confusion about what is going on

Summarize review the main events or ideas

Evaluate give opinions and conclusions from evidence

Connect connect something in the play to another part of the play, another selection, or something in your own life

A page in your Reading Log might look like this:

Left Side of Page	Right Side of Page
MRS. FRANK. We've never done anything illegal. (p. 543)	**Evaluate:** Ironic—hiding is illegal—and sad—she's an innocent victim.

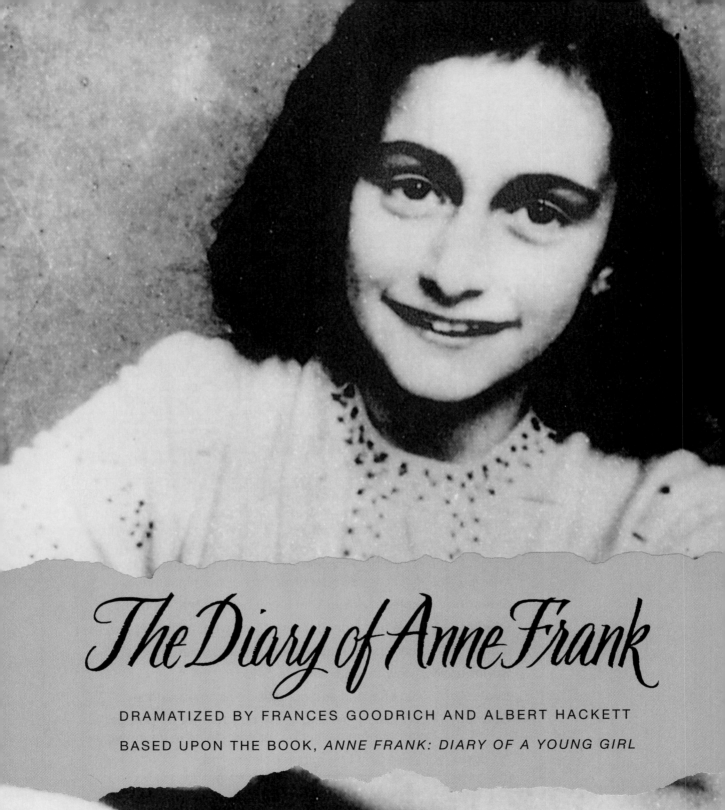

The Diary of Anne Frank

DRAMATIZED BY FRANCES GOODRICH AND ALBERT HACKETT

BASED UPON THE BOOK, *ANNE FRANK: DIARY OF A YOUNG GIRL*

CHARACTERS

MR. OTTO FRANK (frängk)
MIEP (mēp) GIES (hēs)
MR. VAN DAAN (fän dän′)
MRS. PETRONELLA (pet′rə nel′ə) VAN DAAN
PETER VAN DAAN

MRS. EDITH FRANK
MARGOT (mär′gət) FRANK
ANNE FRANK
MR. KRALER (krä′lər)
MR. DUSSEL (düs′əl)

Time *During the years of World War II and immediately thereafter.*

Place *Amsterdam.*
There are two acts.

Act One

SCENE ONE

The scene remains the same throughout the play. It is the top floor of a warehouse and office building in Amsterdam, Holland. The sharply peaked roof of the building is outlined against a sea of other rooftops, stretching away into the distance. Nearby is the belfry of a church tower, the Westertoren, whose carillon rings out the hours. Occasionally faint sounds float up from below: the voices of children playing in the street, the tramp of marching feet, a boat whistle from the canal.

The three rooms of the top floor and a small attic space above are exposed to our view. The largest of the rooms is in the center, with two small rooms, slightly raised, on either side. On the right is a bathroom, out of sight. A narrow steep flight of stairs at the back leads up to the attic. The rooms are sparsely furnished with a few chairs, cots, a table or two. The windows are painted over, or covered with makeshift blackout curtains. In the main room there is a sink, a gas ring for cooking, and a woodburning stove for warmth.

The room on the left is hardly more than a closet. There is a skylight in the sloping ceiling. Directly under this room is a small steep stairwell, with steps leading down to a door. This is the only entrance from the building below. When the door is opened we see that it has been concealed on the outer side by a bookcase attached to it.

The curtain rises on an empty stage. It is late afternoon, November, 1945.

The rooms are dusty, the curtains in rags. Chairs and tables are overturned.

The door at the foot of the small stairwell swings open. MR. FRANK *comes up the steps into view. He is a gentle, cultured European in his middle years. There is still a trace of a German accent in his speech.*

He stands looking slowly around, making a supreme effort at self-control. He is weak, ill. His clothes are threadbare.

After a second he drops his rucksack on the couch and moves slowly about. He opens the door to one of the smaller rooms, and then abruptly closes it again, turning away. He goes to the window at the back, looking off at the Westertoren as its carillon strikes the hour of six; then he moves restlessly on.

From the street below we hear the sound of a barrel organ and children's voices at play. There is a many-colored scarf hanging from a nail. MR. FRANK *takes it, putting it around his neck. As he starts back for his rucksack, his eye is caught by something lying on the floor. It is a woman's white glove. He holds it in his hand and suddenly all of his self-control is gone. He breaks down, crying.*

We hear footsteps on the stairs. MIEP GIES *comes up, looking for* MR. FRANK. MIEP *is a Dutch girl of about twenty-two. She wears a coat and hat, ready to go home. She is pregnant. Her attitude toward* MR. FRANK *is protective, compassionate.*

MIEP. Are you all right, Mr. Frank?

MR. FRANK (*quickly controlling himself*). Yes, Miep, yes.

MIEP. Everyone in the office has gone home . . . It's after six. (*Then pleading.*) Don't stay up here, Mr. Frank. What's the use of torturing yourself like this?

MR. FRANK. I've come to say good-by . . . I'm leaving here, Miep.

MIEP. What do you mean? Where are you going? Where?

MR. FRANK. I don't know yet. I haven't decided.

MIEP. Mr. Frank, you can't leave here! This is your home! Amsterdam is your home. Your business is here, waiting for you . . . You're needed here . . . Now that the war is over, there are things that . . .

MR. FRANK. I can't stay in Amsterdam, Miep. It has too many memories for me. Everywhere there's something . . . the house we lived in . . . the school . . . that street organ playing out there . . . I'm not the person you used to know, Miep. I'm a bitter old man. (*Breaking off.*) Forgive me. I shouldn't speak to you like this . . . after all that you did for us . . . the suffering . . .

MIEP. No. No. It wasn't suffering. You can't say we suffered. (*As she speaks, she straightens a chair which is overturned.*)

MR. FRANK. I know what you went through, you and Mr. Kraler. I'll remember it as long as I live. (*He gives one last look around.*) Come, Miep. (*He starts for the steps, then remembers his rucksack, going back to get it.*)

MIEP (*hurrying up to a cupboard*). Mr. Frank, did you see? There are some of your papers here. (*She brings a bundle of papers to him.*) We found them in a heap of rubbish on the floor after . . . after you left.

MR. FRANK. Burn them. (*He opens his rucksack to put the glove in it.*)

MIEP. But, Mr. Frank, there are letters, notes . . .

MR. FRANK. Burn them. All of them.

MIEP. Burn *this*? (*She hands him a paper-bound notebook.*)

MR. FRANK (*quietly*). Anne's diary. (*He opens the diary and begins to read.*) "Monday, the sixth of July, nineteen forty-two." (*To* MIEP) Nineteen forty-two. Is it possible, Miep? . . . Only three years ago. (*As he continues his reading, he sits down on the couch.*) "Dear Diary, since you and I are going to be great friends, I will start by telling you about myself. My name is Anne Frank. I am thirteen years old. I was born in Germany the twelfth of June, nineteen twenty-nine. As my family is Jewish, we emigrated to Holland when Hitler[1] came to power."

(*As* MR. FRANK *reads on, another voice joins his, as if coming from the air. It is* ANNE'S VOICE.)

MR. FRANK *and* **ANNE.** "My father started a business, importing spice and herbs. Things went well for us until nineteen forty. Then the war came, and the Dutch capitulation,[2] followed by the arrival of the Germans. Then things got very bad for the Jews."

(MR. FRANK'S *voice dies out.* ANNE'S VOICE *continues alone. The lights dim slowly to darkness. The curtain falls on the scene.*)

ANNE'S VOICE. You could not do this and you could not do that. They forced Father out of his business. We had to wear yellow stars. I had to turn in my bike. I couldn't go to a Dutch school any more. I couldn't

---

1. **Hitler,** Adolph Hitler (ā′dôlf hit′lər), 1889–1945, German National Socialist leader, dictator of Germany from 1933 to 1945.
2. **capitulation** (kə pich′ə lā′shən), *n.* a surrender on certain terms or conditions.

go to the movies, or ride in an automobile, or even on a streetcar, and a million other things. But somehow we children still managed to have fun. Yesterday Father told me we were going into hiding. Where, he wouldn't say. At five o'clock this morning Mother woke me and told me to hurry and get dressed. I was to put on as many clothes as I could. It would look too suspicious if we walked along carrying suitcases.

It wasn't until we were on our way that I learned where we were going. Our hiding place was to be upstairs in the building where Father used to have his business. Three other people were coming in with us . . . the Van Daans and their son Peter . . . Father knew the Van Daans but we had never met them . . .

(During the last lines the curtain rises on the scene. The lights dim on. ANNE'S VOICE *fades out.)*

▲ Anne's diary.

SCENE TWO

It is early morning, July, 1942. The rooms are bare, as before, but they are now clean and orderly.

MR. VAN DAAN, *a tall, portly man in his late forties, is in the main room, pacing up and down, nervously smoking a cigarette. His clothes and overcoat are expensive and well cut.*

MRS. VAN DAAN *sits on the couch, clutching her possessions, a hatbox, bags, etc. She is a pretty woman in her early forties. She wears a fur coat over her other clothes.*

PETER VAN DAAN *is standing at the window of the room on the right, looking down at the street below. He is a shy, awkward boy of sixteen. He wears a cap, a raincoat, and long Dutch trousers, like "plus fours."[3] At his feet is a black case, a carrier for his cat.*

The yellow Star of David[4] is <u>conspicuous</u>[5] on all of their clothes.

MRS. VAN DAAN *(rising, nervous, excited).* Something's happened to them! I know it!

MR. VAN DAAN. Now, Kerli![6]

MRS. VAN DAAN. Mr. Frank said they'd be here at seven o'clock. He said . . .

MR. VAN DAAN. They have two miles to walk. You can't expect . . .

MRS. VAN DAAN. They've been picked up. That's what's happened. They've been taken . . .

(MR. VAN DAAN indicates that he hears someone coming.)

MR. VAN DAAN. You see?

(PETER takes up his carrier and his schoolbag, etc., and goes into the main room as MR. FRANK comes up the stairwell from below. MR. FRANK looks much

3. **plus fours,** loose knickers that come down below the knee.
4. **Star of David,** a six-pointed star, a religious symbol of the Jewish people. In Nazi-occupied countries all Jews were required to wear a Star of David prominently displayed on their clothing.
5. conspicuous (kən spik′yŭ əs), *adj.* easily seen.
6. **Kerli** (ker′lē), a nickname.

▲ Mr. and Mrs. Van Daan and Mr. Kraler.

younger now. His movements are brisk, his manner confident. He wears an overcoat and carries his hat and a small cardboard box. He crosses to the VAN DAANS, *shaking hands with each of them.*)

MR. FRANK. Mrs. Van Daan, Mr. Van Daan, Peter. (*Then, in explanation of their lateness.*) There were too many of the Green Police[7] on the streets . . . we had to take the long way around.

(*Up the steps come* MARGOT FRANK, MRS. FRANK, MIEP—*not pregnant now*—*and* MR. KRALER. *All of them carry bags, packages, and so forth. The Star of David is conspicuous on all of the* FRANKS' *clothing.* MARGOT *is eighteen, beautiful, quiet, shy.* MRS. FRANK *is a young mother, gently bred, reserved. She, like* MR. FRANK, *has a slight German accent.* MR. KRALER *is a Dutchman, dependable, kindly.*

As MR. KRALER *and* MIEP *go upstage[8] to put down their parcels,* MRS. FRANK *turns back to call* ANNE.)

MRS. FRANK. Anne?

(ANNE *comes running up the stairs. She is thirteen, quick in her movements, interested in everything, mercurial[9] in her emotions. She wears a cape, long wool socks and carries a schoolbag.*)

MR. FRANK (*introducing them*). My wife, Edith. Mr. and Mrs. Van Daan (MRS. FRANK *hurries over, shaking hands with them.*) . . . their son, Peter . . . my daughters, Margot and Anne.

(ANNE *gives a polite little curtsy as she shakes* MR. VAN DAAN'*s hand. Then she immediately starts off on a tour of investigation of her new home, going upstairs to the attic room.* MIEP *and* MR. KRALER *are putting the various things they have brought on the shelves.*)

MR. KRALER. I'm sorry there is still so much confusion.

MR. FRANK. Please. Don't think of it. After all, we'll have plenty of leisure to arrange everything ourselves.

MIEP (*to* MRS. FRANK). We put the stores of food you sent in here. Your drugs are here . . . soap, linen here.

MR. FRANK. Thank you, Miep.

MIEP. I made up the beds . . . the way Mr. Frank and Mr. Kraler said. (*She starts out.*) Forgive me. I have to hurry. I've got to go to the other side of town to get some ration books[10] for you.

MRS. VAN DAAN. Ration books? If they see our names on ration books, they'll know we're here.

MR. KRALER. There isn't anything . . .

MIEP. Don't worry. Your names won't be on them.
(*As she hurries out.*) I'll be up later.

} (*Together.*)

MR. FRANK. Thank you, Miep.

MRS. FRANK (*to* MR. KRALER). It's illegal, then, the ration books? We've never done anything illegal.

MR. FRANK. We won't be living here exactly according to regulations.

(*As* MR. KRALER *reassures* MRS. FRANK, *he takes various small things, such as matches, soap, etc., from his pockets, handing them to her.*)

MR. KRALER. This isn't the black market, Mrs. Frank. This is what we call the white market[11] . . . helping all of the hundreds and hundreds who are hiding out in Amsterdam.

(*The carillon is heard playing the quarter-hour before eight.* MR. KRALER *looks at his watch.* ANNE *stops at the window as she comes down the stairs.*)

ANNE. It's the Westertoren!

---

7. **Green Police,** a branch of the Nazi police who wore green uniforms.
8. **upstage,** toward the back of the stage. *Down,* or *downstage,* means toward the front of the stage.
9. mercurial (mər kyùr′ē əl), *adj.* changeable.
10. **ration books,** books of coupons which allowed the bearer to buy a fixed amount of provisions or food.
11. **black market . . . white market.** Black market goods are sold illegally, usually at a very high price. The goods the Franks were receiving (white market) were donated by people wishing to help the Jews.

MR. KRALER. I must go. I must be out of here and downstairs in the office before the workmen get here. (*He starts for the stairs leading out.*) Miep or I, or both of us, will be up each day to bring you food and news and find out what your needs are. Tomorrow I'll get you a better bolt for the door at the foot of the stairs. It needs a bolt that you can throw yourself and open only at our signal. (*To* MR. FRANK) Oh . . . You'll tell them about the noise?

MR. FRANK. I'll tell them.

MR. KRALER. Good-by then for the moment. I'll come up again, after the workmen leave.

MR. FRANK. Good-by, Mr. Kraler.

MRS. FRANK (*shaking his hand*). How can we thank you?

(*The others murmur their good-bys.*)

MR. KRALER. I never thought I'd live to see the day when a man like Mr. Frank would have to go into hiding. When you think—

(*He breaks off, going out.* MR. FRANK *follows him down the steps, bolting the door after him. In the interval before he returns,* PETER *goes over to* MARGOT, *shaking hands with her. As* MR. FRANK *comes back up the steps,* MRS. FRANK *questions him anxiously.*)

MRS. FRANK. What did he mean, about the noise?

MR. FRANK. First let us take off some of these clothes.

(*They all start to take off garment after garment. On each of their coats, sweaters, blouses, suits, dresses, is another yellow Star of David.* MR. *and* MRS. FRANK *are underdressed quite simply. The others wear several things, sweaters, extra dresses, bathrobes, aprons, nightgowns, etc.*)

MR. VAN DAAN. It's a wonder we weren't arrested, walking along the streets . . . Petronella with a fur coat in July . . . and that cat of Peter's crying all the way.

ANNE (*as she is removing a pair of panties*). A cat?

MRS. FRANK (*shocked*). Anne, please!

ANNE. It's all right. I've got on three more.

(*She pulls off two more. Finally, as they have all removed their surplus clothes, they look to* MR. FRANK, *waiting for him to speak.*)

MR. FRANK. Now. About the noise. While the men are in the building below, we must have complete quiet. Every sound can be heard down there, not only in the workrooms, but in the offices too. The men come at about eight-thirty, and leave at about five-thirty. So, to be perfectly safe, from eight in the morning until six in the evening we must move only when it is necessary, and then in stockinged feet. We must not speak above a whisper. We must not run any water. We cannot use the sink, or even, forgive me, the w.c.[12] The pipes go down through the workrooms. It would be heard. No trash . . . (MR. FRANK *stops abruptly as he hears the sound of marching feet from the street below. Everyone is motionless, paralyzed with fear.* MR. FRANK *goes quietly into the room on the right to look down out of the window.* ANNE *runs after him, peering out with him. The tramping feet pass without stopping. The tension is relieved.* MR. FRANK, *followed by* ANNE, *returns to the main room and resumes his instructions to the group.*) . . . No trash must ever be thrown out which might reveal that someone is living up here . . . not even a potato paring. We must burn everything in the stove at night. This is the way we must live until it is over, if we are to survive.

(*There is silence for a second.*)

MRS. FRANK. Until it is over.

MR. FRANK (*reassuringly*). After six we can move about . . . we can talk and laugh and have our supper and read and play games . . . just as we would at home. (*He looks at his watch.*) And now I think it would be wise if we all went to our rooms, and were settled before eight o'clock. Mrs. Van Daan, you

---

12. **w.c.,** water closet, the bathroom.

and your husband will be upstairs. I regret that there's no place up there for Peter. But he will be here, near us. This will be our common room, where we'll meet to talk and eat and read, like one family.

MR. VAN DAAN. And where do you and Mrs. Frank sleep?

MR. FRANK. This room is also our bedroom.

MRS. VAN DAAN. That isn't right. We'll sleep here and you take the room upstairs. } *(Together.)*

MR. VAN DAAN. It's your place.

MR. FRANK. Please. I've thought this out for weeks. It's the best arrangement. The only arrangement.

MRS. VAN DAAN (*to* MR. FRANK). Never, never can we thank you. (*Then to* MRS. FRANK.) I don't know what would have happened to us, if it hadn't been for Mr. Frank.

MR. FRANK. You don't know how your husband helped me when I came to this country . . . knowing no one . . . not able to speak the language. I can never repay him for that. (*Going to* VAN DAAN) May I help you with your things?

MR. VAN DAAN. No. No. (*To* MRS. VAN DAAN) Come along, *liefje*.[13]

MRS. VAN DAAN. You'll be all right, Peter? You're not afraid?

PETER (*embarrassed*). Please, Mother.

(*They start up the stairs to the attic room above.* MR. FRANK *turns to* MRS. FRANK.)

MR. FRANK. You too must have some rest, Edith. You didn't close your eyes last night. Nor you, Margot.

---

13. *liefje* (lēf'hyə), darling.

⋏ Anne Frank (in light coat and hat) with family and friends.

ANNE. I slept, Father. Wasn't that funny? I knew it was the last night in my own bed, and yet I slept soundly.

MR. FRANK. I'm glad, Anne. Now you'll be able to help me straighten things in here. (*To* MRS. FRANK *and* MARGOT) Come with me . . . You and Margot rest in this room for the time being. (*He picks up their clothes, starting for the room on the right.*)

MRS. FRANK. You're sure . . . ? I could help . . . And Anne hasn't had her milk . . .

MR. FRANK. I'll give it to her. (*To* ANNE *and* PETER) Anne, Peter . . . it's best that you take off your shoes now, before you forget. (*He leads the way to the room, followed by* MARGOT.)

MRS. FRANK. You're sure you're not tired, Anne?

ANNE. I feel fine. I'm going to help Father.

MRS. FRANK. Peter, I'm glad you are to be with us.

PETER. Yes, Mrs. Frank.

(MRS. FRANK *goes to join* MR. FRANK *and* MARGOT.)

(*During the following scene* MR. FRANK *helps* MARGOT *and* MRS. FRANK *to hang up their clothes. Then he persuades them both to lie down and rest. The* VAN DAANS *in their room above settle themselves. In the main room* ANNE *and* PETER *remove their shoes.* PETER *takes his cat out of the carrier.*)

ANNE. What's your cat's name?

PETER. Mouschi.[14]

ANNE. Mouschi! Mouschi! Mouschi! (*She picks up the cat, walking away with it. To* PETER) I love cats. I have one . . . a darling little cat. But they made me leave her behind. I left some food and a note for the neighbors to take care of her . . . I'm going to miss her terribly. What is yours? A him or a her?

PETER. He's a tom. He doesn't like strangers. (*He takes the cat from her, putting it back in its carrier.*)

ANNE (*unabashed*).[15] Then I'll have to stop being a stranger, won't I? Is he fixed?

PETER (*startled*). Huh?

ANNE. Did you have him fixed?

PETER. No.

ANNE. Oh, you ought to have him fixed—to keep him from—you know, fighting. Where did you go to school?

PETER. Jewish Secondary.

ANNE. But that's where Margot and I go! I never saw you around.

PETER. I used to see you . . . sometimes . . .

ANNE. You did?

PETER. . . . in the school yard. You were always in the middle of a bunch of kids. (*He takes a penknife from his pocket.*)

ANNE. Why didn't you ever come over?

PETER. I'm sort of a lone wolf. (*He starts to rip off his Star of David.*)

ANNE. What are you doing?

PETER. Taking it off.

ANNE. But you can't do that. They'll arrest you if you go out without your star.

(*He tosses his knife on the table.*)

PETER. Who's going out?

ANNE. Why, of course! You're right! Of course we don't need them anymore. (*She picks up his knife and starts to take her star off.*) I wonder what our friends will think when we don't show up today?

PETER. I didn't have any dates with anyone.

ANNE. Oh, I did. I had a date with Jopie to go and play ping-pong at her house. Do you know Jopie deWaal?[16]

PETER. No.

ANNE. Jopie's my best friend. I wonder what she'll think when she telephones and there's no answer? . . . Probably she'll go over to the house . . . I wonder what she'll think . . . we left everything as if

---

14. **Mouschi** (mūs′kē).
15. **unabashed** (un′ə basht′), *adj.* not embarrassed or awed.
16. **Jopie deWaal** (yo′pē də väl′).

The building containing Mr. Frank's business, in which the Franks and Van Daans lived in hiding. Anne called their rooms in the top floor and attic the "Secret Annex."

we'd suddenly been called away . . . breakfast dishes in the sink . . . beds not made . . . *(As she pulls off her star the cloth underneath shows clearly the color and form of the star.)* Look! It's still there! (PETER *goes over to the stove with his star.)* What're you going to do with yours?

PETER. Burn it.

ANNE *(she starts to throw hers in, and cannot)*. It's funny, I can't throw mine away. I don't know why.

PETER. You can't throw . . . ? Something they branded you with . . . ? That they made you wear so they could spit on you?

ANNE. I know. I know. But after all, it *is* the Star of David, isn't it?

(In the bedroom, right, MARGOT *and* MRS. FRANK *are lying down.* MR. FRANK *starts quietly out.)*

PETER. Maybe it's different for a girl.

*(MR. FRANK *comes into the main room.)*

MR. FRANK. Forgive me, Peter. Now let me see. We must find a bed for your cat. *(He goes to the cupboard.)* I'm glad you brought your cat. Anne was feeling so badly about hers. *(Getting a used small washtub.)* Here we are. Will it be comfortable in that?

PETER *(gathering up his things)*. Thanks.

MR. FRANK *(opening the door of the room on the left)*. And here is your room. But I warn you, Peter, you can't grow any more. Not an inch, or you'll have to sleep with your feet out of the skylight. Are you hungry?

PETER. No.

MR. FRANK. We have some bread and butter.

PETER. No, thank you.

MR. FRANK. You can have it for luncheon then. And tonight we will have a real supper . . . our first supper together.

PETER. Thanks. Thanks.

(He goes into his room. During the following scene he arranges his possessions in his new room.)

MR. FRANK. That's a nice boy, Peter.

The yellow Star of David, which all Dutch Jews were forced to wear by the Nazis.

ANNE. He's awfully shy, isn't he?

MR. FRANK. You'll like him, I know.

ANNE. I certainly hope so, since he's the only boy I'm likely to see for months and months.

*(MR. FRANK *sits down, taking off his shoes.)*

MR. FRANK. Annele,[17] there's a box there. Will you open it?

(He indicates a carton on the couch. ANNE *brings it to the center table. In the street below there is the sound of children playing.)*

ANNE *(as she opens the carton)*. You know the way I'm going to think of it here? I'm going to think of it as a boarding house. A very peculiar summer boarding house, like the one that we—*(She breaks off as she pulls out some photographs.)* Father! My movie stars! I was wondering where they were! I was looking for them this morning . . . and

---

17. **Annele** (än′ə lə), little Anne. *Anneke* (än′ə kə), used later, is a similar term of endearment.

Queen Wilhelmina![18] How wonderful!

MR. FRANK. There's something more. Go on. Look further.

(*He goes over to the sink, pouring a glass of milk from a thermos bottle.*)

ANNE (*pulling out a pasteboard-bound book*). A diary! (*She throws her arms around her father.*) I've never had a diary. And I've always longed for one. (*She looks around the room.*) Pencil, pencil, pencil. (*She starts down the stairs.*) I'm going down to the office to get a pencil.

MR. FRANK. Anne! No!

(*He goes after her, catching her by the arm and pulling her back.*)

ANNE (*startled*). But there's no one in the building now.

MR. FRANK. It doesn't matter. I don't want you ever to go beyond that door.

ANNE (*sobered*). Never . . . ? Not even at night time, when everyone is gone? Or on Sundays? Can't I go down to listen to the radio?

MR. FRANK. Never. I am sorry, Anneke. It isn't safe. No, you must never go beyond that door.

(*For the first time* ANNE *realizes what "going into hiding" means.*)

ANNE. I see.

MR. FRANK. It'll be hard, I know. But always remember this, Anneke. There are no walls, there are no bolts, no locks that anyone can put on your mind. Miep will bring us books. We will read history, poetry, mythology. (*He gives her the glass of milk.*) Here's your milk. (*With his arm about her, they go over to the couch, sitting down side by side.*) As a matter of fact, between us, Anne, being here has certain advantages for you. For instance, you remember the battle you had with your mother the other day on the subject of overshoes? You said you'd rather die than wear overshoes? But in the end you had to wear them? Well now, you see, for as long as we are here you will never have to wear overshoes! Isn't that good? And the coat that you inherited from Margot, you won't have to wear that any more. And the piano! You won't have to practice on the piano. I tell you, this is going to be a fine life for you!

(ANNE*'s panic is gone.* PETER *appears in the doorway of his room, with a saucer in his hand. He is carrying his cat.*)

PETER. I . . . I . . . I thought I'd better get some water for Mouschi before . . .

MR. FRANK. Of course.

(*As he starts toward the sink the carillon begins to chime the hour of eight. He tiptoes to the window at the back and looks down at the street below. He turns to* PETER, *indicating in* pantomime[19] *that it is too late.* PETER *starts back for his room. He steps on a creaking board. The three of them are frozen for a minute in fear. As* PETER *starts away again,* ANNE *tiptoes over to him and pours some of the milk from her glass into the saucer for the cat.* PETER *squats on the floor, putting the milk before the cat.* MR. FRANK *gives* ANNE *his fountain pen, and then goes into the room at the right. For a second* ANNE *watches the cat, then she goes over to the center table, and opens her diary.*

In the room at the right, MRS. FRANK *has sat up quickly at the sound of the carillon.* MR. FRANK *comes in and sits down beside her on the settee, his arm comfortingly around her.*

Upstairs, in the attic room, MR. *and* MRS. VAN DAAN *have hung their clothes in the closet and are now seated on the iron bed.* MRS. VAN DAAN *leans back exhausted.* MR. VAN DAAN *fans her with a newspaper.*

ANNE *starts to write in her diary. The lights dim out, the curtain falls.*

In the darkness ANNE'S VOICE *comes to us*

---

18. **Queen Wilhelmina** (wil′hel mē′nə), queen of the Netherlands from 1890 to 1948.
19. **pantomime** (pan′tə mīm), *n.* gestures without words.

again, faintly at first, and then with growing strength.)

ANNE'S VOICE. I expect I should be describing what it feels like to go into hiding. But I really don't know yet myself. I only know it's funny never to be able to go outdoors . . . never to breathe fresh air . . . never to run and shout and jump. It's the silence in the nights that frightens me most. Every time I hear a creak in the house, or a step on the street outside, I'm sure they're coming for us. The days aren't so bad. At least we know that Miep and Mr. Kraler are down there below us in the office. Our protectors, we call them. I asked Father what would happen to them if the Nazis found out they were hiding us. Pim[20] said that they would suffer the same fate that we would . . . Imagine! They know this, and yet when they come up here, they're always cheerful and gay as if there were nothing in the world to bother them . . . Friday, the twenty-first of August, nineteen forty-two. Today I'm going to tell you our general news. Mother is unbearable. She insists on treating me like a baby, which I loathe. Otherwise things are going better. The weather is . . .

(As ANNE'S VOICE *is fading out, the curtain rises on the scene.)*

▲ View from the attic window of the annex, showing the bell tower of the Westertoren.

---

20. **Pim,** a nickname Anne gave to her father.

After Reading

Making Connections

1. Review the entries you made in your Double-Entry Reading Log. Which of your notes was the most meaningful to you? Explain why.

2. Choose four **characters** and list words you would use to describe their physical appearances and personalities.

3. In Scene One, Anne's voice joins her father's as he reads aloud from her diary. Then her voice continues alone. What is the effect of using her voice in this way?

4. Peter burns the yellow star, but Anne does not. What other differences do you see in these two characters?

5. Review the rules they must all live by. How would you cope with such conditions?

Literary Focus: Flashback

A **flashback** is an interruption in the time order of events to show something that happened earlier. In the play, Scene Two is set three years *before* Scene One. Most of the action of the play takes place before the time of Scene One. Why do you think the authors used this flashback technique here?

Vocabulary Study

**capitulation
conspicuous
mercurial
unabashed
pantomime**

Write the letter of the phrase that best completes each sentence.

1. After the capitulation of the Dutch
   a. they took over from the Germans.
   b. the Germans took over.
   c. there was no real change in government.

2. If the yellow Star of David was conspicuous, it was probably
   a. clearly visible.   b. dirty.   c. well hidden.

3. Anne is "mercurial in her emotions," so she would most likely be
   a. sad and moping around all the time.
   b. confused, but not really caring.
   c. lively, with quickly changing moods.

4. When Anne acted unabashed, she was probably
   a. crying.   b. self-confident.   c. hurt.

5. If Mr. Frank indicated something in pantomime, he
   a. screamed.   b. whispered.   c. was silent.

Otto Frank, Anne's father.

SCENE THREE

It is a little after six o'clock in the evening, two months later.

MARGOT *is in the bedroom at the right, studying.* MR. VAN DAAN *is lying down in the attic room above.*

The rest of the "family" is in the main room. ANNE *and* PETER *sit opposite each other at the center table, where they have been doing their lessons.* MRS. FRANK *is on the couch.* MRS. VAN DAAN *is seated with her fur coat, on which she has been sewing, in her lap. None of them are wearing their shoes.*

Their eyes are on MR. FRANK, *waiting for him to give them the signal which will release them from their day-long quiet.* MR. FRANK, *his shoes in his hand, stands looking down out of the window at the back, watching to be sure that all of the workmen have left the building below.*

After a few seconds of motionless silence, MR. FRANK *turns from the window.*

MR. FRANK (*quietly, to the group*). It's safe now.

The last workman has left.

(*There is an immediate stir of relief.*)

ANNE (*her pent-up energy explodes*). WHEE!

MRS. FRANK (*startled, amused*). Anne!

MRS. VAN DAAN. I'm first for the w.c.

(*She hurries off to the bathroom.* MRS. FRANK *puts on her shoes and starts up to the sink to prepare supper.* ANNE *sneaks* PETER'*s shoes from under the table and hides them behind her back.* MR. FRANK *goes in to* MARGOT'*s room.*)

MR. FRANK (*to* MARGOT). Six o'clock. School's over.

(MARGOT *gets up, stretching.* MR. FRANK *sits down to put on his shoes. In the main room* PETER *tries to find his.*)

PETER (*to* ANNE). Have you seen my shoes?

ANNE (*innocently*). Your shoes?

PETER. You've taken them, haven't you?

ANNE. I don't know what you're talking about.

PETER. You're going to be sorry!

ANNE. Am I?

(PETER *goes after her.* ANNE, *with his shoes in her hand, runs from him, dodging behind her mother.*)

MRS. FRANK (*protesting*). Anne, dear!

PETER. Wait till I get you!

ANNE. I'm waiting! (PETER *makes a lunge for her. They both fall to the floor.* PETER *pins her down, wrestling with her to get the shoes.*) Don't! Don't! Peter, stop it. Ouch!

MRS. FRANK. Anne! . . . Peter!

(*Suddenly* PETER *becomes self-conscious. He grabs his shoes roughly and starts for his room.*)

ANNE (*following him*). Peter, where are you going? Come dance with me.

PETER. I tell you I don't know how.

ANNE. I'll teach you.

PETER. I'm going to give Mouschi his dinner.

ANNE. Can I watch?

PETER. He doesn't like people around while he eats.

ANNE. Peter, please.

PETER. No!

(*He goes into his room.* ANNE *slams his door after him.*)

MRS. FRANK. Anne, dear, I think you shouldn't play like that with Peter. It's not dignified.[1]

ANNE. Who cares if it's dignified? I don't want to be dignified.

(MR. FRANK *and* MARGOT *come from the room on the right.* MARGOT *goes to help her mother.* MR. FRANK *starts for the center table to correct* MARGOT's *school papers.*)

MRS. FRANK (*to* ANNE). You complain that I don't treat you like a grownup. But when I do, you resent it.

ANNE. I only want some fun . . . someone to laugh and clown with . . . After you've sat still all day and hardly moved, you've got to have some fun. I don't know what's the matter with that boy.

MR. FRANK. He isn't used to girls. Give him a little time.

ANNE. Time? Isn't two months time? I could cry. (*Catching hold of* MARGOT) Come on, Margot . . . dance with me. Come on, please.

MARGOT. I have to help with supper.

ANNE. You know we're going to forget how to dance . . . When we get out we won't remember a thing.

(*She starts to sing and dance by herself.* MR. FRANK *takes her in his arms, waltzing with her.* MRS. VAN DAAN *comes in from the bathroom.*)

MRS. VAN DAAN. Next? (*She looks around as she starts putting on her shoes.*) Where's Peter?

ANNE (*as they are dancing*). Where would he be!

MRS. VAN DAAN. He hasn't finished his lessons, has he? His father'll kill him if he catches him in there with that cat and his work not done. (MR. FRANK *and* ANNE *finish their dance. They bow to each other with extravagant formality.*) Anne, get him out of there, will you?

ANNE (*at* PETER's *door*). Peter? Peter?

PETER (*opening the door a crack*). What is it?

ANNE. Your mother says to come out.

PETER. I'm giving Mouschi his dinner.

MRS. VAN DAAN. You know what your father says. (*She sits on the couch, sewing on the lining of her fur coat.*)

PETER. For heaven's sake, I haven't even looked at him since lunch.

MRS. VAN DAAN. I'm just telling you, that's all.

ANNE. I'll feed him.

PETER. I don't want you in there.

MRS. VAN DAAN. Peter!

PETER (*to* ANNE). Then give him his dinner and come right out, you hear?

(*He comes back to the table.* ANNE *shuts the door of* PETER's *room after her and disappears behind the curtain covering his closet.*)

MRS. VAN DAAN (*to* PETER). Now is that any way

---

1. **dignified** (dig′nə fīd), *adj.* having pride and self-respect in manner, style, or appearance.

to talk to your little girl friend?

PETER. Mother . . . for heaven's sake . . . will you please stop saying that?

MRS. VAN DAAN. Look at him blush! Look at him!

PETER. Please! I'm not . . . anyway . . . let me alone, will you?

MRS. VAN DAAN. He acts like it was something to be ashamed of. It's nothing to be ashamed of, to have a little girl friend.

PETER. You're crazy. She's only thirteen.

MRS. VAN DAAN. So what? And you're sixteen. Just perfect. Your father's ten years older than I am. (*To* MR. FRANK) I warn you, Mr. Frank, if this war lasts much longer, we're going to be related and then . . .

MR. FRANK. *Mazeltov!*[2]

MRS. FRANK (*deliberately changing the conversation*). I wonder where Miep is. She's usually so prompt.

(*Suddenly everything else is forgotten as they hear the sound of an automobile coming to a screeching stop in the street below. They are tense, motionless in their terror. The car starts away. A wave of relief sweeps over them. They pick up their occupations again.* ANNE *flings open the door of* PETER*'s room, making a dramatic entrance. She is dressed in* PETER*'s clothes.* PETER *looks at her in fury. The others are amused.*)

ANNE. Good evening, everyone. Forgive me if I don't stay. (*She jumps up on a chair.*) I have a friend waiting for me in there. My friend Tom. Tom Cat. Some people say that we look alike. But Tom has the most beautiful whiskers, and I have only a little fuzz. I am hoping . . . in time . . .

PETER. All right, Mrs. Quack Quack!

ANNE (*outraged—jumping down*). Peter!

PETER. I heard about you . . . How you talked so much in class they called you Mrs. Quack Quack. How Mr. Smitter made you write a composition . . . "'Quack, quack,' said Mrs. Quack Quack."

ANNE. Well, go on. Tell them the rest. How it was so good he read it out loud to the class and then read it to all his other classes!

PETER. Quack! Quack! Quack . . . Quack . . . Quack . . .

(ANNE *pulls off the coat and trousers.*)

ANNE. You are the most intolerable, insufferable boy I've ever met.

(*She throws the clothes down the stairwell.* PETER *goes down after them.*)

PETER. Quack, quack, quack!

MRS. VAN DAAN (*to* ANNE). That's right, Anneke! Give it to him!

ANNE. With all the boys in the world . . . Why I had to get locked up with one like you! . . .

PETER. Quack, quack, quack, and from now on stay out of my room!

(*As* PETER *passes her,* ANNE *puts out her foot, tripping him. He picks himself up, and goes on into his room.*)

MRS. FRANK (*quietly*). Anne, dear . . . your hair. (*She feels* ANNE*'s forehead.*) You're warm. Are you feeling all right?

ANNE. Please, Mother. (*She goes over to the center table, slipping into her shoes.*)

MRS. FRANK (*following her*). You haven't a fever, have you?

ANNE (*pulling away*). No. No.

MRS. FRANK. You know we can't call a doctor here, ever. There's only one thing to do . . . watch carefully. Prevent an illness before it comes. Let me see your tongue.

ANNE. Mother, this is perfectly absurd.

MRS. FRANK. Anne, dear, don't be such a baby. Let me see your tongue. (*As* ANNE *refuses,* MRS. FRANK *appeals to* MR. FRANK.) Otto . . . ?

MR. FRANK. You hear your mother, Anne.

(ANNE *flicks out her tongue for a second, then turns away.*)

---

2. *Mazeltov* (mä′zəl tof), an expression used among Jews to express congratulations or wish good luck.

Floor plan of the office building and the top floors that served as a hiding place for the Franks and Van Daans. (This plan does not show the ground-level rooms. Europeans refer to street level as *groundfloor,* and the next floor as *first floor.*).

MRS. FRANK. Come on—open up! (*As* ANNE *opens her mouth very wide*) You seem all right . . . but perhaps an aspirin . . .

MRS. VAN DAAN. For heaven's sake, don't give that child any pills. I waited for fifteen minutes this morning for her to come out of the w.c.

ANNE. I was washing my hair!

MR. FRANK. I think there's nothing the matter with our Anne that a ride on her bike, or a visit with her friend Jopie deWaal wouldn't cure. Isn't that so, Anne?

(MR. VAN DAAN *comes down into the room. From outside we hear faint sounds of bombers going over and a burst of ack-ack.*[3])

MR. VAN DAAN. Miep not come yet?

MRS. VAN DAAN. The workmen just left, a little while ago.

MR. VAN DAAN. What's for dinner tonight?

MRS. VAN DAAN. Beans.

MR. VAN DAAN. Not again!

MRS. VAN DAAN. Poor Putti![4] I know. But what can we do? That's all that Miep brought us.

(MR. VAN DAAN *starts to pace, his hands behind his back.* ANNE *follows behind him, imitating him.*)

ANNE. We are now in what is know as the "bean cycle." Beans boiled, beans *en casserole,*[5] beans with strings, beans without strings . . .

(PETER *has come out of his room. He slides into his*

---

3. **ack-ack,** slang for antiaircraft fire.
4. **Putti** (pu̇t′ē).
5. *en casserole* (an käs rôl′), prepared and served in a covered baking dish.

The Diary of Anne Frank—Act One, Scene 3   **555**

place at the table, becoming immediately absorbed in his studies.)

MR. VAN DAAN (*to* PETER). I saw you . . . in there, playing with your cat.

MRS. VAN DAAN. He just went in for a second, putting his coat away. He's been out here all the time, doing his lessons.

MR. FRANK (*looking up from the paper*). Anne, you got an excellent in your history paper today . . . and very good in Latin.

ANNE (*sitting beside him*). How about algebra?

MR. FRANK. I'll have to make a confession. Up until now I've managed to stay ahead of you in algebra. Today you caught up with me. We'll leave it to Margot to correct.

ANNE. Isn't algebra *vile*, Pim!

MR. FRANK. Vile!

MARGOT (*to* MR. FRANK). How did I do?

ANNE (*getting up*). Excellent, excellent, excellent, excellent!

MR. FRANK (*to* MARGOT). You should have used the subjunctive here . . .

MARGOT. Should I? . . . I thought . . . look here . . . I didn't use it here . . .

(*The two become absorbed in the papers.*)

ANNE. Mrs. Van Daan, may I try on your coat?

MRS. FRANK. No, Anne.

MRS. VAN DAAN (*giving it to* ANNE). It's all right . . . but careful with it. (ANNE *puts it on and struts with it.*) My father gave me that the year before he died. He always bought the best that money could buy.

ANNE. Mrs. Van Daan, did you have a lot of boy friends before you were married?

MRS. FRANK. Anne, that's a personal question. It's not courteous to ask personal questions.

MRS. VAN DAAN. Oh I don't mind. (*To* ANNE) Our house was always swarming with boys. When I was a girl we had . . .

MR. VAN DAAN. Oh, . . . not again!

MRS. VAN DAAN (*good-humored*). Shut up! (*Without a pause, to* ANNE. MR. VAN DAAN *mim-* ics MRS. VAN DAAN, *speaking the first few words in unison with her.*) One summer we had a big house in Hilversum.[6] The boys came buzzing round like bees around a jam pot. And when I was sixteen! . . . We were wearing our skirts very short those days and I had good-looking legs. (*She pulls up her skirt, going to* MR. FRANK.) I still have 'em. I may not be as pretty as I used to be, but I still have my legs. How about it, Mr. Frank?

MR. VAN DAAN. All right. All right. We see them.

MRS. VAN DAAN. I'm not asking you. I'm asking Mr. Frank.

PETER. Mother, for heaven's sake.

MRS. VAN DAAN. Oh, I embarrass you, do I? Well, I just hope the girl you marry has as good. (*Then to* ANNE) My father used to worry about me, with so many boys hanging round. He told me, if any of them gets fresh, you say to him . . . "Remember, Mr. So-and-So, remember I'm a lady."

ANNE. "Remember, Mr. So-and-So, remember I'm a lady."

(*She gives* MRS. VAN DAAN *her coat.*)

MR. VAN DAAN. Look at you, talking that way in front of her! Don't you know she puts it all down in that diary?

MRS. VAN DAAN. So, if she does? I'm only telling the truth!

(ANNE *stretches out, putting her ear to the floor, listening to what is going on below. The sound of the bombers fades away.*)

MRS. FRANK (*setting the table*). Would you mind, Peter, if I moved you over to the couch?

ANNE (*listening*). Miep must have the radio on.

(PETER *picks up his papers, going over to the couch beside* MRS. VAN DAAN.)

MR. VAN DAAN (*accusingly, to* PETER). Haven't you finished yet?

PETER. No.

---

6. **Hilversum** (hil′vər səm), a health resort and residential area some miles from Amsterdam.

MR. VAN DAAN. You ought to be ashamed of yourself.

PETER. All right. All right. I'm a dunce. I'm a hopeless case. Why do I go on?

MRS. VAN DAAN. You're not hopeless. Don't talk that way. It's just that you haven't anyone to help you, like the girls have. (*To* MR. FRANK) Maybe you could help him, Mr. Frank?

MR. FRANK. I'm sure that his father . . . ?

MR. VAN DAAN. Not me. I can't do anything with him. He won't listen to me. You go ahead . . . if you want.

MR. FRANK (*going to* PETER). What about it, Peter? Shall we make our school coeducational?

MRS. VAN DAAN (*kissing* MR. FRANK). You're an angel, Mr. Frank. An angel. I don't know why I didn't meet you before I met that one there. Here, sit down, Mr. Frank . . . (*She forces him down on the couch beside* PETER.) Now, Peter, you listen to Mr. Frank.

MR. FRANK. It might be better for us to go into Peter's room.

(PETER *jumps up eagerly, leading the way.*)

MRS. VAN DAAN. That's right. You go in there, Peter. You listen to Mr. Frank. Mr. Frank is a highly educated man.

(*As* MR. FRANK *is about to follow* PETER *into his room,* MRS. FRANK *stops him and wipes the lipstick from his lips. Then she closes the door after them.*)

ANNE (*on the floor, listening*). Shh! I can hear a man's voice talking.

MR. VAN DAAN (*to* ANNE). Isn't it bad enough here without your sprawling all over the place?

(ANNE *sits up.*)

MRS. VAN DAAN (*to* MR. VAN DAAN). If you didn't smoke so much, you wouldn't be so bad-tempered.

MR. VAN DAAN. Am I smoking? Do you see me smoking?

MRS. VAN DAAN. Don't tell me you've used up all those cigarettes.

MR. VAN DAAN. One package. Miep only brought me one package.

MRS. VAN DAAN. It's a filthy habit anyway. It's a good time to break yourself.

MR. VAN DAAN. Oh, stop it, please.

MRS. VAN DAAN. You're smoking up all our money. You know that, don't you?

MR. VAN DAAN. Will you shut up? (*During this,* MRS. FRANK *and* MARGOT *have studiously kept their eyes down. But* ANNE, *seated on the floor, has been following the discussion interestedly.* MR. VAN DAAN *turns to see her staring up at him.*) And what are you staring at?

ANNE. I never heard grownups quarrel before. I thought only children quarreled.

MR. VAN DAAN. This isn't a quarrel! It's a discussion. And I never heard children so rude before.

ANNE (*rising, indignantly*[7]). I, rude!

MR. VAN DAAN. Yes!

MRS. FRANK (*quickly*). Anne, will you get me my knitting? (ANNE *goes to get it.*) I must remember, when Miep comes, to ask her to bring me some more wool.

MARGOT (*going to her room*). I need some hairpins and some soap. I made a list. (*She goes into her bedroom to get the list.*)

MRS. FRANK (*to* ANNE). Have you some library books for Miep when she comes?

ANNE. It's a wonder that Miep has a life of her own, the way we make her run errands for us. Please, Miep, get me some starch. Please take my hair out and have it cut. Tell me all the latest news, Miep. (*She goes over, kneeling on the couch beside* MRS. VAN DAAN.) Did you know she was engaged? His name is Dirk, and Miep's afraid the Nazis will ship him off to Germany to work in one of their war plants. That's what they're

---

7. **indignantly** (in dig′nənt lē), *adv.* with anger at something unjust or unfair.

doing with some of the young Dutchmen . . . they pick them up off the streets—

MR. VAN DAAN *(interrupting).* Don't you ever get tired of talking? Suppose you try keeping still for five minutes. Just five minutes.

(He starts to pace again. Again ANNE *follows him, mimicking him.* MRS. FRANK *jumps up and takes her by the arm up to the sink, and gives her a glass of milk.)*

MRS. FRANK. Come here, Anne. It's time for your glass of milk.

MR. VAN DAAN. Talk, talk, talk. I never heard such a child. Where is my . . .? Every evening it's the same, talk, talk, talk. *(He looks around.)* Where is my . . . ?

MRS. VAN DAAN. What're you looking for?

MR. VAN DAAN. My pipe. Have you seen my pipe?

MRS. VAN DAAN. What good's a pipe? You haven't got any tobacco.

MR. VAN DAAN. At least I'll have something to hold in my mouth! *(Opening* MARGOT*'s bedroom door)* Margot, have you seen my pipe?

MARGOT. It was on the table last night.

*(*ANNE *puts her glass of milk on the table and picks up his pipe, hiding it behind her back.)*

MR. VAN DAAN. I know. I know. Anne, did you see my pipe? . . . Anne!

MRS. FRANK. Anne, Mr. Van Daan is speaking to you.

ANNE. Am I allowed to talk now?

MR. VAN DAAN. You're the most aggravating . . . The trouble with you is, you've been spoiled. What you need is a good old-fashioned spanking.

ANNE *(mimicking* MRS. VAN DAAN*).* "Remember, Mr. So-and-So, remember I'm a lady."

(She thrusts the pipe into his mouth, then picks up her glass of milk.)

MR. VAN DAAN *(restraining himself with difficulty).* Why aren't you nice and quiet like your sister Margot? Why do you have to show off all the time? Let me give you a little advice,

young lady. Men don't like that kind of thing in a girl. You know that? A man likes a girl who'll listen to him once in a while . . . a domestic[8] girl, who'll keep her house shining for her husband . . . who loves to cook and sew and . . .

ANNE. I'd cut my throat first! I'd open my veins! I'm going to be remarkable! I'm going to Paris . . .

MR. VAN DAAN *(scoffingly).* Paris!

ANNE. . . . to study music and art.

MR. VAN DAAN. Yeah! Yeah!

ANNE. I'm going to be a famous dancer or singer . . . or something wonderful.

(She makes a wide gesture, spilling the glass of milk on the fur coat in MRS. VAN DAAN*'s lap.* MARGOT *rushes quickly over with a towel.* ANNE *tries to brush the milk off with her skirt.)*

MRS. VAN DAAN. Now look what you've done . . . you clumsy little fool! My beautiful fur coat my father gave me . . .

ANNE. I'm so sorry.

MRS. VAN DAAN. What do you care? It isn't yours . . . So go on, ruin it! Do you know what that coat cost? Do you? And now look at it! Look at it!

ANNE. I'm very, very sorry.

MRS. VAN DAAN. I could kill you for this. I could just kill you!

*(*MRS. VAN DAAN *goes up the stairs, clutching the coat.* MR. VAN DAAN *starts after her.)*

MR. VAN DAAN. Petronella . . . *liefje! Liefje!* . . . Come back . . . the supper . . . come back!

MRS. FRANK. Anne, you must not behave in that way.

ANNE. It was an accident. Anyone can have an accident.

MRS. FRANK. I don't mean that. I mean the answering back. You must not answer back. They are our guests. We must always show the greatest courtesy to them. We're

---

8. **domestic** (də mes′tik), *adj.* devoted to family life.

all living under terrible tension. *(She stops as* MARGOT *indicates that* VAN DAAN *can hear. When he is gone, she continues.)* That's why we must control ourselves . . . You don't hear Margot getting into arguments with them, do you? Watch Margot. She's always courteous with them. Never familiar. She keeps her distance. And they respect her for it. Try to be like Margot.

ANNE. And have them walk all over me, the way they do her? No, thanks!

MRS. FRANK. I'm not afraid that anyone is going to walk all over you, Anne. I'm afraid for other people, that you'll walk on them. I don't know what happens to you, Anne. You are wild, self-willed. If I had ever talked to my mother as you talk to me . . .

ANNE. Things have changed. People aren't like that any more. "Yes, Mother." "No, Mother." "Anything you say, Mother." I've got to fight things out for myself! Make something of myself!

MRS. FRANK. It isn't necessary to fight to do it. Margot doesn't fight, and isn't she . . . ?

ANNE *(violently rebellious).* Margot! Margot! Margot! That's all I hear from everyone . . . how wonderful Margot is . . . "Why aren't you like Margot?"

MARGOT *(protesting).* Oh, come on, Anne, don't be so . . .

ANNE *(paying no attention).* Everything she does is right, and everything I do is wrong! I'm the goat around here! . . . You're all against me! . . . And you worst of all!

(She rushes off into her room and throws herself down on the settee, stifling her sobs. MRS. FRANK *sighs and starts toward the stove.)*

MRS. FRANK *(to* MARGOT*).* Let's put the soup on the stove . . . if there's anyone who cares to eat. Margot, will you take the bread out? *(MARGOT gets the bread from the cupboard.)* I don't know how we can go on living this way . . . I can't say a word to Anne . . . she flies at me . . .

MARGOT. You know Anne. In half an hour she'll be out here, laughing and joking.

MRS. FRANK. And . . . *(She makes a motion upwards, indicating the* VAN DAANS.) . . . I told your father it wouldn't work . . . but no . . . no . . . he had to ask them, he said . . . he owed it to him, he said. Well, he knows now that I was right! These quarrels! . . . This bickering!

MARGOT *(with a warning look).* Shush. Shush.

(The buzzer for the door sounds. MRS. FRANK *gasps, startled.)*

MRS. FRANK. Every time I hear that sound, my heart stops!

MARGOT *(starting for* PETER's *door).* It's Miep. *(She knocks at the door.)* Father?

(MR. FRANK comes quickly from PETER's *room.)*

MR. FRANK. Thank you, Margot. *(As he goes down the steps to open the outer door)* Has everyone his list?

MARGOT. I'll get my books. *(Giving her mother a list.)* Here's your list. *(MARGOT goes into her and* ANNE's *bedroom on the right.* ANNE *sits up, hiding her tears, as* MARGOT *comes in.)* Miep's here.

(MARGOT picks up her books and goes back. ANNE *hurries over to the mirror, smoothing her hair.)*

MR. VAN DAAN *(coming down the stairs).* Is it Miep?

MARGOT. Yes. Father's gone down to let her in.

MR. VAN DAAN. At last I'll have some cigarettes!

MRS. FRANK *(to* MR. VAN DAAN*).* I can't tell you how unhappy I am about Mrs. Van Daan's coat. Anne should never have touched it.

MR. VAN DAAN. She'll be all right.

MRS. FRANK. Is there anything I can do?

MR. VAN DAAN. Don't worry.

(He turns to meet MIEP. *But it is not* MIEP *who comes up the steps. It is* MR. KRALER, *followed by* MR. FRANK. *Their faces are grave.* ANNE *comes from the bedroom.* PETER *comes from his room.)*

MRS. FRANK. Mr. Kraler!

MR. VAN DAAN. How are you, Mr. Kraler?

MARGOT. This is a surprise.

MRS. FRANK. When Mr. Kraler comes, the sun begins to shine.

MR. VAN DAAN. Miep is coming?

MR. KRALER. Not tonight.

(KRALER *goes to* MARGOT *and* MRS. FRANK *and* ANNE, *shaking hands with them.*)

MRS. FRANK. Wouldn't you like a cup of coffee? . . . Or, better still, will you have supper with us?

MR. FRANK. Mr. Kraler has something to talk over with us. Something has happened, he says, which demands an immediate decision.

MRS. FRANK (*fearful*). What is it?

(MR. KRALER *sits down on the couch. As he talks he takes bread, cabbages, milk, etc., from his briefcase, giving them to* MARGOT *and* ANNE *to put away.*)

MR. KRALER. Usually, when I come up here, I try to bring you some bit of good news. What's the use of telling you the bad news when there's nothing that you can do about it? But today something has happened . . . Dirk . . . Miep's Dirk, you know, came to me just now. He tells me that he has a Jewish friend living near him. A dentist. He says he's in trouble. He begged me, could I do anything for this man? Could I find him a hiding place? . . . So I've come to you . . . I know it's a terrible thing to ask of you, living as you are, but would you take him in with you?

MR. FRANK. Of course we will.

MR. KRALER (*rising*). It'll be just for a night or two . . . until I find some other place. This happened so suddenly that I didn't know where to turn.

MR. FRANK. Where is he?

MR. KRALER. Downstairs in the office.

MR. FRANK. Good. Bring him up.

MR. KRALER. His name is Dussel . . . Jan Dussel.

MR. FRANK. Dussel . . . I think I know him.

MR. KRALER. I'll get him.

(*He goes quickly down the steps and out.* MR. FRANK *suddenly becomes conscious of the others.*)

MR. FRANK. Forgive me. I spoke without consulting you. But I knew you'd feel as I do.

MR. VAN DAAN. There's no reason for you to consult anyone. This is your place. You have a right to do exactly as you please. The only thing I feel . . . there's so little food as it is . . . and to take in another person . . .

(PETER *turns away, ashamed of his father.*)

MR. FRANK. We can stretch the food a little. It's only for a few days.

MR. VAN DAAN. You want to make a bet?

MRS. FRANK. I think it's fine to have him. But, Otto, where are you going to put him? Where?

PETER. He can have my bed. I can sleep on the floor. I wouldn't mind.

MR. FRANK. That's good of you, Peter. But your room's too small . . . even for *you.*

ANNE. I have a much better idea. I'll come in here with you and Mother, and Margot can take Peter's room and Peter can go in our room with Mr. Dussel.

MARGOT. That's right. We could do that.

MR. FRANK. No, Margot. You mustn't sleep in that room . . . neither you nor Anne. Mouschi has caught some rats in there. Peter's brave. He doesn't mind.

ANNE. Then how about *this?* I'll come in here with you and Mother, and Mr. Dussel can have my bed.

MRS. FRANK. No. No. *No!* Margot will come in here with us and he can have her bed. It's the only way. Margot, bring your things in here. Help her, Anne.

(MARGOT *hurries into her room to get her things.*)

ANNE (*to her mother*). Why Margot? Why can't I come in here?

MRS. FRANK. Because it wouldn't be proper for Margot to sleep with a . . . Please, Anne. Don't argue. Please.

▲ Margot Frank.

(ANNE *starts slowly away.*)

MR. FRANK (*to* ANNE). You don't mind sharing your room with Mr. Dussel, do you, Anne?

ANNE. No. No, of course not.

MR. FRANK. Good. (ANNE *goes off into her bedroom, helping* MARGOT. MR. FRANK *starts to search in the cupboards.*) Where's the cognac?

MRS. FRANK. It's there. But, Otto, I was saving it in case of illness.

MR. FRANK. I think we couldn't find a better time to use it. Peter, will you get five glasses for me?

(PETER *goes for the glasses.* MARGOT *comes out of her bedroom, carrying her possessions, which she hangs behind a curtain in the main room.* MR. FRANK *finds the cognac and pours it into the five glasses that* PETER *brings him.* MR. VAN DAAN *stands looking on sourly.* MRS. VAN DAAN *comes downstairs and looks around at all the bustle.*)

MRS. VAN DAAN. What's happening? What's going on?

MR. VAN DAAN. Someone's moving in with us.

MRS. VAN DAAN. In here? You're joking.

MARGOT. It's only for a night or two . . . until Mr. Kraler finds him another place.

MR. VAN DAAN. Yeah! Yeah!

(MR. FRANK *hurries over as* MR. KRALER *and* DUSSEL *come up.* DUSSEL *is a man in his late fifties, meticulous, finicky . . . bewildered now. He wears a raincoat. He carries a briefcase, stuffed full, and a small medicine case.*)

MR. FRANK. Come in, Mr. Dussel.

MR. KRALER. This is Mr. Frank.

DUSSEL. Mr. Otto Frank?

MR. FRANK. Yes. Let me take your things. (*He takes the hat and briefcase, but* DUSSEL *clings to his medicine case.*) This is my wife Edith . . . Mr. and Mrs. Van Daan . . . their son, Peter . . . and my daughters, Margot and Anne.

(DUSSEL *shakes hands with everyone.*)

MR. KRALER. Thank you, Mr. Frank. Thank you all. Mr. Dussel, I leave you in good hands. Oh . . . Dirk's coat.

(DUSSEL *hurriedly takes off the raincoat, giving it to* MR. KRALER. *Underneath is his white dentist's jacket, with a yellow Star of David on it.*)

DUSSEL (*to* MR. KRALER). What can I say to thank you . . . ?

MRS. FRANK (*to* DUSSEL). Mr. Kraler and Miep . . . They're our life line. Without them we couldn't live.

MR. KRALER. Please, Please. You make us seem very heroic. It isn't that at all. We simply don't like the Nazis. (*To* MR. FRANK, *who offers him a drink*) No, thanks. (*Then going on*) We don't like their methods. We don't like . . .

MR. FRANK (*smiling*). I know. I know. "No one's going to tell us Dutchmen what to do with our damn Jews!"

MR. KRALER (*to* DUSSEL). Pay no attention to Mr. Frank. I'll be up tomorrow to see that they're treating you right. (*To* MR. FRANK) Don't trouble to come down again. Peter will bolt the door after me, won't you, Peter?

PETER. Yes, sir.

MR. FRANK. Thank you, Peter. I'll do it.

MR. KRALER. Good night. Good night.

GROUP. Good night, Mr. Kraler. We'll see you tomorrow, *etc. etc.*

(MR. KRALER *goes out with* MR. FRANK. MRS. FRANK *gives each one of the "grownups" a glass of cognac.*)

MRS. FRANK. Please, Mr. Dussel, sit down.

(MR. DUSSEL *sinks into a chair.* MRS. FRANK *gives him a glass of cognac.*)

DUSSEL. I'm dreaming. I know it. I can't believe my eyes. Mr. Otto Frank here! (*To* MRS. FRANK) You're not in Switzerland then? A woman told me . . . She said she'd gone to your house . . . the door was open, everything was in disorder, dishes in the sink. She said she found a piece of paper in the wastebasket with an address scribbled on it

. . . an address in Zurich. She said you must have escaped to Zurich.

ANNE. Father put that there purposely . . . just so people would think that very thing!

DUSSEL. And you've been *here* all the time?

MRS. FRANK. All the time . . . ever since July.

(ANNE *speaks to her father as he comes back.*)

ANNE. It worked, Pim . . . the address you left! Mr. Dussel says that people believe we escaped to Switzerland.

MR. FRANK. I'm glad . . . And now let's have a little drink to welcome Mr. Dussel. *(Before they can drink,* MR. DUSSEL *bolts his drink.* MR. FRANK *smiles and raises his glass.)* To Mr. Dussel. Welcome. We're very honored to have you with us.

MRS. FRANK. To Mr. Dussel, welcome.

(*The* VAN DAANS *murmur a welcome. The "grownups" drink.*)

MRS. VAN DAAN. Um. That was good.

MR. VAN DAAN. Did Mr. Kraler warn you that you won't get much to eat here? You can imagine . . . three ration books among the seven of us . . . and now you make eight.

(PETER *walks away, humiliated. Outside a street organ is heard dimly.*)

DUSSEL *(rising).* Mr. Van Daan, you don't realize what is happening outside that you should warn me of a thing like that. You don't realize what's going on . . . *(As* MR. VAN DAAN *starts his characteristic pacing,* DUSSEL *turns to speak to the others.)* Right here in Amsterdam every day hundreds of Jews disappear . . . They surround a block and search house by house. Children come home from school to find their parents gone. Hundreds are being deported[9] . . . people that you and I know . . . the Hallensteins . . . the Wessels . . .

MRS. FRANK *(in tears).* Oh, no. No!

DUSSEL. They get their call-up notice . . . come to the Jewish theatre on such and such a day and hour . . . bring only what you can

carry in a rucksack. And if you refuse the call-up notice, then they come and drag you from your home and ship you off to Mauthausen.[10] The death camp!

MRS. FRANK. We didn't know that things had got so much worse.

DUSSEL. Forgive me for speaking so.

ANNE *(coming to* DUSSEL*).* Do you know the deWaals? . . . What's become of them? Their daughter Jopie and I are in the same class. Jopie's my best friend.

DUSSEL. They are gone.

ANNE. Gone?

DUSSEL. With all the others.

ANNE. Oh, no. Not Jopie!

(*She turns away, in tears.* MRS. FRANK *motions to* MARGOT *to comfort her.* MARGOT *goes to* ANNE, *putting her arms comfortingly around her.*)

MRS. VAN DAAN. There were some people called Wagner. They lived near us . . . ?

MR. FRANK *(interrupting, with a glance at* ANNE*).* I think we should put this off until later. We all have many questions we want to ask . . . But I'm sure that Mr. Dussel would like to get settled before supper.

DUSSEL. Thank you. I would. I brought very little with me.

MR. FRANK *(giving him his hat and briefcase).* I'm sorry we can't give you a room alone. But I hope you won't be too uncomfortable. We've had to make strict rules here . . . a schedule of hours . . . We'll tell you after supper. Anne, would you like to take Mr. Dussel to his room?

ANNE *(controlling her tears).* If you'll come with me, Mr. Dussel?

(*She starts for her room.*)

DUSSEL *(shaking hands with each in turn).*

---

9. **deport** (di pôrt′, di pōrt′), *v.* force to leave a country; banish.
10. **Mauthausen** (mout′houz ən), a Nazi concentration camp located in Austria.

Mr. Dussel. ➤

Forgive me if I haven't really expressed my gratitude to all of you. This has been such a shock to me. I'd always thought of myself as Dutch. I was born in Holland. My father was born in Holland, and my grandfather. And now . . . after all these years . . . *(He breaks off.)* If you'll excuse me.

(DUSSEL gives a little bow and hurries off after ANNE. MR. FRANK and the others are subdued.)

ANNE *(turning on the light).* Well, here we are.

(DUSSEL looks around the room. In the main room MARGOT speaks to her mother.)

MARGOT. The news sounds pretty bad, doesn't it? It's so different from what Mr. Kraler tells us. Mr. Kraler says things are improving.

MR. VAN DAAN. I like it better the way Kraler tells it.

(They resume their occupations, quietly. PETER *goes off into his room. In* ANNE'S *room,* ANNE *turns to* DUSSEL.)

ANNE. You're going to share the room with me.

DUSSEL. I'm a man who's always lived alone. I haven't had to adjust myself to others. I hope you'll bear with me until I learn.

ANNE. Let me help you. *(She takes his briefcase.)* Do you always live all alone? Have you no family at all?

DUSSEL. No one.

(He opens his medicine case and spreads his bottles on the dressing table.)

ANNE. How dreadful. You must be terribly lonely.

DUSSEL. I'm used to it.

ANNE. I don't think I could ever get used to it. Didn't you even have a pet? A cat, or a dog?

DUSSEL. I have an allergy for fur-bearing animals. They give me asthma.

ANNE. Oh, dear. Peter has a cat.

DUSSEL. Here? He has it here?

ANNE. Yes. But we hardly ever see it. He keeps it in his room all the time. I'm sure it will be all right.

DUSSEL. Let us hope so. *(He takes some pills to fortify[11] himself.)*

ANNE. That's Margot's bed, where you're going to sleep. I sleep on the sofa there. *(Indicating the clothes hooks on the wall.)* We cleared these off for your things. *(She goes over to the window.)* The best part about this room . . . you can look down and see a bit of the street and the canal. There's a houseboat . . . you can see the end of it . . . a bargeman lives there with his family . . . They have a baby and he's just beginning to walk and I'm so afraid he's going to fall into the canal some day. I watch him. . . .

DUSSEL *(interrupting)*. Your father spoke of a schedule.

ANNE *(coming away from the window)*. Oh, yes.

It's mostly about the times we have to be quiet. And times for the w.c. You can use it now if you like.

DUSSEL *(stiffly)*. No, thank you.

ANNE. I suppose you think it's awful, my talking about a thing like that. But you don't know how important it can get to be, especially when you're frightened . . . About this room, the way Margot and I did . . . she had it to herself in the afternoons for studying, reading . . . lessons, you know . . . and I took the mornings. Would that be all right with you?

DUSSEL. I'm not at my best in the morning.

ANNE. You stay here in the mornings then. I'll take the room in the afternoons.

DUSSEL. Tell me, when you're in here, what happens to me? Where am I spending my time? In there, with all the people?

ANNE. Yes.

DUSSEL. I see. I see.

ANNE. We have supper at half past six.

DUSSEL *(going over to the sofa)*. Then, if you don't mind . . . I like to lie down quietly for ten minutes before eating. I find it helps the digestion.

ANNE. Of course. I hope I'm not going to be too much of a bother to you. I seem to be able to get everyone's back up.

(DUSSEL lies down on the sofa, curled up, his back to her.)

DUSSEL. I always get along very well with children. My patients all bring their children to me, because they know I get on well with them. So don't you worry about that.

(ANNE leans over him, taking his hand and shaking it gratefully.)

ANNE. Thank you. Thank you, Mr. Dussel.

(The lights dim to darkness. The curtain falls on the scene. ANNE'S VOICE *comes to us faintly at first, and then with increasing power.)*

---

11. fortify (fôr′tə fī), v. strengthen.

ANNE'S VOICE. . . . And yesterday I finished Cissy Van Marxvelt's latest book. I think she is a first-class writer. I shall definitely let my children read her. Monday the twenty-first of September, nineteen forty-two. Mr. Dussel and I had another battle yesterday. Yes, Mr. Dussel! According to him, nothing, I repeat . . . nothing, is right about me . . . my appearance, my character, my manners. While he was going on at me I thought . . . sometime I'll give you such a smack that you'll fly right up to the ceiling! Why is it that every grownup thinks he knows the way to bring up children? Particularly the grownups that never had any. I keep wishing that Peter was a girl instead of a boy. Then I would have someone to talk to. Margot's a darling, but she takes everything too seriously. To pause for a moment on the subject of Mrs. Van Daan. I must tell you that her attempts to flirt with father are getting her nowhere. Pim, thank goodness, won't play.

(As she is saying the last lines, the curtain rises on the darkened scene. ANNE'S VOICE *fades out.)*

▲ Anne writing in her diary.

After Reading

Making Connections

1. What quotation did you add to your Reading Log that you think nobody else was likely to have noted? Explain why you felt it was an important quote to include.

2. Do you like or dislike the new dimensions you see in Anne's **character?**

3. What impact might Mr. Dussel's arrival have?

4. Construct a **character web** with Anne in the center, surrounded by her mother, her father, Peter, Mr. Van Daan, and Mrs. Van Daan. Draw lines to connect her to each, and write a word or two to describe each relationship.

5. What is the effect of finding out what happened to Jopie?

Literary Focus: Conflict in Plot

In a literary work, there can be many kinds of **conflict.** A character can be struggling with outside forces or with another character or characters. These conflicts are usually accompanied by an internal conflict within the character. As you continue reading, note how Anne's external conflicts with other characters affect conflicts within herself. Use a chart like the one below to record your thoughts.

External Conflict		**Internal Conflict**
	➤	

Vocabulary Study

dignified
indignantly
domestic
deport
fortify

Write the word from the list that best completes the meaning of each sentence.

1. The way that Anne wrestled on the floor with Peter was not ____.

2. Food was limited, so the people in hiding had little with which to ____ themselves and keep themselves going.

3. Mr. Van Daan said men want a ____ woman, one who will cook and clean house.

4. Anne reacted ____ when Mr. Van Daan called her rude.

5. The Germans planned to ____ the Jews to concentration camps.

Edith Frank, Anne's mother. ➤

SCENE FOUR

It is the middle of the night, several months later. The stage is dark except for a little light which comes through the skylight in PETER'*s room.*

Everyone is in bed. MR. *and* MRS. FRANK *lie on the couch in the main room, which has been pulled out to serve as a makeshift[1] double bed.*

MARGOT *is sleeping on a mattress on the floor in the main room, behind a curtain stretched across for privacy. The others are all in their accustomed rooms.*

From outside we hear two drunken soldiers singing "Lili Marlene." A girl's high giggle is heard. The sound of running feet is heard coming closer and then fading in the distance. Throughout the scene there is the distant sound of airplanes passing overhead.

A match suddenly flares up in the attic. We dimly see MR. VAN DAAN. *He is getting his bearings. He comes quickly down the stairs, and goes to the cupboard where the food is stored. Again the match flares up, and is as quickly blown out. The dim figure is seen to steal back up the stairs.*

There is quiet for a second or two, broken only by the sound of airplanes, and running feet on the street below.

Suddenly, out of the silence and the dark, we hear ANNE *scream.*

ANNE (*screaming*). No! No! Don't . . . don't take me!

(*She moans, tossing and crying in her sleep. The other people wake, terrified.* DUSSEL *sits up in bed, furious.*)

DUSSEL. Shush! Anne! Anne, . . . shush!

ANNE (*still in her nightmare*). Save me! Save me!

(*She screams and screams.* DUSSEL *gets out of bed, going over to her, trying to wake her.*)

DUSSEL. . . . Quiet! Quiet! You want someone to hear?

(*In the main room* MRS. FRANK *grabs a shawl and*

---

1. **makeshift** (māk′shift′), *adj.* used for a time instead of the right thing.

pulls it around her. She rushes in to ANNE, *taking her in her arms.* MR. FRANK *hurriedly gets up, putting on his overcoat.* MARGOT *sits up, terrified.* PETER*'s light goes on in his room.*)

MRS. FRANK (*to* ANNE, *in her room*). Hush, darling, hush. It's all right. It's all right. (*Over her shoulder to* DUSSEL) Will you be kind enough to turn on the light, Mr. Dussel? (*Back to* ANNE) It's nothing, my darling. It was just a dream.

(DUSSEL *turns on the light in the bedroom.* MRS. FRANK *holds* ANNE *in her arms. Gradually* ANNE *comes out of her nightmare, still trembling with horror.* MR. FRANK *comes into the room, and goes quickly to the window, looking out to be sure that no one outside has heard* ANNE*'s screams.* MRS. FRANK *holds* ANNE, *talking softly to her. In the main room* MARGOT *stands on a chair, turning on the center hanging lamp. A light goes on in the* VAN DAANs' *room overhead.* PETER *puts his robe on, coming out of his room.*)

DUSSEL (*to* MRS. FRANK, *blowing his nose*). Something must be done about that child, Mrs. Frank. Yelling like that! Who knows but there's somebody on the streets? She's endangering all our lives.

MRS. FRANK. Anne, darling.

DUSSEL. Every night she twists and turns. I don't sleep. I spend half my night shushing her. And now it's nightmares!

(MARGOT *comes to the door of* ANNE*'s room, followed by* PETER. MR. FRANK *goes to them, indicating that everything is all right.* PETER *takes* MARGOT *back.*)

MRS. FRANK (*to* ANNE). You're here, safe, you see? Nothing has happened. (*To* DUSSEL) Please, Mr. Dussel, go back to bed. She'll be herself in a minute or two. Won't you, Anne?

DUSSEL (*picking up a book and a pillow*). Thank you, but I'm going to the w.c. The one place where there's peace!

(*He stalks out.* MR. VAN DAAN, *in underwear and trousers, comes down the stairs.*)

MR. VAN DAAN (*to* DUSSEL). What is it? What happened?

DUSSEL. A nightmare. She was having a nightmare!

MR. VAN DAAN. I thought someone was murdering her.

DUSSEL. Unfortunately, no.

(*He goes into the bathroom.* MR. VAN DAAN *goes back up the stairs.* MR. FRANK, *in the main room, sends* PETER *back to his own bedroom.*)

MR. FRANK. Thank you, Peter. Go back to bed.

(PETER *goes back to his room.* MR. FRANK *follows him, turning out the light and looking out the window. Then he goes back to the main room, and gets up on a chair, turning out the center hanging lamp.*)

MRS. FRANK (*to* ANNE). Would you like some water? (ANNE *shakes her head.*) Was it a very bad dream? Perhaps if you told me . . . ?

ANNE. I'd rather not talk about it.

MRS. FRANK. Poor darling. Try to sleep then. I'll sit right here beside you until you fall asleep. (*She brings a stool over, sitting there.*)

ANNE. You don't have to.

MRS. FRANK. But I'd like to stay with you . . . very much. Really.

ANNE. I'd rather you didn't.

MRS. FRANK. Good night, then. (*She leans down to kiss* ANNE. ANNE *throws her arm up over her face, turning away.* MRS. FRANK, *hiding her hurt, kisses* ANNE*'s arm.*) You'll be all right? There's nothing that you want?

ANNE. Will you please ask Father to come?

MRS. FRANK (*after a second*). Of course, Anne dear. (*She hurries out into the other room.* MR. FRANK *comes to her as she comes in.*) *Sie verlangt nach Dir!*[2]

MR. FRANK (*sensing her hurt*). Edith, *Liebe, schau . . .* [3]

---

2. *Sie verlangt nach Dir!* (zē ferˈlängt näkh dir). She wants to see you. (German)
3. *Liebe, schau . . .* (lēˈbə shou). My dear, look . . . (German)

Volunteers search for bodies in the ruins of bomb-wrecked buildings, after the bombing of
Amsterdam by the Nazis in 1940.

MRS. FRANK. *Es macht nichts! Ich danke dem lieben Herrgott, dass sie sich wenigstens an Dich wendet, wenn sie Trost braucht! Geh hinein, Otto, sie ist ganz hysterisch vor Angst.*[4] *(As* MR. FRANK *hesitates) Geh zu ihr.*[5] *(He looks at her for a second and then goes to get a cup of water for* ANNE. MRS. FRANK *sinks down on the bed, her face in her hands, trying to keep from sobbing aloud.* MARGOT *comes over to her, putting her arms around her.)* She wants nothing of me. She pulled away when I leaned down to kiss her.

MARGOT. It's a phase . . . You heard Father . . . Most girls go through it . . . they turn to their fathers at this age . . . they give all their love to their fathers.

MRS. FRANK. You weren't like this. You didn't shut me out.

MARGOT. She'll get over it . . .

(She smooths the bed for MRS. FRANK *and sits beside her a moment as* MRS. FRANK *lies down. In* ANNE*'s room* MR. FRANK *comes in, sitting down by* ANNE. ANNE *flings her arms around him, clinging to him. In the distance we hear the sound of ack-ack.)*

ANNE. Oh, Pim. I dreamed that they came to get us! The Green Police! They broke down the door and grabbed me and started to drag me out the way they did Jopie.

MR. FRANK. I want you to take this pill.

ANNE. What is it?

MR. FRANK. Something to quiet you.

(She takes it and drinks the water. In the main room MARGOT *turns out the light and goes back to her bed.)*

MR. FRANK *(to* ANNE*).* Do you want me to read to you for a while?

ANNE. No. Just sit with me for a minute. Was I awful? Did I yell terribly loud? Do you think anyone outside could have heard?

MR. FRANK. No. No. Lie quietly now. Try to sleep.

ANNE. I'm a terrible coward. I'm so disappointed in myself. I think I've conquered my fear . . . I think I'm really grown-up . . . and then something happens . . . and I run to you like a baby . . . I love you, Father. I don't love anyone but you.

MR. FRANK *(reproachfully).*[6] Annele!

ANNE. It's true. I've been thinking about it for a long time. You're the only one I love.

MR. FRANK. It's fine to hear you tell me that you love me. But I'd be happier if you said you loved your mother as well . . . She needs your help so much . . . your love . . .

ANNE. We have nothing in common. She doesn't understand me. Whenever I try to explain my views on life to her she asks me if I'm constipated.

MR. FRANK. You hurt her very much now. She's crying. She's in there crying.

ANNE. I can't help it. I only told the truth. I didn't want her here . . . *(Then, with sudden change)* Oh, Pim, I was horrible, wasn't I? And the worst of it is, I can stand off and look at myself doing it and know it's cruel and yet I can't stop doing it. What's the matter with me? Tell me. Don't say it's just a phase! Help me.

MR. FRANK. There is so little that we parents can do to help our children. We can only try to set a good example . . . point the way. The rest you must do yourself. You must build your own character.

ANNE. I'm trying. Really I am. Every night I think back over all of the things I did that day that were wrong . . . like putting the wet mop in Mr. Dussel's bed . . . and this

---

4. ***Es macht nichts! . . . vor Angst*** (es mäkht nikhts ikh dängk′ə dām lē′bən her′gôt′ däs zē zikh vān′ikh stəns än dikh ven′dət ven zē trôst broukht gā hin īn ät tô zē ist gänts hü ster′ish fôr ängst). It doesn't matter. Thank God that she at least turns to you when she is in need of consolation. Go, Otto, she is hysterical with fear. (German)

5. ***Geh zu ihr*** (gā tsü ēr). Go to her. (German)

6. reproachfully (ri prōch′fəl lē), *adv.* in a manner full of blame or disapproval.

thing now with Mother. I say to myself, that was wrong. I make up my mind, I'm never going to do that again. Never! Of course I may do something worse . . . but at least I'll never do *that* again! . . . I have a nicer side, Father . . . a sweeter, nicer side. But I'm scared to show it. I'm afraid that people are going to laugh at me if I'm serious. So the mean Anne comes to the outside and the good Anne stays on the inside, and I keep on trying to switch them around and have the good Anne outside and the bad Anne inside and be what I'd like to be . . . and might be . . . if only . . . only . . .

(*She is asleep.* MR. FRANK *watches her for a moment and then turns off the light, and starts out. The lights dim out. The curtain falls on the scene.* ANNE'S VOICE *is heard dimly at first, and then with growing strength.*)

ANNE'S VOICE. . . . The air raids are getting worse. They come over day and night. The noise is terrifying. Pim says it should be music to our ears. The more planes, the sooner will come the end of the war. Mrs. Van Daan pretends to be a fatalist. What will be, will be. But when the planes come over, who is the most frightened? No one else but Petronella! . . . Monday, the ninth of November, nineteen forty-two. Wonderful news! The Allies[7] have landed in Africa. Pim says that we can look for an early finish to the war. Just for fun he asked each of us what was the first thing we wanted to do when we got out of here. Mrs. Van Daan longs to be home with her own things, her needle-point chairs, the Beckstein piano her father gave her . . . the best that money could buy. Peter would like to go to a movie. Mr. Dussel wants to get back to his dentist's drill. He's afraid he is losing his touch. For myself, there are so many things . . . to ride a bike again . . . to laugh till my belly aches . . . to have new clothes from the skin out . . . to

have a hot tub filled to overflowing and wallow in it for hours . . . to be back in school with my friends . . .

(*As the last lines are being said, the curtain rises on the scene. The lights dim on as* ANNE'S VOICE *fades away.*)

SCENE FIVE

It is the first night of the Hanukkah[8] celebration. MR. FRANK *is standing at the head of the table on which is the Menorah.[9] He lights the Shamos, or servant candle, and holds it as he says the blessing. Seated listening is all of the "family," dressed in their best. The men wear hats;* PETER *wears his cap.*

MR. FRANK (*reading from a prayer book*). "Praised be Thou, oh Lord our God, Ruler of the universe, who has sanctified us with Thy commandments and bidden us kindle the Hanukkah lights. Praised be Thou, oh Lord our God, Ruler of the universe, who has wrought wondrous deliverances for our fathers in days of old. Praised be Thou, oh Lord our God, Ruler of the universe, that Thou has given us life and sustenance[10] and brought us to this happy season." (MR. FRANK *lights the one candle of the Menorah as he continues.*) "We kindle this Hanukkah light to celebrate the great and wonderful deeds wrought through the zeal with which God filled the hearts of the heroic Maccabees, two thousand years ago. They fought against indifference, against

7. **The Allies** (al'īz), the countries, including Britain and the United States, that fought against Germany, Italy, and Japan in World War II.
8. **Hanukkah** (hä'nə kə), a Jewish festival usually held in December. The festival commemorates the rededication of the temple in Jerusalem after the Maccabees (mak'ə bēz'), a family of Jewish patriots, led the Jews to victory over the Syrians in 165 B.C.
9. **Menorah** (mə nôr'ə), a candlestick with various numbers of branches used primarily in Jewish religious services. The Shamos (shäm'əs), or servant candle, is lit first, then used to light the Menorah.
10. **sustenance** (sus'tə nəns), *n.* food or provisions; nourishment.

tyranny[11] and oppression, and they restored our Temple to us. May these lights remind us that we should ever look to God, whence cometh our help." Amen. *(Pronounced O-mayn.)*

ALL. Amen.

(MR. FRANK hands MRS. FRANK the prayer book.)

MRS. FRANK *(reading).* "I lift up mine eyes unto the mountains, from whence cometh my help. My help cometh from the Lord who made heaven and earth. He will not suffer thy foot to be moved. He that keepeth thee will not slumber. He that keepeth Israel doth neither slumber nor sleep. The Lord is thy keeper. The Lord is thy shade upon thy right hand. The sun shall not smite thee by day, nor the moon by night. The Lord shall keep thee from all evil. He shall keep thy soul. The Lord shall guard thy going out and thy coming in, from this time forth and forevermore." Amen.

ALL. Amen.

(MRS. FRANK puts down the prayer book and goes to get the food and wine. MARGOT helps her. MR. FRANK takes the men's hats and puts them aside.)

DUSSEL *(rising).* That was very moving.

ANNE *(pulling him back).* It isn't over yet!

MRS. VAN DAAN. Sit down! Sit down!

ANNE. There's a lot more, songs and presents.

DUSSEL. Presents?

MRS. FRANK. Not this year, unfortunately.

MRS. VAN DAAN. But always on Hanukkah everyone gives presents . . . everyone!

DUSSEL. Like our St. Nicholas' Day.[12]

(There is a chorus of "no's" from the group.)

MRS. VAN DAAN. No! Not like St. Nicholas! What kind of a Jew are you that you don't know Hanukkah?

MRS. FRANK *(as she brings the food).* I remember particularly the candles . . . First one, as we have tonight. Then the second night you light two candles, the next night three . . . and so on until you have eight candles burning. When there are eight candles it is truly beautiful.

MRS. VAN DAAN. And the potato pancakes.

---

11. **tyranny** (tir′ə nē), *n.* cruel or unjust use of power.
12. **St. Nicholas' Day.** On December 6, the feast of St. Nicholas, Dutch children are given gifts. St. Nicholas, actually a fourth-century Christian saint, is today a figure like Santa Claus. The feast has no real religious significance.

A Menorah. ➤

MR. VAN DAAN. Don't talk about them!

MRS. VAN DAAN. I make the best *latkes*[13] you ever tasted!

MRS. FRANK. Invite us all next year . . . in your own home.

MR. FRANK. God willing!

MRS. VAN DAAN. God willing.

MARGOT. What I remember best is the presents we used to get when we were little . . . eight days of presents . . . and each day they got better and better.

MRS. FRANK *(sitting down)*. We are all here, alive. That is present enough.

ANNE. No, it isn't. I've got something . . . *(She rushes into her room, hurriedly puts on a little hat improvised from the lamp shade, grabs a satchel bulging with parcels and comes running back.)*

MRS. FRANK. What is it?

ANNE. Presents!

MRS. VAN DAAN. Presents!

DUSSEL. Look!

MRS. VAN DAAN. What's she got on her head?

PETER. A lamp shade!

ANNE *(she picks out one at random)*. This is for Margot. *(She hands it to MARGOT, pulling her to her feet.)* Read it out loud.

MARGOT *(reading)*.
    "You have never lost your temper.
    You never will, I fear,
    You are so good.
    But if you should,
    Put all your cross words here."
    (She tears open the package.) A new crossword puzzle book! Where did you get it?

ANNE. It isn't new. It's one that you've done. But I rubbed it all out, and if you wait a little and forget, you can do it all over again.

MARGOT *(sitting)*. It's wonderful, Anne. Thank you. You'd never know it wasn't new.

(From outside we hear the sound of a streetcar passing.)

ANNE *(with another gift)*. Mrs. Van Daan.

MRS. VAN DAAN *(taking it)*. This is awful . . . I haven't anything for anyone . . . I never thought . . .

MR. FRANK. This is all Anne's idea.

MRS. VAN DAAN *(holding up a bottle)*. What is it?

ANNE. It's hair shampoo. I took all the odds and ends of soap and mixed them with the last of my toilet water.

MRS. VAN DAAN. Oh, Anneke!

ANNE. I wanted to write a poem for all of them, but I didn't have time. *(Offering a large box to MR. VAN DAAN.)* Yours, Mr. Van Daan, is *really* something . . . something you want more than anything. *(As she waits for him to open it)* Look! Cigarettes!

MR. VAN DAAN. Cigarettes!

ANNE. Two of them! Pim found some old pipe tobacco in the pocket lining of his coat . . . and we made them . . . or rather, Pim did.

MRS. VAN DAAN. Let me see . . . Well, look at that! Light it, Putti! Light it.

(MR. VAN DAAN hesitates.)

ANNE. It's tobacco, really it is! There's a little fluff in it, but not much.

(Everyone watches as MR. VAN DAAN cautiously lights it. The cigarette flares up. Everyone laughs.)

PETER. It works!

MRS. VAN DAAN. Look at him.

MR. VAN DAAN *(spluttering)*. Thank you, Anne. Thank you.

(ANNE rushes back to her satchel for another present.)

ANNE *(handing her mother a piece of paper)*. For Mother, Hanukkah greeting.

(She pulls her mother to her feet.)

MRS. FRANK *(She reads)*.
    "Here's an I.O.U. that I promise to pay.

---

13. **latkes** (lät′kəs), potato pancakes.

Ten hours of doing whatever you say. Signed, Anne Frank."

(MRS. FRANK, *touched, takes* ANNE *in her arms, holding her close.*)

DUSSEL (*to* ANNE). Ten hours of doing what you're told? *Anything* you're told?

ANNE. That's right.

DUSSEL. You wouldn't want to sell that, Mrs. Frank?

MRS. FRANK. Never! This is the most precious gift I've ever had!

(*She sits, showing her present to the others.* ANNE *hurries back to the satchel and pulls out a scarf, the scarf that* MR. FRANK *found in the first scene.*)

ANNE (*offering it to her father*). For Pim.

MR. FRANK. Anneke . . . I wasn't supposed to have a present! (*He takes it, unfolding it and showing it to the others.*)

ANNE. It's a muffler . . . to put round your neck . . . like an ascot, you know. I made it myself out of odds and ends . . . I knitted it in the dark each night, after I'd gone to bed. I'm afraid it looks better in the dark!

MR. FRANK (*putting it on*). It's fine. It fits me perfectly. Thank you, Annele.

(ANNE *hands* PETER *a ball of paper, with a string attached to it.*)

ANNE. That's for Mouschi.

PETER (*rising to bow*). On behalf of Mouschi, I thank you.

ANNE (*hesitant, handing him a gift*). And . . . this is yours . . . from Mrs. Quack Quack. (*As he holds it gingerly in his hands.*) Well . . . open it . . . Aren't you going to open it?

PETER. I'm scared to. I know something's going to jump out and hit me.

ANNE. No. It's nothing like that, really.

MRS. VAN DAAN (*as he is opening it*). What is it, Peter? Go on. Show it.

ANNE (*excitedly*). It's a safety razor!

DUSSEL. A what?

ANNE. A razor!

MRS. VAN DAAN (*looking at it*). You didn't make that out of odds and ends.

ANNE (*to* PETER). Miep got it for me. It's not new. It's second-hand. But you really do need a razor now.

DUSSEL. For what?

ANNE. Look on his upper lip . . . you can see the beginning of a mustache.

DUSSEL. He wants to get rid of that? Put a little milk on it and let the cat lick it off.

PETER (*starting for his room*). Think you're funny, don't you.

DUSSEL. Look! He can't wait! He's going in to try it!

PETER. I'm going to give Mouschi his present! (*He goes into his room, slamming the door behind him.*)

MR. VAN DAAN (*disgustedly*). Mouschi, Mouschi, Mouschi.

(*In the distance we hear a dog persistently barking.* ANNE *brings a gift to* DUSSEL.)

ANNE. And last but never least, my roommate, Mr. Dussel.

DUSSEL. For me? You have something for me? (*He opens the small box she gives him.*)

ANNE. I made them myself.

DUSSEL (*puzzled*). Capsules! Two capsules!

ANNE. They're ear-plugs!

DUSSEL. Ear-plugs?

ANNE. To put in your ears so you won't hear me when I thrash around at night. I saw them advertised in a magazine. They're not real ones . . . I made them out of cotton and candle wax. Try them . . . See if they don't work . . . see if you can hear me talk . . .

DUSSEL (*putting them in his ears*). Wait now until I get them in . . . so.

ANNE. Are you ready?

DUSSEL. Huh?

ANNE. Are you ready?

DUSSEL. Oh! They've gone inside! I can't get

them out! (*They laugh as* MR. DUSSEL *jumps about, trying to shake the plugs out of his ears. Finally he gets them out. Putting them away.*) Thank you, Anne! Thank you!

MR. VAN DAAN. A real Hanukkah!

MRS. VAN DAAN. Wasn't it cute of her?

MRS. FRANK. I don't know when she did it.

MARGOT. I love my present.

(*Together.*)

ANNE (*sitting at the table*). And now let's have the song, Father . . . please . . . (*To* DUSSEL) Have you heard the Hanukkah song, Mr. Dussel? The song is the whole thing! (*She sings.*) "Oh, Hanukkah! Oh, Hanukkah! The sweet celebration . . . "

MR. FRANK (*quieting her*). I'm afraid, Anne, we shouldn't sing that song tonight. (*To* DUSSEL) It's a song of jubilation, of rejoicing. One is apt to become too enthusiastic.

ANNE. Oh, please, please. Let's sing the song. I promise not to shout!

MR. FRANK. Very well. But quietly now . . . I'll keep an eye on you and when . . .

(*As* ANNE *starts to sing, she is interrupted by* DUSSEL, *who is snorting and wheezing.*)

DUSSEL (*pointing to* PETER). You . . . You! (PETER *is coming from his bedroom, ostentatiously*[14] *holding a bulge in his coat as if he were holding his cat, and dangling* ANNE'S *present before it.*) How many times . . . I told you . . . Out! Out!

MR. VAN DAAN (*going to* PETER). What's the matter with you? Haven't you any sense? Get that cat out of here.

PETER (*innocently*). Cat?

MR. VAN DAAN. You heard me. Get it out of here!

PETER. I have no cat. (*Delighted with his joke, he opens his coat and pulls out a bath towel. The group at the table laugh, enjoying the joke.*)

DUSSEL (*still wheezing*). It doesn't need to be the cat . . . his clothes are enough . . . when he comes out of that room . . .

MR. VAN DAAN. Don't worry. You won't be bothered any more. We're getting rid of it.

DUSSEL. At last you listen to me. (*He goes off into his bedroom.*)

MR. VAN DAAN (*calling after him*). I'm not doing it for you. That's all in your mind . . . all of it! (*He starts back to his place at the table.*) I'm doing it because I'm sick of seeing that cat eat all our food.

PETER. That's not true! I only give him bones . . . scraps . . .

MR. VAN DAAN. Don't tell me! He gets fatter every day! Damn cat looks better than any of us. Out he goes tonight!

PETER. No! No!

ANNE. Mr. Van Daan, you can't do that! That's Peter's cat. Peter loves that cat.

MRS. FRANK (*quietly*). Anne.

PETER (*to* MR. VAN DAAN). If he goes, I go.

MR. VAN DAAN. Go! Go!

MRS. VAN DAAN. You're not going and the cat's not going! Now please . . . this is Hanukkah . . . Hanukkah . . . this is the time to celebrate . . . What's the matter with all of you? Come on, Anne. Let's have the song.

ANNE (*singing*). "Oh, Hanukkah! Oh, Hanukkah! The sweet celebration."

MR. FRANK (*rising*). I think we should first blow out the candle . . . then we'll have something for tomorrow night.

MARGOT. But, Father, you're supposed to let it burn itself out.

MR. FRANK. I'm sure that God understands shortages. (*Before blowing it out*) "Praise be Thou, oh Lord our God, who has sustained us and permitted us to celebrate this joyous festival."

(*He is about to blow out the candle when suddenly there is a crash of something falling below. They all freeze in horror, motionless. For a few seconds there is complete silence.* MR. FRANK *slips off his shoes. The others noiselessly follow his example.* MR. FRANK

---

14. ostentatiously (os′ten tā′shəs lē), *adv.* in a manner intended to attract notice.

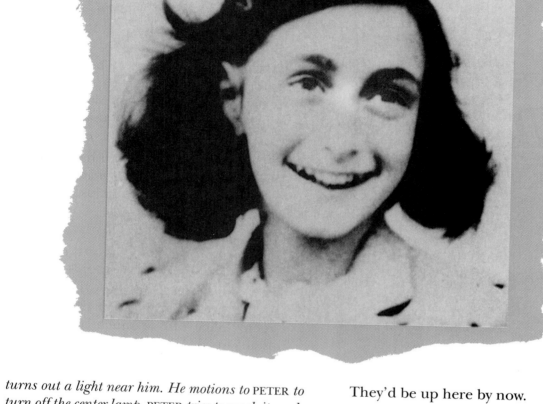

Anne Frank.

turns out a light near him. He motions to PETER to turn off the center lamp. PETER tries to reach it, realizes he cannot and gets up on a chair. Just as he is touching the lamp he loses his balance. The chair goes out from under him. He falls. The iron lamp shade crashes to the floor. There is a sound of feet below, running down the stairs.)

MR. VAN DAAN (under his breath). Oh, no! (The only light left comes from the Hanukkah candle. DUSSEL comes from his room. MR. FRANK creeps over to the stairwell and stands listening. The dog is heard barking excitedly.) Do you hear anything?

MR. FRANK (in a whisper). No. I think they've gone.

MRS. VAN DAAN. It's the Green Police. They've found us.

MR. FRANK. If they had, they wouldn't have left.

They'd be up here by now.

MRS. VAN DAAN. I know it's the Green Police. They've gone to get help. That's all. They'll be back.

MR. VAN DAAN. Or it may have been the Gestapo,[15] looking for papers . . .

MR. FRANK (interrupting). Or a thief, looking for money.

MRS. VAN DAAN. We've got to do something . . . Quick! Quick! Before they come back.

MR. VAN DAAN. There isn't anything to do. Just wait.

(MR. FRANK holds up his hand for them to be quiet. He is listening intently. There is complete silence as

---

15. **Gestapo** (gə stä′pō), the Secret Police of Nazi Germany.

The Diary of Anne Frank—Act One, Scene 5 **577**

▲ A bookcase on hinges and a large wall map hid the door and stairs leading to the attic.

they all strain to hear any sound from below. Suddenly ANNE *begins to sway. With a low cry she falls to the floor in a faint.* MRS. FRANK *goes to her quickly, sitting beside her on the floor and taking her in her arms.*)

MRS. FRANK. Get some water, please! Get some water!

(MARGOT *starts for the sink.*)

MR. VAN DAAN (*grabbing* MARGOT). No! No! No one's going to run water!

MR. FRANK. If they've found us, they've found

us. Get the water. (MARGOT *starts again for the sink.* MR. FRANK, *getting a flashlight*) I'm going down.

(MARGOT *rushes to him, clinging to him.* ANNE *struggles to consciousness.*)

MARGOT. No, Father, no! There may be someone there, waiting . . . It may be a trap!

MR. FRANK. This is Saturday. There is no way for us to know what has happened until Miep or Mr. Kraler comes on Monday morning. We cannot live with this uncertainty.

MARGOT. Don't go, Father!

MRS. FRANK. Hush, darling, hush. (MR. FRANK *slips quietly out, down the steps and out through the door below.*) Margot! Stay close to me.

(MARGOT *goes to her mother.*)

MR. VAN DAAN. Shush! Shush!

(MRS. FRANK *whispers to* MARGOT *to get the water.* MARGOT *goes for it.*)

MRS. VAN DAAN. Putti, where's our money? Get our money. I hear you can buy the Green Police off, so much a head. Go upstairs quick! Get the money!

MR. VAN DAAN. Keep still!

MRS. VAN DAAN (*kneeling before him, pleading*). Do you want to be dragged off to a concentration camp? Are you going to stand there and wait for them to come up and get you? Do something, I tell you!

MR. VAN DAAN (*pushing her aside*). Will you keep still!

(*He goes over to the stairwell to listen.* PETER *goes to his mother, helping her up onto the sofa. There is a second of silence, then* ANNE *can stand it no longer.*)

ANNE. Someone go after Father! Make Father come back!

PETER (*starting for the door*). I'll go.

MR. VAN DAAN. Haven't you done enough?

(*He pushes* PETER *roughly away. In his anger against his father* PETER *grabs a chair as if to hit him with it, then puts it down, burying his face in his hands.* MRS. FRANK *begins to pray softly.*)

ANNE. Please, please, Mr. Van Daan. Get Father.

MR. VAN DAAN. Quiet! Quiet!

(ANNE is shocked into silence. MRS. FRANK pulls her closer, holding her protectively in her arms.)

MRS. FRANK *(softly, praying).* "I lift up mine eyes unto the mountains, from whence cometh my help. My help cometh from the Lord who made heaven and earth. He will not suffer thy foot to be moved . . . He that keepeth thee will not slumber . . . "

(She stops as she hears someone coming. They all watch the door tensely. MR. FRANK comes quietly in. ANNE rushes to him, holding him tight.)

MR. FRANK. It was a thief. That noise must have scared him away.

MRS. VAN DAAN. Thank goodness.

MR. FRANK. He took the cash box. And the radio. He ran away in such a hurry that he didn't stop to shut the street door. It was swinging wide open. *(A breath of relief sweeps over them.)* I think it would be good to have some light.

MARGOT. Are you sure it's all right?

MR. FRANK. The danger has passed. (MARGOT *goes to light the small lamp.*) Don't be so terrified, Anne. We're safe.

DUSSEL. Who says the danger has passed? Don't you realize we are in greater danger than ever?

MR. FRANK. Mr. Dussel, will you be still!

(MR. FRANK takes ANNE back to the table, making her sit down with him, trying to calm her.)

DUSSEL *(pointing to PETER).* Thanks to this clumsy fool, there's someone now who knows we're up here! Someone now knows we're up here, hiding!

MRS. VAN DAAN *(going to DUSSEL).* Someone knows we're here, yes. But who is the someone? A thief! A thief! You think a thief is going to go to the Green Police and say . . . I was robbing a place the other night and I heard a noise up over my head? You think a thief is going to do that?

DUSSEL. Yes. I think he will.

MRS. VAN DAAN *(hysterically).* You're crazy!

(She stumbles back to her seat at the table. PETER follows protectively, pushing DUSSEL aside.)

DUSSEL. I think some day he'll be caught and he'll make a bargain with the Green Police . . . if they'll let him off, he'll tell them where some Jews are hiding!

▲ When the bookcase was swung away, a doorway was revealed that opened onto stairs leading to the secret annex.

(He goes off into the bathroom. There is a second of appalled silence.)

MR. VAN DAAN. He's right.

ANNE. Father, let's get out of here! We can't stay here now . . . Let's go . . .

MR. VAN DAAN. Go! Where?

MRS. FRANK *(sinking into her chair at the table).* Yes. Where?

MR. FRANK *(rising, to them all).* Have we lost all faith? All courage? A moment ago we thought that they'd come for us. We were sure it was the end. But it wasn't the end. We're alive, safe. (MR. VAN DAAN *goes to the table and sits.* MR. FRANK *prays.)* "We thank Thee, oh Lord our God, that in Thy infinite mercy Thou hast again seen fit to spare us." *(He blows out the candle, then turns to* ANNE.) Come on, Anne. The song! Let's have the song!

(He starts to sing. ANNE *finally starts falteringly to sing, as* MR. FRANK *urges her on. Her voice is hardly audible at first.)*

ANNE *(singing).*
"Oh, Hanukkah! Oh, Hanukkah!
The sweet . . . celebration . . ."

(As she goes on singing, the others gradually join in, their voices still shaking with fear. MRS. VAN DAAN *sobs as she sings.)*

GROUP. "Around the feast . . . we . . . gather
In complete . . . jubilation . . .
Happiest of sea . . . sons
Now is here.
Many are the reasons for good cheer."

*(DUSSEL *comes from the bedroom. He comes over to the table, standing beside* MARGOT, *listening to them as they sing.)*
"Together
We'll weather
Whatever tomorrow may bring."

(As they sing on with growing courage, the lights start to dim.)
"So hear us rejoicing
And merrily voicing
The Hanukkah song that we sing.
Hoy!"

(The lights are out. The curtain starts slowly to fall.)
"Hear us rejoicing
And merrily voicing
The Hanukkah song that we sing."

(They are still singing, as the curtain falls.)

After Reading

Making Connections

1. Look back through your Reading Log. What do you think was the most powerful note you made? Explain why it affected you.

2. What is your reaction to Mr. Van Daan's silent trip to the food cupboard at the beginning of Scene Four?

3. **Compare and contrast** Anne's relationship with her mother and her relationship with her father.

4. ☝ What does Dussel's ignorance of Hanukkah show about his **interactions** with Jewish culture and the mainstream Dutch culture in which he has lived?

5. The Hanukkah celebration is interrupted by the noise downstairs. What is the effect on the characters and on the audience?

6. Why do you think the authors end Act One with a song of celebration?

7. Do you think most people have a "good Anne" and a "mean Anne" inside?

Literary Focus: Foreshadowing

Flashback is a return to past events. **Foreshadowing,** another literary technique, involves a suggestion of future events. Foreshadowing creates **suspense** because readers or viewers are made to think about the present and the future at the same time: what is happening and what will happen.

As you continue reading, look for foreshadowing. Pay attention to hints or suggestions about how events might turn out. Notice how these create suspense.

Vocabulary Study

**makeshift
reproachfully
sustenance
tyranny
ostentatiously**

Decide if each of the following pairs of words are synonyms or antonyms. On your paper write *S* for synonym or *A* for antonym.

1. reproachfully—approvingly
2. sustenance—food
3. tyranny—oppression
4. ostentatiously—furtively
5. makeshift—improvised

Act Two

SCENE ONE

In the darkness we hear ANNE'S VOICE, *again reading from the diary.*

ANNE'S VOICE. Saturday, the first of January, nineteen forty-four. Another new year has begun and we find ourselves still in our hiding place. We have been here now for one year, five months and twenty-five days. It seems that our life is at a standstill.

(The curtain rises on the scene. It is afternoon. Everyone is bundled up against the cold. In the main room MRS. FRANK *is taking down the laundry, which is hung across the back.* MR. FRANK *sits in the chair down left, reading.* MARGOT *is lying on the couch with a blanket over her and the many-colored knitted scarf around her throat.* ANNE *is seated at the center table, writing in her diary.* PETER, MR. *and* MRS. VAN DAAN, *and* DUSSEL *are all in their own rooms, reading or lying down.*

As the lights dim on, ANNE'S VOICE *continues, without a break.)*

ANNE'S VOICE. We are all a little thinner. The Van Daans' "discussions" are as violent as ever. Mother still does not understand me. But then I don't understand her either. There is one great change, however. A change in myself. I read somewhere that girls of my age don't feel quite certain of themselves. That they become quiet within and begin to think of the miracle that is taking place in their bodies. I think that what is happening to me is so wonderful . . . not only what can be seen, but what is taking place inside. . . .

(The buzzer of the door below suddenly sounds. Everyone is startled; MR. FRANK *tiptoes cautiously to the top of the steps and listens. Again the buzzer sounds, in* MIEP*'s V-for-Victory signal.[1])*

MR. FRANK. It's Miep! *(He goes quickly down the steps to unbolt the door.* MRS. FRANK *calls upstairs to the* VAN DAANS *and then to* PETER.)*

MRS. FRANK. Wake up, everyone! Miep is here! *(*ANNE *quickly puts her diary away.* MARGOT *sits up, pulling the blanket around her shoulders.* MR. DUSSEL *sits on the edge of his bed, listening, disgruntled.* MIEP *comes up the steps, followed by* MR. KRALER. *They bring flowers, books, newspapers, etc.* ANNE *rushes to* MIEP, *throwing her arms affectionately around her.)* Miep . . . and Mr. Kraler . . . What a delightful surprise!

MR. KRALER. We came to bring you New Year's greetings.

MRS. FRANK. You shouldn't . . . you should have least one day to yourselves. *(She goes quickly to the stove and brings down teacups and tea for all of them.)*

ANNE. Don't say that, it's so wonderful to see them! *(Sniffing at* MIEP*'s coat)* I can smell the wind and the cold on your clothes.

MIEP *(giving her the flowers).* There you are. *(Then to* MARGOT, *feeling her forehead)* How are you, Margot? . . . Feeling any better?

MARGOT. I'm all right.

ANNE. We filled her full of every kind of pill so she won't cough and make a noise.

(She runs into her room to put the flowers in water. MR. *and* MRS. VAN DAAN *come from upstairs. Outside there is the sound of a band playing.)*

MRS. VAN DAAN. Well, hello, Miep. Mr. Kraler.

MR. KRALER *(giving a bouquet of flowers to* MRS. VAN DAAN).* With my hope for peace in the New Year.

---

1. **V-for-Victory signal,** three short buzzes followed by a long one. In the Morse Code the letter V is transmitted by three dots and a dash. It was widely used as a victory symbol during World War II.

Miep Gies.

PETER (*anxiously*). Miep, have you seen Mouschi? Have you seen him anywhere around?

MIEP. I'm sorry, Peter. I asked everyone in the neighborhood had they seen a gray cat. But they said no.

(MRS. FRANK *gives* MIEP *a cup of tea.* MR. FRANK *comes up the steps, carrying a small cake on a plate.*)

MR. FRANK. Look what Miep's brought for us!

MRS. FRANK (*taking it*). A cake!

MR. VAN DAAN. A cake! (*He pinches* MIEP's *cheeks gaily and hurries up to the cupboard.*) I'll get some plates.

(DUSSEL, *in his room, hastily puts a coat on and starts out to join the others.*)

MRS. FRANK. Thank you, Miepia.[2] You shouldn't have done it. You must have used all of your sugar ration for weeks. (*Giving it to* MRS. VAN DAAN) It's beautiful, isn't it?

MRS. VAN DAAN. It's been ages since I even saw a cake. Not since you brought us one last year. (*Without looking at the cake, to* MIEP) Remember? Don't you remember, you gave us one on New Year's Day? Just this time last year? I'll never forget it because you had "Peace in nineteen forty-three" on it. (*She looks at the cake and reads.*) "Peace in nineteen forty-four!"

MIEP. Well, it has to come sometime, you know. (*As* DUSSEL *comes from his room*) Hello, Mr. Dussel.

MR. KRALER. How are you?

MR. VAN DAAN (*bringing plates and a knife*). Here's the knife, *liefje.* Now, how many of us are there?

MIEP. None for me, thank you.

MR. FRANK. Oh, please. You must.

MIEP. I couldn't.

MR. VAN DAAN. Good! That leaves one . . . two . . . three . . . seven of us.

DUSSEL. Eight! Eight! It's the same number as it always is!

MR. VAN DAAN. I left Margot out. I take it for granted Margot won't eat any.

ANNE. Why wouldn't she!

MRS. FRANK. I think it won't harm her.

MR. VAN DAAN. All right! All right! I just didn't want her to start coughing again, that's all.

DUSSEL. And please, Mrs. Frank should cut the cake.

MR. VAN DAAN. What's the difference? } (*Together.*)

MRS. VAN DAAN. It's not Mrs. Frank's cake, is it, Miep? It's for all of us.

DUSSEL. Mrs. Frank divides things better.

MRS. VAN DAAN (*going to* DUSSEL). What are you trying to say? } (*Together.*)

MR. VAN DAAN. Oh, come on! Stop wasting time!

MRS. VAN DAAN (*to* DUSSEL). Don't I always give everybody exactly the same? Don't I?

MR. VAN DAAN. Forget it, Kerli.

MRS. VAN DAAN. No. I want an answer! Don't I?

DUSSEL. Yes. Yes. Everybody gets exactly the same . . . except Mr. Van Daan always gets a little bit more.

(VAN DAAN *advances on* DUSSEL, *the knife still in his hand.*)

MR. VAN DAAN. That's a lie!

(DUSSEL *retreats before the* onslaught[3] *of the* VAN DAANS.)

MR. FRANK. Please, please! (*Then to* MIEP) You see what a little sugar cake does to us? It goes right to our heads!

MR. VAN DAAN (*handing* MRS. FRANK *the knife*). Here you are, Mrs. Frank.

MRS. FRANK. Thank you. (*Then to* MIEP *as she goes to the table to cut the cake*) Are you sure you won't have some?

MIEP (*drinking her tea*). No, really, I have to go in a minute.

(*The sound of the band fades out in the distance.*)

---

2. **Miepia** (mēp′hyə).
3. onslaught (ôn′slôt′, on′slôt), *n.* a vigorous attack.

PETER (*to* MIEP). Maybe Mouschi went back to our house . . . they say that cats . . . Do you ever get over there . . . ? I mean . . . do you suppose you could . . . ?

MIEP. I'll try, Peter. The first minute I get I'll try. But I'm afraid, with him gone a week . . .

DUSSEL. Make up your mind, already someone has had a nice big dinner from that cat!

(PETER *is furious, inarticulate.[4] He starts toward* DUSSEL *as if to hit him.* MR. FRANK *stops him.* MRS. FRANK *speaks quickly to ease the situation.*)

MRS. FRANK (*to* MIEP). This is delicious, Miep!

MRS. VAN DAAN (*eating hers*). Delicious!

MR. VAN DAAN (*finishing it in one gulp*). Dirk's in luck to get a girl who can bake like this!

MIEP (*putting down her empty teacup*). I have to run. Dirk's taking me to a party tonight.

ANNE. How heavenly! Remember now what everyone is wearing, and what you have to eat and everything, so you can tell us tomorrow.

MIEP. I'll give you a full report! Good-by, everyone!

MR. VAN DAAN (*to* MIEP). Just a minute. There's something I'd like you to do for me. (*He hurries off up the stairs to his room.*)

MRS. VAN DAAN (*sharply*). Putti, where are you going? (*She rushes up the stairs after him, calling hysterically.*) What do you want? Putti, what are you going to do?

MIEP (*to* PETER). What's wrong?

PETER (*his sympathy is with his mother*). Father says he's going to sell her fur coat. She's crazy about that old fur coat.

DUSSEL. Is it possible? Is it possible that anyone is so silly as to worry about a fur coat in times like this?

PETER. It's none of your darn business . . . and if you say one more thing . . . I'll, I'll take you and I'll . . . I mean it . . . I'll . . .

(*There is a piercing scream from* MRS. VAN DAAN *above. She grabs at the fur coat as* MR. VAN DAAN *is starting downstairs with it.*)

The back of the building, showing the attic window.

MRS. VAN DAAN. No! No! No! Don't you dare take that! You hear? It's mine! (*Downstairs* PETER *turns away, embarrassed, miserable.*) My father gave me that! You didn't give it to

---

4. inarticulate (in′är tik′yə lit), *adj.* unable to speak.

The Diary of Anne Frank—Act Two, Scene 1   **585**

me. You have no right. Let go of it . . . you hear?

(MR. VAN DAAN *pulls the coat from her hands and hurries downstairs.* MRS. VAN DAAN *sinks to the floor, sobbing. As* MR. VAN DAAN *comes into the main room the others look away, embarrassed for him.*)

MR. VAN DAAN (*to* MR. KRALER). Just a little—discussion over the advisability of selling this coat. As I have often reminded Mrs. Van Daan, it's very selfish of her to keep it when people outside are in such desperate need of clothing . . . (*He gives the coat to* MIEP.) So if you will please to sell it for us? It should fetch a good price. And by the way, will you get me cigarettes. I don't care what kind they are . . . get all you can.

MIEP. It's terribly difficult to get them, Mr. Van Daan. But I'll try. Good-by.

(*She goes.* MR. FRANK *follows her down the steps to bolt the door after her.* MRS. FRANK *gives* MR. KRALER *a cup of tea.*)

MRS. FRANK. Are you sure you won't have some cake, Mr. Kraler?

MR. KRALER. I'd better not.

MR. VAN DAAN. You're still feeling badly? What does your doctor say?

MR. KRALER. I haven't been to him.

MRS. FRANK. Now, Mr. Kraler! . . .

MR. KRALER (*sitting at the table*). Oh, I tried. But you can't get near a doctor these days . . . they're so busy. After weeks I finally managed to get one on the telephone. I told him I'd like an appointment . . . I wasn't feeling very well. You know what he answers . . . over the telephone . . . Stick out your tongue! (*They laugh. He turns to* MR. FRANK *as* MR. FRANK *comes back.*) I have some contracts here . . . I wonder if you'd look over them with me . . .

MR. FRANK (*putting out his hand*). Of course.

MR. KRALER (*he rises*). If we could go downstairs . . . (MR. FRANK *starts ahead,* MR. KRALER *speaks to the others.*) Will you forgive us? I won't keep him but a minute. (*He starts to follow* MR. FRANK *down the steps.*)

MARGOT (*with sudden foreboding[5]*). What's happened? Something's happened! Hasn't it, Mr. Kraler?

(MR. KRALER *stops and comes back, trying to reassure* MARGOT *with a pretense[6] of casualness.*)

MR. KRALER. No, really. I want your father's advice . . .

MARGOT. Something's gone wrong! I know it!

MR. FRANK (*coming back, to* MR. KRALER). If it's something that concerns us here, it's better that we all hear it.

MR. KRALER (*turning to him, quietly*). But . . . the children . . . ?

MR. FRANK. What they'd imagine would be worse than any reality.

(*As* MR. KRALER *speaks, they all listen with intense apprehension.* MRS. VAN DAAN *comes down the stairs and sits on the bottom step.*)

MR. KRALER. It's a man in the storeroom . . . I don't know whether or not you remember him . . . Carl, about fifty, heavy-set, nearsighted . . . He came with us just before you left.

MR. FRANK. He was from Utrecht?

MR. KRALER. That's the man. A couple of weeks ago, when I was in the storeroom, he closed the door and asked me . . . how's Mr. Frank? What do you hear from Mr. Frank? I told him I only knew there was a rumor that you were in Switzerland. He said he'd heard that rumor too, but he thought I might know something more. I didn't pay any attention to it . . . but then a thing happened yesterday . . . He'd brought some invoices to the office for me to sign. As I was going through them, I looked up. He was standing staring at the

---

5. **foreboding** (fôr bō′ding, fōr bō′ding), *n.* a feeling that something bad is going to happen.

6. **pretense** (prē′tens, pri tens′), *n.* a false appearance.

bookcase . . . your bookcase. He said he thought he remembered a door there . . . Wasn't there a door there that used to go up to the loft? Then he told me he wanted more money. Twenty guilders[7] more a week.

MR. VAN DAAN. Blackmail!

MR. FRANK. Twenty guilders? Very modest blackmail.

MR. VAN DAAN. That's just the beginning.

DUSSEL (*coming to* MR. FRANK). You know what I think? He was the thief who was down there that night. That's how he knows we're here.

MR. FRANK (*to* MR. KRALER). How was it left? What did you tell him?

MR. KRALER. I said I had to think about it. What shall I do? Pay him the money? . . . Take a chance on firing him . . . or what? I don't know.

DUSSEL (*frantic*). . . . Don't fire him! Pay him what he asks . . . keep him here where you can have your eye on him.

MR. FRANK. Is it so much that he's asking? What are they paying nowadays?

MR. KRALER. He could get it in a war plant. But this isn't a war plant. Mind you, I don't know if he really knows . . . or if he doesn't know.

MR. FRANK. Offer him half. Then we'll soon find out if it's blackmail or not.

DUSSEL. And if it is? We've got to pay it, haven't we? Anything he asks we've got to pay!

MR. FRANK. Let's decide that when the time comes.

MR. KRALER. This may be all imagination. You get to a point, these days, where you suspect everyone and everything. Again and again . . . on some simple look or word, I'd found myself . . .

(*The telephone rings in the office below.*)

MRS. VAN DAAN (*hurrying to* MR. KRALER). There's the telephone! What does that mean, the telephone ringing on a holiday?

MR. KRALER. That's my wife. I told her I had to go over some papers in my office . . . to call me there when she got out of church. (*He starts out.*) I'll offer him half then. Good-by . . . we'll hope for the best!

(*The group call their good-bys half-heartedly.* MR. FRANK *follows* MR. KRALER, *to bolt the door below. During the following scene,* MR. FRANK *comes back up and stands listening, disturbed.*)

DUSSEL (*to* MR. VAN DAAN). You can thank your son for this . . . smashing the light! I tell you, it's just a question of time now. (*He goes to the window at the back and stands looking out.*)

MARGOT. Sometimes I wish the end would come . . . whatever it is.

MRS. FRANK (*shocked*). Margot!

(ANNE *goes to* MARGOT, *sitting beside her on the couch with her arms around her.*)

MARGOT. Then at least we'd know where we were.

MRS. FRANK. You should be ashamed of yourself! Talking that way! Think how lucky we are! Think of the thousands dying in the war, every day. Think of the people in concentration camps.

ANNE (*interrupting*). What's the good of that? What's the good of thinking of misery when you're already miserable? That's stupid!

MRS. FRANK. Anne!

(*As* ANNE *goes on raging at her mother,* MR. FRANK *tries to break in, in an effort to quiet her.*)

ANNE. We're young, Margot and Peter and I! You grownups have had your chance! But look at us . . . If we begin thinking of all the horror in the world, we're lost! We're trying to hold onto some kind of ideals . . . when everything . . . ideals, hopes . . .

---

7. **Twenty guilders,** a little over $10.00 in American money. The guilder (gil′dər) is the monetary unit of the Netherlands.

everything, are being destroyed! It isn't our fault that the world is in such a mess! We weren't around when all this started! So don't try to take it out on us! (*She rushes off to her room, slamming the door after her. She picks up a brush from the chest and hurls it to the floor. Then she sits on the settee, trying to control her anger.*)

MR. VAN DAAN. She talks as if we started the war! Did we start the war?

(*He spots* ANNE's *cake. As he starts to take it,* PETER *anticipates him.*)

PETER. She left her cake. (*He starts for* ANNE's *room with the cake. There is silence in the main room.* MRS. VAN DAAN *goes up to her room, followed by* VAN DAAN. DUSSEL *stays looking out the window.* MR. FRANK *brings* MRS. FRANK *her cake. She eats it slowly, without relish.* MR. FRANK *takes his cake to* MARGOT *and sits quietly on the sofa beside her.* PETER *stands in the doorway of* ANNE's *darkened room, looking at her, then makes a little movement to let her know he is there.* ANNE *sits up, quickly, trying to hide the signs of her tears.* PETER *holds out the cake to her.*) You left this.

ANNE (*dully*). Thanks.

(PETER *starts to go out, then comes back.*)

PETER. I thought you were fine just now. You know just how to talk to them. You know just how to say it. I'm no good . . . I never can think . . . especially when I'm mad . . . That Dussel . . . when he said that about Mouschi . . . someone eating him . . . all I could think is . . . I wanted to hit him. I wanted to give him such a . . . a . . . that he'd . . . That's what I used to do when there was an argument at school . . . That's the way I . . . but here . . . And an old man like that . . . it wouldn't be so good.

ANNE. You're making a big mistake about me. I do it all wrong. I say too much. I go too far. I hurt people's feelings . . .

(DUSSEL *leaves the window, going to his room.*)

PETER. I think you're just fine . . . What I want

to say . . . if it wasn't for you around here, I don't know. What I mean . . .

(PETER *is interrupted by* DUSSEL's *turning on the light.* DUSSEL *stands in the doorway, startled to see* PETER. PETER *advances toward him forbiddingly.* DUSSEL *backs out of the room.* PETER *closes the door on him.*)

ANNE. Do you mean it, Peter? Do you really mean it?

PETER. I said it, didn't I?

ANNE. Thank you, Peter!

(*In the main room* MR. *and* MRS. FRANK *collect the dishes and take them to the sink, washing them.* MARGOT *lies down again on the couch.* DUSSEL, *lost, wanders into* PETER's *room and takes up a book, starting to read.*)

PETER (*looking at the photographs on the wall*). You've got quite a collection.

ANNE. Wouldn't you like some in your room? I could give you some. Heaven knows you spend enough time in there . . . doing heaven knows what . . .

PETER. It's easier. A fight starts, or an argument . . . I duck in there.

ANNE. You're lucky, having a room to go to. His lordship is always here . . . I hardly ever get a minute alone. When they start in on me, I can't duck away. I have to stand there and take it.

PETER. You gave some of it back just now.

ANNE. I get so mad. They've formed their opinions . . . about everything . . . but we . . . we're still trying to find out . . . We have problems here that no other people our age have ever had. And just as you think you've solved them, something comes along and bang! You have to start all over again.

PETER. At least you've got someone you can talk to.

ANNE. Not really. Mother . . . I never discuss anything serious with her. She doesn't understand. Father's all right. We can talk

▲ Anne's bedroom wall in the secret annex, decorated with her collection of movie stars.

about everything . . . everything but one thing. Mother. He simply won't talk about her. I don't think you can be really intimate with anyone if he holds something back, do you?

PETER. I think your father's fine.

ANNE. Oh, he is, Peter! He is! He's the only one who's ever given me the feeling that I have any sense. But anyway, nothing can take the place of school and play and friends of your own age . . . or near your age . . . can it?

PETER. I suppose you miss your friends and all.

ANNE. It isn't just . . . (*She breaks off, staring up at him for a second.*) Isn't it funny, you and I? Here we've been seeing each other every minute for almost a year and a half, and this is the first time we've ever really talked. It helps a lot to have someone to talk to, don't you think? It helps you to let off steam.

PETER (*going to the door*). Well, any time you want to let off steam, you can come into my room.

ANNE (*following him*). I can get up an awful lot of steam. You'll have to be careful how you say that.

PETER. It's all right with me.

ANNE. Do you mean it?

PETER. I said it, didn't I?

(*He goes out.* ANNE *stands in her doorway looking after him. As* PETER *gets to his door he stands for a minute looking back at her. Then he goes into his room.* DUSSEL *rises as he comes in, and quickly passes him, going out. He starts across for his room.* ANNE *sees him coming, and pulls her door shut.* DUSSEL *turns back toward* PETER*'s room.* PETER *pulls his door shut.* DUSSEL *stands there, bewildered, forlorn.*

The scene slowly dims out. The curtain falls on the scene. ANNE'S VOICE *comes over in the darkness . . . faintly at first, and then with growing strength.)*

ANNE'S VOICE. We've had bad news. The people from whom Miep got our ration books have been arrested. So we have had to cut down on our food. Our stomachs are so empty that they rumble and make strange noises, all in different keys. Mr. Van Daan's is deep and low, like a bass fiddle. Mine is high, whistling like a flute. As we all sit around waiting for supper, it's like an orchestra tuning up. It only needs Toscanini to raise his baton and we'd be off in the Ride of the Valkyries.[8] Monday, the sixth of March, nineteen forty-four. Mr. Kraler is in the hospital. It seems he has ulcers. Pim says we are his ulcers. Miep has to run the business and us too. The Americans have landed on the southern tip of Italy. Father looks for a quick finish to the war. Mr. Dussel is waiting every day for the warehouse man to demand more money. Have I been skipping too much from one subject to another? I can't help it. I feel that spring is coming. I feel it in my whole body and soul. I feel utterly confused. I am longing . . . so longing . . . for everything . . . for friends . . . for someone to talk to . . . someone who understands . . . someone young, who feels as I do . . .

(As these last lines are being said, the curtain rises on the scene. The lights dim on. ANNE'S VOICE *fades out.)*

SCENE TWO

It is evening, after supper. From outside we hear the sound of children playing. The "grownups," with the exception of MR. VAN DAAN, *are all in the main room.* MRS. FRANK *is doing some mending,* MRS. VAN DAAN *is reading a fashion magazine.* MR. FRANK *is going over business accounts.* DUSSEL, *in his dentist's jacket, is pacing up and down, impatient to get into his bedroom.* MR. VAN DAAN *is upstairs working on a piece of embroidery in an embroidery frame.*

In his room PETER *is sitting before the mirror, smoothing his hair. As the scene goes on, he puts on his tie, brushes his coat and puts it on, preparing himself meticulously for a visit from* ANNE. *On his wall are now hung some of* ANNE's *motion picture stars.*

In her room ANNE *too is getting dressed. She stands before the mirror in her slip, trying various ways of dressing her hair.* MARGOT *is seated on the sofa, hemming a skirt for* ANNE *to wear.*

In the main room DUSSEL *can stand it no longer. He comes over, rapping sharply on the door of his and* ANNE's *bedroom.*

ANNE *(calling to him).* No, no, Mr. Dussel! I am not dressed yet. (DUSSEL *walks away, furious, sitting down and burying his head in his hands.* ANNE *turns to* MARGOT.) How is that? How does that look?

MARGOT *(glancing at her briefly).* Fine.

ANNE. You didn't even look.

MARGOT. Of course I did. It's fine.

ANNE. Margot, tell me, am I terribly ugly?

MARGOT. Oh, stop fishing.

ANNE. No. No. Tell me.

MARGOT. Of course you're not. You've got nice eyes . . . and a lot of animation, and . . .

ANNE. A little vague, aren't you?

(She reaches over and takes a brassière out of MARGOT's *sewing basket. She holds it up to herself, studying the effect in the mirror. Outside,* MRS. FRANK, *feeling sorry for* DUSSEL, *comes over, knocking at the girls' door.)*

MRS. FRANK *(outside).* May I come in?

MARGOT. Come in, Mother.

MRS. FRANK *(shutting the door behind her).* Mr. Dussel's impatient to get in here.

ANNE *(still with the brassière).* Heavens, he takes

---

8. **Toscanini . . . Ride of the Valkyries.** Toscanini (tos′kə nē′nē), 1867–1957, was a world-famous Italian musical conductor. "Ride of the Valkyries" (val kir′ēz) is a vigorous musical composition by nineteenth-century German composer Richard Wagner (väg′nər).

the room for himself the entire day.

MRS. FRANK (*gently*). Anne, dear, you're not going in again tonight to see Peter?

ANNE (*dignified*). That is my intention.

MRS. FRANK. But you've already spent a great deal of time in there today.

ANNE. I was in there exactly twice. Once to get the dictionary, and then three-quarters of an hour before supper.

MRS. FRANK. Aren't you afraid you're disturbing him?

ANNE. Mother, I have some intuition.[9]

MRS. FRANK. Then may I ask you this much, Anne. Please don't shut the door when you go in.

ANNE. You sound like Mrs. Van Daan! (*She throws the brassière back in* MARGOT*'s sewing basket and picks up her blouse, putting it on.*)

MRS. FRANK. No. No. I don't mean to suggest anything wrong. I only wish that you wouldn't expose yourself to criticism . . . that you wouldn't give Mrs. Van Daan the opportunity to be unpleasant.

ANNE. Mrs. Van Daan doesn't need an opportunity to be unpleasant!

MRS. FRANK. Everyone's on edge, worried about Mr. Kraler. This is one more thing . . .

ANNE. I'm sorry, Mother. I'm going to Peter's room. I'm not going to let Petronella Van Daan spoil our friendship.

(MRS. FRANK *hesitates for a second, then goes out, closing the door after her. She gets a pack of playing cards and sits at the center table, playing solitaire. In* ANNE*'s room* MARGOT *hands the finished skirt to* ANNE. *As* ANNE *is putting it on,* MARGOT *takes off her high-heeled shoes and stuffs paper in the toes so that* ANNE *can wear them.*)

MARGOT (*to* ANNE). Why don't you two talk in the main room? It'd save a lot of trouble. It's hard on Mother, having to listen to those remarks from Mrs. Van Daan and not say a word.

ANNE. Why doesn't she say a word? I think it's ridiculous to take it and take it.

MARGOT. You don't understand Mother at all, do you? She can't talk back. She's not like you. It's just not in her nature to fight back.

ANNE. Anyway . . . the only one I worry about is you. I feel awfully guilty about you. (*She sits on the stool near* MARGOT, *putting on* MARGOT*'s high-heeled shoes.*)

MARGOT. What about?

ANNE. I mean, every time I go into Peter's room, I have a feeling I may be hurting you. (MARGOT *shakes her head.*) I know if it were me, I'd be wild. I'd be desperately jealous, if it were me.

MARGOT. Well, I'm not.

ANNE. You don't feel badly? Really? Truly? You're not jealous?

MARGOT. Of course I'm jealous . . . jealous that you've got something to get up in the morning for . . . But jealous of you and Peter? No.

(ANNE *goes back to the mirror.*)

ANNE. Maybe there's nothing to be jealous of. Maybe he doesn't really like me. Maybe I'm just taking the place of his cat . . . (*She picks up a pair of short, white gloves, putting them on.*) Wouldn't you like to come in with us?

MARGOT. I have a book.

(*The sound of the children playing outside fades out. In the main room* DUSSEL *can stand it no longer. He jumps up, going to the bedroom door and knocking sharply.*)

DUSSEL. Will you please let me in my room!

ANNE. Just a minute, dear, dear Mr. Dussel. (*She picks up her mother's pink stole and adjusts it elegantly over her shoulders, then gives a last look in the mirror.*) Well, here I go

---

9. **intuition** (in′tü ish′ən, in′tyü ish′ən), *n.* immediate perception or understanding of truths, facts, etc., without reasoning.

Peter Van Daan. ➤

. . . to run the gauntlet. (*She starts out, followed by* MARGOT.)

DUSSEL (*as she appears—sarcastic*). Thank you so much.

(DUSSEL *goes into his room.* ANNE *goes toward* PETER*'s room, passing* MRS. VAN DAAN *and her parents at the center table.*)

MRS. VAN DAAN. . . . Look at her! (ANNE *pays no attention. She knocks at* PETER*'s door.*) I don't know what good it is to have a son. I never see him. He wouldn't care if I killed myself. (PETER *opens the door and stands aside for* ANNE *to come in.*) Just a minute, Anne. (*She goes to them at the door.*) I'd like to say a few words to my son. Do you mind? (PETER *and* ANNE *stand waiting.*) Peter, I don't want you staying up till all hours tonight. You've got to have your sleep. You're a growing boy. You hear?

MRS. FRANK. Anne won't stay late. She's going to bed promptly at nine. Aren't you, Anne?

ANNE. Yes, Mother . . . (*To* MRS. VAN DAAN) May we go now?

MRS. VAN DAAN. Are you asking me? I didn't know I had anything to say about it.

MRS. FRANK. Listen for the chimes, Anne dear.

(*The two young people go off into* PETER*'s room, shutting the door after them.*)

MRS. VAN DAAN (*to* MRS. FRANK). In my day it was the boys who called on the girls. Not the girls on the boys.

MRS. FRANK. You know how young people like to feel that they have secrets. Peter's room is the only place where they can talk.

MRS. VAN DAAN. Talk! That's not what they called it when I was young.

(MRS. VAN DAAN *goes off to the bathroom.* MARGOT *settles down to read her book.* MR. FRANK *puts his papers away and brings a chess game to the center table. He and* MRS. FRANK *start to play. In* PETER's *room,* ANNE *speaks to* PETER, *indignant, humiliated.*)

ANNE. Aren't they awful? Aren't they impossible? Treating us as if we were still in the nursery. (*She sits on the cot.* PETER *gets a bottle of pop and two glasses.*)

PETER. Don't let it bother you. It doesn't bother me.

ANNE. I suppose you can't really blame them . . . they think back to what *they* were like at our age. They don't realize how much more advanced we are . . . When you think what wonderful discussions we've had! . . . Oh, I forgot. I was going to bring you some more pictures.

PETER. Oh, these are fine, thanks.

ANNE. Don't you want some more? Miep just brought me some new ones.

PETER. Maybe later. (*He gives her a glass of pop and, taking some for himself, sits down facing her.*)

ANNE (*looking up at one of the photographs*). I remember when I got that . . . I won it. I bet Jopie that I could eat five ice-cream cones. We'd all been playing ping-pong . . . We used to have heavenly times . . . we'd finish up with ice cream at the Delphi, or the Oasis, where Jews were allowed . . . there'd always be a lot of boys . . . we'd laugh and joke . . . I'd like to go back to it for a few days or a week. But after

that I know I'd be bored to death. I think more seriously about life now. I want to be a journalist . . . or something. I love to write. What do you want to do?

PETER. I thought I might go off some place . . . work on a farm or something . . . some job that doesn't take much brains.

ANNE. You shouldn't talk that way. You've got the most awful inferiority complex.

PETER. I know I'm not smart.

ANNE. That isn't true. You're much better than I am in dozens of things . . . arithmetic and algebra and . . . well, you're a million times better than I am in algebra. (*With sudden directness*) You like Margot, don't you? Right from the start you liked her, liked her much better than me.

PETER (*uncomfortably*). Oh, I don't know.

(*In the main room* MRS. VAN DAAN *comes from the bathroom and goes over to the sink, polishing a coffeepot.*)

ANNE. It's all right. Everyone feels that way. Margot's so good. She's sweet and bright and beautiful and I'm not.

PETER. I wouldn't say that.

ANNE. Oh, no, I'm not. I know that. I know quite well that I'm not a beauty. I never have been and never shall be.

PETER. I don't agree at all. I think you're pretty.

ANNE. That's not true!

PETER. And another thing. You've changed . . . from at first, I mean.

ANNE. I have?

PETER. I used to think you were awful noisy.

ANNE. And what do you think now, Peter? How have I changed?

PETER. Well . . . er . . . you're . . . quieter.

(*In his room* DUSSEL *takes his pajamas and toilet articles and goes into the bathroom to change.*)

ANNE. I'm glad you don't just hate me.

PETER. I never said that.

ANNE. I bet when you get out of here you'll

never think of me again.

PETER. That's crazy.

ANNE. When you get back with all of your friends, you're going to say . . . now what did I ever see in that Mrs. Quack Quack.

PETER. I haven't got any friends.

ANNE. Oh, Peter, of course you have. Everyone has friends.

PETER. Not me. I don't want any. I get along all right without them.

ANNE. Does that mean you can get along without me? I think of myself as your friend.

PETER. No. If they were all like you, it'd be different.

(He takes the glasses and the bottle and puts them away. There is a second's silence and then ANNE *speaks, hesitantly, shyly.)*

ANNE. Peter, did you ever kiss a girl?

PETER. Yes. Once.

ANNE *(to cover her feelings).* That picture's crooked. (PETER *goes over, straightening the photograph.)* Was she pretty?

PETER. Huh?

ANNE. The girl that you kissed.

PETER. I don't know. I was blindfolded. *(He comes back and sits down again.)* It was at a party. One of those kissing games.

ANNE *(relieved).* Oh, I don't suppose that really counts, does it?

PETER. It didn't with me.

ANNE. I've been kissed twice. Once a man I'd never seen before kissed me on the cheek when he picked me up off the ice and I was crying. And the other was Mr. Koophuis,[10] a friend of Father's who kissed my hand. You wouldn't say those counted, would you?

PETER. I wouldn't say so.

ANNE. I know almost for certain that Margot would never kiss anyone unless she was engaged to them. And I'm sure too that Mother never touched a man before Pim. But I don't know . . . things are so differ-

ent now . . . What do you think? Do you think a girl shouldn't kiss anyone except if she's engaged or something? It's so hard to try to think what to do, when here we are with the whole world falling around our ears and you think . . . well . . . you don't know what's going to happen tomorrow and . . . What do you think?

PETER. I suppose it'd depend on the girl. Some girls, anything they do's wrong. But others . . . well . . . it wouldn't necessarily be wrong with them. *(The carillon starts to strike nine o'clock.)* I've always thought that when two people . . .

ANNE. Nine o'clock. I have to go.

PETER. That's right.

ANNE *(without moving).* Good night.

(There is a second's pause, then PETER *gets up and moves toward the door.)*

PETER. You won't let them stop you coming?

ANNE. No. *(She rises and starts for the door.)* Sometime I might bring my diary. There are so many things in it that I want to talk over with you. There's a lot about you.

PETER. What kind of things?

ANNE. I wouldn't want you to see some of it. I thought you were a nothing, just the way you thought about me.

PETER. Did you change your mind, the way I changed my mind about you?

ANNE. Well . . . You'll see . . .

(For a second ANNE *stands looking up at* PETER, *longing for him to kiss her. As he makes no move she turns away. Then suddenly* PETER *grabs her awkwardly in his arms, kissing her on the cheek.* ANNE *walks out dazed. She stands for a minute, her back to the people in the main room. As she regains her poise she goes to her mother and father and* MARGOT, *silently kissing them. They murmur their good nights to her. As she is about to open her bedroom door, she catches sight of* MRS. VAN DAAN. *She goes*

---

10. **Mr. Koophuis** (kōp′hous).

quickly to her, taking her face in her hands and kissing her first on one cheek and then on the other. Then she hurries off into her room. MRS. VAN DAAN looks after her, and then looks over at PETER's room. Her suspicions are confirmed.)

MRS. VAN DAAN. *(She knows.)* Ah hah!

(The lights dim out. The curtain falls on the scene. In the darkness ANNE'S VOICE comes faintly at first and then with growing strength.)

ANNE'S VOICE. By this time we all know each other so well that if anyone starts to tell a story, the rest can finish it for him. We're having to cut down still further on our meals. What makes it worse, the rats have been at work again. They've carried off some of our precious food. Even Mr. Dussel wishes now that Mouschi was here. Thursday, the twentieth of April, nineteen forty-four. Invasion fever[11] is mounting every day. Miep tells us that people outside talk of nothing else. For myself, life has become much more pleasant. I often go to Peter's room after supper. Oh, don't think I'm in love, because I'm not. But it does make life more bearable to have someone with whom you can exchange views. No more tonight. P.S. . . . I must be honest. I must confess that I actually live for the next meeting. Is there anything lovelier than to sit under the skylight and feel the sun on your cheeks and have a darling boy in your arms? I admit now that I'm glad the Van Daans had a son and not a daughter. I've outgrown another dress. That's the third. I'm having to wear Margot's clothes after all. I'm working hard on my French and am now reading *La Belle Nivernaise.*[12]

(As she is saying the last lines—the curtain rises on the scene. The lights dim on, as ANNE'S VOICE fades out.)

▲ A page from Anne's diary, dated October 10, 1942, where she had pasted her photo. In Dutch, she has written, "This is a photo as I would wish myself to look all the time. Then I would maybe have a chance to come to Hollywood."

---

11. **Invasion fever,** the expectation that the Allies would invade Europe to free it from German occupation. The invasion actually began on June 6, 1944, known as "D-Day."
12. *La Belle Nivernaise* (lä bel′ niv ər nez′), a tale by Alphonse Daudet, a nineteenth-century French novelist.

After Reading

Making Connections

1. Review the entries in your Reading Log and choose one that you think would be especially interesting to other readers. Explain why it is interesting.

2. Why do you think the authors chose to open Act Two with Anne's voice reading from the diary?

3. How was the disappearance of Peter's cat **foreshadowed** earlier in the play?

4. How do the incident with the cake and the disappearance of food reflect on the ideals the characters are trying to hold on to?

5. What do you think will happen as a result of the blackmail?

6. Do you think "everyone needs a room to go to"? Explain.

Literary Focus: Mood

The **mood** of a work is its emotional aspect—the atmosphere or feeling of it. The mood may be sad, tense, funny, thoughtful, or any other emotion. Mood is established by settings (a graveyard at midnight), events (a wedding reception), and actions and reactions of characters (two enemies out for revenge on each other). Notice how the mood of the play changes as you continue through the work. Try to identify the moods and the causes for the changes.

Vocabulary Study

onslaught
inarticulate
foreboding
pretense
intuition

Decide if the underlined words are used correctly in the sentences below. On your paper, write *Correct* or *Incorrect,* and if incorrect, explain why.

1. The onslaught began when the German army attacked the Netherlands.

2. Churchill was inarticulate as he clearly explained the seriousness of the war effort.

3. A feeling of foreboding struck the citizens as they watched the fierce enemy soldiers march through their streets.

4. Although they feared the worst, they kept up a pretense of cheerfulness.

5. People became filled with intuition as they waited impatiently for the Germans to be defeated.

SCENE THREE

It is night, a few weeks later. Everyone is in bed. There is complete quiet. In the VAN DAANS' *room a match flares up for a moment and then is quickly put out.* MR. VAN DAAN, *in bare feet, dressed in underwear and trousers, is dimly seen coming* stealthily[1] *down the stairs and into the main room, where* MR. *and* MRS. FRANK *and* MARGOT *are sleeping. He goes to the food safe and again lights a match. Then he cautiously opens the safe, taking out a half-loaf of bread. As he closes the safe, it creaks. He stands rigid.* MRS. FRANK *sits up in bed. She sees him.*

MRS. FRANK *(screaming)*. Otto! Otto! *Komme schnell!*[2]

(The rest of the people wake, hurriedly getting up.)

MR. FRANK. *Was ist los? Was ist passiert?*[3]

*(*DUSSEL, *followed by* ANNE, *comes from his room.)*

MRS. FRANK *(as she rushes over to* MR. VAN DAAN*). Er stiehlt das Essen!*[4]

DUSSEL *(grabbing* MR. VAN DAAN*)*. You! You! Give me that.

MRS. VAN DAAN *(coming down the stairs)*. Putti . . . Putti . . . what is it?

DUSSEL *(his hands on* VAN DAAN*'s neck)*. You dirty thief . . . stealing food . . . you good-for-nothing . . .

MR. FRANK. Mr. Dussel! . . . Help me, Peter!

*(*PETER *comes over, trying, with* MR. FRANK, *to separate the two struggling men.)*

PETER. Let him go! Let go!

*(*DUSSEL *drops* MR. VAN DAAN, *pushing him away. He shows them the end of a loaf of bread that he has taken from* VAN DAAN.*)*

DUSSEL. You greedy, selfish . . . !

*(*MARGOT *turns on the lights.)*

MRS. VAN DAAN. Putti . . . what is it?

(All of MRS. FRANK*'s gentleness, her self-control, is gone. She is outraged, in a frenzy of indignation.)*

MRS. FRANK. The bread! He was stealing the bread!

DUSSEL. It was you, and all the time we thought it was the rats!

MR. FRANK. Mr. Van Daan, how could you!

MR. VAN DAAN. I'm hungry.

MRS. FRANK. We're all of us hungry! I see the children getting thinner and thinner. Your own son Peter . . . I've heard him moan in his sleep, he's so hungry. And you come in the night and steal food that should go to them . . . to the children!

MRS. VAN DAAN *(going to* MR. VAN DAAN *protectively)*. He needs more food than the rest of us. He's used to more. He's a big man.

*(*MR. VAN DAAN *breaks away, going over and sitting on the couch.)*

MRS. FRANK *(turning on* MRS. VAN DAAN*)*. And you . . . you're worse than he is! You're a mother, and yet you sacrifice your child to this man . . . this . . . this . . .

MR. FRANK. Edith! Edith!

*(*MARGOT *picks up the pink woolen stole, putting it over her mother's shoulders.)*

MRS. FRANK *(paying no attention, going on to* MRS. VAN DAAN*)*. Don't think I haven't seen you! Always saving the choicest bits for him! I've watched you day after day and I've held my tongue. But not any longer! Not after this! Now I want him to go! I want him to get out of here!

MR. FRANK. Edith!

MR. VAN DAAN. Get out of here? } *(Together.)*

MRS. VAN DAAN. What do you mean?

MRS. FRANK. Just that! Take your things and get out!

MR. FRANK *(to* MRS. FRANK*)*. You're speaking in

---

1. stealthily (stel′thə lē), *adv.* in a secret manner.
2. *Komme schnell!* (kôm′ə shnel). Come quick! (German)
3. *Was ist los? Was ist passiert?* (väs ist lôs väs ist pä sērt′). What's the matter? What happened? (German)
4. *Er stiehlt das Essen!* (er shtēlt däs es′ən). He is stealing food. (German)

anger. You cannot mean what you are saying.

MRS. FRANK. I mean exactly that!

(MRS. VAN DAAN *takes a cover from the* FRANKS' *bed, pulling it about her.*)

MR. FRANK. For two long years we have lived here, side by side. We have respected each other's rights . . . we have managed to live in peace. Are we now going to throw it all away? I know this will never happen again, will it, Mr. Van Daan?

MR. VAN DAAN. No. No.

MRS. FRANK. He steals once! He'll steal again!

(MR. VAN DAAN, *holding his stomach, starts for the bathroom.* ANNE *puts her arms around him, helping him up the step.*)

MR. FRANK. Edith, please. Let us be calm. We'll all go to our rooms . . . and afterwards we'll sit down quietly and talk this out . . . we'll find some way . . .

MRS. FRANK. No! No! No more talk! I want them to leave!

MRS. VAN DAAN. You'd put us out, on the streets?

MRS. FRANK. There are other hiding places.

MRS. VAN DAAN. A cellar . . . a closet. I know. And we have no money left even to pay for that.

MRS. FRANK. I'll give you money. Out of my own pocket. I'll give it gladly.

(*She gets her purse from a shelf and comes back with it.*)

MRS. VAN DAAN. Mr. Frank, you told Putti you'd never forget what he'd done for you when you came to Amsterdam. You said you could never repay him, that you . . .

MRS. FRANK (*counting out money*). If my husband had any obligation to you, he's paid it, over and over.

MR. FRANK. Edith, I've never seen you like this before. I don't know you.

MRS. FRANK. I should have spoken out long ago.

DUSSEL. You can't be nice to some people.

MRS. VAN DAAN (*turning on* DUSSEL). There would have been plenty for all of us, if *you* hadn't come in here!

MR. FRANK. We don't need the Nazis to destroy us. We're destroying ourselves.

(*He sits down, with his head in his hands.* MRS. FRANK *goes to* MRS. VAN DAAN.)

MRS. FRANK (*giving* MRS. VAN DAAN *some money*). Give this to Miep. She'll find you a place.

ANNE. Mother, you're not putting *Peter* out. Peter hasn't done anything.

MRS. FRANK. He'll stay, of course. When I say I must protect the children, I mean Peter too.

(PETER *rises from the steps where he has been sitting.*)

PETER. I'd have to go if Father goes.

(MR. VAN DAAN *comes from the bathroom.* MRS. VAN DAAN *hurries to him and takes him to the couch. Then she gets water from the sink to bathe his face.*)

MRS. FRANK (*while this is going on*). He's no father to you . . . that man! He doesn't know what it is to be a father!

PETER (*starting for his room*). I wouldn't feel right. I couldn't stay.

MRS. FRANK. Very well, then. I'm sorry.

ANNE (*rushing over to* PETER). No, Peter! No! (PETER *goes into his room, closing the door after him.* ANNE *turns back to her mother, crying.*) I don't care about the food. They can have mine! I don't want it! Only don't send them away. It'll be daylight soon. They'll be caught . . .

MARGOT (*putting her arms comfortingly around* ANNE). Please, Mother!

MRS. FRANK. They're not going now. They'll stay here until Miep finds them a place. (*To* MRS. VAN DAAN) But one thing I insist on! He must never come down here again! He must never come to this room where the food is stored! We'll divide what we have . . . an equal share for each! (DUSSEL *hurries over to get a sack of potatoes from the food safe.* MRS. FRANK *goes on, to* MRS. VAN

DAAN.) You can cook it here and take it up to him.

(DUSSEL *brings the sack of potatoes back to the center table.*)

MARGOT. Oh, no. No. We haven't sunk so far that we're going to fight over a handful of rotten potatoes.

DUSSEL (*dividing the potatoes into piles*). Mrs. Frank, Mr. Frank, Margot, Anne, Peter, Mrs. Van Daan, Mr. Van Daan, myself . . . Mrs. Frank . . .

(*The buzzer sounds in* MIEP's *signal.*)

MR. FRANK. It's Miep! (*He hurries over, getting his overcoat and putting it on.*)

MARGOT. At this hour?

MRS. FRANK. It is trouble.

MR. FRANK (*as he starts down to unbolt the door*). I beg you, don't let her see a thing like this!

MR. DUSSEL (*counting without stopping*). . . . Anne, Peter, Mrs. Van Daan, Mr. Van Daan, myself . . .

MARGOT (*to* DUSSEL). Stop it! Stop it!

DUSSEL. . . . Mr. Frank, Margot, Anne, Peter, Mrs. Van Daan, Mr. Van Daan, myself, Mrs. Frank . . .

MRS. VAN DAAN. You're keeping the big ones for yourself! All the big ones . . . Look at the size of that! . . . And that! . . .

(DUSSEL *continues on with his dividing.* PETER, *with his shirt and trousers on, comes from his room.*)

MARGOT. Stop it! Stop it!

(*We hear* MIEP's *excited voice speaking to* MR. FRANK *below.*)

MIEP. Mr. Frank . . . the most wonderful news! . . . The invasion has begun!

MR. FRANK. Go on, tell them! Tell them!

(MIEP *comes running up the steps, ahead of* MR. FRANK. *She has a man's raincoat on over her nightclothes and a bunch of orange-colored flowers in her hand.*)

MIEP. Did you hear that, everybody? Did you hear what I said? The invasion has begun!

The invasion!

(*They all stare at* MIEP, *unable to grasp what she is telling them.* PETER *is the first to recover his wits.*)

PETER. Where?

MRS. VAN DAAN. When? When, Miep?

MIEP. It began early this morning . . .

(*As she talks on, the realization of what she has said begins to dawn on them. Everyone goes crazy. A wild demonstration takes place.* MRS. FRANK *hugs* MR. VAN DAAN.)

MRS. FRANK. Oh, Mr. Van Daan, did you hear that?

(DUSSEL *embraces* MRS. VAN DAAN. PETER *grabs a frying pan and parades around the room, beating on it, singing the Dutch National Anthem.* ANNE *and* MARGOT *follow him, singing, weaving in and out among the excited grownups.* MARGOT *breaks away to take the flowers from* MIEP *and distribute them to everyone. While this pandemonium[5] is going on* MRS. FRANK *tries to make herself heard above the excitement.*)

MRS. FRANK (*to* MIEP). How do you know?

MIEP. The radio . . . The B.B.C.![6] They said they landed on the coast of Normandy!

PETER. The British?

MIEP. British, Americans, French, Dutch, Poles, Norwegians . . . all of them! More than four thousand ships! Churchill spoke, and General Eisenhower![7] D-Day they call it!

MR. FRANK. . . . It's come!

MRS. VAN DAAN. At last!

MIEP (*starting out*). I'm going to tell Mr. Kraler. This'll be better than any blood transfusion.

MR. FRANK (*stopping her*). What part of Normandy did they land, did they say?

---

5. pandemonium (pan′də mō′nē əm), *n.* wild disorder or confusion.
6. **B.B.C.,** the British Broadcasting Corporation.
7. **Churchill . . . Eisenhower.** Churchill was Prime Minister of England. Eisenhower was supreme commander of the Allied forces in Europe. He later became President of the United States.

MIEP. Normandy . . . that's all I know now . . . I'll be up the minute I hear some more! *(She goes hurriedly out.)*

MR. FRANK *(to* MRS. FRANK*)*. What did I tell you? What did I tell you?

*(*MRS. FRANK *indicates that he has forgotten to bolt the door after* MIEP*. He hurries down the steps.* MR. VAN DAAN, *sitting on the couch, suddenly breaks into a convulsive sob. Everybody looks at him, bewildered.)*

MRS. VAN DAAN *(hurrying to him)*. Putti! Putti! What is it? What happened?

MR. VAN DAAN. Please. I'm so ashamed.

*(*MR. FRANK *comes back up the steps.)*

DUSSEL. Oh, for goodness sake!

MRS. VAN DAAN. Don't, Putti.

MARGOT. It doesn't matter now!

MR. FRANK *(going to* MR. VAN DAAN*)*. Didn't you hear what Miep said? The invasion has come! We're going to be liberated! This is a time to celebrate! *(He embraces* MRS. FRANK *and then hurries to the cupboard and gets the cognac and a glass.)*

MR. VAN DAAN. To steal bread from children!

MRS. FRANK. We've all done things that we're ashamed of.

ANNE. Look at me, the way I've treated Mother . . . so mean and horrid to her.

MRS. FRANK. No, Anneke, no.

*(*ANNE *runs to her mother, putting her arms around her.)*

ANNE. Oh, Mother, I was. I was awful.

MR. VAN DAAN. Not like me. No one is as bad as me!

DUSSEL *(to* MR. VAN DAAN*)*. Stop it now! Let's be happy!

MR. FRANK *(giving* MR. VAN DAAN *a glass of cognac)*. Here! Here! *Schnapps! Locheim!*[8]

*(*VAN DAAN *takes the cognac. They all watch him. He gives them a feeble smile.* ANNE *puts up her fingers in a V-for-Victory sign. As* VAN DAAN *gives an answering V-sign, they are startled to hear a loud sob from behind them. It is* MRS. FRANK, *stricken with remorse.*

She is sitting on the other side of the room.)

MRS. FRANK *(through her sobs)*. When I think of the terrible things I said . . .

*(*MR. FRANK, ANNE *and* MARGOT *hurry to her, trying to comfort her.* MR. VAN DAAN *brings her his glass of cognac.)*

MR. VAN DAAN. No! No! You were right!

MRS. FRANK. That I should speak that way to you! . . . Our friends! . . . Our guests! *(She starts to cry again.)*

DUSSEL. Stop it, you're spoiling the whole invasion.

(As they are comforting her, the lights dim out. The curtain falls.)

ANNE'S VOICE *(faintly at first and then with growing strength)*. We're all in much better spirits these days. There's still excellent news of the invasion. The best part about it is that I have a feeling that friends are coming. Who knows? Maybe I'll be back in school by fall. Ha, ha! The joke is on us! The warehouse man doesn't know a thing and we are paying him all that money! . . . Wednesday, the second of July, nineteen forty-four. The invasion seems temporarily to be bogged down. Mr. Kraler has to have an operation, which looks bad. The Gestapo have found the radio that was stolen. Mr. Dussel says they'll trace it back and back to the thief, and then, it's just a matter of time till they get to us. Everyone is low. Even poor Pim can't raise their spirits. I have often been downcast myself . . . but never in despair. I can shake off everything if I write. But . . . and that is the great question . . . will I ever be able to write well? I want to so much. I want to go on living even after my death. Another birthday has gone by, so now I am fifteen. Already I know what I want. I have a goal, an opinion.

---

8. *Schnapps!* (schnäps) *Locheim!* (lə Hī′əm). Mr. Frank is proposing a toast to life.

American soldiers storm the beach into fire from Nazi defenders, during the D-Day invasion of the French coast.

(As this is being said—the curtain rises on the scene, the lights dim on, and ANNE'S VOICE *fades out.)*

SCENE FOUR

It is an afternoon a few weeks later . . . Everyone but MARGOT *is in the main room. There is a sense of great tension.*

Both MRS. FRANK *and* MR. VAN DAAN *are nervously pacing back and forth,* DUSSEL *is standing at the window, looking down fixedly at the street below.* PETER *is at the center table, trying to do his lessons.* ANNE *sits opposite him, writing in her diary.* MRS. VAN DAAN *is seated on the couch, her eyes on* MR. FRANK *as he sits reading.*

The sound of a telephone ringing comes from the office below. They all are rigid, listening tensely. MR. DUSSEL *rushes down to* MR. FRANK.

DUSSEL. There it goes again, the telephone! Mr. Frank, do you hear?

MR. FRANK *(quietly).* Yes. I hear.

DUSSEL *(pleading, insistent[9]).* But this is the third time, Mr. Frank! The third time in quick succession![10] It's a signal! I tell you it's Miep, trying to get us! For some reason she can't come to us and she's trying to warn us of something!

MR. FRANK. Please. Please.

MR. VAN DAAN *(to* DUSSEL*).* You're wasting your breath.

DUSSEL. Something has happened, Mr. Frank. For three days now Miep hasn't been to see us! And today not a man has come to work. There hasn't been a sound in the building!

MRS. FRANK. Perhaps it's Sunday. We may have lost track of the days.

MR. VAN DAAN *(to* ANNE*).* You with the diary there. What day is it?

DUSSEL *(going to* MRS. FRANK*).* I don't lose track of the days! I know exactly what day it is! It's Friday, the fourth of August. Friday, and not a man at work. *(He rushes back to* MR. FRANK, *pleading with him, almost in tears.)* I tell you

Mr. Kraler's dead. That's the only explanation. He's dead and they've closed down the building, and Miep's trying to tell us!

MR. FRANK. She'd never telephone us.

DUSSEL *(frantic).* Mr. Frank, answer that! I beg you, answer it!

MR. FRANK. No.

MR. VAN DAAN. Just pick it up and listen. You don't have to speak. Just listen and see if it's Miep.

DUSSEL *(speaking at the same time).* . . . I ask you.

MR. FRANK. No. I've told you, no. I'll do nothing that might let anyone know we're in the building.

PETER. Mr. Frank's right.

MR. VAN DAAN. There's no need to tell us what side you're on.

MR. FRANK. If we wait patiently, quietly, I believe that help will come.

(There is silence for a minute as they all listen to the telephone ringing.)

DUSSEL. I'm going down. *(He rushes down the steps.* MR. FRANK *tries ineffectually[11] to hold him.* DUSSEL *runs to the lower door, unbolting it. The telephone stops ringing.* DUSSEL *bolts the door and comes slowly back up the steps.)* Too late. *(*MR. FRANK *goes to* MARGOT *in* ANNE'S *bedroom.)*

MR. VAN DAAN. So we just wait here until we die.

MRS. VAN DAAN *(hysterically).* I can't stand it! I'll kill myself! I'll kill myself!

MR. VAN DAAN. . . . Stop it!

(In the distance, a German military band is heard playing a Viennese waltz.)

MRS. VAN DAAN. I think you'd be glad if I did! I think you want me to die!

---

9. **insistent** (in sis′tənt), *adj.* continuing to make a strong, firm demand or statement; insisting.

10. **succession** (sək sesh′ən), *n.* a group of things coming one after another.

11. **ineffectually** (in′ə fek′chü əl lē), *adv.* without effect; uselessly.

MR. VAN DAAN. Whose fault is it we're here? (MRS. VAN DAAN *starts for her room. He follows, talking at her.*) We could've been safe somewhere . . . in America or Switzerland. But no! No! You wouldn't leave when I wanted to. You couldn't leave your things. You couldn't leave your precious furniture.

MRS. VAN DAAN. Don't touch me!

(*She hurries up the stairs, followed by* MR. VAN DAAN. PETER, *unable to bear it, goes to his room.* ANNE *looks after him, deeply concerned.* DUSSEL *returns to his post at the window.* MR. FRANK *comes back into the main room and takes a book, trying to read.* MRS. FRANK *sits near the sink, starting to peel some potatoes.* ANNE *quietly goes to* PETER*'s room, closing the door after her.* PETER *is lying face down on the cot.* ANNE *leans over him, holding him in her arms, trying to bring him out of his despair.*)

ANNE. Look, Peter, the sky. (*She looks up through the skylight.*) What a lovely, lovely day! Aren't the clouds beautiful? You know what I do when it seems as if I couldn't stand being cooped up for one more minute? I *think* myself out. I think myself on a walk in the park where I used to go with Pim. Where the jonquils and the crocus and the violets grow down the slopes. You know the most wonderful part about *thinking* yourself out? You can have it any way you like. You can have roses and violets and chrysanthemums all blooming at the same time . . . It's funny . . . I used to take it all for granted . . . and now I've gone crazy about everything to do with nature. Haven't you?

PETER. I've just gone crazy. I think if something doesn't happen soon . . . if we don't get out of here . . . I can't stand much more of it!

ANNE (*softly*). I wish you had a religion, Peter.

PETER. No, thanks! Not me!

ANNE. Oh, I don't mean you have to be Orthodox[12] . . . or believe in heaven and hell and purgatory and things . . . I just mean some religion . . . it doesn't matter what. Just to believe in something! When I think of all that's out there . . . the trees . . . and flowers . . . and seagulls . . . when I think of the dearness of you, Peter, . . . and the goodness of the people we know . . . Mr. Kraler, Miep, Dirk, the vegetable man, all risking their lives for us every day . . . When I think of these good things, I'm not afraid any more . . . I find myself, and God, and I . . .

(PETER *interrupts, getting up and walking away.*)

PETER. That's fine! But when I begin to think, I get mad! Look at us, hiding out for two years. Not able to move! Caught here like . . . waiting for them to come and get us . . . and all for what?

ANNE. We're not the only people that've had to suffer. There've always been people that've had to . . . sometimes one race . . . sometimes another . . . and yet . . .

PETER. That doesn't make me feel any better!

ANNE (*going to him*). I know it's terrible, trying to have any faith . . . when people are doing such horrible . . . But you know what I sometimes think? I think the world may be going through a phase, the way I was with Mother. It'll pass, maybe not for hundreds of years, but some day . . . I still believe, in spite of everything, that people are really good at heart.

PETER. I want to see something now . . . Not a thousand years from now!

(*He goes over, sitting down again on the cot.*)

ANNE. But, Peter, if you'd only look at it as part of a great pattern . . . that we're just a little minute in the life . . . (*She breaks off.*) Listen to us, going at each other like a couple of stupid grownups! Look at the sky now.

---

12. **Orthodox,** a follower of the branch of Judaism that keeps most closely to ancient ritual, customs, and traditions.

▲ A German tank corp enters an undefended town during the Nazi invasion of Holland.

Isn't it lovely? (*She holds out her hand to him.* PETER *takes it and rises, standing with her at the window looking out, his arms around her.*) Some day, when we're outside again, I'm going to . . .

(*She breaks off as she hears the sound of a car, its brakes squealing as it comes to a sudden stop. The people in the other rooms also become aware of the sound. They listen tensely. Another car roars up to a screeching stop.* ANNE *and* PETER *come from* PETER'*s room.* MR. *and* MRS. VAN DAAN *creep down the stairs.* DUSSEL *comes out from his room. Everyone is listening, hardly breathing. A doorbell clangs again and again in the building below.* MR. FRANK *starts quietly down the steps to the door.* DUSSEL *and* PETER *follow him. The others stand rigid, waiting, terrified.*

In a few seconds DUSSEL *comes stumbling back up the steps. He shakes off* PETER'*s help and goes to his room.* MR. FRANK *bolts the door below, and comes slowly back up the steps. Their eyes are all on him as he stands there for a minute. They realize that what they feared has happened.* MRS. VAN DAAN *starts to whimper.* MR. VAN DAAN *puts her gently in a chair, and then hurries off up the stairs to their room to collect their things.* PETER *goes to comfort his mother. There is a sound of violent pounding on a door below.*)

MR. FRANK (*quietly*). For the past two years we have lived in fear. Now we can live in hope.

(*The pounding below becomes more insistent. There are muffled sounds of voices, shouting commands.*)

MEN'S VOICES. *Auf machen! Da drinnen! Auf machen! Schnell! Schnell! Schnell!*[13] *etc., etc.*

(*The street door below is forced open. We hear the heavy tread of footsteps coming up.* MR. FRANK *gets two school-bags from the shelves, and gives one to* ANNE *and the other to* MARGOT. *He goes to get a bag for* MRS. FRANK. *The sound of feet coming up grows louder.* PETER *comes to* ANNE, *kissing her good-by, then he goes to his room to collect his things. The buzzer of their door starts to ring.* MR. FRANK *brings* MRS. FRANK *a bag. They stand together, waiting. We hear the thud of gun butts on the door, trying to break it down.*

ANNE *stands, holding her school satchel, looking over at her father and mother with a soft, reassuring smile. She is no longer a child, but a woman with courage to meet whatever lies ahead.*

The lights dim out. The curtain falls on the scene. We hear a mighty crash as the door is shattered. After a second ANNE'S VOICE *is heard.*)

ANNE'S VOICE. And so it seems our stay is over. They are waiting for us now. They've allowed us five minutes to get our things. We can each take a bag and whatever it will hold of clothing. Nothing else. So, dear Diary, that means I must leave you behind. Good-by for a while. P.S. Please, please, Miep, or Mr. Kraler, or anyone else. If you should find this diary, will you please keep it safe for me, because some day I hope . . .

(*Her voice stops abruptly. There is silence. After a second the curtain rises.*)

---

13. *Auf machen . . . Schnell!* (ouf mäkh′ən dä drin′ən ouf mäkh′ən shnel shnel shnel). Open up in there! Open up. Quick! Quick! Quick! (German)

SCENE FIVE

It is again the afternoon in November, 1945. The rooms are as we saw them in the first scene. MR. KRALER *has joined* MIEP *and* MR. FRANK. *There are coffee cups on the table. We see a great change in* MR. FRANK. *He is calm now. His bitterness is gone. He slowly turns a few pages of the diary. They are blank.*

MR. FRANK. No more. (*He closes the diary and puts it down on the couch beside him.*)

MIEP. I'd gone to the country to find food. When I got back the block was surrounded by police . . .

MR. KRALER. We made it our business to learn how they knew. It was the thief . . . the thief who told them.

(MIEP *goes up to the gas burner, bringing back a pot of coffee.*)

MR. FRANK (*after a pause*). It seems strange to say this, that anyone could be happy in a concentration camp. But Anne was happy in the camp in Holland where they first took us. After two years of being shut up in these rooms, she could be out . . . out in the sunshine and the fresh air that she loved.

MIEP (*offering the coffee to* MR. FRANK). A little more?

MR. FRANK (*holding out his cup to her*). The news of the war was good. The British and Americans were sweeping through France. We felt sure that they would get to us in time. In September we were told that we were to be shipped to Poland . . . The men to one camp. The women to another. I was sent to Auschwitz. They went to Belsen.[14]

In January we were freed, the few of us who were left. The war wasn't yet over, so it took us a long time to get home. We'd be sent here and there behind the lines where we'd be safe. Each time our train would stop . . . at a siding, or a crossing . . . we'd all get out and from group to group . . . Where were you? Were you at Belsen? At Buchenwald? At Mauthausen? Is it possible that you knew my wife? Did you ever see my husband? My son? My daughter? That's how I found out about my wife's death . . . of Margot, the Van Daans . . . Dussel. But Anne . . . I still hoped . . . Yesterday I went to Rotterdam. I'd heard of a woman there . . . She'd been in Belsen with Anne . . . I know now.

(*He picks up the diary again, and turns the pages back to find a certain passage. As he finds it we hear* ANNE'S VOICE.)

ANNE'S VOICE. In spite of everything, I still believe that people are really good at heart.

(MR. FRANK *slowly closes the diary.*)

MR. FRANK. She puts me to shame.

(*They are silent.*)

The CURTAIN *falls.*

---

14. **Auschwitz** (oush′vits) . . . **Belsen,** Nazi concentration camps in Poland and Germany, respectively. Buchenwald (bü′khən vält′), mentioned later, was in Germany.

Miep Gies in 1987, reading Anne's diary. ➤

After Reading

Making Connections

1. What are your feelings at the end of the play? Jot down in your notebook the words that express how you feel.

2. What final dimensions of **characters** are brought out as the conflicts over food and possible capture reach their peaks?

3. What effect does news of the invasion have on characters and the audience?

4. What means are used to create the **mood** of increasing tension in Scenes Three and Four as we move to the climax of the play?

5. How is Anne's writing important to her, in this section and throughout the play?

6. In Scene Four, Anne says, "We're not the only people that've had to suffer. There've always been people that've had to . . . sometimes one race . . . sometimes another. . . ." How do **interactions** between people get to this point, of one group seeking to destroy another? What can we do to prevent it from happening again?

7. Do you agree with Anne that "people are really good at heart"? Why or why not?

Literary Focus: Climax and Resolution in the Plot

The **climax** of a work is its turning point, the point at which the outcome of the conflict is determined. The **resolution,** which follows the climax, shows some of the effects of the outcome on characters. In this play, what point is the climax? In the resolution, what do you find out about the effects of the outcome on the characters?

In your notebook, copy the plot structure map shown below. In the places indicated along the rising and falling line, write notes to indicate the following key parts of the plot:

- the central **conflict** of the play,
- the moment of **climax,** and
- the **resolution.**

Climax

Rising Action

Falling Action

Conflict

Resolution

Vocabulary Study

Write the word from the list that is most clearly related to the situation described in each sentence.

1. The Green Police pound on a door repeatedly and refuse to go away.
2. Mr. Van Daan approaches the cupboard to steal food for himself.
3. The characters all dance, sing, and parade around when they find out that the invasion has occurred.
4. The phone rings three times in a row.
5. Mr. Frank tries unsuccessfully to keep Dussel from going downstairs.

Expressing Your Ideas

Writing Choices

Another Point of View *The Diary of Anne Frank* presents clear pictures of several characters besides Anne. Imagine that you are one of those characters. Write a **diary entry** about the events in one scene. Because your character is different from Anne, your account of the same events will use a different way of speaking and may take on a completely different meaning.

Character Profile Select one character and create a **personality profile.** Match words you associate with that character with descriptions, comments, actions, or reactions from other characters. Use five words and accompanying quotes to complete your profile. You might find it helpful to refer to your Reading Log for quotes.

Night and Day Some scenes open at night, while others open during the day. Make a **comparison chart** that shows the different kinds of events, emotions, and moods of the different time settings.

Other Options

Live, On Stage Choose a scene from the play that you find especially dramatic or moving. With other students, divide up the roles and rehearse your lines. Then **dramatize** the scene for the rest of the class. Afterwards, discuss what makes the scene effective.

Music, Please! Select three scenes (or moments in scenes) and find **music** to fit the mood of the scene. If other students are dramatizing scenes, play the music you chose during their performance.

Mr. Frank, Can You Tell Us . . . Working with a partner, act out an **interview** with Mr. Frank after he is released from the concentration camp. Remember that the year is 1945. Keep Mr. Frank "in character"—have him speak as he does in the play.

Expressing Your Ideas

Writing Choices

Personal Time Line Trace the changes in one character from his or her first appearance in the play to the end. Make a **time line** for the character that has one stopping point for each scene in the play (ten scenes in all). At each point on the time line, write a few words to show an important feature of the development of the character.

When You Come to *The Diary*. . . . Tell next year's readers of this book what to expect when they read *The Diary of Anne Frank.* Write a **letter** that will introduce future readers to the events, characters, and ideas of the play.

Quote Map For each character, find one quote from the play that best shows your view of that character. Review your Reading Log first for appropriate quotes. Make a **chart** of the characters and quotes that represent them.

You Made Me Think About. . . . Which character in this play had the greatest impact on you? Write a **dialogue** in which you and the character discuss an issue raised or an idea suggested by the play. When you write the character's lines in this conversation, try to keep to the style of expression the character uses in the play.

Are People Really Good at Heart? Do you agree or disagree with Anne's closing statement? Try to do *both*. Make a comparative **evidence chart** that lists in the left column evidence from the play that people are really good at heart. In the right column list evidence that people are *not* really good at heart. After you finish the lists, write a summary statement to tell which side's evidence seems stronger to you.

Other Options

Heroes in a Desperate Time Find out more about efforts during World War II to stop the Nazi campaign to exterminate the Jews, and **present** your research findings to the class. For example, you could investigate Oskar Schindler, the German businessman portrayed in the movie *Schindler's List,* who saved more than 1,200 Jews from certain death. Or you could learn more about the efforts of people in the Netherlands to protect and hide the Jews of their country. If you have HyperCard or similar software, you could present your findings in an electronic format.

Who Said It? Work with a partner and make up a **quote quiz** for your classmates. Find ten quotes from various characters and present them to your class as an oral quiz. Look for quotes that show something important about the character. Read aloud the quote and ask who said the lines in the play.

Make the Mask In the drama of some cultures, characters wear masks to show something about them. Select three characters from this play and draw or make the **masks** you would have them wear to suggest their personalities and attitudes.

Poster or Postcard Sketch a **poster** or a **postcard** that you think would be representative of the events, people, or ideas of the story. You might want to include elements of the setting and some key events in the drawing. Include the title or Anne's name somewhere in the design.

Writing Mini-Lesson

Summarizing Information

When you take notes during research, you need to summarize. Summarizing is condensing information and putting it into one or two sentences in your own words. Write summary sentences for each section of text you use in your research. Focus on the main idea of the section. Be sure to use your own words. This helps avoid plagiarism. It also helps you make sense of the information. The note card below contains one student's summary of the information gained from looking up *D-day* in an encyclopedia.

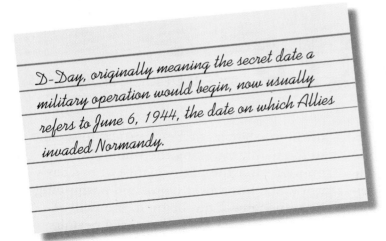

D-Day, originally meaning the secret date a military operation would begin, now usually refers to June 6, 1944, the date on which Allies invaded Normandy.

D-day, the term that has come to stand for the dates of Allied landings on coasts held by the enemy during World War II. The most well-known D-day is June 6, 1944, when Allied forces began the invasion of Normandy. The term originally stood for a secret date on which any military operation would begin. During peacetime, the planning of military operations is based on hypothetical D-days. For example, *D-plus-3* means three days after beginning a military operation.

Activity Options

1. Work with a partner. Skim a chapter from a social studies, health, or science textbook. Write a summary of each section. Confer with your partner to condense the information so that only the main ideas remain.

2. Choose an article from the front page of a newspaper. Write a summary of the article to share with the class.

3. Look back through *The Diary of Anne Frank* to locate terms associated with World War II. Then check an encyclopedia and summarize a portion of the article about the term. Share your summary with a partner. Does your summary communicate the main ideas?

U.S. History Connection

Frederick Douglass was a man shackled by the chains of slavery. His first step toward freedom was learning to read. Knowledge unshackled his spirit, giving him the strength to free himself and others.

A SPIRIT UNSHACKLED

BY FREDERICK DOUGLASS

I have no accurate knowledge of my age. By far the larger part of the slaves know as little of their ages as horses know of theirs, and it is the wish of most masters within my knowledge to keep their slaves thus ignorant. I do not remember to have ever met a slave who could tell of his birthday.

My mother was named Harriet Bailey. My father was a white man. The opinion was also whispered that my master was my father; but of the correctness of this opinion, I know nothing; the means of knowing was withheld from me. My mother and I were separated when I was but an infant.

I never saw my mother, to know her as such, more than four or five times in my life; and each of these times was very short in duration, and at night. She was hired by a Mr. Stewart, who lived about twelve miles from my home. She made her journeys to see me in the night, travelling the whole distance on foot, after the performance of her day's work. She was a field hand, and a whipping is the penalty of not being in the field at sunrise, unless a slave has special permission from his or her master to the contrary.

She was with me in the night. She would lie down with me, and get me to sleep, but long before I waked she was gone.

Very little communication ever took place between us. Death soon ended what little we could have while she lived, and with it her hardships and suffering. She died when I was about seven years old, on one of my master's farms, near Lee's Mill. I was not allowed to be present during her illness, at her death, or burial. . . .

Men and women slaves received, as their monthly allowance of food, eight pounds of pork, or its equivalent in fish, and one bushel of corn meal. Their yearly clothing consisted of two coarse linen shirts, one pair of linen trousers, like the shirts, one jacket, one pair of trousers for winter, . . . one pair of stockings, and one pair of shoes; the whole of which could not have cost more than seven dollars.

The children unable to work in the field had neither shoes, stockings, jackets, nor trousers, given to them; their clothing consisted of two coarse linen shirts per year. When these failed them, they went naked. Children from seven to ten years old, of both sexes, almost naked, might be seen at all seasons of the year.

There were no beds given the slaves, unless one coarse blanket be considered such, and none but the men and women had these. They find less difficulty from the want of beds, than from the want of time to sleep; for when their day's work in the field is done, the most of them have their washing, mending, and cooking to do, and having few or none of the ordinary facilities for doing either of these, very many of their sleeping hours are consumed in preparing for the field the coming day; and when this is done, old and young, male and female, married and single, drop down side by side, on one common bed—the cold, damp floor—each covering himself or herself with their miserable blankets; and here they sleep till they are summoned to the field by the driver's horn.

At the sound of this, all must rise, and be off to the field. There must be no halting; every one must be at his or her post. . . . Mr. Severe, the overseer, used to stand by the door of the quarter, armed with a large hickory stick and heavy cowskin, ready to whip any one who was so unfortunate as not to hear, or, from any other cause, was prevented from being ready to start for the field at the sound of the horn.

Few privileges were esteemed higher, by the slaves of the out-farms, than that of being selected to do errands at the Great House Farm. While on their way, they would make the dense old woods, for miles around, reverberate with their wild songs. I did not, when a slave, understand the deep meaning of those rude and apparently incoherent songs. They told a tale of woe which was then altogether beyond my feeble comprehension; they were tones loud, long, and deep; they breathed the prayer and complaint of souls boiling over with the bitterest anguish. Every tone was a testimony against slavery, and a prayer to God for deliverance from chains.

I have often been utterly astonished, since I came to the north, to find persons who could speak of the singing, among slaves, as evidence of their contentment and happiness. It is impossible to conceive of a greater mistake. Slaves sing most when they are most unhappy. The songs of the slave represent the sorrows of his heart; and he is relieved by them, only as an aching heart is relieved by its tears. At least, such is my experience. I have often sung to drown my sorrow, but seldom to express my happiness. . . .

I was not old enough to work in the field, and there being little else than field work to do, I had a great deal of leisure time. The most I had to do was to drive up the cows at evening, keep the fowls out of the garden, keep the front yard clean, and run of errands for my old master's daughter, Mrs. Lucretia Auld. . . .

Our food was coarse corn meal boiled. This was called *mush.* It was put into a large wooden tray or trough, and set down upon the ground. The children were then called, like so many pigs, and like so many pigs they would come and devour the mush; some with oyster-shells, others with pieces of shingle, some with naked hands, and none with spoons. He that ate fastest got most; he that was strongest secured the best place; and few left the trough satisfied.

I suffered much from hunger, but much more from cold. In hottest summer and coldest winter, I was kept almost naked— no shoes, no stockings, no jacket, no trousers, nothing on but a coarse tow linen shirt, reaching only to my knees. I had no bed. I must have perished with cold, but that, the coldest nights, I used to steal a bag which was used for carrying corn to the mill. I would crawl into this bag, and there sleep on the cold, damp, clay floor, with my head in and feet out. My feet have been so cracked with the frost, that the pen with which I am writing might be laid in the gashes.

Frederick is about eight years old when he is told that he will be sent to live in Baltimore with Hugh Auld, the brother of his owner's son-in-law.

The plan which I adopted, and the one by which I was most successful, was that of making friends of all the little white boys whom I met in the street. As many of these as I could, I converted into teachers. With their kindly aid, obtained at different times and in different places, I finally succeeded in learning to read.

The more I read, the more I was led to abhor and detest my enslavers. I could regard them in no other light than a band of successful robbers, who had gone to Africa, and stolen us from our homes, and in a strange land reduced us to slavery. I loathed them as being the meanest as well as the most wicked of men. It opened my eyes to the horrible pit, but to no ladder upon which to get out. In moments of agony, I envied my fellow-slaves for their stupidity. I have often wished myself a beast. I preferred the condition of the meanest reptile to my own. Any thing, no matter what, to get rid of thinking! It was this everlasting thinking of my condition that tormented me. There was no getting rid of it. It was pressed upon me by every object within sight or hearing, animate or inanimate. The silver trump of freedom had roused my soul to eternal wakefulness. Freedom now appeared, to disappear no more forever. It was heard in every sound, and seen in every thing. It was ever present to torment me with a sense of my wretched condition. I saw nothing without seeing it, I heard nothing without hearing it, and felt nothing without feeling it. It looked from every star, it smiled in every calm, breathed in every wind, and moved in every storm.

Responding

1. Why do you think slave owners did not want their slaves to know their ages or to learn to read?

2. Learning to read was the key that unlocked Douglass's door to freedom. How can education be your key to freedom?

Fine Arts Connection

As Frederick Douglass described, the lives of most slaves were filled with need—need for food, warm clothing, and shelter. In spite of their hardships, the slaves survived. They kept alive the skills and talents they had brought from their native lands. They made beautiful baskets, pottery, and quilts from materials at hand. They made musical instruments, and sang and danced. They remained strong. Theirs was a true triumph of the human spirit in the face of nearly overwhelming pain and degradation.

MUSIC ART CRAFTS

Images top to bottom:

Slave potters from Edgefield, South Carolina, made striking face vessels. This one is only six and a half inches high.

Some African customs survived the rigors of plantation life. In this watercolor by an unknown artist, slaves dance to the music of a drum and banjo.

This musical instrument was made to imitate a native African design. It was made sometime in the early 1800s.

Harriet Powers made her quilt around 1886. Each square shows a scene from the Bible.

Responding

Look carefully at the artifacts pictured above. What did the slave artisans reveal about themselves in their creations?

INTERDISCIPLINARY STUDY

Sociology Connection
Justice eluded most slaves in their lifetime. That can never be changed. However, one woman, Dorothy Redford, found a way to honor her slave ancestors, who contributed so much to the building of a nation.

KIN

JAMES S. KUNEN

Two hundred summers after their ancestors had been dragged there in chains—eighty of them shipped from Africa aboard the brig *Camden*—Dorothy Spruill Redford and perhaps 2,000 other people had come home to Somerset Place, once one of the largest slaveholding plantations in North Carolina. They were descendants of the black men and women who had carved the magnificent estate from the Great Alligator Swamp in the eastern part of the state, who had dug by hand a canal six miles long and twenty feet wide to drain the malarial swamp, who had built a fourteen-room mansion, sawmills, a gristmill. They had cleared and farmed the plantation's 5,870 acres, and many of them had died in the process. Their descendants had come to pay them homage from as far away as California and West Germany. They were doctors, lawyers, teachers, farmers, politicians, and musicians, carrying the variously spelled surnames of their ancestors' original slave masters: Lee and Leigh, Horniblue and Honeyblue, Blunt and Blount.

The reunion was the culmination of nine years' meticulous research by Redford, 43, a social services supervisor in Portsmouth, Virginia. After watching the TV miniseries version of Alex Haley's *Roots* in 1977 with her only child, Deborah, now 23, Redford embarked on the search for her own family origins. "I felt this overwhelming need to know about my past," she says. "I used to think of slavery as ancient history, but I'm only the third generation that wasn't born slave. That's amazing to me."

Working nights, weekends, and vacations, Redford pored through faded local court records for three years before she discovered her link to Somerset Place. In the Chowan County Courthouse, she found a bill of sale showing that her great-great-great-grandmother, Elsy Littlejohn, and Littlejohn's six children had been sold in 1826 by the Littlejohn plantation to the owner of

Two descendants of the Littlejohn slave family, Mereline Moses and Loretta Moore, meet for the first time at the Somerset Place reunion in North Carolina.

Members of four generations of one slave family were photographed on the plantation they worked on in Beaufort, South Carolina.

Somerset, Josiah Collins, Jr., who already owned Elsy's husband, Peter.

Four years later Redford unearthed a 5,000-page collection of Collins family records in the state archives, which provided the names of 21 slave families that had worked the rice-and-corn plantation from its founding in 1785 to the end of the Civil War. In 1865, 328 men, women, and children labored in bondage at Somerset. The indefatigable Redford was able to trace several thousand of their living descendants. Through hundreds of phone calls and letters, she invited them all to this remarkable gathering.

For the most part, the day was festive. By remembering their ancestors' slavery the descendants were celebrating their own freedom.

Some remarked that the achievement and endurance of their shackled forebears had outlived the pain and degradation of slavery. "Think about the strength it took to build this place," said State Senator Blount.

"Talk about true grit. Talk about the right stuff. They had it, and so do we."

Their graves are unmarked. Their one-room, 18-foot-square wooden cabins, in each of which as many as fifteen slaves lived, have long since been torn down. Practically all that remains of the slaves are some broken bricks from the slave hospital. But that seemed not to matter. Today the whole plantation had been transformed into their monument.

"As long as one of us lives, everyone who lived before us lives," Redford told the crowd. "Until the day Somerset plantation crumbles, the slaves will be remembered." The slaves' descendants stood and applauded, and a few whispered, "Amen."

Responding

Remembering the past is painful for many people. The past may call up images of slavery for African Americans, German concentration camps for Jews, and World War II internment camps for Japanese Americans. Why is it important to remember the past, even if it is painful?

617

Reading Mini-Lesson

Using Cause-and-Effect Relationships

The car won't start. What caused that? A rainstorm suddenly appeared out of nowhere. What caused that? This milk tastes spoiled. What caused that? My friend's not acting very friendly this morning. What caused that? We can't get through a day without sorting out the relationships between causes and effects.

You can think of a **cause** as the reason *why* something happened. Sometimes one thing will have many causes. For example, in "A Spirit Unshackled" (page 612), Frederick Douglass reports that he barely knew his mother. Why? There are several causes. She was sold to a different master twelve miles away when Frederick was an infant. She was only able to visit him a few times. Her visits were always at night. She died when he was seven. If you used a semantic web to show these causes, it would look like the top web in the margin.

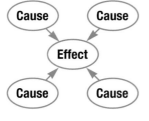

Several Causes Leading to One Effect

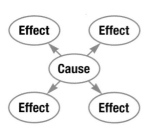

One Cause with Several Effects

Activity Options

1. Although "A Spirit Unshackled" tells of the many hardships of slaves, it is also about Frederick Douglass learning to read. Learning to read was a cause that had many effects. Review the selection and see how many effects you can find. Write them on a cause-effects web like the second one shown here.

2. Another way to look at Douglass learning to read is to place that event in a chain of causes and effects. Write these words at the top of a sheet of paper: "In Baltimore, Douglass makes friends with all the white boys he meets." Take this as the first cause in the chain. The last effect is, "Douglass is tormented by thoughts of freedom." Write this at the bottom of the paper. Complete the chain of causes and effects by writing, in proper order, the rest of the important events between making friends and being obsessed with freedom.

3. Use your social studies book as a resource and see how cause and effect is used to explain a social event. Choose one event related to slavery—perhaps the start of the slave trade, John Brown's Rebellion, or the Civil War—and list both the causes that led up to it and the effects that resulted from it.

Writing Workshop

Research Report

Assignment In a saturation research report, both fictional and non-fictional methods are used to provide factual information in an interesting format. Your assignment is to write a saturation research report in the form of diary entries of someone important in history. Become that person and write a series of diary entries that focus on an event from this person's life. Examples:

—Alexander Graham Bell and the invention of the telephone
—Amelia Earhart and her flight around the world
—Rosa Parks and her famous bus ride

WRITER'S BLUEPRINT

Product	A saturation research report about a specific event presented as three or more diary entries
Purpose	To learn more about a particular individual in history
Audience	Future historians who discover your diary
Specs	To write a successful research paper, you should:

❑ Work with classmates to brainstorm a list of people important in history and major events in their lives. Choose one you'd like to find out more about.

❑ Saturate yourself in your topic by gathering information about this person from every reliable source you can find. These include museums, libraries, letters, books, videos, magazine and newspaper articles, and interviews with experts.

❑ Use the first-person point of view ("I") in your diary entries, as if you were actually living through these moments in time.

❑ Give your reader a clear picture of the event by including details and vivid language.

❑ Double-check your facts and document your sources in a Works Cited list.

❑ Follow the rules of grammar, usage, spelling, and mechanics.

Choose a subject and event for your diary entries. Work with a small group to brainstorm a list of people you've studied from history and the events in which they participated. You might skim a social studies textbook for ideas. Keep track of people and events on a chart. Then choose the person and event that you find most interesting for your diary entries.

Make a list of questions. Now that you have selected your subject, ask yourself: *What information do I already know? What do I need to find out?* List your questions and use them to guide your research. Number your questions. A student wrote these questions before researching Miep Gies.

1. *Why were the people in the attic hiding?*
2. *How did the Germans take over Holland?*
3. *How did Miep and Mr. Kraler manage to get food for the people hiding in the attic?*

Brainstorm research sources. In your original group, make a list of sources of information about your subject. List everything you can think of in your community. Consider categories such as places (libraries, museums), people (librarians, relatives), and organizations (veterans groups, historical organizations). Work with your group to add to these categories.

Do your research. Because you will write diary entries, pay attention to details. First, look for primary sources: letters, photos, diaries, and news accounts. Next look for secondary sources: history books, other books of nonfiction that relate to your subject, encyclopedias, and magazine articles.

Write the name of each source on a 3 x 5 card and then number the card. You will write this number on each note card you write using the source. You can then use the numbers when you list the sources you used. These cards are your source cards.

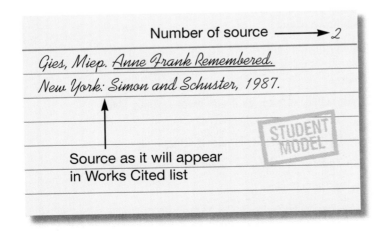

Number of source ⟶ *2*

Gies, Miep. <u>Anne Frank Remembered.</u>
New York: Simon and Schuster, 1987.

Source as it will appear
in Works Cited list

STUDENT MODEL

Next make note cards for the information you want to remember while reading about your subject. The information should answer the questions you wrote. Add any other questions you want answered as you work with your sources. Write the number of your source in the upper right corner of the card. In the upper left corner, write the number of the question the information answers.

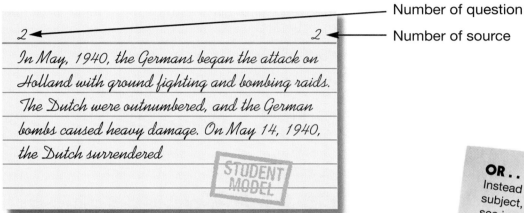

Number of question

Number of source

2   2

In May, 1940, the Germans began the attack on Holland with ground fighting and bombing raids. The Dutch were outnumbered, and the German bombs caused heavy damage. On May 14, 1940, the Dutch surrendered

STUDENT MODEL

OR . . .
Instead of writing as your subject, draw what you see in your scene. Then briefly describe what you have drawn.

OR . . .
Spread your note cards out and arrange them in order. Then think about what your subject might have thought and felt about the event(s).

Try a quickwrite. After you finish your research, try writing a diary entry as your subject. Remember to use first-person point of view ("I" or "me") as you write. The quickwrite will help you figure out if you need to do more research.

Plan your diary entries. Review your note cards. Decide how many diary entries you will need in order to communicate what happened during this important historical event. Consider what your time span will be between your entries: hours? days? weeks?

STEP 2 DRAFTING

Before you write, review the information you gathered in your research and your writing plan. Reread the Writer's Blueprint too.

As you draft, concentrate on getting your ideas on paper. Look ahead to the Revising Strategy on vivid language and imagery. Vivid language and imagery will help your readers visualize what you're describing.

STEP **3** REVISING

Ask your partner for comments on your draft before you revise it.

✔ Have I followed the specs in the Writer's Blueprint?

✔ Do my entries read like diary entries or merely descriptive paragraphs?

✔ Do I use first-person point of view throughout?

✔ Do I use vivid language and imagery?

Revising Strategy

LITERARY SOURCE
"Our stomachs are so empty that they rumble and make strange noises, all in different keys. Mr. Van Daan's is deep and low, like a bass fiddle. Mine is high, whistling like a flute. As we all sit around waiting for supper, it's like an orchestra tuning up. It only needs Toscanini to raise his baton . . . ."
from *The Diary of Anne Frank* dramatized by Frances Goodrich and Albert Hackett

Vivid Language and Imagery

Words that describe what we see, hear, and feel help readers visualize events. For example, "Every time I hear that sound, my heart begins to race" is more likely to make the reader feel fright than "That sound scares me." In the Literary Source, notice Anne Frank's description of hunger.

When you revise, try to include words and phrases that create images in the reader's mind. These images should enable the reader to see, hear, smell, taste, or touch what you're describing.

For practice, try revising these sentences.

I was lonely.   The attic was crowded.

Notice how the writer of the passage below revised a diary entry of Rosa Parks to make the descriptions more vivid.

Thursday, December 1, 1955

It was about 5:00 P.M. I had just finished work at the

Montgomery Fair Department Store, and I had caught the bus home.
dog- *throbbed*
I was tired, and my fingers were filled with blisters from sewing in
collapsed into
the store's tailor shop. I paid my fare and found an empty seat.

Ask a partner to review your revised draft before you edit. When you edit, watch for errors in grammar, usage, spelling, and mechanics. Pay special attention to using the correct form in your Works Cited list.

Editing Strategy

Works Cited

Every research paper includes a list called *Works Cited* or *Bibliography*. This list tells the reader what sources were used in the paper.

- Begin the list of sources on a new page following the last page of your diary entries.

- List only sources from which you took information. List the sources in alphabetical order by author's last name. If the author isn't known, list the work by its title.

- Leave a line of space between entries.

The form changes somewhat for different kinds of sources. The student model shows the correct form for books and encyclopedias. If you're working on a computer, format titles of books and magazines in italic type. Otherwise, use an underscore to indicate italic type as in these examples.

○   Brandt, Keith. Rosa Parks: <u>Fight for Freedom.</u> New York: Troll Associates,

     1993.

○   Garrow, David J., "Parks, Rosa Lee," <u>World Book Encyclopedia,</u> Vol. 15,

     Chicago, World Book, Inc., 1994.

STUDENT MODEL

5 PRESENTING

Here are two ideas for presenting your narrative.

- Dress as your character and read your diary entries aloud to your group. Discuss the events. What new information did you learn?

- Work with a group. Gather your diary entries into a book entitled *Historical Diaries.* Work together to illustrate each entry.

6 LOOKING BACK

Self-evaluate. What grade would you give your paper? Look back at the Writer's Blueprint and evaluate yourself on each point, from 6 (superior) down to 1 (weak).

Reflect. Think about what you learned from writing your diary entries as you write answers to these questions.

✔ What did you learn about your subject that you found especially interesting? Has your view of your subject changed? In what way?

✔ If you could devise another method for doing research, what would you do? How might the research process be improved by using a computer?

For Your Working Portfolio: Add your diary entries and your reflection responses to your working portfolio.

Beyond Print

Storyboard Elements

Composition How will you show the objects and people in the scene? Each panel of the storyboard shows how the people and objects will be photographed. Carefully place panel images so that they achieve the impact that you envision.

Movement What will move in the scene? Will the people move or will the camera move? The storyboard will portray from one panel to the next the movement in the scene.

Color and Lighting What colors will you select for the costumes and the rooms? Draw your storyboard accordingly, using color examples. Remember to make the colors fit the mood of the scene as well as the authenticity of the period.

Sound What sounds other than dialogue will you use in the scene? Will you use music? If so, what music? Or will you use street sounds? Indicate your sounds in notes at the bottom of the storyboard.

Designing a Scale Model of a Set

The Diary of Anne Frank is a powerful story that has as much relevance today as it did when it was first written. Although the story already has appeared in movie form, perhaps it is time to consider making a new movie version. What are some of the plans movie makers must make before actual filming takes place? One job is creating a set. In small groups, help design a set for the new movie version of Anne's diary.

Movie viewers expect films to have action and lots of movement and color. *The Diary of Anne Frank* is a challenge because it is set in a small confined space in a hidden annex of a house. How can you design a set that is authentic, yet still make a gripping movie?

Activity

A good place to begin is to design a three-dimensional scale model of the annex so your director and photographers can visualize the set. This is what most movie makers actually do.

Materials Be creative. Certainly you will need cardboard, wood, and paint. Will you use doll-house furniture?

Making It Look Real For your movie to succeed, you must convince your audience that your set is a replica of the real annex. So, what did the real furniture look like? What decorative elements were on the walls? Paint, wallpaper? What did the windows look like? Find as much information as you can from the text. What you cannot learn from the play will require imagination and research. What furniture was used in the thirties and forties in Europe? When you have finished making your model, present it to your class.

Activity Extension

You may want to do a storyboard based on a scene from the play. A storyboard is a cartoonlike drawing of a scene that gives the movie makers ideas about composition, movement, color and lighting, and sound. (See the margin.) Your storyboard does not have to be a work of art. Stick figures will do.

Projects for Collaborative Study

Theme Connection

Local Justice What situation in your own community, the nation, or the world do you think cries out for justice? In a group, choose an issue you care about and research it to find out the facts. Discuss what you think should be done.

■ Write letters to the editor of your local paper, explaining why the situation is unjust and persuasively arguing for a solution.

■ Prepare posters that identify the problem in words or pictures and urge a solution in an appealing way. Display the posters in your school or community.

Literature Connection

Literature on the Big Screen "Flowers for Algernon" and *The Diary of Anne Frank* are both powerful works of literature that could easily be made into movies. (In fact, both of them *have* been made into movies.) Decide how *you* would present one of these selections as a movie. Working in a group, complete these preparations for the movie:

■ Discuss the **character traits** of the main characters and decide who you would cast to play each character. Then write a casting proposal. You have an unlimited budget, so go for famous stars if you want! You must be prepared to argue for your choices by explaining why they fit the parts.

■ Outline key scenes in the movie, keeping in mind how you will build **suspense** and dramatize the **climax** of the action. You may want to incorporate **foreshadowing** and show a **flashback** also.

Life Skills Connection

Prejudgment of People As you know, **prejudice** is an opinion formed about someone before getting to know the person, based on that person's membership in a group.

■ Can you recall a time when you observed or were a recipient of prejudice? In your notebook, describe the situation and how you felt.

■ In a group, list the factors you think might cause one group of people to be prejudiced toward people of another group. What information or "facts" do you think people would need to alter their perceptions?

■ To wrap up, your group could prepare a skit to dramatize the problem of prejudice and how it can be corrected.

🖐 Multicultural Connection

Inspiring People Sometimes **interactions** between people of different cultures raise issues of fairness or justice. Look through newspapers and magazines to find articles about young people who have encountered an injustice and found a way to overcome it through **individual** spirit. In a small group, choose three individuals of three different cultural backgrounds. Present each person's story to the rest of the class. Discuss:

■ What are the differences between these people?

■ What are the common threads in these three people's lives?

■ Can you make any generalizations about what it takes to overcome injustice?

Read More About Justice

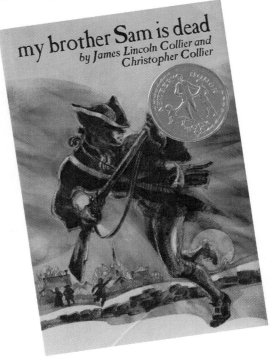

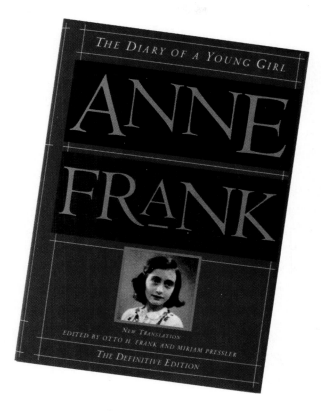

My Brother Sam Is Dead (1974) by James Lincoln Collier and Christopher Collier. In this historical novel set during the Revolutionary War, a family is divided by conflicting national allegiances.

The Diary of a Young Girl (1952; definitive edition 1995) by Anne Frank. Written by a young Jewish girl forced to hide from the Nazis with her family in an Amsterdam warehouse, the diary is a compelling story of the mundane details of daily life in cramped space amid the terror of the world outside.

More Good Books

Farewell to Manzanar (1979) by Jeanne Wakatsuki Houston and James D. Houston. This is a true account of a Japanese American family's experiences while being held in a U.S. internment camp during World War II.

The Upstairs Room (1972) by Johanna Reiss. During World War II, two sisters leave their parents and older sister to hide from the Nazis in a cramped, upstairs room of a farmhouse.

Black Water (1995) by Rachel Anderson. This historical novel, set during Victorian times in England, tells the story of a young

epileptic boy who must cope with his disorder during a time when epilepsy was grossly misunderstood.

To Be a Slave (1968) by Julius Lester. African Americans who served as slaves tell about the auction block, life on the plantation, emancipation, and life after the Civil War.

Zlata's Diary: A Child's Life in Sarajevo (1994) by Zlata Filipović. This diary details the experiences of a young girl whose carefree life was turned upside down by the war in Bosnia between 1991 and 1993.

UNIT **6**

Journeys

Reaching for Your Dream
Part One, pages 632–678

Decisive Journeys
Part Two, pages 679–741

Talking About
JOURNEYS

We all undertake many
kinds of journeys
in life. Fueled by hopes,
dreams, and sometimes
chance, these journeys can
lead us to exciting discoveries about ourselves and
our surroundings. Some
journeys may take us on
side roads that temporarily
delay us in reaching our
destinations. Detours can
even lead us to new goals.

> **I like faraway journeys
> with lots of exciting
> adventures.**
>
> Jenny–Phoenix, AZ

**You must travel high above to the
roof of the universe, find the house
of Sun, Father of All Life...**

from "The Creation of Music" retold
by Donna Rosenberg, page 712

"I enjoy fantasy and adventure stories like Huck Finn, The Hobbit, and Jack and the Bean Stalk."

Michael—Oak Park, IL

I fell asleep on the mountain, and Hendrik Hudson and his crew changed my gun, and everything's changed, and I'm changed, and I can't tell what my name is, or who I am!

from "Rip Van Winkle" by Washington Irving, page 689

"I hate my life!" I yelled. "Then do something about it," she yelled back.

from "A Shot at It" by Esmeralda Santiago, page 637

"I have a dream that I'm going be somebody in life."

Jessica—Denver, CO

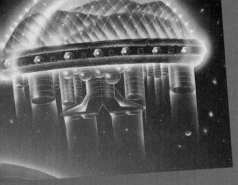

"I like to read about journeys to outer space." Juan—Miami, FL

He did not look back as they began the homeward journey. He could not bear to see the cold glory of the crescent Earth fade from the rocks around him, as he went to rejoin his people in their long exile.

from "If I Forget Thee, Oh Earth..." by Arthur C. Clarke, page 706

631

Part One

Reaching for Your Dream

Being American means different things to different people. Still, one thing most people hold in common is the ability to dream, even though the dreams themselves are different. To many, America means the possibility of realizing those dreams.

 Multicultural Connection **Individuality** involves both belonging to groups and finding your unique place and voice. This sometimes means drawing upon your cultural heritage to discover special ways to express your ideals and beliefs. How do the individuals in these selections relate to their cultural heritage and also maintain their individual voices?

Literature

Esmeralda Santiago	**A Shot at It** ◆ autobiography	.634
	Language Mini-Lesson ◆ Checking Your Spelling	.645
Emma Lazarus	**The New Colossus** ◆ poem	.648
Wing Tek Lum	**Chinese Hot Pot** ◆ poem	.648
Langston Hughes	**Dreams; The Dream Keeper; I, Too** ◆ poems	.650
Naomi Shihab Nye	**My Father and the Figtree** ◆ poem	.652
Abraham Lincoln	**The Gettysburg Address** ◆ speech	.656
Walt Whitman	**O Captain! My Captain!** ◆ poem	.657
Ved Mehta	**from *Sound-Shadows of the New World*** ◆ autobiography	.661

Interdisciplinary Study **School Days**

Frontier Students ◆ U.S. history	.672
Frontier Schools by Russell Freedman ◆ U.S. history	.674
Frontier Trivia ◆ mathematics	.677
Reading Mini-Lesson ◆ Using Graphic Aids	.678

Before Reading

A Shot at It

by Esmeralda Santiago

Esmeralda Santiago
born 1948

Santiago is a graduate of Harvard University and holds a master's degree from Sarah Lawrence College. She has written articles for several national newspapers, including *The New York Times* and *The Christian Science Monitor.* With her husband, Santiago owns a film production company in Boston. They have two children. *When I Was Puerto Rican* is Santiago's first book. You will find out more about her life as you read this story and its epilogue.

Building Background

Setting the Scene "A Shot at It" is from Santiago's autobiography, *When I Was Puerto Rican.* Before arriving in New York City, where the story you are about to read takes place, Santiago lived with her parents and seven brothers and sisters in the rural Puerto Rican town of Macún. Their home was a little tin shack that got so hot, she recalls, that you would burn your fingers if you touched the tin when the sun was out. After her parents divorced, her mother (Mami) moved the family to New York. As the story opens, Esmeralda, who is referred to by her nickname Negi, has just moved with her family into her grandmother Tata's house on Ellery Street. Esmeralda is about to enter the ninth grade. Francisco, who is referred to in the first sentence of the story, was Mami's boyfriend. He later died of cancer.

Getting into the Selection

Writer's Notebook What is it like to be on stage knowing that, for a few minutes, all eyes are on you? What is it like to know that something very important is at stake and that the outcome depends on you? As you read you will find out how Esmeralda Santiago felt during such a situation. Have you ever been in a situation like this? If you have, write about the experience, describing your thoughts, feelings, and the importance of the event to you at the time. If you haven't had such an experience, describe how you imagine such an experience might be.

Reading Tip

Facts About Puerto Rico
Esmeralda Santiago was born in Puerto Rico, an island about one thousand miles southeast of Florida. At the right are a few facts about the island.

PUERTO RICO
Population: 3,522,037
Capital: San Juan
Area: 3,515 square miles
Political Status: U.S. Commonwealth
Languages: Spanish and English

ESMERALDA SANTIAGO

A SHOT AT IT

**TE CONOZCO BACALAO,
AUNQUE VENGAS DISFRAZAO.**

**I RECOGNIZE YOU SALTED CODFISH,
EVEN IF YOU'RE IN DISGUISE.**

While Francisco was still alive, we had moved to Ellery Street. That meant I had to change schools, so Mami walked me to P.S. 33, where I would attend ninth grade. The first week I was there I was given a series of tests that showed that even though I couldn't speak English very well, I read and wrote it at the tenth-grade level. So they put me in 9–3, with the smart kids.

One morning, Mr. Barone, a guidance counselor, called me to his office. He was short, with a big head and large hazel eyes under shapely eyebrows. His nose was long and round at the tip. He dressed in browns and yellows and often perched his tortoiseshell glasses on his forehead, as if he had another set of eyes up there.

"So," he pushed his glasses up, "what do you want to be when you grow up?"

"I don't know."

He shuffled through some papers. "Let's see here . . . you're fourteen, is that right?"

Esmeralda Santiago at age eighteen.

"Yes, sir."

"And you've never thought about what you want to be?"

When I was very young, I wanted to be a *jíbara*.[1] When I was older, I wanted to be a cartographer,[2] then a topographer.[3] But since we'd come to Brooklyn, I'd not thought about the future much.

"No, sir."

He pulled his glasses down to where they belonged and shuffled through the papers again.

"Do you have any hobbies?" I didn't know what he meant.

"Hobbies, hobbies," he flailed his hands, as if he were juggling, "things you like to do after school."

"Ah, yes." I tried to imagine what I did at home that might qualify as a hobby. "I like to read."

He seemed disappointed. "Yes, we know that about you." He pulled out a paper and stared at it. "One of the tests we gave you was an aptitude[4] test. It tells us what kinds of things you might be good at. The tests show that you would be good at helping people. Do you like to help people?"

I was afraid to contradict the tests. "Yes, sir."

"There's a high school we can send you where you can study biology and chemistry which will prepare you for a career in nursing."

I screwed up my face. He consulted the papers again.

---

1. *jíbara* (hē′ba ra), a person from rural Puerto Rico who speaks a specific dialect.
2. cartographer (kär tog′rə fər), *n.* a person who makes maps.
3. topographer (tə pog′rə fər), *n.* a person who studies and charts the surface features (hills, lakes, roads) of a region.
4. aptitude (ap′tə tüd), *n.* natural talent. Aptitude tests are given to people to discover what type of work or studies would best suit them.

"You would also do well in communications. Teaching maybe."

I remembered Miss Brown standing in front of a classroom full of rowdy teenagers, some of them taller than she was.

"I don't like to teach."

Mr. Barone pushed his glasses up again and leaned over the stack of papers on his desk. "Why don't you think about it and get back to me," he said, closing the folder with my name across the top. He put his hand flat on it, as if squeezing something out. "You're a smart girl, Esmeralda. Let's try to get you into an academic[5] school so that you have a shot at college."

On the way home, I walked with another new ninth grader, Yolanda. She had been in New York for three years but knew as little English as I did. We spoke in Spanglish, a combination of English and Spanish in which we hopped from one language to the other depending on which word came first.

"*Te preguntó el* Mr. Barone, you know, *lo que querías hacer* when you grow up?" I asked.[6]

"*Sí, pero,* I didn't know. ¿*Y tú?*"[7]

"*Yo tampoco.* He said, *que* I like to help people. *Pero,* you know, *a mí no me gusta mucho la gente.*"[8] When she heard me say I didn't like people much, Yolanda looked at me from the corner of her eye, waiting to become the exception.

By the time I said it, she had dashed up the stairs of her building. She didn't wave as she ducked in, and the next day she wasn't friendly. I walked around the rest of the day in embarrassed isolation, knowing that somehow I had given myself away to the only friend I'd made at Junior High School 33. I had to either take back my words or live with the consequences of stating what was becoming the truth. I'd never said that to anyone, not even to myself. It was an added weight, but I wasn't about to trade it for companionship.

A few days later, Mr. Barone called me back to his office.

"Well?" Tiny green flecks burned around the black pupils of his hazel eyes.

The night before, Mami had called us into the living room. On the television "fifty of America's most beautiful girls" paraded in ruffled tulle dresses before a tinsel waterfall.

"Aren't they lovely?" Mami murmured, as the girls, escorted by boys in uniform, floated by the camera, twirled, and disappeared behind a screen to the strains of a waltz and an announcer's dramatic voice calling their names, ages, and states. Mami sat mesmerized[9] through the whole pageant.

"I'd like to be a model," I said to Mr. Barone.

He stared at me, pulled his glasses down from his forehead, looked at the papers inside the folder with my name on it, and glared. "A model?" His voice was gruff, as if he were more comfortable yelling at people than talking to them.

"I want to be on television."

"Oh, then you want to be an actress," in a tone that said this was only a slight improvement over my first career choice. We stared at one another for a few seconds. He pushed his glasses up to his forehead again and reached for a book on the shelf in back of him. "I only know of one school that trains actresses, but we've never sent them a student from here."

---

5. academic (ak/ə dem/ik), *adj.* concerned with general studies and education, not technical or professional training.
6. Did Mr. Barone ask you, you know, what you would like to do when you grow up?
7. Yes, but, I didn't know. And you?
8. Me neither. He said, that I like to help people. But, you know, I really don't like people much.
9. mesmerized (mez/mə rīzd/), *adj.* hypnotized.

erforming Arts, the write-up said, was an academic, as opposed to a vocational,[10] public school that trained students wishing to pursue a career in theater, music, and dance.

"It says here that you have to audition."[11] He stood up and held the book closer to the faint gray light coming through the narrow window high on his wall. "Have you ever performed in front of an audience?"

"I was announcer in my school show in Puerto Rico," I said. "And I recite poetry. There, not here."

He closed the book and held it against his chest. His right index finger thumped a rhythm on his lower lip. "Let me call them and find out exactly what you need to do. Then we can talk some more."

I left his office strangely happy, confident that something good had just happened, not knowing exactly what.

"I'm not afraid . . . I'm not afraid . . . I'm not afraid." Every day I walked home from school repeating those words. The broad streets and sidewalks that had impressed me so on the first day we had arrived had become as familiar as the dirt road from Macún to the highway. Only my curiosity about the people who lived behind these walls ended where the façades of the buildings opened into dark hallways or locked doors. Nothing good, I imagined, could be happening inside if so many locks had to be breached to go in or step out.

It was on these tense walks home from school that I decided I had to get out of Brooklyn. Mami had chosen this as our home, and just like every other time we'd moved, I'd had to go along with her because I was a child

I LEFT HIS OFFICE STRANGELY HAPPY, CONFIDENT THAT SOMETHING GOOD HAD JUST HAPPENED.

who had no choice. But I wasn't willing to go along with her on this one.

"How can people live like this?" I shrieked once, desperate to run across a field, to feel grass under my feet instead of pavement.

"Like what?" Mami asked, looking around our apartment, the kitchen and living room crisscrossed with sagging lines of drying diapers and bedclothes.

"Everyone on top of each other. No room to do anything. No air."

"Do you want to go back to Macún, to live like savages, with no electricity, no toilets . . ."

"At least you could step outside every day without somebody trying to kill you."

"Ay, Negi, stop exaggerating!"

"I hate my life!" I yelled.

"Then do something about it," she yelled back.

Until Mr. Barone showed me the listing for Performing Arts High School, I hadn't known what to do.

"The auditions are in less than a month. You have to learn a monologue,[12] which you will perform in front of a panel. If you do well, and your grades here are good, you might get into the school."

Mr. Barone took charge of preparing me for my audition to Performing Arts. He selected a speech from *The Silver Cord,* a play by Sidney Howard, first performed in 1926,

10. **vocational** (vō kā′shə nəl), *adj.* having to do with studies or training for some occupation.
11. **audition** (ô dish′ən), *v.* sing, act, or perform at a try-out that tests the ability, quality, or performance of the performers.
12. **monologue** (mon′l ôg), *n.* part of a play in which a single actor speaks alone.

but whose action took place in a New York drawing room circa 1905.

"Mr. Gatti, the English teacher," he said, "will coach you. . . . And Mrs. Johnson will talk to you about what to wear and things like that."

I was to play Christina, a young married woman confronting her mother-in-law. I learned the monologue phonetically[13] from Mr. Gatti. It opened with "You belong to a type that's very common in this country, Mrs. Phelps—a type of self-centered, self-pitying, son-devouring tigress, with unmentionable proclivities suppressed on the side."

"We don't have time to study the meaning of every word," Mr. Gatti said. "Just make sure you pronounce every word correctly."

Mrs. Johnson, who taught Home Economics, called me to her office.

"Is that how you enter a room?" she asked the minute I came in. "Try again, only this time, don't barge in. Step in slowly, head up, back straight, a nice smile on your face. That's it." I took a deep breath and waited. "Now sit. No, not like that. Don't just plop down. Float down to the chair with your knees together." She demonstrated, and I copied her. "That's better. What do you do with your hands? No, don't hold your chin like that; it's not ladylike. Put your hands on your lap, and leave them there. Don't use them so much when you talk."

I sat stiff as a cutout while Mrs. Johnson and Mr. Barone asked me questions they thought the panel at Performing Arts would ask.

"Where are you from?"

"Puerto Rico."

"No," Mrs. Johnson said, "Porto Rico. Keep your *r*'s soft. Try again."

"Do you have any hobbies?" Mr. Barone asked. Now I knew what to answer.

"I enjoy dancing and the movies."

"Why do you want to come to this school?"

I THINK WE HAVE A SHOT AT THIS.

Mrs. Johnson and Mr. Barone had worked on my answer if this question should come up.

"I would like to study at Performing Arts because of its academic program and so that I may be trained as an actress."

"Very good, very good!" Mr. Barone rubbed his hands together, twinkled his eyes at Mrs. Johnson. "I think we have a shot at this."

"Remember," Mrs. Johnson said, "when you shop for your audition dress, look for something very simple in dark colors."

Mami bought me a red plaid wool jumper with a crisp white shirt, my first pair of stockings, and penny loafers. The night before, she rolled up my hair in pink curlers that cut into my scalp and made it hard to sleep. For the occasion, I was allowed to wear eye makeup and a little lipstick.

"You look so grown up!" Mami said, her voice sad but happy, as I twirled in front of her and Tata.

"Toda una señorita,"[14] Tata said, her eyes misty.

We set out for the audition on an overcast January morning heavy with the threat of snow.

"Why couldn't you choose a school close to home?" Mami grumbled as we got on the train to Manhattan. I worried that even if I were accepted, she wouldn't let me go because it was so far from home, one hour each way by subway. But in spite of her complaints, she was proud that I was good enough to be considered for such a famous school. And she actually seemed excited that I would be leaving the neighborhood.

---

13. phonetically (fə net′ik lē), *adv.* by breaking the words into individual sounds.

14. *toda una señorita,* all a young lady should be.

"You'll be exposed to a different class of people," she assured me, and I felt the force of her ambition without knowing exactly what she meant.

Three women sat behind a long table in a classroom where the desks and chairs had been pushed against a wall. As I entered I held my head up and smiled, and then I floated down to the chair in front of them, clasped my hands on my lap, and smiled some more.

"Good morning," said the tall one with hair the color of sand. She was big boned and solid, with intense blue eyes, a generous mouth, and soothing hands with short fingernails. She was dressed in shades of beige from head to toe and wore no makeup and no jewelry except for the gold chain that held her glasses just above her full bosom. Her voice was rich, modulated,[15] each word pronounced as if she were inventing it.

Next to her sat a very small woman with very high heels. Her cropped hair was pouffed around her face, with bangs brushing the tips of her long false lashes, her huge dark brown eyes were thickly lined in black all around, and her small mouth was carefully drawn in and painted cerise. Her suntanned face turned toward me with the innocent curiosity of a lively baby. She was dressed in black, with many gold chains around her neck, big earrings, several bracelets, and large stone rings on the fingers of both hands.

The third woman was tall, small boned, thin, but shapely. Her dark hair was pulled flat against her skull into a knot in back of her head. Her face was all angles and light, with fawnlike dark brown eyes, a straight nose, full lips painted just a shade pinker than their natural color. Silky forest green cuffs peeked out from the sleeves of her burgundy suit. Diamond studs winked from perfect earlobes.

I had dreamed of this moment for several weeks. More than anything, I wanted to impress the panel with my talent, so that I would be accepted into Performing Arts and leave Brooklyn every day. And, I hoped, one day I would never go back.

But the moment I faced these three impeccably groomed women, I forgot my English and Mrs. Johnson's lessons on how to behave like a lady. In the agony of trying to answer their barely comprehensible questions, I jabbed my hands here and there, forming words with my fingers because the words refused to leave my mouth.

"Why don't you let us hear your monologue now?" the woman with the dangling glasses asked softly.

I stood up abruptly, and my chair clattered onto its side two feet from where I stood. I picked it up, wishing with all my strength that a thunderbolt would strike me dead to ashes on the spot.

"It's all right," she said. "Take a breath. We know you're nervous."

I closed my eyes and breathed deeply, walked to the middle of the room, and began my monologue.

"Ju bee lonh 2 a type dats berry cómo in dis kuntree, Meessees Felps. A type off selfcent red self pee tee in sun de boring tie gress wid on men shon ah ball pro klee bee tees on de side."

In spite of Mr. Gatti's reminders that I should speak slowly and enunciate every word, even if I didn't understand it, I recited my three-minute monologue in one minute flat.

The small woman's long lashes seemed to have grown with amazement. The elegant woman's serene face twitched with controlled laughter. The tall one dressed in beige smiled sweetly.

_____

15. **modulated** (moj′ə lāt əd), *adj.* altered in pitch, tone, or volume for expression.

"Thank you, dear," she said. "Could you wait outside for a few moments?"

I resisted the urge to curtsy. The long hallway had narrow wainscotting[16] halfway up to the high ceiling. Single bulb lamps hung from long cords, creating yellow puddles of light on the polished brown linoleum tile. A couple of girls my age sat on straight chairs next to their mothers, waiting their turn. They looked up as I came out and the door shut behind me. Mami stood up from her chair at the end of the hall. She looked as scared as I felt.

"What happened?"

"Nothing," I mumbled, afraid that if I began telling her about it, I would break into tears in front of the other people, whose eyes followed me and Mami as we walked to the EXIT sign. "I have to wait here a minute."

"Did they say anything?"

"No. I'm just supposed to wait."

We leaned against the wall. Across from us there was a bulletin board with newspaper clippings about former students. On the ragged edge, a neat person had printed in blue ink, "P.A." and the year the actor, dancer, or musician had graduated. I closed my eyes and tried to picture myself on that bulletin board, with "P.A. '66" across the top.

The door at the end of the hall opened, and the woman in beige poked her head out.

"Esmeralda?"

"*Sí*, I mean, here." I raised my hand.

She led me into the room. There was another girl in there, whom she introduced as Bonnie, a junior at the school.

"Do you know what a pantomime is?" the woman asked. I nodded. "You and Bonnie are sisters decorating a Christmas tree."

Bonnie looked a lot like Juanita Marín, whom I had last seen in Macún four years earlier. We decided where the invisible Christmas tree would be, and we sat on the floor and pretended we were taking decorations out of boxes and hanging them on the branches.

My family had never had a Christmas tree, but I remembered how once I had helped Papi wind colored lights around the eggplant bush that divided our land from Doña Ana's. We started at the bottom and wound the wire with tiny red bulbs around and around until we ran out; then Papi plugged another cord to it and we kept going until the branches hung heavy with light and the bush looked like it was on fire.

Before long I had forgotten where I was, and that the tree didn't exist and Bonnie was not my sister. She pretended to hand me a very delicate ball, and just before I took it, she made like it fell to the ground and shattered. I was petrified that Mami would come in and yell at us for breaking her favorite decoration. Just as I began to pick up the tiny fragments of nonexistent crystal, a voice broke in. "Thank you."

BEFORE LONG I HAD FORGOTTEN WHERE I WAS . . .

Bonnie got up, smiled, and went out.

The elegant woman stretched her hand out for me to shake. "We will notify your school in a few weeks. It was very nice to meet you."

I shook hands all around then backed out of the room in a fog, silent, as if the pantomime had taken my voice and the urge to speak.

On the way home Mami kept asking what had happened, and I kept mumbling, "Nothing. Nothing happened," ashamed that, after all the hours of practice with Mrs.

---

16. **wainscotting** (wān′skô ting), wood paneling that goes from the floor to halfway up a wall.

▲ In her first major acting role after graduating from high school, Esmeralda Santiago played a student in the movie "Up the Down Staircase," which starred Sandy Dennis. Esmeralda is the laughing student in the front row. What qualities do you think helped her gain such a high-profile role?

Johnson, Mr. Barone, and Mr. Gatti, after the expense of new clothes and shoes, after Mami had to take a day off from work to take me into Manhattan, after all that, I had failed the audition and would never, ever, get out of Brooklyn.

Epilogue: One of These Days

EL MISMO JÍBARO CON DIFERENTE CABALLO.

SAME JÍBARO, DIFFERENT HORSE.

A decade after my graduation from Performing Arts, I visited the school. I was by then living in Boston, a scholarship student at Harvard University. The tall, elegant woman of my audition had become my mentor through my three years there. Since my graduation, she had married the school principal.

"I remember your audition," she said, her chiseled face dreamy, her lips toying with a smile that she seemed, still, to have to control.

I had forgotten the skinny brown girl with the curled hair, wool jumper, and lively hands. But she hadn't. She told me that the panel had had to ask me to leave so that they could laugh, because it was so funny to see a fourteen-year-old Puerto Rican girl jabbering out a monologue about a possessive mother-in-law at the turn of the century, the words incomprehensible because they went by so fast.

"We admired," she said, "the courage it took to stand in front of us and do what you did."

"So you mean I didn't get into the school because of my talent, but because I had chutzpah?"[17] We both laughed.

"Are any of your sisters and brothers in college?"

"No, I'm the only one, so far."

"How many of you are there?"

"By the time I graduated from high school there were eleven of us."

"Eleven!" She looked at me for a long time, until I had to look down. "Do you ever think about how far you've come?" she asked.

"No." I answered. "I never stop to think about it. It might jinx the momentum."

"Let me tell you another story, then," she said. "The first day of your first year, you were absent. We called your house. You said you couldn't come to school because you had nothing to wear. I wasn't sure if you were joking. I asked to speak to your mother, and you translated what she said. She needed you to go somewhere with her to interpret. At first you wouldn't tell me where, but then you admitted you were going to the welfare office. You were crying, and I had to assure you that you were not the only student in this school whose family received public assistance. The next day you were here, bright and eager. And now here you are, about to graduate from Harvard."

"I'm glad you made that phone call," I said.

"And I'm glad you came to see me, but right now I have to teach a class." She stood up, as graceful as I remembered. "Take care."

Her warm embrace, fragrant of expensive perfume, took me by surprise. "Thank you," I said as she went around the corner to her classroom.

I walked the halls of the school, looking for the room where my life had changed. It was across from the science lab, a few doors down from the big bulletin board where someone with neat handwriting still wrote the letters "P.A." followed by the graduating year along the edges of newspaper clippings featuring famous alumni.

"P.A. '66," I said to no one in particular. "One of these days."

---

17. **chutzpah** (hüts′pə), a Yiddish word meaning boldness and daring.

After Reading

Making Connections

1. Have you ever been in a situation similar to Esmeralda's?

2. What three questions would you ask Esmeralda if you could talk to her today?

3. ☺ How is Esmeralda's cultural heritage part of her **individuality?**

4. Were Mr. Barone, Mr. Gatti, and Mrs. Johnson really helpful? Why or why not?

5. What **writer's techniques** does the author use to maintain suspense throughout the selection?

6. What does it take to give a good performance or audition?

7. What did you learn about being an "outsider" from this selection?

Literary Focus: Situational Irony

Irony is the contrast between what is expected or what appears to be and what actually is. **Situational irony** refers to a happening that is the opposite of what is expected or intended. For example, you want to buy your best friend something really special for her birthday. You want to buy the kind of present that will make her eyes light up so that she'll know just how special she is. Well, three people buy her the *same thing* as you do, and by the time she opens your gift she thinks the whole thing was planned as a joke. That's situational irony.

Esmeralda experiences this irony of situation in her audition. Fill out the chart below with details that explain the differences between Esmeralda's expectations and what actually happens. Then write a brief paragraph on how Esmeralda's audition is an example of situational irony.

Event	Expectation	What Actually Happened
monologue	give in 3 minutes	took 1 minute

Vocabulary Study

cartographer
topographer
aptitude
academic
mesmerized
vocational
audition
monologue
phonetically
modulated

Copy the crossword puzzle and then use the clues to help you fill it in with words from the list.

ACROSS

2. this person knows the "highs" and "lows"

3. a good person to have around when you are lost

5. in a trance

9. knack

10. a long speech spoken by a single actor

DOWN

1. bricklayers and plumbers need this type of training

4. has to do with sounding out words

6. this term is associated with sound quality

7. what you might need to do to get a part in a play

8. a school that offers courses in literature, history, philosophy, etc.

Expressing Your Ideas

Writing Choices

A Letter She'll Keep Forever Write a **letter** that Esmeralda might write to her mentor. Somehow in the letter indicate where Esmeralda is in her life. Is she still in high school or has she graduated? What sorts of things do you think her mentor did for her?

Ahem. May I Have Your Attention Please? Prepare a **monologue** based on the experience you wrote about in your notebook before reading.

Other Options

Silence Is Golden Like Esmeralda, we all sometimes have a difficult time with words. Sometimes it's best to let our actions speak. Create a **pantomime.** Select an activity that you are familiar with and re-create it for an audience.

Laugh It Off Laughter is an essential ingredient in life. Bring these words of wisdom to life by creating a **cartoon** that shows the humorous side of Esmeralda's audition.

Language Mini-Lesson

Checking Your Spelling

Recognize spelling problems. Some words are mispelled again and again. (Did you catch the error in that last sentence?) Sometimes we make spelling mistakes because the words are so familiar that we overlook them when we proofread. Other times, we confuse one word with another that looks or sounds the same. We might also leave the apostrophe out of contractions. These are errors we make because of confusion or carelessness. Find the three misspellings in this lost pet notice.

We lost are pet cat. Have you seen her? She's a gray and white tabby. We dont know where she went, but were offering a reward. Call the Smith family at 555-3333.

Writing Strategy Here are some ways to avoid common misspellings:

- Make sure you include apostrophes in contractions.

- Know the spellings and meanings for words that sound alike.

- Proofread carefully for careless errors. Many times we write *fiend* instead of *friend* or we spell *outside* as two words. Reading aloud helps locate some errors.

Activity Options

1. Be alert to misspelled words on signs and in advertisements. Begin a class chart and bring in or copy mistakes you find. How many can your class find?

2. Write five sentences that include these words: *know, no, their, there, they're, we're, wear, then,* and *than.* Spell them incorrectly in your sentences. Exchange papers with a partner and correct each other's sentences.

3. Work with a partner to make a list of "Careless Errors." Look back through your writing portfolio for words you've misspelled through confusion or carelessness. As you come across other words that fit this category, add them to the list.

Before Reading

The New Colossus by Emma Lazarus

Chinese Hot Pot by Wing Tek Lum

Dreams; The Dream Keeper; and I, Too by Langston Hughes

My Father and the Figtree by Naomi Shihab Nye

Building Background

The American Culture The U.S. population has often been referred to as a "melting pot"—immigrants arrive, settle down, and slowly, their cultural differences melt away. What is left is one culture, identified by a common language, common foods, and a common education, but with some variations according to background and region. However, some people think our culture is more like a "tossed salad," with plenty of individual colors and flavors but held together in one bowl and coated by the same dressing. Others have suggested that a "stew" is a more appropriate description. What do you think?

Getting into the Poetry

Discussion What do you know about the Statue of Liberty? As a class, share what you know about this monument. For example, where is it? Why is it famous? Has anyone in your class seen it?

Reading Tip

Allusion An **allusion** is a reference to a historical or literary person, event, or place, used to heighten the significance of a poetic image or a prose passage. For example, the poem "The New Colossus" refers to a gigantic statue of the Greek god Helios that stood at the entrance to a harbor more than two thousand years ago. However, the poem is not about that statue. It's about a "new" Colossus. As you read the poems in this grouping, see if any of the other authors use allusion.

Emma Lazarus
1849–1887

Emma Lazarus, a Jewish woman from New York City, wrote "The New Colossus" in 1883, as a reaction to anti-Jewish attacks that occurred in Russia in 1881. These attacks forced many Jews to immigrate to the United States. The poem, which celebrates the symbolic nature of the Statue of Liberty as the "Mother of Exiles," is inscribed on a bronze plaque inside the pedestal of the statue. The Statue of Liberty was given to the people of the United States by the people of France in 1884 as a token of friendship and a memorial to those who fought for liberty during the American Revolution.

Wing Tek Lum

Wing Tek Lum is a businessman and poet from Honolulu. In his poetry he often refers to his Chinese ancestry as well as his American upbringing. He is the author of *Expounding the Doubtful Points.*

Langston Hughes
1902–1967

Langston Hughes, born in Joplin, Missouri, became one of America's leading writers during the Harlem Renaissance of the 1930s. An African American, Hughes grew up in Lawrence, Kansas, raised by his grandmother until he was twelve. After her death, Hughes moved first to Illinois and then to Ohio with his mother. Together with other African American artists and writers of the time, Hughes provided information about the daily lives of African American citizens and the immorality of racism. Among his many works that expressed the pride of African Americans in their own history and culture were *Weary Blues* (1926), *Shakespeare in Harlem* (1942), and *Montage of a Dream Deferred* (1951).

Naomi Shihab Nye
born 1952

Naomi Shihab Nye is an American with a Palestinian father and American mother. She was born in St. Louis, Missouri, spent a year in Jerusalem, and then moved to San Antonio, Texas. She has won many awards for her poetry. Among the books she has had published are *Words Under the Words: Selected Poems; The Same Sky: A Collection of Poems from Around the World;* and *Benito's Dream Bottle.*

The New Colossus
Emma Lazarus

Not like the brazen[1] giant of Greek fame,[2]
With conquering limbs astride from land to land;
Here at our sea-washed, sunset gates shall stand
A mighty woman with a torch, whose flame
5 Is the imprisoned lightning, and her name
Mother of Exiles.[3] From her beacon-hand
Glows world-wide welcome; her mild eyes command
The air-bridged harbor that twin cities frame.

"Keep, ancient lands, your storied pomp!" cries she
10 With silent lips. "Give me your tired, your poor,
Your huddled[4] masses yearning to breathe free,
The wretched refuse of your teeming[5] shore.
Send these, the homeless, tempest-tost to me,
I lift my lamp beside the golden door!"

1. brazen (brā′zn), *adj.* 1. bold 2. made of brass.
2. **brazen giant of Greek fame.** Reference is to the Colossus of Rhodes, a gigantic bronze statue of the Greek sun god Helios. It is considered one of the Seven Wonders of the Ancient World.
3. exile (eg′zīl), *n.* a person who must leave his or her country and live somewhere else.
4. huddled (hud′ld), *adj.* crowded close together.
5. teeming (tē′ming), *adj.* full.

Chinese Hot Pot
Wing Tek Lum

My dream of America
is like *dá bìn lòuh*[1]
with people of all persuasions and tastes
sitting down around a common pot
5 chopsticks and basket scoops here and there
some cooking squid and others beef
some tofu or watercress
all in one broth
like a stew that really isn't
10 as each one chooses what he wishes to eat
only that the pot and fire are shared
along with the good company
and the sweet soup
spooned out at the end of the meal.

1. **dá bìn lòuh,** the Vietnamese word for the Chinese hot pot, is a big dish of boiling broth in which meat, fish, poultry, and vegetables are cooked.

◄ Paul Tillinghast, who created this untitled assemblage of the Statue of Liberty, makes a point about our country and its people. What do you think this point is?

649

Dreams

Langston Hughes

Hold fast to dreams
For if dreams die
Life is a broken-winged bird
That cannot fly.

5 Hold fast to dreams
For when dreams go
Life is a barren field
Frozen with snow.

The Dream Keeper

Langston Hughes

Bring me all of your dreams,
You dreamers,
Bring me all of your
Heart melodies
5 That I may wrap them
In a blue cloud-cloth
Away from the too-rough fingers
Of the world.

I, Too

Langston Hughes

I, too, sing America.

I am the darker brother.
They send me to eat in the kitchen
When company comes,
5 But I laugh,
And eat well,
And grow strong.

Tomorrow,
I'll sit at the table
10 When company comes.
Nobody'll dare
Say to me,
"Eat in the kitchen,"
Then.

15 Besides,
They'll see how beautiful I am
And be ashamed—

I, too, am America.

▲ 🐾 *Self Portrait* was painted by Malvin Gray Johnson in 1934. Johnson often included African images in his paintings. Why do you think the artist and the poet believed that it was important to draw upon their cultural heritage to express their artistic **individuality**?

Naomi Shihab Nye

My Father and the Figtree

For other fruits my father was indifferent.
He'd point at the cherry trees and say,
"See those? I wish they were figs."
In the evenings he sat by my bed
5   weaving folktales like vivid[1] little scarves.
They always involved a figtree.
Even when it didn't fit, he'd stick it in.
Once Joha was walking down the road
and he saw a figtree.
10   Or, he tied his camel to a figtree
and went to sleep.
Or, later when they caught and arrested
      him,
his pockets were full of figs.

At age six I ate a dried fig and shrugged.
15   "That's not what I'm talking about!" he
      said.
"I'm talking about a fig straight from the
      earth—
gift of Allah![2]—on a branch so heavy it
      touches the ground.
I'm talking about picking the largest
      fattest sweetest fig
in the world and putting it in my
      mouth."
20   (Here he'd stop and close his eyes.)

Years passed, we lived in many houses,
      none had figtrees.

We had lima beans, zucchini, parsley,
      beets.
"Plant one!" my mother said, but my
      father never did.
He tended garden half-heartedly, forgot
      to water,
25   let the okra get too big.
"What a dreamer he is. Look how many
      things he starts
and doesn't finish."

The last time he moved, I had a phone
      call,
my father, in Arabic, chanting a song I'd
      never heard.
30   "What's that?"
"Wait till you see!"

He took me out to the new yard.
There, in the middle of Dallas, Texas,
a tree with the largest, fattest, sweetest
      figs in the world.
35   "It's a figtree song!" he said,
plucking his fruits like ripe tokens,
emblems, assurance
of a world that was always his own.

---

1. vivid (viv′id), *adj.* bright and colorful.
2. **Allah,** the Muslim name for God.

After Reading

Making Connections

1. Which poem best captures your own experience or vision of America?

2. Compare each poet's vision of America. What **similarities** do the visions share? What **differences** are there?

3. ☞ How do these poems reflect the authors' **individuality** as well as their commitment to their culture?

4. How is the idea of a melting pot **similar** to or **different** from the idea of a Chinese hot pot?

5. Besides "The New Colossus," what other poems in this grouping contain **allusions?** What are they? (If necessary, review the explanation of allusions on page 646.)

6. Which description of American society best matches your own view—melting pot, tossed salad, or stew? Explain.

Literary Focus: Theme

Theme is the underlying meaning of a work. It involves a statement or opinion about the topic. What theme would you say is developed by this group of poems? First, quickly write down in your notebook a few general ideas about each poem. Use a format similar to the one below. After you have done this, try to find an idea that is common to all the poems.

"The New Colossus"
Possible ideas:
Freedom is precious.

"Dreams"
Possible ideas:
Life would be empty without dreams.

Common idea:

Vocabulary Study

Fill in each set of blanks with the correct word from the vocabulary list at the left. Then, for an added bonus, rearrange the circled letters to spell another word relating to the theme of this group of poems.

brazen
exile
huddled
teeming
vivid

1. the sun on a clear day ___ ___ ___ ___ ___
2. the "welcome mat" is not out for this person ◯ ___ ___ ___ ___
3. kittens did this when they wanted to keep warm ___ ___ ◯ ___ ___ ___ ___
4. cutting in at the front of a line could be called this kind of act ___ ◯ ◯ ___ ___ ___
5. the opposite of empty ___ ___ ___ ◯ ___ ___ ___

Expressing Your Ideas _____

Writing Choices

Personal Symbol Write an **essay** or a **poem** about what America means to you. First, choose a symbol to write about, like the American flag, a kind of tree, or your school—whatever represents the United States of America to you. After choosing your symbol, list what it is about that symbol that signifies "America" to you.

Encore! Add another **verse** to "Dreams." Maintain the same rhythm and rhyme scheme established by Hughes.

Dream On Write an **essay** on why dreams are important. Start with a statement of your main idea and then suppy details to support your idea.

Other Options

Details, Details Give an oral **report** on one of the subjects in the poems, such as the Statue of Liberty, immigration, or Ellis Island. Include visual aids such as charts, overheads, and photos.

What Is America? Create a **collage** of American ideas, people, things, and foods. Choose a theme you want to illustrate in your collage, such as "Americans Reach for Dreams." Then find photos that represent that theme.

Mm, Mm, Good! The poems reflect cultural diversity. How diverse is your palate? Create a **menu** of ethnic foods that you like, such as egg rolls, spaghetti, Greek salad, enchiladas, and avocado pudding. Illustrate the menu if you'd like. Next to each food, indicate what country or ethnic group it came from.

Before Reading

The Gettysburg Address

by Abraham Lincoln

Abraham Lincoln
1809–1865

Abraham Lincoln was the six-teenth President of the United States (1861–1865). His election in 1860 sparked the secession of South Carolina from the Union and formation of the Confederacy. As President, Lincoln issued the Emancipation Proclamation in 1863 that marked the begin-ning of the end of slavery in the United States. Lincoln's Gettysburg Address, which he delivered at Gettysburg four months after the historic battle took place, became one of his most enduring legacies. He was assassinated in 1865, five days after the Civil War ended.

Building Background

The Battle of Gettysburg This famous battle, fought from July 1 to July 3, 1863, in southern Pennsylvania, is considered to be a turning point in the Civil War (1861–1865). After Gettysburg the Confederacy never again would be able to mount a major offensive against Northern armies. To honor the 3,155 Union soldiers who died during the battle, the Gettysburg National Cemetery was dedicated on November 19, 1863. It was at this dedication that Lincoln delivered the speech we now call "The Gettysburg Address."

Getting into the Speech

Writer's Notebook
Besides what you have read above, what else do you know about the Civil War? Spend a few minutes writing down everything you can remember about this conflict. After you have warmed up your memory, write a few lines about what President Lincoln must have been feeling or think-ing as he composed the Gettysburg Address.

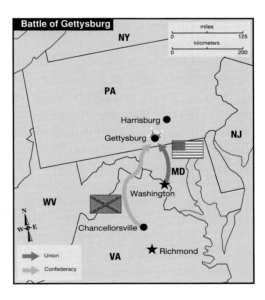

Reading Tip

Antiquated Language The language of this speech is rather **antiquated,** or old-fashioned. Even today, the language of formal speeches is different than the everyday language we use. Speeches are meant to be spoken slowly, with lots of pauses, so that your audience hears every word. That's how you should read this speech, too—slowly.

The Gettysburg Address

Abraham Lincoln

Four score[1] and seven years ago our fathers brought forth on this continent, a new nation, conceived[2] in Liberty, and dedicated[3] to the proposition[4] that all men are created equal. Now we are engaged in a great civil war, testing whether that nation, or any nation so conceived and so dedicated, can long endure. We are met on a great battlefield of that war. We have come to dedicate a portion of that field, as a final resting place for those who here gave their lives that that nation might live. It is altogether fitting and proper that we should do this.

But, in a larger sense, we can not dedicate—we can not consecrate[5]—we can not hallow—this ground. The brave men, living and dead, who struggled here, have consecrated it, far above our poor power to add or detract. The world will little note, nor long remember what we say here, but it can never forget what they did here. It is for us the living, rather, to be dedicated here to the unfinished work which they who fought here have thus far so nobly advanced. It is rather for us to be here dedicated to the great task remaining before us— that from these honored dead we take increased devotion to that cause for which they gave the last full measure of devotion—that we here highly resolve that these dead shall not have died in vain—that this nation, under God, shall have a new birth of freedom—and that government of the people, by the people, for the people, shall not perish from the earth.

---

1. **score** (skôr), group or set of twenty. Four score equals eighty years.
2. conceive (kən sēv′), *v.* think up; form.
3. dedicate (ded′ə kāt), *v.* set apart for a sacred or important purpose.
4. proposition (prop′ə zish′ən), *n.* suggestion or idea.
5. consecrate (kon′sə krāt), *v.* make holy.

Pickett's Charge (detail of a Battle of Gettysburg cyclorama) was painted by Paul Philippoteaux in the early 1880s. What does the painting tell you about this historic 1863 battle?

O Captain! My Captain!

Walt Whitman

O Captain! my Captain! our fearful trip is done,
The ship has weather'd every rack, the prize we sought is won,
The port is near, the bells I hear, the people all exulting,[1]
While follow eyes the steady keel, the vessel grim and daring;
5   But O heart! heart! heart!
      O the bleeding drops of red,
        Where on the deck my Captain lies,
          Fallen cold and dead.

O Captain! my Captain! rise up and hear the bells;
10 Rise up—for you the flag is flung—for you the bugle trills,
For you bouquets and ribbon'd wreaths—for you the shores a-crowding
For you they call, the swaying mass, their eager faces turning;
    Here Captain! dear father!
      This arm beneath your head!
15   It is some dream that on the deck,
        You've fallen cold and dead.

My Captain does not answer, his lips are pale and still,
My father does not feel my arm, he has no pulse nor will,
The ship is anchor'd safe and sound, its voyage closed and done,
20 From fearful trip the victor ship comes in with object won;
    Exult O shores, and ring O bells!
      But I with mournful tread,
        Walk the deck my Captain lies,
          Fallen cold and dead.

---

1. **exult** (eg zult′), *v.* rejoice; celebrate.

After Reading

Making Connections

1. What was the effect of Lincoln's speech on you?

2. Explain in your own words the following three phrases from Lincoln's speech:

   a. "those who here gave their lives that that nation might live"

   b. "these dead shall not have died in vain"

   c. "a new birth of freedom"

3. What would you say is Lincoln's view of the Civil War and the meaning of the soldiers' deaths?

4. The poem "O Captain! My Captain!" was written by Walt Whitman following Lincoln's death. How is Lincoln like the captain in Whitman's poem?

5. What other images or **analogies** (comparisons) could Whitman have used?

6. Could Whitman's poem be applied to any other national leader? Why or why not?

Literary Focus: Writing Style

Writing style is *how* an author writes—the words chosen, the images used, all the decisions the author makes about how to say what he or she has to say. Even the first few words of "The Gettysburg Address"–"Four score and seven years ago"—tell you a lot about Lincoln's style in this speech: somber, dignified, old-fashioned, and momentous. Let's compare the two styles of these texts. First, fill out the chart. Using this information, describe Lincoln's writing style in the speech. Then describe Whitman's. How are they different? How are they similar?

	Gettysburg Address	O Captain! My Captain!
Type of Writing	speech, prose	poetry
Tone	serious	grieving, sad
Images		
Symbols		

Vocabulary Study

Write the word from the list that best completes the meaning of each sentence.

conceive
consecrate
dedicate
proposition
exult

The President had a __(1)__ that was well received by all the veterans. He proposed to __(2)__ the cemetery to the soldiers who died in the battle. Lincoln claimed it was not necessary to bless or __(3)__ the grounds of the cemetery, because the soldiers' deaths had already made those grounds holy. It is hard to __(4)__ of the terrible hardships of the Civil War. We must all __(5)__ in the war's end and hope that such a national crisis never happens again.

Expressing Your Ideas

Writing Choices

Background Check Write a **report** about a person or an incident in Lincoln's life. Possible topics could be his wife Mary Todd Lincoln, his children (and their pets), or the time he walked thirty-four miles in one day just to hear a lawyer's speech. Consult your U.S. history text or library reference materials for other topic ideas.

What's a *Score*? You have been nominated by the President to prepare a new draft of the Gettysburg Address so that young students are able to better grasp its meaning and significance. **Rewrite** the Gettysburg Address using modern language.

O Captain! Write an **explanation** of the comparison of President Lincoln to a captain of a ship. Look first at the biography of Lincoln on page 655. Then examine the poem "O Captain! My Captain!" for similarities between the captain and Lincoln. In your paper, cite specific lines from the poem and explain how they could be applied to Lincoln.

Other Options

Put on Your Stove-top Hat Imagine you are President Lincoln. Practice using the tone of voice you think he may have used in giving the Gettysburg Address. Deliver his famous **speech** to the class. If possible, dress the part.

Sing Out Locate a copy of the **song** "Abraham, Martin, and John." The song, which was sung by Dion, came out in 1968. Listen to it—as a class, if possible—and explain who the three men are and why they are important in the fight for freedom and equal rights. As an alternative, you and a group of students could sing the song for the class.

Speech! Speech! Find other famous speeches or speeches that commemorate famous events. Practice **reading** one aloud to the class. Explain what you think made this speech famous.

Picture History Prepare a **time line** of the Civil War, with pictures and brief explanations of significant events. Examine social studies textbooks to find examples of different ways to present information in a time line. Be sure to include the Battle of Gettysburg.

Before Reading

from Sound-Shadows of the New World

by Ved Mehta

Ved Mehta
born 1934

With the exception of *Sound-Shadows of the New World,* the book from which this selection was taken, and an earlier autobiographical work, Mehta rarely addresses his blindness in his writing. He does not think this fact is important to his readers. Besides his autobiographies, Mehta has written numerous magazine articles, political commentaries, and history books. He has also written several novels, the latest of which is *Three Stories of the Raj.* Mehta has also produced a documentary film, *Chachaji, My Poor Relation,* for which he won the Dupont Columbia Award for excellence in broadcast journalism.

Building Background

Ved Mehta The author was born in India. He contracted meningitis at the age of four, which left him completely blind. His father, a highly educated doctor who trained in England, knew that education was the only way for Ved to avoid the life of most blind Indians—that of a beggar. So Ved was sent to Bombay's Dadar School for the Blind, an American mission school, thousands of miles from his home. When he finished his studies there at the age of fourteen, his father encouraged him to continue his studies elsewhere. Ved eventually was accepted at the Arkansas School for the Blind. He traveled to the United States to begin his studies, which is where the selection begins.

Getting into the Selection

Writer's Notebook In your notebook, divide a sheet in half with a vertical line. On one side of the line write *India.* On the other, write *United States.* As a class, brainstorm what you know about life in India. Then do the same for the United States. Record responses in your notebook. As you read the selection, put additional information in your chart.

India	United States
•was once a British colony	•was once made up of British colonies
•Hinduism is major religion	

Reading Tip

Predict Using your general knowledge, intuition, and information from the chart you and your classmates just completed, write a brief paragraph predicting what Ved, a fifteen-year-old blind Indian boy, will experience on his first day in New York City.

Sound-Shadows

Ved Mehta

At the airport, I was questioned by an immigration[1] official. "You're blind—totally blind—and they gave you a visa?[2] You say it's for your studies, but studies where?"

"At the Arkansas School for the Blind. It is in Little Rock, in Arkansas."

He shuffled through the pages of a book. Sleep was in my eyes. Drops of sweat were running down my back. My shirt and trousers felt dirty.

"Arkansas School is not on our list of approved schools for foreign students."

"I know," I said. "That is why the immigration officials in Delhi gave me only a visitor's visa. They said that when I got to the school I should tell the authorities to apply to be on your list of approved schools, so that I could get a student visa." I showed him a big manila envelope I was carrying; it contained my chest X-rays, medical reports, and fingerprint charts, which were necessary for a student visa, and which I'd had prepared in advance.

"Why didn't you apply to an approved school in the first place and come here on a proper student visa?" he asked, looking through the material.

My knowledge of English was limited. With difficulty, I explained to him that I had applied to some thirty schools but that, because I had been able to get little formal education in India, the Arkansas School was the only one that would accept me; that I had needed a letter of acceptance from an American school to get dollars sanctioned by the Reserve Bank of India; and that now that I was in America I was sure I could change schools if the Arkansas School was not suitable or did not get the necessary approval.

of the New World

---

1. immigration (im/ə grā′shən), *n.* coming into a foreign country or region to live.
2. visa (vē′zə), *n.* official document granting permission to travel to another country.

Muttering to himself, the immigration official looked up at me, down at his book, and up at me again. He finally announced, "I think you'll have to go to Washington and apply to get your visa changed to a student visa before you can go to any school."

I recalled things that Daddyji used to say as we were growing up: "In life, there is only fight or flight. You must always fight," and "America is God's own country. People there are the most hospitable and generous people in the world." I told myself I had nothing to worry about. Then I remembered that Daddyji had mentioned a Mr. and Mrs. Dickens in Washington—they were friends of friends of his—and told me that I could get in touch with them in case of emergency.

CLARIFY: What did Daddyji mean when he said, "In life there is only fight or flight"?

"I will do whatever is necessary," I now said to the immigration official. "I will go to Washington."

He hesitated, as if he were thinking something, and then stamped my passport and returned it to me. "We Mehtas carry our luck with us," Daddyji used to say. He is right, I thought.

The immigration official suddenly became helpful, as if he were a friend. "You shouldn't have any trouble with the immigration people in Washington," he said, and asked, "Is anybody meeting you here?"

"Mr. and Mrs. di Francesco," I said.

Mrs. di Francesco was a niece of Manmath Nath Chatterjee, whom Daddyji had known when he himself was a student, in London, in 1920. Daddyji had asked Mr. Chatterjee, who had a Scottish-American wife and was now settled in Yellow Springs, Ohio, if he could suggest anyone with whom I might stay in New York, so that I could get acclimatized[3] to America before proceeding to the Arkansas

School, which was not due to open until the eleventh of September. Mr. Chatterjee had written back that, as it happened, his wife's niece was married to John di Francesco, a singer who was totally blind, and that Mr. and Mrs. di Francesco lived in New York, and would be delighted to meet me at the airport and keep me as a paying guest at fifteen dollars a week.

"How greedy of them to ask for money!" I had cried when I learned of the arrangement. "People come and stay with us for months and we never ask for an anna."[4]

Daddyji had said, "In the West, people do not, as a rule, stay with relatives and friends but put up in hotels, or in houses as paying guests. That is the custom there. Mr. and Mrs. di Francesco are probably a young, struggling couple who could do with a little extra money."

The immigration official now came from behind the counter, led me to an open area, and shouted, with increasing volume, "Fransisco! . . . Franchesca! . . . De Franco!" I wasn't sure what the correct pronunciation was, but his shouting sounded really disrespectful. I asked him to call for Mr. and Mrs. di Francesco softly. He bellowed, "Di Fransesco!"

No one came. My mouth went dry. Mr. and Mrs. di Francesco had sent me such a warm invitation. I couldn't imagine why they would have let me down or what I should do next.

Then I heard the footsteps of someone running toward us. "Here I am. You must be Ved. I'm Muriel di Francesco. I'm sorry John couldn't come." I noted that the name was pronounced the way it was spelled, and that hers was a Yankee voice—the kind I had heard when I first encountered Americans at home, during the

---

3. **acclimatized** (ə klī′mə tīzd), *adj.* become used to a new place or surroundings.
4. **anna** (an′ə), in India, a former unit of money equal to one-sixteenth of a rupee.

▲ Ved Mehta, age 16, was photographed at a swimming pool in Little Rock, Arkansas, in 1950. Judging from the photograph and from what you have read, would you describe Ved as an optimistic person? Explain your answer.

war—but it had the sweetness of the voices of my sisters.

We shook hands; she had a nice firm grip. I had an impulse to call her Auntie Muriel—at home, an older person was always called by an honorific, like "Auntie" or "Uncle"—but I greeted her as Daddyji had told me that Westerners liked to be greeted: "Mrs. di Francesco, I'm delighted to make your acquaintance."

"You had a terrible trip, you poor boy. What a terrible way to arrive!" Mrs. di Francesco said in the taxi. "Imagine, everything stolen from a bag!"

One bag had contained clothes. The other, a holdall, had contained (in addition to some extra shirts) a number of ivory curios—statues of Lord Krishna,[5] "no evil" monkeys,[6] brooches with a little pattern on them—which Daddyji had bought with the idea that I could sell them at great profit. "You can take the ivory curios to a shop in Little Rock and ask the shop to sell them for you—on commission, of course," he had said. "In America, a lot of people earn and learn. Who knows? Maybe we could start an ivory-export-import business in a year or so, when I retire from government service." He was deputy director general of health services in the Indian government. "I expect there is a great deal of demand over there for hand-carved things." The fact that neither of us had ever sold even a secondhand gramophone didn't stop us from dreaming.

I didn't want Mrs. di Francesco to feel bad, so I made light of the theft. "The other bag is still full," I said.

"The ivory things must have been really valuable," she said. She had helped me fill out the insurance-claim forms. "What a bad introduction to America!"

"But it could have happened in Delhi."

She regaled[7] the taxi-driver with the story, as if she and I were long-standing friends. "And we had to wait at the airport for two whole hours, filling out insurance forms. And he only knew the prices in rubles."

"Rupees," I said.[8]

"Is that right?" the taxi-driver said, from the front seat. "Well, it shouldn't have happened to you, son."

I leaned toward the half-open window and listened for the roar of street crowds, the cries of hawkers, the clatter of tonga[9] wheels, the trot of tonga horses, the crackle of whips, the blasts of Klaxons, the trills of police whistles, the tinkling of bicycle bells—but all I heard was the steady hiss and rush of cars. "In America, you can really travel fast and get places," I said.

Mrs. di Francesco took both my hands in hers and broke into open, unrestrained laughter. I have never heard a woman laugh quite like that, I thought.

"What are you laughing at?" I asked.

"I'd just noticed that all this time you had your hand in your breast pocket. Are you afraid of having your wallet stolen, too?"

I was embarrassed. I hadn't realized what I had been doing.

The taxi-driver took a sharp turn.

"Where are we?" I asked.

"On Broadway," Mrs. di Francesco said.

"Is Broadway a wide road?" I asked.

Here I would travel in taxis amid new friends and have adventures.

---

5. **Lord Krishna,** one of the most important Hindu gods.
6. **"no evil" monkeys,** three monkeys in a row. The first one sees no evil, the second one hears no evil, the third one speaks no evil.
7. regale (ri gāl′), v. entertain.
8. **rubles/rupees,** rubles are the money used in Russia; Mrs. di Francesco is confusing them with rupees, the money used in India.
9. **tonga,** a light, two-wheeled carriage used in India.

She laughed. "A very wide avenue—it's the center of the universe."

At home, the center was a circle, but here the center, it seemed, was a straight line. At home, I often felt I was on a merry-go-round, circling activities that I couldn't join in. Here I would travel in taxis amid new friends and have adventures. I tried to voice my thoughts.

"Poor boy, you have difficulty with the language," Mrs. di Francesco said, gently pressing my hand.

"English is difficult," I said, and I tried to make a joke. "When I was small and first learning English, I was always confusing 'chicken' and 'kitchen.'"

"'Chicken' and 'kitchen,'" Mrs. di Francesco repeated, and laughed.

"I have enough trouble speaking English," the taxi-driver said. "I could never learn to speak Hindu."

"Hindi," I said, correcting him.

"You see?" the taxi-driver said.

Mrs. di Francesco laughed, and the taxi-driver joined in.

After a while, the taxi came to a stop. "Here we are at home, on a Hundred and Thirteenth Street between Broadway and Amsterdam," Mrs. di Francesco said.

Though I was carrying a bank draft for eighty dollars, I had only two dollars in cash, which a family friend had given me for good luck. I handed it to Mrs. di Francesco for the taxi.

"That won't be enough," she said.

"But it is *seven rupees!*" I cried. "At home, one could hire a tonga for a whole day for that."

QUESTION: Why do you think it is so inexpensive to rent a tonga?

"This is New York," she said. She clicked open her purse and gave some money to the taxi-driver.

The taxi-driver put my bags on the curb, shook my hand, and said, "If I go to India, I will remember not to become a tonga driver." He drove away.

We picked up the luggage. Mrs. di Francesco tucked my free hand under her bare arm with a quick motion and started walking. A woman at home would probably have cringed[10] at the touch of a stranger's hand under her arm, I thought, but thinking this did not stop me from making a mental note that the muscle of her arm was well developed.

We went into a house, and walked up to Mr. and Mrs. di Francesco's apartment, on the fourth floor. Mr. di Francesco opened the door and kissed Mrs. di Francesco loudly. Had a bomb exploded, I could not have been more surprised. They'll catch something, I thought. I had never heard any grownups kissing at home—not even in films.

Mr. di Francesco shook my hand. He had a powerful grip and a powerful voice. He took me by the shoulder and almost propelled me to a couch. "This is going to be your bed," he said. "I'm sorry I couldn't come to the airport. Anyway, I knew you wouldn't mind being greeted by a charming lady." He doesn't have a trace of the timid, servile[11] manner of music masters and blind people at home, I thought.

"We had a delightful ride from the airport," I said.

Mr. di Francesco wanted to know why we were so late, and Mrs. di Francesco told him about the theft.

"What bad luck!" he said.

"But I got here," I said.

"That's the spirit," he said, laughing.

"John, thank you for starting dinner," Mrs. di Francesco said from what I took to be the kitchen.

---

10. **cringe** (krinj), *v.* retreat away from.
11. **servile** (sér′vəl), *adj.* like that of slaves; spiritless.

"Oh, you cook!" I exclaimed. I had never heard of a blind person who could cook.

"Yes, I help Muriel," he said. "We don't have servants here, as they do in your country. We have labor-saving devices." He then showed me around the apartment, casually tapping and explaining—or putting my hand on—various unfamiliar things: a stove that did not burn coal or give out smoke; an ice chest that stood on end and ran on electricity; a machine that toasted bread; a bed for two people; and a tub in which one could lie down. I was full of questions, and asked how natural gas from the ground was piped into individual apartments, and how people could have so much hot water that they could lie down in it. At home, a husband and wife never slept in one bed, but I didn't say anything about that, because I felt shy.

"Do you eat meat?" Mrs. di Francesco asked me from the kitchen. "Aunt Rita—Mrs. Chatterjee—didn't know."

"Yes, I do eat meat," I called back to her. I started worrying about how I would cut it.

Mrs. di Francesco sighed with relief. "John and I hoped that you weren't a vegetarian. We're having spaghetti and meatballs, which are made of beef. Is that all right?"

I shuddered. As a Hindu, I had never eaten beef, and the mere thought of it was revolting. But I recalled another of Daddyji's sayings, "When in Rome, do as the Romans do," and said, "I promised my father that I would eat anything and everything in America and gain some weight."

Mrs. di Francesco brought out the dinner and served it to us at a small table. "The peas are at twelve and the spaghetti and meatballs at six," she said. I must have looked puzzled, because she added, "John locates his food on

"There is nothing primitive or backward in India."

a plate by the clock dial. I thought all blind people knew—"

"You forget that India has many primitive[12] conditions," Mr. di Francesco interrupted. "Without a doubt, work for the blind there is very backward."

I bridled.[13] "There is nothing primitive or backward in India."

There was a silence, in which I could hear Mr. di Francesco swallowing water. I felt very much alone. I wished I were back home.

"I didn't mean it that way," Mr. di Francesco said.

"I'm sorry," I said, and then, rallying a little, confessed that Braille[14] watches were unheard of in India—that I had first read about them a year or so earlier in a British Braille magazine, and then it had taken me several months to get the foreign exchange and get a Braille pocket watch from Switzerland.

"Then how do blind people there know what time it is—whether it is day or night?" Mr. di Francesco asked.

"They have to ask someone, or learn to tell from the morning and night sounds. I suppose that things *are* a little backward there. That is why I had to leave my family and come here for education."

"The food is getting cold," Mrs. di Francesco said.

I picked up my fork and knife with trembling fingers and aimed for six. I suddenly wanted to cry.

"You look homesick," Mrs. di Francesco said.

I nodded, and tried to eat. A sense of relief

---

12. primitive (prim′ə tiv), *adj.* very simple, such as people had early in history.
13. bridle (brī′dl), *v.* lift up one's chin or head to express pride or anger.
14. **Braille,** a system of writing for blind people that uses different arrangements of raised dots.

▲ Ved's father, Daddyji, as he appeared in 1921, shortly after attending school in London. What kind of man do you think Daddyji was?

engulfed me: we had mutton meatballs at home all the time, and they didn't require a knife. But the relief was short-lived: I had never had spaghetti, and the strands were long and tended to bunch together. They stretched from my mouth to my plate—a sign of my Indian backwardness, I thought. I longed for the kedgeree[15] at home, easily managed with a spoon.

Mrs. di Francesco reached over and showed me how to wrap the spaghetti around my fork, shake it, and pick it up. Even so, I took big bites when I thought that Mrs. di Francesco was not looking—when she was talking to Mr. di Francesco. Later in the meal, it occurred to me that I was eating the food Daddyji had eaten when he was a student abroad. I resolutely bent my face over the plate and started eating in earnest.

Mrs. di Francesco took away our plates and served us something else, and I reached for my spoon.

"That's eaten with a fork," she said.

I attacked it with a fork. "It is a pudding with a crust!" I cried. "I have never eaten anything like it."

"It's not a pudding—it's apple pie," Mrs. di Francesco said. "By the way, we're having scrambled eggs for breakfast. Is that all right?"

I confessed that I didn't know what they were, and she described them to me.

"Oh, I know—rumble-tumble eggs!" I exclaimed. "I like them very much."

They both laughed. "British—Indian English is really much nicer than American English," Mr. di Francesco said. "You should keep it. In fact, I'll adopt 'rumble-tumble.'"

I felt sad that I had come to America for my studies instead of going to England first, as Daddyji had done. But no school in England had accepted me.

"We've heard so much about India from Uncle Manmath," Mrs. di Francesco said. "It must be a very exciting place."

"Yes, tell us about India," Mr. di Francesco said.

I felt confused. I couldn't think of what to say or how to say it.

"You look tired," Mrs. di Francesco said, patting me on the arm.

"I cannot think of the right English words sometimes," I said.

Mrs. di Francesco cleared some things off the table and said, "Don't worry. Now that you're here, your English will improve quickly."

She went to the kitchen and started washing the plates while Mr. di Francesco and I lingered at the table—much as we might at home.

I asked Mr. di Francesco how he had become self-supporting and independent, with a place of his own.

"You make it sound so romantic, but it's really very simple," he said. He spoke in a matter-of-fact way. "I spent twelve years at the Perkins Institution for the Blind, in Massachusetts. I entered when I was seven, and left when I was nineteen."

"Perkins!" I cried. "I have been trying to go there since I was seven. First, they would not have me because of the war. But after the war they would not have me, either—they said that I would end up a 'cultural misfit.'"

"What does that mean?"

"They said that bringing Eastern people to the West at a young age leads to 'cultural maladjustment'[16]—and they said, 'Blindness is a maladjustment in itself.'"

"But now you're here. I'll call Perkins tomorrow and tell them that the damage is already done, and that your cultural maladjustment would be much worse if you were to end up in Arkansas." He laughed.

---

15. **kedgeree,** a stew.
16. **maladjustment** (mal/ə just/mənt), *n.* poor or unsatisfactory adjustment; not fitting in.

"Do you really think they will take me? Dr. Farrell, the director at Perkins, is a very stubborn man."

"They certainly should. Unlike Massachusetts, Arkansas is a very poor state. Arkansas School for the Blind is a state school. They are required to accept all the blind children in the state free of charge. In fact, you'll probably be the only one there paying for board and tuition. The school is bound to have a lot of riff-raff.[17] It's no place to improve your English. In Arkansas, you'll lose all your nice Britishisms and acquire a terrible Southern drawl. You have to go to Perkins. I know Dr. Farrell."

I was excited. "Perkins is said to be the best school for the blind anywhere. How did you like it? How was your life there?"

"Life at Perkins? It was probably no different from that of millions of other kids. We played and studied." He added obligingly, "It was a lot of fun."

Fun—so that's what it was, I thought. That is the difference between all the things he did at school and all the things I missed out on by not going to a good school.

"And after Perkins?"

"After Perkins, I studied voice at the New England Conservatory, where Muriel and I met. Then I came to New York, started giving voice lessons, married Muriel, and here I am."

"There must be more to tell."

"There really isn't."

"Did Mrs. di Francesco's parents not object? She is sighted."

"I wasn't asking to marry Muriel's parents. She could do what she pleased. This is America."

PREDICT: What do you think happened to Ved?

---

17. **riff-raff** (rif′raf′), *n*. people with bad reputations.

Afterword

No, Ved was not accepted into Perkins Institution for the Blind. The school's enrollment was already filled for the year. Besides, Dr. Farrell suggested to Mr. di Francesco on the phone that accepting such a young student from India would not be good for the young man. Consequently, Ved went on to the Arkansas School for the Blind, where he became president of the school senate and editor of the school paper, which prepared him for a career in journalism. After graduating, he continued his studies at Ponoma College in California, Balliol College in Oxford, England, and earned a master's degree at Harvard University. Then he wrote for the *New Yorker.*

After Reading

Making Connections

1. In your notebook, make a large copy of the head below. Fill it in with everything that you think must be going on in Ved's mind during his first day in New York.

2. "In life, there is only fight or flight. You must always fight." What did Daddyji mean by this? Do you agree?

3. Read the descriptions of Mr. and Mrs. di Francesco. What sort of information do you get through Ved's words? How do you picture them?

4. Explain how this selection fits the **theme** "Reaching for Your Dream."

5. What do you learn about culture and customs in India from the author? How did the author reveal this information?

6. 👁 How did Ved Mehta defend his cultural heritage? What does his defense of his native country show about his **individuality?**

7. If you had been in Ved's situation, what do you think would have been the most difficult thing to do or face?

Literary Focus: Point of View

You are probably already familiar with autobiographies and stories written in the **first person.** You know that literature written in the first person only gives you one person's **point of view.** In the case of the autobiographical piece you just read, the fact that it is told by Ved makes a difference in what you learn and do not learn about Ved's first day in the United States. For example, you do not learn what Mr. and Mrs. di Francesco look like, because Ved doesn't see them. But you *do* learn a lot about how life is experienced by someone who is blind. Go back through the selection and find examples of descriptions the author provides that come from his particular point of view—as an Indian, as a newcomer to New York, and as a blind person. Share and discuss the examples you find with your classmates.

Vocabulary Study

On a sheet of paper, write the word from the list that completes each sentence.

acclimatized
bridle
cringe
immigration
maladjustment
primitive
regale
riff-raff
servile
visa

A. When I left Finland to live in the United States, I learned about __(1)__ firsthand. At the processing center, an official looked at my passport to make sure that I was the right person. Eyes downward, I assumed a __(2)__ role. Another official looked through my baggage to make sure that I didn't have anything illegal. They don't want any __(3)__ to enter the country. The first official stamped my passport, giving me official permission to visit the country. That's called a __(4)__ .

B. A fellow traveler promised to __(5)__ me with stories of adventure and intrigue. You should have seen her __(6)__ with pride when I questioned whether she had really photographed a charging bull elephant. At one point I had to __(7)__ when she told me about the time she almost lost an eye to a bristly boar with a bad attitude.

C. It took me a while to get __(8)__ to my new school. My old school had been a one-room building with eight students. It was __(9)__ compared to this huge building with its two stories. Here, people were nice to me, but I was always afraid of saying something dumb. I guess I was afraid of not fitting in or showing "cultural __(10)__ ."

Expressing Your Ideas ⸺

Writing Choices

Dear Ved Imagine you have been given Ved's name as a pen pal. Write a **letter** welcoming him to the United States. In your letter, include a list of things that Ved should know immediately about life in the U.S.

Dear Diary Write Ved's **diary entry** about his first day in the United States. What would he think was most important to record? What feelings would he write about, that perhaps he could not have shared with his hosts?

Other Options

Background Check Ved's family had to leave Pakistan for India because the country was Muslim and they were Hindi. Use library resources to find out more about one or both of these religions. Present your findings to the class in an **oral report.**

Read Without Eyes Find out more about Braille. Then prepare a **poster** and a **mini-lesson** for your class on the Braille alphabet.

Reaching for Your Dream

School Days

Frontier Students

U.S. History Connection

Common images of America range from the landing of the Pilgrims at Plymouth Rock to the first moon walk. In both cases, a group of people with a common purpose were reaching for a dream. For most Americans, past and present, reaching for a dream begins on a smaller scale than an ocean voyage or a moon walk—it begins with school days.

Sod schoolhouse near Simeon, Nebraska, around 1900

A reading lesson in a one-room schoolhouse

Sharing secrets over lunch.
The girls' lunch boxes are a
tobacco tin and lard pail.

Waiting to board
the school bus

Frontier Schools

by Russell Freedman

" **I remember the first school I attended,**
a room crowded full of big boys and girls, noise and confusion, with
now and then a howl from some boy that was being whipped. I and
my brother, with another boy, occupied a bench with no back, near
the stove. When the stove became too warm, we whirled around and
faced the other side. . . ."

Those are the memories of Roxana Rice, a pioneer girl in Kansas.
With its hard wooden benches and cast-iron stove, her one-room
schoolhouse resembled thousands of others on the western frontier.

When settlers first moved into an area, there were no schools
of any kind. Children were taught at home, or at the home of a
neighbor. . . . As soon as there were enough children in an area,
families would band together to put up a proper school. Everyone
contributed labor and materials for the schoolhouse, which often
served as a church on Sundays.

The first schoolhouse was usually a simple cabin built of logs, sod,
or adobe. Each morning students were called to class by the iron bell
that hung outside the schoolhouse door. They came by foot,
on horseback, and in wagons, carrying their
books, their slates and tablets,
and their dinner pails. Some
of them had to travel several
miles in each direction.

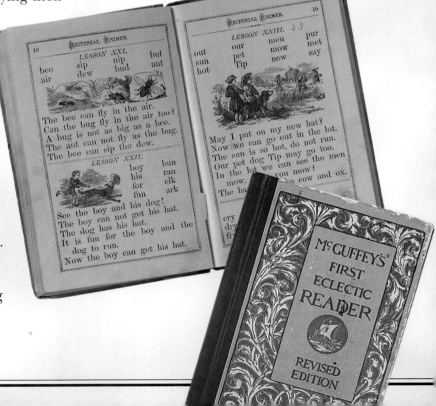

Youngsters of all ages were
taught by a single teacher.
Schools, like frontier homes,
sometimes had dirt floors. Since
there was no running water,
everyone drank from the same
bucket and dipper kept in a
corner of the room. The "playground" was the field outside.
The "rest room" was an outhouse.
Dogs of many breeds and sizes
hung around the schoolhouse,
whining at the door and sneaking
inside to lie at their owners' feet.

Schoolboys pose on a cow

Some early schools had no blackboards, no charts, maps, or globes, no special equipment of any kind. Since textbooks were scarce, students brought whatever books they had at home. They arrived at school with an assortment of dictionaries, histories, encyclopedias, and storybooks. Many had copies of *McGuffey's Readers*, popular schoolbooks of the day that were filled with inspiring stories about hard work, honesty, and piety. . . .

Students memorized grammar rules, recited history dates, practiced penmanship and arithmetic tables, read aloud, and competed in spelling bees. Since the pupils might range in age from seven or eight to sixteen or older, they were not separated into grades. The teacher worked with one or two students at a time, while the others studied by themselves. Older students often tutored younger ones.

The youngsters attended classes only as their chores and the weather allowed. On an ordinary school day, many youngsters were up at 4 A.M., milking cows, chopping wood, toting water, and helping fix breakfast before leaving for school. After a full day of classes, they might do other chores by moonlight so as not to miss the next day's classes. . . .

During the 1860s, fewer than half the youngsters in Oregon received any formal schooling. California did not make education compulsory until 1874, when a law was passed requiring children between the ages of eight and fourteen to attend classes during at least two-thirds of the school year.

Many frontier schools found it difficult to find and keep good teachers. The pay was low. A teacher might earn anywhere from ten dollars to thirty-five dollars a month, paid only while school was in session. In some areas, the school year lasted only three or four months.

To help make up for the low pay, teachers often received free room and board. They lived with the families of their pupils, moving from one home to another, staying longest

Few teachers had any formal training.

with families that had the most children in school. Since so many pioneer families lived in small crowded cabins, this system could be tough on the teacher.

Few teachers had any formal training. To receive a teaching certificate, they had only to pass simple examinations in basic subjects. Some schools were glad to accept almost anyone who was willing to take on the job.

At a mining town in Tuolumne County, an unsuccessful gold-seeker named Prentice Mulford applied for a teaching job. He was examined by the school trustees—a doctor, a miner, and a saloonkeeper. . . . Mulford was asked to spell *cat, hat, rat,* and *mat*. When he did this perfectly, the doctor told him, "Young man, you're hired."

Some teachers were barely older than their pupils. . . . Eventually school boards began to adopt rules that no teacher under sixteen years of age could be hired. As late as 1880, however, the United States Census reported that California still had one boy and two girl teachers under sixteen.

Discipline in the classroom was not usually a serious problem for female teachers. In those days, they were respected because they were women. A male teacher, however, might have to earn the respect of his older students. He might find himself confronted with husky teenagers who had driven oxteams across the continent, fought Indians, mined gold, shot grizzlies, and may have just split a cord of wood before galloping off to class that morning.

These older boys had developed the habits of frontiersmen and were not used to the discipline of a classroom. . . . A school superintendent in Santa Clara, California, demanded an end to "the use of tobacco amongst the grown boys, for the smell is quite disgusting to visitors on entering. Moreover, the constant expectoration [spitting] under the desks renders the room quite filthy. . . ."

At Castroville, California, a young teacher named Tom Clay had no problems at all with discipline. The first day of class, he stood up, smiled at the students before him, and placed a six-shooter on his desk. "We're here to learn," he announced. "If anyone misbehaves, there's going to be trouble."

Responding

1. Consider the differences between school in the nineteenth century and your school today. Make a list of those differences you think matter most. Which differences make school a more positive experience today than it was one century ago?

2. Which elements of nineteenth-century education would you like to see carried over in your school? Give reasons for your answers.

Mathematics Connection

No matter what the year, educators try to make school days reflect the life and times of the students. If you think the following items sound strange, imagine the students from 1876 walking into your school tomorrow! What might they think?

Frontier Trivia

What School Was Like in 1876

In the hallway of P.S. 24, these rules are posted for the students:

1 That any students who are late arriving at school shall be kept in during recess.

2 That whispering is prohibited at all times during school hours. Permission to whisper may be granted only if it concerns school matters.

3 That anyone leaving the seat without permission shall remain after school for 25 minutes.

4 That anyone throwing waste paper on the floor or causing any other untidiness shall be made to sweep the floor after school.

5 That anyone uttering profane words or found fighting shall be locked in the closet for one hour.

Here are some problems from The Common School Arithmetic:

At the General Store a man bought 5 yards of muslin at 12 cents a yard; a wooden bucket for 50 cents and three bags of barley at 6 cents a bag. How much does he owe the storekeeper?

If I sell a goat for $8, how many goats will bring me $96?

If a man's salary is $7 per month and he saves 2% of his salary each year, how much will he have saved in five years?

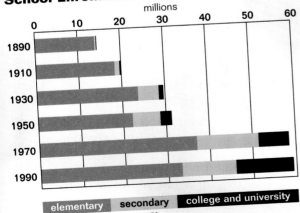

School Enrollment in the United States

millions

	elementary (K-8)	secondary (9-12)	college and university

Source: U.S. Department of Education.

Responding

The mathematics problems on this page reflect the lives of the students who solved them. Write two similar mathematics problems that use contemporary items such as clothing, food, sports equipment, or concert tickets.

677

Reaching for Your Dream

Reading Mini-Lesson

Using Graphic Aids

As you read through a typical day's worth of school assignments, you might come upon a diagram of a plant cell in your science book, a graph of an equation in your math book, a map of physical features in your social studies book, and a pie chart in your health book. These **graphic aids** are used because they help readers understand relationships, proportions, and changes. You can see that "reading" graphic aids can be an important part of completing an assignment.

The **bar graph** shown on page 677 will give you an opportunity to practice your skills. This graph shows how school enrollment in the United States has grown over the last hundred years. Notice that each bar includes three segments that make up the total school enrollment: an elementary (K–8) segment, a secondary (9–12) segment, and a college segment. The furthest extension of the bar shows the total. So, for example, in 1890 there were close to fifteen million students enrolled in school in the United States. Of those, most were enrolled in elementary school. Not very many at all were in high school or college. What conclusions can you draw from this information?

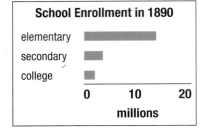

Activity Options

1. If you wanted to examine more closely the proportions of enrollment in one of the years shown, you could make a new graph with a bar for each segment. The bar graph in the margin is for the year 1890. Make one like it for the year 1990.

2. Another form of graphic aid, the **pie chart,** also allows easy visual comparisons. In the margin is a pie chart showing enrollment segments for the year 1910. Make a pie chart for the year 1950.

3. Test your graph interpretation skills by answering these questions about the bar graph on page 677.

   a. What year had the highest enrollment in secondary schools?

   b. Was there a year in which secondary and college enrollment *combined* was greater than elementary school enrollment?

   c. In what year was the difference between elementary and secondary enrollment the *greatest?* In what year was it *smallest?*

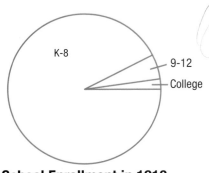

School Enrollment in 1910

Part Two

Decisive Journeys

In each of these stories, someone goes on a journey that leads to a change. However, a change for one person or group will cause changes for others. The journey involving the change will end, but the effects of the changes may continue to be felt for generations to come.

⦿ Multicultural Connection **Group** membership can change over time, as people form new allegiances, create new governments, and travel to new places. In these selections, how do individuals relate to old group ties after they have left those groups behind?

Literature

Washington Irving	**Rip Van Winkle** ◆ play (dramatized by Adele Thane) . .681
Henry Wadsworth Longfellow	**Paul Revere's Ride** ◆ poem 695
Arthur C. Clarke	**"If I Forget Thee, Oh Earth . . ."** ◆ short story . .702
May Swenson	**Orbiter 5 Shows How Earth Looks from the Moon** ◆ poem 707
Donna Rosenberg	**The Creation of Music** ◆ Aztec myth 711
	Writing Mini-Lesson ◆ Preparing Your Presentation Portfolio 716
Paul Yee	**Spirits of the Railway** ◆ American folk tale 718
Li-Young Lee	**I Ask My Mother to Sing** ◆ poem 723

Interdisciplinary Study **Polar Journeys**

Follow Your Dreams by Louise Tolle Huffman ◆ history 726
Six Across Antarctica by Will Steger ◆ history 727
A New Global Outlook by Michael Woods ◆ earth science 729
The North and South Poles ◆ geography 730
　　　Reading Mini-Lesson ◆ Understanding Sequence 732

Writing Workshop **Descriptive Writing**

Exploring Personal Changes 733

Beyond Print **Effective Speaking**

Esmeralda Santiago on Television 739

Before Reading

Rip Van Winkle

by Washington Irving
dramatized by Adele Thane

Washington Irving
1783–1859

Washington Irving was a short story writer, essayist, historian, and biographer. His main contributions were short stories, such as "The Legend of Sleepy Hollow," that contained elements of myth, legend, folklore, and drama. As a youth, he roamed New York City and heard the tales of the Dutch Americans who made up much of the population. He later traveled to the Hudson River Valley where he learned of the local folklore and legends that would later inspire his stories.

Adele Thane
born 1904

Adele Thane has used her experiences as a director, member of various acting companies, and instructor in theaters to help her turn stories into plays for children.

Building Background

The Lazy Husband and the Nagging Wife The stereotype of a nagging wife can be found in many stories and legends. The nagging wife is a negative stereotype, and so is the lazy husband who is often paired with her. The story of Rip Van Winkle shows us both of these stereotypes. Do you think these stereotypes are harmful to relationships between men and women?

Getting into the Play

Writer's Notebook Suppose you fell asleep and, when you woke up, twenty years had passed. How would you look? What would you find changed? In your notebook, list some of the changes you might find in your family, your friends, your neighborhood, and your country.

In Twenty Years, I Would Wake to Find . . .
Family
Friends
Neighborhood
Country

Reading Tip

Picturing the Scene When five or six people are talking, there may be two or three conversations going on. If you were a listener, you probably couldn't catch everything that was said. In a play, however, every line of dialogue is meant to be heard by the audience. If five or six characters are in a scene, only one at a time is speaking aloud to the audience. Since it would seem awkward and unrealistic if five actors stood and waited for the sixth to finish speaking, the other actors engage in business, action that keeps them moving but does not interfere with the dialogue or main action. In Scene 1, Dutcher and Vanderdonk's checker game gives them something to do during others' lines. As you read the play, try to visualize each scene. If you were the director, what business would you have the characters do to make the scene realistic?

RIP VAN WINKLE

WASHINGTON IRVING
DRAMATIZED BY ADELE THANE

CHARACTERS

RIP VAN WINKLE
DAME VAN WINKLE, *his wife*
JUDY, *his daughter*
LUKE GARDENIER ⎫
KATCHEN ⎪
MEENIE, *a girl* ⎬ *Judy's playmates*
JACOB ⎭
NICHOLAS VEDDER, *landlord of the*
　King George Tavern
DERRICK VAN BUMMEL, *the schoolmaster*
PETER VANDERDONK ⎫
BROM DUTCHER ⎬ *men of the village*
OFFSTAGE VOICE
HENDRIK HUDSON
SAILORS, *Hudson's crew*
ORATOR
JONATHAN DOOLITTLE, *proprietor[1] of the*
　Union Hotel
JUDITH GARDENIER, *Judy grown up*
LITTLE RIP, *her son*
TOWNSPEOPLE
CHILDREN

SCENE ONE

Time　*Early autumn, a few years before the Revolutionary War.*

Setting　*A village in the Catskill Mountains.[2] At left, there is an inn with a sign, KING GEORGE TAVERN, and a picture of King George III.[3] A British Union Jack[4] hangs on the flagpole.*

At Rise　NICHOLAS VEDDER, DERRICK VAN BUMMEL, BROM DUTCHER, *and* PETER VANDERDONK *are seated outside the tavern.* VEDDER *is sprawled back in his chair.* DUTCHER *and* VANDERDONK *are at the table, playing a game of checkers.* VAN BUMMEL *is reading aloud from a newspaper. From time to time, a rumble of thunder can be heard in the distance.*

---

1. **proprietor** (prə prī′ə tər), *n.* a person who legally owns something.
2. **Catskill Mountains,** a range of Appalachian Mountains in southeastern New York State.
3. **George III,** 1738–1820, King of England from 1760 to 1820.
4. **Union Jack,** the flag of the United Kingdom.

681

VAN BUMMEL *(reading)*. ". . . and it has been learned that Massachusetts favors a Stamp Act Congress to be held in New York to protest English taxation in the colonies."

DUTCHER *(looking up from his game)*. Good! It's high time we did something about this English taxation.

VANDERDONK. Taxes and more taxes! The English are a pack of rascals with their hands in our pockets.

VAN BUMMEL. There's even a revenue stamp on our newspapers. One of these days the people here in the American colonies will revolt, you mark my words.

VEDDER *(pointing off right as a merry whistle is heard)*. Well, here comes one man who is not troubled by these problems—Rip Van Winkle. (RIP VAN WINKLE *enters, a wooden bucket in one hand, his gun in the other. He props his gun against the tree trunk, then crosses to the group of men.*)

RIP. Good afternoon, Nick Vedder—Brom—Peter. (*To* VAN BUMMEL) Good afternoon, Mr. Schoolmaster. *(They return his greeting. There is a loud rumble of thunder, and* RIP *cocks his head.)* Just listen to that, will you!

DUTCHER. We're probably in for a storm after this heat all day.

VEDDER. Sit down, Rip. Derrick is reading us the news.

VANDERDONK. How about a game of checkers, Rip?

RIP *(hesitating)*. I don't know. Dame Van Winkle sent me for a bucket of water, but—maybe *one* game. *(He sets down the bucket and draws a stool up to the table, as* VANDERDONK *rises.)*

DUTCHER. Your move, Rip. *(Suddenly* DAME VAN WINKLE's *voice is heard from off right.)*

DAME VAN WINKLE *(calling from off right)*. Rip! R-i-p! Rip Van Winkle!

RIP. Oh, my galligaskins![5] It's my wife! *(Before he can get to his feet,* DAME VAN WINKLE *enters with a broom. She looks at men, then crosses directly to* RIP.*)*

DAME VAN WINKLE. So this is how you draw water from the well! Sitting around with a lot of lazy good-for-nothing loafers.[6] *(She tries to hit* RIP *with the broom.)* Pick up that bucket, you dawdling[7] Dutchman, and fill it with water!

RIP *(snatching up the bucket and dodging out of the way)*. Hey there, Dame, I'm not an old rug to be beaten with a broomstick.

DAME VAN WINKLE. Well, you might better be. An old rug is more use than you. At least it would keep our feet warm in winter, which is more than you can do. Little you care that your family is starving and the cow is gone.

RIP. The cow gone?

DAME VAN WINKLE. Aye, the cow is gone, and the cabbage trampled down. When are you going to mend the fence?

RIP. It rained yesterday—

DAME VAN WINKLE. If excuses were shillings, we'd be rich!

RIP. I'll mend the fence—tomorrow.

DAME VAN WINKLE. Tomorrow, tomorrow! All your work is going to be done tomorrow! (RIP *goes to the well as she starts off right, still talking.)* You show enough energy when there's a husking bee[8] or an errand to run for the neighbors, but here at home . . . *(She exits.* RIP *lowers his bucket into the well. The other men rise to go into the tavern.)*

VEDDER. Poor Rip! His wife has the scoldingest tongue in the Hudson Valley.

---

5. **galligaskins** (gal′ə gas′kənz), *n. pl.* a kind of loose trousers or leggings worn in the 1500s and 1600s; here the word is used as a mild exclamation.
6. loafer (lō′fər), *n.* someone who spends time doing nothing; a lazy person.
7. dawdle (dô′dl), *v.* waste time, move slowly.
8. **husking bee,** a gathering of neighbors and friends to husk corn.

VAN BUMMEL. A sharp tongue is the only tool that grows keener with use.

DUTCHER. What would you do, Derrick, if you had a wife like Van Winkle's?

VAN BUMMEL. War could be no worse. I would enlist.

(*They all laugh and exit through the door of the tavern.* RIP *turns to leave, then stops and smiles, as children's voices are heard off left.* JUDY, LUKE, KATCHEN, MEENIE, *holding a kite, and* JACOB, *carrying a bow, run in, left, and shout with delight when they see* RIP.)

CHILDREN (*ad lib*). There he is! There's Rip Van Winkle! (*Etc. They surround him, chattering excitedly.*)

JUDY. Hello, Father, I've brought some of my friends.

RIP. Glad to see you, children.

JACOB (*holding out bow*). Oh, Rip, there's something wrong with my bow. Every time I go to shoot, the cord slips. (RIP *takes the bow, draws his knife from his pocket and cuts the notch deeper for the cord.*)

RIP. There, Jacob, try that, and see if it doesn't work.

JACOB (*pretending to shoot*). Yes, it's all right now.

MEENIE (*holding out kite*). My kite won't stay up, Rip.

RIP (*taking off part of the tail*). Now it will, Meenie—and this breeze is just right for it. (*He hands kite to* MEENIE.)

KATCHEN. My mother wants you to plug up her rain barrel, so she'll be able to wash next week.

RIP. Tell her I'll fix it tonight, Katchen.

LUKE. Rip, will you see what's the matter with my whistle? I made it just the way you showed me, but it isn't any good. (*He hands* RIP *a whistle.*)

RIP (*examining it*). You haven't whittled it right there, Luke. Here, I'll fix it for you. (*He sits on the bench under the tree and begins to whittle.*)

JUDY. Tell us a story, Father!

LUKE. Yes, you tell better stories than anybody in the Catskills.

(*The children all gather around* RIP, *sitting on the ground.*)

RIP. What shall it be about?

JACOB. Indians!

KATCHEN. I like witches and goblins best. (*A long roll of thunder is heard.*)

JUDY. Oh, Father, hear that! Hear the thunder!

RIP. Why, don't you know what that is, Judy? That's Hendrik Hudson and his famous crew, playing ninepins[9] up in the mountains. (*More thunder is heard.*)

MEENIE. Oh, what a noise they make!

RIP. Yes, they are jolly fellows. They sail the wide sea over in their ship, the *Half-Moon,* then every twenty years they come back to the Catskills.

JACOB. What do they do that for?

RIP. Oh, old Hendrik Hudson likes to revisit the country he discovered and keep a watchful eye over his river, the Hudson.

JACOB. I wish I could see Hendrik Hudson and his crew.

RIP. Peter Vanderdonk says his father saw them once in their funny breeches, playing at ninepins up in the hills. (*A loud peal of thunder is heard.*) Listen to their balls rolling! That must be Hendrik Hudson himself, the Flying Dutchman! (DAME VAN WINKLE *enters with broom as* RIP *is speaking.*)

DAME VAN WINKLE. So! Here you are, telling stories without a word of truth in 'em! Oh, *I* could tell a story or two myself—about a shiftless husband who does nothing but whittle and whistle. Whittle and whistle! What a job for a grown man! (*She snatches the whistle from* RIP.)

LUKE (*pleadingly*). It's my whistle! Please don't break it, Dame Van Winkle.

---

9. **ninepins,** game in which nine large wooden pins are set up to be bowled over with a ball.

DAME VAN WINKLE. Take it and begone! *(She gives* LUKE *the whistle and he runs off.)* Judy, you go and ask Dame Vedder for an armful of wood. Your father is too busy spinning yarns to split wood for *our* fire. *(JUDY goes off behind the tavern.)* As for the rest of you, go home if you have any homes, and don't keep hanging around here like stray dogs looking for bones. *(She sweeps the children off the stage with her broom.)* Get along! Begone, all of you! Go home now! *(With arms akimbo, she faces* RIP.*)* Well, what do you have to say for yourself? *(RIP shrugs, shakes his head and says nothing.)* Nothing as usual. *(RIP goes to the tree for his gun.)* What are you getting your gun for? Going off to the mountains, no doubt. Anything to keep you out of the house.

RIP *(good-naturedly).* Well, wife, you have often told me—*my* side of the house is the *out-*side. Where's my dog? Where's Wolf?

DAME VAN WINKLE. Wolf is tied up in the cellar.

RIP. You didn't tie up Wolf?

DAME VAN WINKLE. I certainly did. That dog tracked up my kitchen floor right after I'd finished scrubbing it. Well, if you're going hunting, go, and don't come back until you bring us something for supper. And if you can't bring supper, don't bring yourself.

JUDY *(re-entering from up left, her arms full of logs).* But, Mother, it's going to rain.

DAME VAN WINKLE *(taking the wood).* Pooh! Your father won't get as wet as we will in the house, with the roof leaking and the windows broken. You hurry home now. And bring that bucket of water your father managed to get this far. *(DAME VAN WINKLE starts right, but* JUDY *stays behind with* RIP.*)*

RIP *(calling after his wife).* Wife, turn Wolf loose when you get home. *(DAME VAN WINKLE looks back at him angrily, tosses her head, and exits right.)*

JUDY *(starting to cry as she puts her hand in* RIP'*s).* Father, where will you go if it rains?

RIP. I'll find a place. Don't cry, Judy. Remember your little song? Come, we'll sing it together. *(They sing an appropriate folk song, such as "Rosa, Will We Go Dancing?")*

JUDY *(hugging* RIP*).* Oh, Father, I hope you have wonderful luck. Then Mother won't be so cross.

RIP. I don't blame her for being cross with me sometimes. I guess I don't do much work around here. But I'm going to do better, Judy. I'm going to do all the jobs your mother has been after me about.

DAME VAN WINKLE *(calling from off).* Ju-dee! Ju-dee!

RIP. There's your mother. I'd better be off. Good-bye, Judy dear. *(He walks left, whistling for his dog.)* Come, Wolf! Come, boy! *(A dog's bark is heard off left, as* RIP *turns, waves to* JUDY, *and exits.)*

JUDY *(waving).* Good-bye, Father. *(LUKE enters from right and joins* JUDY *as loud crash of thunder is heard. Startled,* JUDY *clings to* LUKE.*)* Oh, Luke, listen to that thunder!

LUKE. It's only Hendrik Hudson's men playing ninepins. Don't be scared, Judy.

JUDY. I'm not—that is, not very.

DAME VAN WINKLE *(calling from off).* Judy! Ju-dee!

LUKE. You'd better go in or you'll catch it. Your mother is getting awfully free with her broomstick lately. Here, I'll carry your bucket for you. *(He exits right with the bucket of water.* JUDY *lingers behind to look off in direction her father has taken as the thunder gets louder. Then humming softly to herself, she exits right.)*

CURTAIN

All the illustrations of *Rip Van Winkle* are by John Howe. In this one, how has the artist captured Dame Van Winkle's character?

SCENE TWO

Time   *Later the same afternoon.*

Setting   *A forest glade, high in the Catskill Mountains. There is a tree stump at right center, and a large bush at far left. This scene may be played before the curtain.*

At Rise   RIP, *carrying his gun, enters left, dragging his feet wearily. He sinks down on the stump.*

RIP. Whew! That was a climb! All the way up the mountain. How peaceful it is up here. No one to scold me, no one to wave a broomstick. Ah, me! *(He gives a big sigh of contentment.)* I wonder where Wolf is. Wolf! Here, boy! *(He whistles and a dog barks off left.)* That's it, Wolf, sick 'em! I hope we get something this time. We can't go home until we do. *(A loud crash of thunder is heard.)* That thunder sounds much louder up here in the mountains than down in the valley. Maybe it's going to rain after all.

Rip Van Winkle   **685**

▲ The artist must have enjoyed painting Hendrik Hudson and his merry crew! Point out some of the details that make each of these faces different. Which man do you think is Hendrik Hudson?

VOICE *(calling from off, high-pitched, like a bird-call).* Rip Van Winkle! (RIP *looks around wonderingly.)* Rip Van Winkle!

RIP *(rising).* That's my name. Somebody is calling me.

VOICE *(off).* Rip Van Winkle!

RIP. Is it Dame Van Winkle? No—she would never follow me up here. *(Sound of a ship's bell is heard from off right.)* What was that? *(Bell rings again.)* A ship's bell! But how can that be? A ship? Up here in the mountains? *(He gazes off right, in astonishment.)* It *is* a ship! Look at it! Sails all set—a Dutch flag at the masthead. *(Ship's bell is heard again, fainter.)* There, it's gone. I must have imagined it. (1ST SAILOR *with a keg on his back, enters from right and goes to center, as* RIP *watches him in amazement.)* By my galligaskins, what a funny little man! And how strangely he's dressed. Such old-fashioned clothes! (1ST SAILOR *stops at center.* RIP *goes to meet him.)* Hello, old Dutchman. That keg looks heavy. Let me carry it for you. *(He relieves* 1ST SAILOR *of the keg.)* By golly, it *is* heavy! Why did you bring this keg all the way up here to the top of the mountain? And who are you anyhow?

1ST SAILOR (*gruffly*). Don't ask questions. Set it down over there. (*He points left to a spot beside the bush.*)

RIP (*obeying cheerfully*). Anything to oblige. (*There is a commotion off right, and* HENDRIK HUDSON *and his crew enter, capering[10] and shouting. They carry bowling balls and ninepins and a drum.* 2ND SAILOR *has a burlap bag containing drinking mugs thrown over his shoulder.* RIP *turns to* 1ST SAILOR.) Why, bless my soul! Here are a lot of little fellows just like yourself. (*To* SAILORS, *as they gather at center*) Who are you?

SAILORS (*shouting*). Hendrik Hudson and his merry crew!

HUDSON (*stepping forward*). Set up the ninepins, men, and we'll have a game. (*Two or three* SAILORS *set up the ninepins at extreme right.* HUDSON *speaks to the* 1ST SAILOR.) You there, fill up the flagons![11] (2ND SAILOR *opens sack and passes out the mugs.* HUDSON *turns to* RIP.) Now then, Rip Van Winkle, will you drink with us?

RIP. Why, yes, thank you, Captain Hudson. I'm quite thirsty after my long climb up the mountain. (*The mugs are filled from keg.*)

2ND SAILOR (*raising his mug in toast*). To Hendrik Hudson, the *Half-Moon,* and its merry crew!

ALL (*as they raise their mugs*). To Hendrik Hudson, the *Half-Moon,* and its merry crew!

RIP (*lifting his mug*). Well, gentlemen, here's to your good health. May you live long and prosper. (RIP *drinks and smacks his lips.*) Ah! This is the best drink I ever tasted, but it makes me feel very sleepy. (HUDSON *and his men begin to bowl. As they roll the balls, the thunder increases.* RIP *yawns.*) Ho, hum! I can't keep my eyes open. I guess I'll lie down—(*Carrying his gun, he goes behind bush at left, and lies down out of sight.* NOTE: *Unseen by audience,* RIP *may go offstage for necessary costume changes and return in time for his awakening.*)

HUDSON (*to* SAILORS). Now, men, let's stop our game of ninepins, and have a merry dance. Then we'll be off, to return again in twenty years. (*One of the men beats the drum, and* SAILORS *dance. At the end of the dance,* 1ST SAILOR *points to bush where* RIP *is sleeping.*)

1ST SAILOR. Look! Rip Van Winkle is asleep.

HUDSON. Peace be with the poor fellow. He needs to take a good long rest from his nagging wife. Sh-h-h-h! (*He places his finger to his lips and they all go about quietly gathering up the ninepins, balls, mugs, keg, etc., then they tiptoe off the stage, their voices dying away to a whisper. The lights may dim briefly to indicate the passage of twenty years, and recorded music may be played. When the lights come up,* RIP *is heard yawning behind the bush, then he stands up with great difficulty. He limps to center, carrying a rusty gun. His clothes are shabby, and he has a long white beard.*)

RIP (*groaning*). Ouch, my back! It's so stiff. And my legs—just like pokers. My, my, but I'm shaky! I feel as if I'd grown to be an old man overnight. It must be rheumatism coming on. Oh, won't I have a blessed time with Dame Van Winkle if I'm laid up with rheumatism. Well, I'd better get along home to Dame Van Winkle. (*He looks at the gun he is carrying.*) Why, this rusty old thing is not my gun! Somebody has played a trick on me. (*Suddenly recollecting*) It's that Hendrik Hudson and his men! They've stolen my gun, and left this rusty one for me! (*He puts his hand to his head.*) Another scolding in store from the Dame. (*He whistles.*) Wolf! Here, Wolf! Have those scamps stolen my dog, too? He'd never leave me. (*He whistles again.*) Come on, old boy! Maybe he found it too cold and went home to be warmed by his mistress'

---

10. **caper** (kā′pər), *v.* leap or jump about playfully.
11. **flagon** (flag′ən), *n.* a container for liquids.

broomstick. Well, I will follow after and get my hot welcome, too. (*He shoulders the rusty gun and totters off.*)

CURTAIN

SCENE THREE

Time   *Twenty years after Scene 1.*

Setting   *Same as Scene 1, except that the sign above the tavern door reads: UNION HOTEL—PROPRIETOR, JONA-THAN DOOLITTLE. A picture of George Washington has replaced that of King George III. Washington's name is printed below the picture and an American flag flutters on a pole above it.*

At Rise   *An ORATOR is standing on a bench, haranguing a crowd of TOWNSPEOPLE.*

ORATOR. Remember the Boston Tea Party! Remember Bunker Hill! Who saved this country? Who is the father of this country?

TOWNSPEOPLE. George Washington! Washington for President! (*Etc. They sing "Yankee Doodle."*)

> Father and I went down to camp
>   Along with Captain Good'in,
> There we saw the men and boys
>   As thick as hasty puddin'.
>
> Yankee Doodle keep it up,
>   Yankee Doodle Dandy,
> Mind the music and the step
>   And with the girls be handy.

(RIP *enters with a troop of children, who laugh and jeer at him.*)

CHILDREN (*ad lib*). Look at him! He looks like a scarecrow! Where did you come from, Daddy Long-legs? Where did you get that gun? (*Etc.* RIP *and* CHILDREN *go to center.* 1ST CHILD *stands in front of* RIP *and crouches down, pulling on an imaginary beard.*)

1ST CHILD. Billy goat, billy goat! (CHILDREN *begin stroking imaginary beards until* RIP *does the same. He is amazed to find he has a beard.*)

RIP. By my galligaskins, what's this?

2ND CHILD. It's a beard, old Father Time. Didn't you know you had a beard?

RIP. But I didn't have one last night. (CHILDREN *laugh and mock him.*)

ORATOR (*to* RIP). What do you mean by coming here at election time with a gun on your shoulder and a mob at your heels? Do you want to cause a riot?

RIP. Oh, no, sir! I am a quiet man and a loyal subject of King George!

CHILDREN and TOWNSPEOPLE (*shouting, ad lib*). A spy! Away with him! Lock him up. (*Etc.*)

JONATHAN DOOLITTLE (*stepping forward from crowd*). Hold on a minute! We must get to the bottom of this. (*To* RIP) Aren't you a supporter of Washington for President?

RIP (*puzzled*). Eh? Supporter of Washington? (*Shaking his head, wholly bewildered*) I don't understand. I mean no harm. I only want to find my friends. They were here at the tavern yesterday.

DOOLITTLE. Who are these friends of yours? Name them.

RIP (*hesitantly*). Well, one is the landlord—

DOOLITTLE. *I* am the landlord of this hotel— Jonathan Doolittle.

RIP. Why, what happened to Nicholas Vedder?

1ST WOMAN (*pushing her way out of the crowd*). Nicholas Vedder? Why, he's dead and gone these eighteen years.

RIP. No, no, that's impossible! Where's Brom Dutcher? And the schoolmaster, Van Bummel—?

1ST MAN. Brom Dutcher was killed in the war at Stony Point.

2ND MAN. And Van Bummel went off to the war, too. He became a great general, and now he's in Congress.

▲ Rip awakens. What details show how much time has passed?

RIP. War? What war?

2ND MAN. Why, the war we fought against England, and won, of course.

RIP. I don't understand. Am I dreaming? Congress? Generals? What's happened to me?

DOOLITTLE *(impatiently).* Now, we've had enough of this nonsense. Who are you, anyway? What is your name?

RIP *(utterly confused).* I don't know. I mean, I was Rip Van Winkle yesterday, but today—

DOOLITTLE. Don't try to make sport of us, my man!

RIP. Oh, indeed, I'm not, sir. I was myself last night, but I fell asleep on the mountain, and Hendrik Hudson and his crew changed my gun, and everything's changed, and I'm changed, and I can't tell what my name is, or who I am! (TOWNS-PEOPLE *exchange significant[12] glances, nod knowingly, and tap their foreheads.*)

2ND MAN *(shaking his head).* Hendrik Hudson, he says! Poor chap. He's mad. Let's leave him alone.

---

12. **significant** (sig nif′ə kənt), *adj.* full of meaning.

Rip Van Winkle **689**

Rip Van Winkle returns to town after his twenty-year sleep. Review all the art for this play. Why do you think the artist chose these scenes to illustrate? Is there any other scene you would have liked to see illustrated?

RIP *(in great distress).* Isn't there anybody here who knows who I am?

2ND WOMAN *(soothingly).* Why, you're just yourself, old man. Who else do you think you could be? (JUDITH GARDENIER *enters from left, leading* LITTLE RIP *by the hand. He hangs back, whimpering.*)

JUDITH. Hush, Rip! The old man won't hurt you.

RIP *(turning in surprise).* Rip? Who said Rip?

JUDITH. Why, I did. I was just telling my little boy not to be frightened.

RIP *(scanning her face).* And what is your name, my good woman?

JUDITH. My name is Judith, sir.

RIP. Judith? Did you say Judith? *(In great excitement)* And your father—what was his name?

JUDITH. Ah, poor man, his name was Rip Van Winkle. It's twenty years since he went away from home. We never heard of him again.

RIP *(staggered).* Twenty years!

JUDITH. Yes, it must be all of that. His dog

came back without him. I was a little girl then.

RIP. And your mother—where is she?

JUDITH. My mother is dead, sir.

RIP (sighing). Ah, but that woman had a tongue! Well, peace be with her soul. Did you love your father, Judith?

JUDITH. With all my heart. All the children in the village loved him, too.

RIP. Then look at me. Look closely, my dear Judy. I am your father.

JUDITH (incredulously). You? My father?

RIP. We used to sing a little song together, remember? (He sings a few lines from the folksong sung in Scene One.)

JUDITH (slowly). Yes, my father used to sing that song with me, but many people know it.

RIP. Do you remember, Judy, that I told you the story of how Hendrik Hudson and his crew played ninepins in the mountains just before I went off hunting with Wolf?

JUDITH (excitedly). Yes! And Wolf was our dog's name! Oh, Father, it's really you!

RIP (taking her in his arms). Yes, my little Judy—young Rip Van Winkle once, old Rip Van Winkle now. (TOWNSPEOPLE talk excitedly among themselves, as they watch RIP and JUDITH.)

JUDITH. Dearest Father, come home with me. Luke and I will take good care of you.

RIP. Luke?

JUDITH. Luke Gardenier, my old playmate. You used to make whistles for him and take him fishing. We were married when he came back from the war.

RIP. Ah, the war. There is so much I have to catch up with.

JUDITH. You will have plenty of time to do that—and you must tell us what happened to you.

RIP. Maybe you won't believe what happened to me, Judy—it was all so strange. (RIP reaches out a hand to LITTLE RIP, who shyly takes it, and they start off left, JUDITH following. A loud clap of thunder stops them. RIP turns front and shakes his fist toward the mountains.) Oh, no you don't, Hendrik Hudson! You don't get me back up there again. (There is answering roll of thunder that sounds like a deep rumble of laughter as the curtain falls.)

THE END

After Reading

Making Connections

1. Do you sympathize more with Rip or with his wife? Explain your reasons.

2. In your view, what is this story really about: a marriage? a long nap? the Revolution? ghosts? something else? Support your answer.

3. Find a quote that best reflects Rip's **character.** Write it down and explain your choice.

4. 👣 How has **group** identity changed in Rip's town in the twenty years he's been gone? How do the townspeople show that they have changed their loyalties?

5. Do you consider this story to have a happy ending?

6. Why do you think people enjoy fantasies about waking up after a long sleep?

Literary Focus: Developing Plot Through Dialogue

When you read a play, there is no narrator to tell you the action. You must determine everything about the **plot** from the **dialogue** and the **stage directions.** When they speak, characters will often comment on what they are doing and why they are doing it. Review the three scenes of *Rip Van Winkle* and try to find two bits of dialogue for each scene that reveal something important about the action of the play. For each case, write the lines and what they show you about the plot. Use a chart similar to the one started below.

Dialogue	What It Shows About Plot
DAME VAN WINKLE. Well, if you're going hunting, go, and don't come back until you bring us something for supper.	Rip is going out hunting.

Vocabulary Study

caper
significant
proprietor
loafer
dawdle

Write the word from the list at the left that belongs in each group below.

1. frolic, run, ____
2. idler, slacker, ____
3. serious, important, ____
4. wander, stroll, ____
5. owner, landlord, ____

Expressing Your Ideas

Writing Choices

Ours and Theirs Review the play and take notes comparing Rip's attitude toward chores his wife wants him to do with his attitude toward jobs children and neighbors ask him to do. Then write a **persuasive essay** in which Rip explains to his daughter that he really wasn't lazy.

R.I.P. Rip Consider this play from Dame Van Winkle's point of view. Review the play carefully to see what events she would know about. Then write the **eulogy,** or funeral speech, she might say at a service held for Rip seven years after his disappearance.

Quite a Nap You Had There Research the topic of suspended animation to discover more about long-term "naps." Look for information in an encyclopedia, other library resources, or online services. Present your findings in a **research report.**

Other Options

Before and After Make two **sketches** of Rip Van Winkle. Base your first sketch on descriptions you find in the opening scene. Base the second one on his appearance after the sleep, which you will find at the end of Scene 2 and in Scene 3.

The Sound of Symbols You've seen how a character can be associated with an object or symbol: Mike's moustache, Grandpa's medicine bag, Anne's diary. For this play, list five characters and **draw** objects or symbols you associate with each. Explain your reasons for choosing each symbol.

How Many Pins, Hendrik? How do you play ninepins? What does one of the pins look like? Find out by using library resources and/or online services and **demonstrate** the game to the class with a sketch or model.

Before Reading

Paul Revere's Ride

by Henry Wadsworth Longfellow

Henry Wadsworth Longfellow
1807–1882

During his lifetime, Henry Wadsworth Longfellow was probably the best-loved of all American poets. Although he is remembered for his many long story poems such as *Evangeline, The Courtship of Miles Standish,* and *Hiawatha,* he is probably best known for "Paul Revere's Ride." It etched in the minds of Americans a legend from the beginning of the American Revolution.

Longfellow was born in Portland, Maine; was educated at Bowdoin College and abroad; and taught literature and language both at Bowdoin and at Harvard. His poems about Paul Revere, Miles Standish, John and Priscilla Alden, and Hiawatha were once known to every schoolchild.

Building Background

A Legendary Ride Paul Revere left Boston on horseback on April 16, 1775, heading for Lexington and Concord, to warn the colonists that the British planned to destroy their military supplies. He was captured before he got to Concord, but another patriot alerted the Concord colonists, and Revere warned more people on April 18. When the British arrived in Lexington on April 19, they found the minutemen waiting. Shots were exchanged, and the British marched on to Concord. At the bridge into town, minutemen fired on the soldiers, turning them back. The Battle of Lexington and Concord is considered to be the opening of the Revolutionary War.

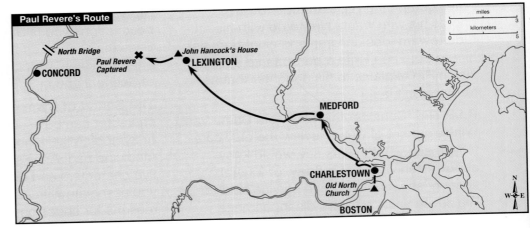

Getting into the Poem

Discussion Do you think it is important for Americans to have "founding heroes"—men and women who helped found our country—to remember in songs, poems, and stories? Would you teach these stories to younger children? Why or why not?

Reading Tip

Narrative Poetry Poems that tell a story are called **narrative poems.** They have some of the traditional elements that short stories do—plot, characters, and setting. In "Paul Revere's Ride," note the main events of the plot and look for details of the setting.

Paul Revere's Ride

A statue of Paul Revere stands before the Old North Church in Boston. Why do you think Revere has become a hero of American history?

Henry Wadsworth Longfellow

In the year 1775, the fervor leading to the Revolutionary War, the war in which the American colonists won independence from Great Britain, centered in and around Boston. Below are some place names to help you read the poem.

Middlesex, *a county in northeastern Massachusetts*
Charlestown, *once a city but now part of Boston*
Mystic, *a river that flows into the Boston harbor*
Medford, *a city near Boston*
Lexington, Concord, *towns near Boston where the first and second battles of the Revolutionary War took place on April 19, 1775*

Listen my children, and you shall hear
Of the midnight ride of Paul Revere,
On the eighteenth of April, in Seventy-five;
Hardly a man is now alive
5 Who remembers that famous day and year.

He said to his friend, "If the British march
By land or sea from the town tonight,
Hang a lantern aloft[1] in the belfry arch
Of the North Church tower as a signal light,—
10 One, if by land, and two, if by sea;
And I on the opposite shore will be,
Ready to ride and spread the alarm

---

1. **aloft** (ə lôft′), *adv.* far above the ground; high up.

Through every Middlesex village and farm,
For the country folk to be up and to arm."

15   Then he said, "Good night!" and with muffled oar
Silently rowed to the Charlestown shore,
Just as the moon rose over the bay,
Where swinging wide at her moorings lay
The *Somerset,* British man-of-war;
20   A phantom ship, with each mast and spar
Across the moon like a prison bar,
And a huge black hulk, that was magnified
By its own reflection in the tide.

Meanwhile, his friend, through alley and street,
25   Wanders and watches with eager ears,
Till in the silence around him he hears
The muster[2] of men at the barrack door,
The sound of arms, and the tramp of feet,
And the measured tread of the grenadiers,[3]
30   Marching down to their boats on the shore.

Then he climbed the tower of the Old North Church,
By the wooden stairs, with stealthy tread,
To the belfry-chamber overhead,
And startled the pigeons from their perch
35   On the somber[4] rafters, that round him made
Masses and moving shapes of shade,—
By the trembling ladder, steep and tall,
To the highest window in the wall,
Where he paused to listen and look down
40   A moment on the roofs of the town,
And the moonlight flowing over all.

Beneath, in the churchyard, lay the dead,
In their night-encampment on the hill,
Wrapped in silence so deep and still
45   That he could hear, like a sentinel's tread,
The watchful night wind, as it went
Creeping along from tent to tent,
And seeming to whisper, "All is well!"
A moment only he feels the spell
50   Of the place and the hour, and the secret dread

---

2. muster (mus′tər), *n.* assembly, especially of troops.
3. **grenadiers** (gren′ə dirz′), Grenadier Guards, a unit of British infantry.
4. somber (som′bər), *adj.* dark, gloomy.

Of the lonely belfry and the dead;
For suddenly all his thoughts are bent
On a shadowy something far away,
Where the river widens to meet the bay,—
55 A line of black that bends and floats
On the rising tide, like a bridge of boats.

Meanwhile, impatient to mount and ride,
Booted and spurred, with a heavy stride
On the opposite shore walked Paul Revere.
60 Now he patted his horse's side,
Now gazed at the landscape far and near,
Then, impetuous,[5] stamped the earth,
And turned and tightened his saddle-girth;
But mostly he watched with eager search
65 The belfry-tower of the Old North Church,
As it rose above the graves on the hill,
Lonely and spectral and somber and still.
And lo! as he looks, on the belfry's height
A glimmer, and then a gleam of light!
70 He springs to the saddle, the bridle he turns,
But lingers and gazes, till full on his sight
A second lamp in the belfry burns!

A hurry of hoofs in a village street,
A shape in the moonlight, a bulk in the dark,
75 And beneath, from the pebbles, in passing, a spark
Struck out by a steed flying fearless and fleet:
That was all! And yet, through the gloom and the light,
The fate of a nation was riding that night;
And the spark struck out by that steed, in his flight,
80 Kindled the land into flame with its heat.

He has left the village and mounted the steep,
And beneath him, tranquil and broad and deep,
Is the Mystic, meeting the ocean tides;
And under the alders that skirt its edge,
85 Now soft on the sand, now loud on the ledge,
Is heard the tramp of his steed as he rides.

It was twelve by the village clock,
When he crossed the bridge into Medford town.
He heard the crowing of the cock,
90 And the barking of the farmer's dog,

---

5. **impetuous** (im pech′ü əs), *adj.* acting with sudden or rash energy.

And felt the damp of the river fog,
That rises after the sun goes down.

It was one by the village clock,
When he galloped into Lexington.
95 He saw the gilded[6] weathercock
Swim in the moonlight as he passed,
And the meeting-house windows, blank and bare,
Gaze at him with a spectral glare,
As if they already stood aghast
100 At the bloody work they would look upon.

It was two by the village clock,
When he came to the bridge in Concord town.
He heard the bleating of the flock,
And the twitter of birds among the trees,
105 And felt the breath of the morning breeze
Blowing over the meadows brown.
And one was safe and asleep in his bed
Who at the bridge would be first to fall,
Who that day would be lying dead,
110 Pierced by a British musket-ball.

You know the rest. In the books you have read,
How the British Regulars fired and fled,—
How the farmers gave them ball for ball,
From behind each fence and farmyard wall,
115 Chasing the redcoats down the lane,
Then crossing the fields to emerge again
Under the trees at the turn of the road,
And only pausing to fire and load.

So through the night rode Paul Revere;
120 And so through the night went his cry of alarm
To every Middlesex village and farm,—
A cry of defiance and not of fear,
A voice in the darkness, a knock at the door,
And a word that shall echo forevermore!
125 For, borne on the night wind of the Past,
Through all our history, to the last,
In the hour of darkness and peril and need,
The people will waken and listen to hear
The hurrying hoofbeats of that steed,
130 And the midnight message of Paul Revere.

---

6. **gilded** (gild′ed), *adj.* covered with gold.

After Reading

Making Connections

1. Does this poem about a past event seem relevant to you? Why or why not?

2. Who is better **characterized,** Paul or his friend in the church tower? What do we learn about each?

3. What elements of the poem create the **mood** surrounding the belfry?

4. Find an example of **irony** in the poem.

5. This poem is part of a group of selections on the **theme** of "Decisive Journeys." What does the poem say is decisive about Paul Revere's ride?

6. ☝ To the victors belong the spoils: the **group** that wins gets to tell the story. In what ways is this clearly a story told by the victors—the winners of the war?

Literary Focus: Rhythm and Rhyme

A good poem read aloud is like a song. Poets who follow the traditional forms use patterns of stressed and unstressed syllables to create the **rhythm** that gives poetry a musical quality. Read the following lines from "Paul Revere's Ride" aloud. The syllables and words that are stressed are underlined. Notice how the pattern of rhythm also emphasizes the important words.

> <u>Lis</u>ten my <u>chil</u>dren, and <u>you</u> shall <u>hear</u>
>
> Of the <u>mid</u>night <u>ride</u> of <u>Paul</u> Re<u>vere</u>,
>
> On the <u>eigh</u>teenth of <u>A</u>pril, in <u>Sev</u>enty-<u>five</u>;
>
> <u>Hard</u>ly a <u>man</u> is <u>now</u> a<u>live</u>
>
> Who re<u>mem</u>bers that <u>fam</u>ous <u>day</u> and <u>year</u>.

Traditional poems are written in **stanzas,** which are groups of lines set off visually from the other lines in a poem. The example above is a five-line stanza.

Poems considered to be traditional generally have **rhyme,** a repetition of syllable sounds at regular intervals. In the lines above, *hear, Revere,* and *year* rhyme. What other rhyme do you notice in the stanza?

Review the poem as if you were preparing to read it aloud. Note the four-beat rhythm of lines, and also pay attention to the rhyme—which lines rhyme with each other?

Vocabulary Study

somber
aloft
impetuous
muster
gilded

For each item below, connect the two words given by writing a sentence that includes them both. For example, you could connect *impetuous* and *aloft* by writing, "The impetuous pilot rushed to get his plane aloft."

1. Use *somber* and *aloft* in a sentence.
2. Use *impetuous* and *gilded* in a sentence.
3. Use *muster* and *somber* in a sentence.
4. Use *aloft* and *gilded* in a sentence.
5. Use *impetuous* and *muster* in a sentence.

Expressing Your Ideas

Writing Choices

Say It in Prose "Paul Revere's Ride" is a poem that tells a story. Write a **summary** of the story told in the poem. Before you begin, make notes to answer the questions *who, what, when, where, how,* and *why.* Then retell the story in your own words. You probably will want to reread the poem to make sure your summary is accurate before writing the final draft.

Just the Facts Longfellow twisted the truth a bit in writing his poem, in order to tell a good story. Find out what *really* happened on Paul Revere's ride. Then prepare a **chart** that compares the events as told in the poem with the real events.

Paul! Paul! Come Here This Minute! There has been a mix-up. Dame Van Winkle is now married to Paul Revere. On the afternoon of April 18, 1775, they talk about his upcoming ride and all the work he has not finished. Write a **dialogue** that shows the different attitudes these two characters would have toward the midnight ride.

Other Options

Listen, My Children Reread the poem and choose your favorite stanza to memorize. Practice reading your lines aloud, emphasizing certain syllables and words to show your **interpretation** of the rhythm and mood of the stanza. Repeat the lines until you know them from memory. Present your interpretation of the poem to your class and compare it with the way others interpret the poem.

Look, My Children, and You Shall See . . . Make a **cartoon** of the poem by dividing it into scenes and drawing a picture for each scene. Begin by reviewing the poem to see how many actions you need to present. Then draw a sketch for each scene to accompany the matching lines from the poem.

As I Climbed the Ladder . . . Work with a friend to prepare a talk show **interview** with the friend in the belfry who gave the signal to Paul Revere. Begin by reviewing the poem for details of the friend's experiences. Then brainstorm the questions that might be asked about such an experience and then conduct the interview for your classmates.

Before Reading

"If I Forget Thee, Oh Earth . . ."

by Arthur C. Clarke

Arthur C. Clarke
born 1917

The British author Arthur C. Clarke first discovered science fiction at the age of twelve when he began reading the pulp magazine *Amazing Stories.* He instantly became addicted to these adventurous tales and began writing short stories for a school magazine. Forced to leave school due to poverty, Clarke worked as an auditor for a time and then enlisted in the Royal Air Force. After World War II, he earned a college degree in physics and mathematics and soon became a full-time writer.

Clarke has won many awards for his writing, including the prestigious Hugo Award and Nebula Award for his science fiction. His best-known work is *2001: A Space Odyssey,* on which he collaborated with movie director Stanley Kubrick.

Building Background

Could We Live on the Moon? The moon is a silent, barren place. It offers little for humans, because there is no air to breathe, no water to drink, and no food to eat. The temperature conditions are not good for human life either. The days are fiercely hot and the nights are bitterly cold. The moon has no atmosphere because its gravity is too weak. Therefore, the moon has no clouds and no rain. There are craters covering the face of the moon, many of them several miles wide. Living on this globe would be emptier and more devoid of life than living in the middle of a desert.

Getting into the Story

Discussion Given the information above about conditions on the moon, what would humans have to do in order to live there indefinitely? In small groups, brainstorm ideas for ways to build a city on the moon. What supplies would be needed? How would humans get water and food? How would they breathe? How would they protect themselves from heat and cold? Your groups might want to sketch or diagram your best ideas.

Reading Tip

Concrete Poems Poets pay careful attention to how their poems sound. Rhythm and rhyme are important elements of the sound pattern a poem will make. Stanzas and line breaks are also important because they help determine how a poem will be read and what will be emphasized. In some poems, the shape or visual appearance will also be important. Such poems, called **concrete poems,** rely in part on their appearance. The poem at the end of this story is an example. Before you read the poem, look at it. What does the shape of the poem suggest to you?

Arthur C. Clarke

"If I Forget Thee, Oh Earth . . ."

When Marvin was ten years old, his father took him through the long, echoing corridors that led up through Administration and Power, until at last they came to the uppermost levels of all and were among the swiftly growing vegetation of the Farmlands. Marvin liked it here: it was fun watching the great, slender plants creeping with almost visible eagerness toward the sunlight as it filtered down through the plastic domes to meet them. The smell of life was everywhere, awakening inexpressible longings in his heart: no longer was he breathing the dry, cool air of the residential levels, purged[1] of all smells but the faint tang of ozone. He wished he could stay here for a little while, but Father would not let him. They went onward until they had reached the entrance to the Observatory, which he had never visited: but they did not stop, and Marvin knew with a sense of rising excitement that there could be only one goal left. For the first time in his life, he was going Outside.

There were a dozen of the surface vehicles, with their wide balloon tires and pressurized cabins, in the great servicing chamber. His father must have been expected, for they were led at once to the little scout car waiting by the huge circular door of the airlock. Tense with expectancy, Marvin settled himself down in the cramped cabin while his father started the motor and checked the controls. The inner door of the lock slid open and then closed behind them: he heard the roar of the great air pumps fade slowly away as the pressure dropped to zero. Then the "Vacuum" sign flashed on, the outer door parted, and before Marvin lay the land which he had never yet entered.

---

1. **purge** (pėrj), *v.* clean or free of an undesired thing or impurity.

▲ *Future Farming* is by Carol Gillot. What does the artist seem to be predicting about the future of farming?

He had seen it in photographs, of course: he had watched it imaged on television screens a hundred times. But now it was lying all around him, burning beneath the fierce sun that crawled so slowly across the jet-black sky. He stared into the west, away from the blinding splendor of the sun—and there were the stars, as he had been told but had never quite believed. He gazed at them for a long time, marveling that anything could be so bright and yet so tiny. They were intense unscintillating points, and suddenly he remembered a rhyme he had once read in one of his father's books:

> Twinkle, twinkle, little
> star.
> How I wonder what
> you are.

Well, *he* knew what the stars were. Whoever asked that question must have been very stupid. And what did they mean by "twinkle"? You could see at a glance that all the stars shone with the same steady, unwavering light. He abandoned the puzzle and turned his attention to the landscape around him.

They were racing across a level plain at almost a hundred miles an hour, the great balloon tires sending up little spurts of dust behind them. There was no sign of the Colony: in the few minutes while he had been gazing at the stars, its domes and radio towers had fallen below the horizon. Yet there were other indications of man's presence, for about a mile ahead Marvin could see the curiously shaped structures clustering round the head of a mine. Now and then a puff of vapor would emerge from a squat smokestack and would instantly disperse.

They were past the mine in a moment: Father was driving with a reckless and exhilarating skill as if—it was a strange thought to come into a child's mind—he were trying to escape from something. In a few minutes they had reached the edge of the plateau on which the Colony had been built. The ground fell sharply away beneath them in a dizzying slope whose lower stretches were lost in shadow. Ahead, as far as the eye could reach, was a jumbled wasteland of craters, mountain ranges, and ravines. The crests of the mountains, catching the low sun, burned like islands of fire in a sea of darkness: and above them the stars still shone as steadfastly as ever.

There could be no way forward—yet there was. Marvin clenched his fists as the car edged over the slope and started the long descent. Then he saw the barely visible track leading down the mountainside, and relaxed a little. Other men, it seemed, had gone this way before.

Night fell with a shocking abruptness as they crossed the shadow line and the sun dropped below the crest of the plateau. The twin searchlights sprang into life, casting blue-white bands on the rocks ahead, so that there was scarcely need to check their speed. For hours they drove through valleys and past the foot of mountains whose peaks seemed to comb the stars, and sometimes they emerged for a moment into the sunlight as they climbed over higher ground.

And now on the right was a wrinkled, dusty plain, and on the left, its ramparts and terraces rising mile after mile into the sky, was a wall of mountains that marched into the distance until its peaks sank from sight below the rim of the world. There was no sign that men had ever explored this land, but once they passed the skeleton of a crashed rocket, and beside it a stone cairn[2] surmounted by a metal cross.

CLARIFY: What do you think the crashed rocket and cairn indicate?

It seemed to Marvin that the mountains stretched on forever: but at last, many hours later, the range ended in a towering, precipitous[3] headland that rose steeply from a cluster of little hills. They drove down into a shallow valley that curved in a great arc toward the far side of the mountains: and as they did so, Marvin slowly realized that something very strange was happening in the land ahead.

The sun was now low behind the hills on the right: the valley before them should be in total darkness. Yet it was awash with a cold white radiance that came spilling over the crags beneath which they were driving. Then, suddenly, they were out in the open plain, and the source of the light lay before them in all its glory.

It was very quiet in the little cabin now that the motors had stopped. The only sound was the faint whisper of the oxygen feed and an occasional metallic crepitation as the outer walls of the vehicle radiated away their heat. For no warmth at all came from the great silver crescent that floated low above the far horizon and flooded all this land with pearly light. It was so brilliant that minutes passed before Marvin could accept its challenge and look steadfastly into its glare, but at last he could discern[4] the outlines of continents, the hazy border of the atmosphere, and the white islands of cloud. And even at this distance, he could see the glitter of sunlight on the polar ice.

It was beautiful, and it called to his heart across the abyss of space. There in that shining crescent were all the wonders that he had never known—the hues of sunset skies, the moaning of the sea on pebbled shores, the patter of falling rain, the unhurried benison[5] of snow. These and a thousand others should have been his rightful heritage,[6] but he knew them only from the books and ancient records, and the thought filled him with the anguish of exile.

Why could they not return? It seemed so peaceful beneath those lines of marching cloud. Then Marvin, his eyes no longer blinded by the glare, saw that the portion of the disk that should have been in darkness was gleaming faintly with an evil phosphorescence: and he remembered. He was looking upon the funeral pyre of a world—upon the radioactive aftermath of Armageddon.[7] Across a quarter of a million miles of space, the glow of dying atoms was still visible, a perennial[8] reminder of the ruinous past. It would be centuries yet

2. **cairn** (kern, karn), pile of stones heaped up as a memorial, tomb, or landmark.
3. precipitous (pri sip'ə təs), *adj.* very steep.
4. discern (də zėrn', də sėrn'), *v.* see clearly.
5. **benison** (ben'ə zən, ben'ə sən), a blessing.
6. heritage (her'ə tij), *n.* what is handed down from one generation to the next.
7. **Armageddon** (är'mə ged'n), *n.* **1** (in the Bible) the great and final conflict between the forces of good and evil at the end of the world. **2** any great and final conflict.
8. perennial (pə ren'ē əl), *adj.* lasting for a very long time; enduring.

before that deadly glow died from the rocks and life could return again to fill that silent, empty world.

And now Father began to speak, telling Marvin the story which until this moment had meant no more to him than the fairy tales he had once been told. There were many things he could not understand: it was impossible for him to picture the glowing, multicolored pattern of life on the planet he had never seen. Nor could he comprehend the forces that had destroyed it in the end, leaving the Colony, preserved by its isolation, as the sole survivor. Yet he could share the agony of those final days, when the Colony had learned at last that never again would the supply ships come flaming down through the stars with gifts from home. One by one the radio stations had ceased to call: on the shadowed globe the lights of the cities had dimmed and died, and they were alone at last, as no men had ever been alone before, carrying in their hands the future of the race.

Then had followed the years of despair, and the long-drawn battle for survival in this fierce and hostile world. That battle had been won, though barely: this little oasis of life was safe against the worst that Nature could do. But unless there was a goal, a future toward which it could work, the Colony would lose the will to live, and neither machines nor skill nor science could save it then.

EVALUATE: Do you think it is true that people need a goal to work toward?

So, at last, Marvin understood the purpose of this pilgrimage. He would never walk beside the rivers of that lost and legendary world, or listen to the thunder raging above its softly rounded hills. Yet one day—how far ahead?—his children's children would return to claim their heritage. The winds and the rains would scour the poisons from the burning lands and carry them to the sea, and in the depths of the sea they would waste their venom until they could harm no living things. Then the great ships that were still waiting here on the silent, dusty plains could lift once more into space, along the road that led to home.

That was the dream: and one day, Marvin knew with a sudden flash of insight, he would pass it on to his own son, here at this same spot with the mountains behind him and the silver light from the sky streaming into his face.

He did not look back as they began the homeward journey. He could not bear to see the cold glory of the crescent Earth fade from the rocks around him, as he went to rejoin his people in their long exile.

Another Voice

May Swenson

ORBITER 5 SHOWS
HOW EARTH LOOKS FROM THE MOON

There's a woman in the earth, sitting on
her heels. You see her from the back, in three-
quarter profile. She has a flowing pigtail. She's
holding something — some holy jug. Her left arm is thinner,
in her right hand. She's the Indian Ocean. Asia is
in a gesture like a dancer. Her pigtail points to Europe
light swirling up out of her vessel. Her pigtail points to Europe
and her dancer's arm is the Suez Canal. She is a woman
in a square kimono, bare feet tucked beneath the tip of Africa. Her tail of long hair is
bare feet tucked beneath the tip of Africa. Her tail of long hair is
the Arabian Peninsula.

A woman in the earth.

A man in the moon.

This NASA photograph shows Earth from the surface of the moon. What aspects of the Earth from this perspective might look like a woman? ➤

After Reading

Making Connections

1. What did you think was the most memorable image or scene in this story?

2. Do you think the ending of this story is pessimistic or optimistic?

3. What is the effect of the narrator *not* telling you where you are?

4. What was the purpose of the journey Marvin was taken on? How was it decisive in his life?

5. How is the perspective in the poem "Orbiter 5 Shows How Earth Looks from the Moon" the same as the perspective in the story? How is it different from our usual perspective?

6. **Science fiction** often shows science as the hero, the villain, or as both. Do you think science and technology will save us or destroy us?

7. 👣 Marvin's father takes him on a journey to remind him of his "roots." Can you think of any ethnic or national **groups** that may have experienced a situation similar to that of the Colony in this story?

Literary Focus: Imagery

Imagery is the use of words to create sensations that usually have to be experienced: sights, sounds, tastes, smells, and touches. In a poem or story, imagery is an effective way to contrast two settings. Concentrate on visual imagery. Review the story and contrast the visual imagery of the Colony and the moon on which it exists with the imagery of Earth as Marvin sees it and his father describes it. List three descriptions of each setting to show how they are contrasted. Here's an example:

Moon Colony	Earth
a fierce sun in a jet-black sky	the hues of sunset skies

Vocabulary Study

**purge
precipitous
discern
heritage
perennial**

Find the unrelated word in each group below.

1. **a.** eliminate   **b.** clean   **c.** purge   **d.** soil
2. **a.** heritage   **b.** heirloom   **c.** heroism   **d.** inheritance
3. **a.** notice   **b.** ignore   **c.** determine   **d.** discern
4. **a.** flat   **b.** steep   **c.** precipitous   **d.** sheer
5. **a.** perennial   **b.** transitory   **c.** eternal   **d.** enduring

Expressing Your Ideas

Writing Choices

Reflections on Earth In Unit 5, you saw how Anne Frank used a diary to record her thoughts and reflections about her confinement, a kind of exile. Marvin is also in exile. Write a **diary entry** in which he reflects on his feelings about his exile from Earth. What are his thoughts about the future?

Life in Space Working in a group, use library and/or online resources to research living conditions in space for a **report** to your class. Be sure to explain extremes of temperature, lack of oxygen, and other features of the space environment that humans must be protected from.

Marvin to Marvin, Jr. The story comes to a close, but the conflict doesn't really end. Write a **continuation** of the story to show what happens long in the future, when the exiles make their first effort to return to their planet. Keep the same point of view and style as the original story.

Other Options

The Colony Construct a **model** (or make a sketch) of the setting of this story. Show the features of the Colony the story describes. You might include a part to show Earth as it appears to the exiles.

Earth Images, from Afar Make a **comparison chart** that shows the images of Earth found in the two selections, "If I Forget Thee, Oh Earth. . ." and "Orbiter 5 Shows How Earth Looks from the Moon."

Time Capsule Travel back in time to the point when the battle raged on Earth. You are a teacher of history. You know that Earth will be uninhabitable for some time to come. You select four items to be buried in a **time capsule** to be preserved for the return of future generations. Tell the class what items you would select and why you think they should be preserved.

The Creation of Music

retold by Donna Rosenberg

Donna Rosenberg
born 1934

Donna Rosenberg has taught mythology at all levels from kindergarten to adult. She became interested in mythology by looking at the stars. As she was teaching a youth group about the constellations, she began to research the myths behind the constellations, starting with the story of Orion, the Hunter. She began by reading myths aloud to her students, and then went on to create her own retellings, always trying to preserve the spirit of the original myth.

What do people have to learn from myths? She says, "The power of myth is that it deals with the relationship between the individual and the universe in which he or she lives. To really experience the power of myth, you need to be in an environment that is beyond your control."

Building Background

The Aztecs of Mexico A thousand years ago, the Toltec people dominated northern Central America. Then civil war broke out and destroyed Toltec power, leaving the capital city, Tula, in ruins. Later, the Aztecs settled near this site, in the area that has become Mexico City. The Aztecs had great respect for the Toltecs, and adopted many elements of their language and myths. In fact, the first Aztec ruler claimed to be descended from **Quetzalcoatl,** the chief god and founder of the Toltecs.

Literature, architecture, sculpture, metal crafts, mosaics, and other arts were important in Aztec culture. In the 1500s, when Hernán Cortés came to Central America, he found a city larger and grander than any city in Spain. How did Cortés overthrow this great empire so quickly? One thing that helped him immensely was that some Aztecs, including the ruler, believed Cortés to be the god Quetzalcoatl—returning to them, as tradition promised.

Getting into the Story

Writer's Notebook Try your hand at myth writing. **Myths** are stories that explain the origin of important events (such as the creation of the world) or natural phenomena (such as a mountain). Myths can also explain how a human activity first began. In your notebook, write notes or an outline for a myth that explains how music was first created. Be sure to list who or what created it, the reason for creating it, and the good or bad effects music has had on the world.

Reading Tip

Retelling a Myth Donna Rosenberg always tries to preserve the spirit of the culture embedded in the myth she is retelling. In "The Creation of Music," she also tries to preserve the language of the original myth, which had been recorded as a poem. As you read this story, find examples of the poetic elements of imagery, figurative language, and rhythm. Try reading some parts aloud to hear the rhythm.

THE CREATION OF MUSIC

retold by Donna Rosenberg

▲ This Mexican mask of the god Quetzalcoatl is a turquoise mosaic. What makes the mask look like a god?

ONE DAY TEZCATLIPOCA,[1] GOD OF THE HEAVENS, CAME DOWN TO EARTH AND wandered from place to place, observing all the beauties of nature. As he walked, he said to himself, "Earth Monster has brought forth mountains and valleys, rivers and streams, forests and meadows. In the light of Sun's rays, her flowers sparkle like brilliant jewels among her blades of grass. Clearly, there is much on Earth to please the hearts of human beings. Yet creation is not complete. Something is missing. Animals roar and people talk, but I hear no music! My heart is heavy with sadness, for music delights the soul as nothing else can."

---

1. **Tezcatlipoca** (tes kät′li pō′kä), *n.* the chief Aztec god.

So Tezcatlipoca summoned Quetzalcoatl,[2] in his form as Wind. "Wind, hear my voice and come to me!" he called to each of the four corners of the world.

Wind groaned complainingly and reluctantly[3] gathered himself together from where he lay scattered over Earth's surface. He rose higher than the tallest tree and the mightiest mountain, and in the form of a great black bird, he came forth to meet the god of the heavens.

Tezcatlipoca heard the waves rise in tumult[4] from the ocean depths and crash with a roar upon the sandy shore. He heard the branches of the trees creak and moan as their leaves tossed and touched. He smiled. Quetzalcoatl had heard his voice, and he was coming.

Quetzalcoatl arrived quickly. As usual, his tempestuous disposition gave him an angry look even when he was quiet. He rested at Tezcatlipoca's feet without complaint.

"Quetzalcoatl," Tezcatlipoca began, "I find that ripe fruits, colorful flowers, and the brightness of Sun's rays make the whole earth beautiful. Yet, in spite of such beauty, Earth is sick with sadness! Not one beautiful sound fills the silence. Not one animal, bird, or human being can sing! Even you know only how to whine and howl, or moan and groan!

"Life must contain music! Music must accompany the awakening dawn. It must inspire[5] the dreaming man. It must comfort the waiting mother. One must be able to hear it in the wings of the bird overhead and in the waters of the nearby brook.

"You must travel high above to the roof of the universe, find the house of Sun, Father of All Life, and ask him to give you musicians to live on Earth and add their beauty to the world. Surely Sun can do this, for he houses many musicians and a flaming choir whose brilliance sheds light upon the earth. Choose the best among both and return to Earth with them.

"When you reach the shore of the ocean," Tezcatlipoca concluded, "you will find my three servants, Water Monster, Water Woman, and Cane and Conch. Command them to unite their bodies and create a bridge on which you can travel up to Sun."

Quetzalcoatl agreed. As he traveled across the face of Earth, he heard what Tezcatlipoca had described, either sad silence or harsh, raucous[6] chatter. When he reached the seashore he found Tezcatlipoca's three servants, who created the bridge for him. Even with the bridge, it took all of his mighty breath to bring him to the house of Sun.

Sun's musicians strode about the halls in colors appropriate to the music they played. Those who played cradle songs and melodies for children wore gleaming white. Those who played songs accompanying the epics of love or war wore brilliant red. Those who wandered with their music as minstrels among the clouds wore bright blue, and those who sat in the golden rays of Sun playing their flutes wore radiant yellow. Quetzalcoatl could not find a musician dressed in a dark, sad color, for there were no sad songs.

As soon as the Father of All Life saw Quetzalcoatl, he exclaimed, "Musicians! I see Wind, that turbulent pest who annoys Earth,

. . . EVERY LIVING THING COULD CREATE ITS OWN KIND OF MUSIC.

---

2. **Quetzalcoatl** (ket säl′kō ät′l), *n.* an Aztec god, associated especially with the arts and learning.
3. **reluctantly** (ri luk′tənt lē), *adv.* unwillingly.
4. **tumult** (tü′mult, tyü′mult), *n.* noise or uproar.
5. **inspire** (in spīr′), *v.* fill with thought, feeling, life, force, etc.
6. **raucous** (rô′kəs), *adj.* harsh sounding.

approaching our peaceful kingdom. Be silent! I want to hear no singing! I want to hear no playing of instruments! Whoever makes a sound when Wind speaks will have to return to Earth with him, and you will find no music there."

Wind climbed the stairways to the halls of Sun. As soon as he saw the musicians, he raised his deep voice and shouted, "Musicians! Singers! Come with me!"

Not one musician or singer replied to his call.

Wind shouted again, more harshly, "Come, musicians! Come, singers! The Supreme Lord of the Universe summons you to join him!"

Again, not one musician or singer replied to his call. They remained in frozen silence in obedience to the wishes of flaming Sun, like a colorful array of dancers suspended in the midst of their dance.

Then Tezcatlipoca, God of the Heavens, expressed his rage. From the four corners of the sky, flocks of black storm clouds rumbled ominously toward the house of Sun, lashed forward by the whip of their lord's lightning bolts. Mighty roars of thunder poured from the great god's throat, engulfing the house of Sun in torrential[7] sound.

The storm clouds swallowed Sun, Father of All Life, who drowned like a flaming beast. Shivering with terror, the musicians and singers flew into the lap of Wind, who lifted them gently—so as not to crush their music—

and happily carried them down to Earth, who was waiting far below.

Meanwhile, Earth scanned the heavens with her dark eyes, watching for the first appearance of Wind. Her face shone with a special radiance and she smiled with delight upon seeing that Quetzalcoatl's quest had been successful. All life welcomed the wanderers. Trees lifted their leafy branches, birds fluttered their wings, people and animals raised their voices, and flowers and fruits lifted their faces in greeting.

Sun's musicians and singers landed happily upon Earth and wandered off in small groups. One could not travel to the most distant corners of the world without meeting singers and musicians all along the way. Even Wind was now happy. No longer did he sadly sigh, moan, and groan as he had in former days. He now sang along with the rest of all life, refreshing the trees of the forest, the meadows, and the ocean waters with his gentle breezes.

So it came to pass that Tezcatlipoca and Quetzalcoatl helped one another to create music upon Earth. Music accompanied the awakening dawn. It inspired the dreaming man. It comforted the waiting mother. One could hear it in the wings of the bird overhead and in the waters of the nearby brook. From that time forth, every living thing could create its own kind of music.

_____

7. **torrential** (tô ren′shəl), *adj.* violently rushing.

Music was an important part of early Mexican society. The Aztec people sang, danced, and played instruments such as this horizontal drum, a hollowed log with beautiful carvings. ▼

After Reading

Making Connections

1. Of the purposes of music listed in the last paragraph of page 713 of the selection, which do you think is the most important? Why?

2. This myth was originally told in the form of a poem. Give an example of a passage from the myth that sounds poetic.

3. Does this story remind you of any other quest or adventure story?

4. What is shown by Quetzalcoatl's response to Tezcatlipoca's summons?

5. What is the effect of the arrival of music on Earth?

6. 👏 Myths often express the central values of a **group's** culture. What do you think this myth says about the Aztec view of music?

7. Do you think it would be better if there were no sad songs?

Literary Focus: Setting

The **setting** of a work helps to create the atmosphere and mood for the reader. Besides naming a time and place, an author will use description to give the reader a sense of when and where the story takes place and what kinds of things can happen there. For example, the eerie setting of the church belfry in "Paul Revere's Ride" helps to create a feeling of tension and danger.

In this selection, there are several settings. Review the myth to discover how many settings there are, and then look for specific words that describe each setting in the work. Use a chart similar to the one started below to record your ideas.

Setting 1: ___Earth___	Setting 2: ___The House of Sun___
flowers sparkle like brilliant jewels among blades of grass	

Vocabulary Study

reluctantly
tumult
inspire
raucous
torrential

On your paper, write the letter of the word that is most nearly opposite in meaning to the capitalized word.

1. TUMULT: **a.** noise **b.** quiet **c.** uproar **d.** slow **e.** scarce
2. RELUCTANTLY: **a.** gladly **b.** haltingly **c.** lazily **d.** unwillingly **e.** disagreeably
3. RAUCOUS: **a.** harsh **b.** mean **c.** grinding **d.** loud **e.** pleasant
4. INSPIRE: **a.** terrify **b.** entertain **c.** love **d.** bore **e.** threaten
5. TORRENTIAL: **a.** still **b.** rushing **c.** busy **d.** enclosed **e.** chosen

Expressing Your Ideas

Writing Choices

Your "Creation" Retell "The Creation of Music" as a **poem.** Find key sentences from the myth that you want to include. Then turn these sentences into lines of poetry by keeping only words and phrases that create images. You will have to decide what rhythm and rhyme your poem should have. Aim for a poem of ten to twenty lines.

One Day. . . . The Aztec drawing at right is of one of the most popular Aztec gods, Tlaloc, the god of rain. In the drawing he is holding a corn plant. Take the role of myth-maker and create your own **myth,** explaining the origin of corn. In the myth, give Tlaloc a role in bringing corn to Earth and portray Tlaloc with the characteristics you imagine a rain god would have.

Other Options

What Does a God Look Like? Select three characters from this myth and either draw **sketches** or make **masks** of what these characters might look like. Try to imitate the style of the Aztec art on this page.

Tezcatlipoca's Disk Jockey Plan the **sound track** for a movie based on this myth. For each paragraph, list either specific musical titles or the kind of music you would add to the dialogue to produce an effective movie.

Heavenly Drama With a group of classmates, perform "The Creation of Music" as a **dance** or **play** for another group of students. You will need to decide how to translate into dance or drama such images as Wind "gathering himself together from where he lay scattered over Earth's surface."

Writing mini-Lesson

Preparing Your Presentation Portfolio

Now is the time to change your **working portfolio** into your **presentation portfolio**. This is the collection of written work that will be presented to others to show how you have met your goals for the year.

Reviewing and Selecting Samples

- Start by checking with your teacher to find out the requirements for the presentation portfolio.

- Next, decide which pieces you will include in your presentation portfolio. Divide your work into three stacks: **definitely use, definitely not use,** and **unsure.** Use your goal statements as a guide to review each piece of work. You might also consider your reflections, your self-evaluations, and comments from others.

Arranging Your Portfolio

There are several ways to arrange your portfolio.

- Chronological—Arrange your samples from the beginning of the year to the end. This order helps show what you have learned.

- By category—Group the same kinds of writing together, such as narratives, reports, essays, and so forth. This arrangement shows your growth on each kind of writing separately.

- By theme—Sort your pieces by mood or topic. This arrangement highlights the major themes in your writing.

Completing the Package

- Write an introduction that first explains the entire folder and then each piece. This will help readers see your work the way you want them to see it. Use your goal statements as a guide.

- Finalize the cover.

- Skim over the portfolio to make sure no pages are missing, and that they're ordered the way you'd like.

Before Reading

Spirits of the Railway

by Paul Yee

Paul Yee
born 1956

Paul Yee grew up "caught between two worlds," in the Chinatown section of Vancouver, British Columbia. Besides writing stories for children, he is a noted historian and the author of *Saltwater City: An Illustrated History of the Chinese in Vancouver.*

    Paul Yee's Aunt Lillian, born on the West Coast in 1895, provided him with stories about the early Chinese immigrants to America. From her came details such as the potato sacks for protection from the cold. Yee was particularly interested in the construction of the railway because so many workers had died from landslides, dynamite blasts, disease, and bad weather. Much of his information was obtained from newspapers, letters written by travelers, or from contractors' ledgers. His stories are the combinations of many different people's stories.

Building Background

The Chinese Who Helped Build America "Spirits of the Railway" combines historical fact with imaginative fantasy. The factual aspect of the story deals with the hardships and prejudice encountered by Chinese immigrants who worked on the construction of the transcontinental railroad. These immigrants had fled from poverty and war in southern China, endured a long and uncomfortable journey across the Pacific, and lived in crowded tenements in the "Chinatowns" of the West. In addition, Chinese workers faced discrimination on the job. They were scorned for being different and ridiculed for their unfamiliar diet, long pigtails (which they had been required to wear by their Manchu overlords in China), wide straw hats, and pajamalike clothing.

Getting into the Story

Discussion Do you like ghost stories? Do you have a favorite one? Ghost stories are marked by spirits, eerie settings, and hauntings or other events that are hard to explain by scientific means. Many of these stories are set in the dark, either at night or in dark and frightening places. In small groups, have a volunteer tell a favorite ghost story. Then discuss the story. What parts of it are typical of such stories? What elements in the story make it especially scary? Together make a concept web of the typical features of ghost stories.

- night
- weird sounds — **Ghost Stories**

Reading Tip

Elements of a Ghost Story A common idea in ghost stories is that the dead cannot rest in peace if they are not buried or otherwise given the proper rituals of a funeral. Another typical idea is that the ghost wants justice or revenge. For example, the ghost of a person who was murdered may come back to haunt the murderer. As you read "Spirits of the Railway," notice the elements that are typical of a ghost story.

Spirits of the Railway

Paul Yee

One summer many, many years ago, heavy floodwaters suddenly swept through south China again. Farmer Chu and his family fled to high ground and wept as the rising river drowned their rice crops, their chickens, and their water buffalo.

With their food and farm gone, Farmer Chu went to town to look for work. But a thousand other starving peasants were already there. So when he heard there was work across the ocean in the New World, he borrowed some money, bought a ticket, and off he sailed.

Long months passed as his family waited to hear from him. Farmer Chu's wife fell ill from worry and weariness. From her hard board bed she called out her husband's name over and over, until at last her eldest son borrowed money to cross the Pacific in search of his father.

For two months, young Chu listened to waves batter the groaning planks of the ship as it crossed the ocean. For two months he dreaded that he might drown at any minute. For two months he thought of nothing but his father and his family.

▲ Ron Chan created the art for this story. Could the activities shown here have taken place at the same time? Why do you think the artist combined images of the workers and the train?

Finally he arrived in a busy port city. He asked everywhere for his father, but no one in Chinatown had heard the name. There were thousands of Chinese flung throughout the New World, he was told. Gold miners scrabbled along icy rivers, farmers ploughed the long low valleys, and laborers traveled through towns and forests, from job to job. Who could find one single man in this enormous wilderness?

Young Chu was soon penniless. But he was young and strong, and he feared neither danger nor hard labor. He joined a work gang of thirty Chinese, and a steamer ferried them up a river canyon to build the railway.

Who could find one single man in this enormous wilderness?

When the morning mist lifted, Chu's mouth fell open. On both sides of the rushing river, gray mountains rose like walls to block the sky. The rock face dropped into ragged cliffs that only eagles could ascend and jutted out from cracks where scrawny trees clung. Never before had he seen such towering ranges of dark raw rock.

The crew pitched their tents and began to work. They hacked at hills with hand-scoops and shovels to level a pathway for the train. Their hammers and chisels chipped boulders into gravel and fill. Their dynamite and drills thrust tunnels deep into the mountain. At night, the crew would sit around the campfire chewing tobacco, playing cards and talking.

From one camp to another, the men trekked up the rail line, their food and tools dangling from sturdy shoulder poles. When they met other workers, Chu would run ahead and shout his father's name and ask for news. But the workers just shook their heads grimly.[1]

"Search no more, young man!" one grizzled old worker said. "Don't you know that too many have died here? My own brother was buried alive in a mudslide."

"My uncle was killed in a dynamite blast," muttered another. "No one warned him about the fuse."

The angry memories rose and swirled like smoke among the workers.

"The white boss treats us like mules and dogs!"

"They need a railway to tie this nation together, but they can't afford to pay decent wages."

"What kind of country is this?"

Chu listened, but still he felt certain that his father was alive.

Then winter came and halted all work. Snows buried everything under a heavy blanket of white. The white boss went to town to live in a warm hotel, but Chu and the workers stayed in camp. The men tied potato sacks around their feet and huddled by the fire, while ice storms howled like wolves through the mountains. Chu thought the winter would never end.

When spring finally arrived, the survivors struggled outside and shook the chill from their bones. They dug graves for two workers who had succumbed[2] to sickness. They watched the river surge[3] alive from the melting snow. Work resumed, and Chu began to search again for his father.

Late one afternoon, the gang reached a mountain with a half-finished tunnel. As usual, Chu ran up to shout his father's name, but before he could say a word, other workers came running out of the tunnel.

---

1. **grimly** (grim′lē), *adv.* in a serious way, not offering hope; sternly, harshly, or fiercely.
2. **succumb** (sə kum′), *v.* die.
3. **surge** (sėrj), *v.* rise and fall; move like waves.

▲ How has the artist created a ghostly setting for this scene?

"It's haunted!" they cried. "Watch out! There are ghosts inside!"

"Dark figures slide soundlessly through the rocks!" one man whispered. "We hear heavy footsteps approaching but never arriving. We hear sighs and groans coming from corners where no man stands."

Chu's friends dropped their packs and refused to set up camp. But the white boss rode up on his horse and shook his fist at the men. "No work, no pay!" he shouted. "Now get to work!"

Then he galloped off. The workers squatted on the rocks and looked helplessly at one another. They needed the money badly for food and supplies.

Chu stood up. "What is there to fear?" he cried. "The ghosts have no reason to harm us. There is no reason to be afraid. We have hurt no one."

"Do you want to die?" a man called out.

"I will spend the night inside the tunnel," Chu declared as the men muttered unbelievingly. "Tomorrow we can work."

Chu took his bedroll, a lamp, and food and marched into the mountain. He heard the crunch of his boots and water dripping. He knelt to light his lamp. Rocks lay in loose piles everywhere, and the shadowy walls closed in on him.

At the end of the tunnel he sat down and ate his food. He closed his eyes and wondered where his father was. He pictured his mother weeping in her bed and heard her voice calling his father's name. He lay down, pulled his blankets close, and eventually he fell asleep.

Chu awoke gasping for breath. Something heavy was pressing down on his chest. He tried to raise his arms but could not. He clenched his fists and summoned[4] all his strength, but still he was paralyzed. His eyes strained into the darkness, but saw nothing.

"We have no final resting place."

Suddenly the pressure eased and Chu groped for the lamp. As the chamber sprang into light, he cried, "What do you want? Who are you?"

Silence greeted him, and then a murmur sounded from behind. Chu spun around and saw a figure in the shadows. He slowly raised the lamp. The flickering light traveled up blood-stained trousers and a mud-encrusted jacket. Then Chu saw his father's face.

"Papa!" he whispered, lunging[5] forward.

"No! Do not come closer!" The figure stopped him. "I am not of your world. Do not embrace me."

Tears rose in Chu's eyes. "So, it's true," he choked. "You . . . you have left us . . ."

His father's voice quivered with rage. "I am gone, but I am not done yet. My son, an accident here killed many men. A fuse exploded before the workers could run. A ton of rock dropped on us and crushed us flat. They buried the whites in a churchyard, but our bodies were thrown into the river, where the current swept us away. We have no final resting place."

Chu fell upon his knees. "What shall I do?"

His father's words filled the tunnel. "Take chopsticks; they shall be our bones. Take straw matting; that can be our flesh. Wrap them together and tie them tightly. Take the bundles to the mountain top high above the nests of eagles, and cover us with soil. Pour tea over our beds. Then we shall sleep in peace."

When Chu looked up, his father had vanished. He stumbled out of the tunnel and blurted the story to his friends. Immediately they prepared the bundles and sent him off with ropes and a shovel to the foot of the cliff, and Chu began to climb.

---

4. **summon** (sum′ən), *v.* call; stir to action; rouse.
5. **lunge** (lunj), *v.* make a sudden forward movement.

When he swung himself over the top of the cliff, he was so high up that he thought he could see the distant ocean. He dug the graves deeper than any wild animal could dig, and laid the bundles gently in the earth.

Then Chu brought his fists together above his head and bowed three times. He knelt and touched his forehead to the soil three times. In a loud clear voice he declared, "Three times I bow, three things I vow. Your pain shall stop now, your sleep shall soothe you now, and I will never forget you. Farewell."

Then, hanging onto the rope looped around a tree, Chu slid slowly back down the cliff. When he reached the bottom, he looked back and saw that the rope had turned into a giant snake that was sliding smoothly up the rock face.

"Good," he smiled to himself. "It will guard the graves well." Then he returned to the camp, where he and his fellow workers lit their lamps and headed into the tunnel. And spirits never again disturbed them, nor the long trains that came later.

Another Voice

I Ask My Mother to Sing

Li-Young Lee

She begins, and my grandmother joins her.
Mother and daughter sing like young girls.
If my father were alive, he would play
his accordion and sway like a boat.

5 I've never been in Peking, or the Summer Palace,
nor stood on the great Stone Boat to watch
the rain begin on Kuen Ming Lake, the picnickers
running away in the grass.

But I love to hear it sung;
10 how the waterlilies fill with rain until
they overturn, spilling water into water,
then rock back, and fill with more.

Both women have begun to cry.
But neither stops her song.

After Reading

Making Connections

1. Does "Spirits of the Railway" bring comfort or fear? Why would it have been told by Chinese who came to America?

2. In what ways does this seem like a typical ghost story to you?

3. 👣 What aspects of Chinese culture are revealed in this selection?

4. How does young Chu's journey **compare** with his father's?

5. What is the cause of his father's anger?

6. Compare the poem with the story. How are they alike? How do they differ?

7. A proper burial is important in every culture. Why do you think this is so?

Literary Focus: Plot

Every story has a **plot,** a sequence of events that shows the characters in action. The elements of the plot usually follow this pattern:

Background	the setting and characters are established
Conflict	the story is set in motion with a problem
Rising Action	the characters do things to try to solve the problem
Climax	the turning point is reached; the outcome is decided
Falling Action/ Resolution	loose ends are wrapped up; effects on characters told

Copy the plot structure map below into your notebook, and fill it in for "Spirits of the Railway" by summarizing the key events of the story that match up with each part of the plot.

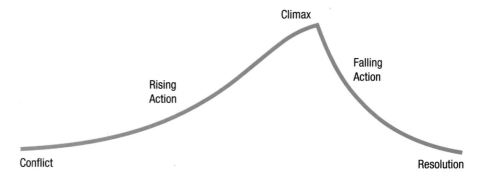

Vocabulary Study

grimly
succumb
summon
lunge
surge

Write the listed word that best completes each sentence.

1. When Chu ran up and yelled his father's name in a cave, the others shook their heads ____, thinking there was no hope.

2. The people who survived the winter dug graves for the people unfortunate enough to ____ to the cold.

3. The sight of the spirit made fear ____ through young Chu.

4. After he saw his father's face, he started to ____ forward, but his father told him to stay back.

5. Chu had to ____ all of his strength, calling it to help him.

Expressing Your Ideas

Writing Choices

Mother, I Have News While young Chu has been searching for his father, his family in China has been waiting for news. Now that Chu knows what has happened to his father, he decides to write to his family. Write the **letter** you think he would write, explaining the fate of his father. Write in the style you think Chu would use to address his family.

The Gold Mountain Many thousands of Chinese immigrants worked on the building of the railroads in the West. Research the topic and prepare a **report** to your class. Use library resources as well as online services to gather information.

Long Division This story could easily be dramatized. Review the story and decide how many scenes you would need in a play based on the story. Then write a **scene summary** that lists the scenes and the main action involved in each.

Other Options

Model Railroad Young Chu was amazed at the size of the mountains: "Never before had he seen such towering ranges of dark raw rock." To give your class an idea of the size of the project of tunneling through these mountains, build a **model** that shows, in relative size, a typical mountain, a tunnel with a train in it, and a railroad worker. You will need to do some research to find the sizes of the mountains and trains.

The Acting Spirit Working in a group, select an important **scene** from the story to act out for your classmates. After you assign parts, you will probably have to rewrite some narration into dialogue. Rehearse the scene together until you can present it with the proper timing. You may wish to use props, costumes, and simple scenery.

Best Spirit in a Starring Role There is a contest for the best ghost story, and you are entering this selection. Each entry consists of a story and an illustration of the most powerful or dramatic moment of the work. Make the **sketch** or **illustration** you would submit to the contest.

Decisive Journeys

Polar Journeys

History Connection

To many people around the world, an image of Americans is an image of adventurers. Polar explorer Will Steger certainly fits that description. He has traveled to polar regions few people have seen. Steger's journeys are not just for adventure, however. He works to make the planet a better place for all of us.

Follow Your Dreams

by Louise Tolle Huffman

Will Steger is one of a few men who have been to both the North and South Poles. In 1986, Steger organized an expedition team made up of seven men and one woman. Their goal was to reach the North Pole by dog sled. On May 1, 1986, six of the original eight members triumphantly stood at the top of the world. Steger and teammate Ann Bancroft talk about the expedition:

Ann, you were the first woman to reach the North Pole. Do you have any special advice for girls?
Don't limit your thinking. It's not just a man's world. Anybody can do this. Your thinking will be your biggest barrier. If you think you can't do something because you are a girl, you won't be able to do it. My advice to girls is the same as to boys—follow your dreams.

Will, what would you like to say to young people?
If you want to be an explorer or whatever, just go out and do it. It takes time to become a doctor or an explorer. You've got to put a lot of effort into it, but it's the effort that makes dreams come true.

Young people definitely need to be aware of the planet and take responsibility for it, maybe even more than adults. They may need to set aside some personal goals for the good of the earth. They should educate themselves to become aware of how we are all connected to this world.

Six Across Antarctica

Into the Teeth of the Ice

by Will Steger

I was first fascinated by Antarctica as a boy, reading about Fuchs and Hillary in *National Geographic.* Poring over pictures of crevasses and mountains and scientific camps, I wondered how men dealt with this wild environment, how they survived. I knew then that Antarctica was a place I had to see.

I dreamed of it for thirty years. The reality was triggered by a one-in-a-million meeting in the middle of the frozen Arctic Ocean, when the path of my 1986 dogsled trek to the North Pole crossed that of Frenchman Jean-Louis Etienne, who was skiing solo to the Pole. We sat that night in a tent and drank tea and found that we shared the same dream.

We wanted to prove that six men from six different nations, who had grown up with starkly different cultural backgrounds, could work together toward a common goal under some of the cruelest conditions on the planet.

We hoped our expedition would help focus the world's attention, and similar cooperation, on the icy continent. The next few years will be crucial to Antarctica's future. Increasingly it is beset by pollutants; tourists are clamoring to visit. Most important, the international treaty that governs Antarctica comes up for review in 1991, leaving open to discussion such vital issues as scientific research, mining, military presence, and territorial claims.* As the world's greatest

On October 31, 1991, thirty-one nations signed the Madrid Protocol, which bans gas and oil exploration in Antarctica for the next fifty years.

remaining pure wilderness, Antarctica's harsh yet surprisingly delicate environment must be preserved.

Asked why six men, one each from the United States, France, the Soviet Union, China, Japan, and Britain, would attempt such a challenge, Jean-Louis spoke for us all when we announced Trans-Antarctica: "You dream about exploration or you do not, but if you do, then the attraction is very strong, all of your life."

Trans-Antarctica officially got under way at sunrise on July 27, 1989; six men, three sleds, forty dogs. We spent the first week establishing a traveling rhythm for the next seven months. Keizo Funatsu, Geoff Somers, and I were each responsible for a dog team; Victor Boyarsky skied ahead of the sleds, acting as a scout; Jean-Louis would maintain radio contact; Qin Dahe did daily scientific studies.

After a quick breakfast of tea and oatmeal, we would dig the sleds out from under the drifted snow, harness the dogs, and travel until 1 P.M. Spread out along the trail, we had little opportunity for conversation; we welcomed the chance to gather at lunch, even if the winds were too strong to talk. On those rare occasions when the sun shone during a lunch break, Antarctica seemed almost peaceful.

Day 161, January 3, 1990: "Essentially our days have little pain or suffering to them now. It's a lot easier getting up in the morning,

time passes a lot quicker. Day after day of blue sky, very calm at night. Occupying your mind is now the real challenge."

We arrived at Vostok January 18, the first to cross the area of inaccessibility on foot. We were greeted by fireworks and the forty Soviets who work there. Vostok is close to the coldest spot in the world, where an incredible minus 128.6° F was recorded in 1983. The morning

we arrived, it was 48 below and dropping fast. I knew it would only get colder until we neared the coast, 850 miles away. Indeed, on February 6 we recorded our coldest day—54 below—and on the 15th, the worst windchill, minus 125. Windstorms like those on the peninsula swept us again, though thankfully they were now at our backs.

Two days out of Mirnyy the storms came back with a vengeance. As always in such conditions, we staked skis and poles every few yards between the tents. It was here that Keizo, looking after his dogs in the blizzard, lost his way between ski markers and had to bury himself to survive.

His own journal tells the story best:
"Once I was in my snow ditch, blowing snow covered me in five, ten seconds. I could breathe through a cavity close to my body, but the snow was blowing inside my clothes, and I was getting wet. I knew my teammates would be looking for me. I believed I would be found; it was just a matter of time. I had to believe that.

"Very few people have that kind of experience, lost in the blizzard. I said to myself, 'Settle down, try and enjoy this.' In my snow ditch I truly felt Antarctica. With the snow and quiet covering me, I felt like I was in my mother's womb. I could hear my heart beat— boom, boom, boom—like a small baby's. My life seemed very small compared to nature, to Antarctica."

Finding Keizo alive was the greatest relief I have ever known. The storms calmed the next day, and on March 3, 1990—after 220 days and 3,741 miles—we arrived at the other side of the continent.

It wasn't until we stepped off the Soviet ship that carried us from Mirnyy to Perth, Australia, that we became aware of all the changes that had occurred while we were away. We stepped off into a new world: The Berlin Wall had tumbled, San Francisco had been rocked, Nelson Mandela was free, Eastern Europe was tasting liberty.

Perhaps our expedition—as a small example of multinational effort focused on the last great frontier—would be accepted as a contribution toward the world's new awakening.

Responding
1. Will Steger set out to prove that many nations can work together for the betterment of the planet. Do you think that all nations of the world will ever be able to put aside their differences and really work together for the good of all people? Explain your answer.

2. In his interview, Will Steger says that young people have a responsibility to care for the Earth. What can you do, starting now, to take care of the Earth for your generation and those that follow?

Earth Science Connection

Polar journeys are more than adventures for a handful of explorers. They have become critical scientific expeditions that study how Earth began and how it is changing. The survival of the planet in the future may depend in part on information that can be gathered by studying the polar regions.

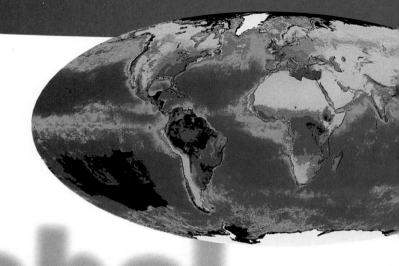

A New Global Outlook

by Michael Woods

As late as 1950, Antarctica remained the most mysterious land on Earth. More than half of the continent had never been explored.

But Antarctic science has evolved in scope, and now looks outward to the rest of the Earth, and deep into the universe. It focuses on using the Antarctic to understand much broader scientific problems. The research still helps to expand knowledge about Antarctica. But it also has important applications elsewhere, in understanding global processes like climate change, ocean levels, the effects of industrial pollutants, and even the origin and fate of the universe.

Antarctica has become an early-warning system for detecting global environmental change. Modern studies of Antarctic organisms are providing early information about the damaging effects of ozone depletion. The *ozone hole,* a thinning of the atmospheric layer that protects Earth from the sun's *ultraviolet light,* was discovered in Antarctica. Studies of the massive West Antarctic Ice Sheet are helping to establish worldwide consequences of another global environmental threat, the *greenhouse effect.* This warming of Earth's climate is caused by a buildup of carbon dioxide and other gases in the *atmosphere* that block the release of Earth's heat. If global warming should melt polar ice sheets, sea levels would rise, flooding many coastal areas.

Scientists also are establishing the global importance of the southern ocean, formed by the South Atlantic, South Pacific, and Indian oceans, which surround the Antarctic. The southern ocean contains only about ten percent of Earth's water. But exchanges of heat, water, and gas between the ocean and the atmosphere influence global weather and regulate the world's climate.

In addition to helping humanity explore Earth and the universe, Antarctic science may prepare men and women for actual exploration of other worlds. The Antarctic is so remote, so cold, so dry, so hostile that it can be used to simulate conditions that astronauts would encounter on other planets.

Responding

Imagine that you are a scientist who is going on an expedition to Antarctica. You have your choice of studying any of the environmental topics mentioned in this reading. You choose what you think is the most critical problem. What will you study? Explain your choice.

Geography Connection

The polar regions are some of the last frontiers on Earth. Unlike frontiers explored by earlier adventurers such as Marco Polo and Leif Erikson, they are far from ideal for human habitation. However, some species of plants and animals have adapted to the harsh environments.

THE North POLE

- is known for its extremely cold temperatures.

- is somewhat warmer than the South Pole.

- is in the Arctic Ocean.

- is at the center of a permanent ice mass that can be as thick as 164 feet.

- has many life forms, including microscopic plants, shrimps, fish, seals, and walruses.

- is the only area of the world to have polar bears.

- offers scientists the opportunity to study weather, wildlife, and the history of our planet.

THE South POLE

- is known for its extremely cold temperatures.

- has an average annual temperature of −70° F.

- is on land, the continent of Antarctica, which is the largest desert on earth, having hardly any precipitation.

- is covered by an ice sheet that averages about 8,000 feet and is more than 15,000 feet deep at its thickest point.

- has a few land life forms, including bacteria, lichen, and insects.

- is the only area of the world to have penguins.

- offers scientists the opportunity to study weather, wildlife, and the history of our planet.

Responding

Research the plant and animal species that can be found at either the North or South Pole. Draw a picture and write a short description of one species. With classmates, make a bulletin board display of your work.

Reading Mini-Lesson

Understanding Sequence

What do you think of when you think of history—all those names and dates, right? History books often cover great spans of time, and it is easy to get confused about the time period if you don't read carefully. Understanding **sequence** is especially important in reading history texts because what happens in one year may have an effect on what happens the next year. As you read a history article, notice that the order of events is often marked by dates and even times. To keep those dates in your mind as you read and study, it helps to take notes, perhaps in the form of a time line or an outline.

The article "Six Across Antarctica" (pages 727–728) describes a sequence of events that results in a major accomplishment: Six men from different nations work together to cross Antarctica by dog sled. Starting with the chance encounter in 1986 that sparked the idea for the expedition, you learn about the key events of the expedition in a clear chronological order.

Here is a time line of key dates mentioned in the article. You can see that whole months have been left out of the report.

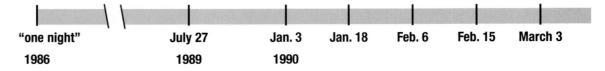

| "one night" 1986 | | July 27 1989 | Jan. 3 1990 | Jan. 18 | Feb. 6 | Feb. 15 | March 3 |

Activity Options

1. Copy and complete the time line by writing in, at each point, the important event reported on or associated with that date.

2. Summarize each paragraph of the article, starting with when the expedition begins, and create an ordered list of events. Then review one paragraph and make a list of the details that "flesh out" that event for you and make it vivid in your mind.

3. As well as specific dates and times, time markers can be words such as *then, after,* and *later.* Work with a partner to find ten words or phrases that serve as time markers in "Follow Your Dreams" and "Six Across Antarctica."

Writing Workshop

Exploring Personal Changes

Assignment Characters in these selections took journeys that resulted in personal or historical changes. Write about a journey you might take that could cause an important change in your life or in the lives of others. See the Writer's Blueprint for details.

WRITER'S BLUEPRINT

Product	Five entries in a travelogue
Purpose	To describe an imaginary journey, as you experience it, that results in an important change in your life or in the lives of others
Audience	People who want to learn about your journey
Specs	As the writer of a successful travelogue, you should:

❑ Brainstorm possible journeys. Choose one that you feel would bring an important change in your life or the lives of others. This journey might be a trip to another country or a series of experiences leading to a goal, such as graduating from high school or preparing for a career.

❑ Begin your travelogue with an entry which describes the start of your journey. Write as if you have just started out. Address questions such as where you're going and why and who (if anyone) is going with you.

❑ Go on to write three more entries at different points on your journey. These might be places you stop along the way or events on the way to your goal, and they should contribute to the important change you believe will be a result of your journey.

❑ Conclude with a final entry at the end of your journey. Explain what the journey has meant to you and what change it will cause in your life or in the lives of others.

❑ Keep your writing lively by using verbs that are in the active voice.

❑ Follow the rules for grammar, usage, spelling, and mechanics. Use the correct comparative forms of adjectives and adverbs.

The following instructions are designed to lead you to a successful travelogue.

Explore journeys of different characters in the literature to spark ideas for your own journey. Why did each character make the journey? What important changes resulted from it? If you had made such a journey, how might you have reacted? Enter your information in a chart like this one.

Character	Journey	Reason	Change that resulted	How I might have reacted
Marvin in "If I Forget Thee, Oh Earth . . ."	To an open plain on another planet	To see Earth	Marvin realizes he must pass on the dream of returning to Earth.	Mixed feelings of sadness and hope

OR . . .
If you already know what journey you want to write about, you can cluster words and phrases connected to that destination.

Cluster the journeys you'd like to make. Can you remember any journeys you've dreamed about taking? It might have been a trip to a foreign country or another planet. Maybe yours is a mental journey, something you've dreamed about that hasn't really happened. Cluster your dreams of travel. Do one for journeys to actual places and one for mental journeys. Your clusters might look like this.

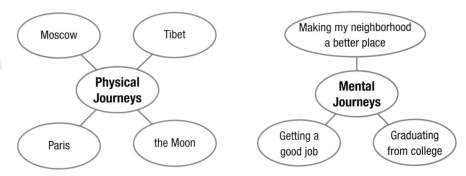

Plan the travelogue. Use a photocopy or sketch of a map showing your starting point and your destination. Draw a line that represents your journey. Along the line, plot five points to show the stages of the trip at which you'll write your entries. Number the points from one to five. Then sketch a scene or write a few sentences to remind yourself about the focus of each entry. Refer to your charts and notes as you create your travelogue plan.

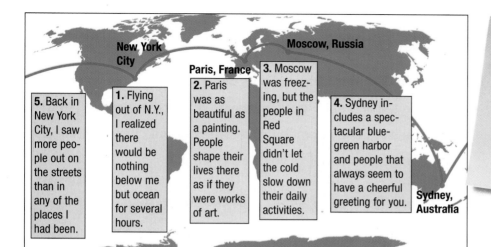

1. Flying out of N.Y., I realized there would be nothing below me but ocean for several hours.

2. Paris was as beautiful as a painting. People shape their lives there as if they were works of art.

3. Moscow was freezing, but the people in Red Square didn't let the cold slow down their daily activities.

4. Sydney includes a spectacular blue-green harbor and people that always seem to have a cheerful greeting for you.

5. Back in New York City, I saw more people out on the streets than in any of the places I had been.

OR . . .
If your destination is a goal rather than a place, you might sketch yourself as you are now for the starting point and as you will look after achieving your goal.

LITERARY SOURCE
"For two months, young Chu listened to waves batter the groaning planks of the ship as it crossed the ocean. For two months he dreaded that he might drown at any minute. For two months he thought of nothing but his father and his family."
from "Spirits of the Railway" by Paul Yee

Ask yourself: *Do I have all the material I need?* Look at what you've done so far. If you still need more material, you might:

• Discuss your journey idea with a partner. Focus on why it interests you and how such a journey might change you.

• If possible, look up your destination in an encyclopedia or library book. Note details you can use in your travelogue.

• Consult the *Reader's Guide to Periodical Literature,* which can be found in most libraries. See if any recent magazines have articles about your destination.

DRAFTING

Before you write, review your steps from the Prewriting stage and the Writer's Blueprint. Then, begin your draft. Remember to use active voice verbs in your writing. It will make your writing livelier. Look ahead to the Revising Strategy for tips on using the active voice.

As you draft, concentrate on getting your ideas on paper. Here are some ideas for getting started.

• Begin as if you are packing the things you'll need on your journey.

• Describe your ideas about the place you're visiting.

• If you're visiting several places, start with an itinerary of your trip which shows where you're going and when you'll be there.

Write in the active voice to give the feel of a traveler going places and doing things.

Ask your partner for comments on your draft before you revise it.

✔ Does the first entry explain where I'm going and why?

✔ Does each entry contribute to the important change at the end?

✔ Have I used the active voice consistently?

Revising Strategy

Active and Passive Voice

A verb is active when the subject performs the action. A verb in the active voice has a direct object.

Sam **hailed** the only taxi.

Sam is the subject and performs the action of hailing a taxi. *Taxi* receives the action and is the direct object of the sentence.

A verb is in the passive voice when the subject receives the action.

The taxi **was hailed** by Sam.

Taxi still receives the action, but now it's the subject. *Was hailed* is the passive verb. A passive verb has some form of *be* as an auxiliary verb followed by a past participle.

Most writers prefer active verbs because they express action in a more natural and direct way. The writer of the draft below keeps verbs active.

LITERARY SOURCE

"Tense with expectancy, Marvin settled himself down in the cramped cabin while his father started the motor and checked the controls. The inner door of the lock slid open and then closed behind them: he heard the roar of the great air pumps fade slowly away as the pressure dropped to zero."
from "If I Forget Thee, Oh Earth" by Arthur C. Clarke

STUDENT MODEL

August 23, 1999: I am really scared now! When I woke up this morning, I went to my brother's room to wish him a happy birthday. He was under the covers but when he lifted the blanket off his face, he was a she! She smiled at me and said, "I'm so happy I'm thirteen. Now you'll let me go to the mall with you, right?" I said, "Sure," and ran out of the room.

STEP **4** EDITING

Ask a partner to review your revised draft before you edit. When you edit, watch for errors in grammar, usage, spelling, and mechanics. Pay special attention to using the correct comparative forms of adjectives and adverbs.

Editing Strategy

Comparative Forms of Adjectives and Adverbs

Travel writing often includes comparisons. Here are a few tips on using the correct forms of adjectives and adverbs to make comparisons.

Adjectives and adverbs have three degrees of comparison: positive, comparative, and superlative.

Positive	Comparative	Superlative
cold	colder	coldest
delicious	more delicious	most delicious
quickly	more quickly	most quickly
bad	worse	worst

Most adjectives and adverbs of one syllable form their comparative and superlative degrees by adding -er and -est. Adjectives of more than two syllables and adverbs ending in -ly form their comparative and superlative degrees by adding *more* or *most*. Adjectives and adverbs such as *bad, good, well, many,* and *much* have irregular comparative and superlative forms. Check a dictionary if you're not sure how to form a comparative or superlative.

Notice how the writer of the draft below used comparative forms.

> August 23, 1999: It's me again. It's still Zena's birthday and things are weirder than ever! It's as if she has Geo's personality. I found her in my room, reading my magazines, and talking on my phone! But she's worse than Geo! I just found her in the bathroom using my makeup and hairbrush! This has to stop.
>
> STUDENT MODEL

FOR REFERENCE... More rules for using comparative forms of adjectives and adverbs are listed in the Language and Grammar Handbook.

STEP **5** PRESENTING

Here are two ideas for presenting your travelogue.

- Keyboard your travelogue entries and add maps, photographs, or sketches to illustrate them. Make photocopies of the completed travelogue for your class.

- Turn your travelogue entries into postcards from the road. Use 3 x 5 or 4 x 6 cards to create illustrated postcards of different points on your journey. On the backs of these cards, use your travelogue entries to provide information about each place.

STEP **6** LOOKING BACK

Self-evaluate. What grade would *you* give your paper? Look back at the Writer's Blueprint and evaluate yourself on each point, from 6 (superior) down to 1 (weak).

Reflect. Think about what you learned from writing your travelogue as you write answers to these questions.

✔ How would you improve your travelogue if you wrote it again?

✔ Could you experience the same change in your life that you described in your travelogue without traveling? Explain your answer.

For Your Working Portfolio: Add your travelogue entries and your reflection responses to your working portfolio.

Beyond Print

Talk Show Tips

Remember the following tips while doing this activity.

Make Eye Contact Talk shows succeed because the hosts look at the camera and, thus, the viewer. Keep those eyes where they ought to be—on the camera, the guests, or the host. Do not look down.

Keep It Moving TV programs succeed because they are paced quickly and do not bore a restless audience. Therefore, do not read prepared speeches. Work from notes.

Talk Clearly and Conversationally Watch how the pros do it. You can hear every word. Yet, on talk shows, the hosts make what they say appear to be very spontaneous. Sometimes they are reading off cue cards held above the camera, so the host can look at the camera and speak directly to the viewers at the same time. You may use cue cards if you wish.

Esmeralda Santiago on Television

Esmeralda Santiago, the author of "A Shot at It," seems to be the kind of person most people would like to know. She'd probably do well on a TV talk show where she could inspire millions of viewers.

Activity

Plan a talk show that features Esmeralda Santiago as a guest.

- Divide the class into two groups. One group will be the host group and the other half will be the Santiago group.

- The job of the host group is to write an introduction for the guest and to make up as many questions as possible for her.

- The job of the Santiago group is to make up a brief statement for Santiago to say at the beginning of the show and to develop background information about her.

- Both groups must base their activities on "A Shot at It." It is okay to make up information that is not available in the story, but the information must fit what everyone knows about Santiago.

After completing the above steps, put on the talk show.

- The Santiago group will appoint a member to represent Santiago, who will be seated on "stage" and give a statement about her life.

- After Santiago has given her statement, members of the host group will take turns asking a few questions.

- Santiago and members of her group will collaborate to answer the questions posed by the host group.

Activity Extensions

1. Practice a show. Then do it again, this time videotaping it. Critique the tape and do it again. See if practice can improve it.

2. Rehearse giving statements directly into a camera. Keep redoing it, until you achieve the "polish" of a seasoned TV personality.

Projects for Collaborative Study

Theme Connection

Dream Journeys Everyone dreams of making a journey someday—to explore an exotic place, to learn new things, or to return to a place you once lived. In a small group, choose a destination for a dream journey and plan your trip. Divide up these parts of the project among members of your group:

- Make a map showing where you'll travel.

- Prepare a guidebook, with advice on local customs, sights to see, and places to stay.

- If your destination is a place where people speak a language other than English, prepare a dictionary of useful words and phrases that will help you communicate.

- Write a fictitious diary, with entries for each day of your journey.

Literature Connection

Sharing Poetry You've read poems by quite a few poets in this unit. Which poem did you like best? Find another poem by the same poet or in the same style. Then divide into Sharing Groups of three to five students.

- Read your poem aloud to your Sharing Group. The other members of the group, after listening to the poem, should share what they liked most about the poem.

- On your own, write a poem modeled after the poem you read aloud. Try to follow the **rhythm** and the **rhyme** pattern (or lack of rhyme) of your model poem. Share your poem with your group.

- Your group might want to publish a collection of poems written by group members.

Life Skills Connection

Twenty Years Later . . . It happened to Rip Van Winkle; imagine it just happened to you! Your class went on a field trip, got tired, and took a nap. You all awaken to discover it is twenty years later. In your notebook, respond to these questions:

- What are your family and friends (who were not on the field trip) doing?

- How has your community changed?

- What will you do now?

As a class, compare your responses to the above and discuss these questions:

- What changes did you expect?

- What changes surprised you?

- What can you do together to respond to these changes?

- What ideas come to mind regarding how you might prepare for your future?

Multicultural Connection

Belonging You belong to many groups—a family, an ethnic group, a religious group, an age group, and perhaps social groups such as the Scouts or a youth group.

- In your notebook, reflect on what you have learned by being a part of these **groups.** How have these various groups made you into the unique **individual** you are today?

- As a class, create a bulletin board display or a collage that shows the many different groups to which members of your class belong. With pictures, photographs, drawings, or words, tell what you have learned from these groups.

Read More About Journeys

Johnny Tremain (1943) by Esther Forbes. In this award-winning novel, set during the Revolutionary War, a young man with a severely burned hand learns that he can play an important role in the drive for independence despite his injury.

Walk Two Moons (1994) by Sharon Creech. This novel explores a teenager's attempt to understand why her mother had to leave home suddenly on a spiritual quest.

More Good Books

Walt Whitman (1995) by Catherine Reef. This biography explores the life of one of America's greatest poets.

Lincoln: A Photobiography (1987) by Russell Freedman. This award-winning work, featuring many rarely seen period photographs and drawings, covers the life of Abraham Lincoln.

Bull Run (1993) by Paul Fleischman. In this fictional work, sixteen people, eight from the North and eight from the South, present their feelings and observances of the Civil War through journal entries. Their paths all meet at the Battle of Bull Run.

When I Was Puerto Rican (1993) by Esmeralda Santiago. This autobiography follows the author from her childhood in the countryside of Puerto Rico to New York's School of Performing Arts.

The Ear, the Eye and the Arm (1994) by Nancy Farmer. Set in Zimbabwe in 2194, this science fiction tale follows the perilous exploits of a thirteen-year-old boy and his younger brother and sister after they leave their high-tech home.

Glossaries, Handbooks, and Indexes

Understanding Fiction 744

Understanding Nonfiction 746

Understanding Poetry 748

Understanding Drama 750

Glossary of Literary Terms 752

Glossary of Vocabulary Words 756

Language and Grammar Handbook 765

Index of Skills and Strategies 783

Index of Fine Art and Artists 790

Index of Authors and Titles 792

Text Acknowledgments 794

Illustration Acknowledgments 796

Understanding Fiction

Fiction is writing that comes from an author's imagination. Its purpose is to illustrate some truth about life or to entertain. A **novel** is a long work of fiction dealing with characters, actions, and scenes that copy those of real life in a complex plot. A **short story** is shorter than a novel. It often describes just one event, and the characters are usually fewer in number and not as fully developed as those in a novel. Short stories can usually be read in one sitting.

Fiction shapes our own imaginations because it provides glimpses into the past, ideas about life in the future, and understanding of the world as it is today. Fiction has several important elements.

Characters

The **characters**—the people or animals—are one of the most important elements in fiction. Authors make their characters seem real by describing such things as what they look like (Anna was tall and wore jeans), the way they speak or act (Tony spoke calmly but his hands shook), and sometimes even what they are thinking (Norman wondered why his parents disagreed).

Plot

The **plot**—what happens to the characters—is a second important element in fiction, and it is carefully worked out by the author so that one event flows logically after another. In most fiction, the plot is built around a **conflict,** a problem or struggle of some sort. The conflict may be between characters, between a character and some object or event, or between a character and that character's inner self. The conflict builds to an emotional moment called a **climax,** or turning point, when the main character takes an action to end the conflict, or when the way events are working out causes some important change.

Usually the turning point comes close to the end of the story and sometimes it is at the very end. The conclusion of a story, where the complications of the plot are worked out, is called the **resolution.** The events before the climax are often referred to as the *rising action,* while the events after the climax are called the *falling action.*

Setting

The **setting**—when and where the action takes place—is a third important element in fiction. Sometimes the setting is crucial to what happens, and then it is described in detail by the author. If the particular city or town and the exact season or year are important to the action, an author usually states them directly (New York City on a cold December Monday in 1996). Often authors do not need to be so definite. If all that happens occurs in one room and involves a character with an inner conflict, then the setting may not be described in detail because it is irrelevant to the story.

Theme

Another important thing to look for in fiction is **theme,** or underlying meaning. A theme may be directly stated by the author or only implied. Theme is not the same as subject, or topic, in that it involves a statement or an opinion about the topic. Not every work of fiction has a theme, and various readers may discover different themes in the same selection.

Mood/Tone

The author's choice of words and details to describe setting, characters, and events contributes to two additional elements of fiction—mood and tone. **Mood** refers to the atmosphere or feeling created in the reader by the author. **Tone** is the author's attitude toward the subject or toward the reader.

Strategies for Reading Fiction

When reading fiction, it is helpful to consider the following things:

- **Think about the characters.** What happens to each one? Who is your favorite character and why?

- **Think about the events.** What is the central problem or conflict? What is the moment of greatest suspense? Is the order of events important? Do you like the ending?

- **Think about when and where the action takes place.** Often the **setting** will be explained in the first few paragraphs. What are some of the other things that create a sense of time and place?

As you read, think about what the author suggests as well as what he or she actually states. When the information about the characters, events, and setting is only suggested, rather than stated, you must make **inferences.** An inference is a reasonable conclusion based on clues provided by the author. Looking for clues and making inferences will help you become a better reader.

If a story is not too long, read it through without stopping. What is it about? To become involved, **visualize** the characters and the place. After reading, it is often necessary to go back and reread sections. Try it. Be sure you know who the main characters are and what they are like. Be sure you understand where the action takes place and what the main problem is and how it is solved.

You'll also want to consider the **narrator,** or who is telling the story. Is the narrator a character participating in the events, or someone outside the story who is simply observing what happens? The two most common **points of view** are first person (a character in the story) and third person (an outsider). Ask yourself: From whose point of view am I seeing the characters, events, and setting?

As you read, stop occasionally and think about what you are reading.

Question yourself about the characters and events. "Why is this character such a bully? Is she jealous or just plain mean?"

Predict what may happen next. "Will the girl come out of the coma?"

Clarify what is happening by trying to explain things to yourself. "The carpet design helps me understand the game the boy has made up to amuse himself."

Summarize what has happened so far, an especially important step when you are reading a long story or difficult novel.

Evaluate by making judgments about the quality of the author's work. You can also evaluate such elements as a character's actions. "This story seems true to life, because I think it's possible for a dog to save a person's life."

Connect the story with your own experiences—do you think the character is doing the right thing? Do you identify with the way the character feels? "I felt exactly the same way—scared and lonely—when I moved last year."

Understanding Nonfiction

Nonfiction is about real people, real places, and things that actually happened. It includes many kinds of writing but can be divided into two general groups—**informational nonfiction,** such as newspaper articles, and **narrative nonfiction,** such as biography, which has many of the same literary elements as fiction. Although narrative nonfiction may tell a story, the story should be true and based on facts.

Below are descriptions of some of the most common types of nonfiction.

Autobiography

An **autobiography** is an account of all or part of a person's life written by that person. Feelings and observations about life's experiences are often important in an autobiography. Because the author is the narrator, an autobiography is almost always told from the first-person point of view.

Shorter forms of autobiography include **diaries, memoirs,** and **journals.** Today some autobiographies of people noted for contributions in special fields, such as politics or sports, are written with the help of a professional writer. The selection from *The Autobiography of Eleanor Roosevelt* and "A Shot at It" by Esmeralda Santiago are examples of autobiography found in this book.

Biography

A **biography** is an account of a real person's life written by another person. Biographers try to learn about a noteworthy person and then help readers get to know that person. A biography can take us back in time or around the world to learn about fascinating people and their remarkable lives.

Doing research is part of a biographer's job, and books, letters, and journals all can be a source of details for a biography. If possible, a biographer interviews the subject of the biography, or people who have known the person. To help readers visualize time periods, places, and people, a biography may have a setting and characterization, just as fiction does. Although the goal of a biographer is to provide a truthful account, sometimes imagined details are drawn from the facts available. "A President's Wife" by Russell Freedman is a biography of Eleanor Roosevelt. "Beni Seballos" by Phillip Hoose is another example of biography included in this book.

Essay

An **essay** is a discussion about a specific topic, and it often expresses an opinion on the topic. Some essays are primarily expository, or informative. They explain something or give more information about a subject. Essays may be classified as formal or informal. A formal essay has a serious tone and is generally intended to persuade the reader. An informal essay, more concerned with entertaining than persuading, has a personal, friendly tone. Sometimes an informal essay is humorous. "Inequalities" by Nereida Román is an essay.

Speech

A **speech** is written to be given as a public talk, usually for a particular occasion such as a graduation, a memorial service, or a political rally. It may be formal or informal, and the topic will depend upon the intended audience. The Gettysburg Address by Abraham Lincoln is a well-known speech you will find in this book.

Strategies for Reading Nonfiction

When reading nonfiction, it is helpful to consider the following strategies:

- Before you actually begin reading nonfiction, **warm up by previewing.** Consider the title and read the first paragraph. Also look at any illustrations. What clues to the subject do you find? Knowing what to expect should help you better understand what you read.

- **Think about the facts and opinions presented.** Since accuracy is important in nonfiction you'll want to distinguish between statements of fact and statements of opinion. Remember that a statement of fact can be proved while a statement of opinion expresses personal feelings, beliefs, or evaluations. Any statement about a future event is an opinion since it cannot be proved that it will happen.

- **Consider the author's purpose**. Why do you think this author wrote this particular work of nonfiction? Is it simply to inform you by providing facts? Is it to persuade you to an idea? Or is the purpose to entertain?

- **Consider your own purpose for reading.** It can allow you to read with **flexibility.** For example, if you are reading a difficult article about a recent discovery in space in preparation for reporting on it in science class, you will want to slow down and pay careful attention to the details. On the other hand, if you are looking for the name of the scientist who made the discovery, you might skim the article by glancing quickly at the material to find the specific information you want.

- **Use the time-order relationships in the material.** Paying attention to when things happen is particularly important when you read a history textbook, a biography, or an autobiography. Dates and clue words, such as *in 1900,* will help you find the order of events.

- **Think about cause-and-effect relationships.** Noticing how events are linked in a pattern, one event happening as the result of another, will help you follow narrative nonfiction. Using cause-and-effect relationships is also very useful in reading the directions for a science experiment or a history text.

- **Looking for the main idea, topic, and details** in nonfiction can be a help in remembering as well as understanding what you read. Recall that the topic is the subject of the selection and the main idea is the "big" idea about that topic. Details are included to support the main idea.

Understanding Poetry

Poetry is a type of literature that creates an emotional response through the imaginative use of words. It helps you experience what you might not otherwise notice. It can surprise or delight you, and it often will suggest some new ideas for thought. Poetry dates back to the beginning of human communities when poetic forms were used in tribal ceremonies. Later, stories were told in verse and passed along from one generation to the next.

Traditional poems are written in **stanzas,** or groups of lines that are set off visually from the other lines in a poem. Many traditional poems are **narrative poems,** poems that tell stories. They have the same literary elements you find in fiction, such as plot, characters, and setting. The **repetition** of sounds is another characteristic of traditional poems.

A modern poem characteristically is written in the language of everyday speech, and it may be about a variety of subjects, from rattlesnakes to homework. Often a modern poem creates a single **image** that appeals to your senses. Many modern poems are written in **free verse,** meaning they are free from any fixed or repeated patterns.

Below are descriptions of several important elements in poetry.

Rhythm

The pattern of sounds that are stressed and not stressed in a poem provides the **rhythm.** As you read the following stanza from Henry Wadsworth Longfellow's "Paul Revere's Ride," what syllables do you emphasize, or pronounce louder?

Listen my children, and you shall hear
Of the midnight ride of Paul Revere,
On the eighteenth of April, in Seventy-five;
Hardly a man is now alive
Who remembers that famous day and year.

The pattern of stressed syllables gives you a feeling for the beat of the stanza. Notice that the rhythm is not quite regular. In the first line, these syllables are stressed: *Lis-, chil-, you,* and *hear.* There are two unaccented syllables (*-ten, my*) between *Lis-* and *chil-,* but only one (*shall*) between *you* and *here.* Rhythm makes poetry enjoyable to read. It may be regular, or it may be slightly irregular to emphasize certain words.

Rhyme

The repetition of a sound in two or more words is called **rhyme.** In poetry, the last words of lines often rhyme. In the stanza from "Paul Revere's Ride," there is end rhyme in lines 1, 2, and 5 (*hear, Revere, year*) and also in lines 3 and 4 (*Seventy-five, alive*).

Figurative Language

Figurative language goes beyond the ordinary meanings of words in order to achieve a new effect or to express an idea in a fresh way. **Simile, metaphor, personification,** and **hyperbole** are four kinds of figurative language often used by poets. Notice how the night wind is portrayed in the following lines from "Paul Revere's Ride." To what is the night wind compared? What human qualities are given to the wind?

Beneath, in the churchyard, lay the dead,
In their night-encampment on the hill,
Wrapped in silence so deep and still
That he could hear, like a sentinel's tread,
The watchful night wind, as it went
Creeping along from tent to tent,
And seeming to whisper, "All is well!"

Imagery

When writers help us experience what can be seen or heard, they are using images, or

imagery. Writers also use imagery to help readers experience the way things smell, taste, and feel. You can almost hear the striking of the village clock and feel the dampness of fog in these lines from "Paul Revere's Ride."

It was twelve by the village clock,
When he crossed the bridge into Medford
town.
He heard the crowing of the cock,
And the barking of the farmer's dog,
And felt the damp of the river fog,
That rises after the sun goes down.

Alliteration

Sound devices are an important part of poetry. The repetition of consonant sounds at the beginnings of words or within words is called **alliteration,** as shown in these lines from "Paul Revere's Ride" with the repeated sound of the letter *b.*

He heard the bleating of the flock,
And the twitter of birds among the trees,
And felt the breath of the morning breeze
Blowing over the meadows brown.

Strategies for Reading Poetry

When we read poems, it's important to listen to the words. Often they say more than they directly tells us. Keep in mind the following tips as you read poetry.

• **Use the title** to get a clue to the topic of the poem.

• **Do not pause or stop at the end of a line** unless there is a mark of punctuation indicating that you should do so.

• **Look for the meaning.** One way to do this is to pay attention to the punctuation. Although lines may flow from one to the next, ideas are often expressed as statements or questions.

• **Try to see in your mind the pictures** created by the words.

• In a poem that tells a story, **look for the action and visualize the characters** who determine the action.

• In reading poetry that focuses on an image or an emotion, **listen for the voice of the poem.** Notice how the word choices of the poet help you visualize an object or experience an emotion.

• **Give careful attention to each word in a poem.** Because poets use words precisely and sparingly, each word is significant.

• With any poem, it helps to **try reading aloud.** By listening to the poem's sounds you will get insight into the meaning. Hear the beat of the rhythm, the pattern of rhyme, and the repetition of sounds.

• **Keep in mind that the speaker of a poem is not necessarily the poet** but rather the voice the poet has chosen to communicate the experience.

Understanding Drama

A **drama** is a literary work that is written for presentation to an audience. It tells a story through the speech and actions of the characters. It may be written in verse or in prose. Generally, plays are fictional, but occasionally they are based on true events and real people. Even a play that tells the story of something that actually happened will probably not re-create the exact words that were spoken. This happens because no one may remember just what was said at a particular moment.

As is true for fiction, the **characters** in a drama are developed in several ways. You can learn about them from what the playwright tells you, from what the characters say about themselves, from what others say about the characters, and from what the characters do.

Most plays have the same elements of **plot** that you find in fiction. There will be a problem, a conflict, and a resolution.

Below are the common forms that drama takes and some important terms to know as you learn about drama.

Stage Plays

In the nineteenth and early twentieth centuries, the **stage** was seen as a room with one wall removed. The audience viewed all that happened through this invisible "fourth" wall. Before the performance and during intermissions, a curtain replaced the invisible wall. Recently the traditional stage has become less confined, and some theaters have been built with the stage in the center and seating on all sides. Stage plays are acted in front of live audiences.

Television Plays

A **television play** is performed on a stage for broadcast to television viewers. You will see this form of drama most frequently on public or educational television networks.

Movies

Usually filmed at different locations and over a period of time, **movies** can include more action than is possible in a stage or television play. Movies are produced for both large public theaters and for first-time viewing on television.

Radio Plays

The two most significant features of **radio plays** are dialogue between characters and sound effects that add to the drama. Although radio plays are not common today, they were very popular before the days of television.

Cast of Characters

If you go to the performance of a play, you will likely get a program that lists all of the **characters** who have parts in the production. The script for a play you read will have a similar list of characters at the beginning, before the scene is described or the action starts. Sometimes this list not only names the characters in the play but also describes or identifies them for you. Here is the beginning of the cast of characters from *Back There* by Rod Serling.

CHARACTERS

PETER CORRIGAN, *a young man*
JACKSON, *member of the Washington Club*
MILLARD, *member of the Washington Club*
WHITAKER, *member of the Washington Club*

Script

A play, whether it is performed live on stage or filmed by a camera, starts with a **script** made up of the stage directions and dialogue. In a play of more than one scene, the script shows how the play is divided into parts.

Stage Directions

Stage directions are the playwright's instructions to the performers. The setting may be described in detail in stage directions at the beginning of a play. You will notice that stage directions are usually printed in a different type, as in the following example from *Back There*.

SCENE 1

Exterior of club at night. Near a large front entrance of double doors is a name plaque in brass which reads "The Washington Club, Founded 1858." In the main hall of the building is a large paneled foyer with rooms leading off on either side.

Stage directions also provide information for the actors on how to interpret lines and how to move. When you read a play, the stage directions help you visualize the **characters' actions**. As in this example from *Back There*, stage directions may be set apart in parentheses as well as different type.

CORRIGAN (*takes a step down the stairs, staring at the* LIEUTENANT). You're going to a play tonight?

(*The* LIEUTENANT *nods.*)

Dialogue

Since the story in the play is revealed through the words of the characters as they perform on stage, **dialogue** makes up most of the text of a play. It is the chief means of moving the plot along in a play and is made up of the lines, or speeches, of the various characters. The following conversation is from *Back There*.

POLICE OFFICER. I was going to suggest, sir, that if perhaps we place extra guards in the box with the President—

CAPTAIN. The President has all the guards he needs. He's got the whole Federal Army at his disposal and if they're satisfied with his security arrangements, then I am too and so should you. Next case!

Strategies for Reading Drama

Reading a play is different from viewing it because you must picture the scene, imagine the characters, and interpret the actions.

- **Use the stage directions to visualize.** The information the playwright provides in the stage directions will help you picture the **setting** and the actions of the characters.

- **Read the stage directions carefully.** It's important to read the stage directions carefully because they help you imagine the scene and the action. You may be tempted to skip over the directions and focus on the dialogue, but if you do this you will miss some things you would see or hear if you were viewing the play or movie.

- **Try reading the characters' lines aloud.** Work with a partner or small group of classmates. Choose a scene from a play or movie script and assign individuals to the different parts. Read the dialogue as you imagine the character would say the words. Consider your tone of voice as well as the signals the playwright has included in the punctuation.

- **Be alert to special terms.** A play written for filming will usually include some specific directions for the person doing the camera work. For example, *fade in* means "to become slowly more distinct" and *pan* means "to move horizontally or vertically to take in the larger scene."

Glossary of Literary Terms

Words within entries in SMALL CAPITAL LETTERS refer you to other entries in the Glossary of Literary Terms.

alliteration The repetition of consonant sounds at the beginnings of words or within words. Alliteration is used to create melody, establish MOOD, and call attention to important words in a poem or sentence. "Lonely and spectral and somber and still" is an example ("Paul Revere's Ride," page 697).

biography Any account of a real person's life. "A President's Wife" by Russell Freedman (page 78) is a biography. An autobiography is the story of part or all of a person's life written by the person who lived it. Esmeralda Santiago's *A Shot at It* (page 634) is an autobiography.

characterization The methods an author uses to acquaint a reader with the characters in a work. An author may develop a character through describing the character's physical appearance, as Maya Angelou does in describing Mrs. Flowers (page 152). A character's speech and behavior may be described, as are those of the grandmother in "The Horned Toad" (page 446). The thoughts and feelings of a character may be told, as are Al's in Saroyan's "The Parsley Garden" (page 142). The author may also develop a character by revealing the attitudes and reactions of other characters, as Kurt Vonnegut does in showing the reactions of Helmholtz and Quinn to Jim in "The Kid Nobody Could Handle" (page 45).

connotation The emotional associations surrounding a word, as opposed to the word's DENOTATION, or literal meaning. The word *home,* for example, has a warmer, cozier connotation than the word *house.* In "The White Umbrella," Gish Jen uses words with strong connotations to describe the attractiveness of the umbrella. It was "pure white," it "glowed like a scepter," and it had a "slender silver handle" (pages 245–246).

denotation The strict, literal meaning of a word; the definition in a dictionary. (See also CONNOTATION.)

dialogue The conversation between two or more people in a literary work. Dialogue can serve to develop CHARACTERIZATION, as in Langston Hughes's "Thank You, Ma'am" (page 254), or it can help create the MOOD, as in Gwendolyn Brooks's "Home" (page 39). Dialogue can also advance the PLOT, as it often does in plays, such as *The Diary of Anne Frank* (page 538).

drama A composition in prose or verse written to be acted on a stage, before motion-picture or television cameras, or in front of a microphone. *Back There* (page 93), *The Diary of Anne Frank* (page 538), and *Rip Van Winkle* (page 681) are examples of drama.

end rhyme The rhyming of words at the ends of lines of poetry.

> Your world is as big as you make it.
> I know, for I used to aBIDE
> In the narrowest nest in a corner,
> My wings pressing close to my SIDE.
> —Georgia Douglas Johnson, "Your World," page 89

essay A brief composition that presents a personal point of view. "Animal Craftsmen" (page 302) is a good example of an essay.

fantasy A work that takes place partly or entirely in an unreal world. Often, there are incredible characters and the plot concerns events that cannot be scientifically explained. "The Enchanted Raisin" (page 315) is a fantasy.

fiction A story, novel, or play about imagined people and events. Examples are "Viva New Jersey" (page 6) and *Rip Van Winkle* (page 681).

figurative language Language expanded beyond its ordinary literal meaning. It uses comparisons to achieve new effects, to provide fresh insights, or to express a relationship between things that are essentially different. The most common figures of speech are SIMILE, METAPHOR, and HYPERBOLE.

flashback An interruption in the action of a story, play, or piece of nonfiction to show an episode that happened at an earlier time. A flashback is used to provide background information necessary to understanding the characters or plot. By using a flashback, an author can have some freedom to rearrange the events of a story in an order that has the strongest effect. There is a flashback toward the beginning of "Viva New Jersey," when Lucinda, after finding a lost dog, recalls the journey she and her family took six months earlier, when they left Cuba for the United States (page 6).

foreshadowing The author's use of hints or clues to suggest events that will occur later in the narrative. In "Flowers for Algernon" (page 485), what happens to the mouse Algernon often foreshadows what will happen to Charlie.

free verse A type of poetry that is "free" from a fixed pattern of RHYTHM or RHYME. Poems in free verse in this book include "The Dust Will Settle" (page 27) and "Rice and Rose Bowl Blues" (page 162).

hyperbole An exaggerated statement, sometimes involving FIGURATIVE LANGUAGE, used chiefly to heighten the effect of a statement. Examples of hyperbole include Howie saying, "I love her with a deep, burning, eternal flame of passion" in "Liverwurst and Roses" (page 66) and Mona saying, "We're going to catch *pneumonia*" in "The White Umbrella" (page 247).

imagery Concrete words or details that appeal to the senses of sight, sound, touch, smell, taste, and to internal feelings. Gwendolyn Brooks's "Home" (pages 39–41) is rich in specific, concrete details that appeal to the senses.

inference A reasonable and intelligent conclusion drawn by a reader or viewer from hints or implications provided by the author or artist. For example, early in "Flowers for Algernon" (pages 489–492) the reader can infer that Charlie's co-workers aren't really his friends, even though he thinks they are.

irony A contrast between what appears to be and what really is. *Verbal irony* occurs when one says the opposite of the intended meaning, as when Jim says "Aren't you the lucky one?" to Helmholtz in "The Kid Nobody Could Handle" (page 48). *Irony of situation* exists when what happens is the opposite of what is expected or intended. In *Back There* (page 93), it is ironic that Corrigan tries to prevent Lincoln's assassination but instead changes the fortunes of a minor character. *Dramatic irony* occurs when the reader or spectator knows more about the true state of affairs than a character does. For example, there

is dramatic irony in "Flowers for Algernon" when Charlie says, "all my friends are smart people but there good. They like me and they never did anything that wasn't nice" (page 494). As readers, we know that Charlie's friends are not very nice and have treated him badly.

metaphor A figure of speech that involves an implied comparison between two basically unlike things. In a metaphor there is never a connective such as *like* or *as* to signal a comparison is being made. (See SIMILE.) The comparison may be stated (She was a stone) or implied (Her stony silence filled the room). In "The Sidewalk Racer," for example, Lillian Morrison compares the rider of a skateboard to a sailor on the sea (page 163). (See also SIMILE and FIGURATIVE LANGUAGE.)

mood The atmosphere or overall feeling within a work. The choice of setting, objects, details, images, and words all contribute to create a specific mood. The mood can change during the course of a story. In *The Diary of Anne Frank,* for example, the mood can shift suddenly from celebration to terror (as in Act One, Scene 5) or from anger to joy (as in Act Two, Scene 3).

myth A traditional story connected with the religion or beliefs of a people, usually attempting to account for something in nature. "The Creation of Music" (page 711) is an Aztec myth.

narrative A story or account of an event or a series of happenings. It may be true or fictional. "Prisoner of My Country" (page 31) and "The Kid Nobody Could Handle" (page 45) are both narratives.

narrator The teller of a story. The teller may be a character in the story, as in Poe's "The Tell-Tale Heart" (page 262); an anonymous voice outside the story, as in London's "To Build a Fire" (page 176); or the author, as in Maya Angelou's *I Know Why the Caged Bird Sings* (page 152). (See also POINT OF VIEW.)

nonfiction Any writing that is not fiction; any type of literature that deals with real people and events. BIOGRAPHY, ESSAY, and speech are types of nonfiction. "Animal Craftsmen" (page 302), "The Gettysburg Address" (page 656), and "Sound-Shadows of the New World" (page 661) are examples of nonfiction.

Glossary of Literary Terms   **753**

novel Long works of FICTION dealing with characters, situations, and settings that copy those of real life. *The Outsiders* by S. E. Hinton is an example of a novel.

onomatopoeia Words used to imitate the sound of a thing. *Hiss, smack, buzz,* and *hum* are examples of words whose sounds suggest their sense. There are several examples of onomatopoeia in these lines from Longfellow's "Paul Revere's Ride" (page 698):

> He heard the bleating of the flock,
> And the twitter of birds among the trees,
> And felt the breath of the morning breeze
> Blowing over the meadows brown.

parody A humorous imitation of serious writing. It follows the form of the original, but often changes the sense to ridicule the writer's style or message. "Variations on a Theme by William Carlos Williams" by Kenneth Koch (page 383) is a parody of William Carlos Williams's poem, "This Is Just to Say" (page 382).

personification A figure of speech or FIGURATIVE LANGUAGE in which human characteristics are given to nonhuman things. In the poem "Primer Lesson" (page 392) Carl Sandburg personifies proud words when he describes them as wearing boots and walking off.

play (See DRAMA.)

plot In the simplest sense, a series of happenings in a literary work. The term is also used to refer to the action as it is organized around a *conflict* and builds through complication to a *climax* followed by a RESOLUTION. "The Treasure of Lemon Brown" (page 362) has all the elements of a fully developed plot.

poetry Composition in verse. The words in poetry are arranged in lines that have RHYTHM and, sometimes, RHYME.

point of view The vantage point from which an author presents the actions and characters of a story. The story may be related by a character (the *first-person* point of view), as in "Prisoner of My Country" (page 31) or "The Tell-Tale Heart" (page 262), or the story may be told by a narrator who does not participate in the action (the *third-person* point of view). Further, the third-person narrator may be *omniscient*—able to see into the minds of all characters, as in "To Build a Fire"

(page 176)—or the third-person narrator may be *limited*—confined to a single character's perceptions, as in "The Treasure of Lemon Brown" (page 362). An author who describes only what can be seen, like a newspaper reporter, is said to use an *objective* point of view. (See also NARRATOR.)

repetition A word or phrase used over and over again for emphasis, especially in poetry but also sometimes in folk tales. Repetition is used in the last few lines of the poem "The Dust Will Settle" (page 27).

resolution The tying up of the PLOT; the conclusion, where the complications in a plot are resolved.

rhyme The repetition of syllable sounds. End words that share a particular sound are called END RHYMES. Rhyming words within a line of poetry are called *internal rhymes.* In "The Sidewalk Racer" (page 163), *swerve* and *curve* and *sound* and *ground* are internal rhymes.

rhyme scheme The pattern of END RHYMES in a poem. You can chart a rhyme scheme with letters of the alphabet by using the same letter for end words that rhyme, as in this example:

> Listen my children, and you shall hear   a
> Of the midnight ride of Paul Revere,   a
> On the eighteenth of April, in Seventy-five;   b
> Hardly a man is now alive   b
> Who remembers that famous day and year.   a
> —Longfellow, "Paul Revere's Ride," page 695

rhythm The arrangement of stressed and unstressed sounds in writing and speech. Rhythm may be regular or it may be varied. In "Your World," by Georgia Douglas Johnson (page 89), the rhythm is regular (capital letters indicate stressed words or syllables):

> Your WORLD is as BIG as you MAKE it.
> I KNOW, for I USED to ABIDE
> In the NARROWest NEST in a CORner,
> My WINGS pressing CLOSE to my SIDE.

science fiction A fictional literary work that uses scientific and technological facts and ideas as a basis for fantastic stories. Science fiction often involves adventures in the future or on other planets—as in Arthur C. Clarke's short story "If I Forget Thee, Oh Earth . . ." (page 702)—or about travel through time—as in Rod Serling's play, *Back There* (page 93). Science fiction is a form of FANTASY. However, it can also be set in our own time, in a not-too-distant future in which some technological or scientific breakthrough has occurred—as in "Flowers for Algernon" (page 485).

setting The time and place in which the events of a narrative occur. The setting may be specific and detailed and introduced at the very beginning of the story, or it may be merely suggested through the use of details scattered throughout the story. In some stories the setting is vital to the narrative: it may have an effect on the events of the PLOT, reveal character, or create a certain MOOD. In other stories the setting is relatively unimportant. The setting is important in *Back There* (page 93), "To Build a Fire" (page 176), and "The Banana Tree" (page 194).

short story A story shorter than a NOVEL. Although it generally describes just one event, it most often has a beginning, a middle, and an end. The characters are usually fewer in number and not as fully developed as those in a novel. William Saroyan's "The Parsley Garden" (page 142) and Robert Cormier's "The Moustache" (page 410) are examples of a short story.

simile A comparison in which the word *like* or *as* is used to point out a similarity between two basically unlike things. Gary Paulsen uses a simile in "Stop the Sun" when he describes Terry's father's breath "coming in short, hot pants like some kind of hurt animal" (page 20). (See METAPHOR.)

speaker The same as a NARRATOR. Often the narrator of a poem is called the speaker.

stanza A group of lines set off visually from the other lines in a poem. Julio Noboa Polanco's poem "Identity" (page 164) has five stanzas.

stereotype A fixed, generalized idea about a character or situation. An example of a stereotyped character is the wicked stepmother in "The Enchanted Raisin" (page 315). A stereotyped situation might be a plot about a small boy and a brave dog.

suspense The method or methods an author uses to maintain a reader's interest. In *Back There* (page 93), Rod Serling creates suspense by placing obstacles in the way of Corrigan's attempt to prevent Lincoln's assassination. We don't know till very late in the play whether Corrigan will succeed or fail, and that keeps us interested.

symbol An object, action, person, or situation that suggests a meaning beyond its obvious meaning. In "The Kid Nobody Could Handle" (page 45), Jim's boots are a symbol of the appearance he gives of being tough and mean.

theme The underlying meaning of a literary work. A theme may be directly stated, but more often it is merely implied. In Gerald Haslam's short story "The Horned Toad" (page 446), the topic or subject of the story is a grandmother's visit, but an important theme is the importance of family ties.

tone An author's attitude toward the subject of a literary work or toward the reader. That attitude may be serious, bitter, humorous, sympathetic, cynical, or ironic. Tone is conveyed through the author's particular choice of words and details in describing setting, portraying characters, and presenting events. Yoshiko Uchida's tone in "Prisoner of My Country" (page 31) is indignant. Ellen Conford's tone in "Liverwurst and Roses" (page 65) is humorous and lighthearted: the main character may be suffering, but the author's tone implies that what he's going through is really not a tragedy.

Glossary of Vocabulary Words

a	hat	o hot	ü rule
ā	age	ō open	ch child
ä	far	ô order	ng long
e	let	oi oil	sh she
ē	equal	ou out	th thin
ė	term	u cup	ŦH then
i	it	ù put	zh measure
ī	ice		

ə { a in about / e in taken / i in pencil / o in lemon / u in circus

A

abide (ə bīd′), *v.* continue to live (in a place); dwell.

abyss (ə bis′), *n.* a very great bottomless depth.

academic (ak′ə dem′ik), *adj.* concerned with general studies and education, not technical or professional training.

acclimatized (ə klī′mə tīzd), *adj.* become used to a new place or surroundings.

accusation (ak′yə zā′shən), *n.* charge of wrong-doing.

acute (ə kyüt′), *adj.* sharp; keen.

adrift (ə drift′), *adj.* floating without direction.

advocate (ad′və kit, ad′və kāt), *n.* person who pleads or argues for; supporter.

affirm (ə fėrm′), *v.* declare to be true.

agitated (aj′ə tāt əd), *adj.* disturbed, upset.

ail (āl), *v.* be the matter with; trouble.

ajar (ə jär′), *adj.* slightly open.

allegiance (ə lē′jəns), *n.* faithfulness to a person or thing.

aloft (ə lôft′, ə loft′), *adv.* far above the ground; high up.

alternate (ôl′tər nāt), *v.* take turns with.

ambition (am bish′ən), *n.* desire to rise to a high position.

amnesia (am nē′zhə), *n.* partial or total loss of memory caused by injury to the brain, or by disease, shock, etc.

anachronism (ə nak′rə niz′əm), *n.* anything out of keeping with a specified time.

antiseptic (an′tə sep′tik), *adj.* having a sterilized or sterile quality; cold, barren, lifeless, etc.

anxiety (ang zī′ə tē), *n.* uneasy thoughts or fears over the possibility of coming misfortune.

aperture (ap′ər chər, ap′ər chùr), *n.* opening or hole.

appalled (ə pôld′), *adj.* filled with horror or alarm.

apprehension (ap′ri hen′shən), *n.* expectation of misfortune; dread of impending danger.

aptitude (ap′tə tüd), *n.* natural talent.

aristocrat (ə ris′tə krat), *n.* a person who holds a high position in society.

aroma (ə rō′mə), *n.* distinctive fragrance.

artillery (är til′ər ē), *n.* weapons, usually large.

ashamed (ə shāmd′), *adj.* feeling shame; disturbed or uncomfortable because one has done something wrong, improper, or foolish.

asphalt (as′fôlt), *n.* a mix of tar and stones that is used for road surfaces; blacktop.

audacity (ô das′ə tē), *n.* reckless daring; boldness.

audible (ô′də bəl), *adj.* loud enough be heard.

audition (ô dish′ən), *v.* sing, act, or perform at a tryout that tests the ability, quality, or performance of the performers.

aura (ôr′ə), *n.* an atmosphere that surrounds something or someone.

authentic (ô then′tik), *adj.* real, not copied.

avalanche (av′ə lanch), *n.* a large mass of snow and ice, or dirt and rocks, loosened from a mountainside and descending swiftly into the valley below.

awed (ôd), *adj.* filled with wonder and amazement.

B

baffle (baf′əl), *v.* bewilder.

barrack (bar′ək), *n.* a large, plain building in which many people live.

belligerent (bə lij′ər ənt), *adj.* fond of fighting; warlike.

benefactor (ben′ə fak′tər, ben′ə fak′tər), *n.* person who has given money or kindly help.

benign (bi nīn′), *adj.* kindly and gentle.

betray (bi trā′), *v.* be disloyal to.

bitterly (bit′ər lē), *adv.* painfully.

blasphemy (blas′fə mē), *n.* contempt for a holy or sacred thing; profanity.

brazen (brā′zn), *adj.* **1.** bold. **2.** made of brass.

bridle (brī′dl), *v.* lift up one's chin or head to express pride or anger.

browse (brouz), *v.* look at casually.

bungalow (bung′gə lō), *n.* a small house, usually of one story.

butte (byüt), *n.* a steep, flat-topped hill standing alone.

C

cajole (kə jōl′), *v.* persuade by pleasant words or flattery; coax.

calamity (kə lam′ə tē), *n.* a great misfortune.

campaign (kam pān′), *n.* series of connected activities to do or get something, such as to win an election.

canvas (kan′vəs), *n.* a piece of strong cloth to be painted on.

caper (kā′pər), *v.* leap or jump about playfully.

capitulation (kə pich′ə lā′shən), *n.* a surrender on certain terms or conditions.

caravan (kar′ə van), *n.* group traveling together for safety.

cartographer (kär tog′rə fər), *n.* a person who makes maps.

cerebral (sə rē′brəl), *adj.* of the brain.

civil rights (siv′əl rīts), the rights guaranteed to all citizens.

clairvoyant (kler voi′ənt, klar voi′ənt), *adj.* supposedly having the power of seeing or knowing things that are out of sight.

commence (kə mens′), *v.* begin.

commotion (kə mō′shən), *n.* bustle or confusion.

comply (kəm plī′), *v.* act in agreement with a request or command.

compressed (kəm prest′), *adj.* squeezed together.

conceited (kən sēt′əd), *adj.* having too high an opinion of oneself.

conceive (kən sēv′), *v.* think up; form.

condense (kən dens′), *v.* make more compact.

confront (kən frunt′), *v.* face boldly.

consecrate (kon′sə krāt), *v.* make holy.

console (kon′sōl), *n.* a cabinet that stands on the floor and houses, in this case, a television.

conspicuous (kən spik′yü əs), *adj.* easily seen.

conspiratorial (kən spir′ə tôr′ē əl), *adj.* having to do with secret plans with others to do something wrong; plotting or scheming.

cordial (kôr′jəl), *adj.* warm and friendly in manner.

craggy (krag′ē), *adj.* rough; uneven.

cringe (krinj), *v.* retreat away from.

D

dawdle (dô′dl), *v.* waste time; move slowly.

debris (də brē′), *n.* fragments; litter.

decathlon (di kath′lon), *n.* a track-and-field contest with ten different events. The person who scores the most points for all ten parts is the winner.

dedicate (ded′ə kāt), *v.* set apart for a sacred or important purpose.

deft (deft), *adj.* quick and skillful in action.

degrading (di grā′ding), *adv.* bringing into dishonor or contempt.

deport (di pôrt′, di pōrt′), *v.* force to leave a country; banish.

deprive (di prīv′), *v.* keep from having.

derision (di rizh′ən), *n.* ridicule.

desolation (des′ə lā′ shən), *n.* barren or deserted condition.

deterioration (di tir′ē ə rā′shən), *n.* when something wears down and becomes lower in quality.

detest (di test′), *v.* intensely dislike; hate.

devise (di vīz′), *v.* think out, plan, or invent.

devour (di vour′), *v.* eat very hungrily.

dignified (dig′nə fīd), *adj.* having pride and self-respect in manner, style, or appearance.

diminish (də min′ish), *v.* make smaller.

discern (də zėrn′, də sėrn′), *v.* see clearly.

discreet (dis krēt′), *adj.* very careful and sensible in speech and action.

dispatch (dis pach′), *v.* send off to some place or for some purpose.

dispel (dis pel′), *v.* drive away and scatter.

dissection (di sek′shən), *n.* the act of cutting apart an animal in order to study its structure.

diversion (də vėr′zhən, dī vėr′zhən), *n.* distraction.

dolt (dōlt), *n.* a dull, stupid person.

domestic (də mes′tik), *adj.* devoted to family life.

E

eerie (ir′ē), *adj.* something that is weird or strange and causes fear.

elegant (el′ə gənt), *adj.* graceful; showing good taste.

eloquence (el′ə kwəns), *n.* flow of forceful speech.

embossed (em bôst′), *adj.* decorated with a design that stands out from the surface.

empathy (em′pə thē), *n.* quality of entering into another's feelings.

emphatic (em fat′ik), *adj.* strongly expressed.

encampment (en kamp′mənt), *n.* place where a group, such as soldiers, make a camp.

endurance (en dùr′əns), *n.* power to last and to withstand hard wear.

ennui (än′wē), *n.* boredom.

essence (es′ns), *n.* that which makes a thing what it is; the necessary part.

evict (i vikt′), *v.* remove from a building by legal means.

evoke (i vōk′), *v.* call forth; bring out.

excruciating (ek skrü′shē ā′ting), *adj.* causing great suffering; very painful.

exile (eg′zīl), *n.* a person who must leave his or her country and live somewhere else.

extension (ek sten′shən), *n.* an additional amount of time.

extremities (ek strem′ə tēz), *n.* the hands and feet.

exult (eg zult′), *v.* rejoice, celebrate.

F

familiar (fə mil′yər), *n.* intimate friend.

fast (fast), *v.* go without food; eat little or nothing.

fatigue (fə tēg′), *n.* weariness caused by hard work or effort.

fauna (fô′nə), *n. pl.,* the animals of a particular region or period.

fertile (fėr′tl), *adj.* soil that is rich and productive.

flexible (flek′sə bəl), *adj.* mentally able to adapt to changing circumstances.

flounder (floun′dər), *v.* struggle awkwardly without making much progress.

fodder (fod′ər), *n.* coarse food, such as hay and cornstalks, for a horse, cattle, etc.

foreboding (fôr bō′ding, fōr bō′ding), *n.* a feeling that something bad is going to happen.

foresight (fōr′sīt′), *n.* power to see or know beforehand what is likely to happen.

fortify (fôr′tə fī), *v.* strengthen.

founder (foun′dər), *v.* fail.

fragile (fraj′əl), *adj.* delicate; frail.

fugitive (fyü′jə tiv), *n.* person who runs away or attempts to escape.

furtive (fėr′tiv), *adj.* sly, secret.

futility (fyü til′ə tē), *n.* uselessness.

G

generation (jen′ə rā′shən), *n.* all of the people born about the same period. Parents belong to one generation and their children to the next.

gesticulation (je stik′yə lā′shən), *n.* excited gesture.

gilded (gild′ed), *adj.* covered with gold.

gnarled (närld), *adj.* twisted; knotted.

grimly (grim′lē), *adv.* in a serious way, not offering hope; sternly, harshly, or fiercely.

H

habitable (hab′ə tə bəl), *adj.* fit to live in.

handiwork (han′dē wėrk′), *n.* work done by a person's hands.

harass (har′əs, hə ras′) *v.* trouble by repeated attacks.

harness (här′nis), *v.* tie or strap to something.

heritage (her′ə tij), *n.* what is handed down from one generation to the next.

homage (hom′ij, om′ij), *n.* respect.

homely (hōm′lē), *adj.* not good looking; having an ordinary appearance; plain.

huddled (hud′ld), *adj.* crowded close together.

humiliated (hyü mil′ē āt id), *adj.* made to feel lowered and shamed in the eyes of others.

hypocritical (hip′ə krit′ə kəl), *adj.* insincere.

I

immensity (i men′sə tē), *n.* very great size or extent.

immigration (im′ə grā′shən), *n.* coming into a foreign country or region to live.

impaired (im perd′), *adj.* damaged; weakened.

impassively (im pas′iv lē), *adj.* without feeling or emotion.

impede (im pēd′), *v.* stand in the way of; hinder.

imperative (im′pər′ə tiv), *adj.* necessary; urgent.

impetuous (im pech′ü əs), *adj.* acting with sudden or rash energy.

improvise (im′prə vīz), *v.* make up on the spur of the moment.

inadequacy (in ad′ə kwə sē), *n.* a being not adequate, not as much as is needed.

inarticulate (in′är tik′yə lit), *adj.* unable to speak.

inaugural (in ô′gyər əl), *adj.* of or for the ceremony of installing a person in office.

incarcerate (in kär′sə rāt′), *v.* imprison; put in prison.

incentive (in sen′tiv), *n.* thing that urges a person on.

incessantly (in ses′nt lē), *adv.* always; without stopping.

inclusively (in klü′siv lē), *adv.* including everyone.

incomprehensible (in′kom pri hen′sə bəl), *adj.* impossible to understand.

incredulously (in krej′ə ləs lē), *adv.* doubtfully; without being able to believe.

indignantly (in dig′nənt lē), *adv.* with anger at something unjust or unfair.

indomitable (in dom′ə tə bəl), *adj.* unbeatable; unconquerable.

ineffectually (in′ə fek′chü əl lē), *adv.* without effect; uselessly.

inevitable (in ev′ə tə bəl), *n.* not to be avoided.

ingenious (in jē′nyəs), *adj.* skillful in making; clever.

insistent (in sis′tənt), *adj.* continuing to make a strong, firm demand or statement; insisting.

inspire (in spīr′), *v.* fill with thought, feeling, life, force, etc.

instability (in′stə bil′ə tē), *n.* being unstable; being unpredictable.

instinctively (in stingk′tiv lē), *adv.* of or having to do with instinct, intuition, or unlearned behavior.

insurmountable (in′sər moun′tə bəl), *adj.* that cannot be overcome.

inter (in tėr′), *v.* put into a grave or tomb; bury.

intern (in tėrn′), *v.* force to stay in a certain place.

intolerable (in tol′ər ə bəl), *adj.* too much to be endured; unbearable.

intricately (in′trə kit lē), *adv.* in a complex or complicated way.

introspective (in′trə spek′tiv), *adj.* having to do with looking inward to examine one's own thoughts and feelings.

intuition (in′tü ish′ən, in′tyü ish′ən), *n.* immediate perception or understanding of truths, facts, etc., without reasoning.

invariably (in ver′ē ə blē), *adv.* without changing; always in the same way.

involuntary (in vol′ən ter′ē), *adj.* not controlled by one's will.

irritability (ir′ə tə bil′ə tē), *n.* impatience; unnatural sensitivity; annoyance.

L

lacerated (las′ə rāt′əd), *adj.* torn roughly; mangled.

lair (ler), *n.* den or resting place of a wild animal.

lament (lə ment′), *v.* express grief.

lilt (lilt), *n.* a light, graceful rhythm.

linger (ling′gər), *v.* be slow to pass away or disappear.

loafer (lō′fər), *n.* someone who spends time doing nothing; a lazy person.

lucid (lü′sid), *adj.* clear; sane.

luminous (lü′mə nəs), *adj.* full of light; shining.

lunge (lunj), *v.* make a sudden forward movement.

M

makeshift (māk′shift′), *adj.* used for a time instead of the right thing.

maladjustment (mal′ə just′mənt), *n.* poor or unsatisfactory adjustment; not fitting in.

maneuver (mə nü′vər), *v.* to move with great skill.

menial (mē′nē əl), *adj.* low; humble.

mercurial (mər kyur′ē əl), *adj.* changeable.

mesmerized (mez′mə rīzd′), *adj.* hypnotized.

mirage (mə razh′), *n.* an optical illusion.

modulated (moj′ə lāt əd), *adj.* altered in pitch, tone, or volume for expression.

molding (mol′ding), *n.* decorative wood used along the walls of a room.

mongrel (mung′grəl), *n.* a dog of mixed breed.

monologue (mon′l ôg), *n.* part of a play in which a single actor speaks alone.

monotony (mə not′n ē), *n.* lack of variety; sameness.

mosaic (mō zā′ik), *adj.* resembling a decoration made of small pieces of glass, wood, etc., to form a picture or design.

motivation (mō′tə vā′shən), *n.* the reason or force that makes people act.

muse (myüz), *v.* be completely absorbed in thought.

muster (mus′tər), *n.* assembly, especially of troops.

mutinous (myüt′n əs), *adj.* rebellious; uncontrollable.

muzzle (muz′əl), *n.* **1.** the projecting part of the head of an animal, including the nose, mouth, and jaws. **2.** a cover or cage of straps or wires to put over an animal's head or mouth to keep it from biting or eating.

N

naively (nä ēvʹ lē), *adv.* without question; like a child.

O

obligation (obʹlə gāʹshən), *n.* duty due to a promise, contract, or relationship; responsibility.

obscure (əb skyu̇rʹ), *v.* cloud; darken.

obstinate (obʹstə nit), *adj.* hard to control.

ominous (omʹə nəs), *adj.* threatening.

onslaught (ônʹslôtʹ, onʹslôt), *n.* a vigorous attack.

opinionated (ə pinʹyə nāʹtid), *adj.* firm, even stubborn, with regard to one's opinion.

opportunist (opʹər tüʹnist), *n.* a person who uses every opportunity to gain some advantage, regardless of right or wrong.

ornament (ôrʹnə mənt), *v.* to decorate or add beauty to.

ostentatiously (osʹten tāʹshəs lē), *adv.* in a manner intended to attract notice.

P

pandemonium (panʹdə mōʹnē əm), *n.* wild disorder or confusion.

pantomime (panʹtə mīm), *n.* gestures without words.

parody (parʹə dē), *n.* a humorous imitation of a serious writing.

perennial (pə renʹē əl), *adj.* lasting for a very long time; enduring.

perilous (perʹə ləs), *adj.* dangerous.

periphery (pə rifʹər ē), *n.* an outside boundary.

petition (pə tishʹən), *n.* a formal request to an authority to have something done.

phonetically (fə netʹik lē), *adv.* by breaking the words into individual sounds.

pigment (pigʹmənt), *n.* a coloring matter that is used to dye paint.

plateau (pla tōʹ), *n.* a period or state of stability or little or no growth.

platform (platʹfôrm), *n.* a plan of action or statement of principles for a political party or group.

poignant (poiʹnyənt), *adj.* stimulating to the mind, feelings, or passions; intense.

postponement (pōst pōnʹmənt), *n.* delay.

pouch (pouch), *n.* small bag or sack.

precipitous (pri sipʹə təs), *adj.* very steep.

pretense (prēʹtens, pri tensʹ), *n.* a false appearance.

primer (prīʹmər), *n.* paint that is used for the first coat of paint as a sealer or base.

primitive (primʹə tiv), *adj.* very simple, such as people had early in history.

probe (prōb), *v.* search.

profound (prə foundʹ), *adj.* capable of having great knowledge or understanding.

progeny (projʹə nē), *n.* children; offspring.

proposition (propʹə zishʹən), *n.* suggestion or idea.

proprietor (prə prīʹə tər), *n.* a person who legally owns something.

protest (prə testʹ), *v.* object to.

pungent (punʹjənt), *adj.* a taste or smell that is very sharp.

purge (pėrj), *v.* clean or free of an undesired thing or impurity.

purifying (pyu̇rʹə fī ing), *adj.* making pure, clean, or free from evil.

Q

quadrant (kwodʹrənt), *n.* (in geometry) one of the four parts into which a plane is divided by two straight lines crossing at right angles.

quarrel (kwôrʹəl), *v.* disagree angrily.

quest (kwest), *n.* search or hunt.

quirky (kwėrʹkē), *adj.* peculiar or odd.

quivering (kwivʹər ing), *adj.* trembling; shaking.

R

radiant (rā′dē ənt), *adj.* shining; beaming.

rapture (rap′chər), *n.* a strong feeling, especially of delight or joy.

raucous (rô′kəs), *adj.* harsh sounding.

receipt (ri sēt′), *n.* a written record of money that has been received.

refined (ri fīnd′), *adj.* well-bred.

refuse (ref′yüs), *n.* waste; rubbish; trash.

regale (ri gāl′), *v.* entertain.

regally (rē′gəl lē), *adv.* royally; like a king or queen.

regression (ri gresh′ən), *n.* a return to an earlier way of thinking or acting.

relent (ri lent′), *v.* become less harsh or cruel; be more tender and merciful.

reluctantly (ri luk′tənt lē), *adv.* unwillingly.

remnant (rem′nənt), *n.* small part left; fragment.

remorse (ri môrs′), *n.* deep, painful regret for having done wrong.

rendition (ren dish′ən), *n.* the performance or interpretation of a piece of music.

replicate (rep′lə kāt), *v.* copy exactly or reproduce.

reproachfully (ri prōch′fəl lē), *adv.* in a manner full of blame or disapproval.

resemblance (ri zem′bləns), *n.* similar appearance; likeness.

reservation (rez′ər vā′shən), *n.* land set aside by the government for a special purpose.

resolve (ri zolv′), *n.* firmness in carrying out a purpose; determination.

resounding (ri zoun′ding), *adj.* sounding loudly.

respectively (ri spek′tiv lē), *adv.* as regards each of several persons or things in turn or in the order mentioned.

revelation (rev′ə lā′shən), *n.* the act of making known.

riff-raff (rif′raf′), *n.* people with bad reputations.

S

sagacity (sə gas′ə tē), *n.* sharp mental ability; shrewdness.

sage (sāj), *n.* a small shrub whose leaves are used for seasoning and medicines.

savor (sā′vər), *v.* enjoy or appreciate.

scepter (sep′tər), *n.* the rod carried by a ruler as a symbol of royal power.

scoundrel (skoun′drəl), *n.* wicked person; someone without honor or principles.

senility (sə nil′ə tē), *n.* the mental and physical deterioration often characteristic of old age.

serenity (sə ren′ə tē), *n.* peace and quiet.

servile (sėr′vəl), *adj.* like that of slaves; spiritless.

shabby (shab′ē), *adj.* much worn.

sibling (sib′ling), *n.* a brother or sister.

significant (sig nif′ə kənt), *adj.* full of meaning.

simmer (sim′ər), *n.* process of cooking something at or just below boiling point.

slurred (slėrd), *adj.* pronounced unclearly, indistinctly.

solder (sod′ər), *n.* metal that is melted and used to connect other metal parts.

solitary (sol′ə ter′ē), *adj.* alone or single.

somber (som′bər), *adj.* dark; gloomy.

sophistication (sə fis′tə kā′shən), *n.* worldly experience.

sparse (spärs), *adj.* thinly scattered.

spontaneity (spon′tə nē′ə tē), *n.* the quality of being natural, unplanned, and unforced.

staccato (stə kä′tō), *adj.* when the beats of a rhythm (such as a person's footsteps) are abrupt and disconnected.

stealthily (stel′thə lē), *adv.* in a secret manner.

stern (stėrn), *adj.* harshly firm; strict.

strut (strut), *v.* walk in a self-important manner.

subtle (sut′l), *adj.* so fine or delicate as to be unnoticed.

succession (sək sesh′ən), *n.* a group of things coming one after another.

succumb (sə kum′), *v.* die.

summon (sum′ən), *v.* call; stir to action; rouse.

supposition (sup′ə zish′ən), *n.* belief or opinion.

surge (sėrj), *v.* rise and fall; move like waves.

surrogate (sėr′ə gāt, sėr′ə git), *adj.* substitute.

suspect (sus′pekt, sə spekt′), *adj.* open to suspicion.

sustenance (sus′tə nəns), *n.* food or provisions; nourishment.

syndrome (sin′drōm), *n.* a group of symptoms considered together to be characteristic of a particular disease or condition.

systematically (sis′tə mat′ik lē), *adv.* according to a method; in an organized way.

T

tangible (tan′jə bəl), *adj.* something that is real, actual, and definite.

tattered (tat′ərd), *adj.* ragged.

taunt (tônt), *v.* jeer at; mock.

taut (tôt), *adj.* tightly drawn.

teeming (tē′ming), *adj.* full.

tempestuous (tem pes′chü əs), *adj.* stormy.

tenant (ten′ənt), *n.* person who rents the place where he or she lives.

tenement (ten′ə mənt), *n.* apartment building, especially in a poor section of town.

tentatively (ten′tə tiv lē), *adv.* hesitatingly; with caution.

thesis (thē′sis), *n.* statement to be proved or maintained against objections.

thicket (thik′it), *n.* shrubs and small trees growing close together.

thrash out, *v.* settle by thorough discussion.

topographer (tə pog′rə fər), *n.* a person who studies and charts the surface features (hills, lakes, roads) of a region.

tormented (tôr ment′əd), *adj.* tortured.

torrential (tô ren′shəl), *adj.* violently rushing.

trace (trās), *n.* very small amount; a little bit.

transformation (tran′sfər mā′shən), *n.* a change in form or appearance.

transformed (tran sfôrmd), *adj.* changed.

treacherous (trech′ər əs), *adj.* having a false appearance of strength, security, etc.; not reliable; deceiving.

trod (trod), *v.* walk on or trample.

tumult (tü′mult, tyü′mult), *n.* noise or uproar.

turbulent (tėr′byə lənt), *adj.* disorderly; violent.

tyranny (tir′ə nē), *n.* cruel or unjust use of power.

U

unabashed (un′ə basht′), *adj.* not embarrassed or awed.

uncanny (un kan′ē), *adj.* strange and mysterious.

unceremonious (un′ser ə mō′nē əs), *adj.* informal; not as polite as would be expected.

unconstitutional (un′kon stə tü′shə nəl), *adj.* against the Constitution of the United States, which guarantees certain rights.

unnerving (un nėrv′ing), *adj.* making someone lose his or her nerve or self-control.

unpretentious (un′pri ten′shəs), *adj.* modest.

unreliable (un′ri lī′ə bəl), *adj.* not to be depended on.

unseemly (un sēm′lē), *adj.* not suitable; improper.

uprooting (up rüt′ ing, up rùt′ ing), *n.* removal from one's home.

V

vacuous (vak′yü əs), *adj.* showing no thought or intelligence; stupid.

varmint (vär′mənt), *n.* unliked animal or person (DIALECT).

vehemently (vē′ə mənt lē), *adv.* forcefully; with strong feeling.

veteran (vet′ər ən), *n.* person who has served in the armed forces.

vie (vī), *v.* compete; strive for superiority.

vigil (vij′əl), *n.* a staying awake for some purpose; a watching.

visa (vē′zə), *n.* official document granting permission to travel to another country.

vivid (viv′id), *adj.* bright and colorful.

vocational (vō kā′shə nəl), *adj.* having to do with studies or training for some occupation.

vulnerable (vul′nər ə bəl), *adj.* sensitive to criticism.

W

wedge (wej), *v.* squeeze.

wince (wins), *v.* draw back suddenly; flinch.

Language and Grammar Handbook

The following Language and Grammar Handbook will help you as you edit your writing. It is alphabetically arranged, with each entry explaining a certain term or concept. For example, if you can't remember when to use *accept* and *except,* look up the entry **accept, except** and you'll find an explanation of the meaning of each word and a sentence (many from selections in this book) using each word.

A

a, an The choice between *a* and *an* depends on the beginning sound, not the beginning letter, of the following word. *A* is used before a consonant sound, and *an* is used before a vowel sound.

◆ . . . on the Arkansas summer days it seemed she had *a* private breeze which swirled around, cooling her.
   from *I Know Why the Caged Bird Sings* by Maya Angelou

◆ It grew like *an* avalanche, and it descended without warning. . . .
   from "To Build a Fire" by Jack London

Tiffany thought it was *a* useful idea.

accept, except *Accept* means "to take or receive; consent to receive; say yes to." It is always a verb. *Except* is most commonly used as a preposition meaning "but."

◆ I later learned that my great-grandmother . . . had been moving from house to house within the family, trying to find a place she'd *accept.*
   from "The Horned Toad" by Gerald Haslam

◆ You don't want anything from me *except* my happiness.
   from "Coretta and Edythe: The Scott Sisters" by Carol Saline

adjective Adjectives are modifiers that describe nouns and pronouns. Adjectives tell *what kind, which one,* or *how many.*

What kind:	*red* rose	*powerful* surf	*heavy* load
Which one:	*this* cassette	*that* skateboard	*those* tents
How many:	*three* ships	*few* passengers	*many* miles

See also **comparative forms of adjectives and adverbs.**

adverb Adverbs modify verbs, adjectives, or other adverbs. They tell *how, when,* or *where.*

How:	carefully	cautiously	slowly
When:	later	now	today
Where:	there	near	outside

See also **comparative forms of adjectives and adverbs.**

affect, effect *Affect* is usually a verb. It is most frequently used to mean "to influence." *Effect* is mainly used as a noun meaning "result or consequence."

◆ A medical encyclopedia said that both diseases *affect* the brain's ability to function.
    from "Beni Seballos" by Phillip Hoose

◆ . . . seeing how an animal makes its nest or egg case or food storage vaults has the *effect* of increasing our amazement.
    from "Animal Craftsmen" by Bruce Brooks

agreement

1. Subject-verb agreement. When the subject and verb of a sentence are both singular or both plural, they agree in number. This is called subject-verb agreement. Usually, singular verbs in the present tense end in *s*. Plural verbs do not have the *s* ending.

Andy drives. (singular subject; singular verb)
Jo and Andy drive. (plural subject; plural verb)

Pronouns generally follow the same rule. However, the singular pronouns *I* and *you* always take plural verbs.

	Singular	Plural
1st person	**I drive**	we drive
2nd person	**you drive**	you drive
3rd person	he/she/it drives	they drive

Changes also occur with the verb *to be* in both the present and past tense:

Present Tense		Past Tense	
I am	we are	I was	we were
you are	you are	you were	you were
he/she/it is	they are	he/she/it was	they were

a. Most compound subjects joined by *and* or *both...and* are plural and are followed by plural verbs.

◆ Then Mona and my mother were getting out of the car.
    from "The White Umbrella" by Gish Jen

b. A compound subject joined by *or, either...or,* or *neither...nor* is followed by a verb that agrees in number with the closer subject.

Either the teacher or the *students present* the award.

Neither the students nor the *teacher wants* to do it.

Problems arise when it isn't obvious what the subject is. The following rules should help you with some of the most troublesome situations:

c. Phrases or clauses coming between the subject and the verb do not affect the subject-verb agreement.

> The footprints of the dog *were* found in the snow.

d. Singular verbs are used with the singular indefinite pronouns *each, every, either, neither, anyone, anybody, one, everyone, everybody, someone, somebody, nobody, no one*.

> ◆ Although I was upset, *neither* of the women *was* in the least *shaken* by what I thought was an unceremonious greeting.
> from *I Know Why the Caged Bird Sings* by Maya Angelou

e. Plural indefinite pronouns take plural verbs. They are *both, few, many,* and *several.*

> *Few* of the cast members *know* their lines.

f. The indefinite pronouns *all, any, most, none,* and *some* can be either singular or plural depending on their meaning in a sentence.

Singular	Plural
Most of the trip *was* exciting.	*Most* of the cookies *were* eaten.
Some of the fruit *was* spoiled.	*Some* of the problems *were* easy.

g. Unusual word order does not affect agreement; the verb generally agrees with the subject, whether the subject follows or precedes it.

> ◆ Parked at the curb were rows of trucks being loaded. . . .
> from "Prisoner of My Country" by Yoshiko Uchida

> ◆ On top of this ice were as many feet of snow.
> from "To Build a Fire" by Jack London

NOTE: When writing dialogue, an author may intentionally use *there's* incorrectly for effect.

◆ Now using that prior knowledge, *there's* a hundred things you can do to protect yourself.
from *Back There* by Rod Serling

In informal English you may often hear sentences like "There's a book and some paper for you on my desk." *There's* is a contraction for *There is.* Technically, since the subject is *a book and some paper,* the verb should be plural and the sentence should begin, "There are. . . ." Since this may sound strange, you may want to revise the sentence to something like "A book and some paper are on my desk." Be especially careful of sentences beginning with *There;* be sure the verb agrees with the subject:

> ◆ There *are* no *walls,* there *are* no *bolts,* no locks that anyone can put on your mind.
> from *The Diary of Anne Frank* by Frances Goodrich and Albert Hackett

> ◆ There *was* a *pair* of elk horns over the top. . . .
> from "Strong but Quirky: The Birth of Davy Crockett" retold by Irwin Shapiro

2. Pronoun-antecedent agreement.

a. An antecedent is a word, clause, or phrase to which a pronoun refers. The pronoun agrees with its antecedent in person, number, and gender.

>   antec.   pron.
> ◆ *Eleanor* seemed to go everywhere. Since *she* could travel more freely
>
>   antec.   pron.
> than *Franklin*, she again became *his* "eyes and ears."
> from "A President's Wife" by Russell Freedman

b. Singular pronouns are generally used to refer to the indefinite pronouns *one, anyone, each, either, neither, everybody, everyone, somebody, someone, nobody,* and *no one.*

> ◆ Both women have begun to cry,
>
>   antec.   pron.
> But *neither* stops *her* song.
> from "I Ask My Mother to Sing" by Li-Young Lee

Now look at the following sentence:

> *Everybody* brought *his* ticket to the gate.

This sentence poses problems. It is clearly plural in meaning, and "everybody" may not refer to men only. To avoid the latter problem, you could write "Everybody brought his or her ticket to the gate." This solution gets clumsy and wordy, though. Sometimes it is best to revise:

> The students brought their tickets to the gate.

This sentence is now clear and non-sexist.

all right *All right* is generally used as an adjective and should always be spelled as two words.

> ◆ Are you *all right?* I mean do you feel *all right?*
> from *Back There* by Rod Serling

among, between *Among* implies more than two persons, places, or things. *Between* usually refers to two, followed either by a plural or by two expressions joined by *and*—not by *or.*

> ◆ And when there were little frictions *among* my staff, you were always careful to keep negative things away from me so that I wouldn't worry.
> from "Coretta and Edythe: The Scott Sisters" by Carol Saline

> Sam couldn't decide *between* the two classes.

> Sam couldn't decide *between* the acting class and the storytelling class.

See also **between you and me.**

apostrophe An apostrophe is used in possessive words and in contractions. It is also used to form the plurals of letters and numbers if the plurals would be confusing without it.

Jason's backpack Chris's jacket
can't Mind your p's and q's.
but: In the 1880s, . . .

appositive An appositive is a noun or phrase that follows a noun and identifies or explains it. It is usually set off by commas.

◆ Today Miss McIntyre, *our guidance counselor,* said, "You have to decide who you are and where you're going."
from "Who You Are" by Jean Little

◆ She told them about Frederick Douglass, *the most famous of the escaped slaves.*
from *Harriet Tubman* by Ann Petry

awkward writing A general term (abbreviated *awk*) sometimes used in theme correcting to indicate such faults as inappropriate word choice, unnecessary repetition, clumsy phrasing, confusing word order, or any other weakness or expression that makes reading difficult.

B

bad, badly Be careful in using the modifiers *bad* and *badly. Bad* is an adjective. Use it to modify a noun or a pronoun. Use the adverb *badly* to modify a verb, adjective, or adveb.

◆ The days aren't so *bad.* . . . What's the use of telling you the *bad* news when there's nothing you can do about it?
from *The Diary of Anne Frank* by Frances Goodrich and Albert Hackett

◆ His feet must be *badly* frozen by now. . . .
from "To Build a Fire" by Jack London

between you and me After prepositions such as *between,* use the objective form of the personal pronouns: *between you and **me,** between you and **her,** between you and **him,** between you and **us,** between you and **them:***

Just *between you and me,* I know she'll be back.

C

capitalization

1. Capitalize all proper nouns and adjectives.

Asia Asian
Elizabeth Elizabethan

NOTE: If an article or possessive pronoun comes before a family title, the title is not capitalized: *My dad's* hobby is bungi jumping. *A sister* can be a real pest sometimes.

2. Capitalize peoples' names and titles.

Harry S. Truman Senator Carol Mosley Braun
Justice Thurgood Marshall the Secretary of State
Ms. Kathleen Cross Grandma
President of the United States Uncle Benjamin

NOTE: Do not capitalize *god* when it refers to those found in ancient myths and legends.

3. Capitalize the names of races, languages, religions, and religious figures and writings. Also capitalize any adjectives made from these names.

French bread	German
African	Russian folk tale
the Bible	Biblical prophet
Allah	the Koran
the Lord God	the Torah

NOTE: Do not capitalize directions of the compass or adjectives that indicate direction: Go *north* three blocks. The storm came from the *southeast.*

NOTE: *Earth* is capitalized when used with other planet names but not when preceded by *the*: On a clear night Venus and Mars can be seen from *Earth.* The *earth* has a core of molten lava.

NOTE: Do *not* capitalize the names of the seasons: *spring, summer, fall, winter.*

NOTE: Some modern poetry does not begin each line with a capital letter.

4. Capitalize geographical names (except for articles and prepositions).

Australia	South America
the Gulf of Mexico	Lake Michigan
the South	the Sahara Desert

5. Capitalize the names of structures, organizations, and bodies in the universe.

Democratic Party	the Empire State Building
the United Way	Jefferson High School
Jupiter	the Milky Way

6. Capitalize the names of historical events, times, and documents.

| the Bill of Rights | the Battle of the Bulge |
| the Dark Ages | the Declaration of Independence |

7. Capitalize the names of months, days, holidays, and time abbreviations.

| January | Thursday | Thanksgiving | A.M., P.M. |

8. Capitalize the first words in sentences, lines of poetry, and direct quotations.

Because she forgot to save her work, Judy lost her entire report when her computer froze.

◆ Listen my children, and you shall hear
    Of the midnight ride of Paul Revere,
        from "Paul Revere's Ride" by Henry Wadsworth Longfellow

Professor Bowen said, "Read chapters six and seven and be ready for a quiz."

9. Capitalize certain parts of letters, outlines, and the first, last, and all other important words in titles.

Dear Sir or Madam: Dear Grampa Curt,
Sincerely yours,   Very truly yours,
I. Popular pets
    A. Dogs
        1. Breeds
        2. Care and feeding
    B. Cats

Book Title	*The Outsiders*
Newspaper	*The Des Moines Register*
Play	*The Miracle Worker*

Television Series	*Star Trek: The Next Generation*
Short Story	"Raymond's Run"
Song	"America, the Beautiful"
Work of Art	*Whistler's Mother*
Magazine	*Wired*

clause A clause is a group of words that has a subject and a verb. A clause is *independent* when it can stand alone and make sense. A *dependent* clause has a subject and a verb, but it can not stand alone. The reader is left wondering about the meaning.

Independent clause: Rip Van Winkle slept for twenty years.

Dependent clause: Although Rip slept for twenty years, . . .

colon (:) The colon is used after the greeting of a business letter and between the hour and minutes when you write time in numbers.

Dear Mr. Wells: 6:15 A.M.

A colon is also used after phrases that introduce a list or a quotation.

◆ Because I felt, as only a young girl can, all the pain of being an ugly duckling, I was afraid . . . of almost everything, I think: of mice, of the dark, of imaginary dangers, of my own inadequacy.
from *The Autobiography of Eleanor Roosevelt* by Eleanor Roosevelt

◆ She sighed. "The Chinese have a saying: one beam cannot hold the roof up."
from "The White Umbrella" by Gish Jen

NOTE: (1) Some writers leave out the comma before the *and*. (2) If the items in the series are all separated by a word like *and,* no comma is necessary.

◆ She and Leeza went straight to work . . . picking bell peppers and tomatoes and cucumbers and a great deal of parsley for the salad.
from "The Parsley Garden" by William Saroyan

comma Commas are used to show a pause or separation between words and word groups in sentences, to avoid confusion in sentences, to separate items in addresses and dates, in dialogue, and in figures and friendly letters.

1. Use commas between items in a series. Words, phrases, and clauses in a series are separated by commas.

◆ Above the tormented trees a zinc sheet writhed, twisted, and somersaulted in the tempestuous flurry.
from "The Banana Tree" by James Berry

◆ I can run faster, jump higher, squat lower, dive deeper, stay under water longer, and come up drier that any man in these here United States.
from "Strong but Quirky: The Birth of Davy Crockett" by Irwin Shapiro

2. Use a comma after certain introductory words and groups of words, such as clauses and prepositional phrases of five words or more.

◆ When I was twelve, my mother went to work without telling me or my little sister.
from "The White Umbrella" by Gish Jen

◆ In the spring of 1852, she went back to Cape May, New Jersey.
from *Harriet Tubman* by Ann Petry

3. Use a comma to set off nouns in direct address. The name or title by which persons (or animals) are addressed is called a noun of direct address. It is set off by commas.

◆ "I was wondering if we could talk about something, Dad. . . ."
from "Stop the Sun" by Gary Paulsen

◆ The eldest boy, Gustus, sat farthest from his father.
from "The Banana Tree" by James Berry

4. Use commas to set off interrupting words and appositives. A phrase or clause that interrupts the general flow of a sentence is often set off by commas.

◆ One evening, when I was about five, I climbed up a ladder on the outside of a rickety old tobacco barn at sunset.
from "Animal Craftsmen" by Bruce Brooks

◆ And the rabbit, representing the slave in the animal tales, knows from experience to fear man.
from "He Lion, Bruh Bear, and Bruh Rabbit" by Virginia Hamilton

5. Use a comma before the conjunction in a compound sentence. A comma is generally used before the coordinating conjunction (*and, but, for, or, nor, yet, so*) that joins the parts (independent clauses) of a compound sentence.

◆ I don't think I ever saw Mrs. Flowers laugh, but she smiled often.
from *I Know Why the Caged Bird Sings* by Maya Angelou

6. Use a comma after a dependent clause that begins a sentence. Do not use a comma before a dependent clause that follows the independent clause.

◆ As Mona began to play, I jumped up and ran to the window. . . .
from "The White Umbrella" by Gish Jen

◆ Mona came tearing up to my side as my mother neared the house.
from "The White Umbrella" by Gish Jen

7. Use commas to separate items in a date. If a date is within a sentence, put a comma after the year.

The artist was born on April 15, 1960, in a small farmhouse.

8. Use a comma to separate items in an address. The number and street are considered one item. The state and Zip Code are also considered one item. Use a comma after the Zip Code if it is within a sentence.

Jeff Carpenter	Angelina Cortez
513 E. Jefferson Avenue	7468 Broadway
Joliet, IL 60411	Tulsa, OK 74129

The letter is addressed to Sara Smith, 5019 Topanga Avenue, Los Angeles, California 98421, but was delivered to me by mistake.

NOTE: If the compound parts are very short, no comma is needed.
◆ Uncle Roarious let out a yelp and Davy leaned down.
from "Strong but Quirky: The Birth of Davy Crocket" by Irwin Shapiro

9. Use a comma to separate numerals greater than three digits.

84,600   1,156,825 $21,000

10. Use a comma after the greeting in a friendly letter and after the closing in all letters.

Dear Michael,   Yours truly,

11. Use commas in punctuating dialogue. *See* **dialogue.**

comma splice *See* **run-on sentence.**

comparative forms of adjectives and adverbs Most adjectives and adverbs have three forms to show comparison. The **positive** form does not make a comparison, the **comparative** form compares two things, and the **superlative** form compares three or more of anything.

Most adjectives and adverbs form the comparative and superlative in regular ways.

1. Most one- and two-syllable modifiers add *-er* and *-est* to make the comparative and superlative forms. Note the slight spelling changes that occur with some words.

Positive	Comparative	Superlative
big	bigger	biggest
cool	cooler	coolest
fine	finer	finest
handy	handier	handiest
pretty	prettier	prettiest
gentle	gentler	gentlest

2. Longer modifiers use *more* and *most* to make comparisons

Positive	Comparative	Superlative
beautiful	more beautiful	most beautiful
quickly	more quickly	most quickly
practical	more practical	most practical

3. Some adjectives and adverbs do not follow the usual rules. Their comparative and superlative forms are made differently.

Positive	Comparative	Superlative
good	better	best
bad	worse	worst
much	more	most
little	less	least
well	better	best
badly	worse	worst
much	more	most

conjunction A conjunction is a word that links one part of a sentence to another. It can join words, phrases, or entire sentences.

D

dash (—) The dash is used to show a sudden change in thought or to set off words that interrupt the main thought of a sentence.

◆ "You're blind—totally blind—and they gave you a visa?"
from "Sound-Shadows of the New World" by Ved Mehta

◆ All Lucinda had were her memories—and now this dog whom she untied from the tree.
from "Viva New Jersey" by Gloria Gonzalez

dialogue Dialogue is often used to enliven many types of writing. Notice the paragraphing and punctuation of the following passage. *See also* **quotation marks.**

◆   She heard the familiar guttural voice say, "Who's there?"
She answered quickly, "A friend with friends."
He opened the door and greeted her warmly. "How many this time?" he asked.
"Eleven," she said and waited, doubting, wondering.
He said, "Good. Bring them in."
from *Harriet Tubman* by Ann Petry

E

ellipsis (. . .) An ellipsis is used to indicate that words (or sentences or paragraphs) have been omitted. An ellipsis consists of three dots, but if the omitted portion would have completed the sentence, a fourth dot is added for the period.

◆ It was hard to exchange the security offered by that clean warm kitchen for the darkness and the cold of a December night. . . . Harriet had found it hard to leave the warmth and friendliness, too.
from *Harriet Tubman* by Ann Petry

exclamation point (!) An exclamation point is used at the end of an exclamatory sentence—one that shows excitement or strong emotion. Exclamation points can also be used with strong interjections. *See also* **quotation marks.**

◆ The old man's terror must have been extreme!
from "The Tell-Tale Heart" by Edgar Allan Poe

◆ "Oh! That was stupendous," she said without hugging me.
from "The White Umbrella" by Gish Jen

F

fragment *See* **sentence fragment.**

good, well *Good* is used as an adjective to modify a noun or pronoun. Do not use it to modify a verb. Use the adverb *well* to modify a verb, adjective, or adverb.

◆ She had told them about the place where they would stay, promising warmth and *good* food. . . .
from *Harriet Tubman* by Ann Petry

◆ Life had treated him *well*.
from "The Kid Nobody Could Handle" by Kurt Vonnegut, Jr.

NOTE: When you are referring to health, both *good* and *well* can be used. They mean different things. If the meaning is "not ill," use *well*. If the meaning is "pleasant" or "in good spirits," use *good*.

◆ He wasn't a *well* man.
from "The Kid Nobody Could Handle" by Kurt Vonnegut, Jr.

◆ It was a bright, sunny day, and he felt *good*.

hopefully This is often used to mean "it is hoped" or "I hope," as in the following sentence,

Hopefully, you'll have wonderful luck.

However, in formal writing, avoid this usage and write the sentence as follows:

◆ Oh, Father, *I hope* you have wonderful luck.
from "Rip Van Winkle" by Washington Irving

however Words like *however, moreover, nevertheless, consequently,* etc. (known as conjunctive adverbs) require special punctuation. If the word comes within a clause, it is generally set off by commas.

◆ He was surprised, *however,* at the cold.
from "To Build a Fire" by Jack London

If the conjunctive adverb separates two independent clauses, a semicolon is used preceding the word and a comma after.

He works very hard; *however,* he doesn't earn much money.

interjection An interjection is a word or phrase used to express strong emotion.

Yes! We made the play-offs!

Oh no, I'm late again.

NOTE: In handwritten or non-computer writing, underlining takes the place of italics.

italics Italics are used to indicate titles of whole works such as books, magazines, newspapers, plays, films, and so on. They are also used to indicate foreign words and phrases. *See* **capitalization,** rule 9, for examples of italicized titles.

◆ He was a newcomer in the land, a *chechaquo,* and this was his first winter.
from "To Build a Fire" by Jack London

its, it's *Its* is the possessive form of the personal pronoun *it; it's* is the contraction meaning "it is."

◆ In the hours the hurricane stayed, *its* presence made everybody older.
from "The Banana Tree" by James Berry

Language and Grammar Handbook   **775**

◆ "Who told you it belongs to Eugenie? *It's* not Eugenie's. *It's* mine. And now I'm giving it to you, so *it's* yours."
from "The White Umbrella" by Gish Jen

L

lay, lie This verb pair presents problems because, in addition to the similarity between the words, the past tense of *lie* is *lay*. The verb *to lay* means "to put or place something somewhere."

Present	Past	Past Participle	Present Participle
lay	laid	(has) laid	(is) laying

Please *lay* the papers on the desk.

◆ Impassively, he *laid* it on the table in front of Helmholtz.
from "The Kid Nobody Could Handle" by Kurt Vonnegut, Jr.

The verb *to lie* means "to rest in a flat position."

Present	Past	Past Participle	Present Participle
lie	lay	(has) lain	(is) lying

Notice the way the verb is used in the following sentences:

◆ . . . I did not hear him *lie* down.
from "The Tell-Tale Heart" by Edgar Allan Poe

◆ As he grimaced and covered his ears, he was forcefully slapped against a coconut tree trunk that *lay* across the road.
from "The Banana Tree" by James Berry

◆ It took me an hour to place my whole head within the opening so far that I could see him as he *lay* upon his bed.
from "The Tell-Tale Heart" by Edgar Allan Poe

◆ They reached the top of the stairs, and Greg felt Lemon Brown's hand first *lying* on his shoulder. . . .
from "The Treasure of Lemon Brown" by Walter Dean Myers

NOTE: When the meaning you intend is "not to tell the truth," *lie (lied, has lied)* is the verb to use.

◆ "I'm not avoiding you," he *lied.*
from "Liverwurst and Roses" by Ellen Conford

lose, loose *Lose* (to lose one's way, to lose one's life, to lose a watch) is a verb; *loose* (to come loose, loose-fitting) is an adjective.

◆ . . . the boy's weight and the weight of the purse caused him to *lose* his balance.
from "Thank You, Ma'am" by Langston Hughes

◆ "We were crossing a rice paddy in the dark," he said, and suddenly his voice flowed like a river breaking *loose.*
from "Stop the Sun" by Gary Paulsen

HINT: Remember that *lose* often means the opposite of *gain.* Each word has just four letters.

◆ . . . we don't want to *lose* our sense of wonder just because we *gain* understanding.
from "Animal Craftsmen" by Bruce Brooks

M

myself (and himself, herself, etc.) Be careful not to use *myself* and the other reflexive and intensive pronouns when you simply need to use the personal pronoun *I* or its objective form *me.*

Incorrect: John and myself are going to the game.
Correct: John and I are going to the game.

Incorrect:	Luis told Amy and myself the joke.
Correct:	Luis told Amy and me the joke.

Reflexive pronouns reflect the action of the verb back to the subject. An intensive pronoun adds intensity to the noun or pronoun just named.

◆ We gathered around the warmth of the hot plate . . . wondering how we had gotten *ourselves* into such an intolerable situation. (the reflexive pronoun *ourselves* refers back to *we*.)
from "Prisoner of My Country" by Yoshiko Uchida

◆ I brought chairs into the room . . . while *I myself* . . . placed my own seat upon the very spot. . . .
from "The Tell-Tale Heart" by Edgar Allan Poe

N

noun A noun is a word that names a person, place, thing, or idea. Most nouns are made plural by just adding -*s* or -*es* to the singular. When you are unsure about a plural form, check a dictionary.

P

parallel construction Items in a sentence that are of equal importance should be expressed in parallel (or similar) forms. These can take the form of noun phrases, verb phrases, and among others, prepositional phrases.

◆ But here was a boy *without fear, without dreams, without love.*
from "The Kid Nobody Could Handle" by Kurt Vonnegut, Jr.

◆ It rose *from* the creases in his hands, *from* permanent white lines rimming his fingernails, *from* the paint-motes he sometimes missed with thinner. . . .
from "Elegy Written at the County Junkyard" by James D. Houston

◆ I can *run faster, jump higher, squat lower, dive deeper, stay under water longer, and come up drier* than any man in these here United States,
from "Strong but Quirky: The Birth of Davy Crockett" by Irwin Shapiro

parentheses ( ) Parentheses have two uses: 1) to enclose words that interrupt the thought of the sentence, and 2) to enclose references to page numbers, chapters, or dates.

The finest food in town (and the most expensive) can be found at Le Champignon Restaurant.

Edgar Allan Poe (1809–1849) led a troubled life.

NOTE: Apostrophes are not used with personal pronouns to show possession.

◆ These things might soon be *theirs* no longer.
from "Home" by Gwendolyn Brooks

possessive case The possessive case is formed in various ways. For singular nouns and indefinite pronouns, add an apostrophe and *s*. *See also* **apostrophe.**

my brother's car	no one's notebook	everybody's children

For plural nouns ending in an *s,* add only an apostrophe:

the doctors' office	the babies' pool	the teachers' rooms

However, if the plural is irregular and does not end in *s,* add an apostrophe and then an *s.*

women's children's men's

preposition Prepositions are words that show the relationship between a noun or pronoun and some other word in a sentence.

Common prepositions include:

about	at	down	near	to
above	before	during	of	toward
across	behind	except	off	under
after	below	for	on	underneath
against	beneath	from	onto	until
along	beside	in	out	up
among	between	inside	over	upon
around	but	into	since	with
as	by	like	through	without

prepositional phrase Prepositional phrases are groups of words that begin with a preposition and end with a noun or pronoun. These phrases act as modifiers and create more vivid pictures for the reader. Notice the four prepositional phrases (marked with parentheses) in the following sentence:

◆ Lucinda traveled the route each day (on her way) (to the high school) (along the New Jersey side) (of the river).
from "Viva New Jersey" by Gloria Gonzalez

pronoun Subject pronouns are used as subjects of sentences. Object pronouns can be used as direct objects, indirect objects, or objects of prepositions.

When a pronoun is used as the subject of a sentence, the pronoun is in the nominative case and is called a subject pronoun.

Subject Pronouns

Singular	I	you	he, she, it
Plural	we	you	they

When a pronoun is used as an object, the pronoun is in the objective case and is called an object pronoun.

Object Pronouns

Singular	me	you	him, her, it
Plural	us	you	them

quotation marks Quotation marks enclose a speaker's exact words. They are also used to enclose some titles.

NOTE: To check that you are using the correct pronoun in a compound subject or object, say the sentence with just one pronoun. For the compound subject *She and I,* you would say *I went* (Not: *me went*). In a compound subject with *I,* the *I* is always second.

She went to the mall.
I went to the mall.
She and *I* went to the mall.

The waiter served *me* lunch.
The waiter served *him* lunch.
The waiter served *him* and *me* lunch.

1. The first word of a direct quotation begins with a capital letter. When a quotation is broken into two parts, use two sets of quotation marks. Use one capital letter if the quote is one sentence. Use two capital letters if it is two sentences.

◆ "Better had let me tell you somethin," Bruh Rabbit said, "for I've seen Man and I know him the real king of the forest."
from "He Lion, Bruh Bear, and Bruh Rabbit" by Virginia Hamilton

◆ "Maybe we better hurry up," she went on, looking at the sky. "It's going to pour."
from "The White Umbrella" by Gish Jen

2. Use a comma between the words that introduce the speaker and the words that are quoted. Place the end punctuation or the comma that ends the quotation inside the quotation marks. Begin a new paragraph each time the speaker changes.

◆ "But why shouldn't I?" she argued. "Lots of people's mothers work."
"Those are American people," I said.
"So what do you think we are? I can do the Pledge of Allegiance with my eyes closed."
from "The White Umbrella" by Gish Jen

3. Put question marks and exclamation points inside the quotation marks if they are a part of the quotation. Put question marks and exclamation points outside the quotation marks if they are not part of the quotation. *See also* **dialogue.**

Alvin asked, "Who's going to play third base?"

Did Susan say, "I'll be absent tomorrow"?

Sebastian shouted, "Everyone out!"

4. Enclose titles of short works such as stories, songs, poems, and book chapters in quotation marks. *See* **capitalization,** rule 9.

R

raise, rise Use *raise* to mean "lift"; use *rise* to mean "get up."

Present	Past	Past Participle	Present Participle
rise	rose	had risen	is rising
raise	raised	had raised	is raising

◆ Several times he stumbled. . . . When he tried to *rise*, he failed.
from "To Build a Fire" by Jack London

◆ When she *rose* to speak, she prayed silently that she would have something meaningful to say to the people in front of her.
from "A President's Wife" by Russell Freedman

◆ She didn't want to be caught staring, so she *raised* her menu a little higher. . . .
from "At the Avenue Eatery" by Gayle Pearson

NOTE: Often, in narrative writing, authors purposely choose to use run-ons for effect, such as in the following passage:

◆ He passed the Kennedy's, he passed the vacant lot, he passed Mrs. Blakemore's.
from "Home" by Gwendolyn Brooks

S

run-on sentence   This occurs when there is only a comma (known as a comma splice) or no punctuation between two independent clauses. Separate the clauses into two complete sentences, join them with a semicolon, or join them with a comma and a coordinating conjunction *(and, but, or, nor, yet, so, for).*

Notice the use of capital and lower-case letters in each correct example. You only need a capital letter when you break the run-on into two complete sentences.

Run-on: The student received her schedule, then she went home.
Correct: The student received her schedule. Then she went home.
Correct: The student received her schedule; then she went home.
Correct: The student received her schedule, and then she went home.

semicolon (;)   Use this punctuation mark to separate the two parts of a compound sentence when they are not joined by a comma and a conjunction.

◆ Terry wanted it that way; he wanted his father alone.
from "Stop the Sun" by Gary Paulsen

sentence fragment   A fragment, like a run-on sentence, should be avoided because it signals an error in the understanding of a sentence. A fragment often occurs when one sentence is finished, but another thought occurs to the writer and that thought is written as a complete thought. A fragment may be missing a subject, a verb, or both.

Fragment: I loved the book. Especially when Huck is trying to free Jim.
Correct: I loved the book, especially when Huck is trying to free Jim.

As with run-ons, fragments are sometimes used by writers for effect or emphasis.

◆ He would give all of them a new pair of shoes. Everybody.
from *Harriet Tubman* by Ann Petry

◆ I breathe deep. Close the suitcase slowly. Prepare to heave it once and for all. This time with both hands.
from "Elegy Written at the County Junkyard" by James D. Houston

sit, set   *Sit* means "to sit down"; *set* means "to put something somewhere."

Present	Past	Past Participle	Present Participle
sit	sat	had sat	is sitting
set	set	had set	is setting

Sit down and let me tell you what happened.

Set the groceries on the counter, please.

T

than, then   *Than* is used to point out comparisons; *then* is used as an indicator of time. Notice the use of *than* and *then* in the following examples.

◆ Mrs. Flowers deserved better *than* to be called Sister.
from *I Know Why the Caged Bird Sings* by Maya Angelou

◆ He sat awhile, watching the sign blink first green *then* red, allowing his mind to drift to the Scorpions, *then* to his father.
from "The Treasure of Lemon Brown" by Walter Dean Myers

Be careful of punctuation with the word *then.* If it separates two independent clauses, be sure to punctuate them to avoid creating a run-on sentence.

◆ All day the Jamaican sun didn't come out. Then, ten minutes before, there was a swift shower of rain. . . .
from "The Banana Tree" by James Berry

their, there, they're *Their* is a possessive, *there* is an introductory word or adverb of place, and *they're* is the contraction for *they are.*

◆ They took *their* sandwiches, along with an orange soda to share, and sat at the kitchen table. (possessive)
from "The Mechanical Mind" by Gary Soto

HINT: Remember that *there* has the word *here* in it; these two words are related in that they can both be indicators of place.

◆ "I was announcer in my school show in Puerto Rico," I said. "And I recite poetry. *There,* not here." (reference to place)
from "A Shot at It" by Esmeralda Santiago

◆ . . . those grey hairs are mistakes I made
and spun into lessons
of silver thread. Besides
I think *they're* rather attractive.
(contraction of *they are*)
from "Keepsakes" by Deloras Lane

to, too, two *To* is a preposition that means "toward, in that direction" or is used in the infinitive form of the verb (e.g., *to follow*); *too* means "also" or "more than enough"; *two* means "more than one."

◆ He opened a door *to* the hall that led *to* the alley. . . .
from "The Parsley Garden" by William Saroyan

◆ . . . the future seemed far *too* distant *to* address it.
from "Viva New Jersey" by Gloria Gonzalez

◆ Babe planted his large hoofs between *two* mountains and waited.
from "Paul Bunyan Digs the St. Lawrence River" by Dell J. McCormick

verb A verb is a word that tells about an action or a state of being. The form or *tense* of the verb tells whether the action occurred in the past, the present, or the future. *See also* **agreement, 1. Subject-verb agreement.**

verb shifts in tense Use the same tense to show two or more actions that occur at the same time.

Incorrect: Rolanda *woke* (past) the boys and *fixes* (present) them breakfast.

Correct: Rolanda *woke* (past) the boys and *fixed* (past) them breakfast.

W

HINT: Many people find it difficult to figure out whether to use *who* or *whom*. You may want to rewrite a sentence to avoid the word.

◆ The children, *whom* I had arranged in a circle, immediately began to move around the room.

◆ Immediately after I arranged the children in a circle, they began to move around the room.

who, whom *Who* is used as a subject. *Whom* is used as a direct object or the object of a preposition.

◆ There entered three men, *who* introduced themselves. . . .
   from "The Tell-Tale Heart" by Edgar Allan Poe

◆ All Lucinda had were her memories—and now this dog, *whom* she untied from the tree.
   from "Viva New Jersey" by Gloria Gonzalez

who's, whose *Whose* is a possessive; *who's* is a contraction meaning "who is."

Whose life is it, anyway? (possessive)

Who's going out? (contraction of *who is*)

would of This incorrect expression is often used mistakenly because it sounds like *would've,* the contraction for *would have.* In formal writing, write out *would have,* and you won't be confused.

I *would have* gone to bed earlier if I had known what today would be like!

Y

your, you're *Your* is the possessive form of the personal pronoun *you; you're* is a contraction meaning "you are."

◆ Now that *you're* here, *your* English will improve quickly.
   from "Sound-Shadows of the New World" by Ved Mehta

Index of Skills and Strategies

Literary Genres, Terms, and Techniques

Alliteration, 165, 749, 752
Allusion, 308, 646, 653
Author's purpose, 409, 484, 747
Autobiography, 84, 151, 159, 746
Biography, 84, 746, 752
Characterization, 84, 148, 159,
    229, 231–234, 298, 331, 379,
    418, 470, 567, 608, 610, 692,
    699, 744, 752
    and plot, 14
    and setting, 122
    character development, 17, 24
    character traits, 148, 214, 275,
        282, 418, 493, 551
    compare/contrast, 418
    through dialogue, 24, 42
Characters
    first-person narrator, 260
    stereotyped, 322
    stock, 314
Climax, 323, 608, 626, 724
Concrete poem, 701
Conflict, 165, 323, 567, 724
Connotation, 159, 752
Denotation, 159, 752
Dialect, 193, 216, 387, 393
Dialogue, 24, 42, 64, 193, 403,
    751, 752
Diction, 159, 345, 359
Drama, 92, 680, 692, 750–751, 752
Elegy, 269
End rhyme, 752
Essay, 477, 746, 752
Exaggeration. See Hyperbole.
Fable, 91
    moral of, 91
Fantasy, 314, 752
Fiction, 744–745, 752
Figurative language, 87, 426, 710,
    748, 752.
    See also Hyperbole, Metaphor,
    Personification, Simile.
Flashback, 25, 275, 551, 581, 726, 752
Folk tale, 106, 108, 216, 387, 517
Foreshadowing, 175, 190, 514,
    581, 596, 626, 753

Free verse, 748, 753
Humor, 75, 407, 644
Hyperbole, 75, 76, 521, 527, 753
Idiom, 29, 118, 345, 359
Imagery, 24, 26, 114, 190, 275,
    301, 307, 338, 432, 622, 708,
    710, 748, 753
Informal language, 345
Irony, 139, 643, 699, 753
    dramatic, 493, 753
    of situation, 643, 753
    verbal, 753
Line breaks, 308, 428
Metaphor, 87, 90, 166, 312, 338,
    432, 753
Monologue, 129
Mood, 214, 267, 338, 361, 363,
    432, 596, 699, 714, 744, 753
    and setting, 361
Moral, 91, 338, 520
Motivation, 258
Myth, 106, 710, 753
Narrative, 753
Narrative poem, 694, 748
Narrator, 753
Nonfiction, 746–747, 753
Novel, 744, 754
Onomatopoeia, 754
Oral history, 387
Parody, 381, 385, 754
Personification, 202, 277, 282,
    407, 754
Perspective. See Point of view.
Plays. See Drama.
Plot, 14, 75, 76, 105, 371, 409,
    567, 724, 744, 754
    climax, 90, 323, 608, 626, 724
    conflict, 371, 567, 608, 724
    elements of, 608, 626, 724
    resolution, 323, 608, 724, 754
    through dialogue, 692
Poetry, 26, 54, 55, 87, 91, 161, 308,
    428, 694, 740, 748–749, 754
    See also Concrete poem, End
    rhyme, Free verse, Line breaks,
    Narrative poem, Rhyme,
    Rhythm, Stanza.
Point of view, 37, 43, 63, 122, 236,
    251, 267, 269, 298, 306, 331,

    443, 444, 455, 482, 514, 609,
    670, 708, 754
    first-person, 260, 670, 754
    objective, 754
    third-person, 754
        limited, 754
        omniscient, 754
Repetition, 29, 482, 699, 748, 754
Resolution, 608, 724, 754
Rhyme, 91, 428, 699, 740, 748,
    752, 754
Rhythm, 26, 29, 277, 384, 699,
    710, 740, 748, 754
Science fiction, 92, 104, 484, 708,
    754
Setting, 36, 42, 104, 122, 190, 454,
    714, 744, 755
    and mood, 361
    compare/contrast, 714
Short story, 25, 515, 744, 755
Simile, 312, 338, 419, 755
Slang, 345, 359
Sound devices. See Alliteration,
    Onomatopoeia, Repetition,
    Rhyme, Rhythm.
Speaker, 755
Speech, 746
Stage directions, 92, 692
Stanza, 699, 748, 755
Stereotype, 322, 680, 755
Stock character, 314
Style, 108, 159, 277, 345, 658
Suspense, 267, 306, 581, 626,
    643, 755
Symbolism, 54, 251, 443, 755
Theme, 14, 64, 90, 122, 132, 148,
    236, 258, 322, 409, 418, 443,
    470, 493, 527, 626, 653, 670,
    699, 744, 755
    definition of, 132, 258, 653, 744,
        755
    vs. topic, 132, 258, 744
Title, 29, 75, 148, 258, 418, 419,
    454
Tone, 222, 312, 426, 427, 658, 744,
    755
Turning point. See Climax.
Word choice. See Diction.

Writing Forms, Modes, and Processes

Audience, 115, 229, 331, 463, 619, 733

Creative writing, 15, 54, 76, 91, 105, 108, 202, 203, 216, 223, 276, 283, 299, 301, 307, 313, 408, 419, 433, 444, 514, 520, 527, 609, 654, 671, 709, 715, 725, 740

Descriptive writing, 15, 36, 37, 44, 55, 150, 160, 172, 191, 204, 307, 419, 455, 733–738, 740

Drafting, 117, 231, 333, 465, 621, 735

Editing, 119, 233, 335, 467, 623, 737
   strategies for, 119, 233, 335, 467, 623, 737

Expository/informative writing, 5, 15, 29, 30, 37, 43, 85, 106, 133, 140, 191, 203, 229–234, 259, 268, 408, 433, 444, 463–468, 515, 520, 610, 654, 671, 709, 725, 740

Forms
   advertisement, 323, 394
   autobiographical incident, 5
   bibliography, 385, 623
   biographical sketch, 259, 268, 380, 427
   captions, 276, 483
   character sketch, 122
   commendation, 215
   comparison/contrast, 122, 160, 203, 444, 609
   continuation of story, 15, 299, 419, 470, 515, 709
   conversation, 300
   critique, 259, 385
   description, 37, 160, 166, 260, 307, 419, 444, 731
   dialogue, 149, 313, 408, 610, 700
   diary entry, 91, 203, 609, 671, 709, 740
   dictionary, 740
   directions, 15, 140
   e-mail dialogue, 86
   encyclopedia entry, 215
   epilogue, 55, 203

essay, 133, 229–234, 483, 520, 654
eulogy, 455, 693
evidence chart, 610
explanation, 15, 37, 659
fable, 91, 283
folk tale, 223, 283
food diary, 169
found poem, 191
guide to fauna, 455
guidebook, 252, 740
guidelines, 408
how-to, 15, 140
introduction, 716, 739
invention (description), 172
job description, 85
journal, 55, 515
legend, 394
letter, 15, 43, 76, 85, 133, 140, 149, 191, 252, 372, 427, 463–468, 515, 610, 626, 644, 671, 725
list, 37, 76, 140, 283, 299, 427, 531
math problems, 677
memoir, 276
menu, 299, 654
message, 520
mini-lesson, 671
monologue, 331–336, 644
mood piece, 268
myth, 715
new verse, 654
news article, 191, 268
outline, 76
parody, 385
personality profile, 299, 609
persuasive essay, 323, 693
plan, 61
play, 115–120
plot line, 105, 323
poem, 54, 91, 166, 202, 276, 307, 338, 372, 385, 394, 433, 654, 715
portfolio, 16
prediction, 5, 25
prescription, 25, 61
questions, 215, 620
quote quiz, 610
rebuttal, 313
recipe, 15

report, 29, 105, 133, 223, 252, 433, 444, 470, 619, 659, 725
research paper, 215, 693
response, 149, 380
rewrite, 160, 283, 455, 520, 659
scene, 408
script, 419
sequel, 323
speech, 468
stanza, 313
story, 15, 25, 43, 105, 122, 394, 433, 470, 515, 527
story ending, 372
summary, 228, 229, 443, 610, 611, 700, 725
tall tale, 527
travelogue entries, 733–738

Narrative writing, 15, 25, 30, 43, 55, 115–120, 191, 259, 276, 291, 610, 619, 700

Note-taking, 228, 289, 330, 461, 469, 611, 620

Organization
   chronological, 115, 733

Outlining, 76, 228, 231, 330, 462

Paragraphs
   details, 229, 231, 232, 331, 333
   main idea, 229, 230, 331, 333
   ordering, 117, 231, 333, 465, 621
   transitions, 331, 334

Peer review/editing, 117, 119, 232, 233, 300, 334, 335, 465, 467, 622, 623, 736, 737

Personal expression, 5, 77, 92, 129, 133, 141, 243, 252, 291, 299, 339, 421, 427, 468, 536, 624, 626, 632, 654, 738

Persuasive/argumentative writing, 215, 313, 323, 626, 693

Portfolio
   presentation portfolio, 716
   working portfolio, 16, 120, 234, 300, 336, 386, 468, 516, 624, 738
      getting started on, 16
      maintaining, 386
      setting up, 16

Presenting, 120, 234, 336, 468, 624, 716, 738

Prewriting, 76, 115–117, 230–231,

331–333, 464–465, 620–621, 734–735

Process writing. *See* Drafting, Editing, Presenting, Prewriting, Revising.

Proofreading. *See* Editing.

Purpose, 115, 229, 331, 463, 619, 733

Quickwrite, 230, 332, 464, 621

Revising, 117–118, 232, 300, 334, 465–466, 516, 622, 736
    strategies for, 118, 232, 334, 466, 622, 736

Self-evaluate, 120, 234, 336, 468, 624, 738

Sentence structure, varying, 466

Thesis statement, 230

Transitional words and phrases, 334

Vivid language, 622

Voice (active/passive), 736

Works cited, 619, 623

Writer's Blueprint, 115, 229, 331, 463, 619

Writer's notebook, 5, 17, 30, 44, 64, 77, 92, 106, 129, 141, 161, 204, 214, 216, 243, 277, 291, 301, 308, 421, 434, 445, 484, 521, 536, 633, 655, 680, 710

Writing with computers, 86, 119, 234, 738
    using a spell-check program, 86, 645
    using graphics, 738

Reading/Thinking Strategies

Bias and propaganda, 337

Cause and effect, 387, 421, 426, 454, 520, 581, 596, 608, 618, 714, 724, 747

Clarify, xxiii, 90, 104, 108, 139, 159, 165, 180, 190, 198, 202, 214, 222, 251, 258, 267, 275, 282, 288, 296, 298, 312, 322, 369, 407, 411, 426, 432, 443, 454, 482, 484, 492, 493, 507, 514, 520, 527, 537, 596, 626, 658, 662, 670, 692, 699, 705, 714, 724, 745

Compare/Contrast, 29, 44, 62, 84, 87, 90, 108, 111, 122, 165, 214, 222, 251, 260, 261, 275, 298, 306, 312, 322, 397, 407, 418, 426, 432, 482, 514, 527, 534, 551, 581, 653, 658, 676, 692, 708, 724

Comprehension. *See* Cause and effect, Compare/Contrast, Details, Draw conclusions, Fact and opinion, Infer, Judgments, Main idea, Sequence, Visualize.

Connect, xxiii, 14, 24, 36, 43, 54, 58, 72, 84, 90, 111, 122, 132, 139, 148, 154, 190, 194, 202, 214, 222, 251, 258, 267, 282, 286, 298, 306, 312, 314, 322, 327, 418, 426, 432, 454, 459, 462, 484, 493, 514, 515, 527, 537, 581, 608, 617, 641, 658, 670, 676, 692, 699, 714, 724, 745

Context clues. *See* Vocabulary and Study Skills index.

Critical response. *See* Clarify, Connect, Evaluate, Predict, Question, Summarize.

Details, 36, 42, 54, 75, 84, 90, 104, 108, 111, 102, 148, 159, 173, 190, 202, 214, 222, 258, 267, 268, 298, 301, 307, 322, 407, 419, 426, 462, 477, 482, 493, 527, 534, 551, 596, 653, 694, 699, 714, 732

Draw conclusions, 29, 42, 54, 58, 75, 104, 134, 159, 202, 251, 258, 288, 291, 322, 401, 407, 418, 443, 514, 551, 581, 608, 613, 658, 708, 724

Evaluate, xxiii, 21, 24, 48, 54, 60, 75, 84, 90, 104, 108, 132, 139, 148, 159, 165, 184, 190, 202, 214, 222, 251, 267, 294, 322, 407, 432, 443, 482, 484, 493, 514, 533, 537, 551, 567, 581, 596, 643, 676, 708, 714, 729, 745

Fact and opinion, 482, 534, 670, 747

Generalizations, 134, 401.
    See also Draw conclusions.

Independent reading (bibliographies), 123, 237, 339, 471, 627, 741

Infer, 14, 24, 29, 42, 54, 90, 132, 148, 159, 202, 214, 258, 282, 298, 322, 403, 407, 418, 426, 432, 443, 454, 514, 581, 596, 608, 670, 692, 708, 714, 745, 753

Judgments, 14, 24, 36, 58, 84, 90, 104, 139, 148, 202, 227, 251, 298, 306, 418, 531, 643, 692, 714

Main idea, 173, 306, 307, 462, 477, 611, 747

Opinion, 14, 482, 534, 670, 747

Personal experience, xxiii, 14, 24, 36, 42, 54, 58, 60, 61, 75, 90, 132, 165, 202, 222, 275, 288, 298, 306, 322, 407, 418, 426, 432, 443, 454, 459, 482, 514, 520, 533, 551, 567, 596, 608, 613, 643, 653, 670, 699, 714, 728

Predict, xxiii, 5, 51, 68, 104, 132, 148, 177, 187, 253, 258, 264, 312, 364, 412, 426, 449, 452, 484, 488, 497, 508, 514, 537, 567, 596, 660, 669, 745

Prereading. *See* Preview, Set purpose, Use prior knowledge.

Preview, 5, 17, 26, 30, 38, 40, 46, 64, 87, 106, 129, 134, 141, 151,161, 175, 193, 204, 216, 243, 253, 261, 269, 277, 291, 301, 308, 314, 403, 409, 421, 428, 434, 445, 477, 484, 517, 521, 536, 633, 646, 655, 660, 680, 701, 717, 747

Question, xxiii, 36, 58, 84, 139, 156, 190, 200, 258, 264, 267, 288, 414, 426, 443, 482, 484, 494, 502, 514, 533, 537, 581, 643, 658, 665, 745

Reading rate, 289, 462, 611, 716

Sequence, 139, 204, 275, 306, 322, 275, 432, 454, 514, 692, 708, 724, 732, 747
    time markers for, 732

Set purpose, 2, 30, 44, 58, 64, 77, 87, 92, 106, 141, 151, 175, 204, 216, 243, 253, 261, 269, 301,

314, 403, 409, 421, 477, 517, 581, 680, 717, 747

Summarize, xxiii, 84, 173, 312, 482, 484, 486, 499, 503, 510, 534, 537, 567, 658, 670, 699, 732, 745

Supporting details, 173, 307, 462, 477

Topic, 132, 462

Use prior knowledge, 5, 17, 26, 30, 38, 44, 58, 77, 122, 175, 193, 291, 308, 484, 633, 646, 655, 660, 694

Visualize, 108, 111, 114, 161, 165, 267, 275, 298, 301, 306, 312, 403, 407, 432, 454, 521, 527, 670, 680, 708, 745

Vocabulary and Study Skills

Analogies, 91, 252

Antiquated language, 655

Antonyms, 160, 268, 306, 323, 506, 581, 715

Bibliography, preparing, 619, 623

Charts

    cause/effect chart, 421

    compare/contrast chart, 44, 323, 609, 660, 709

    creating, 115–116, 122, 331, 333, 397, 427, 464, 470, 517, 610, 620, 678, 700, 709, 734

    for note-taking, 14, 17, 24, 29, 42, 64, 84, 87, 106, 134, 148, 165, 173, 251, 338, 397, 426, 445, 482, 514, 567, 658, 660, 692, 714

    interpreting, 59, 110, 173, 226, 227

    K-W-L chart, 77, 462

    main idea chart, 307, 477

    pie chart, 173, 678

    pre-writing chart, 115–116

Classifying, 106, 330, 716

Clustering. *See* Semantic map.

Computer, 86, 121, 234, 427, 610, 645, 693, 709, 725, 738

Context clues, 15, 25, 85, 151, 191, 261, 445

    foreign languages, 445

Diagrams

    cause/effect, 618

    creating, 15, 38, 140, 228, 269, 332, 394, 397

    open mind, 230

    plot structure, 323, 608, 724

    Venn, 62, 418

    See also Charts, Graphs, Semantic map.

Dictionary, 86

Encyclopedia, 215, 611, 619, 692

Graphic organizers. *See* Charts, Diagrams, Graphs, Maps, Note-taking, Reading log, Scene map, Semantic map, Spectrum, Time line, Venn diagram.

Graphs, 59, 133, 253, 312, 323, 427, 470

    bar graph, 59, 677, 678

K-W-L chart, 77, 462

Library, 338, 433, 520, 619, 659, 671, 693, 708, 725

Magazines, 235, 289, 327

Maps, 5, 110, 141, 204, 215, 228, 537, 655, 694, 730, 734–735

Newspapers, 235, 323, 516, 611

Note-taking, 228, 289, 330, 461, 469, 611, 620–621

Outlining, 76, 228, 330, 462

Pie chart, 173, 678

Prefixes, 92

Reader's Guide To Periodical Literature, 735

Reading log, 484, 536–537, 551, 567, 581, 596

Reading rate, 289, 462, 611, 716

Research, 29, 43, 85, 105, 121, 122, 140, 171, 173, 215, 223, 227, 252, 268, 289, 299, 307, 313, 427, 470, 619, 693, 700, 725, 731

    electronic research, 121, 427, 610, 693, 709, 725

Scene map, 104

Semantic map, 90, 114, 129, 159, 190, 193, 267, 268, 282, 314, 330, 407, 443, 462, 618, 717, 734

Skimming/Scanning, 289, 462, 611, 716

Source cards, 620

Spectrum, 14, 190, 298

Synonyms, 37, 160, 306, 506, 581

Time line, 91, 105, 204, 528–531, 610, 659, 732

Unfamiliar words, 434

Venn diagram, 62, 418

Vocabulary study, 15, 25, 37, 43, 55, 76, 85, 91, 105, 121, 140, 149, 160, 166, 191, 203, 214–215, 223, 252, 268, 276, 283, 299, 306, 313, 360, 372, 393, 408, 419, 427, 433, 444, 455, 483, 515, 551, 567, 596, 609, 644, 654, 659, 671, 693, 700, 709, 725.

    See also Analogies, Antonyms, Context clues, Synonyms.

Word web. *See* Semantic map.

Works Cited list. *See* Bibliography.

Grammar, Usage, Mechanics, and Spelling

a and *an,* 765

accept and *except,* 765

Active verbs, 736

Adjectives, 765

    as modifiers, 335, 765

    comparative forms, 737, 773

    or adverbs, 335

Adverbs, 765

    as modifiers, 765

    comparative forms, 737, 773

    or adjectives, 335

affect and *effect,* 766

Agreement

    pronoun-antecedent, 332, 768

    subject-verb, 300, 766–767

all right, 768

among and *between,* 768

Apostrophes, 645, 768–769

    in contractions, 768–769

    in possessives, 768–769, 777–778

Appositives, 769

Awkward writing, 769

bad and *badly,* 769

Capitalization, 769–771

    in a script, 119

    in dialogue, 770, 779

    in letters, 467, 770

    in outlines, 770

in quotations, 779
of buildings, structures, 770
of geographical names, 770
of historical events, times, and documents, 770
of months, days, holidays, 770
of names and titles of people, 769
of organizations, institutions, 770
of proper nouns and adjectives, 769–770
of races, ethnic groups, languages, nationalities, 769–770
of religious beings and sacred writings, 769–770
of sentences, 770
of titles, 770–771
Clauses, 771
dependent, 771
independent, 771
Colons, 771
in a script, 119
Commas, 771–773
in a compound sentence, 772
in a date, 772
in a series, 420, 771
in addresses, 772
in dialogue, 774, 779
in direct address, 772
in letters, 467, 772–773
in quotations, 779
with appositives, 772
with dependent clauses, 772
with numerals, 773
Comma splice, 780
Comparative forms of adjectives and adverbs, 773
Conjunctions, 774
Contractions, 768–769
Dash, 774
Dependent clauses, 771
Dialogue, 774
Ellipses, 774
Exclamation points, 774
good and *well,* 775
Homophones, 86
hopefully, 775
however, 775
Independent clauses, 771

Interjection, 775
Italics, 775
its and *it's,* 775–776
lay and *lie,* 776
lose and *loose,* 776
Misspellings, common, 645
Modifiers, misplaced,192
Nouns, 777
capitalization of proper nouns, 769–770
forming possessives of, 768–769, 777–778
Parallel construction, 777
Parentheses, 777
Past tense, 766
Periods
in a script, 119
Possessives, 768–769, 777–778
Preposition, 778
Prepositional phrase, 778
Present tense, 766
Pronouns, 778
agreement with antecedents, 233, 332, 768
as object, 778
as subject, 778
between you and me, 769
indefinite, 300, 767
intensive, 776–777
myself, himself, herself, etc., 776–777
reflexive, 776–777
Punctuation, 119, 768–769, 771–773, 774, 777–779, 780
Quotation marks, 778–779
and end punctuation, 779
and titles, 779
in direct quotations, 779
raise and *rise,* 779
Run-on sentence, 780
Semicolons, 780
in a series, 420
with compound sentences, 780
Sentence fragment, 780
sit and *set,* 780
Spelling
contractions, 768–769
homophones, 86, 645
possessives, 768–769, 777–778
prefixes, 92
proofreading for, 461, 645

Subject-verb agreement, 300, 766–767
than and *then,* 780–781
their, there, and *they're,* 781
to, too, and *two,* 781
Transitional words and phrases, 334
Verbs, 781
active, 735, 736
agreement with subject, 300, 766–767
lay and *lie,* 776
lose and *loose,* 776
passive, 736
raise and *rise,* 779
shift in tenses, 781
sit and *set,* 780
tenses, 766
vivid, 735
Voice, active and passive, 736
who and *whom,* 782
who's and *whose,* 782
would of, 782
your and *you're,* 782

◼

Speaking, Listening, and Viewing

Analyzing art, 10–11, 19, 23, 27, 40, 45, 51, 67, 71, 74, 89, 97, 102, 107–108, 479, 615, 703, 711, 717
composition, 89, 97, 102, 130–131, 133, 153, 201, 207, 293, 317, 441, 504–505, 519, 522, 686, 689, 721
context, 113, 195, 285, 293, 297
critical viewing, 107, 113, 133, 176, 183, 199, 207, 244, 263, 293, 297, 299, 301, 363, 389, 391, 410, 428, 439, 447, 649
Beyond Print, 121, 235, 337, 469, 625, 739.
Collaborative learning
brainstorming, 76, 105, 116, 132, 139, 171, 314, 419, 517, 620
debate, 313
dramatization, 105, 120, 203, 283, 408, 419, 444, 609, 725

group activities, 105, 252, 275, 323, 420, 433, 493, 506
group discussion, 16, 169, 260, 517, 646, 670
interview, 133, 215, 469, 609, 700
oral reading, 268, 313
partners, 76, 108, 133, 215, 232, 233, 260, 268, 299, 300, 313, 334, 335, 386, 419, 444, 465, 467, 469, 516, 609, 610, 611, 622, 623, 700, 732, 735, 736, 737
peer review
  editing, 119, 233, 300, 335, 467, 623, 737
  revising, 117, 232, 334, 465, 622, 736
prewriting, 115–117, 620, 735
projects
  thematic, 122, 236, 338, 470, 626, 740
  life skills, 122, 236, 338, 470, 626, 740
  literature, 122, 236, 338, 470, 626, 740
  multicultural, 122, 236, 338, 470, 626, 740
research, 709
share writing in small groups, 234, 336
Creating art, 15, 16, 25, 43, 55
before and after pictures, 15
board game, 43
brochure, 140, 236
bulletin board display, 372
cartoon, 283, 644, 700
collage, 16, 55, 133, 166, 235, 483, 654, 740
comic strip, 91, 140, 223, 283
diagram, 15
drawing, 16, 43, 165, 191, 252, 338, 360, 408, 433, 455, 621, 693, 731
family tree, 455
illustration, 25, 360, 520, 624, 725
map, 215, 228, 444, 740
mask, 114, 610, 715
medicine bag, 444
model, 114, 149, 215, 307, 625,
693, 709, 725
montage, 235
mural, 37
painting, 252
photograph, 16, 307
picture book, 149, 223, 235
political cartoon, 385
portfolio cover, 716
postcard, 610, 738
poster, 105, 160, 191, 276, 338, 515, 610, 626, 671
scale model, 625
sketch, 91, 105, 203, 215, 307, 433, 693, 709, 715, 725
storyboard, 117, 625
tessellation, 329
t-shirt, 223
Debate, 313, 338, 483, 515
Discussion
group, 17, 26, 37, 38, 59, 87, 121, 122, 129, 134, 151, 193, 253, 261, 269, 314, 338, 403, 409, 428, 470, 477, 517, 609, 626, 646, 694, 701, 740
panel, 444
Dramatization, 122, 283, 470, 515
conversation, 160, 372
dialogue, 307, 372
job interview, 133
pantomime, 166, 203, 644
play, 120, 715
puppet show, 283
radio play, 336
role play, 149, 323, 483
scene, 76, 105, 252, 360, 408, 419, 609, 725
skit, 25
tale, 527
Evaluating art, 107–108, 293
Exhibiting art, 29, 55, 140, 235, 731, 740
Interview, 15, 37, 43, 215, 236, 252, 259, 276, 313, 380, 460, 469, 493, 609
poll, 133
talk show, 191, 506, 700, 739
Listening, effective, 469
Media literacy, 337, 625.
  See also Media and Technology index.
Multimodal activities. *See* Creating

art, Debate, Discussion, Dramatization, Interview, Music, News report, Oral report, Read aloud, Speech.
Music, 76, 108, 203, 515, 609
and dance, 166, 715
song, 338, 385, 408, 659
News report
news panel show, 37
press conference, 191
Oral report, 25, 259, 313, 380, 493, 520, 610, 654, 671
demonstration, 259, 693
explanation, 268, 433
time capsule contents, 709
visual report, 276
Read aloud, 54, 108, 160, 222, 223, 234, 277, 420, 520, 710
dramatic reading, 268, 624
oral interpretation, 268, 313, 700
play, 120
poetry, 91, 740
speech, 659
Relating art to experience, 16, 29, 40, 45, 67, 130–131, 137, 145, 271, 276, 285, 305, 377, 480, 483, 615
Relating art to literature, 19, 37, 40, 102, 142, 153, 155, 223, 249, 255, 259, 279, 391, 406, 415, 444, 485, 491, 501, 509, 512–513, 524, 625, 651, 663, 685, 690, 707
Responding to art, 394, 483, 715
Speaking, effective, 468, 739
oral reading, 268, 313
oral report, 25, 259, 313, 380, 493, 520, 610, 654, 671
Speech, 468
first lady's speech, 85
Gettysburg address, 659
on insanity defense (pro or con), 268
storytelling, 299, 470
visiting speaker, 122, 338
Visual literacy, 235.
  See also Analyzing art, Creating art, Evaluating art, Exhibiting art, Relating art to experience, Relating art to literature.

Interdisciplinary Connections

Anthropology
  Native Americans, 395–397
Art, 29
  Native American, 398–400
  slave, 615
Community service, 236
  volunteering, 236
Geography, 5, 110, 141, 204, 521, 537, 633
  North/South Poles, 730–731
Health, 261
  diet, 167–169, 172
  hypothermia, 175
History
  Armenia, 141
  Mexico, 710
  Nazi Germany, 536–537
  polar exploration, 726–728
  World War II, 536, 610
  See also U. S. History.
Math
  bar graph, 59, 677, 678
  charts, 59
  survey, 380
  tessellations, 328–329
  word problems, 677
Music, 29, 55
Photography
  Jacob Riis, 284–285
Psychology, 26, 493, 495
  family relationships, 456–459
  self-esteem, 60–61
Religion
  and art, 398–400
  and nature, 395–400
Science
  astronomy, 701
  earth science, 224–227, 729
  life science, 301, 324–327, 445
Sociology, 56–58, 253, 284, 286, 616–617, 532–533
Special text focus
  all work, no play, 528
  brainstorms, 167
  deceiving to the eye, 324
  forces of destruction, 224
  generations together, 456
  high jumpers, 56
  in harmony, 395
  polar journeys, 726
  reformers, 284
  school days, 672
  trailblazers, 109
  unshackled, 612
U. S. History, 17, 30, 77, 81–83, 97, 105, 106, 115, 161, 204, 215, 216, 261, 421, 434, 517, 521, 655, 694, 717
  child labor laws today, 532–533
  Frederick Douglass, 612–614
  Jane Addams, 286–288
  Mother Jones, 528–531
  nineteenth-century
    child labor, 528–531
    frontier schools, 672–677
    inventions, 170–171
    pioneer women, 109–113
    reformers, 284–288
  oral history, 460–461
  slavery, 612–617

Media and Technology

Audiotaping, 460–461
Camera, 625
Color, 625
Computer, 86, 121, 234, 427, 610, 645, 693, 709, 725, 738
  CD-ROM, 121
  computer terms, 121
Electronic research, 121
Lighting, 625
Media literacy, 337, 625
  critical thinking, 337
  interacting with media, 337, 521
    recognizing bias/propaganda, 337, 444
    recognizing purpose, 337
    relating media to literature, 24, 29, 30, 444, 515, 626
Online services, 121
Sound track, 203, 625, 715
Storyboard, 625
Videotaping, 739
Writing with computers, 86, 234, 738
  using a spell-check program, 86, 645
  using graphics, 738

Multicultural Awareness and Appreciation

Cultural awareness, 4, 15, 29, 36, 122, 166, 193, 222, 517, 724
  Armenia, 141
  Chinese Americans, 717
  India, 660
  Mexico, 710, 712, 715
  Native Americans, 395–400
  Philippines, 373
  Puerto Rico, 633
Exploring similarities, 15, 626, 660
Prejudice, 626
Recognizing/respecting differences, 4, 15, 193, 251, 338, 434, 626, 660
Special text focus
  change, 4, 7, 14, 29, 36, 42, 122, 174, 185, 202, 214, 236
  choice, 128, 130–131, 132, 148, 159, 165, 236
  communication, 338, 344, 359, 371, 379, 470
  group/groups, 242, 251, 258, 282, 338, 431, 679, 692, 699, 740
  individuality, 476, 479, 480, 482, 514, 520, 626, 632, 643, 651, 653, 670, 708, 714, 740
  interaction, 402, 418, 431, 443, 454, 470, 514, 535, 581, 608
  perspective, 63, 75, 84, 88–89, 90, 105, 108, 122, 290, 298, 312, 322, 338, 517
Stereotypes, 322, 680, 755

Life Skills

Change, 4, 7, 14, 26, 29, 30, 36, 42, 54, 56, 122, 456–459, 484, 680, 740
Community service, 236
Conflict and resolution, 338, 428, 456–459
First impressions, 470
Journeys/dreams, 733–738, 740
Personal management, 4
Pledges, 338
Prejudice, 626
Problem solving, 373, 626
Relationships, 456–459, 470
Values, 236, 338, 428, 520

Index of Fine Art and Artists

Adoquei, Sam, *Portrait of Rockney C.,* cover (detail), ii
African American art (anonymous), Face vessel, 615; Watercolor, 615; Musical instrument, 615
American Indian art (anonymous), Mohawk mask, 398; Dance shirt, 398; Cherokee mask, 399; Hopi buffalo Kachina doll, 399; Crow shield cover, 399; Drum (Northern tribes), 400; medicine bag, 435; Tohono O'odham baskets, 479
Arriazola, Sandra, *Self-Portrait,* 131
Auth, Dennis, Illustration, 137
Aztec art (anonymous), Mosaic mask of Quetzalcoatl, 711; Drum, 713; Drawing of Tlaloc, 715

Barnet, Will, *Soft-Boiled Eggs,* 321
Beallor, Fran, *Light Year's Returning,* 133; *Studio Arch,* 509
Bearden, Romare, Untitled painting, 6–7; *Before Dawn,* 153
Ben, Herbert, *The Skies,* 400
Bernardin, James, Illustration, 522
Birmelin, Robert, *The Moment I Saw the Man with a Rifle,* 259
Bono, Mary, Illustration, 501
Brown, Monin, and/or **Mitchell, Hattie,** *Improvisational Blocks,* 431

Calero, Oswaldo Guayasamín, *My Brother,* 451
Carter, Clarence Holbrook, *Shivered Glass,* 363
Chagall, Marc, *Equestrian* (detail), 74
Chan, Ron, Illustrations, 719, 721
Christen, Maria, *Chouette au Coucher de Soleil,* 394
Cordero, Helen, Storyteller sculpture, 483

Dana, Richard, *Hard Listening,* 19
Delessert, Etienne, Illustration, 491
Deurloo, Robert, *King Thunder,* 107
Dine, Jim, *20 Hearts,* 71; *The Art of Painting No. 2* (detail), 142
Dollman, J. C., Painting, 183

Escher, Maurits, Drawing, 328

Gallen-Kallela, Akseli, *Landscape Under Snow,* 176
Garza, Carmen Lomas, *A Medio Dia/Pedacito de mi Corazón (At High Noon/A Little Piece of My Heart),* 447
Gile, Selden, *Woman of Taos,* 391
Gillot, Carol, *Future Farming,* 703

Goings, Ralph, *Country Girl Diner,* 293; *Diner Still Life,* 297
Gorky, Arshile, *The Artist and His Mother,* 145
Green, Jonathan, *The Sand Bar,* 340–341

Hopper, Edward, *Adam's House,* 40
Howe, John, Illustrations, 685, 686, 689, 690

Johnson, Lonni Sue, Illustration, 310
Johnson, Malvin Gray, *Self-Portrait,* 651

Kaufmann, Isidor, *Girl with Flowers in Her Hair,* 299
Kopilak, G. G., *Still Life #3,* 415

Lawrence, Jacob, *Harriet Tubman* series: Plate 10, 213; Plate 16, 207; Plate 20, 211
Lempa, Mary, Illustration, 406
LeVan, Susan, Illustration, 1
Lindneux, Robert, *Portrait of Davy Crockett,* 219
Ling, Lauren, Collage, 23

Magritte, René, *Le Modèle Rouge,* 51
Mak, Kam, Rice bowl and origami bird, 162; Painting, 441
Manning-Carner, Hyacinth, *Fruit Stand Vendor,* 199
Marshall, Alvin, *Journey to the Butterfly World,* 397
Momaday, Al, *Buffalo Dream,* 106

NASA, Photograph of Earth from the moon, 707
Nez, Redwing T., *Her Precious Time,* 27

Ong, Diana, *Señorita #1,* 10; *Together,* 67; *Portrait 3,* 244; *The Piano Lesson,* 249

Philippoteaux, Paul, *Pickett's Charge,* 656
Picasso, Pablo, *Weeping Woman,* 317; *Flowers,* 485, 513
Pierre, Christian, *Emma's Lion,* 279
Pinkney, Jerry, Illustration, 524
Powers, Harriet, Quilt, 615

Ramírez, Manuel Ibarra, Clay puppets, 480
Ray, Gayle, *Owl and Snake,* 389
Richbourg, Lance, *Sliding in Yankee Stadium,* 238–239
Riis, Jacob, Photographs, 284–285
Rousseau, Henri, *Tropical Storm with Tiger-Surprise,* 124–125

Scott, Jeanne Filler, *The Veteran-Eskimo Husky,* 188
Shahn, Ben, *Liberation,* 472–473
Shakito, *Runaway Beach,* 195
Shuptrine, Hubert, *Ben,* 367; *The Tribesman,* 439
Silverman, Sherri, *Ladders of Light #7: Yellow Hands,* 504–505
Speight, Francis, *King's Mountain, North Carolina,* 628–629

Thomas, Maryann, Painting, 410
Thompson, John, Illustration, 262–263
Tillinghast, Paul, Untitled assemblage, 649
True, David, *Wind and Geometry,* 201

U.S. art (anonymous), Woodcut of Lincoln's assassination, 102

Uchida, Yoshiko, Painting of a dust storm, 37

Van Gogh, Vincent, *Old Peasant,* 519
Van Hulsdonck, Jacob, *Plums, Apricots, in a Bowl,* 382
Vickrey, Robert, *Portrait of Scott,* 45

Wilson, John, *My Brother,* 255
Wood, Grant, *Spring Plowing,* 429
Wyeth, Andrew, *Albert's Son,* xxiv; *Soaring,* 88–89

Yerka, Jacek, *Metropolis II,* 271
Young, Stephen Scott, *Easter Bonnet,* 155

Index of Authors and Titles

Acosta, Teresa Palomo, 428
Alvarez, Julia, 274
Anaya, Rudolfo A., 517
Angell, Judie, 345
Angelou, Maya, 151
Animal Craftsmen, 302
At the Avenue Eatery, 292
Aunty Misery, 220
Autobiography of Eleanor Roosevelt, The, from, 82

Back There, 93
Balcells, Jacqueline, 314
Banana Tree, The, 194
Batten, Mary, 324
Ben Carson: A Man of Action, 56
Beni Seballos, 374
Berry, James, 193
Boy and His Grandfather, The, 518
Brand, Dionne, 201
Brooks, Bruce, 301
Brooks, Gwendolyn, 38
Bruchac, Joseph, 106

Caduto, Michael J., 106
Camouflage: The Big Cover-Up, 324
Catalogue, 406
Changeling, The, 481
Chinese Hot Pot, 648
Clarke, Arthur C., 701
Cofer, Judith Ortiz, 216, 478
Colman, Penny, 528
Conford, Ellen, 64
Coretta and Edythe: The Scott Sisters, 422
Cormier, Robert, 409
Corn Flake Kings: The Kellogg Brothers, 167
Creation of Music, The, 711

Dear Marsha, 346
Deloria, Vine, Jr., 395
Diary of Anne Frank, The, 538
Douglass, Frederick, 612
Dream Keeper, The, 650
Dreams, 650
Dust Will Settle, The, 27
Dusting, 274

Elegy Written at the County Junkyard, 270
Elwood, Ann, 460
Enchanted Raisin, The, 315

Fable for When There's No Way Out, 88
Flowers for Algernon, 485

Follow Your Dreams, 726
Forgotten Language, 28
Frank, Anne, 536
Freedman, Russell, 77, 674
Frontier Schools, 674
Frost, Robert, 428

Gettysburg Address, The, 656
Go Down, Moses, 213
Gonzalez, Gloria, 5
Goodrich, Frances, 536
Greeting Disorder, 404

Hackett, Albert, 536
Hamilton, Virginia, 277
Harriet Tubman, from, 205
Haslam, Gerald, 445
He Lion, Bruh Bear, and Bruh Rabbit, 278
Home, 39
Hooper, Meredith, 167
Hoose, Phillip, 373
Horned Toad, The, 446
Houston, James D., 269
How Does a Hurricane Develop?, 224
How the Snake Got Poison, 388
Huffman, Louise Tolle, 726
Hughes, Langston, 253, 647
Hurricane, 201
Hurston, Zora Neale, 387

I Ask My Mother to Sing, 723
I Know Why the Caged Bird Sings, from, 152
I, Too, 650
Identity, 164
"If I Forget Thee, Oh Earth . . .," 702
In Balance with Nature, 395
Indians, 479
Inequalities, 480
Irving, Washington, 680

Jacob, Rahul, 532
Jane Addams, 286
Jen, Gish, 243
John Henry, 524
Johnson, Georgia Douglas, 87

Keepsakes, 309
Keyes, Daniel, 484
Kid Nobody Could Handle, The, 45
Kin, 616
Koch, Kenneth, 381
Kunen, James, S., 616

Lane, Deloras, 308
Lazarus, Emma, 647
Lee, Li-Young, 723
Lincoln, Abraham, 655
Little, Jean, 129
Liverwurst and Roses, 65
London, Jack, 175
Longfellow, Henry Wadsworth, 694
Lum, Wing Tek, 647

Mark, Diane Mei Lin, 161
Markoe, Merrill, 403
McCormick, Dell J., 521
Mechanical Mind, The, 135
Medicine Bag, The, 435
Mehta, Ved, 660
Moore, Rosalie, 406
Morrison, Lillian, 161
Mother in Mannville, A, xxv
Mother Jones Seeks Justice for the Mill Children, 528
Moustache, The, 410
My Father and the Figtree, 652
My Mother Pieced Quilts, 430
Myers, Walter Dean, 361

New Colossus, The, 648
New Global Outlook, A, 729
Nye, Naomi Shihab, 647

O Captain! My Captain!, 657
Ohrn, Deborah Gore, 286
Orbiter 5 Shows How Earth Looks from the Moon, 707
Orsag, Carol, 460

Parsley Garden, The, 142
Passing of the Buffalo, The, 107
Paul Bunyan Digs the St. Lawrence River, 522
Paul Revere's Ride, 695
Paulsen, Gary, 17
Pearson, Gayle, 291
Petry, Ann, 204
Poe, Edgar Allan, 261
Polanco, Julio Noboa, 161
President's Wife, A, 78
Primer Lesson, 392
Prisoner of My Country, 31

Rawlings, Marjorie Kinnan, xxv
Rice and Rose Bowl Blues, 162
Rip Van Winkle, 681
Rivas, Ophelia, 478
Román, Nereida, 478
Roosevelt, Eleanor, 82
Rosenberg, Donna, 710
Ross, Gayle, 387

Saline, Carol, 421
Sandburg, Carl, 392
Santiago, Esmeralda, 633
Saroyan, William, 141
Search for Your "Roots," 460
Sellers, Patricia, 56
Serling, Rod, 92
Shapiro, Irwin, 216
Shaw, Anna Howard, 109
Shot at It, A, 634
Sidewalk Racer, The, 163
Silverstein, Shel, 26
Six Across Antarctica, 727
Smith, Howard E., 224
Sneve, Virginia Driving Hawk, 434
Soto, Gary, 134
Sound-Shadows of the New World, from, 661
Spirit Unshackled, A, 612
Spirits of the Railway, 718
Steger, Will, 727
Stop the Sun, 18
Strawberries, 390
Strong but Quirky: The Birth of Davy Crockett, 217
Survival of the Stronghearted, 109
Swenson, May, 87, 707

Tapahonso, Luci, 26
Tarshis, Lauren, 456
Tell-Tale Heart, The, 262
Thane, Adele, 680
Thank You, Ma'am, 254
They Won't Let Me Grow Up, 456
This Is Just to Say, 382
Time to Talk, A, 429
To Build a Fire, 176
Too Much Work=Poor Grades, 532
Transformación, 481
Treasure of Lemon Brown, The, 362

Uchida, Yoshiko, 30

Variations on a Theme by William Carlos Williams, 383
Viva New Jersey, 6
Vonnegut, Jr., Kurt, 44

Walker, Alice, 308
White Umbrella, The, 244
Whitman, Walt, 657
Who You Are, 130
Williams, William Carlos, 381
Without Commercials, 310
Woods, Michael, 729

Yee, Paul, 717
Your World, 89

Acknowledgments

continued from page iv

161 From "Rice and Rose Bowl Blues" by Diane Mei Lin Mark. Reprinted by permission of the author. **162** "Rice and Rose Bowl Blues" by Diane Mei Lin Mark. Reprinted by permission of the author. **163** "The Sidewalk Racer" from *The Sidewalk Racer and Other Poems of Sports and Motion* by Lillian Morrison. Copyright © 1965, 1967, 1968, 1977 by Lillian Morrison. Reprinted by permission of Marian Reiner for the author. **164** "Identity" by Julio Noboa Polanco. Copyright © 1973 Julio Noboa Polanco. Reprinted by permission of the author. **167** From "Corn Flake Kings: The Kellogg Brothers" from *Everyday Inventions* by Meredith Hooper. Copyright © 1972 by Meredith Hooper. Reprinted by permission of the author. **172** Abridged excerpt from *Steven Caney's Invention Book* by Steven Caney. Copyright © 1985 by Steven Caney. All rights reserved. Reprinted by permission of Workman Publishing Company, Inc. **193** Susan M. Trosky, *Contemporary Authors,* Vol. 135. Detroit: Gale Research Inc., 1992, p. 37. **194** "The Banana Tree" from *A Thief in the Village and Other Stories* by James Berry. Copyright © 1987 by James Berry. Reprinted by permission of the Publisher, Orchard Books, New York. **201** "Hurricane" by Dionne Brand. Reprinted by permission of the author. **204** Pamela S. Dear, *Contemporary Authors,* Vol. 46. Detroit: Gale Research Inc., 1995, p. 299. **205** From *Harriet Tubman: Conductor on the Underground Railroad* by Ann Petry. Copyright © 1955 by Ann Petry, renewed 1983 by Ann Petry. Reprinted by permission of Russell & Volkening as agents for the author. **216** James G. Lesniak, *Contemporary Authors,* Vol. 32. Detroit: Gale Research Inc., 1991, p. 89. **217** "Strong but Quirky: The Birth of Davy Crockett" from *Yankee Thunder* by Irwin Shapiro. Copyright © 1972 by Julian Messner, an imprint of Silver Burdett Press, Simon & Schuster Elementary. Reprinted by permission. **220** "Aunty Misery" by Judith Ortiz Cofer. Copyright © 1988 by Judith Ortiz Cofer. Reprinted by permission of the author. **224** From *Weather* by Howard E. Smith. Copyright © 1990 by Howard E. Smith. Reprinted by permission of Doubleday, a division of Bantam Doubleday Dell Publishing Group, Inc. **244** "The White Umbrella" by Gish Jen. Copyright © 1994 by Gish Jen. First published in *The Yale Review.* Reprinted by permission of the author. **254** "Thank You, Ma'am" by Langston Hughes from *The Langston Hughes Reader.* Copyright © 1958 by Langston Hughes. Renewed © 1986 by George Houston Bass. Reprinted by permission of Harold Ober Associates Incorporated. **270** "Elegy Written at the County Junkyard" from *Three Songs for My Father* by James D. Houston. Copyright © 1974 by James D. Houston. Used by permission of Capra Press. **274** "Dusting" from *Homecoming* by Julia Alvarez. Copyright © 1984 by Julia Alvarez. Published by Plume, an imprint of New American Library, a division of Penguin USA, New York. First published by Grove Press in 1984. Reprinted by permission of Susan Bergholz Literary Services. **278** "He Lion, Bruh Bear, and Bruh Rabbit," from *The People Could Fly: American Black Folktales* by Virginia Hamilton. Copyright © 1985 by Virginia Hamilton. Reprinted by permission of Alfred A. Knopf, Inc. **286** "Jane Addams" by Deborah Gore Ohrn from *HerStory* by R. Ashby and Deborah Gore Ohrn, editors. Copyright © 1995. Reprinted by permission of Viking Penguin, a division of Penguin Books USA, New York. **288** Stephanie Sammartino McPherson, *Peace and Bread: The Story of Jane Addams.* Minneapolis: Carolrhoda Books, Inc., 1993. **292** "At the Avenue Eatery" from *One Potato, Tu* by Gayle Pearson. Copyright © 1992 by Gayle Pearson. Reprinted by permission of Atheneum Books for Young Readers, an imprint of Simon & Schuster. **302** Text from "Animal Craftsmen" from *Nature by Design* by Bruce Brooks. Copyright © 1991 by the Educational Broadcasting Corporation and Bruce Brooks. Reprinted by permission of Farrar, Straus & Giroux., Inc. **309** "Keepsakes" by Deloras Lane. Used by permission of the author. **310** "Without Commercials" from *Horses Make a Landscape Look More Beautiful: Poems by Alice Walker.* Copyright © 1984 by Alice Walker. Reprinted by permission of Harcourt Brace & Company. **312** From "Keepsakes" by Deloras Lane. Used by permission of the author. **312, 337** From "Without Commercials" from *Horses Make a Landscape Look More Beautiful: Poems by Alice Walker.* Copyright © 1984 by Alice Walker. Reprinted by permission of Harcourt Brace & Company. **315** "The Enchanted Raisin" by Jacqueline Balcells, translated by Janice Molloy in *Landscapes of a New Land: Short Fiction by Latin American Women,* 1989, 1992, pp. 154–162. Edited by Marjorie Agosin. Reprinted by permission of White Pine Press, Fredonia, NY. **324** From "Camouflage: The Big Cover-Up" from *Nature's Tricksters* by Mary Batten. Text copyright © 1992 by Mary Batten. Reprinted by permission of Little, Brown and Company. **328** "Tessellations" from *Transition Mathematics.* Copyright © 1995 Scott, Foresman and Company. Reprinted by permission. **346** "Dear Marsha" by Judie Angell. Copyright © 1989 by Judie Angell from *Connections: Short Stories* by Donald R. Gallo, Editor. Reprinted by permission of Delacorte Press, a division of Bantam Doubleday Dell Publishing Group, Inc. **362** "The Treasure of Lemon Brown" by Walter Dean Myers, *Boy's Life,* March 1993. Copyright © 1983 by Walter Dean Myers. Reprinted by permission of Miriam Altshuler Literary Agency as agent for Walter Dean Myers. **374** "Beni Seballos" from *It's Our World, Too!* by Phillip Hoose. Copyright © 1993 by Phillip Hoose. Reprinted by permission of Little, Brown and Company. **382** "This Is Just to Say" from *Collected Poems: 1909–1939,* Volume I by William Carlos Williams. Copyright 1938 by New Directions Publishing Corp. Reprinted by permission of New Directions Publishing Corp. **383** "Variations on a Theme by William Carlos

Williams" from *Thank You and Other Poems* by Kenneth Koch. Copyright © 1962, 1994 by Kenneth Koch. Reprinted by permission of the author. **388** "How the Snake Got Poison" from *Mules and Men* by Zora Neale Hurston. Copyright 1935 by Zora Neale Hurston. Copyright renewed © 1963 by John C. Hurston and Joel Hurston. Reprinted by permission of HarperCollins Publishers, Inc. **390** "Strawberries" by Gayle Ross. Reprinted by permission of the author. **392** "Primer Lesson" from *Slabs of the Sunburnt West* by Carl Sandburg. Copyright © 1922 by Harcourt Brace & Company and renewed 1950 by Carl Sandburg. Reprinted by permission of the publisher. **395** Excerpt from "Foreword" by Vine Deloria, Jr., from *Keepers of the Animals* by Michael J. Caduto and Joseph Bruchac. Reprinted by permission of Fulcrum Publishing. **404** "Greeting Disorder" from *How to Be Hap-Hap-Happy Like Me* by Merrill Markoe. Copyright © 1994 by Merrill Markoe. Reprinted by permission of Viking Penguin, a division of Penguin Books USA, Inc. **406** "Catalogue" by Rosalie Moore, *The New Yorker,* May 25, 1940. Copyright 1940 The New Yorker. Reprinted by permission. **410** "The Moustache" from *Eight Plus One* by Robert Cormier. Copyright © 1975 by Robert Cormier. Reprinted by permission of Pantheon Books, a division of Random House, Inc. **422** "Coretta and Edythe: The Scott Sisters" from *Sisters.* Text copyright © 1994 by Carol Saline. Reprinted by permission from Running Press Book Publishers. **429** "A Time to Talk" from *The Poetry of Robert Frost,* edited by Edward Connery Lathem. Copyright 1916, 1939, © 1967, 1969 by Holt, Rinehart and Winston. Copyright 1944 by Robert Frost. Reprinted by permission of the Estate of Robert Frost and Jonathan Cape Ltd. **430** "My Mother Pieced Quilts" by Teresa Palomo Acosta. Reprinted by permission of Teresa Palomo Acosta. **432** From "My Mother Pieced Quilts" by Teresa Palomo Acosta. Reprinted by permission of Teresa Palomo Acosta. **435** "The Medicine Bag" by Virginia Driving Hawk Sneve. Copyright © 1975 by Virginia Driving Hawk Sneve. Reprinted by permission. **446** "The Horned Toad" by Gerald Haslam. Copyright © 1983 by Gerald Haslam. Reprinted by permission of the author. **456** From "They Won't Let Me Grow Up" by Lauren Tarshis in *Scholastic Choices,* October 1994. Copyright © 1994 by Scholastic Inc. Reprinted by permission. **460** "Search for Your 'Roots'" from *The Macmillan Illustrated Almanac for Kids* by Ann Elwood, Carol Orsag and Sidney Solomon. Copyright © 1981 by Ann Elwood, Carol Orsag and Sidney Solomon. Reprinted by permission of Simon & Schuster. **480** "Inequalities" by Nereida Román from *Hispanic, Female and Young,* 1994. Reprinted by permission of the publisher, Arte Público Press, University of Houston. **481** "The Changeling" by Judith Ortiz Cofer from *Prairie Schooner,* Vol. 6, No. 3, Fall 1992. Copyright © 1992 University of Nebraska Press. Reprinted by permission of University of Nebraska Press. **481** "Transformación" by Judith Ortiz Cofer, translated by Johanna Vega. From *Cool Salsa* by Lori M. Carlson, Ed. Copyright © 1994 by Lori M. Carlson. Reprinted by permission of

Henry Holt & Company, Inc. **485** *Flowers for Algernon* by Daniel Keyes. Short story version. Copyright © 1959, 1987 by Daniel Keys. Reprinted by permission of the author. **518** "The Boy and His Grandfather" from *Cuentos: Tales from the Hispanic Southwest* by José Griego y Maestas and Rudolfo A. Anaya. Copyright © 1980 by the Museum of New Mexico Press. Reprinted by permission of the Museum of New Mexico Press. **522** "Paul Bunyan Digs the St. Lawrence River" by Dell J. McCormick from *Legends of Paul Bunyan* by Harold Felton. Copyright © 1947 by Alfred A. Knopf, Inc. Reprinted by permission of Alfred A. Knopf, Inc. **528** From *Mother Jones and the March of the Mill Children* by Penny Colman. Copyright © 1994 by Penny Colman. Reprinted by permission of The Millbrook Press, Inc. **532** Abridged from "Too Much Work=Poor Grades" by Rahul Jacob, *Fortune,* April 5, 1993, p. 92. Copyright © 1993 Time Inc. All rights reserved. Reprinted by permission of Fortune. **533** "Child labor and rules of reason" from *Chicago Tribune,* 8/5/95. Copyright © 1995 Chicago Tribune Company. All rights reserved. Reprinted by permission of Chicago Tribune. **538** *The Diary of Anne Frank* by Frances Goodrich and Albert Hackett. Copyright 1954, © 1956 as an unpublished work. Copyright © 1956 by Albert Hackett, Frances Goodrich Hackett and Otto Frank. Reprinted by permission of Random House, Inc. **612** From *Escape from Slavery* by Frederick Douglass, edited by Michael McCurdy. Copyright © 1993 by Michael McCurdy. Reprinted by permission of Alfred A. Knopf, Inc. **616** From "Two Hundred Summers Later, Slavery's Descendants Honor the Ghosts of a Plantation" by James S. Kunen & Jane Sims Podesta, *People,* Sept. 15, 1986, pp. 175–177. Copyright © 1986 Time, Inc. Reprinted by permission of People Magazine. **634** "A Shot at It" from *When I Was Puerto Rican* by Esmeralda Santiago. Copyright © 1993 by Esmeralda Santiago. Reprinted by permission of Addison-Wesley Publishing Company. **648** "Chinese Hot Pot" from *Expounding the Doubtful Points* by Wing Tek Lum. Copyright © 1987 by Wing Tek Lum. Reprinted by permission of the author. **650** "Dreams" from *The Dream Keeper and Other Poems* by Langston Hughes. Copyright 1932 by Alfred A. Knopf, Inc. and renewed © 1960 by Langston Hughes. Reprinted by permission of the publisher. **650** "I, Too" from *Selected Poems* by Langston Hughes. Copyright 1926 by Alfred Al Knopf, Inc. and renewed 1954 by Langston Hughes. Reprinted by permission of the publisher. **650** "The Dream Keeper" from *The Dream Keeper and Other Poems* by Langston Hughes. Copyright 1932 by Alfred A. Knopf, Inc. and renewed © 1960 by Langston Hughes. Reprinted by permission of the publisher. **652** "My Father and the Figtree" from *Different Ways to Pray* by Naomi Shihab Nye. Copyright © 1980 by Naomi Shihab Nye. Reprinted by permission of the author. **661** From *Sound-Shadows of the New World* by Ved Mehta. Copyright © 1985 by Ved Mehta. Originally published by W. W. Norton. Reprinted by permission of Wylie, Aitken & Stone, Inc. **674** "Frontier Schools" from *Children of the Wild West* by Russell Freedman.

Copyright © 1983 by Russell Freedman. All rights reserved. Reprinted by permission of Clarion Books/Houghton Mifflin Co. **677** From *Going to School in 1876* by John J. Loeper. Copyright © 1984 by John J. Loeper. Reprinted by permission of Atheneum Books for Young Readers, an imprint of Simon & Schuster. **681** "Rip Van Winkle" by Washington Irving from *Famous Stories and Fairy Tales* by Adele Thane. Copyright © 1967 Adele Thane. Reprinted by permission of Plays, Inc. **702** "If I Forget Thee, Oh Earth . . ." by Arthur C. Clarke. Copyright 1954, renewed © 1979 by Arthur C. Clarke. Reprinted by permission of Scovil, Chichak & Galen Literary Agency, Inc. **707** "Orbiter 5 Shows How Earth Looks from the Moon" by May Swenson. Copyright © 1969 by May Swenson. Reprinted by permission of The Literary Estate of May Swenson. **711** "The Creation of Music" retold by Donna Rosenberg from *World Mythology* by Donna Rosenberg. Copyright © 1994, 1956 by NTC Publishing Group. Reprinted by permission of National Textbook Company, a division of NTC Publishing Group. **718** "Spirits of the Railway" from *Tales from Gold Mountain* by Paul Yee. Text copyright © 1989 Paul Yee. Reprinted by permission of Simon & Schuster Books for Young Readers and Groundwood/Douglas & McIntyre Children's Books. **723** "I Ask My Mother to Sing" from *Rose* by Li-Young Lee. Copyright © 1986 by Li-Young Lee. Reprinted by permission of BOA Editions, Ltd., 92 Park Ave., Brockport, NY 14420. **726** From "Follow Your Dreams" by Louise Tolle Huffman from *Of Cabbages and Kings,* pp. 118–120. Copyright © 1992 by Reed Publishing Inc. Reprinted by permission. **727** From "Six Across Antarctica: Into the Teeth of the Ice" by Will Steger from *Of Cabbages and Kings,* pp. 123–125. Copyright © 1992 by Reed Publishing Inc. Reprinted by permission. **729** Michael Woods, *Science on Ice.* Brookfield, CT: The Millbrook Press, 1995, pp. 19–21.

Illustrations

Unless otherwise acknowldged, all photographs are the property of Scott, Foresman and Company. Page abbreviations are as follows: (t)top, (c)center, (b)bottom, (l)left, (r)right, (ins)inset.

Cover (detail), **ii,** Sam Adoquei, "Portrait of Rockney C.," 1992, Collection of the artist **vii** Susan LeVan, "The Gardener," digital medium, LeVan/Barbee Studio **ix** Henri Rousseau, "Tropical Storm with Tiger-Surprise," Superstock, Inc. **xi** Lance Richbourg, "Sliding in Yankee Stadium," Superstock, Inc. **xiii** Jonathan Green, "The Sand Bar," 1991, oil on canvas 72" x 55", Jonathan Green Studios, Inc., Naples, FL **xv** Ben Shahn, "Liberation," 1945, © 1996 Estate of Ben Shahn/Licensed by VAGA, New York, NY **xvii** Francis Speight, "King's Mountain, North Carolina," c. 1940, Hickory Museum of Art purchase funded by the Kenneth K. Milholland family in memory of Mildred J. Gifford. Photograph courtesy of Schwarz Gallery, Philadelphia **xxiv** Courtesy Museet for Samtidskunst, Oslo, Norway **0–1** Susan LeVan, "The Gardener," digital medium (detail), LeVan/Barbee Studio **1, 4, 16, 56, 62(icon)** M. C. Escher, "Study for Rind," (detail) © 1995 M. C. Escher/Cordon Art-Baarn-Holland. All rights reserved. **1, 63, 86, 109, 114(icon)** Diana Ong, "Harmony," (detail), Superstock, Inc. **3(t)** © 1996 Robert Vickrey/Licensed by Vaga, New York, NY **3(b)** © David Young-Wolff/PhotoEdit **6–7** Collection Leonard Bates, New York **11** Superstock, Inc. **19** Courtesy Richard Dana **23** Lauren Ling/Courtesy Cliff Knecht **26(t)** Courtesy Luci Tapahonso **26(b)** AP/Wide World Photos **27** Photo by Jerry Jacka **30** Photo by Deborah Stone **33** War Relocation Authority/National Archives **35, 37** Courtesy, The Bancroft Library **38** Courtesy HarperCollins Publishers **44** Photo by Jill Krementz **45** © 1996 Robert Vickrey/Licensed by Vaga, New York, NY **51** © 1996 C. Herscovici, Brussels/Artists Rights Society (ARS), New York. Ex-Edward James Foundation, Sussex, England/Bridgeman Art Library, London/Superstock, Inc. **57** © Max Aguilera-Hellweg **60** © David Young-Wolff/PhotoEdit **67** Superstock, Inc. **71** Courtesy Pace Gallery **74** Stedelijk Museum, Amsterdam, © 1995 Artists Rights Society (ARS), New York/ADAGP, Paris **77** Photo by John Elari **78** Stock Montage, Inc./Historical Pictures **81** UPI/Corbis-Bettmann **83** Franklin D. Roosevelt Library **87(t)** UPI/Corbis-Bettmann **87(b)** Schomburg Collection, New York Public Library, Astor, Lenox and Tilden Foundation **88–89** Shelburne Museum, Shelburne, Vermont. Photo by Ken Burris **92** From the Estate of Rod Serling **97(l)** Culver Pictures Inc. **97(r)** © Rick Brady/Uniphoto **102** Frank & Marie-Therese Wood Print Collections, Alexandria, VA **106(t)** Photo by John Sheldon/H-O Photographers **106(b)** Photo by Carol Bruchac **106(r)** Courtesy Patricia Janis Broder, from AMERICAN INDIAN PAINTING & SCULPTURE. **107** Courtesy Robert Deurloo **109** Courtesy Lane County Historical Museum **112(t)** Solomon D. Butcher Collection/Nebraska State Historical Society **112–113, 113(r)** Wyoming State Archives, Museums & Historical Department **113(bl)** California Historical Society, Title Insurance & Trust Co. (L.A.) Collection of Historical Photographs **113(tl)** San Diego Historical Society, Title Insurance & Trust Collection **124-125** Henri Rousseau, "Tropical Storm with Tiger-Surprise," Superstock, Inc. **125, 128, 150, 167, 173(icon)** Superstock, Inc. **125, 174, 192, 224, 228(icon)** Superstock, Inc. **131** Courtesy Sandra Arriazola **133** Courtesy Fran Beallor **134** Photo by Carolyn Soto **137** © Dennis Auth/Stock Illustration Source, Inc. **141** Photo by Jerry Bauer, © Time/Life, Inc. **142** The Art Museum, Princeton University. Presented in memory of Helen B. Seeger on the date of her birthday by her son, Stanley J. Seeger, Jr., through the Helen B. Seeger Fund. Photo by Clem Fiori **145** Collection of Whitney Museum of American Art, New York. Gift of Julien Levy for Maro and Natasha Gorky in memory of their father. 50.17. **151** AP/Wide World Photos **153** Courtesy of the Public Library of Mecklenburg County and The Romare Howard Bearden Foundation **155** Courtesy John H. Surovek Gallery **161(t)** Photo by George Dean **162** © Kam Mak/Stock Illustration Source, Inc. **163** © Jonathan Elderfield

167 Kellogg's Corn Flakes® advertisement is a registered trademark of the Kellogg Company 168 Kellogg Company 170(cl) Courtesy Jill Ruter 170(bc), 171(cl) Culver Pictures Inc. 171(c) Henry Ford Museum and Greenfield Village 176(t) Superstock, Inc. 176(b) Courtesy The Antell Collection, Helsinki, The Central Art Archives. Photo by Jukka Romu 182–183 E. T. Archive/Collection of the Cavalry Club 185 © Jeff Schultz/AlaskaStock 188 Applestock Art Archives 193 Courtesy, Harcourt Brace & Co. 195 Superstock, Inc. 199 Superstock, Inc. 201 Lilja Art Foundation 204 AP/Wide World Photos 207, 211, 213 Hampton University Museum, Hampton, Virginia 216 Courtesy of Arte Publico Press 219 Superstock, Inc. 224, 225 © Philippe Mazellier 226 © Black Star 226–227 National Oceanic and Atmospheric Administration, National Environmental Satellite, Data, and Information Service, National Climatic Data Center, Satellite Data Services Division 227(t) © Jim Pickerell/Black Star 227(b) Superstock, Inc. 238–239 Lance Richbourg, "Sliding in Yankee Stadium," (detail), Superstock, Inc. 239, 242, 260, 284, 289(icon) Vincent Van Gogh, "Self-Portrait in Gray Felt Hat," (detail), Van Gogh Museum, Amsterdam/Superstock, Inc. 239, 290, 300, 324, 330(icon) Rene Magritte, "Le Chant D'Amour," (detail), © 1996 C. Herscovici, Brussels/Artists Rights Society (ARS), New York. Christie's, London/Superstock, Inc. 240(t) © Michael Newman/PhotoEdit 240(b) Courtesy Lonni Sue Johnson 241(t) © David Young-Wolff/PhotoEdit 241(b) Superstock, Inc. 243 AP/Wide World Photos 244 Superstock, Inc. 249 Superstock, Inc. 253 UPI/Corbis-Bettmann 255 Smith College Museum of Art, Northampton, Massachusetts, purchased 1943 259 Courtesy A. Robert Birmelin 261 Manuscripts Department, Lilly Library, Indiana University, Bloomington, IN 262–263 Courtesy John Thompson 269 Photo by Watson, Courtesy of the Scribner Book Companies 271 From MIND FIELDS published by Morpheus International 277 Courtesy Virginia Hamilton 279 Superstock, Inc. 284(t) Library of Congress 284(c, b), 284-285, 285(b) The Jacob A. Riis Collection, Museum of the City of New York 285(t) Library of Congress 286–288 University of Illinois at Chicago, The University Library, Jane Addams Memorial Collection 291 Courtesy Gayle Pearson 293, 297 Courtesy O. K. Harris Works of Art, New York 299 Superstock, Inc. 301 Courtesy HarperCollins Publishers 302(t) © Stephen Dalton/Photo Researchers 302(b), 303, 304, 305(t) © Stephen Dalton/Animals Animals 304–305 © Robert Maier/Animals Animals 305(b) © Hans Reinhard/Photo Researchers 308(t) Courtesy Deloras Lane 308(b) AP/Wide World Photos 310 Courtesy Lonni Sue Johnson 317 © 1996 Estate of Pablo Picasso/Artists Rights Society (ARS), New York. Courtesy Tate Gallery, London/Art Resource, NY 321 © 1996 Will Barnet/Licensed by VAGA, New York, NY 324(t) © Stan Way Man/Photo Researchers 324(tc) © Larry Tackett/Tom Stack & Associates 324(bc) © Breck P. Kent/Animals Animals/Earth Scenes 324(b) © Rod Planck/Photo Researchers 326(t) © Lawrence Migdale/Photo Researchers 326(b) © David G. Barker/Tom Stack &

Associates 327(t) © Peter C. Aitken/Photo Researchers 327(b) © Dr. Paul A. Zahl/Photo Researchers 328(t) © M. A. Chappell/Animals Animals/Earth Scenes 328(b) © 1995 M. C. Escher/Cordon Art-Baarn-Holland. All rights reserved. 340–341 Jonathan Green, "The Sand Bar," 1991, oil on canvas 72" x 55" (detail), Jonathan Green Studios, Inc., Naples, FL 341, 344, 386, 395, 401(icon) Superstock, Inc. 341, 402, 420, 456, 462(icon) Superstock, Inc. 343(t) © Myrleen Ferguson/PhotoEdit 345 Courtesy of Orchard Books 349 Courtesy Susan Cohen 350–351 © Robert P. Comport/Animals Animals 352–353 Superstock, Inc. 354–355 Superstock, Inc. 356 © Ron Rovtar/FPG International Corp. 361 Courtesy of Scholastic 363 National Museum of American Art, Smithsonian Institution, museum purchase, Robert Tyler Davis Memorial Fund. Art Resource, NY 367 © 1976 Hubert Shuptrine. Courtesy of the Collection, Mr. and Mrs. Harold R. McLaughlin, Jr. All rights reserved. Used with permission. 373 Photo by Richard Connelly, Courtesy Little, Brown and Company 377 From IT'S OUR WORLD, TOO! by Phillip Hoose, © 1993 Phillip Hoose. By permission of Little, Brown and Company. 381(t) Photo by John D. Schiff 381(b) © Larry Rivers 382 Christie's, London/ Superstock, Inc. 387(t) Courtesy The Estate of Carl Van Vechten 387(b) Courtesy HarperCollins Publishers 389 Superstock, Inc. 390–391 Superstock, Inc. 391 Jonathan Chriss Collection. Courtesy of THE SOCIETY OF SIX: CALIFORNIA COLORISTS, by Nancy Boas, Chronicle Books, San Francisco, 1988 394 Bridgeman Art Library, London/ Superstock, Inc. 396 © Jerry Jacka 397 Photo by Jerry Jacka 398(t, bl), 399(t), 400(r) San Diego Museum of Man, photos by John Oldenkamp 398–399 The National Museum of Denmark, Department of Ethnography, photo by Kit Weiss 399(br) Field Museum of Natural History, photo by Diane Alexander White, neg. #A111803C, cat.# 69633 400(l) Courtesy Peter Furst 403 Courtesy Viking Press, photo by Bonnie Schiffman 404–405 Bronze dogs by Roberta Laidman, photos by Philip Cohen 406 © 1993 Mary Flock Lempa 409 Courtesy Bantam Publishing, photo by Beth Bergman 410 Courtesy Maryann Thomas 415 Superstock, Inc. 421 Courtesy Running Press 423 UPI/Corbis-Bettmann 428(t) Dartmouth College 428(b) © 1983 Sharon Stewart 429 © 1996 Estate of Grant Wood/Licensed by VAGA, New York, NY 430-431 Courtesy of the San Francisco Craft and Folk Art Museum 434 AP/Wide World Photos 439 © 1982 by Hubert Shuptrine. Courtesy of The Blount Collection, Montgomery Museum of Art. All rights reserved. Used with permission. 441 © Kam Mak/Stock Illustration Source, Inc. 445 Courtesy University of Nevada Press 447 © Carmen Lomas Garza, photo by Wolfgang Dietze 451 Oil on wood, 15⅞" x 12¾" (40.3 x 32.4 cm). The Museum of Modern Art, New York. Inter-American Fund. Photograph © 1995 The Museum of Modern Art, New York. 456 © Arthur Tilley/FPG International Corp. 457 © R. Sidney/Image Works 458(t) © Nathan Nourok/PhotoEdit 458(b) © John Henley/Stock Market 459 © Myrleen Ferguson/PhotoEdit 472-473 Ben

Shahn, "Liberation," 1945 (detail), © 1996 Estate of Ben Shahn/Licensed by VAGA, New York, NY **473, 476, 516, 528, 534(icon)** Superstock, Inc. **473, 535, 611, 612, 618(icon)** © AFF/AFS, Amsterdam, The Netherlands **478(t)** Courtesy Nereida Roman **478(b)** Courtesy of Arte Publico Press **479** Baskets by Rose and Norma Antone, Dorina and Ruby Garcia, and Charlene Juan. Photo by Jerry Jacka **480** © David Lavender **483** Photo by Jerry Jacka **484** AP/Wide World Photos **485, 513** © 1996 Estate of Pablo Picasso/ Artists Rights Society (ARS), New York. A. K. G., Berlin/Superstock, Inc. **491** Courtesy Etienne Delessert **495** From Rorschach, PSYCHODIAGNOSTIK Verlag Hans Huber Bern, © 1921, renewed 1948 **501** © Mary Bono/ Stock Illustration Source, Inc. **504–505** Superstock, Inc. **509** Courtesy Fran Beallor **517** Courtesy Rudolfo A. Anaya **519** Bridgeman Art Library, London/Superstock, Inc. **521** Courtesy of Caxton Printing **522** Courtesy James Bernardin **524** From *John Henry* by Julius Lester, illustrated by Jerry Pinckney. Copyright © 1994 by Jerry Pinckney on Illustrations. Used by permission of Dial Books for Young Readers, a division of Penguin Books USA Inc. **528, 530(b)** Courtesy of The Newberry Library, Kerr Co. Archives **529** Courtesy United Mine Workers of America **530(t), 531(t)** Library of Congress **531(b)** Photo by Lewis Hine. Courtesy Albin O. Kuhn Library and Gallery, University of Maryland **532** © Tony Freeman/PhotoEdit **536** AP/Wide World Photos **538–547, 550–568, 577–595, 607** © AFF/AFS, Amsterdam, the Netherlands **548** Courtesy of The Holocaust Memorial Foundation of Illinois, Skokie, IL **570, 604** UPI/Corbis-Bettmann **601** Corbis-Bettmann **614** North Carolina Collection, UNC Library at Chapel Hill **615(cl, b)** Smithsonian Institution **615(cr)** Abby Aldrich Rockefeller Folk Art Center, Colonial Williamsburg Foundation **615(t)** Courtesy the Acacia Collection of African Americana **617(l)** People Weekly © Will McIntyre **617(r)** Library of Congress **628–629** Francis Speight, "King's Mountain, North Carolina," c. 1940 (detail), Hickory Museum of Art purchase funded by the Kenneth K. Milholland family in memory of Mildred J. Gifford. Photograph courtesy of Schwarz Gallery, Philadelphia **629, 632, 645, 672, 678(icon)** Superstock, Inc. **629, 679, 716, 726, 732(icon)** Superstock, Inc. **630** From RIP VAN WINKLE by John Howe. Copyright © 1988 by John Howe. By permission of Little, Brown and Company **631(b)** Courtesy Carol Gillot **633** © Benno Friedman/Vintage Books **635** Courtesy Cantomedia **641** Kobal Collection **647(t)** Corbis-Bettmann **647(c)** UPI/Corbis-Bettmann **647(b)** Photo by Michael Nye **649** © Paul Tillinghast/ Stock Illustration Source, Inc. **651** National Museum of American Art, Washington, DC/Art Resource, NY, 1967.57.30 **655** Library of Congress **656** Gettysburg National Military Park **660** Courtesy W. W. Norton and Company, Inc., photo by Jerry Bauer **663** Copyright © 1985 by Ved Mehta, from SOUND SHADOWS OF THE NEW WORLD (W. W. Norton & Co.), reprinted with the permission of Wylie, Aitken & Stone, Inc. **667** Copyright © 1972 by Ved Mehta, from DADDYJI (W. W. Norton & Co.), reprinted with the permission of Wylie, Aitken & Stone, Inc. **672(br)** Library of Congress **672(c)** Solomon D. Butcher Collection, Nebraska State Historical Society **672(bl), 673(b)** Denver Public Library, Western History Department **673(t)** Roy Andrews Collection, Special Collections, University of Oregon Library **675** National Archives **680** Sleepy Hollow Restorations **685, 686, 689, 690** From RIP VAN WINKLE by John Howe. Copyright © 1988 by John Howe. By permission of Little, Brown and Company **694** Longfellow House Trust **695** © Julie Houck/Stock Boston **701(l)** UPI/ Corbis-Bettmann **701(r)** NASA **702, 705** © Cynthia Clampitt **703** Courtesy Carol Gillot **704, 706** © Corrine Johns **707** NASA **710** Courtesy Donna Rosenberg **711** Bridgeman Art Library, London/Art Resource, NY **713** CNCA.-INAH.-MEX, photo by José de los Reyes Medina **715** Library of Congress **717** Courtesy James Ho Lim **718–722** Ron Chan **726–728** © Will Steger/ Black Star **729** NASA **730(b)** Superstock, Inc. **730** Arctic Region Map © 1983 by Instituto Geografico De Agostini, R. L. 95-S-333 **731** Antarctic Region Map © HarperCollins Cartographic 1995. Reproduced with permission. **731(t)** Superstock, Inc.